D0207081

Strange Piece
of Paradise

Terri Jentz

Strange Piece
of Paradise

Farrar, Straus and Giroux

New York

Farrar, Straus and Giroux
19 Union Square West, New York 10003

Copyright © 2006 by Terri Jentz
All rights reserved
Printed in the United States of America

Grateful acknowledgment is made for permission to reprint the following material:

Lyrics from "Sisters of Mercy" by Leonard Cohen, copyright © 1967 (renewed) by Sony/ATV Songs LLC. All rights administered by Sony/ATV Music Publishing, 8 Music Square West, Nashville, TN 37203. All rights reserved. Used by permission.

Excerpt from *An Explanation of America* by Robert Pinsky, copyright © 1979 by Princeton University Press. Reprinted by permission of Princeton University Press.

Lines from Poem XI of "Twenty-One Love Poems" by Adrienne Rich, copyright © 2002 by Adrienne Rich, copyright © 1978 by W. W. Norton & Company, Inc., from *The Fact of a Doorframe: Poems 1950–2001* by Adrienne Rich. Used by permission of the author and W. W. Norton & Company, Inc.

Historical photograph of the Golden Pioneer, courtesy of the Oregon State Library.

ISBN-13: 978-0-7394-7532-4

Designed by Michelle McMillian

For Donna,
who saw me through

They make us parents want to keep our children
Locked up, safe even from the daily papers
That keep the grisly record of that frontier
Where things unspeakable happen along the highways.

In today's paper, you see the teen-aged girl
From down the street; camping in Oregon
At the far point of a trip across the country,
Together with another girl her age,
They suffered and survived a random evil.

—ROBERT PINSKY, *AN EXPLANATION OF AMERICA*

Contents

Part One

It has sometimes taken me ten years to understand even a little of some important event that happened to me. Oh, I could have given a perfectly factual account of what happened but I didn't know what it meant until I knew the consequences.

—KATHERINE ANNE PORTER

A Dangerous Summer's Night

Poised on that twilight edge between life and death, I felt intimately the part of me that was flesh, and I knew also that I was something more.

I came to that insight early on. I was scarcely twenty.

IT WAS 1977, a drought year in the American West, the driest year in recorded history, although history in those parts went back only a hundred years.

Back then, all of America was in a drought. The fever dream of the sixties had simmered down and the country had lost its way. The national mood was dispirited, in recovery from shocks and traumas, pinched by stagnation and inflation. Fatalism shadowed sunny American optimism.

Gas prices had never been higher. But I didn't care. I was riding a bike.

America was hardly past its two hundredth birthday as I was nearing my twentieth. Its bicentennial year called for celebrations to restore a sense of the nation's magic and promise. Out of that came a bicycle trail, the BikeCentennial, forged from coast to coast through America's most spectacular countryside. My college roommate and I were riding the trail on our summer vacation. Encouraged by the 1970s culture to strive for self-discovery, we were hoping that the song of the open road would enlarge life's meaning.

In the Cascades of the Northwest, drought conditions were melting the glaciers left from the last ice age. The mountain passes cleared unusually early in the summer of '77 and allowed us to scale the highest pass. On the seventh day of our journey, we rode up through green rain forest. At the summit, a field of lava, night-black, surrounded us from every direction, as if a devastating fire had burned through only yesterday. Breathing in the air of the heights, we headed down. Trees abruptly appeared again. Only now they were reddish desert trees.

We set up our tent along a river in a small park in a desert of juniper and sage, and bedded down for the night. It was Wednesday, June 22, the summer solstice. As the earth slowly turned in the dark, Americans in one time zone after the next settled in front of their TVs, safe in their living rooms. They watched the CBS Wednesday-night movie, the world television premiere of a dark and unsettling Western, one of those edgy films made in the seventies that reflected the mood of national cynicism. It was a film complete with psychopaths and moral degeneracy, a new American mythology that turned the romantic version of the Old West on its head.

The sound of screeching tires woke me. It was near midnight, and we had just gone to sleep. A stranger deliberately drove over our tent, then attacked us both with an axe. I saw his torso. He was a meticulous cowboy who looked like he had stepped off a movie set.

My great voyage across America ended abruptly there. And that was how I reached young adulthood, with a certain knowledge of life at its farthest edges.

Its Long Life

I entered young adulthood with a story that cast a spell on me. The details of the attack and of how we managed to survive gave me a dramatic tale to tell. But to make a full accounting of this event and its aftershocks seemed for many years impossible. Could I ever apply meaning to what had long seemed a senseless act, one that happened without pattern or reason? Was there even a "why" to it?

It took fifteen years before I finally realized that a long-ago incident had transformed me, divided my life into a before and an after. My personal history bewildered me, but two questions kept surfacing. The first was elusive: How could I get the recurring dreams to stop, the ones that haunted me through the years—dreams in which I was captive at the age of twenty, unable to progress to another stage of life? What dislocation of spirit had arrested a part of my psyche?

The second question was easier to grasp: Who was the man who emerged that night in a desert park, bent on destruction? This question had but one simple answer: an individual with a name. A man with his own history—a past, a present, and, impossible to imagine, a future. Fifteen years had passed, and the crime had never been solved. Its reckoning was long overdue.

Both questions converged in a flashbulb image that struck deep into my memory: the headless torso of a fit, meticulous young cowboy suspending an axe over my heart. The image conjured for me a villain out of myth and legend.

I began an education in such mythic imagery early on, when for my fourth birthday I received a 3-D Viewmaster that came with a package of sample discs. I remember holding the Viewmaster to my eyes and clicking the button on its right side. I clicked my way through 3-D views of beautiful American landscapes and frames of iconic American imagery until I froze at one: a headless torso wearing a costume out of the Old West, a holster slung around his waist, his hand training a revolver on me, the viewer—which, in its startling three-dimensionality, forced me to stare down the gun's cold gray barrel.

The image stayed with me until that summer of '77, when I conflated in my mind what I remembered from my childhood toy, a cowboy torso trying to shoot me, and what I actually saw in the flesh. The memory of my attacker—that cowboy torso trying to axe me—crystallized at the margins of my consciousness as the nocturnal visitation of a villain out of legend.

It was the gripping power of this image that would compel me to set out to solve a crime—one that I hoped could solve me.

IN 1992, I RETURNED to the scene of the incident, a place in the Oregon desert called Cline Falls. The visit turned out to be catalytic. If my vision had before been blinded by the trauma of the attack, now I was keen to see. What was the panorama that surrounded me? What lay across the river and across the highway? Who else happened to be in Cline Falls Park that night? Who lived in the surrounding ranches, and in the town four miles away? Who were the souls of this rugged community of the American West: the courageous ones who rescued us that night? the passive ones who wouldn't speak up?

I took frequent journeys back to the scene of the crime over a period of several years, and the questions continued to unfold. Why did the community still remember an event from long ago as though it happened only yesterday, as if it were an open wound? Why did some tell me that the event had devastated them? Why were others indifferent? And what about the people who, I would discover, claimed they knew the identity of the attacker all those years?

Conversations were seldom journalistic interviews. Often they turned into infused encounters, my story forging an intimacy among strangers. People were, for their own reasons, eager to look through my eyes, and into what might have been my last moments—sometimes it was a far-out symbol of their own worst trauma, which if not life-threatening was at least soul-diminishing. They answered my questions; they made valiant attempts to resurrect the past; they helped me with my investigation, which they understood as my personal mission. When I met someone for the first time, I learned always to begin with the story.

I realized the tale I had to tell wasn't mine alone. The events of that long-ago summer night had driven deep into others in that desert community. Mine was not a solitary, isolated experience in one person's life. It was a collective experience, even for those who hadn't witnessed it. On some subterranean level it was as though they were waiting for me to return, to tap their potent remembrances, and by doing so to bring some kind of integration to a memory that never fit into any narrative they knew.

As I excavated my personal history over many years of returning to Oregon, questions kept arising, still more troubling questions that brought to the surface the violent and extreme in our culture. The first time around, America's dark underside found me. Later, I went looking for it. And it wasn't hard to find. Of all developed nations, America is especially violent. It is violent by habit. My 3-D Viewmaster warned me of this when I was just four years old.

But I also found the other extreme. John Steinbeck said it just right in *The Grapes of Wrath*, our archetypal tale about lost American dreams: strange things happen to people in America. Some bitterly cruel. And some so beautiful that faith is refired forever.

The First Years

Fifteen long years elapsed between the attack itself and my compulsion to investigate it. It was a period of dormancy—incubation for what was to come later.

At first, I wore my story like an odd appendage, a Siamese twin. It was surely affixed to me, too freaky to ignore, yet not incorporated in any way into the rest of my life. Instead of pursuing its deeper implications, I would trot out the pain in my past for dramatic purposes. The cicatrix that snaked around my left forearm mellowed from scarlet to rose, but it was still strikingly visible when I rolled up my shirtsleeves. "It's a perfect axe cut," I'd say to those bold enough to ask, explaining that the coil around my left forearm was not a surgical incision, but the precise tracing left by an axe-wielding maniac whom I encountered one night. I knew that few people would have an opportunity to view such a thing in their entire lives, and I wanted them to appreciate fully this door into the dark. Then I might be inspired to uncloak the whole collection of hidden scars: ridges in my right shoulder where the truck first struck my body—"tire treads etched into my skin," I would explain—and the knob in the middle of my collarbone where it had broken and healed, subtracting an inch and a half of chest span. Pulling up the bottom of my shirt, I would reveal a line of gentle bumps where the ribs had snapped in half.

There was nothing in my appearance to say "victim." The contrast between my bright, open face without a blemish and the concealed scars made for great mystery. I could keep my picturesque scars hidden. Or raise a curtain on them as I wished. They were great show-and-tell, visual aids for "The Story" of just how they had arrived on my body.

The story was both my grand disclosure and my secret. I had no qualms about blurting it out to strangers. But I was more secretive with new friends. For them, my narration was an initiation. I withheld it sometimes for months, until new friends turned into good friends—then I'd pop the story on them, suggesting that I was infinitely more complex than they had ever imagined. I formed bonds according to how they reacted. A particular empathy or fascination might mean a lifelong friendship, or even a love affair. I'd form a special rapport—it seemed a predestined friendship—if someone remembered the incident from the media attention it got in 1977, as it was reported in newspapers across the country and broadcast by Walter Cronkite himself, a fact I didn't mind noting. I knew I had a good tale, but I didn't understand precisely what listeners found compelling other than the obvious sensational details, nor did I have the insight to comprehend my nagging compulsion to tell it.

In the early years, I narrated my story with great levity, punctuating the recitation with laughter, a breezy chirp in my voice. I didn't catch on that it was not only the tale itself but also my way of telling it that left my listeners with queer scrutinizing expressions on their faces. As I progressed through the cheerful beats of my narrow escape, I got to the part where I described the condition the axeman had left me in: I had no movable arms. I described myself, with those silly, useless arms that wouldn't do what I asked them to do, as a "scarecrow." I even would picture Ray Bolger singing and dancing.

IN HINDSIGHT, I can see that the dispassionate way I told the story (and the scarecrow image) was, in the therapeutic idiom, a dissociative numbing similar to how some war veterans I'd heard about would spin their battle stories—but it was also a metaphor offered up from the deep folds of the psyche. I had split into two distinctly separate selves that summer night in June 1977.

There was the official self: the bright and independent woman right out of Yale, an aspiring artist in New York City, coming of age with the rest of her baby-boom peers, playing at being hip, trying to develop social poise, personal charm and style, and striving with ambiguous direction to fulfill that singularly twenty-something desire to make something of herself overnight. True, my upper body was torqued, concave; my breathing was fast and shallow from bearing the weight of an invisible truck; my right shoulder curled forward, and my right arm was so stiff I couldn't grasp the loops that hung from the ceilings of the subway cars I took each day. And I would freeze while crossing city streets if a car came on too fast. Still, I fancied myself no different from the rest of my ambitious peers, and I tripped about the metropolis day and night thinking that this shining city, with its canyons of tall buildings that glittered with sun by day and then turned black and mysterious by night, where one had the sense that marvelous life-altering events might happen at any moment, held all the promise befitting my destiny.

But there was also a scarecrow self—an unacknowledged, angry, aggrieved shadow, who lived in a scarecrow body. It was plotting from the beginning to sabotage the other self. That took a long time. But, meanwhile, she was sending messages in a bottle.

The way a psyche tries to make sense of things, the way it tries to stitch itself back together after a violent criminal attack is as unique as a fingerprint or a crystal structure. This other creature spoke an odd language—an encrypted language of unconscious knowledge, calling out to be recognized:

She must be the one who scrawled a mysterious reference in my daily calendar for 1980, on the day of July 24. *Murder in the Met*, she wrote. Today, I only vaguely remember what this news story referred to. A young ballerina ambushed by a malevolent janitor backstage after hours? It's a strange reference in this calendar, which otherwise is filled with notations of every lunch, brunch, and dinner date, every book read and movie seen, every incident that might possibly be relevant to a young artist in New York City in the early 1980s. But it is surely there: *Murder in the Met*, scribbled next to the notation about my having taken in the Picasso exhibit at MOMA.

Certainly it was this exiled self who, after I wrote an article for a magazine about the mysterious death of a model who fell from the window of a fashion photographer's loft, decided to enter only one line in my journal about the incident, a quote from the girl's autopsy report: *The entire body is covered with a thin film of black dirt.* She was also the one who jotted, in the midst of other journal entries about my various attempts at dating, an isolated reference, apparently apropos of nothing: *The smell of my blood-encrusted body.*

Some motivation from this unknown district of the mind, from the porous unconscious, inspired me to perform the curious ritual of rummaging through the closet of my Brooklyn brownstone apartment looking for a bag stashed there. I would yank the fabric out of the sack until it unfurled on my living room floor: the mummy sleeping bag, the same one that three years before, when the police gave it back to me, I had instructed my father to wash in a Laundromat, so that the surf of pink suds slapping against the round glass porthole of the washing machine might restore it to a usable condition. I'd search the bag's silky interior to find all that was left of the blood—a few dark stains only I could identify. I wished there were more of them, and bigger. What might be repellent to most— were there others who would save the very sleeping bag they were almost murdered in?—was oddly satisfying to me. I wasn't afraid of the blood. I had developed an overnight fearlessness about blood. Reconnecting with it filled me with a contentment I couldn't comprehend then and didn't question. Blood was no longer "gore" to me. It was life itself. I would hold the fabric to my nose and try to recall the singular smell—like copper pennies held in a damp palm.

During the same era, I kept a clipping file labeled VIOLENCE, in which I collected stories about those who, unlike me, didn't live to tell the tale: my college classmate whom I met only once, Sarai Ribicoff, a young journalist, pictured in *Newsweek* under a body blanket just after she was murdered outside a Venice, California, restaurant; a young actress mutilated and raped on the roof of a New York City apartment building, her body found beside a *Playbill*; a waiter, Richard

Adan, stabbed to death outside a Lower East Side restaurant (while I was asleep in an apartment just blocks away) by convicted killer Jack Abbott, who so charmed Norman Mailer with his jailhouse scrawlings that Mailer had lobbied to spring him from prison just weeks before the crime; "Princess Doe," a teenage girl found beaten to death in a creek bed and buried by a small New Jersey community as a symbol of "the death of all youth"; various news clippings of people murdered with axes.

I also was fixated on the ten-speed bicycle I'd kept, along with the mummy sleeping bag, from the storied bicycle trip. I compulsively took it apart and re-assembled it, and named it the Bicycle of Doom. It was this bicycle's dark affinities, my shadow self believed, that encouraged whispers from the unconscious, instructing me to take off for a location unknown to my rational mind and landing me at the scene of other people's untimely tragedies. It was not a coincidence, I believed, that one day I was seized with the inspiration to drop whatever I was doing, hop on the saddle, and head off toward the Brooklyn Bridge, where just before I arrived a cable had snapped and killed a tourist. My bicycle, I believed—if I got up close to its battered frame and leather seat—still bore a smell like blood.

I actually have a photograph of this second self, the estranged angel with the dark obsessions. She appears in my passport picture taken in 1982. I don't remember what triggered her appearance, but this other, more troubled twin revealed herself to the camera one day in a photo studio in Brooklyn. White heat radiating from pale skin on my high forehead, peaked brows knitted into a scowl, bulges between my eyes, nostrils flared, my thick lips forming a half smile—any impartial person would have thought this young woman had it on her mind to do someone in.

Though I kept up a disguise of "normalcy" as well as I could, the persona was cracking. The other self in its various guises was making ever more frequent appearances. One moment, I was all swaggering manic energy—gesticulating, smiling, flirting, cracking a joke—filled with buoyant enthusiasm. In an instant, I was cut off. Brooding or totally blank. Drained of life.

A soundman on a film crew I was working on knew me only a few days when he gave me the deepest image I have of the split self of that era.

He said, "Terri, you look like the puppeteer just left."

I wasn't fully inhabiting my body. Maybe you could say part of my soul fled into the desert that night back in June 1977, fled the instant the truck struck my chest; maybe you could say it abandoned my fragile, mortal body, and it hadn't yet climbed back in.

THEN THE WHISPERS of the second self got more persistent than the curious notations that turned up in my journal. The cryptic messages tore off their mask and presented themselves for what they really were: terror.

One might expect a girl who found herself under an axe to feel plenty of terror right away. But I had lived through the seemingly unsurvivable, and in the first years following the attack I imagined myself impervious to destruction: airtight, watertight, weather-stripped, puncture-proof, bulletproof, flameproof . . . in a word, immortal.

But reactions to trauma change shape with the passage of years. The fears began imperceptibly, almost comically. I looked around and perceived that danger might be lurking in what appeared, on the surface, to be completely benign. I decided that something as seemingly innocuous as polyester fabric sort of scared me—as though, if you were wearing it and came too close to a match, you'd end up a fuse. Ordinary fly zappers, with their eerie columns of neon blue light, seemed especially sinister. One hung from a porch where I was chatting one day, and I couldn't hear what was being said because my ear was cocked to the buzzing zaps at slightly irregular intervals, signaling the sudden and random annihilation of a fly.

Some part of me at the edges of consciousness had lost trust in the order of things. The facts of the world broke faith with me. I was no longer deceived that life was following a script in which certain things would never happen.

Evidence of this truth turned up in the newspaper one day: the story of a boy on vacation in Yellowstone Park who walked onto a dock to view the geyser pools. When a vapor kicked up, obscuring his vision, he stumbled into the water. By the time they fished him out—a matter of minutes—his bones were boiled clean. This last detail really made an impression on me—that something so out-of-the-world horrific could happen on vacation in one of America's glorious national treasures like Yellowstone. It reminded me of the time years before, months after the press had made me notorious on my college campus, when, at lunch one day, I overheard one student whispering to another: *Isn't she the girl who got mauled by a bear in Yellowstone?*

I might as well have been the girl who got mauled by a bear in Yellowstone. I was fixated only on the *randomness* of how we all could be taken out—the "accidental" aspect of the incidents of fate, that something you could never invent in a fiction if you were plotting your own fate could happen from nothing and nowhere, even in the places that seemed most innocent.

The exact instrument of fate—geyser pool, bear, murderous psychopath—seemed beside the point. But then I stopped circling around generalized notions of tragic destinies and realized why some part of me had lost faith in the order of things—because a malignant human being could bring on the startling eruption that ends your life as you know it: somebody might even want to kill you.

Concrete data began to accrue. Living in dicey New York City in the 1980s meant the likelihood of crossing paths with someone who might not have your best interests in mind: I was mugged by three young men in Brooklyn who surrounded me one evening, said they had a gun, and demanded my wallet, which I handed over without further incident. But I spent the next two days in terror of a greater magnitude than my friends had experienced from their muggings. And what my female friends considered typical harassment—young studs making hissing sounds as women passed them on the street—didn't just annoy me; it sent a primal chill down my spine, inspiring an atavistic instinct that annihilation might result from this hiss, as from a rattle you hear in the grass. When a bullet careened through a window of the Brooklyn Public Library and whizzed past my eyeballs, in front of the table where I was quietly reading, I was actually surprised that the bullet didn't have my name on it.

By the end of my twenties, I began to notice something. I was no longer certain of myself as a young woman for whom the lights would always turn green. I was mysteriously debilitated. My concentration was dispersed. My personal will, once strong and focused, flapped back and forth, easily deflected. My breathing was shallow and erratic. In one journal entry, I described my body, with its inconvenient indentations left by truck and hatchet, as "trampled grass that had lost its spring." In another entry, I described "a sense of being always on the edge—of what? Death?" Before I was twenty, I had never been concerned about my physical well-being. But closeness to death had left its mark. My mother lived half a continent away from me, but that didn't stop me from calling her in a panic whenever I had the slightest ailment, for each seemed to threaten my very survival.

A flicker of self-knowledge told me I needed repair, though I couldn't, or wouldn't, specifically attribute the damage—symptoms I understood only obscurely—to the violence I had endured at age twenty. No one in my circle could understand my misplaced stoicism. Friends, even acquaintances, who watched my curiously distraught behavior told me they worried about me, asked me how I was coping—and for a long time I didn't know there was any coping to do, other than to deal with the usual stuff of life, which wasn't too tough. Mercifully, I had been spared other deep traumas: serious illness and the death of loved ones hadn't touched me at all. Because I could lower the curtains on my scars, they were easy to forget. I ignored the task of coming to understand how one violent event might have diverted me. For several years no one thing happened to make me touch bottom. I didn't sink into the oblivion of drugs or alcohol. Not once did I pop a Valium. I never had what others vaguely referred to as a "nervous breakdown," to describe their susceptibility to life's dazzling array of turmoil.

But fear had fused with flesh. The exquisite responsiveness of my stress hormones made me susceptible to even small frights. I entered a new phase of living my life with tremendous caution. It seemed to me that it was a great risk to inhabit a body. Often I felt flashes of panic just to find myself encased in one. It was like those moments everyone has while careening down a five-lane freeway—that instant when you wake up to the certainty that barreling at high speed in a skin of metal, at the mercy of the strangers around you, can't be anything but perilous to tissue and bone.

Once, some time around the age of thirty, I did the math: seventy percent of my energy, I wagered, went to worrying about the omnipresent threats, anticipating how to protect myself from them—which, of course, was impossible, as I couldn't script their arrival. To withstand the adrenaline charge that accompanied the anxiety, I doped myself with sleep. My life swung between heart-pounding panic and deep drowse on the couch. Sleep, sleep, sleep—as though I were living in a fairy tale in which a witch had placed a spell on me.

BY MY MID-THIRTIES, the fever had broken, and I was no longer so frightened. I evaluated the planet's dangers like "normal" people—in other words, I was in denial.

Maybe I couldn't feel the fear because it had frozen me solid. Repetitive dreams were a staple of my night life: Walking on ice, I could get no forward traction. I screamed but found myself mute. I was stuck at the age of twenty, unable to leave that stage of life. There would be nothing but college, forever. Nothing but living in dormitories or off-campus housing, taking endless classes I would never complete, studying lessons I couldn't learn. There could be no graduation. There would be no future.

In these dreams, my own classmates had moved on, and I was still twenty. I looked into the fresh faces of the new twenty-year-olds, and there was no face I recognized. The new twenty-year-olds found no kinship with me, and left me to eat alone in the dining hall, because though I was twenty, I was an old, old twenty.

Once, in real life, when I still lived in New York City, I took a train to New Haven, Connecticut, and trod the college campus where I had spent most of my twentieth year. I stood in front of Freshman Commons and muttered some incantations, asking that the dreams stop. As I headed back to the station, I happened to catch sight of a postcard on a student housing bulletin board. Someone deep in my psyche, someone who wanted housing on campus because she needed to reside there a very long time—in fact for all eternity—scrutinized that postcard to see if there were anyplace she might want to live. I was fully awake but had to rouse myself as though from a dream, to remind myself that I lived in New York City and had for almost a decade. The dreams didn't stop after that. They only gathered urgency until I knew that it was time to return.

Part Two

Anthropologist Godfrey Lienhardt describes the animistic understanding of the Dinka tribe in the Sudan. A Dinka believes his own memories and daydreams to be external to himself, as external as the hills, and quick with substance. A man who was imprisoned in Khartoum named his infant daughter Khartoum in order to placate Khartoum, which seized him from time to time vividly. He believed that as he walked about his village, Khartoum itself, the city with its prison, overwhelmed him with the force of its presence.

—ANNIE DILLARD, *THE WRITING LIFE*

Escape from the Dead Zone

How red the Fire rocks below—
How insecure the sod

—EMILY DICKINSON

I yanked from the garage a cardboard box filled with memorabilia. I pawed through the stuff, which exuded a musty odor. But more than that, it all bore the scent of sadness: the get-well cards from friends, newspaper clippings carrying banner headlines like HUNT AXE ATTACKER OF SUBURBAN COED; the few items of camping gear that I'd saved, like a fluorescent orange handlebar pack, the tiny camp stove, and the aluminum mess kit in which I'd cooked what was nearly my last supper.

I had reduced my somber reliquary in 1990 when I moved from New York to California at the age of thirty-three, and I regretted it now. I had divested myself of the bloodstained mummy sleeping bag. I sent it on to its next life by ditching it in a plastic garbage bag and heaping it in the alley. Then I posted an ad in the neighborhood deli to sell the Bicycle of Doom. I remembered the day a woman of about my age arrived to look at it. I wheeled the battered red-and-white ten-speed out of the closet (so that I might preserve one keepsake from the bicycle, I had removed its old leather saddle). She paid me forty bucks, and as she wheeled it away, I felt guilty. I considered that I was doing a very bad thing, a downright immoral thing, passing on, with no disclosure, this object of weighty provenance.

Sleeping bag and bicycle were gone forever, but I had very consciously preserved the flashlight I'd saved my life with. Now I opened the bag that contained it. The flashlight especially emanated a scent of something strong. I fit my hand around the plastic handle, deformed after melting on a hot radiator in my New York City apartment. The flashlight's associations connected me to a trace of a wild, rushing emotion, which disturbed me. I quickly put the flashlight back into its plastic bag and tied it up tight.

Something about the contents of the cardboard box, all these items with their charged memories, cooking for fifteen years, mingling their juices, brought to mind something my father told me about Abraham Lincoln when I was a child. He read somewhere that the corpse of this poet and president, whose deepest desire was to keep the Union together, was exhumed several decades after his death. An American flag had been draped on his face, and the dyes of the flag, stripes of red and white, had stained his skin. The contents of my box had mingled a bit like that: they had congealed into a tangy essence of that night in 1977. I couldn't face up to looking through the artifacts thoroughly. The box lay in the middle of my living room for weeks, untouched. All traffic had to move around it. The disinterment could proceed only a little at a time. But the glacial emotions that had surrounded the attack for years began to thaw.

It was the summer of 1992, and I was trying to think up stories for movies that might touch people. But no story I could imagine had any guts or soul whatsoever, let alone any authenticity. Mostly what was missing was an attitude of compassion, an author's tenderness for her characters and their fates. Then one day an old idea resurfaced. An idea shot through my head so electrifying that the fog in my mind dissolved and the bougainvillea outside the window turned a vibrating color of pink I could describe only as hallucinogenic. It was a kind of seizure: I would write my own story.

I had a sudden insight that maybe my creative dry spell had a deeper-lying cause. Some shadowy part of me had choked off the pipeline to the fertile unconscious so that only this one story could sluice through. Maybe I could never tell another story until I had told this one. Unless I could purge this one impelling piece of psychic business, my own guts, my heart, would be locked away forever. This story, one that *only* I could tell, was the *only* story that could . . . what? Rescue, redeem, resurrect, restore me? Mining the past for what it might yield, I hoped, could be a recipe for repair.

Not only would I write about my misadventures one night fifteen years before, I would also embark on an odyssey into the western American desert where the incident took place. This journey would traverse the earth as well as the mind, and in so doing, would stitch my past into my present life. It was a heady idea.

I TALKED TO my mother. It was an interview of sorts, the first of several we'd have over the course of the summer, now that we both lived in the West. Through the years, we had spoken openly about the event. It wasn't something we pushed away, denied, pretended hadn't happened. But I'd never wrapped my mind around what the experience might have been for her; it had never even occurred to me to try. I had no children of my own. How could I comprehend what it was to know intimately the vulnerability of your child, and to lose control of her until she returned to you in the aftermath of her decisions, to salve ruptured flesh and mend broken bones?

"It never leaves your mind, really," she said.

That I could understand. The event had been running in a loop just underneath the surface of my awareness for fifteen years.

She remembered as if it were yesterday when she and my dad first arrived at the hospital in Oregon, walked into intensive care, and saw me lying there, "all banged up," as she described me.

"And you said to us, 'You didn't *both* have to come!'—as though you thought it was crazy we came at all! Then you said, 'Give me your hand.' "

"I asked you to take my hand?"

"Yes, and that was so unlike you and me, you know." I knew it was. I'd guessed I hadn't held my mother's hand beyond the age of ten.

"I did, huh?"

"You did . . . you held out your hand, and I remember it was all dirty and you had blood under your fingernails."

Blood under my fingernails. It came as a revelation that my mother was a historic archive of details I was suddenly hungry for. I could feel pressure around my heart.

"That night, I went back to my hotel room and cried." Her usually strong voice was drained of energy. "Oh, how close that was. But we got through it, didn't we? Somehow. Some way."

Then she turned the heat back on me: "But you never had any interest in wanting to look into what happened. Way back then, I always wondered why you never cared. I always told your father we should pursue this. But he didn't stay with it. It bothered me that we weren't taking an interest in it." It was so like my mother not to take action on her preternatural powers of intuition. "Why has it taken you fifteen years to want to go back? Why now?" she asked.

Why now? I had no answer at hand. True, from the outset I was downright apathetic about wanting to know the larger story around my attack in Oregon in 1977. When I related the events of that period, a mental density always thickened around what I considered an insignificant detail: "Well? What happened to the guy?" my listeners unfailingly wanted to know. I'd tell them as an afterthought, "Oh, they never caught him."

It was remarkable: for all the fears I had developed in my adult life, the agent of this incident, the germ of it all, inspired no fear at all. It had always seemed to me that this headless horseman from Cline Falls was just some kind of "force" out there—no life, no soul, no past, no future—a phantom energy that I wrestled with on a cool June night in the desert of Oregon.

I found a page from an old 1980 notebook where I had scrawled, *He looked like a Wrangler jean torso. Shirt neatly tucked.*

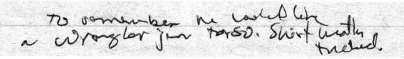

That piece of concrete evidence, a journal entry from as early as 1980, validated the flashbulb memory I had preserved since 1977—of the meticulous cowboy torso, his body so specific in recall that his headlessness seemed almost unimportant. Now I would at last begin to speculate: *Who did it? Who was this axeman?*

MY NEIGHBOR Mary came by one day, and I told her about my upcoming trip to Oregon. "That was you!" She'd remembered the event vividly from fifteen years before, as she lived in Northern California at the time, just over the Oregon border.

"I just remember really identifying with the girl with the broken arm that had been cut up with an axe . . . it was a really powerful image. I felt such rage." And I wondered as she spoke: Why has this woman, whom I've only recently met, carried the rage about my broken body all these years when I myself couldn't access it?

Where was the outrage I might have felt because the perpetrator of the crime had escaped judgment? When it came to the axeman, I blanked. I knew there was meaning in the absence, and I would have to discover it. Logically, I might expect the rage actually was so white-hot that it obliterated any picture of itself.

How could I access the rage? The first requirement, it seemed to me, was to come face-to-face with the instrument of torture, to look squarely at its cutting edge. I sought out the tool department in a Hollywood hardware store and picked out a handsome axe with a long blond-wood handle and a shiny red blade. A salesman told me he didn't know its price, so he'd give me a really good deal.

"I deserve it," I said.

"I'm sure you do." He smiled. I smiled back. And by the way, he asked, why was I shopping for an axe? I told him I was going on an adventure to Oregon. He didn't note that my answer didn't quite follow, and he said, "Oh, you've gotta go to Bend, Oregon! Up there, it's killer hiking, killer fishing, killer skiing . . ."

Bend, Oregon, happened to be just miles down the road from the crime scene itself, and was the location of the hospital that pieced me back together again. In my mind, Bend was synonymous with the attack.

"Killer camping?" I asked brightly.

"Yeah, killer camping!" he said, playing along with a joke he was unaware of. I assured him I'd check it out.

I left the store with my axe and headed over to a Clinton-Gore campaign stand. One bystander saw me and immediately broke into song: "Lizzie Borden took an axe. Gave her mother forty whacks! When she saw what she had done, she gave her father forty-one!"

Another bystander asked me, "Are you an axe murderess?"

"Yes," I said, collecting my campaign pin.

As if that weren't enough, farther down the mall, I passed a guy who shouted at me, "Hey, you gotta see the movie *Killing in a Small Town*!"

"What's that about?"

"An axe murderess who chops up her husband's girlfriend!"

I hollered back that I would check it out, for sure.

I was astounded by the popularity of my axe. I held it at my side in the parking garage, and two women grimaced at me. Finally, I concealed it in my trunk.

I once read about an African woman who danced in her father's military uniform to exorcise his malignant influence over her. In that same spirit—of inhabiting the fear in order to tame and control it—I began to collect many axes over the next few years. As I wore the precise imprint of the implement on my arm, its influence was unmistakable; so in order to free myself of its dominion, I figured I must flaunt it. I combed flea markets and garage sales for any handsome axe or hatchet I could find. A stash accumulated in my house and in the trunk of my car. Once, I actually needed to use the first red-bladed axe to cut wood, and couldn't find it anywhere. Later I found out that when my mother had come to visit she was horrified to find it on display in my house, and she'd hidden it under my front porch. The pathos of a mother's experience of her daughter's ordeal in Oregon came thunderously home to me as I fixed the image in my mind of Mom laying eyes on that axe in my living room and spiriting it away without saying a word to me.

"WHAT DO YOU MEAN, the files have been purged! I can't believe you'd throw out the files on a case like this. This was a major event in Oregon fifteen years ago. I was nearly murdered!"

"But you weren't murdered."

"So you're telling me, if I were dead, you'd still have the files?"

That's what she was telling me.

I had screwed up my courage to phone the Deschutes County, Oregon, District Attorney's Office to locate any existing police records, and found myself on the line with the Victims' Assistance program, talking to a haughty young woman who had little appreciation for my mission.

"Look. This was a heinous, gruesome, unbelievably horrific crime. I really think the files must exist somewhere—"

She cut me off and asked in a tart, disparaging voice, "Was this a rape or something?"—as though plain old ordinary rapes are a dime a dozen around here, honey.

This dismissive young voice—female at that—made my hackles rise. I boomed through the receiver, cutting to the quick: "No, it was not a rape. A man chopped me up with an axe."

Without another syllable, the younger woman handed the phone to a polite older woman with a reassuring deep voice. She listened patiently and then said, "Hopefully we can find these records and *put this to rest.*"

I got a call back the next day. The older woman had figured out which police agency in Oregon handled the case and had located the allegedly destroyed police reports. The case was closed. Therefore, I was welcome to pick up the reports any weekday from the Records Department of the Oregon State Police, in Salem.

I'D CAST MY LINE; the hook had sunk in deep waters and was now irretrievable. Police records awaited me in Oregon, a straight shot up Interstate 5, one thousand miles north of my home. This prospect staggered me: I would return to that particular place for the very first time since I was taken out of there on a stretcher. I never thought I would, not until the very moment the idea arose in my glowing brain.

Oregon seemed an infinitely faraway place—hardly a place on the geographical earth—because for fifteen years it had existed only in brilliant memory drenched in explosive associations.

Maybe my second self, the dark double, was responsible for the abrupt emotional decision to pack up my New York life in an old Volvo and drive clear across the country to the western seaboard, where I would live within driving distance of those old police files. Maybe my recent move to California was meant to provide a launching pad for Oregon; surely I would never have sought out those police files if I had stayed in New York. Maybe this was the whole point: to move to the Ring of Fire, land of earthquakes and volcanoes, where the landscape's violence constantly unsettles the status quo; where change is forced upon you by the earth's plates careening around on the liquid magma, the Pacific plate relentlessly pushing north and forcing itself under the North American plate, so that, willing or not, I would move closer to Oregon by inches every year.

I studied myself in the mirror and tried to hold in one steady glance all the parts of my life. The self I had been at twenty: a chubby girl with a round face, no cheekbones yet visible, with long, stringy hair parted in the middle. An edgy, assertive young woman, heart sealed away under quite a lot of female adolescent anger, but whose strong will was fully intact.

And the self reflected back in the mirror: at thirty-five, I seemed milder than when I was twenty. My edges were tempered, I supposed, because I had learned to access my heart. I had a streak of silver hair that I was especially proud of, a silver shock that in my early twenties grew from a scar in my hairline. It literally sprang from one of the blows—or so it seemed—and I liked that. I thought it gave me a kind of halo, and I had a secret pride in thinking that I was lit by some divine source derived from adversity.

I held my skinny left arm in front of the mirror to view the entire length of the smooth scar. Faded now from rose to white, it wound around the landscape of my forearm like a meandering river. I was fond of this scar. Because after the years when my will was afflicted, when I couldn't fulfill the promises I'd made to myself, when at times I couldn't defend my own integrity, it reminded me of a night when my will was potent, when it orchestrated precise action guided by compassion.

I placed a battered Fleetwood Mac record on the turntable and dropped the needle. The band's *Rumours* album was number one on the airwaves for all of 1977, and certain passionate songs that sprang from the band's personal torments had so fused with my past that a single note could conjure the events of June 22 in a multisensory flood. I sprawled on the couch and stared at the ceiling. Instead of trying to push the memory out of my head, I tried to get it back in my head, remembering that time as life in the extreme, emotion pushed to a fierce maximum: acts of will, acts of love, and a privileged glimpse of life near the edge of death.

I tried to recall the visual contours of that landscape, the spooky desert oasis by the river where we camped one night. Then the memory of that most elusive emotional sense: the smell of the resin from a western juniper tree and how, that night, the sharp scent of juniper resin mingled with the scent of blood. The string of those associations brought a tactile memory, and it had to do with Shayna. I had never stopped dwelling on the friend and college roommate with whom I had set out to cross America on bicycle. Our mutual calamity had pulled us apart long ago, and I had no idea where she was or what she was doing. It was she who came to mind during those times when I tried to confront the consequences of that night. I had long ago suppressed any compassion I might have felt for what I myself had endured. But when I thought of Shayna's injuries, my sorrow was arterial, a dull heartache as accessible as my pulse. My fingers still felt her head wound. It wasn't a visual memory, because I never saw it; I only touched it, and that fingertip remembrance was more vivid than anything my eyes could have reported. I felt her wound as a kind of Braille. It was, ironically, the closest I'd ever come to knowing how the blind perceive.

Shayna was a key figure in the recurring dreams in which I could never escape the age of twenty. In those dreams, she, too, was a captive at that tender age. And in our mutual entrapment was a message—something unresolved about the role she played in my life's story, some yearning I had to reckon with. What would I need from her now, to calm the restless layers of my psyche?

The past arose before my eyes: I pictured two girls on bikes, alone on a highway in the lonesome desert, one wearing a gold T-shirt with the word ORYGUN emblazoned across the front, the other in an identical red T-shirt. I tried to replay the beats in the story that led us down that road. I had no trouble conjuring the girl I was at nineteen going on twenty. Those months leading up to the events of the summer of '77 were branded in my memory with a bright ferocity.

Bright College Years

... How bright will seem
Through mem'ry's haze
Those happy, golden bygone days.

—OLD YALE SONG

Fluorescent lights glared in my eyes. I
was trying to get some sleep, but the room wasn't designed for comfort. It was
3:30 a.m., and I was lying on a table in a study room in the bowels of my dormitory—my psychology paper on "Cognitive Schemas" due in precisely five and a
half hours, into which I had yet to fit a couple of days' worth of hard thinking. After fifteen minutes of dubious rest, I hunkered over my manual typewriter again.
I drained my cup of tea, stuck the tea bag into my mouth, chewed it until it lique-
fied into a cud, and swallowed the tea leaves and a bit of the paper whole. I had to
keep my mind large and alert until I laid a stack of pages on my professor's desk
at 9:00 a.m.

As fluorescence dissolved to daylight and muffled sounds from the dining hall
signaled that breakfast was being served, I finished the final page. I didn't have a
clue about what I'd written on the last three pages. I'd simply let my brain take off
on its own to create lofty intellectualizations I myself didn't fully understand but
that I hoped could be decoded by a professor who would grant me an A, because
getting a B would shatter my ego. I clipped the pages together and shoved them
into my backpack, climbed to the attic of the dormitory library, crawled through
a trapdoor, and hoisted myself onto the roof.

A tall, broad-shouldered girl whose recognizably Anglo-Saxon features were
padded with baby fat, I was wearing white painter's pants, a blue work shirt, socks
dyed pink in the laundry, and a bandanna that lent a semblance of order to my
stringy hair. I looked out with bloodshot eyes at the Yale campus that spread
nearly to the distant rocky bluffs. Bells tolled from a neo-medieval confection
called Harkness Tower; scads of ivy smothered the buildings—Gothic spires,
Colonial red brick and shutters—now enlivened with blooming wisteria and dog-
wood. The campus appeared from above like a knitting sampler of the last six

centuries of architecture. No doubt about it, I thought to myself, these towers of the Ivy League were impressive, and I felt special to be standing among them. But however much I might love the aesthetics of the place, I had little in common with the provenance of this American makeover of Cambridge and Oxford—its flagstone walkways still populated with the ghosts of rich and entitled Protestant white boys in Brooks Brothers suits.

The upheavals of the 1960s—the civil rights movement, the Vietnam War protests, and the sexual revolution—had convulsed Yale, like the nation in microcosm, and brought about the most radical changes in the university's history. I indirectly owed my admittance to this esteemed institution to the women's movement, which was brought about by a fairly small group of impassioned, mostly young women who, in an astonishingly short period of time between 1968 and 1975, radically changed the landscape for the mass of women in America. By the fall of 1975, my freshman year, the women's liberation movement was at its height. The Equal Rights Amendment seemed destined to pass. My classmates and I took completely for granted the emancipation our elder sisters had won for us. The campus pathways were now filled with women clattering with hasty steps in their blocky Frye boots and clogs toward early classes. They were a resilient pack of pioneering spirits to have launched themselves into Yale, these women of every class, race, and ethnicity who scrawled cryptic messages to one another on the toilet stalls: GROW UP, YOU NEUROTIC, SELF-CENTERED, IMMATURE YALIES. I THINK YOU ALL ARE A BUNCH OF FASHIONABLY LIBERAL BITCHES WHO DON'T KNOW WHAT THE SHIT YOU ARE TALKING ABOUT OR WHO YOU ARE.

Even so, by 1975, women had been at Yale only since 1969, a mere six years in the life of a university founded in 1701. Yale was still an entrenched male playground in the scale of giants, where reading rooms were lined with immense oak tables at which generations of analytical masculine minds had studied (I had only to spread my books out over their gently worn, polished oak expanses, and my wild, chaotic brain seemed to organize itself into neat little grids); where the gloomy stone gymnasium built in the architectural vernacular of the witch-burning era required that I drag myself up endless flights of dungeon steps to get to my infrequent workouts, as square-jawed flowers of manhood bounded past me four stairs at a time; where secret societies of men, called forbidding names like "Skull and Bones" and "Wolf's Head," hid out in windowless tombs on campus, concealing arcane rituals from the eyes of women; where all-male singing groups like the Whiffenpoofs put male bonding to music.

At nineteen, a sophomore at the end of spring term, I stood alone on the rooftop, something I did often, because the bird's-eye perspective on the esteemed institution that was spread out before me gave me a feeling of conquest over a place with which I was already out of sync. In truth, it had gotten the better of me. After only a couple of years, I was plotting to take a break.

The chiseled bluffs on the horizon were blurred with spring green, and that meant freedom. It was April, and soon I would be heading into a greater, more magnificent horizon than anything that Connecticut could serve up: I was heading to the Far West.

WHEN I FIRST arrived in New Haven in the fall of 1975, I could not have imagined I might later want to escape this Eastern bastion of privilege by hopping on a bicycle and pedaling through long stretches of western desert. As a young girl in the Middle West, I had strived to get out of the sticks and into the urbane power centers of the East. From a humble family farming the Great Plains, I had no pedigree to live up to—no doctors or lawyers, no industrialists or professors in my background, no one with much wealth. I wanted to do what no one in my family had ever done. I was hooked on the American aristocracy, and I set my sights on the Ivy League because of Caroline Kennedy. She was my age and my idol. At fourteen, I headed to the local library with the mission of researching every magazine article ever written about her. As I studied her freckled face framed by a headband, I decided that surely Caroline would be the sort of girl to continue her patrilineage and attend Harvard. A singular resolve built inside me: however slim the odds, she would see me there. From that moment, I corralled my manic, restless energies into creating the teen résumé that would land me in an elite school, and I began the process of introducing my father to the idea that, a few years up the road, he might have to invest his small inheritance in an astronomical college tuition. I felt no pangs of conscience doing this. I knew the man well enough; this voracious reader sought every spare moment to bury himself in weighty novels and histories. He would surely embrace this chance for his daughter to get the ultimate classical education. By the time I actually applied to colleges, three years later, thoughts of Caroline had fallen away, and New Haven had replaced Cambridge on my wish list. I knew for sure I had no interest in a "girls' school." I wanted to tough it out with the boys.

As soon as I reached the Ivy, I sanded off my Midwestern vowels. College is the classic ground to reinvent the self, its culture a feeding frenzy of new possibilities. I costumed myself in an arty antique-black woolen cape, which snapped in the brisk New Haven air as I whirled across campus, meeting for dinner or a play or a concert this or that new friend. I was popular in a way I had never been among the anti-intellectual jocks of my suburban high school; I was finally among peers who appreciated my edgy, sardonic self. I wrote home to my parents on Yale letterhead illustrated with an etching of Harkness Tower: *I love this place! Wild horses couldn't drag me away!* My mother wrote back: *I sent you some tea bags. Please don't eat them!*

IT WAS MY first day at Yale when I met Shayna. "I'm Shayna," she said, unaffected and friendly, with a winsome smile, flashing perfect white teeth.

"S-h-a-y-n-a." She spelled her name for me, assuming correctly that it was more exotic than anything that had heretofore reached my midwestern ears. We stood in the hallway outside the suite of rooms where we had just unpacked the possessions we thought might help us in our transition from childhood. For me that meant my typewriter, bicycle, thirty-five-millimeter camera, and Rolleiflex, together with a mandolin and a zither I didn't play. I noticed that Shayna had a guitar and a few Joan Baez songbooks.

Shayna and I both had been assigned to Silliman College, one of twelve colleges that divided the university into intimate communities. We lived in adjoining quads, four girls to a suite of rooms on the same floor in one of the many vertical entryways in the Georgian-style college. This architectural design was intended to foster intimacy among floormates, which would lead to the mythic Yale friendships for which the institution was known. Shayna and her bunkmate, Ellen, slept in a suite identical to mine, through a fire door labeled EMERGENCY in red letters.

Shayna was pretty in a way that some girls, especially bookish ones, are pretty at eighteen: utterly modest, unself-conscious, with no inkling of the power they hold over others. She had shining dark eyes, smooth olive skin that makeup had never touched, fleshy cheeks as pinchable as a child's, and dark shoulder-length hair, straight and glossy, pulled off her face with a simple bobby pin. She walked with a sway of her hips that was as sensuously alluring as it was completely uncontrived.

My life to that point had been filled with big, blondish Germans and Scandinavians, and Shayna's looks were as exotic to me as her name. Small and girlish in her smock, corduroys, and flip-flops, she had to look up at me as she spoke. She told me she was from the Boston area and that both her parents were professors—her pedigree as a child of Eastern liberal intellectuals was clearly a key point of her identity. She described her impressive background with such charm that she didn't annoy me or make me jealous. In fact, it intrigued me even more than Caroline Kennedy's; Jewish intellectuals were nowhere to be found in my prairie childhood. Accustomed to the slurs I'd heard whispered as a child, I'd grown up viewing Jews as forbidden fruit. I was immediately magnetized toward Shayna.

I told her my name and didn't have to spell it. "I'm from Chicago," I said, leaving out the "suburb" part, as it seemed so square.

Shayna and I shortly became friends. We could sense in each other that we were more virginal, more wholesome, than many other members of the class of '79, just from a quick assessment of the girls on the floor below us. The dorm bathrooms were coed, and Donna Summer's fifteen-minute orgasmic moan in "Love to Love You, Baby" was blasting from stereos all over campus. But we were not the sort of girls to let sexual rites of passage distract us from our studies. Rather, we were the sort who gave rise to the cliché "It's easier to get into Yale than to get into a Yale woman." It was probably safe to say that, in all our days, a cigarette would never be posed between our fingers; that kind of "cool" was out of the question. Yet we were as temperamentally different as the clothes we wore in our bunks each night: for me, a stained, tattered, oversize T-shirt; for her, a spotless Lanz of Switzerland nightgown patterned with neat, sweet rows of hearts, a scalloped bib around the neck and a ribbon bow at the throat.

That I was drawn to Shayna was a refreshing break in my social pattern, which was to seek out other encrusted adolescents with whom I could avert much true connection by sprinkling talk with wisecracks and facetious statements. I clung to my cynical armor because it was all I had to protect the inchoate mush inside my throbbing heart—I didn't like the messy feelings that overwhelmed me any time I came close to admitting affection for someone, spilling out in the form of red splotches that began on my chest and moved up my neck.

Shayna appeared to me preposterously sweet and good-natured. In her parlance, things were "peachy" or they were "sad," and people were "sweeties," unless they transgressed the parameters of the "nice," and then they were "obnoxious." She was always exhorting everyone to be "cheery," often while carrying brain-racking books from her depth psychology courses that would imply a different cast of personality. Her screaming-red, thick copy of Emile Durkheim's *Suicide* I remember in particular.

One day in the freshman dining room, I noticed that Shayna had a string tied around her index finger. "What's the string for, Shayna?"

She guilelessly admitted to the string's true purpose: she called it her "intentional kindness" string. "It reminds me to pay attention to other people and their feelings. I always want to be reminded about how my words and actions affect others."

Maybe all those yellow happy faces, those smiles of perpetual cheer that showed up everywhere in the seventies, had devalued the quality of "niceness" for me. Shayna's mastery of good cheer and courtesy was a social virtue that eventually, much later, I myself would try hard to acquire. But that day in the dining hall, her un-ironic attempt at goodness inspired its nasty opposite in me. I declared that wearing a string to remember to be nice was "useless and silly." She didn't appear to take offense. The cynic in me seemed to amuse Shayna. I aimed my next cutting remark at her droll roommate Ellen. Shayna leaned into my arm and rested her head on my left shoulder. I sat rigid at the onset of this agreeable physical contact, having had so little in my adolescence. Then she let out a peal of laughter, one of her delightful musical laughs that ended in the lowest vocal registers, implying conspiratorial agreement. She collapsed into me, and I leaned back, holding her up.

IF COLLEGE was the classic ground to reinvent the self, with self-discovery its primary task, who was I inventing or discovering? At age seventeen, I wrote in an essay to the Yale admissions committee that I was constantly seeking to uncover new perspectives, "even to the point of passing forbidden boundaries." But I was stumbling without guidance toward something I had only a dim awareness of wanting: a total education, a moral education—for mind, body, and spirit. I riffled through the five-hundred-page Yale Programs of Study and wondered how I might fashion my destiny from these coolly cerebral and therefore daunting offerings.

My wilder longings were satisfied by my photo safaris beyond the protected quads of campus. I rode my bicycle, an old Rolleiflex hanging from my neck, through New Haven's mean streets, looking to grab a portrait in the style of my chosen mentor in spirit, Diane Arbus, portrayer of the dark and extreme. I was looking for humanity at the edges of society, the human oddities who didn't look "normal," who didn't resemble my neighbors in suburban Chicago or my classmates at Yale. I thought I might decipher some secret code from their lives that I knew I wouldn't learn in that five-hundred-page course book. When I brought these photos back from the darkroom and proudly displayed them to my classmates, Shayna would tell me it was "obnoxious" to push my camera so close into people's faces, especially disadvantaged ones. She couldn't fathom what drew me to these quirky pursuits. When Shayna ventured out into the New Haven community, it was to mentor kids from the ghetto or cheer sick children in the hospital.

That winter, Shayna invited her sardonic neighbor from the heartland home to meet her family in a wealthy, woodsy Massachusetts suburb. I felt like a fish out of water with her boisterous Jewish clan, and I wrote a long description of the weekend in a letter to my conservative midwestern parents, wanting to impress them with my new friends, and the new identity they were granting me by association.

I must admit, the weekend's best entertainment was observing the Weisses. They are an extremely driven family, but apparently good-natured and certainly were hospitable to me. The pressure in that family for achievement (they seemed to know half the people mentioned in *The New York Times* Sunday morning) is incredibly intense. I knew I couldn't escape a few pointed queries as to my educational plans. "Why did you decide to go to Yale?"—the economist asked me three times during the course of the weekend. "What courses are you taking?" "English, photography, art history—" He cuts me off. "What are you taking that's substantial?" "Daddy!" (Shayna in the background.) He proceeds to lecture on the importance of taking an economics course. Mrs. Weiss is a spacey professor, playing mother, who ran around constantly, asking questions and not waiting for the answers. I guess she's gradually learning to cook. (Shayna, outside the Kosher Star Meat store, "Moira, you bought turkey—are you sure you know how to fix it?")

Shayna was a sweetie—as usual. It was interesting to see her with her family. The Humanitarian and the Great Arbitrator—she has to be the model child.

Back in Shayna's dorm room, I delighted her with stories of the weekend. Doubling over and choking with laughter, she admitted that I had nailed her family just right. I loved her for laughing at my antics, as I wanted desperately to be thought of as a young woman abounding in wit, barely masking my melancholic, artistic soul. I represented to Shayna the sort of person who would always be disaffected, and she bought my fabricated image wholesale, and professed sympathy for it: "Terri dear," she'd say to me, "I realize that with your cynical, rather refreshingly cynical, outlook, you'll never let yourself be truly happy. Ah well." As the school year drew on, her sympathy for me, her many admonitions to "be happy," her motherly coaxing ("I wish you'd go to the doctor to find out why you fall asleep during the day!") began to activate something inside me, hollow and aching and cut off.

WHEN I TRY to recapture one weekend in the spring of that first year, I picture our band of friends lounging in the sheltering Silliman courtyard. For a brief respite, we were all at ease in the limpid air. Shayna, in jean cutoffs, sneakers, and a red bandanna, sat cross-legged on an Indian blanket strumming her guitar. She was singing an Appalachian death ballad from her Joan Baez songbook in a lilting, untrained voice. In my innermost secret heart, tucked away from everyone, I remember being infatuated with her. And I wasn't Shayna's only admirer. She had many: Mark and Ellen, Damon, Eric, Peter, Charlie, and others still. She touched something in all of us. Her open face, the high arch of her brows, her sparkling laugh, her niceness, drew us all in. Her consistent sweetness, her inscrutable true feelings, made her into a blank screen that allowed us all to project onto her our deepest needs. And when she withheld from us, as we all eventually discovered she would do, we sat around the dining hall comparing notes on how to make her love us more.

FRESHMAN YEAR came to a close. Shayna and I became roommates and moved into the gloomy stone entrance tower of Silliman to begin sophomore year. Then the academic pressure weighed in and never let up. If relentless ambition—the success myth, the idea that everything exists to be improved—was an essential element of the American character, then this elite institution was a caricature of America. At Yale, the success myth was ramped up to a mania. A notorious pressure cooker, the university was reputed to have the most competitive culture of any in the nation. President Kingman Brewster, Jr., even warned us of these "terrible pressures" in his Freshman Address in the fall of '75. His voice rang out across Woolsey Hall, exhorting us not to miss out on the freewheeling experimentation that a liberal arts education had to offer.

Brewster had presided over Yale when New Haven was one of the flash points for the sixties civil rights and antiwar movements. It was hard to believe, but only a scant five years before, on May Day 1970, students barricaded themselves inside classrooms to protest the arrest of one of the Black Panthers, and the National Guard tried to smoke them out with tear gas. Our soon-to-retire president saw with clear eyes that the student body, mirroring society as a whole, was taking a turn toward self-absorption and careerism. My classmates, the "Me Generation" in the making, trudged off diligently to the library to build their transcripts, as I supposed they would later build their bank accounts and the letters after their names. But I wasn't prelaw or premed; I wasn't even planning to go to graduate school. During freshman year, I took a desultory attitude toward grades and experimented to my heart's content. Then as a sophomore, as the pressures multiplied, I fell lockstep into formation and grade-grubbed with masochistic fanaticism.

And my brain was ballooning out of bounds. The cool, cerebral courses of study were feeding that bright elastic sponge, my eager, ambitious brain cells, but something was left behind: other parts of me—instinct, intuition, the capacity for passion and wonder, the spiritual growth that is the natural impulse of adolescence. My ardent girl self, accustomed to following whims and inspiration, was dispirited by what struck me as bloodless intellectualization. I wrote in my journal, *And so, is it a reflection on me or on my Yale education that after a year at Yale, I can no longer think of original ideas? The creativity has run dry.*

I was required as a sophomore to declare a major: I chose the Art major. But the rigid modernism of Yale's Bauhaus-inspired program was making mincemeat of my figurative sensibilities. In January 1977, I committed myself to the English major, precisely because I was perversely drawn to its rigors. Yale's heavyweight English Department was in flux between New Criticism and postmodern deconstruction—methods so forbidding to my nineteen-year-old soul that my decision to immerse myself in such thinking led to an outbreak of shingles over my entire lower body, a sure sign of inner rebellion, and I knew it even then.

Then one day in the Silliman dining hall, as I was sitting among my social group arranged around a big oak table—Shayna, Malcolm, Heather, and some others—my ears were buzzing from the din in the dining room: from every direction, a clattering of cutlery and precocious adolescent minds running amok, theorizing in precise and affected tones. Like the clear ring of a fork tapping a crystal glass, something refreshing drew my attention, uttered from somewhere at the end of my table: a student we hardly knew was going on about how he and a group of friends had taken the BikeCentennial "TransAmerica Trail" the previous summer, in 1976, its inaugural year.

We all turned to listen. As a celebration of America's two hundredth anniversary, a group of hardy bikers put together a route of America's most scenic blue roads, mostly two-lanes stretching 4,200 miles from ocean to ocean. In the late seventies there was nostalgia for a mythic American crossing. Highway 66, the "mother road," the legendary road of flight, was finally replaced by the interstate system. In the winter of '77, the familiar black-and-white Route 66 shield was ceremoniously removed from the terminus in downtown Chicago.

Good student that I was, I knew my American history. The idea of traversing the expansive land had evolutionary roots. Lewis and Clark crossed it, then the railroad crossed it, then Americans motored across it, including my family, and John Steinbeck and his poodle Charlie. Why not bicycle across it? Pedaling through America was a way to get to know the big place up close, intimately.

The voice at the end of the table told us that you could take the trail with an official BikeCentennial group, or you could order their guidebooks and go independently. The route was marked with special signs, and at intervals of no more than a day's journey apart were specially reserved campgrounds or bike inns.

"You can start in the West or in the East. We started in Oregon, at the trailhead on the Pacific. We biked on into Idaho, then Wyoming and Montana. Climbed the Rockies, crossed the Continental Divide, coasted down onto the prairies and into Kansas, Missouri, Kentucky. Over the Appalachians and up the Shenandoahs. After two and a half months we ended up in Yorktown, Virginia, on the Atlantic."

This little preppie was no triathlete. He seemed more like a typical Yale nerd who'd hit on a great antidote to academic life.

"It's hard. *Physically* hard. Different from what it's like here."

Someone asked him why he started in the West.

"The prevailing winds are out of the West, so usually the winds will be at your back. Also, the mountains are half as high in the East, but the grades are twice as steep as they are in the West. The Appalachians are cruel. The old roads go straight up and straight down. Start in the West, and you work up to it."

Every one of us, in our mind's eye, could picture ourselves on this transcendental journey into unknown parts, powering our bodies across glorious vistas with the wind in our lungs. This action-packed adventure would build our bodies, our whole selves, as academia had built our brains. This would be the ultimate abandon, a soul flight of adolescence, freedom for our rebel selves. We were children of our moment. In spite of this grade-grubbing we'd found ourselves mired in, we had inherited from the sixties an ethos of pursuing the unbeaten path, of taking chances. The rock lyrics were screaming at us: Go your own way. Take it to the limit. All of us present at the table declared that we would form our own independent group and go the following summer.

Then one by one, over the following weeks, everyone dropped out.

When it got down to brass tacks, riding a bike across America rather than working a summer job was about as feasible for most of us as tracking the snow leopard in the Himalayas.

One person besides me stayed in: Shayna. On the face of it, she was the most unlikely one—the girl who might be expected to spend the summer doing something goal-oriented or useful to society, like taking premed courses at Harvard or volunteering for some disadvantaged group. Shayna was never like me, one with a reputation for seeking the odd experience: she and all my roommates raised their eyebrows the day they heard I cut classes to ride an elephant through New Haven while photographing the circus. Yet she was the one who most wanted to go. I remember quite clearly, as others dropped out, that my desire was not as great as hers. At that early stage, a bicycle trip across America seemed not farfetched—never that—but like an awful lot of work. As a fairly athletic girl, I was recruited into Yale women's crew freshman year. I lasted exactly one week on that grueling regimen.

At this incipient stage, when the idea was a dream, it was Shayna who kept the dream alive, and I, alone among her secret admirers, felt honored to go with her. I didn't ask her why she yearned to go. I knew academic pressures were crushing her, too; we suffered together through a brain-grinding cognitive psych course that spring. Both of us, in opposite bedrooms of our quad, had sweated out papers on how the brain stores memory. Still, looking back, it's hard for me to understand why Shayna so wanted to take that trip. I searched her old letters for clues and found only one, written in three colors of ink—orange, pink, and blue. She admitted she was haunted by a feeling that she was disconnected, "floating" through life. Maybe she longed for more introspection. Maybe the meditative solitude of this cross-country excursion would be the first time in a life freighted with expectations and pedigrees to live up to when her very own voices would be able to speak to her.

I set about informing my parents of the plan. My father was a traveling man and a permissive parent when it came to adventure. He had no problem accepting that his spirited daughter wanted to ride a bike across America with just one other girl. My mother got a firm set to her jaw and her blue eyes turned steely— it was the face she always wore when a big worry set in, and that was often. She said it was a crazy and dangerous thing for a girl to do, and spun off what I thought was a predictable litany of disasters that could occur. My father "overruled" her on the matter of the bicycle trip—*overruled*, a word used jokingly between my parents to refer to the obvious power imbalance between them—and when they voiced their final verdict, which I considered purely ceremonial, it was "go ahead, but we're not paying for it."

So I got a job washing dishes in one of the college dining rooms, tossing plates and cups into the gaping mouth of a dish machine and watching them be spit out clean on the other side—a task that gave me a sweet sense of completion I seldom got at Yale. Our dining hall acquaintance loaned us his BikeCentennial Trail guidebooks. I researched the latest technology in bicycles. I spent hours poring over bike equipment catalogues. I ordered helmets, packs, rain gear, sleeping bags, ground rolls, repair tools—an enterprise that seemed very naughty when Milton's *Paradise Lost* beckoned.

Then one day the first portent occurred, number one in a series of subtle yet persistent omens that led up to the night of June 22: I pulled an all-nighter writing a paper in the grim basement study room of Silliman College. In the morning, bleary and disoriented, I stepped out for breakfast, leaving my backpack behind. I returned to find that an unsigned money order for $160 had been stolen from my pack, a sum earmarked for bike equipment for both Shayna and me. It was one in a succession of burglaries that had afflicted Silliman for two years. The nation's crime wave had reached Yale's ivory towers.

When I moaned to Shayna about the theft, she seemed disinterested. She hadn't taken part in any pre-voyage preparations. She wasn't the sort to digress from her studies to figure out what camping equipment to take—she who'd never seen the inside of a tent. Nor did she need to put aside her studies to take a job. The finances, I presumed, were already in place for her, though she made no offers to reimburse me for my loss. I might have taken her apathy as a strong hint that, as the months had passed, she was no longer all that committed to the reality of our dream—but she told me she still wanted to go, and I intended to make it happen. Undaunted, I put on my white uniform and washed more dishes.

A Girl and Her Bike

Bicycle:—Bicycles often make their appearance in contemporary dreams.

1. As a means of transport bicycles differ from other vehicles . . . Forward progress is determined solely and exclusively of any other source of energy by the rider's personal and individual efforts.
2. Balance can only be maintained by forward motion, just as in the development of the external or inner life.
3. Only one person at a time can ride a bicycle— tandems are a separate subject.

—THE PENGUIN DICTIONARY OF SYMBOLS

I stand and rejoice every time I see a woman ride by on a wheel . . . The moment she takes her seat she knows she can't get into harm while she is on her bicycle, and away she goes, the picture of free, untrammeled womanhood.

—SUSAN B. ANTHONY

Answering the call of the open road wasn't farfetched to me. I came from a classic itinerant American family. We migrated around the country most of my childhood, following my father's promotions within his company to towns all over the flat heartland. His job, as best as I understood it, was to cover the prairie with more shiny *red* International Harvester tractors and combines than John Deere could cover the prairie with shiny *green* tractors and combines. We had moved three times by the time I was two. I cried a lot after this third move to a tiny North Dakota hamlet and told my mother I wanted to go "home." But within a few months, I flipped to the radical extreme. One day barely past my second birthday, I was left unattended for a minute, and I toddled off past the few buildings that made up downtown, then kept right on going. My frantic mother found me on the highway heading out into the treeless plains.

As I grew, we never stayed put for very long. My early childhood was a chronology of dislocation. Small wonder I developed an early affinity for bicycles. I learned that by hopping on my bike, I could allay my fears by thoroughly figuring out the new terrain between home and school, and even ranging into the great beyond. I had a bike for each stage of girlhood, and each one I adored.

The first I got at six, in Fargo, North Dakota. My older brother had just gotten his first red Schwinn, with balloon tires and a bar stretching from the seat to the handlebars. I demanded of my father equal status, and eventually he presented me with a tiny blue bike with snazzy red pedals and training wheels. Soon I yearned for the exhilaration of fast motion, so Dad took the training wheels off. Still, something was not quite right about this bike: it didn't look like my brother's. The anatomical wisdom of having no bar running from seat to handlebars (if you happened to be a girl) was explained to me, and it festered in my six-year-old brain that this was insane logic. I was even less impressed that the dropped frame of a girl's bike was meant to allow me to ride it while wearing a dress.

I was a girl resisting confinement, of the same tribe as American women of the past, suffragists of the late nineteenth century, who co-opted the bicycle as soon as the new contraption appeared on the scene. For them, it was a tool for emancipation: bicycles allowed those of the supposedly weaker sex to travel well beyond their previous limits, and women on wheels became a grave threat to the social order. Apoplectic men with red splotches traveling from their tight Edwardian collars to their bowler hats would watch helplessly as their newly independent womenfolk, in their newly unfettered clothing, pedaled off into the wider world.

I begged for a bigger bike, and finally, one birthday morning, I awoke to a shiny blue bike with silver fenders and glittery streamers flowing from its handlebars. When we took up residence in the capital of North Dakota, I rode this new bike to orient myself with the grids of our new neighborhood. Still, I felt a disconnect with this latest set of wheels, with its dropped frame. That didn't matter, because its days were numbered. We packed up before the year was out and unpacked in yet another flat town, and I'd hardly peeled the Allied moving van sticker from the bike's frame when it was stolen from our backyard. Crime statistics for a place like Grand Forks, North Dakota, in 1966 would no doubt point to this theft's being rather bad luck. Although, in retrospect, it made perfect sense. People my age could plot the rise in crime precisely as they marked their birthdays, beginning in the late 1950s.

Days after the burglary, I happened to be looking out the picture window of our little box house. I saw a boy a bit older than I riding what looked suspiciously like my bicycle. He was standing up on the pedals, moving fast. Yes, I recognized those streamers glittering from the handlebars. How dare this little delinquent taunt me by riding *my* bike past *my* house? What was a boy doing, I wondered, stealing a *girl's* bike?

For my eighth birthday my parents took me to select my next bike personally. I made a radical choice for a girl my age. Though still a girl's bike, this one was sleek—not one of those typical Schwinn Hollywood model pink-and-white, feminine toys the other girls rode. It had extra-thin tires and a second gear that kicked in when you pedaled backward. And it was jet black—not a color for girls in the mid-1960s.

I rode this gender-bending freedom machine in ever-widening concentric circles around my flat, treeless neighborhood, exhausted myself riding against the hard winds toward the horizon line and pure expanse that opened up at the end of every street. I was still riding this bike when we moved to a nice frame house with a white picket fence in a charming hilly town in South Dakota. There, I pedaled through my leafy neighborhood campaigning for my dad's favorite candidate. "Nixon's the one!" I hollered, going against my own developing political affiliations: I harbored a secret crush on Bobby Kennedy.

By late summer 1968, Bobby was dead and Dad had been promoted again, this time to company headquarters. At the end of that tempestuous year, we moved from our storybook Dakota town to the hotbed of the entire turbulent decade: Chicago during the urban riots. But Dad sheltered his family from those days of rage in an especially tame suburb west of the city, with neat grids of old houses, immaculately kept, an area zoned so that no RV or truck could mar the town's suburban perfection. There I replaced the black bike with a much less practical set of wheels, a fad at the time: a metallic green tandem with silver fenders, which I had saved up baby-sitting money to buy. Its allure to me was that it made me trendy, but I had no intention of having anyone ride in the second seat. I didn't have the social skills to make the compromises a tandem required. When a friend took the second seat late one night, I threw her off in a tantrum and made her walk home.

Within the safe embrace of Western Springs, my friends and I rode our bikes through quiet streets overarched with hardwood trees in the overwhelming summer green, and when darkness fell, we flipped on our bike lights. We had no thought of lurking danger. But then I ventured farther—biked the trail to the zoo in distant Brookfield, which ran through stretches of woodland called "forest preserves." Enough Chicago news had filtered into my consciousness, enough talk of bodies found in "shallow graves," that I figured I might one day spot a flash of flesh under a pile of fresh dirt, and was ever ready to alert my girlfriends— though they surely did not share my preoccupations—to any suspicious mounds our bicycles might traverse on our sylvan trail.

Next came an apple-green Schwinn ten-speed Super Sport, with an impressive leather saddle and, finally, a straight bar running across its frame. This bicycle served as my serious transportation to and from high school. It was also my therapy of choice: I'd vault into the saddle and set out at night to the freeway overpass, where I'd settle my brain by watching the car lights, swimming incandescent streams that led to points elsewhere in America.

I brought the Schwinn east, but in the spring of 1977, when Shayna and I began planning our trip, I realized that this old hunk of green metal could never propel me across the continent. I researched new models for both of us, and together we went to a bike shop to pick them up. The ten-speed I'd chosen, white with a dash of red, with brushed aluminum forks, was one slick piece of machinery—the pinnacle of 1970s bicycle technology. A brochure claimed that the frame had been forged using "aerospace technology." I picked it up by its crossbar and hoisted it on my shoulder to test its weight. No chain guard. No kickstand. No fenders. This bike would float me across America like a magic carpet.

Shayna didn't question my seasoned judgment in bicycles. She commented only that hers looked fine, and we wheeled them away. Back in our dorm, we got out all the gear I'd ordered and arranged it on the bikes—identical orange side panniers, sleeping bags, ponchos, helmets; identical everything.

IT STARTED WITH a phone call from my father sometime during the spring term. What did I think about leaving school for a semester or two? He had an adventure to propose.

My father and I shared a romantic temperament. Love of adventure, or at least the *idea* of adventure, was one of our primary bonds. Now one had finally materialized. After moving up through the corporate ranks, he was now responsible for the sale of the company's equipment throughout the world. But he had never been assigned the foreign post he coveted. Now he'd been offered the job that would assure him a life out of a cold-war spy thriller: making sure that International Harvester machines were harvesting Russian steppes and mining Siberian tundra. He and my mother would be moving to Moscow in the summer.

"Are you kidding, Dad? I'd go in a heartbeat!" I must have responded, with the no-holds-barred exuberance of my teen self. This was, after all, the logical trajectory of my transcendent bike ride across America: I'd just keep heading east, on to further adventure.

A few weeks later, coincidentally, Shayna learned that her father had been invited to teach economics in Moscow for one semester, and he asked her if she wanted to spend the next fall in the Soviet Union with him. There was no question that she would go; Shayna, too, was ready for a break from academe. She and I both were giddy about this odd confluence. The perfect escape from the Yale grind had just fallen into our laps.

Our strange destinies were now hurtling along precisely the same subterranean track.

SPRING SEMESTER ended in May. While other students packed their books and hauled old couches from their dorm rooms into storage and took off for summer internships with senators in Washington and magazines in New York, Shayna and I stayed behind to earn our passage across the United States by cleaning rooms the others had left behind. Five bucks an hour was a lot of money to me, and taking a custodial job was, for Shayna, yet another refreshing digression from her routine. Together, we heaved mops over floors soaked with beer, and imagined the glorious vistas that lay ahead.

We weren't so foolish to think that we could ride our bikes over four thousand miles without so much as a trial run. Our plan for regular training fell apart, but we set aside a single weekend and pedaled into the hills north of New Haven— matching red-and-white bikes each loaded with matching orange packs and thirty pounds of gear.

The first day was sticky and hot. The old Connecticut roads went straight up and straight down. We had sore thighs, aching knees, stiff hands, upper backs that pulsed with pain. When tires went flat and chains fell off, I plunked myself by the side of the road to fix them, glowering with subtle resentment that Shayna hadn't bothered to learn bike mechanics. Finally we churned up the last hill and pulled into a campground by a small waterfall.

Before setting up our tent among other campers, we hobbled over to the waterfall to rest our bones. We were contemplating water sliding over rock when abruptly, appearing from nowhere, a skinny young man with long, greasy blond hair and a distinct unpleasantness loomed near us. We ignored him and moved farther along the rocky ledge to avoid him, but he materialized in front of us. This time he shook a beer can, arched his back, held it to his crotch, flipped the top. The beer shot out in a piss stream into the water.

"Obnoxious!" Shayna declared. This guy had definitely gone beyond the parameters of nice.

"Gross. Let's get away from this jerk."

We hurried back to the campground to pitch our tent.

"Do you think that creep will bother us again?" Shayna asked, and I shared precisely the same intuition. Yeah, that lowlife was likely to hit on us again— might even try to break into our tent.

Together we brainstormed a plan to confuse him: we reversed the direction of the tent. Instead of facing the door toward the center of the circle of tents, which the other campers had arranged as in a community, we turned it the other way, opening out onto the trees. Convinced that we'd shielded ourselves inside a magic bubble, we relaxed, negotiated for space inside the cramped and clammy nylon, and fell asleep.

Some time in the night, the back tent walls began to rustle. Somebody was try-ing to break in but couldn't find the door.

Shayna screamed, a sharp, authoritative command: "Leave us alone!"

The intruder stopped, foiled. We kept watch for a while on the tent walls, until they held reliably still, then we let our heavy bodies surrender to sleep.

At the first light, the offensive man was nowhere to be seen. As we loaded our bikes, Shayna and I made a pact: during our upcoming trip across America, we would *always, always, always* stay in campgrounds, where the presence of a group would protect us. Never would we camp by the side of the road, where we might be preyed upon by whoever happened by. That day we pedaled back to New Haven. Our enthusiam for bike touring was dimmed, but we chalked it up to just bad luck. It would be different when we got to the West.

Overland, to a Strange Piece of Paradise

A trip, a safari, an exploration, is an entity different from all
other journeys. It has personality, temperament, individuality,
uniqueness. A journey is a person itself. No two are alike.
And all plans, safeguards, policing, and coercion are
fruitless. We find after years of struggle that we do not take
a trip; a trip takes us.

—JOHN STEINBECK,
TRAVELS WITH CHARLIE IN SEARCH OF AMERICA

"Rhi-aaaa-nnon" blared from the stereo
atop my little-girl white French Provincial chest of drawers in my upstairs bedroom of our English Tudor suburban Chicago homestead. My racing adrenaline
fueled the compulsive organization of my expedition gear, the obsessive arrang-
ing and rearranging of the things on the floor, chosen for their efficiency and
light weight: a two-ounce rain poncho, my dad's red International Harvester
windbreaker with the slogan RED POWER emblazoned across the back, one beige
woolen sweater, one pair of long pants, one bandanna, two T-shirts, one pair of
bike shorts with a chamois crotch, three pairs of underwear and no more, a tiny
camp stove, a mess kit, aluminum camp cutlery, a foam ground roll, a mummy
sleeping bag, a nylon two-man pup tent, repair tools including large vise-grip pli-
ers and a miniature plastic flashlight. I packed and repacked all of it, finding just
the right position for every item in the panniers that would hang on either side of
the rear wheel of my new ten-speed, with which I had become deeply intimate. I
studied every bolt and screw, knew the precise tension needed on the brake
calipers, understood the tender finessing of a derailleur, recognized the sweet
smell of just the right amount of WD-40 on the moving parts.

"There'll be long stretches in the desert—maybe even one hundred miles between towns. We have to be *completely* self-reliant—carry our own water, fix our
own bikes . . ." I told my high school friends, playing up the rigors of the undertaking, this self-proving ritual, casting myself as one who could endure peril and
asceticism, as one who would court risk as a source of vigor.

Shayna was due in two weeks, and I counted every day. She would fly to Chicago with her parents to visit her grandparents, then we would depart by bus for the West. That left me only a few final days in the suburb I had often regarded as a tame and sheltered prison. During my cross-country trip, my parents would be pulling up stakes again. But this time they wouldn't be dispatching the Allied moving van to rumble into another leafy suburban street elsewhere in the heartland. Home and parents would vanish altogether, only to reappear in some transmuted form in Moscow, behind the mysterious Iron Curtain during the height of the Cold War. I liked that notion. It very much appealed to my love of the outré.

I had but a few days of ordinary life to endure, so I practiced patience, watched a bloated Elvis prance his last dance around a Vegas stage on TV with my mother, and boxed up my bicycle for the bus trip across country. Even that was a ritual pleasure, the way you disassembled the parts—removed the drop-style handlebars and saddle, wrapped the pedals, taped stiff cardboard around the delicate derailleur—so the bike would remain in its virgin state at the other end of the continent.

WHEN THE DAY of Shayna's arrival finally came, my adrenaline rush was supplanted by a queasy unease that arose in the pit of my stomach as I drove my family's powder blue Mercury Monarch to collect her from her grandparents' house. I hadn't seen her parents since my visit to their home the year before. This time Milton and Moira Weiss were less convivial than I remembered, courteous but distant. Perhaps they thought I was culpable for entering this far-fetched and possibly dangerous escapade into their daughter's field of awareness.

Shayna said her goodbyes. Her absentminded professor mother, girlish with straight dark hair and bangs, hugged her daughter and planted a big kiss on her forehead. I watched from a distance and lowered my head. This display made me uncomfortable. Saying goodbye to my own family was always an awkward, undemonstrative affair.

Shayna's mother turned to me and said pointedly, "Take good care of Shayna, Terri."

Shayna sighed, as she often did. "Oh, Moira!"

I blushed and fled into myself. Such a loaded petition, this laying on me of a parental obligation. It weighed heavily on me; I sensed it asked more of me than I had in reserve. At the same time I received it like a benediction, this passing of responsibility from the mother herself, for the girl I so admired.

Soon we were in the Mercury Monarch, and I was making off with Shayna— or that's how I felt, almost surprised that Shayna's parents had let me drive away with her. We were moving closer to our journey, but we had one last hurdle, the awkward moment of introducing her, by now my symbol of East Coast sophistication, to my roots.

However I might worry about culture clash, my midwestern-friendly parents could always be counted on to be gracious to my friends. My father rattled the ice in his Scotch and bantered on in his bluff, jovial way about our move to the Soviet Union, about how coincidental it was that both our families would end up there, and what grand adventures we would all have. My mother piped in about how she hated the idea of going to such a dreadful place: What was a housewife to do with herself in Moscow?

My mother told Shayna she'd been given no choice in the matter of moving to Moscow, the closed society where only a handful of students, teachers, and journalists, and fewer still businessmen, went to live during the Cold War. She wasn't intrigued by the peculiar kismet that she was returning to her own obscure roots: her father was born a Volga German north of Moscow in the days of the czars. "I'd better not have to wait in long lines with those poor Russians!" she exclaimed, and Shayna laughed politely until avenues for conversation were exhausted, and Shayna pulled out *The New York Times* crossword puzzle.

The day of departure, I awoke in gloom. I told my mother about a bad dream I'd had during the night—as she reminded me many years later—but as deeply as I have excavated for details of that summer, the memory of that dream has eluded me.

I have no recollection of taking in the finality of that goodbye to my childhood home, or to the family beagle, or to the sheltered suburb that had allowed, though I didn't know it then, my adolescent self to flourish in self-confidence and entitlement. Exploring the neighborhood's hushed streets, arched over with big hardwood trees, I rode my bike late into the night without fear. It must not have registered in my awareness to pause and bless this place for what it had given me. "See you in Moscow!" I called out as I bade farewell to my parents, and got a thrill saying it.

My old high school boyfriend Dave threw our expedition gear into his pickup and drove us downtown, to the bus station on Randolph Street. I heaved both Shayna's bike box and my own into the cargo area, praying that our pristine cycles would survive the trip uninjured. Soon the Sears Tower on the Chicago skyline was disappearing behind us. Ahead lay the great prairie and four days and three nights on a Greyhound bus. We could have taken the plane, but we wanted to ride the bus. Riding the bus was part of the point, part of this Americana adventure of feeling the miles and getting the lay of the land and rubbing up against people we would never encounter at the snack machines in the library at Yale.

I hardly glanced out the grimy bus window as we crossed the treeless prairie. Shayna and I were absorbed in the mini-universe inside the Greyhound. We whispered wry commentary to each other about our fellow sojourners: the goofy driver who cracked dumb jokes; the girl named Wildflower, on her way to the Rajneeshes, who expounded hippie-trippy metaphysics; Mary, the serious endocrinology student who educated us on hormones and glands and all their functions. I remember also a lonely woman in gradual conquest of a shy and darkly handsome Iranian student. When the woman finally let herself sink onto his manly chest, Shayna elbowed me and we broke into giggles.

Darkness fell and we both assumed a dozen positions to try to sleep. Shayna slumped against my shoulder and then finally surrendered to my lap as a pillow. I sat upright and still, keeping myself from falling asleep so she wouldn't awaken. Listening to her peaceful exhalations, I felt content.

The bus lurched to a stop early the second morning. Groggy and with unbrushed teeth, we peered out the bus window: here in Cheyenne, Wyoming, real cowboys, shooting wads of tobacco through stained teeth, swaggered along bus bays in their high-heeled boots with pointed tips sharp as weapons.

We stepped out into the strong, full western light and onto pavement littered with tobacco wads fired from the mouths of a thousand cowboys.

I asked Shayna, "Do you have any idea what those are?"

"Gross. Let's not get into the lurid details."

These cowboys were a breed apart, I thought. Even in the Badlands of North Dakota, where my mother grew up, they didn't grow 'em like they did here, deeper in the West. We hopscotched off the pavement and whiled away our time window-shopping gaudy displays of silver-studded saddlery, vestments of a culture far removed from our own, until our next bus arrived. I watched with an eagle eye, as I did during every bus change, that our precious bike cargo was transferred. The bus pulled west out of Cheyenne, and in a gauzy reverie of anticipation, I watched as the expanse of the high desert unfolded.

This was the beginning of the real West.

I'D WILLFULLY reinvented myself as an Ivy League Easterner, but the West had had a grip on my imagination ever since I was a young girl and caught a glimpse of a wild white mustang darting over a plat in the Badlands near my mother's parents' farm. The towns where I grew up on the eastern, prairie side of the state of North Dakota were culturally the Middle West, and that, to me, meant placid and ordinary. Visiting Grandma and Grandpa's house on the Montana border meant heading into something more exotic. Every year, our family drove a Ford across the entire state of North Dakota, a journey of eight hours on two-lane blacktop, and along the way my father lurched off the road to read every historical marker ("hysterical markers," my brother called them, because the constant detours brought my mother to her wit's end). He lectured to us about the history of the land we were passing over. He'd point out the gentle mounds and piles of rocks in the corners of square fields and tell us they were Indian burial mounds, left alone by farmers out of respect for the deceased—and I loved to imagine the skeletons under the soil, rich beads wrapped around their neck vertebrae and threaded through their rib cages. When our car had crossed the Missouri River, the prairie rolled into the Great Plains, and flat grasslands congealed into dramatic buttes.

This rougher landscape excited me because it marked the beginning of the Far West, which made my girl's heart stir, because (as I had been taught in small Dakota towns at points along the Lewis and Clark Trail) the West was a place with possibilities. It was a vast open space imbued with the magic of wilderness, a place where you could renew yourself and reinvent yourself, a place where physical strength counted and self-reliance was a virtue, where you could range into unknown territory and test your limits, like Teddy Roosevelt had done ("I never would have been president if it had not been for my experiences in North Dakota," he once said). In short, the West was where something wonderful was always about to happen. Hadn't the verse of a 1920s-vintage picture postcard I kept told me so?

Out where the world is in the making,
Where fewer hearts with despair are aching;
That's where the West begins . . .
Where there's more of singing and less of sighing,
Where a man makes friends without half trying . . .

Out where the world was in the making—across the high desert of Wyoming, and Idaho, into Eastern Oregon along the dry basalt breaks of the Columbia River, until, in a jarring transformation, the yellow bluffs gave way to the lush Columbia River Gorge, where tall waterfalls crashed down mossy cliffs—two girls jostled in a Greyhound bus toward the western horizon.

OUR HOME on wheels for three days arrived in Portland. There our fellow traveler Mary, the endocrinology student, took us to tour the rose gardens in her town, high atop a hill with a splendid outlook to the north, where two volcanic cones in receding perspective rose dramatically above the earth, well above the clouds, as though suspended in the sky in a realm all their own. I felt a stab of awe. The Dakota prairie girl had seen nothing like this before. I imagined I was viewing a fifth dimension, something like paradise.

We had only a minute to linger before Mary delivered us back to the station and we said our final farewells. Shayna and I would board another bus bound for the Pacific.

AS WE SNAKED along the Columbia, en route to the coastal village of Astoria at the mouth of the great river, our impending bike trip left the realm of reverie and acquired material form: in the seat in front of us were two bike pilgrims setting out on the very same cross-country crusade. Mark and Kathy Rentenbach were a young married couple from Virginia, he a law student and she a high school teacher. They were only five years older than we, but the age gap made them real adults in our eyes.

"We're only going as far as Pueblo, in eastern Colorado. That's two thousand miles," Mark told us, adding that they were marathon runners and had trained for weeks to prepare for the hundred-mile days that lay ahead.

"We're going all the way across," I said, quickly suppressing any self-doubt. Shayna seconded that, just as enthusiastically.

Seven Days

Day One: June 16

In an oyster light, we arranged everything in its allotted place in our packs, slipped on our red plastic helmets, mounted our bikes, which were now so heavy they felt like small motorcycles, and pushed off down Oregon coastal Route 1. We'd left without our new friends, Kathy and Mark, whose bikes had gotten lost in transit.

Drizzling mist dampened our faces. We pedaled slowly, side by side, in sync with the low thunder of the surf that we could hear but not see. I settled into my comfortable old leather bicycle seat (the one I'd taken from my old high school bike, as it bore the imprint of my body) and surrendered to a euphoric daze, loving the open, raw exposure of bicycle travel. I could feel changes in temperature, smell the changing palette of fragrances, integrate the changing elevations in my muscles. I spun my pedals and my thoughts expanded: Eighty days and 4,200 miles lay ahead. My mind would be free to roam, to absorb earth and sky.

Suddenly the swirling, low-lying fog lifted like a stage curtain, opening a vista of sun shining on mossy cliffs, which slipped down to surf roiling against monolithic offshore rocks. I pulled my wool sweater over my head and looked around, startled by the oversize scale of the landscape. By comparison, the geographies of the East seemed small and skimpy.

After a leisurely pace, we knocked off well before the day was over and pulled into a campground forested with firs the size of skyscrapers. We walked our bikes among aboriginal giants draped in phosphorescent moss, as shafts of light pierced the forest canopy, throwing spotlights on giant sword ferns. We rhapsodized to each other about the natural beauty of the place. That was how Shayna and I best related to each other. Love of natural beauty was our greatest affinity.

We found a campsite, and I figured it was time to school Shayna on camping techniques, specifically on the wisdom of digging a rain ditch around our little red-and-green two-man tent.

"This is nothing like that creepy campground in Connecticut," one of us said as we attended to our camp chores.

The complete perfection of our first day of biking in Oregon augured well. Exultant, we chatted confidently with people camping around us. (*You girls are sure a long way from home. All the way across America on bicycles? All by yourselves? You girls sure are brave.*) Shayna wrote in a spiral notebook while I read my BikeCentennial Trail guide, which was packed with detail about the flora and fauna and points of history and roadside kitsch on the route across the continent. When night fell, we zipped ourselves into our cocoon and fell asleep to the sounds of the forest. Day one had been an idyll.

Day Two: June 17

While we pedaled south on the coast road through tendrils of mist, a caravan of logging trucks swept by, massive trunks of old-growth firs and spruce chained to their truck beds, all felled by axe and chain saw. We tightened our grip and kept our balance through a wobble.

Then a narrow tunnel loomed directly in front of us. We stopped at its mouth. Our instincts for danger were in sync. Would we have time to push our bikes through before the next truck blasted through? We dismounted, entered the darkness, clung to the clammy walls until we reached the light—just as a pile of logs on wheels barreled through.

The sour taste of fear was in our throats: one dissonant chord in utopia. But soon the sun broke through the fog, precisely as it had the day before. We plunked ourselves down by the side of the road. We were indolently munching strawberries and tanning our limbs when two familiar faces emerged from the top of the hill: Mark and Kathy.

"Hey, you guys!" Kathy squealed. They were delighted to see us, and made fun of our helmets, teasing that we looked like miniature linebackers on bicycles. It felt companionable to ride in a group, and we set off down the road together, now a foursome. Kathy, lively and with a ready laugh, whose blond pigtails hung down under a funny fishing hat that she wore instead of a helmet, bantered on about the logging trucks and other hazards of the road.

"We were riding along quietly when all the sudden a bird flew right into the side of my head. It scared the daylights out of me. I think it was some kind of hawk attack."

"It was just a grouse," Mark said. "A bewildered grouse." Mark was a diminutive man with a trim, dark beard and intense blue eyes that registered moods that swung between brooding and playful. He didn't wear a helmet, either. Instead, he sported a train conductor's cap.

"So Mark tells me, 'It's *just* a grouse, Kathy.' "

They were an especially attractive couple, lean and wiry athletes whose training showed. I envied their buff physiques and spiffy gear. By comparison, we were woefully unprepared, pretty makeshift in our bike attire, and we both needed to turn some baby fat into toned muscle.

To keep up with our new friends, we were obligated to step up our pace and push beyond our threshold. We downshifted and upshifted, and when our legs turned to rubber we stood on our pedals and guzzled water from bottles lashed to our frames—all that just to bring up the rear. Early evening, we collapsed into tents pitched in a fog-shrouded campground at the edge of the sea.

Day Three: June 18

En route again the next day, I noticed that Mark had slowed way down to ride alongside Shayna. He hated law school, and the two were commiserating on the cruel rigors of academia. Here was yet another admirer in the making, another encumbered soul drawn to Shayna's sweetness, I thought, as I fell into pace with Kathy.

I enjoyed biking in this merry band—but was it my imagination, or was Shayna avoiding me? Subtle tensions had been building between us since the bus trip. It had been a while since I had heard a motherly admonition or an exhortation to "be happy." I watched how she would banter with Mark and Kathy, just as she had always done with me. Only now she didn't.

We pulled off the coast road at Neskowin to pose for a portrait in front of the pounding surf at Proposal Rock. We had to mark this moment because it would be our last day on the Pacific before we headed east over the Coast Range, toward the Cascade Mountains, then the great American desert, the Rockies, and the rolling prairies. Mark got the idea that we four should strike a Napoleonic pose, arms stiffly held across our waists, would-be conquerors of the continent. He set the camera on a timer a distance away. I posed along with the other three, but alienation from the group was building inside me. I watched Shayna closely. No, it wasn't my imagination. She was abrupt with me and directed more and more of her attention to our new friends. If I had still been a teenager, I would have sulked. But as I was almost twenty, I feigned an air of superior aloofness. *Click!*

We dipped our front wheels in the Pacific waters, swung our legs over our saddles, and headed eastward to the Coast Range. Three days into our trip, the inevitable occurred in the Pacific Northwest: a deluge. We donned our rain ponchos and climbed hard through towers of dripping conifers. The physical struggle for which we had contracted was upon us.

FALLING BEHIND AGAIN, Shayna and I found ourselves riding side by side in the dark rain.

"I don't know about getting all the way to Virginia." Shayna's tone wasn't especially friendly.

That rattled me. I must have bristled at her suggestion. Quitting was not feasible to me. Although she had been the first to push the dream, I had designed and equipped our journey. My zeal for adventure had outstripped my still-undeveloped judgment. I can picture myself as she might have silently viewed me, this girl with annoying bravado charging forth without a single reservation. Maybe she was waking up to how outlandish our plan really was. Maybe she was thinking, but could not say to me, *Have we lost our minds to be out here doing this?*

At that age, on that day, I couldn't face her second thoughts. I couldn't say anything resembling "If you feel that way, let's talk about it."

I could only fasten onto the idea that Shayna was rejecting me, for something I had said or done. But what? Was I too possessive of her attention? Were we growing apart? Paranoid thoughts pestered me. Imagining the worst, I pictured her not talking to me at all, shutting me out altogether. Without her mothering solicitation, where was I to turn for comfort on this endless ribbon of road?

Exertion sharpened my mind to focus on my burning leg muscles, and we steamed on in the pelting rain, over sixty miles of mountain passes, before bedding down for the night under weeping cedars. "Oh, God, I can't even touch my muscles, they hurt so bad," Kathy said in a mock whimper as she unloaded her bike. "Three days feel like three weeks."

Day Four: June 19

A billboard along the road announced, VISIT BUT DON'T STAY! Oregon was only the first state of many on our expedition, but it made a profound impression on us as a very strange piece of paradise. We'd passed this message more than once, and it wasn't exactly welcoming, this temporary visa in the garden of Eden with its subtle threat of punishment if we lingered. The Oregonians themselves were folksy friendly, but would snap at us in a second if we mispronounced the state's name: "It's not Or-e-gone, it's OR-Y-GUN!"

Day Five: June 20

After another seventy-mile day traversing the mercifully flat Willamette Valley, our convoy pedaled into the college town of Eugene. We checked into a cheap neon-and-stucco motel and celebrated our first night in a real bed by bouncing up and down on a mattress—all four of us. Then we biked downtown to wash our clothes, shop, share a beer, and reacquaint ourselves with city life. Guided by that invisible imperative to wear identical gear in spite of the growing strain between us, Shayna and I bought matching T-shirts in the university bookshop. The shirt announced in big letters that we'd learned our lesson well: OR-Y-GUN.

Day Six: June 21

Striking out east under radiant skies into the hills that roll up to the Cascade Mountains, we witnessed the landscape morphing from bucolic to dynamic along the McKenzie River, a wild, exhilarating tumult of water that charged down from the high mountains. We were beginning to climb. I rounded a bend in the road and caught a glimpse of Three-Fingered Jack, an eroded volcano that graced the summit, a white fang that appeared, then quickly disappeared, then reappeared at the next bend, only to vanish again—as though beckoning me on. Anticipation blazed inside me. I studied the BikeCentennial Trail guide under plastic on my handlebar pack.

Our goal was to reach the base of the summit that evening, to position ourselves for the following day, when we would traverse the craggy peaks at their highest point, McKenzie Pass—4,050 feet of switchbacks to the top. Our trail guidebooks warned us about McKenzie Pass. It would be a grueling climb. Most bikers would opt to take a gentler pass, the Santiam, with a summit at three thousand feet. Shayna and I, along with our marathon-running comrades, chose McKenzie without question. McKenzie was the crucible through which we would test our mettle, and because of drought conditions, we were in luck: the pass usually opened on Independence Day. This year it had opened early.

We labored steadily uphill behind Mark and Kathy, but by mid-afternoon our stamina gave out. Sheer exhaustion forced us both to confess to our friends for the first time: we had to quit. But they, whose well-conditioned hearts beat more slowly than ours, wanted to push on. So we summoned resources we hadn't known we possessed and slogged up yet another hill behind them, until together we reached base camp.

Day Seven: June 22

A clanging pot woke us at 5:45 a.m. Shayna and I clambered out of our tent into the chilly predawn green and wet alongside the churning McKenzie River. Shayna pulled on her red ORYGUN T-shirt. I pulled on my gold one. We stuffed our packs, snapped bungee straps in place over our loads, and headed up the road for the assault on the summit. Mark by now had emerged as the leader of our pack. His self-denying discipline thrust him ahead of the three of us. Though he was sick with strep throat he would coach us over the summit. He ordered us not to stop until the summit was achieved.

Sweat stung my eyes. My thighs began to cramp. I slid my numb hands down the curl of the handlebars and stared straight at the red-toned road under my wheels. I pushed right, then left, every revolution a victory over gravity. One serpentine left curve led inexorably to a right curve. We were at the bottom of a canyon of steamy spring green towering so high that the sky was hardly visible. The big trees barely parted for the road, and seemed to close behind us, giving us no choice but to proceed.

Mark was ahead of us, out of sight, Kathy just ahead, and Shayna just behind me. I distracted myself with stories I'd heard about bikers on this transcontinental voyage who'd tossed out the contents of their packs to lessen the tyranny of gravity. First the radio. The extra wrench. Finally it would get down to the third pair of underwear, flung into the trees along the roadside. I amused myself thinking that an extra pair of underwear could make a difference. I was lugging a thirty-five-millimeter camera that weighed a ton, and I wasn't about to surrender it.

A few more switchbacks, under blessedly rainless skies, and then I gave out and dropped my feet to the ground, hoping Mark wouldn't notice. Shayna caught up, and I pulled out my Minolta to squeeze off a shot of her.

A curled black-and-white photo catches her in an exposed moment, so different from the photos I snapped at college, where her bright dark eyes were ever camera-ready. Cheeks flushed, hair matted with perspiration, a depression of sweat just above her breast visible through her ORYGUN T-shirt. She scratches a bite on her arm. She's smiling. But there's something about her eyes. The perfect arc of her eyebrows doesn't match them. The right eye is squinting. The left focuses on a different sight line. Both eyes are filled with misgiving.

"We're holding Mark and Kathy back," I said, and Shayna agreed. We both felt guilty about slowing them down. The day before, they had wanted to go on without us. Besides, they were a married couple. The idea of overhearing sounds of lovemaking from the next tent was compelling motivation for both of us to give our new friends some elbow room. So, there on the side of the road we formulated a plan to split up with them: We would make it clear that they weren't stuck with us. We'd have a loose arrangement. Sometimes we'd meet up. Sometimes we wouldn't. Tonight we'd let them go on alone, and we would catch up with them the following night. I was relieved that Shayna had agreed to split off from them. Our mutual plan reassured me that the tension between us was but a temporary thing. We pushed our heavy loads forward and hauled up the next switchback.

Eventually we reached the barricade that blocked access to snowy roads for most of the year. Only now, because of the drought, the gates were swung open, as though welcoming us, or daring us.

As we climbed higher, rock outcroppings began to appear, and the presence of the sky returned. The firs and spruce lost their warmth and turned blue gray, ever smaller and more desperate, until finally the stands of trees disappeared altogether. The air was thin and cold. It seemed that the bonds of gravity had released us. Thirty miles straight up and we'd reached the summit.

Streams of black lava from an ancient eruption surrounded us—a quiet tumult of dark jagged rock, an occasional patch of snow, and isolated skeletal trees, bone white, pushing up from the earth. Beyond this endless black sea, five white volcanic cones shimmered on the horizon. Mark and Kathy were out of sight. Shayna and I pedaled, one in front of the other, awed and silent. This extraterrestrial place was drained of color, so the fluorescence of our orange packs glowed electric, vibrating with hallucinatory intensity. Spooky and exhilarating, I thought as I looked around me at this dreamlike landscape and inhaled a deep breath of the thin air.

Farther along the summit, we caught up with Kathy and Mark, along with a throng of tourists frolicking at a scenic overlook, their huge RVs parked in a lot carved out of the lava. I hated RVs, with their long, greedy side-view mirrors that nearly forced us off the road. I erased them from view. There were no such things in my imaginary West.

Picking up velocity, we dropped from the summit and coasted several miles without turning a pedal, banking expertly around curves, feathering our rear brakes. Then the snow vanished and the air turned warm and dry. Our surroundings utterly changed. The trees were wholly different. Fir and spruce had disappeared; stands of straight ponderosa pines lined a red-colored road. They were reassuring in their dignity, with their bark glowing warmth. We were in the high desert now.

Almost nowhere in America do so few miles mark so complete a transformation of landscape. We had journeyed from the rain forest to something like the North Pole and down into a desert in a few short hours. I felt a shift. Breathing in the fragrance of the land, feeling the elevation in my muscles, I'd dissolved into the landscape—and as it changed, my thoughts expanded with the open stretch of desert.

ON A FLAT ROAD colored a gorgeous chalky red, lined on either side by tall ponderosas, our foursome pedaled slowly into Sisters, a tiny town with Old West storefronts. We pulled into a Dairy Queen, ordered ice cream cones, collapsed on the grass, and rolled on our stomachs to even the tan on the backs of our legs.

I whispered to Shayna that it was time to tell Mark and Kathy of our plan to separate. She began to equivocate. She wasn't sure if she was ready to leave them yet.

"But they're going to camp by the side of the road in the next town tonight. Didn't we decide on our Connecticut trip that it was safer to stay in campgrounds?" I said, even though I knew deep down it was hypocritical to stick to the letter of our law. We'd already spent one night in a pasture, and one in a city park with Mark and Kathy. "The guidebook says there's a campground just a few miles up the road—not as far as the town of Redmond, where they're heading. Let's stay there. Besides, we have to split from them sometime, don't we? Isn't that what we decided? We'll see them tomorrow night. Okay?"

"Okay," Shayna said.

"You guys ready?" Mark wanted to rock and roll.

"Hey, we're going to let you guys go on by yourselves tonight," I said. "There's a campground just sixteen miles away."

"*Sure* you don't want to come with us?" Kathy pleaded.

"No, no, you go on," we said. "We're too exhausted to ride a whole twenty miles to Redmond. We'll meet you tomorrow night in Mitchell."

"Well, all right," Mark and Kathy both said, and they pedaled off.

"Have a great ride!" Shayna called out enthusiastically.

"Bye!" I yelled.

"Tomorrow night in Mitchell!" they shouted back.

I could feel relief decompressing my body when they vanished down the road. Maybe now I could find out what was bothering Shayna.

We shopped for our evening meal and visited a tiny museum about life on the frontier. Then we mounted our steeds, fastened our helmets, and spurred on.

Cline Falls

Over my handlebars, opening in front of my tires, the arid plateau stretched to the horizon. The pretty green places were behind us. The stately ponderosas, standing like sentinels, abruptly disappeared, as quickly as the firs and spruces had vanished before them, and now the yellow desert, overexposed under a full-bodied sun, was dotted with western junipers, curiously stunted and gnarled.

The desert instilled in me a peculiar euphoria. Its sun-drenched nothingness touched a chord deep inside me. Now I could streak across boundless two-lane roads, and with each mile my body would grow stronger, my mind more focused, and I would reconnect with something essential within myself. The bigness of this land, the wide reach of my vision, evoked memories of the fractured plateaus and long horizons of the Dakota plains where I traipsed as a child. It sent me back to the young girl in brown jeans and cowboy boots, and into the thrumming synchrony of mind and muscle, will and emotion, that I knew then, before the chipping away began, the scaling down into the claustrophobic parameters of being a woman, if I could call myself that at nineteen. In these last six days, I sweated myself out from the inside, so that my perspiration would mingle with this atmosphere, and the power of this land would enter into me, infusing every pore and cell.

I fell into a rhythm, worked up a cadence where my feet revolved in perfect time with the shifting gears, in flawless sync with the elevations of the hills. It was as though a rhythm had been beating all along, the real rhythm of life, and finally, in this empty desert, I had discovered it and was beating along with it. I bolted off, steadily gaining ground on Shayna until I couldn't see her when I looked back. As recently as a day or two before, I would have gladly sacrificed the thrill of finding my second wind to keep pace with Shayna. But the tension between us had given me an excuse to think only of myself, of pushing my strength to its maximum.

Some minutes passed and the euphoria subsided. My conscience kicked in. I braked to a stop and waited for Shayna. I unstrapped my helmet, wiped the perspiration from my forehead, and breathed in the sweet aroma of sweat and sun that arose from my baking brown skin. It was closing on three o'clock in the afternoon at the height of summer, and the sun cast no shadows.

Eventually she came into view, her short torso stretched awkwardly over her bicycle. She didn't fit her frame properly; the geometry wasn't right. She couldn't push her energy into the road like I could.

She pulled up in a mood so dark she was unrecognizable as Shayna.

"I can't believe you took off like that. I couldn't even see you!" To look at me she had to squint into the sun. I was taken aback. I had never seen Shayna express strong emotion before.

"I was just trying out that pedaling technique Mark taught us . . ." I tried to tell her that I was merely fulfilling the goal of effective cycling by maintaining a constant number of pedal revolutions per minute regardless of the changes in the terrain, the rhythm we *both* had sought for the entire previous week—and I was actually getting results.

"I couldn't even see you, Terri! There's nothing out here. We're *alone*. We're supposed to ride together."

I mumbled lame apologies as I pulled on my helmet and pushed off.

Chastened, I pedaled more slowly, and we rode in a strained file the last ten miles to the campground listed in our guidebooks.

AN HOUR BEFORE, the prospect of the empty desert exhilarated me. Now the fantasy had crumbled and the emptiness felt desolate. We pulled up to a brown sign that read CLINE FALLS STATE PARK, and looked down.

A road dipped into the park, following the curve of a small white-water river rushing through reeds and among boulders. Down below, a few picnic tables were scattered on desert dust and patches of yellow crabgrass. On the other side of the river, a dry bluff rose up, carpeted with juniper and sage.

The expanse of open desert we had just come through didn't feel as lonely and forbidding as did this little hollow bleached by yellow light, where humanity had tried to carve out a resting place.

A sign on the road warned us that the park was for DAY USE ONLY. I pulled my BikeCentennial Trail guide from under the plastic map case on my handlebar pouch. Sure enough, the guidebook had sent us here to spend the night. But there had been a mistake. Cline Falls State Park was not an overnight campground after all.

We looked down on the godforsaken place and forced ourselves to paper over our differences long enough to work out what to do: bike to the next town, try to find Mark and Kathy and sleep outside somewhere along the side of the road with them? Or did it make more sense to stay here and camp alone?

I laid out my argument: We'd just climbed over the most grueling mountain pass. It was true that we could count on several more hours of daylight. But even if we could muster the energy to push another four or five miles to the next town, who knew if we could find Mark and Kathy? Besides, hadn't we decided they needed their privacy for one night?

Shayna said she really didn't want to stay.

I could feel dread forming in my gut. Something felt awry. We had pushed ourselves beyond our own natural pace to keep up with our friends, and then we hadn't stayed with them. Now we were off their pace and we, as traveling companions, were off our own pace. We weren't sticking to any plan at all. Our rhythms were erratic, running against the flow you feel when things are going right.

We'd made an agreement to separate from Mark and Kathy, I said again. If we had any notions of making our way across the country, we'd have to learn to ride by ourselves sooner or later. Besides, it made sense to stay here, to get off these bikes and get some rest rather than ride off into the unknown.

Shayna turned her wheel into the down slope, and we descended into Cline Falls State Park.

SHE HAD CONSENTED to stop in this place, but I could feel the miles that separated us now—as though the whole panorama of desert we'd just ridden through had gotten pushed in between us. It was the most estranged moment of our friendship, and our estrangement made us mute to each other. And yet, down in the park as we looked for a place to pitch our tent, one of us said, "I feel we're being watched." And the other said, "I feel something, too."

With shared instincts we scanned the horizon for anyone suspicious. A bald older man with coke-bottle glasses zigzagged on foot away from the bathrooms at the park entrance.

Doesn't he look like a weirdo?

Yeah, but maybe we're just being paranoid.

The feeling didn't go away. We felt the fear small animals feel and we instinctively looked for a safe place to pitch our little tent, to hide it from whatever predator the radar in our limbic brains was picking up. We spotted a small utility building at the edge of the river, thinking its concrete walls could somehow shield us from this invisible presence we thought we felt, but when we walked around the back side of it we found a marshy river's edge teeming with mosquitoes.

"We can't camp back here, we'll be eaten alive," we both agreed.

"Maybe we're just being paranoid," we agreed again, and settled on another spot to pitch our tent—right out in the open, but along the riverbank, where we assumed no one on the highway could see us. We snapped the bungee cords off our heavy packs and dumped our loads onto a patch of crabgrass near a couple of picnic tables.

I threaded a chain around both bikes and locked them to a picnic bench—the safekeeping of our bicycles was one of my prevailing obsessions, for without them our trip would have abruptly ended—while Shayna pulled the stakes out of the tent bag. We discussed: Were we being paranoid to think someone might try to break into our tent that night? No, we decided, in perfect harmony. Let's revive the strategy that had foiled our midnight intruder in our Connecticut trial run: face our tent in a counterintuitive direction. Here that meant setting it up with its door opening toward the brushy river's edge, when the far more practical position, one that would have allowed us more room to maneuver, was facing the park road.

Others began to arrive: families in square pickups rolled up near picnic tables and unloaded feasts we envied, and we exchanged the usual road chatter with them. *Where you from? . . . Well, you sure are a long way from home . . . You girls are biking all the way across America? Gee, you're brave. I seen a lot of bikers come through around here, but not two girls goin' alone . . . Jim, these girls are headin' all the way to Virginia on their bikes . . . Oh, 's that right? You girls sure have strong legs . . .*

Then we went about our dinner chores in silence, exchanging only the monosyllables required to attend to the business at hand. We emptied a box of macaroni into a tiny aluminum camp pot. Turned up the blue flames of our tiny Sterno camp stove until the macaroni softened. Dumped out the water. Dumped in a can of tuna. Dumped in some salt and pepper. Dinner.

Wordlessly we ate, our saddle-sore bottoms aching on the planks of the picnic table, our little tin forks pinging on the bottom of our aluminum mess kits to spear just enough macaroni to sate our terrific hunger. As the sun sloped westward, I washed the gook out of our mess kits in an outdoor sink and watched Shayna from a distance, on the ground, hunched over a spiral notebook. I longed to be closer to her, but it seemed my every word was having the opposite effect, and I had no repository of skills for bringing her around. Back at the campsite, I asked her a friendly question, but the sentiment miscarried. She answered without lifting her eyes from the careful letters she was inscribing on the page.

IN HIGH LATITUDES at the summer equinox, the shortest night of the year, it was nearly ten o'clock when the gathering dusk finally closed in over the bluffs surrounding us in all directions. Shayna let out an audible yawn—the most I'd heard from her in a while—and pushed her spiral notebook into her pack. "I'm going to bed." She dragged her packs into the tiny tent, and zipped herself in.

Feeling hollow and lonely, I sat alone in the crisp air scented with juniper and listened to the murmur of the river. By now the picnicking families had packed up and driven away. Teenagers cruised the looped park road in cars and trucks, and shadowy couples kissed under cover of darkness in cars parked in a lot down the road to my right.

Half an hour passed and the parked cars drove away one by one, until only two or three were still there. I felt reassured by the presence of others in the park, relieved we were not alone in this bleak place.

A chill crept down my chest. A film of dried sweat tightened on my skin, and I pulled my red windbreaker more closely around me, cradled my bare knees in my arms, and looked up at the big western sky—not enlarging me now but dwarfing me. I unzipped the tent as quietly as I could, felt for the edges of Shayna's sleeping bag so as not to poke her accidentally and make matters worse, peeled off my bike shorts, and slithered into the clinging synthetic folds of my mummy sleeping bag. I lit up a dark corner with my small flashlight, popped out my contact lenses, stowed the light and lens case in a pocket hanging from the tent wall, and filled my lungs with a couple of breaths of the stuffy air. The gravity of my own spent body pulled me heavily onto the hard ground.

Orygun, 1992

My gut clenched as we approached the state line. California lay behind us. WELCOME TO OREGON just ahead. The big brown sign cut into the shape of the state looked ordinary enough. To others crossing this border, the sign meant a state in America. To me, it meant a darkening state of mind, an alien place where I knew hardly anyone, a malevolent landscape that would surely trigger an incendiary blast of memory.

My traveling companion, Robin, and I pulled abruptly off the road on a sharp uphill grade. A small color photo shows me holding myself up against the sign, hair pulled back off my face, revealing my high forehead pulsing with determination. My eyes are protected by a pair of dark Ray Bans. I'm frowning and I look quite fierce, as though expecting a physical threat. I'd survived this place one time, but was I pressing my luck to come here a second time?

Twelve hours of road lay behind us—five more to Salem and the police investigation files, which would shed light on the larger mystery of what happened to me on the night of June 22, 1977. I half expected to see those uncordial VISIT BUT DON'T STAY billboards I remembered lining the interstate, but there wasn't a single one.

Maybe it was guilt by association, but Oregon's state capital struck me as a gloomy place, a clutch of gray government buildings under a washed-out sky. The tilted light, already diffuse at this high latitude in autumn, was almost gone at the end of the business day. We found the Oregon State Police Department of Records in the city center. Robin got out the video camera to record this initiatory moment—beginning my investigation into my own crime—but she balked at bringing the camera onto police premises. They're going to throw us out, she said, but I insisted, and made my dramatic entrance. A woman at the reception desk glared at us when she spotted Robin with the camera. She let me sign for the paperwork, while another woman indeed threw us out, but we got the footage and a slim stack of pages entitled "Crime Report." We took this file over to the capital mall and set up the tripod to document every nuance of my reaction to the revelations I expected to receive about the events of a summer's night fifteen years and three months before.

MY TRAVELING COMPANION was the first intimate friend I'd made when I started my life over in California two years before. Robin had noticed immediately a shadow trailing me. I was one whom she would expect to have "fire and focus"— the words she used. But something had gone missing. When I first embarked on this journey, she was eager to join me. The injustice that hadn't fully registered with me outraged her from my first flip recitation of the story. She wanted to dig into it with me, and agreed to shoot some footage that we might turn into a short documentary.

But that wasn't the real reason I wanted to record myself reading the police file. I wanted Robin to tape me so that I could watch myself registering emotion, so that my defenses couldn't push it underground again. This recording would provide forensic evidence of what simmered beneath the surface.

Oregon's statehouse loomed behind us under leaden skies. The building seemed to me especially sinister, a 1930s-vintage marble pile topped by a weird cylindrical rotunda that looked like a landing dock for a spaceship.

"Are you scared?" Robin asked as she began to shoot.

"I don't think so," I said hesitantly. "I guess I'll find out when I read it."

The file was skinny. Little more than thirty pages. "ATTEMPTED MURDER" was typed next to my name at the top of the first page.

On the videotape, I'm leaning forward with my hand on my high forehead, as though to protect my brain from an influx of more than it can handle.

" 'Attempted Murder,' with *my* name attached. It just blows my mind!"

The base facts of what had really happened to me were shearing through the fossilized story I had concocted long ago. I watched myself intentionally shiver. Was I defending myself from the real shiver coursing from the inside out?

Time: 11:30 P.M. to 11:45 P.M., June 22, 1977
Location of Victim at Time of Crime: In small tent
Victim's Activity at Time of Crime: Sleeping.

The distillation of my story into this haunting objectivity brought a bemused smile to my lips.

Method and Point of Entry: N/A
Instrument and Force Used: Hatchet or similar weapon.

Robin trained the camera on me as I read on, a deep furrow in my brow and my mouth down-turned.

On the late evening of June 22, 1977 two young female bicyclists, camping at the Cline Falls State Park near Redmond, were assaulted. The victims had retired to bed in a small camp tent near the Deschutes River. A vehicle operated by an unknown male subject was driven over a curb, across the lawn area and into the tent occupied by the two victims. The assailant subsequently attacked the victims with an axe type weapon, causing severe head wounds and fled the scene.

Before now, I had had an exclusive point of view of the attack. Shayna and I were the only ones there that night. The experience was ours alone.
Now there were police. I was seeing through their eyes.

Cline Falls Park is located five miles west of Redmond on Highway 126. The park is a state controlled rest area on the east bank of the Deschutes River. It is used both by local residents and the traveling public as a picnic facility, swimming and fishing. There is an access road about ¼ mile in length leading from Highway 126 to the grounds. There is a one way circular driveway through the park with restrooms at the north end and a large parking area at the southern portion . . . The victims had situated a two man tent near the riverbank.
    Tire impressions were noted leaving the paved roadway over a 7" curb and traveling in a near ½ circle type maneuver. The tracks led back to the roadway to the curb and pavement. Near the apex of the turning tire impressions was a large quantity of blood in the grassy portion of the park.

My brain was reeling: I read back over the description of the tire tracks forming a 180-degree circle in the grass, the apex of which was intersected by a "large quantity of blood." It was a graphic image I could easily hold in my mind. I pictured the queer geometry—like mathematics chalked on a blackboard, only it wasn't a vector but blood that intersected the apex of this 180-degree curve.
    Perhaps this half circle with blood at its apex signified something beyond a description of a mere crime scene? I imagined it as some sort of encrypted message in the grass, perhaps the sophisticated scribbling of some providential presence. Was it a puzzle to figure out? Something having to do with why certain people meet with particular fates?
    The spare, evocative prose of this police report and its poetic implications excited me, played tricks on my mind. I imagined it was possible to discover the transcendent and metaphysical in the jolting, stripped-down formality of its lan-

guage. I caught my thoughts heading off in this lunatic direction, sobered up, and read on:

Received from the Oregon State Police the personal property of TERRI LEE JENTZ and SHAYNA LEA WEISS listed below:

1—Solar CB-AM-FM receiver model number 322.
1—35 MM camera and black case.
1—Kodak instamatic 20 camera.
1—Timex Electric wristwatch
1—5 Francs, miniature knife and scissors set. $18.82 cash. $930.00 Traveler's Checks.
1—Pr. prescription glasses & blue case.
1—Yellow wire bound notebook.
1—Mastercharge card in name of Shayna L Weiss.

It all flooded back to me in startling specificity: The solar radio Shayna's father had made her take, because he believed access to news would save us in an emergency. The heavy camera I lugged so I could be an *artiste*. Shayna's Instamatic (she had no such pretensions). The watch I wore in case we needed to know the hour and minute, on a trip that was meant to release us from the tyranny of our class schedules. My glasses, so I could still see in the event that I lost a contact lens. The yellow spiral notebook in which Shayna inscribed her neat letters before she went to bed. A miniature knife and scissors—the closest things to weaponry we carried. Could we really have crossed America in two and a half months with less than a thousand dollars in cash? (I guessed that Shayna's credit card would pull us through if we came up short.) I'd forgotten about the five French francs I carried in my handlebar pouch just under the map case. They belonged to the Citizen of the World: an image of myself I cherished.

I suddenly felt like a professional observer, an archaeologist excavating traces of disappeared lives: an inventory of the artifacts of two girl travelers locked quietly away to molder in police archives. It all struck me as awfully sad—these shattered remains of some past existence.

At 5:45 AM, 6-23-77 a request was made for the Prineville Patrol to observe for a young female and male bicyclists . . . At 8:35 AM, Corporal Bussey advised that he had located the couple on the old Prineville highway approximately ½ way between Redmond and Prineville . . . Mr. and Mrs. Rentenbach advised that they had shipped their bicycles from their home state of Virginia to Astoria, Oregon. They traveled to Astoria by plane and bus to attempt a cross country bicycle trip. On the bus from Portland they became acquainted with the victims. They began their cross country journey on June 16, 1977 and traveled as far as Sisters with the two girls. They split up in Sisters at about 3:00 PM, 6-22-77 and intended to meet again at Mitchell the evening of 6-23-77.

I remembered Kathy and Mark's stricken faces staring down at me in my hospital bed. They had seen me brimming with vigor only the day before.

The Rentenbachs were advised of the assault on the two girls and were questioned regarding any encounter they had experienced along the trip that would aid in identifying a suspect. Both agreed that nothing had occurred that would give them a hint as to whom the attacker might be.

I pictured Mark and Kathy being "advised of the assault on the two girls." How might that advisory have taken place? It had been fourteen years since I last heard from them.

I read back over the line, "On the bus from Portland they became acquainted with the victims." I was struck by the suggestion of fate embedded in the language. That even on the bus heading toward the trailhead in Astoria we were "victims" waiting to be.

I continued to read, and a wider vision of the events of June 22, 1977, opened up. My youthful perception was that once we got east of the Cascade Mountains we found ourselves in a desert wilderness. Truth was, we were anything but alone in Cline Falls State Park. The place was hopping with locals, families having picnics, and kids cruising the park road. Now they came alive with voices.

Several reported seeing a guy in a red or maroon pickup with a white canopy—maybe a Chevy, maybe a Ford—parked near the tent site that night. Some said he was in his twenties. Others said thirties. Most described him as standing between five foot nine and six feet. He was wearing a T-shirt and jeans, and maybe a plaid shirt. Two people said he had a beard.

"Remember I said plaid shirt?" I asked Robin, referring to the time I had regaled her with my story. That the cowboy with the axe might have worn a plaid shirt was one of those details that had remained sketchy in my memory, a detail I was uncertain of—unlike other details that were vivid.

"Do you remember a beard?" Robin asked me.

I'd always described a headless torso. But I sent my mind back into the dark hole of memory and said, out of somewhere, "No, I remember clean-shaven."

SURELY THERE was a guy in blue jeans driving a reddish pickup in Cline Falls State Park the night of June 22, 1977. Interviews elicited five similar descriptions of what might have been one man, but curiously the document in my hands suggested that police had done no further investigation to learn the man's identity.

According to this crime report, however, people called in with still other leads. One woman phoned police when she heard news of the attack on the radio and related that she'd been in a motel the night it happened, and bikers driving Harleys were behaving suspiciously in the room next door. One of them stamped his foot four times and said, "Hey, baby" when he saw her. Later, there was a loud party going on in their room, with shouting and arguing and banging on the wall. One of the men told the other, "I'm going to cut your fucking head off." Another was heard to say, "I've got the wrench." In the morning they pushed their Harleys out of their rooms, and one of the bikers looked at the woman observing from the next room and stamped his foot four times again.

Exactly four times? A spell or hex?

The detectives didn't follow up on the bikers with the foot-tapping ritual, but the "I'm going to cut your head off" line must have seemed sufficiently like a signature that they did bother to enter it in the police report.

They noted also that one Stephen Douglas Malick had attacked two young female hitchhikers with a wrench near the Santiam Summit in the Cascades several years before, in 1974. The wrench-as-weapon theme apparently made sense to them—the wrench belonging in the same toolbox, presumably, as a hatchet or an axe. Furthermore, they noted that one Joseph Hamilton Segner was in custody in Curry County, charged with the beating death of a young female hitchhiker—weapon unspecified. Segner was also a suspect in another murder of a female in a park in another Oregon county, and he was known to have good knowledge of most parks in the entire state. But police did not bother to investigate further either Malick or Segner as suspects.

I turned the pages of the file to a description of various exhibits—pieces of physical evidence collected by the crime lab. There were samples from a damaged picnic table that had been swiped by the perpetrator's vehicle; paint from the curb that the vehicle had jumped; several soil samples. There were axes and hatchets of various sorts listed, with no references to where they had been obtained. All had been tested for the presence of blood, and there was none. One hatchet was found in a van in Clackamas County, far away from the crime scene, but only animal hair was detected on it.

Exhibit 5: —two T-shirts, red and yellow, which are heavily blood stained, received from Investigator Cooley. Both shirts are cut which appears to be for medical treatment. The right back shoulder of the yellow T-shirt has nine partially cut and torn holes measuring from ⅛ to ½ inch. The right shoulder of the red shirt has seven cut and torn holes measuring from ⅛ to 1 inch.

Exhibit 6: —a red and green tent which is torn and bloodstained in several areas. A partial shoe print is noted.

Red and yellow T-shirts, red-and-green tent, soaked in blood and tattered. These minute particulars, including the colors, were vivid in my recollections. There were times in anticipation of this trip to Oregon when I wondered whether the truth of what was pulling me north was not just police reports but a substance of my girl's body that I knew existed still somewhere in these northern latitudes. And here was proof in these police files that some part of my body was actually present there. I could picture blood from both of us, stiff and dried on an aged piece of nylon tent stored in a plastic bag on the shelves of a crime lab. In the same bag, I imagined a gold T-shirt, cut to tatters, with the word ORYGUN across the front. And a second identical red T-shirt, also stained. I had to admit that this was, in part, what I had come for, longed to make contact with, perhaps run through my fingers.

By now, I'd leafed through almost the entire document. Only a couple pages remained. I was getting the sinking feeling that the inquiry into the attempted double murder of two girls had never been a matter of gravity for the investigating agency.

A balding middle-aged man in a business suit walked by swinging a briefcase. Noting the video camera, he called back just after he passed us, "I don't want to see your movie unless there's violence!"

Could this man in a business suit really have just said, *"I don't want to see your movie unless there's violence"*? Is violence so threaded into the warp and weave of the American culture that even a random joke could uncannily hit the mark?

"Oh, there's plenty of violence!" I shot back.

It was all too much for one sitting. I closed the document.

I HAD A pilgrimage to undertake: we would retrace the BikeCentennial Trail, drive by car the very same itinerary Shayna and I had pedaled by bicycle fifteen years before. Our destination would be Cline Falls State Park.

As we drove away, I flipped open my Oregon guidebook, figuring I'd educate myself on the peculiar architecture of the Oregon state capital building—which struck me as reminiscent of some kind of Soviet edifice out of the Stalin era. I read: *Atop the capitol dome is a gold-leafed bronze statue of a bearded, axe-wielding pioneer.*

Axe-wielding pioneer? I squinted to sharpen my vision.

Sure enough, our camera had been trained on it, but we hadn't noticed: perched on the top of the cylindrical dome was an axeman, gleaming gold, a cape tossed over his puffed-out chest. He held the axe in his stiff right arm.

The guidebook said that this figurine, known as the "Golden Pioneer," stood twenty feet high, his axe fully seven feet long.

There was a deep strangeness in seeing the contents of my psyche—the memory of a meticulous axeman standing in a rigid posture with legs astride—converge with the statue sheathed in gold and perched atop the capital building of the state that, in my mind, was wholly associated with axe murder. It was at once unnerving and exhilarating: data toward a theory that life might be knotted into an inexorable pattern, that things had a deeper order beneath the appearance of randomness. I was always one to watch for these coincidences. I considered them a breakthrough of awareness, assigned meaning to them, as if to reassure myself of the existence of an invisible plane, one that supported this one, a manifestation of divine care. At other times I was sure it was only make-believe to think that isolated events were bound by hidden symmetries. Often I dismissed those "synchronicities" as the stuff of fiction, manic fantasies born from the need to believe in an ultimate coherence, to make life more than a series of discontinuous, arbitrary incidents that made little sense. A feeling of destiny can offer comfort in the face of the wild contingency of things.

But did that mean that my doomed 1977 bicycle trip had been nothing but a rendezvous with fate, a stitch in a preexisting pattern? Who wants a life story like that?

AS WE DROVE AWAY, I mused to Robin that the very first time I ever registered a car in my own name, in New York City a few years ago, I was given a license plate that contained the letters *AX*.

"I wouldn't make too much of that," Robin said soberly.

Okay, maybe it was a coincidence, but nonetheless, it was significant to me. I felt marked with a scarlet *AX*.

A car swerved in front of us at that very moment. We could read the letters *AX* clearly on the back plate. "See? See?" I said triumphantly to my dubious companion.

And then it kept happening. In the space of a few minutes, two more license plates containing some variation of letters that spelled *ax* or *axe* pulled in front of our car. It was some kind of cosmic prank. Even the skeptic's eyes were widening.

Dreamscape, Deathscape

Seest thou yon dreary plain, forlorn and wild,
the seat of desolation?

—MILTON, *PARADISE LOST*

Our car climbed through a tunnel of bright green, heading up Highway 242 to McKenzie Pass, and with each sharp turn I marveled that I had once hauled my own body and thirty pounds of gear against this much gravity.

It was gratifying, in a queer way, to have the remembered imagery of the road now sharpen into a tight focus outside the window. I knew that as we drove, the humid green rain forest would dissolve to a cool, treeless tundra of black lava, and as we descended, the tundra would dissolve to a hot, dry desert. I knew if I followed this road deeper into the desert I would end up in Cline Falls. And I knew that that vaguely remembered place would suddenly become real again, and I would breathe in its molecules, and the memory of that night would rush back, fresh and alive. This landscape would conjure that memory, would pierce to the core of the experience buried beneath the calcified strata of so many tellings of the story.

I gazed out the windshield, lulled into a trance by Native American flute music playing in the car, when at the edge of my field of vision I caught a glimpse of something amid the backward rush of the firs and spruce. I jerked my head to the right, but we were past him. I swiveled to catch a glimpse out the back window: a huge man in heavy work boots walking methodically and swinging a long axe. He was alone. His appearance had been sudden, apparition-like. I watched him in the rear window until he disappeared. We were in logging country, after all.

As we gained elevation, I watched my expectations unfold: the trees grew ever more stunted until we arrived at the summit, and then they disappeared altogether.

Here was that field of chaotic lava, black as pitch, frozen in some specific moment of turmoil. A few trees clung to life, so stunted it was impossible to guess their age. The dead ones, white snags emerging from the blackness, reminded me of skeletons frozen in rigor mortis.

This chain of high volcanoes, these fire-born mountains of ice, mark the spot where change is inexorable. It's the place where the Pacific Ocean floor grinds under the North American continent, pushing up capricious cones that stretch from Canada to California. Usually there's a wide expanse of land between them, and they reign alone over their domain. But here in Oregon, there's a whole gang of them. Here the earth is seriously on the move, and by setting foot here, I would be forced along with it.

This unsettled land had gotten mixed up with my fate, was inextricably intertwined with my destiny. Maybe, I thought, it wasn't just the events of the night of June 22, 1977, that had divided my life into a before and an after. I entertained a notion: the landscape was complicit, too. The very blackness of this place brought to mind the idea that it was black as in "FADE TO BLACK": as though it had the power to wipe from the screen my beliefs about the world's order; surely that had happened when I passed by here an age ago.

ROBIN AND I descended the summit and dropped eight miles into drier land, where ponderosa pines clung to rocky outcrops—and though we were traveling east, we entered the mythic West.

We pulled into the town of Sisters, at the base of the Cascades—the town where Shayna and I left Mark and Kathy and ventured alone into our rough future. Though the hamlet had grown in fifteen years, it took but two minutes to pass through, and we found ourselves in the high desert. I recognized the stately ponderosas lining the highway, the way they abruptly disappeared, with junipers taking their place.

I rolled down the window and breathed juniper on the wind. My pulse quickened.

I looked out over miles of rugged plateau covered with juniper and sage. It occurred to me how appallingly heedless we had been at nineteen—bookish, sheltered girls who weren't paying attention to the newspaper headlines. We thought that what lay out over our handlebars was the untroubled landscape of romantic imaginings, a series of American idylls, images from postcards, calendars, puzzle pictures, and decks of cards. We dreamed we would pedal past Fourth of July parades in small towns, American flags snapping in breezes, and friendly folks waving from their porches; we dreamed we would bed down to serene nights under star-spangled skies.

Didn't we know that something had irrevocably changed since our descent from the summit? Didn't we surmise, on some shadowy level, that we had left behind our greenness with the pretty green places—and we would never have it back?

The desert is a holy void, all essentials burned away. It has a presence as powerful as the ocean, a raw force that acts on us, that puts us under the influence of what we cannot control.

Smells of juniper crowded in. My stomach was queasy. I turned off the flute music and sank down in the seat of the car. I was moving into dread. My body could feel its presence, close in the distance. A couple of miles more, and there it was. A sign: CLINE FALLS STATE PARK.

I remembered with sharp clarity the very instant we descended into Cline Falls State Park the late afternoon of June 22, 1977. I looked down into the hollow. I remembered that Shayna and I could see into the park from the road. I remembered Shayna hesitating on the brink of her fate. I remembered the moment we turned our wheels downhill.

Now the junipers had spread and obscured the overlook. We drove our car down an asphalt road—wasn't it gravel before, and the descent steeper? At the bottom, the park opened up: several acres of flat land borrowed from the floodplain of the Deschutes River, and then this strange river. Strange because it flowed from south to north, reversing the usual course of rivers. Strange because it had a subterranean cataract, the "Lost River," a dark twin of itself that flowed through catacombs of lava.

There was a groomed patch of green in the center of the park, where a large flock of redbreast robins pecked. Then a horseshoe-shaped paved road followed the curve of the water, a narrow band of sliding silver, flowing quickly through the motionless desert. The sight of it—fast water, still desert—gave me vertigo.

Between the looped road and the river was a crescent of grass with evenly spaced picnic tables cemented to the ground. I tried to make the scene before me jibe with memory. The template was the same: Curved road matching the bend in the river. Picnic tables scattered about. But the place no longer had the sun-bleached, forbidding atmosphere I remembered. Trees had grown tall, and lush grass cloaked the dry soil. This park, as parks tended to be, was a half-shaded place. Its caretakers had subdued the desert, had made the park a friendly oasis. I expected sinister. Instead, it felt inviting.

I tried consciously to conjure the place in my memories—to bring back its real character, parched and dreary. I squinted away the autumn light and summoned a shadowless drench of summer solstice sun. I shrank the trees. Dissolved the green grass to yellow.

I began to walk and, as though led by a divining rod, crossed the lawn and headed straight to a patch of grass by the river.

The patch was dry. All around, the grass was green as in an Easter basket, but here, on the ground I felt I recognized, the grass was sparse and yellowed, just as it was back then.

I so wanted to believe there was meaning in this yellow patch. I was here to make sense of this experience, and this fit: the grass here was surely dry. I wanted to think that this bone-dry patch had resisted change because it marked a spot where something of us remained.

I held in my mind a precise image of dark pools of blood in the nylon folds of the deflated tent. Our blood soaked the earth that night, and surely it hadn't left. I filled my nostrils with a memory of an overwhelming odor: it wasn't a stench; there was nothing foul or rank. Rather, the scent of blood was heady and pungent, and all-pervasive in the earth and air.

I got down on my knees and stretched out on the ground, wanting to pull up what was still there of me in the earth. The ground felt soft against my belly. I breathed in the scent of the soil.

I turned over and looked up at the black locust tree above me and thought I recognized the pattern the branches made, framed against the sky.

Yes, it happened here.

Acts of Will (June 22, 1977, Night)

Screaming tires: that's what wakes me.

In a millisecond a colossal weight strikes my shoulder and pounds my chest. The pain is searing and brief. Instantly the soul of my body takes flight. And the pain seems to take flight with the soul.

What remains is some vestige of the body, left to feel the intense weight—not the pain of it, but the heaviness of it. It is a weight so heavy it's like a deep grief, the way it constricts the heart. Heavy like that, even heavier.

The cool night air surrounds me—tent walls are torn away and no longer close me in. My lungs gasp under this weight, which my mind—now cut loose, floating in the blackness, surprisingly clear and aware—is trying to identify. Reason tells me I am pinned under the wheels of a vehicle. But why?

A picture arises in my mind: drunk teenagers. I'd watched them mindlessly cruise the looped park road after dark. Surely they careened over the curb and dumbly struck our tent, ignorant of their malevolence. A flash of anger: the dumb asses had better figure it out and get the hell off my body . . . But why is it taking so long? My lungs suck in another thimble of air. My ears reach into the darkness, anticipating their sloppy laughter. But there is only silence.

I wait in the darkness and listen for a sound that will tell me anything at all. It comes from above. I hear someone stepping down from a place high above.

The silence is peculiar now. The silence is ominous. No, this is not a band of drunks. Sounds drift to my ears from a single point, telling me that only one person is here with me now. I picture a man. What does he want?

There is Shayna's voice. Sharp. High-pitched. Aggressive. *Leave us alone!*

It flits through my brain that her words are the same as those she shouted in the Connecticut campground a month before.

Then a thudding sound. Something soft absorbing a blow. Several more thuds.

Seven in all, I later tell police. Truthfully, I'm not certain how many there are. But many more than are needed to silence her.

Then more silence. Intense, physical silence.

My surreally agile mind is sure of the answer now: the lone man is a psycho, and the psycho is a murderer. That insight doesn't fill me with terror. I'm aware that terror is irrelevant just now. Rather, I'm puzzled: Why hasn't the tonnage flattened me dead? I wait for death to come.

Ears click on: more sounds. I make out that the man is stepping up into the thing above me. An engine revs. The impossible weight moves, releases me. My chest heaves, gulping air. I'm giddy with oxygen; life flows back. Busy now with breathing, I pay no attention to him.

A starburst explodes in my head. Then another. I'm thrashing from side to side; my eyes flutter open to a piece of wood laying blows on me. Darkness again. I forget my eyes; my fingers are alert, grabbing the end of what is striking me, feeling not wood but the curve of cool metal. The screen in front of my retina displays a brilliant show of light. A warm tingle rushes and spreads across my body. Consciousness darkens, ebbs away. Yet a flicker remains alive to take note: this is what dying is.

The blows stop, and the abrupt change arouses my mind from the warm, darkening dream. More sounds: the man getting back in the vehicle. An engine turns over, moves away, stops. He has moved a short distance away for reasons I can't make out. But his departure grants me a moment of reprieve, and I am able to reflect.

How awfully young I am to die. What a great waste it would be to end this nineteen-year flash of life here, just now, in this strange desert. That thought gives rise to an apprehension of loss: an instant of mourning for myself. So this is it?

No: I must pull myself away from the siren call of oblivion and make a bid for my life.

I open my eyes wide.

To the torso of a cowboy. A pair of pointed boots straddle me, and in them, lean, muscular legs tightly wrapped in a pair of neat, dark blue jeans. Farther up, two shapely forearms hold the wooden handle of a hatchet, suspended motionless above me, and I note the perfect symmetry in this pose—long legs apart, elbows akimbo, hands together on the handle. Just above the shoulders the head disappears, the face dissolves in darkness.

He's not moving. The moment is frozen, and I scan the fit torso and linger on one detail: his shirt tucked meticulously into jeans so that not one wrinkle, not one bulge of fabric, mars the surface of his flat stomach.

I take a beat to think: such an attractive cowboy. Then my response catches me off guard and I take another beat to observe the irony that I find the cowboy attractive. I don't feel terror lying underneath his strange weapon.

He lowers the axe. He lowers it slowly. My eyes watch as it descends to a point just above my chest and pauses. I cup my hands over my heart, clasp the blade, and from somewhere in my body summon a voice. Firm, with a touch of politeness.

"Please leave us alone," I say. "Take anything. Just leave us alone."

He says nothing.

I can see quite clearly, inches in front of my eyes, both my hands just over my heart, folded like a prayer around the blade.

Then gently, ever so gently, he lifts the hatchet from my grasp, steps over me, and walks away.

I hear him climb into his vehicle. The engine revs. He peels away.

I LIE ON my back in a strangely euphoric solitude—eyes wide open, fully a part of this outer world and aware that I have come up against a most unthinkable thing, and have crossed over.

Above me the branches of a tree frame the sky. The world rushes in with intensity. The sharp desert air is pungent with juniper and heavy with the scent of blood. The river rushes and crickets chirp, and I think: this would be any ordinary cool summer night if it weren't for the fact that I am lying here, cut open, with a raw sensation deep inside, in places I have never known. I feel wind blowing through my veins.

I feel wet like I've never felt wet before. Wet with my own blood, viscous and sticky. I'm cold, and it's my blood that chills me. The chill of blood feels different from the chill of water.

Until now I've had thoughts only for myself, but now he's gone. My friend is somewhere near me. I hear sounds I have never heard before. Not human sounds, not quite animal sounds. I know they come from deep suffering, that they are the very essence of suffering. Something like keening, wailing, moaning.

I turn my attention to where those awful sounds come from. Somewhere behind me, near the river. My geography is all off. We are not where we went to sleep, but several feet from that spot. I'm still in my mummy sleeping bag.

I crawl out of the slippery nylon, grope over to where I find her, close to the river's edge, curled on her side in her T-shirt, her sleeping bag draped over her legs.

Her face is pale and unblemished in the moonlight. She looks untouched. Her skin calls to mind the white porcelain of a doll's cheek. But what of the many blows I'd heard? My hand reaches to the back of her head, my fingers trace a hole, a piece of skull punched in. I run my fingers over the jagged edge, touch the soft tissue of her brain. The wound feels mortal. My mind stretches to the unimaginable: she is dying. Emotion, with its explosive power, wells up to fill my mind with only one thought coalesced into will: I won't let her.

I become aware of time passing, aware that time is life, and I spring to action, now a pure force dedicated to her living. Nothing can happen until I see clearly. I fumble through the torn and deflated tent and with uncanny precision locate my contact lens case. I try to maneuver the tiny hard lens from the case, but lifting my right arm isn't working. I wedge my right elbow on the ground for support, scoop the little disc onto the sticky tip of my right index finger, and, using the lubrication that drips from my hair, maneuver a lens into first one eye and then the next.

I blink away the blood, and now the scattered campsite is sharp under a dim moon.

I paw through the tent fabric for my small yellow flashlight and find it quickly, as my racing, logical mind formulates a plan to ride my bicycle four miles to the next town. My legs surprise me—they still carry my weight, catapult me over to the two bicycles leaning against the picnic table, chained together as we'd left them.

I set out to spin the barrels of the lock, but cannot lift either of my arms to the task. I ask my body to act, command my arms to move, but both dangle helplessly at my side. It dawns on me that the bones in my upper body are broken. I cannot ride my bike. So I scan my mind for another plan.

Are we all alone in this place? I look to the right. No cars left in the parking lot. The kissing couples have gone.

But from the left, a pair of wide-set headlights moves toward me along the curve of the park road. Alertness ratchets up another notch. It's a moment of pure attention: The cowboy coming back to finish us off? Or someone who will take us out of here?

My fingers have sent a picture to my mind—a piece of skull punched in, the soft tissue of Shayna's brain—and I wager that there's no time for caution.

My legs power me after the truck, my dangling right arm swinging the flashlight in bizarre arcs, my voice making noises about help.

The headlights sweep across me, illuminating my left hand, and I glimpse a muscle, bright red, spilling from a deep gash in the fleshy part of my palm. It occurs to me how very odd it is to see my insides pouring out of my skin.

The truck pulls past me, rounds the bend in the road, lurches to a stop, and I can see in the window of the cab the face of a teenage girl.

Her huge eyes stare at me from under a bandanna wrapped around her forehead. A long-haired teenage boy peers around the girl from the driver's side, his mouth dropped open.

Leaving Cline Falls, 1992

I pulled my face away from the dry grass, got to my knees, and stood up. This was something wondrous: getting up from the ground, standing solidly on my own two feet, here in this place, Cline Falls. I could be in this place and have full use of my arms. My eyes were clear instead of seeing through my own blood into the dark.

I walked away from that spot as though taking my first steps, first my left foot, then my right, each behind the other. My companions—Robin, along with two New York friends recently moved to Portland, who had joined me on this side of the mountain—watched me as I walked away. They, too, knew this was no ordinary walk.

I got into the car, and we drove the road that followed the curve of the river, up and out of the park. This was a potent act. I was leaving Cline Falls State Park—by my own sweet will. During this revisitation, I had slipped out of time, and for this moment at least the past seemed undone. This would be a ritual of maturation. The past would fuse with the present. And that alchemy would forge a new psychic terrain.

RETRACING PRECISELY the events of June 22, 1977, Robin and I turned east toward Redmond. My eyes were wide—my consciousness recording everything—not like before, when I traveled this road in the back of a truck and saw only the stars swirling in the night sky. Everything I couldn't see then I wanted to see now, as though I were taking back possession of my faculties. Several volcanoes lay to the west. It was near sunset, and their flanks turned pink with alpenglow as the sun fell behind snowy peaks. I perceived this landscape through a scrim of my dark associations of the place, through optics of pain and sadness; it was as though the atmosphere were washed with gray, and yet it was achingly beautiful, achingly sad, and gave me the peculiar bittersweet thrill that sadness can bring.

In the three miles from Cline Falls we passed ranches and a farm that raised reindeer called Operation Santa Claus, and then, finally, we reached a low wooden sign surrounded by gay flower beds: REDMOND EST. 1910. It was a town you might see anywhere in the American West: two parallel arteries, one heading north and one heading south, lined with low-slung buildings and an old frontier hotel. Humble bungalows were laid out on a grid, which was bisected by railroad tracks and an irrigation canal. A gas station jumped out at me. It wasn't as you might expect, named, say, Gas 'n' Suds or Value Gas. No, here in Redmond, Oregon, the local independent gas station was named, none too reassuringly, TRU-AX.

We sought out the Redmond Hospital, where our rescuers had first taken Shayna and me. I recognized nothing about it, as I had never seen the outside. But I replayed the specific moment of pulling up in the back of the pickup just before midnight. I remembered hearing pounding on the hospital's doors, shouts to wake up the doctors.

Now we turned southwest on Highway 97 and followed the route the sirens took at two o'clock in the morning on June 23.

Twenty miles later, we pulled into Bend and filed through a commercial strip of squat businesses lining U.S. 97. The desert pressed in around the town. On the streets of Bend, the scent of juniper and sage was on the wind. We turned east into the desert, and soon St. Charles Hospital came into view.

I summoned the memory of it then, such an impression it had made on me. It commanded the desert, this solidly shaped six-story structure, dun-colored like the sands and topped by a cross—reminiscent of a Coptic monastery in the Sahara. To the west, pine forests sloped up to the volcanoes. To the east were arid lands of juniper and sagebrush. The hospital was designed in the seventies with the intention of lifting patients' spirits, so there was a picture window in every room. Shayna's room had the desert rolling east. That volcanoes hadn't floated on the horizon outside her window seemed obscurely significant to me now.

I left Robin in the car and, with trepidation, headed for the lobby. I wanted a private communion with this place. There was a room in this building where I had left something behind, and I might now take it back. I entered the lobby, a seventies time capsule—the purple décor bore the unmistakable aesthetics of that era—looking dated now. Enormous windows let in views of the landscape. An elevator brought me to the fifth floor. And, yes, the room I sought was still there: 505. The door was open, and it was empty. I stood just outside and looked in. It was the same as any private hospital room, with its single bed, chair, TV. But this was a room with a difference. Outside the huge window loomed the silhouettes of five volcanoes.

NO DOUBT about it—something of me was still in this room.

A weird, wistful, morphine-drenched memory broke through as I looked at the long twilight outside the snowy peaks: my younger self confined to a hospital bed, under the influence of painkillers coursing through me. It was a day or two after the attack, and I was replaying a moment from that dangerous first hour.

This moment had been confined to the margins of my waking mind. I seldom made it a part of the official story I told others. But it was the crowning moment in the story I told myself. The memory had taken on an air of unreality, as it was hidden in my private world. I was carrying it like a burden.

It was just after the cowboy had squealed off. Shayna was near the river, curled on her side. I called her name and got no answer. I pulled myself close to her face. She was quiet now, unconscious.

And I thought to myself that I loved this girl. *Love* was a word I had never dared used, not even to myself. But I remember thinking I could indulge myself right now. Love was what this presence was. A tangible thing.

Then this enigmatic moment: I knew we had no moments to spare. I remember thinking maybe I was stealing a moment from her, but I needed to make contact. I figured this would be my only chance. Both my arms were broken: I can't even think how I was able to touch the back of her head. I was spilling blood. Had we together formed this large quantity of blood in the grass, near the apex of the circle?

I gave her a kiss on her pale cheek.

Her cheek was cool. Too cool. A thermal sense gave me vital information: the living heat was leaving her. The intense blue-whiteness of her skin surrounded by darkness broke in two incongruous directions: toward the whiteness of innocence, and toward the whiteness of horror. She was a dying child. A precise sorrow filled me. I had passed off the edge of the map, alone in a strange desert with the presence of love and the presence of death. I thought: if she is dead, I will stay with her. I wouldn't leave her alone in this bleak place. The next thought crowded out the last: a certainty that she wouldn't die. I was too young to know hopelessness. I couldn't picture the end of her. And I remember thinking, I won't let happen what I can't picture. The heart gathered the body into a single sense, and under its influence, one single purpose: that we both would live.

I hovered outside the hospital room door, recalling this moment that had been bottled up inside me for fifteen years, this moment of pure feeling. Pure pain. That kiss. Flesh touching flesh—the natural language of the heart for a creature who was suffering. I had never been able to share this memory with her. From the third day of the bicycle trip, distance had already overtaken our friendship.

Every now and then I glanced toward the nurse's station. I was mildly concerned that a nurse might throw me a suspicious glance, and if she did, I would have to tell the truth, regardless of whether she understood: that I'd returned in the hope that my heart would break for my younger self, that I could soothe a deep grief by superimposing my present pain upon the past.

"Take care of Shayna, Terri." Her mother had made me promise. I was a child myself. Now I wondered, with a glimmer of compassion for myself, who would take care of me?

Alive

The teenage girl with the bandanna around her forehead and her boyfriend with the long blond hair stared at me wide-eyed and slack-jawed from the window of the truck. I had to make them understand that it wasn't just me standing there dripping blood and dangling limbs. There was a girl dying by the river, and I couldn't lift her because my arms didn't work.

I wondered for the space of a second whether they'd heard me, believed me. Then they dashed from the truck in a blur of action.

I told them to pick everything up. The bikes, too. I called out the combination to the lock, and they tried to tell me it wasn't important—but I issued a command: *Get everything. I want everything out of here.* They sprang to do my bidding, and I lurched after them, hard on their heels, my body a manic marionette pulled by the strings of an invisible power, back and forth at a fever pitch between campsite and truck. We bounded over to where Shayna lay by the river, and I watched them as they acted as my arms—one lifted her legs, the other her shoulders. I trailed them back to the truck, where the teenage girl lifted Shayna onto her lap. I felt thwarted that I couldn't care for her. I wanted to squeeze into the cab with them, cradle her head in my own lap, but there was no room for me. So I struggled into the open truck bed, with the bicycles and the camp gear, and collapsed on my back as the truck took off out of the park and flew down the highway.

My consciousness drifted upward into the pleasantly whirling darkness, but my body yanked me back to earth. Now that my mission was done, now that I was in the hands of others, my body allowed itself to ache and throb.

Then a picture arose in my mind—Mom and Dad, Shayna's mom and dad; they crept into my awareness with a trickle of guilt and embarrassment. *How in the world am I going to explain this to them?*

The truck braked to a stop, and there was loud pounding on a door. I opened my eyes to a pool of sickly yellow light. The anxious voice of the teenage girl said something about waking up the doctors. Mindful of the passing moments, I fretted about how long it might take to call a doctor here in the boonies. Finally, blessedly, the door opened.

I LAY ON a gurney in a room painted green while a nurse shaved my drenched hair, pinched the contact lenses out of my eyes, took scissors and snipped up the middle of my gold ORYGUN T-shirt, now soaked red, until it peeled away from my chest.

"Hey, that's my Orygun T-shirt!" I said loudly. I couldn't surrender my honorary affiliation to this place called Oregon, even under these circumstances.

The nurse said dryly: "You can get another one."

The pain got worse—it wasn't like before, in the desert, when I blazed with warmth. Now the pain seared, as the nurse shunted me around on the X-ray machine and I felt my bones rattle and poke.

Then people arrived and drew out of me the very first telling of the story.

I LIFTED MY head so I could look to my right, where Shayna lay on her gurney. We each had a bag of blood suspended above us, a vital thread of red circulating into our veins. A white-coated doctor stuck another tube into Shayna's besieged body, and she jerked away from the prick and called out, "Terri, stop it! Leave me alone!"

Her anger sliced into my wide-open heart. I didn't understand that she and I were in separate realms, on different temporal planes: she had been unconscious during most of the attack; she was still inhabiting the day, the afternoon, still registering her anger about my leaving her alone on the open road. The events of the last hour didn't exist for her.

I felt my heart heave. *Please don't think I'm inflicting this pain on you. I would not have left you to die there.*

Then she was awake, giving her name and address to the doctor. When he walked away, I called out her name.

"What?" she answered, in a gruff tone I had never heard her use.

Then she let out a low moan and we lay quietly side by side, taking in the blood of others to restore what had been stolen from us. Voices above told me we were lucky. We might be in the middle of the desert in a tiny hospital, but this was not the end of the world. There was a large hospital in a nearby town where a rare repository of great doctors would save us.

We were packed into an ambulance and sent flying down another dark desert road.

I WAS IN no danger of dying. My consciousness was fully present. Ever since I took my life back, my head was screwed on tight. No way was I sliding into oblivion again: I was solidly here, sensorium intact, taking mental notes on how different it felt inside the stuffy four walls of a hospital after reveling for seven days in the open air.

My mind quickly developed strategies for rejecting the gravity of what had just happened.

"Doctor," I said to the white-coated presence above me, "I don't think you have to call my parents right now. I don't think you have to get them involved, do you?" He smiled and didn't debate the question with me.

Privately I concocted plans for getting back on the road. It would take only a day or two to put this regrettable incident behind us, then we'd catch up with Mark and Kathy. (Isn't that why, during our rescue, I had made sure the bicycles and all our gear remained in my meticulous keeping?) These strategies calmed me until I was overtaken by intense exhaustion. I lolled into a druggy delirium until, in that submerged place, a memory arose: the moment I touched Shayna's brain. And that memory rocked me like depth charges.

"Is Shayna going to die?" I asked the nurse.

"She's in surgery now. They don't know yet. But she might not make it through."

I was overwhelmed by awe and terror. Until now, death had not touched my young life. I couldn't grasp that Shayna, quick with life just an hour ago, might be gone in the next.

Take care of Shayna, Terri. Her mother's words resounded in my ears. I nodded off and soon felt the presence of the nurse near me again.

"Is Shayna going to die?" I asked.

"We don't know. She's still in surgery." The answer floated in my ears with the same air of doom.

My own wounds called me back to myself. In the desert, the blows had acted as their own anesthetic, but now the pain had come on full bore. I had the cogency to know physical from emotional pain; they were separate, but both pounded me at the same time.

I was wheeled into a room where lights blitzed my eyes and a female voice by my side explained that one of the bones in my left forearm had been chopped through by a hatchet—a fact I was unaware of, had not even noticed—and the doctor would put it back together again. The kindly older doctor told me he didn't want to make my cut any worse, so he would simply slip a narrow plate— which he exhibited to me—into the existing slash in my arm. My left arm turned into a construction site, and I stared up into what seemed like klieg lights as vibrations pierced my ear and sent tickles up my bones, and after a while it was over.

"How is Shayna now?" I asked.

"She's still in surgery."

Still? How many hours? Five. Six. Seven.

"Is Shayna going to die?" I asked again. And again. Not aware that the year's shortest night had long ago turned to day.

Finally the voice told me Shayna was out of surgery. It had been hours.

"She's alive?"

"Yes, she's alive."

AS ANOTHER blood transfusion flowed into my body, I opened my eyes again and Mom and Dad were standing there. These familiar faces—Mom trying to assemble her features into a mask of calm, Dad standing behind Mom with a furrowed brow—looked peculiar here, in this improbable place. I flushed with embarrassment. "You didn't *both* have to come," I said sheepishly, feeling really guilty that Dad had had to leave work for something like this.

So the doctor had called them when I asked him not to. Events were unfolding beyond my control. My parents were here, catapulted from the faraway Chicago suburbs, injected into my grand adventure, to this remote place where I had come to find myself, to rescue me from the really dumb thing I felt I had done.

"Give me your hand," I said to my mother, relief spreading over me.

I slipped into slumber and when I awoke my mother was by my side. Now I could ask her about Shayna's welfare.

"Terri, when Shayna woke up earlier . . . she couldn't see," she told me.

"She can't see?"

"They don't know whether her full sight will come back . . . or whether she'll be blind . . . They just don't know."

Blind? This news demolished me. This was not part of the plan. Yes, I could by now acknowledge that we had been through a terrible thing, but my plan was that we would survive as we had been before: whole. Not *blind*.

My mother told me that the doctors believed Shayna might recover her vision when the swelling in her brain tissues healed. Tomorrow she might be able to see a little. Maybe more the day after that. We would just have to wait.

Tomorrow she will see ran through my head like a mantra, as I lolled back into a drug-induced oblivion.

When I came to, I opened my eyes to sunburned, stricken faces looking down at me over the bed rail: Kathy and Mark. They looked terribly out of place here in the hospital. They told me they were pulled off the road early that morning by police, just a few miles outside Redmond, where they had spent the night. They were en route to Mitchell, where they'd expected to meet up with us again. The police gave them scanty but grim information. The sight of me filled in the missing details: I knew I looked like a bald, black-eyed, bruised pulp with tubes sticking out of my body.

Kathy had to sit. Mark left the room.

OUTSIDE THE LARGE WINDOW of this hospital room a line of five snowcapped volcanoes shimmered on the horizon, and I was camping out among their summits, under the moon and stars, on my hospital bed.

Great emotion swept over me. Squalls of rage and bursts of euphoria balled up in a morphine drug haze. I couldn't discern one state from another, with this energy coursing through my veins—which still felt open to the air, though now they were stitched up, giving off a faint smell of dried blood, slightly nauseating.

Rage: induced by the pain and the memory of the blows. Bursts of euphoria: arising from gratefulness at having survived, at having helped Shayna survive.

I was nothing but a chain of moods, one sliding away and replaced by its opposite. I laughed. I sobbed. I wanted to talk. I wanted silence. I wanted to sleep. I wanted to be awake. I wanted to be left alone. I wanted to be loved.

MY MOTHER'S blue-gray eyes fixed on me, the daughter she scarcely recognized, as she adjusted the scarf on my shaved head. *Hovering* was the word she used to describe these ministrations. Her light brown hair just beginning to fleck with gray was brushed to either side of her high forehead, which seemed to pulse with worry, and tight knots hardened on either side of her smile. I was impressed at how well she'd held up, how composed she'd been—how brave. I hadn't even seen her cry. I knew how well she could hold up in a crisis; it had always been so. As long as I could remember, my mother was always distracted with worry, and it seemed to take her away from me. Especially when she was home alone with her two kids while my father traveled, worry coursed through her like a steady current. It showed on her high forehead, in the firm set of her jaw, in the way her eyebrows hooded her clear eyes, which glazed over in a distant gaze.

By the time I was six I'd developed into a first-rate worrier just like she was, and it showed on my forehead just the same. For a while, in my grade-school years, she and I were locked into a complicity of imaginary fear. (As a third grader in another new town, every morning before I left for school I repeated to my mother the same mantra, *Be home when I get home*, because I knew if she wasn't, the terror of existing unprotected in the world would engulf me.)

Maybe my original nature was to seesaw between fear and fearlessness, shyness and boldness, because I could count on my timid self to eventually do the most daring things in a dramatic counterreaction. That had put me and my mother at odds during my teen years, when I chose to wear a somewhat make-believe identity of tough fearlessness, a time when even my best friend's mother had to tell me, "Terri, sometimes it's good to be afraid."

Now I had done the most outrageously daring thing, a thing she hadn't wanted me to do, and the worst *had* happened. The unimaginable apotheosis of all her worries had come to pass—and yet she was present and calm. This version of my mother reminded me of when I was very young and sick with asthma that was so bad I couldn't breathe, times when imaginary worry had turned real, and she was calm and grounded and attentive, and the distracted look in her eye would go away and I would bask in her love.

Now I felt that same love and full attention as she hovered over me, adjusted my bed, rearranged a bandage—and since something in my heart had broken open in the last few days, I could finally let her in.

AS DOCTORS weaned me away from morphine, I acquired new clarity about my circumstances. I was in a Catholic hospital, St. Charles Memorial in Bend, Oregon, some twenty miles from Cline Falls State Park, a brand-new facility that had attracted highly skilled doctors because of the beauty of the landscape. The superb quality of the medical care had saved Shayna's life and pieced me together again.

I came to understand the full nature of my injuries. When the truck rolled over my body, my right upper arm broke and the flesh was shredded by the tire treads; my right lung collapsed, my right collarbone fractured and overlapped; the right side of my rib cage was crushed and the lowest ribs cracked in half.

The rain of blows from the hatchet left two-inch gashes all over my scalp, a broken nose, a chip in the skull over my left eye, and a fixed and dilated left pupil. One of the bones in my left forearm was sliced through, the fleshy part of my left palm was slashed, and my little finger was broken.

It went without saying that I had survived against enormous odds. If the weight of the truck or the blows of the hatchet had landed an inch or two in any direction other than where they had, my injuries might have been fatal. That I scarcely lost consciousness throughout the assault was perhaps unusual, though I considered it an ordinary response, a response any other person would have had. And no one told me otherwise.

Doctors had restored my blood. They had operated on my nose, on my left forearm, and on the shoulder muscle of my right arm. I would have to breathe into a machine for a few days to revive my crushed right lung. But the rest of my injuries would heal on their own. The prognosis for my complete and speedy recovery was excellent. That I was young and in great physical condition—that I had biked strenuously for a week and scaled a mountain only the day of the attack—worked in my favor.

My mother kept me posted on all that was unfolding outside my room. Shayna was now alert. The punched-in piece of skull turned out to be her salvation, as it had pushed into her brain and wedged itself into an artery, damming the blood flow and forestalling her death. When the vascular surgeon removed the piece of bone, a major vein burst. He stopped the flow with his finger, while inserting a new vein that would carry her blood. It was fortuitous—it might even have been a miracle—that of all the folding surfaces of her brain, only the cells responsible for vision had been traumatized by the blows to the back of her head. She'd sustained no other damage to her head or to any other part of her body. She was hardly in any pain. Moreover, the optic cells in her brain were only injured; as the swelling diminished over the coming weeks, her sight would gradually return. Her peripheral eyesight was already coming back, but she still had no frontal vision. With luck, her frontal eyesight would return entirely as the optic cells healed.

I lay in bed and imagined her traumatized brain tissues healing. I willed her optic cells to once again take messages from her eyes. This information revived my dream that each one of us would survive this ordeal without any permanent losses.

Shayna's parents dropped by my room briefly to check in on me. They arrived many hours after my own parents, having been alerted to what had happened to their daughter by the cruelest means: radio news reports had gone out on the wire early Thursday morning and were broadcast in Boston before the doctors had had a chance to call them. When they flew to Portland, they changed planes in Chicago, where they happened upon the banner headlines of a Chicago newspaper, which told them a more precise story of excruciation. They arrived in Portland at night, and exactly like my parents, they followed a lonely route that wound into the mountains and down into the desert, not knowing if they would find their daughter alive at the end of a strange road.

Now I had the presence of mind to contemplate the two sets of parents thrown together here in Bend, Oregon. They were so different that the very thought of them together made me squirm. I learned, though, that Shayna's father and my mother discovered an ally in each other: they had both opposed the bike trip from the very beginning, thinking all along it was an insane idea. My father and Shayna's mother were the more permissive parents who had permitted us our folly. Then, too, both families shared common ground in the future life behind the Iron Curtain in Moscow that would follow this untimely meeting in the Oregon desert. Ultimately, though, they would not bond over their shared tragedy.

I YEARNED TO see Shayna, to share with her the story of that night, and I inquired about her more or less constantly. She was on the other side of the nurse's station, in room 520, but I knew only what I heard from others—from the hospital chaplain, who spoke with a kindly Irish brogue; from my parents; and from our mutual friends who phoned—that she had no memory of the events of that night because her head trauma had caused amnesia. Further, she considered herself extremely fortunate that she didn't remember anything at all, and she didn't want to know. Shayna did not care to hear the story of what transpired in those hours lost to oblivion.

My mother took note of the discrepancy between my preoccupation with Shayna's welfare and Shayna's seeming indifference to mine. But my mother had witnessed this behavior from me all my life: I was a deeply impressionable and serious child who formed unusually intense bonds with teachers and friends. She'd say that I got "wound up" over any little relationship. But the pulsing beam I directed toward Shayna was exponentially greater than anything she'd seen so far.

I felt shut out by Shayna, and her rejection plunged me into blackness. In school, I had delighted in our playful sparring, which sprang from our opposite personalities. Now we were polarized by our differences: I was the rageful, weepy one, with black eyes and scarlet gashes, bearer of the gory details of our shared history. My mother confided in me that the nurses—the ones who gave me my pills, turned my body over, and cleaned my sutures—were afraid of me, of my sullen moods and tyrannical demands.

It hadn't escaped my observant mother that the nurses preferred fluttering around in room 520, administering to the sweet Shayna, who said "thank you" a lot and whose face was without a scratch. A gauze bandage was wrapped around her head; there wasn't a wound in sight.

POLICE SURROUNDED my bedside as soon as the nurse sentinels allowed them. One was a tall, jovial, manly type with a dimple in his square chin. Another detective made less of an impression.

"Did any young man try to approach you while you were biking?"

"No."

"Nobody stopped you on the road? You don't remember a guy talking to you in the park that afternoon?"

"Definitely not."

I gave them what I thought was a strong description of the attacker. I described his pointed cowboy boots; his new blue jeans, tight on his shapely legs, pressed and clean; his shirt—I thought I remembered plaid—tucked neatly into his jeans, not a bulge of fabric to mar the smooth surface of his stomach. He was an attractive, meticulous cowboy. I told them he seemed about my age. He seemed a bit taller than me, but not by much. I estimated five foot ten to five foot eleven. He was lean, physically fit, but not muscle-bound.

"So you're sure you can't remember anything about his face?"

"No. But I didn't have my contacts in and I'm really nearsighted. I couldn't see anything above the neck."

I said I thought he drove a pickup.

"Did you see a pickup?"

No, I didn't remember seeing a pickup. I heard a pickup. I sensed a pickup.

I saw his weapon vividly. I called it a hatchet. But it also seemed bigger than a hatchet, so sometimes I called it an axe. I described a wooden handle—I was sure about the wooden handle. I remembered grasping my hands around the wood itself. And I remembered distinctly that at one moment my hands clasped a rounded hunk of cool metal on the pounding end.

The next day, two detectives filed into my room again, stood at the foot of my bed and snapped open a case to a handsome display of hatchets, all lined up, as though they were trying to sell them like Fuller brushes.

"Was the weapon you saw anything like any one of these?" The image of these cops with their display case of hatchets struck me as hilarious, but I suppressed the urge to laugh and carefully studied each tool in turn.

I was certain I didn't recognize any of them.

"None of them? Are you *sure*?" One of the detectives was visibly surprised. I could tell he had information he was holding back.

"None of them," I insisted.

He selected a tiny hatchet that looked like a toy. Its handle wasn't wooden. "You're sure this wasn't the one you were attacked with?"

So of all the hatchets he showed me, this toy was the one he was most interested in?

"No," I told him. These wounds are for real.

They folded up their display case.

Over the next couple days, talk filtered through to me that local law enforcement was by no means as state of the art as the hospital I was in. The cops around these parts were trained to chase taillights, not axe murderers. Still, I half expected that any day they would yank the desert rat out of his hidey-hole and trot him in front of me, so I could say: yeah, that's him. I know the bend of his legs. The sinew of his muscles. His meticulous habits.

One day a man showed up who identified himself as a hypnotist; he was to try to pull a "better" description from my unconscious mind. He told me to close my eyes and imagine tiny balloons lifting up my fingers. He leaned in close and counted backward. Instead of getting heavy and sleepy, I smelled garlic breath, and that struck me as funny and I didn't go into a trance. But it didn't matter. I wasn't in a stupor that night of June 22. I was hyper-alert and super-awake. I'd told the police exactly what I'd seen, and I believed no more could be extracted from me.

The detectives never even came up with a photo display to show me. But I didn't give their investigation much thought. I was more concerned about the daily progress of Shayna's eyesight.

A WEEK PASSED. My body eased up on the pain, and the outpouring of attention was pulling me out of the blackness. Bouquets lined my room, and I sat upright in bed trying to make gestures with both my injured arms as best I could while chatting on the phone to my friends about my near-death experience. I described how profoundly I had been affected: I had cut through all that was superficial and had touched the core of something deeper than everyday life and its prosaic worries. "It just wasn't your time," those of a metaphysical bent speculated to me.

A male nurse came to visit and told me a detail that fed my tale of heroism. He had heard doctors say that Shayna had had only minutes to live when she arrived at the first emergency room. And my lifeline hadn't been much longer: I was spilling a lot of blood. This cheerful blond nurse wearing blue-green hospital scrubs made me feel good about myself, and when he left he presented me with a pair of my own souvenir blue-green hospital scrubs. Another nurse gave me an identical replica of the ORYGUN T-shirt that had been snipped off my body. Yet another managed, where others had failed, to reach though my defenses by nicknaming me "Sherman," after the thirty-four-ton tank used in World War II, manned by a gun crew of four. Presumably she got the idea from my bodily stamina under siege—to say nothing of my emotional armor, still under discussion among the nursing crew.

People wrote in from all over the state, and I felt privileged to be embraced by these xenophobic Oregonians who had put up the VISIT BUT DON'T STAY billboards. "Last Saturday I saw three girls on bikes go by our place, and we exchanged smiles and waves," wrote one woman. "I was mowing the lawn while my husband was out logging. Just wonder if this could of been you kids." Another woman inscribed on her card, "We want you to know how deeply distressed Oregonians are over what has happened. That such things can happen in any state of our great land is deplorable, but when it happens here it brings pain and shame to all who love it. We can only hope that time will ease the pain and dim the memory, and that someday in years to come you will come back and enjoy the beauties of our state."

Children from the nearby Lutheran church sent me homemade cards with big hearts drawn on them. "I hope they catch that man soon!" enthused a justice-seeking little girl named Ceci in gold sparkles on pink construction paper.

Then one day I got a phone call from our bus companion, Mary, the endocrinology student who'd seen us off, hale and hardy, at the Portland bus station only two weeks before. She caught me on an upward swing, jacked on adrenaline and in an ebullient mood, and I gave the events of the last few days an especially uplifting spin. A couple of days later I got a letter from her. She told me that she could relate to the story I'd told. She herself had had a close shave a few years before, on her college campus in Portland: three guys tried to abduct her and her roommate one night at gunpoint. Her roommate started to run, and the guy with the gun tried to pull Mary into a car by knocking her unconscious with the gun, until someone yelled and scared the guys off.

I must have told Mary that I thought what had happened to me was an isolated incident. She warned me that, although there didn't seem to be a motive for my attack, a "redneck" angered by two "uppity" young women traveling by their own muscle power was enough of a motive. She didn't want fear to inhibit me as I moved through the world, but she counseled that I should always keep in mind how this type of man would view my actions.

I appreciated Mary's concern. But what happened to me had not swayed me one iota from my given assumptions—that I wouldn't in any way curtail my ranging ways just because I happened to be a woman.

A get-well card arrived from a classmate. Pictured on the card were three nuns in black-and-white habits riding bicycles. "Did you ever consider wearing habits for protection on the highways?" the friend had jotted inside.

Then a letter arrived from Doreen, a member of the Yale community who sang with Shayna in the Slavic Chorus but whom I'd never personally met:

> Lots of well-meaning people will try to convince you it was your fault for being where you were—even the newspaper report back here implied as much—but the kind of violence you suffered is something we cannot be protected against . . . Neither you nor Shayna is in any way responsible for what happened, but people who care for you and are still frightened, after the fact will try to find a reason for it and fasten on the place, etc. as an easy scapegoat. We are angry at having been so frightened and we strike out at the only visible agent involved—often the victim. This happens in rape cases all the time, as I'm sure you know already . . .

As it turned out, Doreen had been rather prescient. Now that the immediate crisis was over, a public relations official at the hospital suggested to my mother that people might actually blame me for the attack. Apparently information had leaked out that a letter or diary entry police found in Shayna's spiral notebook indicated that I was the one who had insisted on our staying in the Cline Falls State Park that night. Whispered indictments came from some anonymous quarters that I was at least partially at fault. The hospital official advised my mother that I should always be reminded that I had helped to save Shayna's life in spite of my own serious injuries.

But I loaded myself with guilt because I was the one less injured. The pride I felt about my heroics shriveled in the face of the enormity of Shayna's loss of sight: *Was* I to blame? Did I save her from what I got her into in the first place? It's true that Shayna's parents had been frosty with me. They hardly visited my room. Were they mad at me?

My mother came unhinged one day when one of her relatives called her and imitated a well-known public service announcement: "Do you know where your children are?" he had asked her with an insinuating tone.

Then my father grumbled about the insinuations made by at least one newspaper reporter: any girls camping overnight in a place designated for day use only had to be girls looking for trouble. He rose to our defense by spouting off to the local Bend *Bulletin*:

> Marvin Jentz . . . described his daughter as an experienced camper and bicyclist who "knows how to take care of herself. These were two very respectable, bright Yale coeds who were camping and minding their own business." Jentz said the two women "weren't traveling with boys like a lot of people do" and that he didn't want "any innuendoes" on their character

. . . Jentz vowed that when his daughter, Terri, recovers, "she'll never set foot in the state of Oregon because it's safer in downtown New York or Chicago."

Ten days floated by, and I was informed that Shayna would soon be discharged. A family friend with a private jet would fly her back to Boston. I'd asked to see her several times—appointments were made, and delayed. Finally her parents wheeled her into my room to say goodbye.

Raw sunlight poured in the window to my left. She sat in her wheelchair on my right, next to the aluminum rail of my hospital bed. I couldn't see her wound, which was concealed by white gauze wrapping her entire head above her eyebrows. Her skin looked smooth and dark next to her white turban. Her eyes were unfocused and a little ethereal, so that in her white turban she looked like a holy woman, some kind of female sadhu from the Far East.

I reached for her hand. She held the weight of my fingers limply, which told me I was merely being tolerated by her. My heart retracted in shame.

Shayna vanished and the hospital felt cavernous and hollow. I fell into a misery and wanted to be left alone. But during my remaining days, my mother continued her ministrations, gently coaxed me out of bed to regain my strength. Mother and daughter (in hospital gown, arm in sling) padded down the hospital corridors together.

MARK AND KATHY had lingered in Bend for days, incessantly talking over the unimaginable sequence of events with both sets of parents, then retiring at night to a basement room in a hostel where they slept with the lights on. Finally they were ready to get back in the saddle. My father lashed their bicycles to his car and drove them to the crest of a hill outside of Prineville, just beyond the point where the detective had stopped them, a lifetime before.

My father returned to my bedside and reported to me how he'd watched the two slowly pedaling away, disappearing into the dry lands ahead, and how he felt sad leaving them out there alone. "They're good kids," he said.

Over the next few weeks I would get postcards from them. They would cycle ninety-mile days across the sagebrush uplands in a heat wave, with burning backs and parched lips, only two water bottles to sustain them for seventy-mile spans. They would ride sun-beaten roads littered with reeking carcasses of decomposing antelope. They would push through dust storms and hailstorms, caked with mud up to their waists, with not even a tree for shelter. They would pedal against terrific head winds, be forced off the road by colossal trucks, fall into cattle guards and sustain injuries that would require stitches. "After our grueling day today, we can't even imagine going all the way across," they wrote to me.

At the end of a journey that began with a kiss and a handshake in Astoria, Oregon, on June 16, they reached Pueblo, Colorado, on July 24—2,125 miles and halfway across the continent—swollen, stiff, hardly able to walk. They declared that never again would they attempt such a long ride. But when it was over, they knew they would miss those full, strenuous days, and they felt better about themselves for having experienced them.

As I read their letters, I felt a deep sense of regret for what I had missed.

ON JULY 3, after twelve days in the hospital, I was discharged. The cops released my camp equipment—minus the ripped tent—to me.

"What do you want me to do with the sleeping bag?" my father asked me, adding that it was covered in blood.

I told him to take it to the Laundromat, and he didn't argue. The bike, the mummy sleeping bag, the orange bike packs, the flashlight—I wanted it all with me.

Mom and Dad pushed me outdoors in a wheelchair. We'd retrace our route back over the Cascade range in a jeep provided by International Harvester. From Portland we'd fly United Airlines to Chicago.

I paused in the parking lot of the hospital to sniff the heady high desert air, and glanced back at the volcanic cones, snowcapped and sparkling under a blueing sky.

To me, Oregon was a dark and strange piece of paradise.

Afterlife

Only three weeks before, my high school friend Dave had left us at the Greyhound bus station. Now he studied the brooding girl propped up with pillows on the floral sofa in her parents' home. The pupil of her left eye was frozen wide open, a pool of darkness that did not match the pupil of her right eye. She stared with an odd gaze at once hyper-alert and absent.

Anger radiated from this girl, an anger deeper than the adolescent angst of the tough teen Dave had known—it was exponentially more intense, of another category altogether. He wanted out of the room, but he couldn't leave her alone until her parents had returned from their errands.

Sunlight slanted in through the small panes of the lead-glass windows. It was the Fourth of July holiday, one of the most humid summer afternoons the Chicago suburbs could dish up.

An hour passed, thick and still, and my friend Kathy relieved Dave. Kathy expected to find her childhood friend despondent and depressed, a broken girl. Instead she found her filled with a manic, elated energy, taking off her headscarf and pointing to the gashes in her scalp, wanting to show them off. She was actually proud of those gashes.

Kathy left quickly, uncomfortable with this bandaged creature she didn't recognize in face or spirit.

I DIDN'T KNOW it then, but there was a new presence in the room that day: my shadow self, the estranged angel, in her first public appearance.

My body was jacked with adrenaline. My pulse was racing. The scent of blood was on me still. My nostrils were filled with juniper. Recalling the bleached desert charged me with currents of emotion I didn't understand, a kind of euphoria, as though I'd gotten a "contact high" from the cowboy, and now that rush had come back full-force. We had matched audacious acts of will, the cowboy and I. He was angry as hell, and through his blows he transmitted his rage to me. And now my rage coursed through me like endorphins.

Night came as I lay in my childhood bed. Darkness brought no relief from the day's stifling heat. I was on my back so I wouldn't disturb my clavicle splint and my tender rib cage. I labored to breathe in the muggy air until I drifted into sleep. The effort to fill my lungs morphed into a nightmare of a terrifically heavy weight crushing my chest. I awoke and called out for my mother.

I SAT PROPPED UP on the couch in the family room, where I would convalesce for only a week while the contents of my childhood home were packed up and shipped behind the Iron Curtain, including, at my insistence, my bicycle and mummy sleeping bag. My mother's anxiety about moving to Moscow and into the cradle of the Cold War was now compounded by my condition. But my father was a corporate man on the rise. He was much relieved that the Oregon mishap would not delay him. I, too, wanted to continue the adventure. I was aware that no form of therapy, emotional or physical, would be available to me in a remote outpost like Moscow, but I didn't think I needed any. It didn't occur to me that I had any "demons to exorcise." I liked my demons, unique as they were.

As my mobility was limited, there was little to do but brood about Shayna's eyesight, wonder about her progress, continue to visualize optic cells healing in the back of her head. Within the week, a letter arrived from Boston. Shayna made light of her condition, describing herself as an "old blind mole" pecking away at the family typewriter. She hoped that her letter would be legible, and she hoped, too, that everything had calmed down and that things were back to a semblance of normality, as she put it matter-of-factly. She detailed for me the normality of her days, and closed with "Stay healthy and cheery and take care."

Stay healthy and cheery and take care. I reread the line, flabbergasted. Was it conceivable that in spite of the events of the past two weeks, Shayna had scarcely missed a beat of the ongoing flow of everydayness from which I had so veered?

In increments, life's gravitational pull to "normality" reasserted itself even on me. My fixed and dilated left pupil began to respond to light again, and I could feel my body healing: the black sutures crisscrossing my scalp began to itch something furious, and I couldn't scratch them. I felt like I was wearing a head full of those old-fashioned metal curlers stuffed with plastic spikes (though I had no hair). Worse, it felt like someone had stretched a tight rubber bathing cap over the curlers until the pinpricks bore into my scalp. I wanted to rip the whole thing off but could only practice patience with my body as it mended itself.

I began to pick up a few threads of the old Terri. I sent back the BikeCentennial Trail guides my dining hall acquaintance had lent me. (It never occurred to me that he might no longer want them.) My college roommates Ellen and Nancy flew in from the East Coast to visit, and I re-injured my ribs on the big laughs tiny Ellen was always able to arouse in me. By the end of the week I was ambulatory and even went to see *Annie Hall* with my friend Kathy, giving my ribs another workout.

Finally I reentered the outer world to the extent that I was keenly interested in how the media told my story. I was glad that the Chicago papers considered the event important enough to give it front-page billing. "Hunt Ax Attacker of Suburb Co-ed," the *Daily News* screamed in banner headlines. But use of the word *co-ed* distressed me—this duplicitous put-down, this label assigning females to a secondary category. I never knew the word held currency until there it was, thirty-six-point boldface, describing me to a circulation of three million people. I was even more annoyed that my high school graduation photo used in the piece was captioned "Terri Jentz: *'We need help.'* " I felt compromised by the vulnerability, the helplessness, those words broadcast. Vulnerability and helplessness didn't square with the image I needed to hold of myself. I didn't like how my survival had been turned into a tired old damsel-in-distress story—that I had been cast as a typical female victim. It galled me that the papers had misquoted me. They had me saying to my rescuers on the night of June 22: "We need help. My friend is hurt *bad.*" I was now obliged to "annotate" the text of my quote before sending clippings to friends on the East Coast. I underlined that sentence and drew an arrow to a handprinted commentary in the margin: "Misquotation! Not even hysteria would bring on such poor grammar."

My friends back East sent more newspaper clippings to me. As it turned out, the Chicago press treated me well compared with my own *Yale Daily News*. The university reporter described me as running away from my axe-wielding attacker, screaming until my hysterical shrieks supposedly scared him off. A fabricated quote had me saying, "All I could do was stay by her and protect her and wait for help to come." I cringed that this writer had dared put his own script into my mouth! It occurred to me that if I wanted the truth of my own story to be told, I would have to tell it myself.

ON ANOTHER humid afternoon, when the house was nearly packed up, I got a phone call from a Yale friend with news of a classmate just murdered in another sheltered suburb, Scarsdale, New York. When her boyfriend, Yale classmate Richard Herrin, found out she was leaving him for another man, he bludgeoned Bonnie Garland with a hammer while she lay sleeping in her childhood bedroom. I didn't know Bonnie, but I had seen her perform in an all-girl a cappella singing group; surely I had passed the redheaded girl—tall and zaftig as I was—countless times on the flagstone walkways of campus. She had a beautiful soprano voice. Her boyfriend knew how to make her songless. He hammered her throat.

It was a chilling synchronicity, a coincidence I stored away, thinking that one day I might be able to decode what it all meant.

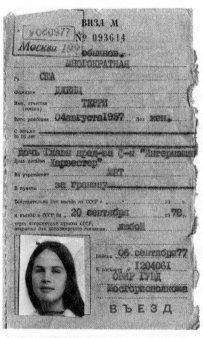

July 17, 1977

I sat alone in a room high in the Intourist Hotel in Moscow overlooking the Kremlin's golden domes bathed in an amber light. If it felt bizarre to be abruptly airlifted from a hospital in the western desert back to midwestern suburbia, it was downright surreal to be abruptly airlifted over the Iron Curtain to this drab Soviet room with its exotic Byzantine view—all in the space of three weeks.

In this room, I sensed what I had known from Russian literature and history: Russia was a place where sorrows could be fully enjoyed. It was a country with an exceptional familiarity with death and suffering. In Russia, it was appropriate to marinate yourself in melancholy. And that was what I was in the mood to do.

Ecstasy and injury—who but the Russians would devise a word describing feelings the mind thinks of as incompatible but the heart knows belong together: *umilenie*. It is an old-fashioned word you might find in Russian Bibles and Dostoyevsky, describing a state of being in which you have been taken down, brought to your knees, humbled—when kaleidoscopic emotions of tenderness, humility, sadness, and rapture all wash through you. *Umilenie* described the new stirrings I didn't recognize: the rush of rage had now morphed into an exhilarating sadness.

Out of darkness and passion came an insight I hadn't before understood: I had been raised in a family that taught basic morals, a strong spirituality that invested life with meaning, and a faith in something beyond the material. But I was allowed to be an especially self-centered child, growing up in a self-indulgent generation, and something was missing in my development. Now I had glimpsed another quality of being residing within me that was capable of self-sacrifice in service of another human being. I was awash in the insight that every human life is intricately connected to every other, and what inside me had been sullen and cynical, hollow and aching, was now crying out for connection. I replayed that June night over and over. I read and reread letters from friends and strangers expressing their love, praising my courage and strength. My heart was twisting and turning; I felt the organ so acutely I figured everyone could see it, as though it were pinned on my shirt, exposed and throbbing. I felt vulnerable, and locked myself in my room alone.

. . .

MY VIGOR INCREASED. I could leave my room at the Intourist Hotel and venture to a bench in nearby Alexander Gardens, beneath the red Kremlin walls. There I watched huge blocks of floral color ebbing and flowing, crowds of Russian women on outings, all wearing identical polyester dresses. And when I felt stronger still, I began to take a daily walk across the vast open expanse called Red Square.

Every day they stared: One-armed war veterans with ribbons and medals hanging from soiled coats. Baby-faced soldiers. Babushkas in shawls. For sure, I was different from Soviet girls my age. But never had they seen, not even among other American girls in baggy corduroys and tight T-shirts, one who looked quite like this: a girl especially tall by Russian standards, with a shaved head, fresh gashes, and one arm in a sling. Brazen souls equipped with a smattering of English would approach me: "*Devushka!*" they would call out. "What has happened to you?" Or they would cackle derisively, "*Malchik!*" as they often mistook me, with my shorn hair, for a gender-confused oddity, something between a boy and a girl.

I was given to answering candidly. And my answer invariably incited a lecture: what happens in the morally bankrupt West would *never* happen in the Soviet Union, at least not according to *Pravda*. In letters to friends in the States, I dared hyperbolize, describing myself as "the second attraction on Red Square, after Lenin's Tomb."

And Lenin's Tomb was an attention-getter, for sure: back and forth in front of the black granite tomb the honor guard goose-stepped in their shiny jackboots, like Nazis in those documentaries about Hitler. Stiffly holding guns bristling with shiny knives, they kicked their legs unnaturally high, their knee-length coats swinging like skirts. Tourist kids imitated the weird, stiff march, then fell to the ground giggling.

The display in front of Lenin's Tomb seeped into me, its totalitarian aesthetic conflated with my biography: One night in July, a white night in these high latitudes, the sun shone outside my bedroom window at 3:00 a.m. But inside my dreaming head it was black night on Red Square. The cobblestones were lit by an electric glow. Our humble little two-man tent was pitched in front of Lenin's Tomb. Two bicycles leaned on kickstands nearby. A military truck emerged from the darkness and careened over the tent. The tent collapsed on the cobblestones. A Soviet soldier wearing shiny jackboots above his knees emerged from the truck. I recognized him. He was one of Lenin's goose-stepping honor guards. Instead of a bayonet, he had an axe. With a stiff arm, he swung at a body. Maybe mine. It wasn't clear. But I awoke in a sweat.

IN EARLY AUGUST, around the time of my twentieth birthday, my parents and I moved from the hotel into an enclave south of the city center, meant to isolate foreigners from Soviet citizens. Inside this crumbling Soviet edifice surrounded by concertina wire, we settled into an enormous apartment provided by my father's company. There our rooms were bugged and there we were spied on by KGB sentinels in guard boxes in the parking lot. Several days a week, I was tutored in Russian by a Soviet spy named Galina, who taught me to inscribe letters in Cyrillic, while slipping in sly inquiries about just who my Russian friends were. Study kept me busy, but I worried obsessively about Shayna. I couldn't hide the panic that would seize me at moments—a spike of cold fear that she might suddenly die. My mother calmed me on these occasions. "It's not possible that Shayna will suddenly drop dead like that!" she would console me, bringing me back to my senses.

Often I would fixate on one particular memory I had of the bike trip, the day before the ascent to the summit, one day before the assault. Shayna and I were buying groceries in a country store when she looked up at me and asked, "Which canned soup do you want for dinner?" I looked down into her eyes and perceived them as liquid pools, dark and deep. I remember thinking in just that instant, why has this mundane moment separated itself from the flow of others? Of all the times I looked at her, answered a simple question, why now, looking into her eyes, had *this* moment pierced my awareness? In hindsight, I read it as a portent, one I hadn't missed but couldn't interpret.

I couldn't bear the uncertainty over whether Shayna would regain her complete eyesight. Dozens of times I reran the attack scenario with our fates reversed. Picturing myself blind, I imagined the death of all that defined me: my wanderlust, my visual eye, my independence.

"Terri, it's Shayna who lost her sight, not you," my mother had to say to me.

But now my infatuation with Shayna had turned into something else, something I didn't understand that locked into my psyche the night of the attack and rearranged me. During those potent hours when I was so close to her life and to her death, some part of me had merged boundaries and couldn't let go.

For moments I had been released from the cramped quarters of my usual heart space and I was utterly confused by this reach of feeling. It had to do with love. That much I knew—but a more complicated notion of love than anything I'd experienced.

What I had experienced were warm currents of feeling tinged with pain that I learned to conjure up out of thin air. It started in my early teens, when I learned to will these feelings to overtake me. This adolescent love—love in the abstract, fantasy love, being in love with love—heightened my senses, made me feel intensely alive, but stopped way short of physical desire. I can say this because merely listening to sad songs about lost love in other languages, particularly in French, could trigger these feelings as easily as any flesh-and-blood human being.

I remember precisely the moment it struck with Shayna: not long after we met during our freshman year, we were chatting in the hallway outside our dormitory suites. A voice inside my head made a decision: I would make this girl the object of warm currents of feeling. She would work on me like a powerful drug. The reasons I chose Shayna were largely unconscious. But she wasn't the first and she wouldn't be the last.

What I experienced the night of June 22 was different. The complexity of feeling told me it wasn't just one type of love but many combined into a thick weave. I was a bookish girl, so I found a copy of Erich's Fromm's *The Art of Loving*. I sat on park benches and dutifully made my way through chapters on the many varieties of love: brotherly, motherly, erotic, love of self, love of God. I learned that love is not a warm, fuzzy feeling that visits you by chance, but rather an act of will. It is an art, and like other arts, it demands practice. I wondered what that meant in regard to Shayna—that love is an art, and demands work and practice. I wasn't sure.

But there was no question in my mind that my friendship with Shayna would endure. Thanks to the extreme event we had shared, I felt sure that our friendship had evolved from the typical friendship of young people who stay together only as long as their proximity to one another lasts. I had in mind a friendship of the rarest type, which reached deeply into two people, would require attention and sacrifice, would survive any test.

I wrote her a letter: "As far as I am concerned a lifelong friendship is sealed in blood. If you don't feel that way, please tell me quickly, so I can start changing my mindset." And I leveled with her about how deeply she had hurt my feelings. "I have to purge myself of something while the memory is still fresh. As I clumsily tried to explain in the hospital, my being at one point so close to your life had a powerful psychological effect on me. My maternal passions are flaming for you. Also, because of the way events happened, I've carried pretty much the whole emotional burden of this thing, and it was no small matter for me. But I think I've handled it well. I've suffered none of those insidious psychological scars that everyone wrote to warn me about, and I'm sure that I'm a stronger, more sensitive person as a result . . ." But, I continued, in a time of acute emotional stress, "unrequited affection in the hospital was far more painful than a chest full of broken ribs."

I knew that Shayna's sister read her letters aloud to her. This embarrassed me. In a perfect world my infatuation would never have seen the light of day. I didn't even want to acknowledge the implications of these feelings to myself.

I decided not to send the letter. But then I couldn't help myself. On that crucible night, my adolescent love had been alchemized into something higher and deeper, something that could not be denied expression. I mailed it anyway.

Shayna wrote back that she was sorry I felt the way I did. She herself had noticed that she was treating me differently before the accident. She guessed it was because whenever she spent a great deal of time with any one person, even little things could get on her nerves. And she admitted that she wasn't "completely on the ground" in the hospital. But, she assured me, she was eternally grateful for my actions in Oregon. And she urged me to see a psychiatrist, a doctor who specialized in traumatic cases, someone I could talk to about my memories.

She wrote also that her strength had returned to normal. She could jog again. She could see the time on a clock, and though she couldn't yet read, she could make out individual letters in a book. She would arrive in Moscow the second week of September, as planned. The surgery she required—to have a plate inserted over the opening where the skull had been punched through—would wait until after she returned from the Soviet Union. Another classmate regularly in touch with Shayna lifted my spirits by reaffirming that, as far as he knew, Shayna would most certainly join me in Moscow. "Shayna is glad she won't be returning to Yale until the spring, so people will forget what happened," he wrote to me, as though this news was of ordinary interest.

MY FATHER remembers that he and I met Shayna and her father when they arrived in Moscow in September. Although I can recall studying *The Art of Loving* in the waiting room of shabby Sheremetyevo Airport, I cannot reproduce the reunion in the sickly light of that place. My own memory chooses to stage the encounter in a more dramatic Russian Cold War setting:

The sky was a thick slab of slate, the sun in total eclipse, and the gaudy floral dresses had dissolved into shapeless black coats by late September. My heart was heavy as I rode a red tramcar that carved through filthy slush, past one colossal red propaganda billboard after the next—brandishing hammers and sickles, calling the workers to march toward Leninism—and I wondered, would the reunion with Shayna bring the mutual bond I sought? My gloom warned me no.

I changed streetcars three times, until one of Stalin's seven architectural monstrosities that looked like wedding cakes appeared on the dull horizon. This one housed MGU, Moscow University, where Shayna would live while her father taught classes. Then I spotted them, Shayna and Milton, waiting for me in the shadow of the forbidding pile, as the biggest snowflakes I'd ever seen fell from the sky. So we meet again, I thought to myself, in this unlikely place, with our two unlikely families, whose destinies have briefly converged.

She was bundled in a long coat, a scarf wrapped tightly around her neck. Her round face was pale, her eyes unfocused, and she didn't express delight when she saw me—or rather, when she heard my voice. Absent was her fresh and clear face. It seemed out of character for the girl I had once known that she looked at the ground when she walked.

No, the moment of my reunion with Shayna and her father was not the warm embrace I had sought. It was as chilly as the air and colored like the sky.

We saw each other only a few times over the next few weeks. Occasionally our families shared a meal, or a contact with a dissident or a journalist, or a Soviet adventure—such as the October night of the Jewish holiday Simchat Torah, when I tagged along with Shayna and her father to a synagogue and watched the dancing spill out into the street, knowing the KGB goons in plastic raincoats were milling in the crowd, incognito, with their cameras.

I didn't get to see her often, but was relieved to be closer to news of her recovery. Doctors speculated it would take up to six months for her frontal vision to be completely restored. September and October brought little progress from one day to the next, until finally progress stopped altogether. Spots of darkness would remain in her visual field for the rest of her life.

MY PARENTS planned a vacation in Paris for one week in late October. As it happened, during that same week Shayna's father would be needed in the States, and he asked me to be her caretaker. Paris was a dream destination for me. But nothing would have brought deeper contentment than the chance to care for Shayna. Eagerly I accepted what felt like an honor, and she moved into my parents' apartment for that week. We were alone together for the first time since the bike trip.

Every day we hoofed it past the uniformed KGB guard in his little booth whose watchful eye followed us and who presumably noted our comings and goings to the Department of Comings and Goings, as we filled our hours with wanderings around Moscow. As Shayna's wary guardian who held an unusually privileged memory, I kept my eye fastened on the back of her head. I knew enough about Russian crowds to fear them—the unyielding bodies en masse that left casualties crushed against barricades and walls at soccer games and state events, even in subways—so I let Shayna walk in front of me. I kept sight of that vulnerable spot, skin stretched over an open head wound, soft brain, covered now with shocks of short dark hair. As we swooshed out of the subway tunnel at Red Square in an inexorable rush, I plotted to tackle any of the thick black coats that might shove between her and me.

Under a rare blue sky, we crossed the great plaza to Saint Basil's Cathedral (named for a Russian Holy Fool named Basil who apparently lay buried beneath it), a confection of domes and bell towers that rose from Red Square with a thirteenth-century solidity and playfulness that Soviet Russia lacked. Shayna lifted her Instamatic to her right eye, aimed somewhere toward the domes, and snapped.

I watched her and wondered: How much could she see? What was she framing? The enormity of her loss seized me with sorrow. Nothing could ever restore to us the days when our eyes would alight on the world in the same way.

Throughout that week Shayna and I spoke nothing at all of Oregon—nothing at all—except a passing reference to our biking companions, Kathy and Mark. I scrutinized the events of each day for traces of our original bond, but our rapport was clearly different.

A single day remained before my parents were due from Paris. All afternoon I anticipated my last opportunity to disburden myself.

Night came. I was in my bed, under soft lamplight, and she on a mattress next to me on the floor. I bantered on, small talk, then:

"You know, I really want to tell you everything that happened that night in Oregon."

"No! Don't . . . I'm not kidding you. I don't want to hear it."

"Oh, come on."

"No."

"Still? You don't want to ever hear it?"

"No."

I insisted to Shayna that I would just have to tell her anyway. I switched off the lamp. She covered her ears with her pillow, and I began to recount the details of that night. I figured if I just kept talking she would take the pillow away out of her determined politeness.

She did not. She also did not run out of the room and set up a bed on the comfortable sectional couches in the living room. Her staying was one concession to my desperation to connect, but her ears remained deeply buried, and I droned on for some time. I think I told the whole story, maybe even those parts I might not have revealed had I thought she was listening. I remember being annoyed with her for not listening, I remember thinking unkind thoughts: a picture of three monkeys, hear-no-evil, see-no-evil, speak-no-evil, sailed through my mind as I looked down at Shayna under her pillow. Neither one of us seemed to be especially tormented by our cruelty toward the other. I think we both fell right to sleep, and we awoke in our stalemate. She had succeeded in living another day without letting me push onto her what she abhorred hearing. I began another day with the pain of the unheard story.

SHAYNA LEFT MOSCOW after a couple of months, determined to attend the spring term at Yale. She could now read painstakingly with large magnifiers, and intended, regardless of her disability, to finish premedical studies. I planned to stay in Moscow through the entire school year, to continue my self-study of Russian culture and provide companionship for my lonely mother, still distraught over the events in Oregon.

That I was one of the few Westerners whom the regime permitted to move around Moscow unescorted gave me powerful motivation to recover my full strength, and I began to cavort around town with a new Russian friend, dodging the all-seeing eye and all-hearing ear. But by December, the circus of the macabre had begun to wear me out. I'd seen enough fiendish imagery: a glowing Lenin's corpse, goose-stepping soldiers, even menacing tank parades on city streets. Yale's ivory towers were looking like shelter. I decided to return for the spring semester.

Besides, I'd stirred up trouble for my father. At the ballet one night, he drew me out of earshot of my mother and confided to me that a subtle threat from the KGB had reached his ears: the spooks didn't like that I was in possession of the children's book *Eloise in Moscow*, with its clever illustrations of the overprivi-leged, ill-mannered little Eloise on her tour of the Soviet capital, trailed every-where by dark figures peering out of spyglasses. I had made a copy of the book on a Xerox machine in my father's office. I thought I was making only one copy. But there was a soul in this machine: it was actually making two. The "shadow" copy fell into the hands of the KGB. Furthermore, the KGB goons didn't like the friends I had made, the dissidents I associated with, specifically the *Jewish* dissi-dents. The particular KGB agent assigned to spy on my father's company was pre-sumptuous enough to voice his disapproval of our contact even with "that Jewish family whom we knew from the States." At Christmas, I effused in a letter to fel-low bikers Mark and Kathy Rentenbach, "What a life I've been leading . . . victim of an axe attack in June and KGB harassment in December. And I'm only a callow 20-year-old!"

For our Christmas holiday, we took, in the language of Westerners living aus-terely behind the Iron Curtain, a "rest and recovery" trip to cushy Western Eu-rope. On our last night in Vienna, my mother and I were together in our hotel suite. Suddenly, out of a moment of inner anguish having nothing to do with outer circumstances, I let out a hair-raising scream that unwound my diaphragm over a count of ten. Then I shrieked that I would hurl myself out the window of this very room. My loyally attentive mother sat with me on the bed with a firm set to her jaw, gazing into the middle distance, and waited until the last decibel had fallen into the heavy draperies. For months now, she had been observing me, try-ing to fathom the black moods and flashes of rage that swept through me in the aftermath of that night in June. But she knew me this well: I had no intention of hurling myself out the window of this very room or any other. She sat with me quietly until my show of histrionics was over, and we left to meet my father for dinner.

I SHRUGGED OFF Russian melancholy as soon as I arrived back at school. In New Haven, the sun blazed brilliantly and the snow glittered. The housing committee had awarded me an unofficial "psychological single"—a cozy room with a great east-facing view of the stately mansions of Hillhouse Avenue.

Those who had read the grisly headlines could hardly believe I might come back from such an ordeal intact and, to outward appearances, with such a great attitude. To some, I became a "victim hero." Not a *victim*, mind you. Nobody likes victims very much—the ones who *look* freakish and scare you with reminders of the world's cruelties and horrors. I was a victim *hero*: not only was I a survivor, but also I had survived looking great, with no hooks for hands, no eye patch, no gash marring rosy cheeks. In fact, I looked better than before, as I had dropped fifteen pounds and now sported a chic gamine hairstyle and stylish Austrian clothing.

I quickly became the subject of great interest. I would catch passing whispers of conversation about me: *"Isn't she the one who got mauled by a bear in Yellow-stone Park last summer?"* One of the titans of the English Department included me in his list of after-hours phone calls to pretty young undergrads. Another young English professor researched all the news articles about the attack, and wrote romantic poetry about his vision of me: a solitary, compulsive wanderer, "core-riven by desire and loss." I got unlimited extensions on papers from whatever professor I asked. My suffering had been transmuted into privilege, something to be coveted. Surely, they thought, my bloodbath had taught me something about what it meant to be *alive*, had revealed to me some special *gnosis*, a mysterious knowledge. A classmate sitting next to me in the dining hall told me one day that, though it might seem weird, she actually *envied* me my experience. I told her soberly and with subtle pride that no, it didn't seem weird to me at all. Indeed, I felt that my experience had in some sense anointed me.

DURING THE SUNNY, snow-bright winter of 1978, Shayna and I saw each other infrequently. We made no special plans to meet, but when our paths happened to cross, Shayna always urged me to get psychiatric counseling, since she believed that, of the two of us, I was the one in need of professional help to process the traumatic memories.

By February, eight months had transpired since the incident, but adrenaline still powered me by day and nightmares fueled my nights. The dreams had morphed into scenes of natural devastation: I was clinging for life on jagged offshore rocks, as foaming seas washed away the bags and boxes containing all my worldly belongings.

One day I caved in to Shayna's advice and requested psychiatric treatment from the Yale Health Center. They assigned me to a lean, pale, bearded man in a white coat. He looked like a doctor in a Chekhov play, the decent man who arrives to give succor to the depressed, delicate lady languishing in her decaying country estate—he himself too soft and ineffectual to face the brutalities he is seeking to exorcise. The doctor began by asking what I wanted to talk about. I told him my story in its rawest and cruelest form: all I had to do was glance down at my Frankenstein arm with its still-crimson gash to summon into the psychiatrist's office the essence of that night—ruptured flesh, severed bone, agonized heart.

The Chekhovian doctor couldn't help himself. His training crumbled under the story. He may have thought I was absorbed only in my tale, but I watched him carefully as his eyes moistened and a tear slid down his sallow cheek and disappeared into his beard. He recovered himself but said very little. It didn't matter to me what he said, because I had already decided that the man was weak. Shedding tears for me wasn't what I needed. Tears only incensed me. I decided that I wouldn't be counseled by this man, or by anyone else. Who could possibly understand the shadows I was navigating? The glimpse of an awakened heart that had blasted open months before was shuttered now. I was shut down, severed from compassion for myself.

But I pressed on with Shayna. As she became more opaque and ever more remote, I became more demanding. I insisted that we had to clear up unfinished business. Finally she agreed, showing up in my room one night, bracing herself for a tough talk.

Outside the sash windows, a heavy snow fell on the eighteenth-century mansions that lined Hillhouse Avenue. Inside, a fire crackled and Billie Holiday sang the blues. We two students were back at the hearth, sheltered by this old institution, this fairy-tale place that we had sought to escape months before. We had found in the unprotected world the most extreme transgression, and had brought it back with us, into this room, buried in our psyches—and in our bodies in the form of metal plates substituting for bone.

She said it right from the start: no, she still didn't want to hear the story of that night, if that just happened to be the agenda I had set for the evening.

I sat quietly and deliberated about what to discuss, if not that.

Billie wailed. The embers smoldered in the fireplace.

"You know," I said after a while, "I couldn't have saved you if I hadn't cared for you so deeply."

I'm certain I used the word *saved* that snowy February night. I'm certain because, in 1979, I scrawled this half of a sentence in my journal: *But I couldn't have saved you if.*

In 1979, I still remembered clearly the second half of the sentence I had said to her, the part about caring deeply, but I didn't commit it to paper because it was too painful to contemplate. I remembered just as clearly what she had said next:

"Maybe you shouldn't have."

I did document that line in my '79 journal, along with what had followed: she had said that she believed that her disability was her "penance" for the pain she had caused me.

I think what she meant was: she would rather have died than feel an obligation to me that she couldn't fulfill. Because she truly did not want to give back.

Her disability was her penance for not having been able to return to me what I relentlessly pushed toward her. She must have felt intense guilt in that precise moment. For one who once wore a string on her finger to remind herself to be kind, her hardness of heart toward me must indeed have caused her pain.

Oddly, I can easily imagine being in Shayna's shoes that night. Hardness of heart is a state I know well. More often than having my heart pinned on my shirt, exposed and throbbing, I have felt it like a stone, inert in my chest.

What was I looking for that she did not want to give? What would have satisfied me? *But I couldn't have saved you if . . .* Perhaps an element of yearning for an acknowledgment that I had helped save her life? Yes, but not, I think, because I wanted her to be beholden to me. Rather because I wanted her to pay attention; I wanted her to reach in and touch me in response to this life-changing event. (And anyway, hadn't she helped to save me, too? Without her energizing presence fighting for life, I might have bled to death in that place.) No. It wasn't about the saving. I wanted her to let me into her psyche, as she had lodged in mine.

Something, however small, was missing in the room that night—an unrequited something or another—a missing moment that followed me with the fidelity of a shadow for a very long time. That night, a haunting was hatched, and in the overall design of life, this is an irony, considering one of my childhood fantasies. When I was a little girl, six years old, night after night I reran in my mind one of my favorite fantasies: I imagined a round pit dug deep in the ground, three times my height. Another little girl my age was trapped inside. The pit was on fire, flames licking the edges. I would somehow muster great courage to jump in and rescue the little girl before the flames closed in. We would bond around the experience we had shared, happily ever after.

Shayna and I never said goodbye when she graduated in the spring of 1979 with the rest of our class. If there was a figure in the underworld responsible for our destinies, for a time, careening along the same subterranean path, by now that phantom had thrown a switch and sent us hurtling onto two wildly diverging tracks, on into the years to come.

I STAYED ON into the next fall semester to finish up my degree. Without Shayna there, the university felt as empty as the hospital in Bend, Oregon, the day after she left. I was taking a poetry writing class that fall of 1979, and I absorbed what I was taught: all art is about degrees of woundedness; from this a poem springs. Now it was too late to grieve with Shayna, so I grieved into verse. I stayed up all night recalling the incident of nearly two years before, when she'd developed her snapshots from our tour of Moscow. Proudly she had displayed them to me: pictures of blurs and blobs.

> *"I just got back*
> *my pictures of Russia."*
> *Fellow traveler, newly blind,*
> *home from sightseeing.*
> *I might expect*
> *the usual Kodak instamatic*
> *stipple-surface square*
> *portraits of red eyes—*
> *if not for a vision that*
> *held the plastic black*
> *box up to the face to snap*

two onions of Saint Basil's—
I think. A blurry face
of a monument at a tilt.
A study in blue of a
Russian sky and a
blob in the corner that
hints of a Kremlin
tower or maybe
a portico of the Bolshoi.
All neatly under plastic in
Stipple-surface, gold-trimmed
"My Photo Album."

"Do you remember this time?"
"And this?" I can only see,
(for tears blur my eyes),
a will that made
of what you could not see
a record that you still cannot
see. But will just
because you cannot.
"Yes, I remember."—the sky and
the blob and a time when
you would have seen the Bolshoi.

That same fall of 1979, my father called me. He'd just gotten off the phone with one of the detectives from Oregon. Finally they had a suspect: a guy in jail had confessed the Cline Falls crime. The suspect, however, had taken a polygraph to determine his guilt, and the results pointed to his innocence. This should not trouble us, the detective told my father, because he was, nonetheless, most likely the man responsible. He assured us that the suspect had done some very bad deeds and would accordingly be in jail a "very long time," so we should feel some closure. The lawman gave my father the impression that possibly an indictment and trial would be forthcoming, and he would let us know if they needed me to fly back to Oregon.

I envisioned an all-expenses-paid trip back to that high-altitude landscape, to a courtroom drama like something out of *Perry Mason*. I pictured myself on the witness stand surrounded by lots of dark oak, facing the axeman across the room. This news provided an opportunity for me to write another poem. Now I would versify that other individual with whom my fate was intertwined in a three-strand braid. "To the Axeman Finally Caught Two Years After the Crime":

So we'll meet again. Only
This time (if you don't mind)
I'll stand. I want to be
More dignified than previously
When you came like a flash and
Tried to abscond with my life.

Mythological monster interrupting
My sleep, Green Knight with an axe
Headless horseman (substitute Chevy
Pick-up), seen from below in the dark
with legally blind without glasses
20/400 vision, as you chopped
Through my ulna, unbeknownst to me,
And battered my cranium—funny
I remember thinking what
An attractive physique you had.
(And thanks for using a classy tool.
Me and Raskolnikov's old lady)

If you meant to offend me—
In the bliss of warmth at the edge
Of life, known only to a privileged
Few who return to tell,
My spine wasn't bristling with
Indignity. In truth I didn't care.

And I won't bother to ask you why.
I won't ask you: But why?
. . .
Instead I toss the flame to you.
I've already brushed my Waterloo.
It's time you sampled yours.

No need to worry. It would seem
(By virtue of my being)
that the proverbial balance of life
And death tilts a touch towards life
But won't it be ironic—that when your
Neck hangs on the scale, you
who dwell on the lighter pan will have
Permission to high-tail to the other?

Society sure enough will keep
You around (we're civilized in most
States). Life clings even to its blunders.
I survived in spite of you.
And you'll survive in spite of yourself.

My spine wasn't bristling with / Indignity. In truth I didn't care. At that age, a need for justice didn't preoccupy me. I wasn't thinking that the meticulous cowboy had left his mark on me. In fact, my scars and broken bones by now seemed to have nothing whatsoever to do with him; these scars and broken bones seemed my very own creation, markings that had *individuated* me.

In any case, we never heard from the detective again. I stopped thinking about that town in Oregon, and about those people who sent me flowers and cards. I hardly remembered the two local kids who answered my cries for help.

Not Mine Alone

In a Bend motel room on an overcast October day in 1992, I sat down to study again the scrappy written record of the investigation into the Cline Falls attack. I was astonished to find that the inquiry had petered out by the end of the summer of '77. The final two pages of the crime report then jumped ahead two years, to the late summer of 1979. On September 4, a felon at the Oregon State Penitentiary by the name of Floyd Clayton Forsberg told the Oregon police that his cellmate, Richard Wayne Godwin—aka "Bud" Godwin—had confessed the Cline Falls attack to him:

> Floyd Forsberg stated that he had gotten the following information from Richard "Bud" Godwin during conversations he had with him on or about July 4, 1979 while at the Oregon State Penitentiary. Floyd Forsberg stated while in contact with Bud Godwin he was detailing his past criminal involvement to him at the Oregon State Penitentiary and described the following incident. Godwin told him that he has a niece or cousin, Forsberg could not remember which it was, who resided in Eastern Oregon. Bud told him that he had been involved in past sexual relations with this individual. During the time of the incident, he heard that this girl was camping out at a park with her boyfriend. Bud said that after finding this information out, he became jealous and decided to teach them both a lesson. On the night of the incident, he drove to the particular park where the girl and her boyfriend were alleged to be camping. He was driving his pickup and found what he thought to be her camp tent. He said he then drove over and through the tent, attempting to run over the occupants. However he discovered that this was not his niece or cousin's tent . . .

Forsberg told police that "Bud" turned over to him a handwritten, signed confession admitting to the Cline Falls attack. Forsberg gave police the impression that this alleged written confession contained still more explicit details than those Forsberg himself was willing to provide. However, when police asked Forsberg to turn over the document, he declined—"for reasons of his own." In other words, no official had ever laid eyes on it.

I remembered when the Oregon State Police detective called my father in the fall of 1979 and told him about the man in jail who had confessed to the Cline Falls crime, even though he had taken a polygraph that pointed to his innocence. At the time, I wasn't engaged by this development in the case. I didn't call the police myself to ask why they had dropped the case after they learned of this confession. I didn't ask what had led them to believe the man was guilty if a polygraph had indicated otherwise. I wasn't curious about what grievous deeds had landed him in jail or how long his sentence would be. The matter just trailed off while I pushed the whole subject out of my awareness. I relegated the news to a footnote in a story that, in my mind, revolved almost exclusively around my special adolescent rite of passage.

Clearly the "Bud" Godwin mentioned in the record of the investigation was the same suspect the detective had been referring to in 1979. I studied his description: He stood five foot six and weighed 140 pounds. Brown and gray hair. Blue eyes. Born 1945. That made him thirty-two years old in 1977. I remembered a guy who was taller and younger: at the time of the attack I told the police five ten to five eleven, early twenties. Oddly, there were no documents included in the report indicating that Godwin had taken a polygraph to determine his involvement in the Cline Falls attack. In fact, it seemed that the detective hadn't followed up on Godwin at all. That the meager file ended there disturbed me. How could there have been no follow-up? Wouldn't they have wanted to close the case? Didn't they care that they were leaving the community with an axe murderer in their midst?

Now I was staring into the bright lights of the second question that had inspired my quest. Who was this person with a history, a face, a future, at the center of my story? Aside from the mystery of the attacker's identity, I had to confront a possible motive for my near murder fifteen years before. I was forced to wrap my mind around the gnarly question: *Why?* Why would someone, on a hair-trigger whim, target two girls for destruction, complete strangers to him? For the first time in fifteen years, I gathered my mental energies and pushed through the density that always thickened around the question of the perpetrator.

I dilated that moment when our attacker put pedal to metal and sent his pickup careening over our tent. *Why?* He thought we were someone he knew? No. I didn't buy it: whoever took the hatchet to us could clearly see whom he was swinging at. Neither of us could have been mistaken for someone's "boyfriend." If it had been Godwin, I did believe he might have wanted to teach someone "a lesson." I knew such men abounded—the ones who hated women as a category, and who vented their rage on any vulnerable member of the gender.

Still, perhaps there was some truth in this story. I imagined that Shayna and I had traded destinies with a girl we didn't know. A twitch of emotion crossed my heart. The insight grew on me—yes, we must have swapped fates with a stranger, a young woman close to us in age, and I felt a sudden intimacy with her. The question of whether or not Godwin was our mutual nemesis dangled limply at the conclusion of this investigation that ended in 1979. Involuntarily, I touched my hand to my heart.

"You know, I'm feeling a lot of anger. This is an investigation?" I spouted to Robin. "This is bullshit!"

For many years I had disguised my avoidance and denial behind spiritually vacuous notions that I was vibrating on a higher plane because I was not angry at my attacker. Now, finally, rage so long repressed flared up with a muscular spasm.

"Do you feel ripped off?" Robin asked. She was measuring my reactions to this revelation, looking for fissures in the façade, as though the fact that I hadn't cared about the identity of my attacker all these years had been responsible for the low vitality and scattered focus she'd observed in me.

Yeah. I felt ripped off. As if the police hadn't given a damn.

After a decade and a half of not caring who my attacker was, now I was incensed: somewhere out there was a man who remained uncharged, untried, unrepentant—a man who had been allowed to get away with it.

"TWO COUNTS of sodomy. One count of murder," the voice over the phone told me.

I winced. A sex killer. This guy was worse than I had expected. Then I caught myself. What *had* I expected?

"Yes, he is still in jail," said the woman from the Oregon State Penitentiary. According to her records, Godwin had been sentenced to life, but had been given a release date of March 1995. That date was approximately two and a half years away. I didn't get it. Didn't life mean *life*?

I asked her, "What were the circumstances of his crimes?"

She told me her records showed only his convictions.

"Of course," I said.

Hearing the disappointment in my voice, she suggested I search the court archives in Lane County, Oregon. That's where Godwin had been sentenced in 1979.

Again I called the woman who had helped me acquire the state police crime report—Marie in Victim's Assistance at the Deschutes County District Attorney's Office. I told her I felt certain I hadn't been given the entire file. Perhaps the slim stack of papers had been purged of other documents? Surely there had to be other reports. Crime lab exhibits? Pieces of physical evidence? Photos? More information on suspect Richard Wayne Godwin? A record of his polygraph test? I pressed her: Could pieces of the investigation reside in places other than the Records Department of the Oregon State Police in Salem? Might some documents have remained locally in Bend?

"Look. I've got violent men beating up women, and these women are calling me *four times a day*. This can't be a priority for me." She paused. "I guess I don't know why you want to do this. The statute of limitations has expired on this case. It can't be prosecuted anymore. What are you looking to do?"

This was the second time I had heard that the statute of limitations had expired on my case. Marie had told me on the phone when I first called, but I wasn't listening carefully. The implication that my attacker could never be prosecuted for this crime was just beginning to hit me.

"Is it revenge you want?" she asked me.

Revenge sounded so ugly. She had meant it to sound ugly.

I wondered to myself, was I vengeful?

If I were vengeful I might have expected those hot fires to have erupted long ago. I believed my motivations were lofty: a dangerous man might be sprung from prison in two years, I told her. Though neither she nor I knew the circumstances surrounding his convictions of sodomy and murder, surely that particular cocktail of deeds meant he might still be dangerous after sixteen years in jail. Furthermore, this same man may also have driven over a tent containing two girls and taken a hatchet to them. Perhaps if people knew the full extent of his crimes, they wouldn't be so cavalier about releasing him. I believed public safety might be seriously at stake.

"And besides," I sputtered, "as someone who was nearly murdered, I don't feel this case was ever handled properly, and I want to find out why."

The words that came out of my mouth surprised me. Why this sudden zeal after years of not caring?

Marie got defensive. "The investigation was done the way it was supposed to be done. Excellent people were working on it." She suggested I drop by the courthouse to see her in person. In the meantime, she would try to turn up more pieces of the investigation.

UPSTREAM FROM Cline Falls, the sinuous Deschutes River winds through the city of Bend on its course to the Columbia. It snakes past several resort motels as a wild river, with steep, boulder-strewn banks and rushing white water, until, in the center of town, it makes an S curve—the bend for which the town was named—and then flattens out into placid waters called Mirror Pond. Near Mirror Pond are a couple of parallel main streets anchored by brick and stone buildings dating from the turn of the century. I understood from reading the *Bulletin* that Bend had developed as a ponderosa mill town prior to World War II, and though the two huge lumber mills had closed by the early nineties, Main Street grew prosperous housing trendy businesses that catered to a recreational crowd flocking to ski Mount Bachelor, a dormant volcano. One of the town's oldest restaurants maintained two thick ponderosa trees growing through its center. Thanks to the recreational crowd, Bend was a fairly liberal outpost in otherwise conservative Central Oregon. With a population of twenty thousand, it had more in common with Eugene, in the Willamette Valley, than with tiny Redmond twenty miles away.

I found the Deschutes County District Attorney's Office on Wall Street, housed in an old courthouse constructed of somber black volcanic rock. I mounted a long stone staircase, then climbed more stairs inside to the second floor. Behind me, a giant modern window spanning both stories framed the Cascades on the western horizon. The volcanoes were sharp and distinct against dry blue skies.

Marie, a tall, deep-voiced woman in her sixties, led me to her office and informed me that, regrettably, she had been unable to find any paperwork other than the slim crime report she and I both now had copies of.

"No physical evidence?"

"This case is very old."

It couldn't be possible. The crime scene had such a physical presence in my memory—with a full complement of textures and scents—that surely the tiny green-and-red two-man tent, some tatter of gold T-shirt, some snippet of red T-shirt, had survived in a plastic bag tagged with identification wires, stored on the shelf of a crime lab somewhere. Even if the case had been closed, I simply would not accept that these relics had entirely vanished from the earth.

Marie sat at her desk and paged through the crime report with avid interest. Battered women may have been vying for her attention, but some curiosity, albeit morbid, would detain her for a while.

"By the way, how is the other girl doing now?" she asked me after absorbing the details of the report. "The Weiss girl?"

I had to admit, I didn't know.

AFTER WE GRADUATED, Shayna and I made no effort to stay in touch. Then one raw late-winter day in 1981, I was slouched at the wheel of a station wagon at a red light on Fifty-seventh Street and Fifth Avenue in the brash cacophony of a New York City rush hour, watching in an absent daze as throngs of pedestrians washed across my windshield.

A young woman bundled in a heavy coat caught my attention. She wasn't rushing with the crowd. She measured her steps, and I suspected she couldn't see well.

In a moment I recognized her. I pulled to the curb and leaped out of the car.

"Shayna!"

Startled, she turned and blinked.

"Shayna!"

She turned her head toward the sound, looked straight at me, but her dark brown eyes didn't focus.

"It's me!"

Her face was blank.

"Terri," I said, and it was painful to have to state my name.

She made a show of recognition, spoke my name, but didn't light up like old friends do when you run into them in places out of the context of your relationship. She looked weary.

In a matter of minutes—traffic and an unresolved past pressing us to rush from each other—we exchanged news: we both were living in New York City, almost neighbors without knowing it. She was studying at a New York medical school. I was working in TV. She told me that life as a medical student was hard for her because of her sight loss. In the last few years, she said, she'd had hard times, the hardest she'd ever known in her life—and I imagined that she had gotten through them as she always had, by sheer force of will.

Drivers leaned on their horns to force me to move. Shayna and I hugged politely and said goodbye, with no promises to stay in touch.

For a long time afterward, I reran the scenario in my mind: Shayna measuring her steps in front of my windshield on that chilly day. I even pictured her with an orange-tipped cane, although I was never certain whether or not this prop was an embellishment of memory. After all, maybe I could no longer view her accurately—since I would forever see her through the prism of her injury.

I thought about how odd it was that our reunion should have taken place in precisely that way, in the cold anonymity of a New York City crowd—that I would have paid attention to the careful steps of one stranger among the multitude of strangers with their multitude of afflictions, and that suddenly the paradigm shifted and the stranger was an intimate, whose affliction I knew only too well. Whose affliction I had held in my very own hands.

Our paths crossed once more. At my college boyfriend's wedding on Long Island, in 1982, my old college roommates tapped me on the shoulder to tell me, "Shayna's here. She wants to see you." They threaded me through the guests until I saw her standing still, smiling warmly but not brightly, as I remembered from that other life. We were formal and said nothing of consequence, but it didn't matter. Just laying eyes on her ratcheted my senses to a sharp alertness.

As it turned out, she needed a ride back to Manhattan, and I could drive her. I had a flash of the same contentment I had felt years before in Moscow, knowing I had a week alone to take care of her. Now I would have two hours. We walked to my car and I pointed to an ancient hardwood tree on the lawn. I recalled from years before how I had learned to reach into her by sharing something of beauty in the natural world. She turned her head to the left and then to the right. I realized she couldn't locate the tree, and I was embarrassed that I'd forgotten about her handicap.

In the car we traded news of our families. Then she brought it up again: had I been in therapy yet? I hadn't. But I must get help to "heal the memories," she insisted. She picked up a magnifying glass and labored through a paragraph from one of her medical textbooks, about posttraumatic stress disorder—the malady that hadn't even been named at the time of our attack, that only since 1980 had been defined into existence by the bible of psychiatric diagnosis, the third edition of the *Diagnostic and Statistical Manual of Mental Disorders*, the *DSM-III*. "The person has experienced an event that is outside the range of human experience," Shayna read, then listed categories of symptoms: "flashbacks, nightmares, psychic numbing, heightened psychological arousal, a distracted mind . . ."

I didn't listen to what she was reading. (Had she brought her homework to a wedding in case she might find a spare moment for study?) I could think only how remarkable it was that she was in the car, sitting beside me. I occasionally took my eyes off the road to watch her poignant figure hunched over her medical book, making out the clinical definition of what she believed must surely be troubling me.

"You really ought to talk to a therapist," she said again, parceling out the very same advice as she had five years before.

At twenty-four, I saw no reason to repeat my experience with the weeping psychiatrist at the Yale Health Center. I perceived Shayna's concern for my psychological welfare only in light of her refusal to hear my story. Did she mean for the therapist to be her proxy? Did she want me to tell my story to a professional, someone with a degree in the ways of psychic wounds, so that my memories would heal over, my haunted mind would dissolve into a serene tabula rasa, and the narrative might cease to exist altogether?

MARIE DREW MY attention to a letter included in the crime report, from a Boston psychic who had written to Shayna's father on July 7, 1977. The psychic had seen Shayna appear on a talk show with her parents, and she was impressed by Shayna's lack of anger. "Most victims of lesser situations will rant and rave, and cry 'why me?' endlessly, never accepting that there is no rational reason for an irrational act." The psychic explained that she was writing to Milton Weiss because her second sight had picked up clues to the crime: the man responsible was a habitual drunk; he had an association with farming; he was a wife beater; he was already known to police. He was drunk when the incident took place, and didn't really remember it now. Although he'd had some thoughts about the attack, he had decided it was a bad dream he'd had, planted in his head by a news broadcast he'd heard. "If he is found before much time passes, there is a cloth—perhaps a bit of clothing or something from the tent—caught underneath his truck." Then the psychic made more apologies for the violent man's irrational acts. "He is a violent man, but not deliberately dangerous. When he jumped out of his truck, he first thought he was chopping down the brush or small tree that had hung him up. He hit before he even knew what he was striking at."

Another woman from the office joined us and listened while Marie finished reading the psychic's letter. "I think the psychic was right . . . he was drunk. He just thought you were a bush, and started chopping," the woman declared.

"I was there," I said bluntly. "And he knew what he was chopping. He did not mistake me for a bush."

The woman began to twitch. Her legs were crossed, and the top leg bobbed up and down. "But an axe. Maybe that's what attracts the extra horror of it . . . the sadistic feeling of enjoying it . . . that'd be quite a different type of mentality," she said through a tight jaw.

WHEN DESCHUTES COUNTY District Attorney Mike Dugan heard that the victim of the unsolved Cline Falls attack had turned up after fifteen years, he was curious. Though he'd occupied his office only since 1989, the storied 1977 incident was well known to him. With his long beard and slicked-down hair parted in the middle, Dugan cultivated the look of a lawyer of the Old West you might see staring out of a tintype.

"You have to know that this case is not prosecutable. The statute of limitations for attempted murder in Oregon is three years," he told me pointedly. The full force of this fact struck me only now. Now I would have to come to grips with the breathtaking reality: the axeman had been off the hook since 1980.

Of course, Dugan explained, crimes of murder have no statute of limitations.

"So just because by some miracle we lived, this case was dropped?"

He shrugged his shoulders. "What *are* you looking for?"

I'd driven a long way with the vaguest of ambitions. Now I wanted answers. I didn't care if the case was prosecutable or not. I asked who else might still be around who would know something about this investigation.

Dugan advised that it was pointless to contact the district attorney from that era—Louis Selkin was in his dotage and indisposed. And unfortunately, the head of the investigating agency, Lieutenant Lamkin of the Oregon State Police, died several years before. But Lamkin's two detectives Bob Cooley and Clayton Durr were retired and living in the area. And I might also pay a visit to Bob Chandler, the editor in chief of the Bend *Bulletin*. He'd been around forever, one of the town patriarchs.

"YOU WERE ONE of *those* girls?"

The librarians in the Bend Public Library were astir. I had walked in and identified myself as one of the two girls attacked in Cline Falls State Park in 1977. They all remembered the incident vividly, and at first they were incredulous that one of the characters in the oft-told tale could be, at this very moment, standing in front of the desk in the library looking so bright-eyed and normal. My presence seemed to animate them, and they rushed to locate the news clips I'd requested from the archives.

Nola, one of the librarians, told me she wasn't even living in the area when it happened. She was living in New York State in June of 1977, planning to move to Bend later that the summer.

"It was shocking; it was something that affected me a great deal. It made a memory that was unsettling to me, and I never let go of it. It's always in my head. And I always wanted any kind of resolution to it."

Something about Nola's words stuck in my mind: *It made a memory*—as though a shard of the past had lodged itself in her mind, one that lived there still, breathing out emotion.

"Well, there's no resolution to it," I told her.

"There's no resolution to it," she repeated.

Here it was again: the collective memory of this story. It had always astonished me that I could meet someone of my generation or older, from any part of the country, who might remember even the particulars of that axe attack. Two girls on a bike. A tent. An axe.

Why, I asked Nola, had *this* memory stayed with her for fifteen years?

She answered only after she considered carefully. "It was the randomness of the event, the violence of the event, the fact that it made me as a woman feel vulnerable . . . Other people I've spoken to remembered it because they were engaged in similar activities. Biking. Camping. Things where we always felt safe. And we didn't like the fact that it had happened in our community—that there was no prosecution, the fact that it made a stain on our community. It was a part of our history that we regretted and couldn't do anything about.

"It has *always* been in the back of my memory . . . It bothered me," she added as she handed me a stack of microfiche boxes.

It was curious. Local Central Oregon coverage of the incident wasn't nearly so eye-catching as that in my hometown of Chicago, where the story made it into all three major newspapers; banner headlines in the *Chicago Sun-Times* and the *Chicago Daily News* ran for three days, morning and evening editions. The *Chicago Daily News* first screamed, "Suburb Girl on Bike Trip Axed in Tent," then "Hunt Ax Attacker of Suburb Co-ed."

The Bend *Bulletin*, however, a paper with a circulation of about twenty thousand, carried stories that were anything but sensational. In fact, the word *axe* never once made it into the headlines, the first of which, on June 23, 1977, read—in small type and no initial caps, in the self-consciously unpretentious style of the paper—"2 women seriously hurt in attack at Cline Falls."

The brief breaking story gave a status report on the investigation: police had released a pared-down version of my description of the assailant (a guy five foot nine to five foot eleven, wearing blue jeans), and told reporters they had no description of the car, no eyewitnesses, and no fingerprints. Coverage in the next three days focused on Shayna's and my daily improvement and, with somewhat less emphasis, on news of the unfolding investigation.

Lieutenant Ken Lamkin of the state police reported that investigators had no leads and had found no trace of a weapon. "Without a motive, we're in pretty bad shape," Lamkin told the *Bulletin*. "We just don't know what would set a person off for as violent and vicious an attack as this."

On June 25, the third day after the attack, police investigators said they still had no suspects, and they were checking manufacturers' specifications to see if they could identify the assailant's vehicle from tire marks made in the park.

Then something caught my attention: an editorial entitled "Someone knows."

Someone knows

Someone in this part of the state either knows or has a strong and probably correct suspicion of the name of the young man who attacked two Yale students at Cline Falls State Park Wednesday.

The assailant knows, of course. It seems obvious that anyone who would engage in such an attack is in need of psychiatric help. He should turn himself in to state or local police officers.

If he's slow to come forth, someone else should. Some friend or relative of the young man who committed the attack either knows the name of the assailant or suspects strongly his identity.

Such attacks are not unknown in this area, although they are rare. Quick apprehension of the perpetrator is necessary to ease the fears of thousands of park, forest and backyard campers in this part of the state at this time of the year. That apprehension may be much quicker if anyone who has any knowledge, or strong suspicion based upon fact, will contact police officers.

This piece amazed me, for a couple of reasons. It seemed slanted toward a belief that the attacker was a local. Then, too, it presented curiously limited reasoning for why he should be apprehended: to ease the fears of the recreational crowd.

The fifth day after the attack, June 27, in an article in the *Bulletin*, investigator Bob Cooley told the paper that they'd "like to think it's a local person, but that's only a gut feeling." Cooley also said he planned to talk that day with a local seventeen-year-old youth charged the previous Friday with assaulting his girlfriend. But apparently Cooley wasn't terribly excited about this lead. He "doesn't expect to tie the youth to the Cline Falls attack," the reporter wrote. This article was curious, too. Here was another indication that the attacker was a local.

Why would Cooley have interviewed this local boy if the investigator already had information that would lead him to expect not to tie the youth to the attack?

Two days later, on June 29, the *Bulletin* featured a story, "Victims of Cline Falls attack look forward to trip home." Illustrated by our high school graduation photos, the article quoted state police as saying that they were still having a hard time finding clues. "But there's a bright side to this story," the article glowed. "The victims may be able to go home with their parents at the end of the week." And better yet, according to the parents, "each will remember Oregon—its beauty and its people—fondly, despite the vicious assault last week."

I spun through issues from the weeks of July and August, but it seemed, as far as the *Bulletin* was concerned, the Cline Falls attack had already fizzled out, been forgotten or suppressed, submerged by the next news cycle.

I expected the news to make the biggest impact on the small community of Redmond. Cline Falls State Park, situated but four miles east of the town, was Redmond's backyard, one of its family watering holes. On Wednesday, June 22, 1977, the weekly *Redmond Spokesman*, in print since 1910, had already gone to press. On that day, the paper featured an article about how crime statistics in Redmond were in keeping with national trends. A diagram demonstrated that the crimes of burglary, theft, vandalism, traffic violations, and disturbances topped the charts. Armed robbery was minuscule. Spousal abuse, rape, and homicide weren't even mentioned. The police blotter for the previous week recorded arrests for "disobeying a traffic signal," "careless driving," "exceeding maximum speed," and "tandem axle overload."

News of the Cline Falls attack had to wait one week. The following Wednesday, June 29, a tiny article appeared—six and a half column inches—tucked into the lower half of an inside page, captioned (in small letters, in the manner of its sister newspaper, the *Bulletin*) "Injured girls improve." That story was deemed of lesser importance than the feature on that page: "Birdman will stay: Riverside residents divided on proposal to reopen quarry," which told of a local character known as the Birdman, who had been granted a license for life to live peaceably in his shack on the river upstream from Cline Falls State Park, but was now threatened by a quarry that might disturb him and the wildlife he cared for.

The lacunae in this paper's coverage struck me as fantastical. Nowhere in *The Redmond Spokesman* that week was there an article about fear among a populace living with an unidentified would-be axe murderer in their midst. Nowhere was there an honest reckoning of whether the assailant who struck at this *local* park might indeed be homegrown. Nowhere was there a quote from a mayor or city council member. There was no call for police and community to work together to solve the crime.

Instead there were two editorials printed that week—one about management of wild horses, another about a spelling bee. And there was a telling advertisement, printed on an inside page, selling work boots. It pictured a cartoon drawing of a barrel-chested lumberjack in plaid shirt and jeans, leaning on a huge double-headed axe. TOUGH, MEAN & RUGGED, the ad copy read.

Finally, in a letter to the editor, one cry in the wilderness issued forth from a local resident: "What is this country coming to? Two innocent girls on a tour of America on bicycles are unnecessarily and brutally beaten?"

Unnecessarily beaten?

The story of the attack cropped up in newspapers in other parts of Oregon in an understated fashion. A couple of articles tried to assure their readership that the state's vaunted recreational wilderness areas were still safe, even though only two weeks before, on June 9, two teenagers, a boy and a girl, were shot to death in broad daylight as they picnicked in a state park near Eugene. Reporters made much of the fact that the victims of the Cline Falls attack had stayed overnight in an area designated for "Day Use Only." The Salem *Statesman Journal*, a newspaper of Oregon's capital, featured an article: "Parks safe, says official. Coeds were attacked in Park day use area":

> Two Yale University coeds who were brutally beaten while on a bicycling trip Wednesday did not heed signs at Cline Falls State Park and camped in a day use area which offered only minimal security, a state park official said Friday. "The problem with the girls was that they were not camping in a designated camp area. They went off into a day use area that was not chained for the night. Anyone could have gone in there."

Since there was no apparent motive for the crime on the part of the assailant—since the real culprit had disappeared altogether—the responsibility had shifted to us: a motive on our part had to be the cause of the whole bloody mess. The state park official said it best: "The problem with the girls . . ."

Six months later, on New Year's Eve 1977, the story resurfaced. The *Bulletin* published an article lamenting that "1977 was a year of trial and tribulation for Central Oregon residents. Residents languished in the drought of the century and watched crime increase." Bend editors and readers were polled on their top local stories of '77. "Women attacked" made the top ten.

And here was something I had not remembered: in the summer of 1978, on the one-year anniversary of the event, an AP reporter caught up with Shayna and me in summer school. A follow-up article appeared in the *Bulletin*, illustrated by a photo of us—two chubbettes (we'd gained back our weight loss), our shaved heads grown out into shocks of hair sticking out in several directions, standing against a backdrop of the gothic towers of Yale.

"Hardly a month goes by without us checking some sort of lead," Lieutenant Lamkin told the *Bulletin*. "But motive is the problem. They don't follow a pattern," he insisted. "There might not be another incident like this for another 10 years."

When the AP reporter asked me if I thought about a motive, I advanced the theory that it was an example of the age-old contempt for women who dare act like men. "He probably was watching us from the road. There was no sexual or robbery motive. The act was pure violence. He just wanted to kill us." Then I went on, philosophizing to the reporter: "I'm not bitter. Not too much frightens me now. Something like that helps put things in perspective."

I studied my own picture, this twenty-one-year-old in baggy corduroys with the awkward hairdo, and could just hear my young self talking. Always so cocksure with unearned certainty.

Shayna had added that she didn't remember anything at all about the attack. "I'm happy about that," she'd said.

THE EDITOR OF the Bend *Bulletin*, Bob Chandler, a man in his sixties with a large florid face, didn't get up from his desk when Robin and I walked into his office.

"I'm here to talk to you about an unsolved crime that happened in this community fifteen years ago—"

I hardly had the words out of my mouth when he interrupted: "You were one of the girls conked on the head in Cline Falls."

That unnerved me, for three reasons: His arch tone. The odd phrase "conked on the head." And that he'd figured out who I was, with an uncanny instinct, from the key words "fifteen years ago" and "unsolved crime."

"Sit down," he ordered.

I told Chandler how astounded I was by how little investigation had been done on this case, considering the magnitude of the crime and the scar it had left on the community, even its impact on the whole nation at the time. I told him that Walter Cronkite, America's most respected newsman of the day, had deemed the incident important enough to make mention of it on the evening news. Why hadn't this community thought it important enough to solve?

"It was a heinous crime, and Walter liked to have a heinous crime a week," Chandler said, fixing me with a haughty look, and puncturing my dream of Walter's personal interest in my destiny.

"You have to understand, motiveless crime was rare. Most often people know the people they kill, and know 'em darn well. You have a ninety percent better chance of getting killed by your brother-in-law who gets mad at you than by a stranger." With his stentorian voice, Chandler sounded like the narrator of a 1940s newsreel.

"But this case was rare. Nobody was even arrested. The investigator had to have something to go on. Investigation really is the gathering of huge bits of little pieces of information. But he had no leads. He had no bloodstained auto found twenty miles away. He had no eyewitness. He had no license plate. He had nobody who was stopped at a service station two hours later and acted insane when he put nickels into the pay phone. Nobody dropped his personal effects at the scene; nobody dropped his wallet, no receipts from a motel where he stayed the night before. This case had absolutely not one thing to work on. You're going to have a different perspective than what I have . . . but I really don't know what else they would have done. Nothing that I can think of. There were tire tracks—but then you've got to find a car with those tires on them. They spread those tire tracks over the state—if anyone's car was involved in something funny, they'd take a look at these tracks. The tire tracks were the only physical evidence at all they had that was identifiable."

I told Chandler that I suspected our attacker would have to have been familiar with Cline Falls State Park to have driven down there at night and known his way around. Did Chandler have a hunch that the perpetrator was a local?

"But anybody could have been there that day and driven off the highway between Sisters and Redmond and seen you, and gone into Redmond, had supper and come back. And they could have been from three thousand miles away. I would have thought that if it'd been somebody from around here, there would have been enough talking—enough this, that, and the other—that someone would have gotten wind of it. Police operate on snitches! What they really operate on is people calling up on the phones or people coming to the police station—on which they can act. That's why I wrote an editorial, to try and shake something loose."

Then it was Chandler who had written the "Someone knows" editorial. At least one editorial voice in Bend had spoken up, even if the editors of the newspaper closest to the event, *The Redmond Spokesman*, had been mute.

"Unfortunately, it didn't work," Chandler added.

"It's a mystery," I stated with obvious irony. Agreeing with Chandler, admitting that this mystery was unsolvable—that I was fated to live forever haunted by the unknown identity of the man who had tried to kill me—seemed to soften the ornery old newspaper man.

"It is. It was a mystery at the time. It was a terrible thing. It did shake up things. It did leave reactions on people," he said, with something like compassion in his voice. "Enough of a reaction so when you came and said 'I was here fifteen years ago,' I knew what you were talking about."

I thanked him for his time, and Chandler, now cheerful and warm, told me he had all the time in the world and sent me out of the office with an offer to help at any time.

I left still astonished that I had only had to say to him "unsolved crime fifteen years ago," and he had known what I was talking about—as though time in this region could be measured by the distance from that particular event, as though my personal history had a claim on the present here.

FROM A PAY PHONE at a lunch spot in Bend, I called Marie at the DA's office. Earlier in the week I had asked a favor of her; it was an important favor, crucial to my ceremonial replay of the events of '77. Could she track down one of my rescuers, Bill Penhollow, so that I might thank him, these many years later, for daring to pick up a bloody apparition in a dark park at night? I didn't know how to find Darlene, the girl who was with Bill that night—her name wasn't in the phone books, and she'd probably married—but I had been told the Penhollows were a large, respected clan in the Redmond community.

I recalled when the couple visited me in the Bend hospital, their sweet faces shyly peering at me over the rail of my hospital bed: Bill with his long white-blond hair that curled up at the ends, and Darlene with her huge, expressive eyes. They were tentative with me, tongue-tied. They gave me a small terrarium, something green and growing. I was polite, but not bubbling over with warmth and gratitude. I didn't feel especially connected to these local kids from this rural culture so far from my Ivy League world. That they happened by that night seemed to me only a convenient stroke of luck. And it was surely they, I had privately groused, who had provided the misquotation to the media "My friend is hurt *bad!*"—causing my snobby ego a certain public humiliation. Now, after fifteen years, I was embarrassed by the way I had once regarded them—as local yokels—and I wanted to thank them from the heart.

"He doesn't want to see you," Marie told me bluntly.

She had talked to Bill's mother, who related that what her son saw that night in the park where he had played as a child had changed his life. In the days after the summer night of June 22, 1977, Bill was a hero in town. He'd helped to save two lives, and the adrenaline rush from his heroism carried him along until it ran out and he had a hard fall to earth. After that, the eighteen-year-old boy moved back into his parents' house, where he'd wake up in the middle of the night screaming, haunted by nightmares. Bill once hit a rough patch in his life, and the family suspected that the vision he saw that night an age ago—in a place he had thought was safe and familiar—was maybe partly to blame. Among the Penhollow clan, Cline Falls wasn't talked about.

I went back to our table in the Bend café and told Robin about this unforeseen twist. Emotion involuntarily welled up until I couldn't hold it back, even in this public place. I cried openly and covered my eyes with my Ray Bans.

We *were* connected, Bill and I. We had both preserved the same white-hot memory of that night. What I saw was a vision most people couldn't fathom. But Bill saw something that I didn't see: me. I knew now, irrevocably, what had never occurred to me before my return to Oregon: this story wasn't mine alone.

Near the Apex of the Turning Tire Impressions Was a Large Quantity of Blood

It is in this rather violent mood that the Deschutes [River] exits from the Bend area.

—RAYMOND R. HATTAN, *BEND IN CENTRAL OREGON*

This time I was not engaged in a grieving ritual. Back in Cline Falls State Park, I was carrying on an investigation at the crime scene fifteen years after the yellow tape was taken down, surveying the grounds with the cool eye of a detective. Camouflaged in Tony Llamas boots and a cowboy hat, I traced the route the perpetrator took on his rampage: Highway 126 travels west to east between Sisters and Redmond. Four miles shy of Redmond, a sign points out the access road, which dips down into the park. This road had been paved and slightly rerouted since 1977, but it originated now as it had then, at a higher elevation on Highway 126, then descended a quarter mile into the park, into a hollow of level terrain bordering the east bank of the Deschutes River. Restrooms constructed of cinder block stood at the bottom of this road. Originating at the restrooms, a paved one-way lane looped around the park, following the horseshoe-shaped bend of the river. Our tent had been pitched in the middle of that bend.

Police had found clear tire impressions in the dirt, indicating that a vehicle had jumped the curb alongside the curved part of the lane. Once on the grass, it had made a semicircle, hit one green picnic table—the police noted fresh damage to one corner of its attached bench and that the table had moved eight and a half inches from its original location—then struck our tent, situated a few feet from the river, where "near the apex of the turning tire impressions was a large quantity of blood in the grassy portion of the park."

Then the vehicle accelerated from the location of the tent, leaving deep ruts,

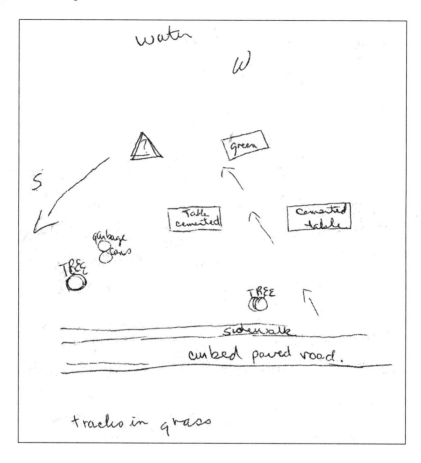

and continued rolling in a semicircle back to the curb farther along the curved one-way lane.

Physical evidence pointed to the moment when the perpetrator jumped the curb. But that moment was preceded by the moment he decided to slam the pedal to the floor. This moment interested me now. How did he know two women were sleeping in the tent? Had he seen us outside the tent just before we retired? Or had he spied on us as we set up camp? When had he first seen us? Had he trailed us across the mountains?

Police had interviewed a handful of people who were in Cline Falls State Park the night of June 22, 1977. The crime report, written by one of the investigating officers, Senior Trooper Robert Cooley, was a digest of what they said:

A Mrs. Gilbert told police that she was having a picnic with her family between 6:30 and 9:00 p.m., just west of the girls in the tent. She and her family observed a man in his thirties, wearing new jeans and a red-and-blue-plaid shirt. He was between her party and the two girls. The man's jeans were dusty and looked as if he may have been working in cement. He cooked his dinner and entered a camper affixed to a light-red pickup with a bed inside. Mrs. Gilbert and her group noted a light-colored canopy and Washington license plates. When her party left at nine o'clock this man was still at the same location.

Two local girls, Dana Walters and Lori Gregory, drove their red Ford Pinto through Cline Falls State Park at 7:30 p.m., then crossed over to the north side of Highway 126, to a swimming hole. A newish red Chevrolet pickup was parked to the rear of their vehicle. The girls got out and walked to the river to swim. The subject in the pickup followed them and sat on a rock watching them. He didn't say or do anything. They described him as about twenty-five years old, maybe wearing a beard, with curly dark hair falling just below his ears. He was wearing a white T-shirt and blue jeans. The girls swam until 8:00 p.m., then left the area and didn't see the man again.

At 6:50 a.m., on June 23, the morning after the attack, an eighteen-year-old teen, Adolph Wende, heard about the assault over the radio and called the police. He said he was in the park at around 11:30 p.m. with a friend, Richard Sala of Redmond. He recalled seeing the small tent in the park and observed a red pickup with a white camper bearing Washington license plates parked nearby. He and Sala crossed to the other side of the highway where local teenagers congregated, then cruised back into the park five minutes later. This time Wende didn't remember seeing the tent, but he claimed that the red pickup was in another location, slightly farther into the park. A white male about twenty-seven years old, about five foot eleven or six feet tall, wearing blue jeans and a white T-shirt, was getting into the pickup.

A girl named Robin Williams also contacted police, saying she had been in the park the night of the attack. She claimed that she and her brother, James Williams, were there with Adolph Wende, Richard Sala, and William Jonas at around 11:00 p.m. They saw an orange pup tent and two bicycles leaning against a picnic table. Parked nearby was a newer-model red Ford pickup with a white canopy. The man standing by the pickup appeared to be thirty-five years old. He stood five foot nine or five ten and wore a light shirt and faded blue jeans. Because the roadway was narrow, they were obliged to pass close to the parked pickup. The driver stood by the door, waiting for them to go by. He wore metal-rimmed sunglasses. His hair was combed back over his ears and was relatively long in back. After they passed by, they heard him start his engine.

Police talked to William Jonas, who had accompanied Robin and James Williams, Adolph Wende, and Richard Sala when they entered the park at around 11:00 p.m. Jonas remembered spotting an orange two-man tent near the river and two bicycles nearby. He also noticed a lone male entering a maroon Ford pickup with a white canopy. Jonas said that the man was in his twenties, about five nine to five eleven and wore a dark, well-trimmed beard. He was dressed in blue jeans and a white T-shirt.

The cops contacted Richard Sala on June 24, and he remembered accompany-ing Adolph Wende during the evening of June 22, and recalled joining James Williams, his little sister, Robin Williams, and William Jonas—but Sala could not recall driving through Cline Falls park.

Actually, it was significant that a fourteen-year-old girl named Robin Williams was present in Cline Falls State Park the night of June 22, 1977. She was the niece of Richard Wayne Godwin, the girl whom Floyd Forsberg claimed Godwin was seeking in a jealous rage.

> On the night of the incident, he [Godwin] drove to the particular park where the girl and her boyfriend were alleged to be camping. He was driv-ing his pickup and found what he thought to be her camp tent. He said he then drove over and through the tent, attempting to run over the occu-pants. However he discovered that this was not his niece or cousin's tent. *Godwin told Forsberg that he later found out that his niece or cousin was at the park and recognized his pickup after he had run over the tent. He said he also found out that the police had questioned his niece or cousin about this in-cident and that she had intentionally given a false description of the suspect's vehicle to conceal his identity* [italics are mine].

My first instinct was to dismiss the motive of mistaken identity. Whoever at-tacked us could see clearly that we were strangers to him. And yet Floyd Forsberg possessed knowledge that Godwin's niece was indeed in Cline Falls State Park the night of June 22. That Godwin knew she was there made Forsberg's allegations of Godwin's guilt somewhat more believable to me.

But Robin was in the company of her brother and three other teens and had *voluntarily* called the police to furnish them with a description of a possible sus-pect and vehicle. Robin's description of a possible suspect was of someone slightly older and a few inches taller than her uncle. Presumably the girl would have known her own uncle if she'd seen him.

If Godwin was present in Cline Falls, did Robin change her description to pro-tect him?

The various descriptions of the man people observed in the park the night of June 22, 1977, were so similar that it was logical to assume they were all describ-ing the same individual: He was maybe in his twenties, maybe thirties. He stood anywhere from five eight to six feet. He wore a T-shirt and jeans, and maybe a plaid shirt. Possibly he had long curly hair, possibly a beard. Possibly he was wear-ing sunglasses at night. Probably he drove a red or light-red pickup with a white camper bed, though the pickup might have been maroon. Maybe the pickup was a Chevy. Maybe it was a Ford.

Was Richard Wayne Godwin the man people had described seeing? One detail didn't fit: police described Godwin as five foot six inches tall. Could cowboy boots with a high heel make a diminutive man, if seen from a distance, look medium height to tall?

MARIE OF THE DA's office was acquainted with one of the two Oregon state police detectives in charge of my case in the late seventies, and she arranged for me to call him.

"I hardly remember anything. And I'm retired now. Been retired since eighty-six," Clayton Durr told me over the phone, in a gruff tenor. His partner, Bob Cooley, had retired even longer ago, in 1980. I could try talking to him, but he was away on a fishing trip.

I pressed Durr, insisting that any detail—any at all—would be gratifying to my psyche, and finally I secured an invitation to his home in Bend.

A burly, balding man with a gunshot scar near his ear on one side of his head, Clayton Durr reluctantly met us at the door of his bungalow in a modest Bend neighborhood. The presence of Robin's video camera rattled him, and he wouldn't let her tape the interview. In speaking of the morning after the attack, he related how he had been called at 5:00 a.m. and given orders by his commander to wade knee-deep in the cold Deschutes River near the crime scene to look for the axe. At nine o'clock that same morning he was ordered to stay in the office for the next two days and man the phones.

"I should never have been called off." As Durr's wife sat quietly behind him, strenuously listening, Durr groused that it had been a waste of his investigative energies to sit in the patrol office fielding calls from crackpots from all over the country with theories on what had happened.

"We never got one decent phone call out of the whole deal. They had things to say, they didn't know what they were talking about. I had one woman from Albany call. She said she knew who did it. Of course your ears perk up. 'Well, I seen a black man throwing a knife against a tree last week.' 'Where's he at?' 'Well, he's in Albany somewhere.' " Durr had asked where in Albany. The woman said she didn't know.

"Everyone in the nation was calling up saying who did it; meanwhile there were no leads."

I pressed Durr to tell me anything at all about the suspect Richard Wayne Godwin and his supposed confession.

Durr remembered no investigative clues that would have linked Godwin to the crime other than Forsberg's claim of Godwin's confession. Durr and his partner, Cooley, never found evidence, circumstantial or otherwise, that Godwin had been trolling Cline Falls State Park on the night of June 22.

But he remembered plenty about Godwin himself: "They found a skull in Godwin's trailer."

"Skull?"

"Of a little girl."

Durr sketchily related that it was inmate Floyd Forsberg who helped law enforcement link the skull to Godwin. Godwin confessed to the murder of a five-year-old girl, Andrea Tolentino, to Forsberg; he had even drawn a map. Forsberg then led police to the remains of a child's body on a remote logging road.

Forsberg tried to attribute other crimes to Godwin. There was Cline Falls, along with a couple of other crimes.

Durr picked up steam as he talked about "Frosty," rattling on like one of those cops with a fondness for colorful crimes. "Forsberg ought to be on screen in Hollywood." He had pulled off a bank robbery in Reno, Nevada. He had a friend by the name of Clark Gable Timmons who, with a female partner, plotted to break him out of jail. They set up a ladder that went from a hotel window to the jail. The girl held the ladder. Forsberg escaped, then all three of them showed up in Bend and robbed another bank. Then Forsberg killed the girl who'd helped him escape. And that's how he ended up in the pen, where he met Godwin. "Frosty" Forsberg was a notoriously unreliable, smooth-talking con who would stop at nothing to turn circumstances to his advantage.

Durr's filmic recall of Forsberg's criminal escapades caused me to question his claim that he recalled little about the Cline Falls case itself. I asked him if he had ever talked to Robin Williams, Godwin's niece.

He told me that he and Cooley tried to talk to her after Godwin's name surfaced in connection with Cline Falls. "She denied any involvement with her uncle and didn't want anything to do with us."

"So that was it? They dropped it?"

Durr shrugged. He had nothing more to offer, and the edgy feeling in the room told me it was time to pack it up.

The retired cop left us at the door with "I never had a decent suspect on this. If anything, maybe it was Godwin."

My friend and I left the desert lands the next morning, bound for Lane County, Oregon: Godwin country. We retraced our path across the snowy summits of the Cascades, until the firs and rhododendrons reappeared and we were in the damp marine climate, gliding into Eugene, past the playing fields of the local high school, where the Eugene Axemen (their football team) played—until we found the public institutions in Lane County that contained the historical record of the crimes of Richard Wayne Godwin.

IN MARCH 1979, a child's skull was found in Godwin's trailer by a relative in Springfield, Oregon, while Godwin was away in jail. The thirty-four-year-old drill press operator had been arrested two weeks before for molesting his five-year-old daughter. At the time of his arrest, Godwin was already on probation for another sex crime: a 1977 conviction for sodomizing his five-year-old niece.

Within days of its discovery, law enforcement in Lane County tentatively linked the skull to Summer Rogers, a five-year-old girl who had disappeared nearly three years before, in July of 1976, while playing near the Willamette River in Eugene. Then forensic experts determined that the skull likely belonged to Andrea Tolentino, a five-year-old girl missing for nearly three years: in the early morning hours of October 2, 1976, Andrea was abducted from her mother's car while it was parked outside the Cougar Room Bar in Blue River, Oregon, along the McKenzie River in the foothills of the Cascades. Prosecutors would not speculate to the media on how the skull ended up in Godwin's trailer, and he was not yet charged with the crime.

Two months later, on August 15, headlines in the *Register-Guard* announced that a prison inmate had provided a break in the Andrea Tolentino case. Convicted killer Floyd Forsberg, an inmate at the Oregon State Penitentiary, told authorities that Richard Wayne Godwin had given him explicit directions for finding the remains of the child's body.

His hands and legs bound in chains, Forsberg led law enforcement to a remote mountainside three miles south of Blue River. On a steep embankment off a logging road under several inches of dirt, they found nine human bones and two human teeth. Forsberg was "absolutely accurate," Lane County District Attorney Pat Horton told reporters. "He indicated he could take us to within 50 feet. And the bones were indeed within 50 feet of where he pointed for us to begin our search."

The two teeth fit perfectly into empty cavities in the skull found in Godwin's trailer.

Forsberg hooked up with Godwin at the Oregon State Penitentiary. There he devised a scheme to provide Godwin's confession of the Tolentino murder to law enforcement officials in return for their help in an unrelated scheme of his own: to obtain a new trial for an associate who, Forsberg claimed, had been wrongly accused of a Portland murder.

To gain the confidence of the police, the deal-making convict managed to lead authorities to the precise location of Andrea Tolentino's remains. Forsberg went on to make claims that Godwin had confessed to two additional murders and two attempted murders. Forsberg insisted that Godwin had told him he had drowned a six-year-old boy in his own bathtub, on October 15, 1977, and later dumped the child's body in a nearby mill pond. Police had previously treated that death as an accidental drowning.

Forsberg also turned in a "confession," written in Godwin's hand, that claimed responsibility for the murder of a thirty-five-year-old Eugene woman who had disappeared from a resort in the Cascades the day before Christmas 1978. Kaye Turner, a former teacher and marathon runner from Eugene, was on her daily six-mile run through the ponderosas along the Metolius River near Camp Sherman when she vanished. Her partial remains were found in the nearby woods eight months later.

Godwin gave up his right to a trial. He pleaded guilty to kidnapping and murdering Andrea Tolentino. The *Register-Guard* reported, "Wearing a pale, blue-denim suit and speaking so softly that he could barely be heard, the 34-year-old Godwin admitted taking the sleeping girl from her mother's car outside a Blue River tavern, driving her to the woods in his pickup truck, and then choking her to death."

He was sentenced to life in prison. In return for a plea of guilty, Godwin was allowed to serve his life sentence in a state other than Oregon, where he was known publicly as a child molester, the lowest rung on the prisoner hierarchy, and would be subject to attacks by other inmates.

Through his attorney, Godwin denied that he had had anything to do with any disappearances or deaths other than that of the Tolentino girl. He claimed that he had agreed to implicate himself falsely in the deaths of Kaye Turner and the boy who drowned. Godwin's motive for these confessions was self-serving. He was seeking Forsberg's protection from other inmates in the prison. Godwin insisted that Forsberg had dreamed up the stories, sat him down, and had him copy the fictions in his own handwriting.

Indeed, the handwritten "confession" of Kaye Turner's murder had a few suspicious elements to it, according to people who knew her. They insisted that Kaye would never have accepted a ride from a strange man in the woods. "Getting in the pickup would be highly untypical, I would think. She knew a lot about people," said one friend who had helped organize a search for her body.

According to the *Register-Guard*, months after confessing to the murder of Tolentino, Godwin passed a polygraph test, seemingly clearing himself of responsibility for the death of the six-year-old boy. He passed two further polygraph examinations that, along with a good alibi from his wife, convinced the Jefferson County district attorney that Godwin had not killed Kaye Turner.

Though it was not mentioned specifically in the newspapers in 1979, the crime report on the Cline Falls assault did outline a statement given by Forsberg claiming that Godwin had confessed to the axe attack. Had Forsberg forced Godwin to write a confession, just as he apparently had in the cases of the six-year-old boy and Kaye Turner? When Godwin took the polygraph test relating to the murder of the jogger and the boy, presumably he also answered questions regarding Cline Falls. The Oregon State Police told my father in 1979 that an unnamed suspect in the Cline Falls case had taken a polygraph, though the scant crime report included no record of it.

AS ROBIN and I drove down Interstate 5, en route home, to California, my thoughts were doing somersaults on the ribbons of asphalt: I'd come to Oregon expecting to find vague information, colorful clues of a literary nature, that might help me imagine a villain. But my imagination back then, in my naïveté, had ended in hollow concepts, cinematic ideas of a psycho killer. Now I'd stumbled upon the life and crimes of a real fiend.

The Andrea Tolentino case received relatively little media attention in 1979 because no trial took place, and newspapers reported that the murderer got sentenced to life in prison. The citizenry of Lane County presumably took the life sentence at face value and gratefully pushed Godwin out of their awareness. I assumed that they had forgotten Andrea Tolentino, an unknown child passing through their community one night, and wouldn't have kept track of her killer. The public would not be informed that Godwin was due for an exit interview sixteen years into his incarceration for "life." No one was likely to show up to protest his parole. It seemed possible that he had been a model prisoner and might very well be released into the quiet, leafy streets of his hometown, where no one would recognize the small, quiet man or remember his deeds.

This attitude would change by 1994, thanks to highly publicized cases of child abduction at the hands of released felons. But this was only 1992. I'd learned a secret about an impending disaster. Whether or not Godwin was the man in Cline Falls that summer night in 1977, I felt responsible for the danger his release posed, and that knowledge brought a fresh emergency to my life.

FROM CALIFORNIA a few days later, I called the second investigator of the Cline Falls attack, Robert Cooley, home in Bend after his fishing trip.

"The reason I'm calling you is, I'm one of those girls who was chopped up in Cline Falls all those years ago." I used the phrase "chopped up" intentionally. I figured Cooley, a seasoned cop, might enjoy this hard-boiled talk, just as newspaper editor Bob Chandler had favored his "conked on the head" approach.

Cooley paused. My hard-boiled talk seemed to throw him off.

"Oh yeah, yeah." His voice was soft, with the slow cadence of a kindly older man. "Which one are you?"

I told him I wasn't the girl who lost her eyesight. (I always assumed Shayna's injuries were more memorable than mine.)

"Okay, I remember you now." He was genial. He asked if my parents were doing well and inquired about Shayna's welfare.

Relieved that he seemed more forthcoming than his old partner, Durr, I asked Cooley what he recalled about suspect Richard Wayne Godwin.

"Okay, he's the one who killed the little girl . . . You're aware that Godwin's name came up through Frosty Forsberg, and Godwin denied any involvement in it? And I assume you're aware of what Forsberg is, and what his connection to this whole thing is. He was in the habit to get criminals to confess things. Godwin was in because he had sodomized his own children. This type of person in the pen is leading a charmed life if he can stay alive. Well, Forsberg was the head con over there in the penitentiary, and Godwin went to Forsberg for help to keep from being killed in the pen, I guess. Forsberg claimed that Godwin was responsible for another murder of a girl in Camp Sherman—"

"Kaye Turner," I said right away. This athletic woman from Eugene—murdered so close in time and place to my own attack and who reminded me of myself—had already begun to capture my attention.

"Well, Godwin wasn't in on the Kaye Turner murder. Two other people are in custody awaiting trial on that murder right now."

So Godwin's confession to the Kaye Turner crime was definitely not true.

"But at least one crime that Forsberg pinned on Godwin *was* true," I said. "The murder of Andrea Tolentino. Then it may or may not have been true that he committed the Cline Falls crime against us." One fact that made Godwin's guilt more convincing to me, I told Cooley, was the presence of Godwin's niece in Cline Falls State Park on the night of June 22, 1977. She came forward *voluntarily*.

"I was aware of that, too. So when you want an answer as to whether my hunch was that he was the one, why, at the time I felt good that he was."

Two years after the Cline Falls attack, Cooley said, when Forsberg's allegation came to light, Cooley tried to interview Robin at home, with her mother present, but the girl cried and denied any involvement with her uncle. There were no other significant leads.

I asked Cooley again whether he had a gut instinct about whether Godwin was involved.

"I wouldn't know one way or another. It looked good, yes. It looked great."

"So you never proved Godwin *wasn't* the guy?"

"Oh, no."

"It's still a question mark then?"

"What looked good was: whoever attacked you was some sort of a fiendish person who was really mad at someone, and that's what Forsberg indicated to us, that it flipped Godwin off to see this girl he'd been having an affair with, with someone else. That was a good start. Why, I felt good that he was the one at the time, because I think I called your dad, and Mr. Weiss, too, just to give them some feeling that something was being done, I guess.

"Our biggest problem was there was so much going on at the particular time," Cooley continued. "Twenty-four hours wasn't enough time in the day to do what we needed to do. We had that assault on you, then we had the Kaye Turner thing, then we had a dismemberment death, and a couple more homicides besides that—"

"When was that dismemberment death?" I asked. Dismemberment deaths put my newly attuned investigative mind on red alert.

Cooley told me that the body parts of a woman in her mid-forties named Mary Jo Templeton were found in Mirror Pond in downtown Bend in 1978. That case was still unsolved. Then there was another dismemberment death in the Snake River, on the border of Idaho. A "coed" was biking or hiking south from her college at Washington State. Her body parts ended up in the Snake River.

"Body parts in the Snake River," I repeated, my voice weakening a little. "And those two murders happened right around the same time?" I was suddenly fashioning myself into a criminal "profiler," looking for patterns in killings across state lines.

"In the same general span of time."

"Is that still an unsolved crime, too?"

"As far as I know."

"According to the crime report, a lot of people in the park that night remembered a guy in a red pickup with a white canopy. A couple people said he had Washington plates—and you're talking about a dismemberment in Washington. Did you ever check up on that?"

"No."

"Did you ever check the kind of vehicle Godwin was driving?"

"I'm sure we knew at the time."

I asked him if he had ever talked to Godwin personally.

"No. And I don't recall who did . . . I just can't recall. We were involved in so darn many things."

I eased up on Cooley. I had exhausted his ability to summon the past, at least for this interview.

"Well, it's good to hear from you," he said. "When I retired, there were about three cases I wished we could have gotten to the bottom of, and yours was one of them. We just never quite got that magic piece of evidence that we needed. If we could have found that vehicle—because we had the tire tracks, the width of the tires, the wheel base, the whole thing—"

"He could have unloaded that vehicle fast."

"Even if he'd kept it," Cooley said, "the main thing we needed—the tires—they'd be gone."

I brought the topic back to Godwin, delicately suggesting that it was "too bad" his possible link to the Cline Falls attack hadn't been investigated more thoroughly. If it were known for certain that he committed the Cline Falls attack, perhaps his "life" sentence wouldn't have been reduced to a mere sixteen years. Didn't Cooley believe that a man who kills a girl and preserves her remains has all the earmarks of a serial killer in the making?

"Well, he's a pervert. What a serial killer is . . . what the profile is on that, I don't even know. We didn't even use that word back then."

HARD TO BELIEVE, but when I looked into it I found that nobody even uttered the term *serial killer* back in quaint 1977. A series of murders of strangers without a known motive were called "stranger killings" until finally, in the late seventies, the FBI coined the label that trips off our tongues so easily today. Yet the galaxy of rogues who would achieve notoriety some years later were already hard at work in the summer of '77. During the summer *Star Wars* hit movie screens, the summer Elvis died, "Son of Sam" David Berkowitz terrorized New York City; Ted Bundy escaped a Colorado jail and headed to Florida for another killing spree; Kenneth Bianchi and Angelo Buono deposited nude female corpses on unpopulated hillsides of East Los Angeles; in that same town, William Bonin, the "Freeway Killer," cruised for young male hitchhikers, and Patrick Kearney, the "Trashbag Murderer," was convicted of killing and dumping in the garbage the remains of more than twenty-eight men. Just a few miles from my suburban Chicago home, John Wayne Gacy buried bodies of young boys under his house. The year 1977 happened to be an off-year for midwestern boy Jeff Dahmer, a period sandwiched between his first killing spree, in 1976, and his second, in '78.

America had seen some high-profile atrocities starting in the late fifties and continuing into the sixties and early seventies. I noted with irony that the year of my birth, 1957, is often cited as the beginning of the trend of "motiveless" crimes that were once considered rare and then eventually became a kind of national obsession. In 1957, *Life* and *Time* magazines told America about one particular farmhouse in the bucolic dairy country of Wisconsin where furniture was made from human body parts by ghoul Ed Gein. Three years later, Gein would be the inspiration for Norman Bates in Hitchcock's *Psycho*, the film that kicked off the "slasher" movie genre. After that, we heard about the Boston Strangler, we heard about Juan Corona, who killed twenty-five transient farm workers in California in the sixties. We heard about the Manson Family zombies, and of the Zodiac Killer, who left random victims with astrological signs carved into their bodies. But no label for the phenomenon had yet made it into the culture. Murders of strangers still baffled law enforcement agencies.

"Without a motive we're in pretty bad shape," Lieutenant Lamkin of the Oregon State Police—the commanding officer in charge of Detectives Cooley and Durr—told the Bend *Bulletin* in June 1977.

In the minds of most detectives trying to solve a homicide back then—and even now to some extent—you had to be able to think up a story behind the murder to figure out who did it, a story that arose out of a relationship between the victim and the perpetrator: a guy didn't like the color of another's skin so he plugged a bullet through him; or his wife was threatening to leave him, so he knifed her; or she wanted her husband's money, so she poisoned him. Without a motive to weave a story around—without jealousy, greed, or revenge; without racial, class, religious, or gender hatred—police were in the dark.

That motiveless crime baffled most local law enforcement back in 1977 implied that the bygone era of the seventies was more innocent than now, when so-called motiveless malice is old news.

It amazed me that the Chicago newspapers would lavish so much attention on a suburban girl who crossed paths with an axe murderer somewhere in the distant West. Not even the anticipated march of uniformed neo-Nazis on the Fourth of July in the predominately Jewish suburb of Skokie captured as much front-page Chicago press in the last week of June of that year. Just why did this particular assault on two women traveling by bicycle and camping out in the American West carve itself deep into the collective psyche that summer of 1977?

I wondered about those people abroad in the land, those by and large optimistic, sheltered Americans who watched Walter Cronkite or read their newspapers the last week of June. People must have been puzzled, as the story was a peculiar alchemy of American cultural iconography—the elite East Coast Ivy League, the frontier West, the axe murderer running amok: elements you don't often find in the same little tale.

Did coverage point to a growing social phenomenon that people were beginning to notice but could not yet name, something mysteriously emblematic that jolted them out of their mental comfort?

Perhaps those headlines worked to explode the myth of American innocence that was already unraveling in that troubled decade. Maybe our misbegotten road trip had punctured one of America's founding myths that ran subliminally in the nation's psyche: America was once an eastern-seaboard nation with a boundless paradise stretching westward. That virgin land of plenty had remained in the American imagination, as though it still existed out there, in perfect harmony, eternally waiting to embrace us. If we chose to escape the disharmony and sickness of civilization, the godly wilderness was always there to renew our spirits.

That same month of June 1977, the Oregon axe attack shared newspapers with stories about how three girl scouts were strangled in their sleeping bags in a wilderness camp in Oklahoma.

This was not how it was supposed to be. The myth had gone awry. Killers were trolling not only the dark urban alleys. They had infiltrated our paradise.

IT WAS OCTOBER 1992—the year the crime rate had reached its peak in America—and I had survived my second journey to that strange piece of paradise called Oregon. I had returned home, sound in mind and body, and I marveled at that fact.

But one image from my recent journey kept rising before my eyes and pulsed with pictorial power: a gentle boy with long blond locks lurching awake from a fevered dream of a girl bathed in blood erupting from the dark. How ironic, I thought, that I should be haunted by Bill's memory of me—that my autobiography, as I told it to myself, did not include this particular self-portrait. I realized that I needed this boy to hold a looking glass squarely in front of my eyes.

The Specifics of the Atrocity

One year went by after my first glimpse into the larger story of my near death under a truck and an axe in a desert park. Then I blew a fuse. My return to Cline Falls, the twists and turns in my investigation, generated in me spikes of emotion that eventually sapped me of any spark. By late 1993, whenever I thought about the new disclosures I'd gathered, I felt nothing at all.

To find the will to proceed, I had to rewind and replay the question: What was I looking for in the first place? I thought back to the moment when my mother directed the question to me: "Why has it taken you fifteen years to want to go back? Why now?"

I knew I was trying to understand the heavy weight of my past on my present; I was trying to restore myself to full dimensions of feeling with regard to the past, to register the force of an experience not yet fully owned. And I had managed to summon a deeper response, even if it had fled once again.

I remembered when inspiration first struck: I believed that my investigation at the scene of the crime would yield truths about what happened that night. I could bear to contemplate, after so many years, that the "force" who attacked me, that phantom energy, was actually an individual with a past, present, and future. I also imagined that this truth-seeking might restore something vital in my core. But the very idea of restoring something vital in my core was then the vaguest of abstractions.

I couldn't mourn for the girl I was before that June night. Could I ever have an awareness of how different I might have become had the attack never occurred? I could easily summon an image of myself on the morning of June 23, 1977, after a peaceful sleep. I woke to the sun lighting tent walls, unzipped the door, stretched, and soaked up the dry heat on my skin. I loaded my red-and-white bicycle and continued down the road with Shayna under an immaculate cobalt sky, feeling proud that my body was stronger than it was the day before. Then I pictured this same girl moving through the years. I tried to figure out who she might have been with no bloodstained sleeping bag in her closet. I called on the full powers of my imagination, but—nothing. That other girl had pedaled over the horizon and was nowhere in sight.

What seemed concrete was the intensity of the experience I had in the fall of 1992 when I first returned to Cline Falls. Perhaps some mysterious process of repair had begun during my ritual of lying on the patch of desert ground where my blood had once flowed: Prior to June 22, 1977, I had been a broad-shouldered, big-boned girl who took up her space on the earth. There was nothing dainty about the body that endeavored to ride a bicycle 4,200 miles across the country. Afterward, I had gradually become incorporeal and scrawny, with an ethereal sort of presence, all my energy flowing up out of the top of my head—not at all grounded into the earth.

After that ritual of lying on the earth in 1992, day by day while on Oregon soil, I started to put on weight—startlingly unusual for me. And as the pounds added up, I liked the way gravity pulled me down. I liked my heavier footfalls on the ground. This was how I remembered myself at the age of twenty. I thought I felt the presence of a phantom body, solid and fleshy, as though something or somebody who hadn't been around for a while had climbed back in. A return of a part of me that fled into the desert that night? Or is that just what I wanted to believe? Did it matter?

My seesawing extremes of emotion between numbness and intense arousal clued me in to the fact that reason alone wasn't capable of guiding me to the right questions. I would have to consult the more mysterious parts of the self, the exiled parts of me that once searched the inside of a sleeping bag for dark stains. It seemed to me this estranged angel was the one who had brought an electric question to my awareness: What was the *literal horror* of what had happened to me?

How could I view my fate as others saw it?

THE PAPERBACK TRADER on Santa Monica Boulevard was filled with thousands of well-thumbed true-crime paperbacks. True crime dwarfed all other categories. Legions had been here before me, delving into grisly pages. I felt a little seedy as I piled yellowing paperbacks on the counter. But I would read them to rouse myself out of sedation.

Crimes that would sicken others provoked little response in me. That serial killer Arthur Shawcross had devoured the vaginas of prostitutes did have me spinning for a while. A photo of Elizabeth Short (called the "Black Dahlia" by the media), her body severed at the waist and drained of blood, provoked a few tremors in my heart. But not much else pierced my blunted emotions. When I heard about a woman held hostage and raped in the house next door to a friend of mine, I poked at my feelings by trying to imagine her captive for hours. But nothing. The wall was too thick. I felt like a failure and thought of giving up.

Then I carried on a debate with myself: why was I expecting so much of myself? I could always quit this entire exploration. The whole quest was self-propelled. It wasn't an assignment from school or God or a boss. I could simply change the channel on the subject matter. Drop it. Everything would go back to untroubled normality.

Then the mood got apocalyptic in Los Angeles. On January 17, 1994, the Northridge earthquake struck the Los Angeles Basin in the dead of night. To the sound of a mountain breaking apart, I emerged from my house with my bike helmet on and hunkered down on the floor of my neighbor's house. The ground stopped heaving, and I had suffered no injuries to body or home—only one crack in one pot—but my psyche had cracked open wide enough to allow in a state of mind I recognized: the posttraumatic stress disorder of the *Diagnostic and Statistical Manual of Mental Disorders.*

In the weeks following the quake, Southern California rebuilt itself, and others I knew recovered their equilibrium. But there was a black patch over my spirit that spring. I remained in a debilitating torpor, with a crisis of will deeper than any I had known before. I would awaken from sleep unrefreshed. My thinking was a morass. I could be reduced to tears for no apparent reason. Everyday sirens on the street induced spasms of panic. I scrawled in my journal, *Move through this period of feeling like there's doom up ahead and no hope.* I was convinced that planning for the future was fruitless, because the world would self-destruct, if not in the next moment, then in the moment after that. An invisible restraining force hampered me from taking action. Simple tasks were daunting. I sat in my garden and commanded my pale, skinny arms to pick up the shovel, and they would not. I felt deader than ever—a marionette after the puppeteer has just left, jointed limbs dangling limply by strings. Although I had a stable love relationship, good health, a calm domestic life, and a nice home where wild green parrots visited me regularly in the tropical jungle of my backyard, demons were alive and well and living in the netherworld of my psyche.

Clearly I needed professional help. And it wasn't the first time I realized it. But it took me until the age of twenty-seven to finally take Shayna's advice and seek therapy.

By the late eighties there were experts around who understood more about what I'd been through than the Chekhovian doctor at Yale had in 1978. Society had taken a very long time to respond to the emotional aftermath of trauma, but a confluence of forces—the needs of Holocaust survivors and Vietnam veterans; the attention the women's movement had brought to the consequences of rape, battery, and incest, along with sky-rocketing crime—had finally brought trauma to the forefront. In 1994, the *DSM-IV* even revised its definition of posttraumatic stress disorder. It was finally understood that the condition, with its array of disturbances, was not a disorder that occurred as a result of a terrifying event that was "outside the range of human experience." It is not outside the range of usual human experience to be raped or battered, to be a victim of incest, violent crime, or political torture. The stark, miserable truth is that it is quite common. The new definition of PTSD required only that the sufferer be exposed to actual or threatened death or serious injury, even if that meant witnessing or learning about such an experience.

I experimented with therapies of every stripe. The late twentieth century was a good time to find a cure—everything the Eastern and Western Hemispheres had to offer. One self-defense course—in which I learned the will and the skill to kill for self-preservation—had particular resonance for me. Most women couldn't outmuscle a man, so they taught us to drop to the ground and kick. The thighbone is the longest, strongest bone in a woman's body. We were taught to unleash our maximum power by kicking the attacker to the ground, then raising our leg high over his head and slicing down with a deadly smash. While executing this final destroying blow, we were taught to shout at the top of our lungs, "AXE! AXE! AXE!" Yes, it's true.

In the spring of 1994, I sought out yet another therapist, a man who had an ordinary degree in counseling but who was something of a mystic. He agreed that the experience of being hacked out of my physical prime and given a glimpse of my early death by an unapprehended perpetrator had put a lock on my will for decades after. This therapist didn't brook accepting paralysis. There was only one way to strengthen the will: exercise it daily. "Forget about talking therapies right now," he said to me in the very first session. "The real way to overcome fear is to take action. You have to systematically desensitize yourself to these resistances by overcoming them." It would feel like a death, he told me, to push through the gravity of these resistances. But on the other side: "resurrection." That meant a release of energy, tapping into a power with potency beyond the ordinary. He gave me a mantra: "Action is your salvation."

And there was action to take. My conscience nagged me. Bud Godwin was scheduled for release into the public in March 1995, and it was already the winter of 1994. Though law enforcement in the era in which he had been convicted, the late 1970s, may have been naive as to the depth of his killing capacity, by the nineties we had a context for the likes of a man who kidnapped, raped, and murdered a five-year-old girl and then saved her skull as a trophy. He surely ranked in the pantheon of serial ghouls. As one whose capacity for indignation was slow to mature—I had never been one to fight for causes—I knew this time I had to rally my will.

When twelve-year-old Polly Klaas was raped and murdered in October 1993 by a parolee who had snatched her from her peaceful Petaluma, California, home, the public began to tune into the consequences of releasing felons who'd committed acts that beggared the imagination, and committed them again and again.

Then, in the summer of 1994, Nicole Simpson was murdered close to my own home in Los Angeles—not so close that I was able to hear the howling Akita, but very close indeed—and almost overnight the public keenly focused on murder and justice. The collective surge gave me momentum to reanimate myself. I pushed through my resistance and forced myself to reread court papers about Richard Wayne Godwin that I'd obtained from the Lane County, Oregon, archives the year before. I tried to figure out which Oregon officials to alert about his impending release. (I was ignorant about the criminal justice system, but I was learning through the O. J. Simpson trial, along with everyone else in America.)

I couldn't banish the vision of Godwin preying on five-year-old Andrea Tolentino. I needed ten, twelve hours of bed rest a night, then would pull myself from my bed to my desk, make a phone call, follow a new lead—which would overexcite me and unleash another collapse. Then I would lie dormant for two days again until my next arousal. Something would always get me going again—an event in the outer world or a dream bubbling up from my unconscious. The recurring dreams in which I was stuck at the age of twenty were coming more frequently now, sometimes several times a week. I forgave myself the inaction of the past year. Maybe this was how my inquiry would have to proceed.

FIND THE GIRL with hooks for hands! I scrawled in my journal. She was the girl Lawrence Singleton had left for dead in a ditch after he severed her forearms with five swings of a hatchet. That happened in 1978, somewhere in Northern California—a crime that exploded into the national media at the time. Mary Vincent survived and struggled to the road. Presumably, meeting her would be for me like finding the portrait in the attic of what I really looked like—not the unblemished persona I presented to the world, but the portrait of my wounded doppelgänger self, struggling to make her presence felt.

I brought to mind my Yale classmate Bonnie Garland, murdered by her boyfriend in her own home in July 1977. I wanted to know, what was Bonnie thinking as she waited to die, that summer night. Had she felt the hammer blows falling on her? Was there pain or no pain?

I would dwell on the fate of other victims of violence. I was beginning to punch through my defenses, to denude myself of denial. I was deliberately forcing myself into dark places, and my newly inflamed emotions were finally dissolving years of apathy and numbness. I was prepared to ramp up the voltage: I tried to imagine how I might have looked had I died that night. Would I have resembled the woman in a crime scene video that a homicide detective once showed me? Strangled by her husband with yellow polypropylene rope, she lay in rigor mortis on the floor of their bedroom. Her body, marbled purplish like painted chiaroscuro, resembled a beautiful sculpture in repose. I imagined my own perimortem state, as I lay half in my sleeping bag amid the nylon folds of my tent, pooled with my blood by the murmuring Deschutes River on that cool summer night, my face bearing the precise emotion I was feeling at the moment death came. I imagined this still tableau as seen from an altitude of a few feet.

This disturbing image inspired in me a devout desire to get closer, finally, to the specifics of my atrocity. I tried to get my X-rays from St. Charles Hospital in Bend, but was crestfallen to learn that they had been destroyed.

In *The Killing of Bonnie Garland*, by Willard Gaylin, M.D., I read that defense attorneys in the trial of Richard Herrin tried to block the prosecution from influencing a jury with graphic images of a dead Bonnie. The defense wanted to keep the gore out of the courtroom. After all, Herrin's counsel said at the trial, "she was dead. Nothing was going to bring her back."

And I realized: I *wanted* to see the gore. My rational self would censor these desires; I would catch myself in such thinking, then wonder if I hadn't gone beyond the pale. I had taken it right to the edge. Was this morbid curiosity or the moral high ground? Then I decided, who among us can say where prurient eagerness to view horror ends and compassion begins?

I had written in my journal only weeks before, *I need to be able to scrape off the scar tissue that everyday life imposes!* By now I had scraped off so much scar tissue, I was traveling so deep under the skin—examining the viscera—that it was hard for me to have an ordinary conversation. My partner was on an extended business trip, and I was alone at home for weeks dwelling on these borderland preoccupations, actively seeking intrusions of horror into my daily life. I read widely and absorbed vivid accounts of times, places, and people flooded with blood: the Holocaust, the Khmer Rouge. One detail struck with particular force: during the war, there were places at Auschwitz/Birkenau where reddish fluids seeped from below the ground and pooled on the soil. This was not a metaphor. It was a physical fact.

As it happened, the most rapid bloodshed in the bloodiest century—the genocide in Rwanda—was taking place at just the time of these preoccupations, although I knew nothing of it.

Trying to immerse myself in the pain of others, to tap into this reservoir of feeling, was wholly new to me. Before, I had been fixated on the violence of the world, and I made cool, uncomprehending notations of it in my notebooks. But this was different. I'd never before tried to imagine the suffering that exists, to look deeply at human misery without flinching. I had to trust that it was the dark wisdom of the deeper self that had set me off on this study, to dwell on the "specifics of the atrocity."

THE SOUNDS SHE made that night, the lament of a dying girl, were a piece of the story I had never told Shayna, not even in Moscow, when she held that pillow over her ears. The story had stood between us for seventeen years. We remained at an impasse, holding alive a dialectic of remembrance and amnesia.

By 1994, I had unpacked my story quite a few times in the therapeutic context. But that I had never been able to tell Shayna the story continued to distress me. I was holding onto the idea that there was a perfect listener. And that perfect listener was Shayna. That I was unable to tell her the tale seemed to call its very existence into question. Alone with my memories, I sometimes entertained the notion that the event wasn't real. That it hadn't taken place at all. Maybe our attacker was just a chimera ejected from deep in my unconscious where nightmares dwelt.

Twelve years had passed since Shayna and I had last seen each other. I didn't know where she was living, what she was doing, whether she was thriving or not. I crossed the breach by writing first to her father—of all her family members, he had taken the most interest in finding the perpetrator—to let him know that I had taken up the case again and was investigating a suspect. He responded immediately with interest, and eventually I got a letter from Shayna herself, in her own hand on lined paper torn from a spiral notebook.

It was a chatty letter, first with news of friends: she regretted she hadn't been in touch with some of her very best friends from Yale, including me. She brought me up-to-date on her life: she had, in those many years since our last encounter, married, become a doctor, a teacher, and a mother of three.

She assured me, at the end of her brief letter, that she supported me in my quest for the perpetrator, that she felt fortunate to have lived, and that she wanted to speak for those who had not. So she would write the Oregon parole board and lend her voice to helping keep behind bars the dangerous individual who might have been our attacker.

But she made no mention of the special circumstances of our connection. Nor did she comment on how unusual it was, given our singular history, that we'd been completely out of touch. By the end of her letter, I felt something was left wanting.

I wrote back. I had many questions to ask her, heavy questions: I wanted to know how she explained her impaired eyesight, to her patients, to acquaintances, especially to her children. I wondered how people, intimates and strangers, responded to her disability. I wanted to know how confined her life was. I wanted to know if her partial blindness had been a purification, a cleansing of the visual dominance of the external world that was always grabbing us and distracting us—I wondered if it made her life more like a meditation, if it sharpened her intuition and the other more neglected senses.

But I wrote instead that I thought it was sad we had lost our connection. I acknowledged that we had experienced that event in the summer of '77 in two dramatically different ways, and afterward had responded to it in two dramatically opposite ways. I supposed that the "atomic force of such a tragedy can either bond people together for life, or send them careening out of one another's orbits." I told her that I still desired to "mull over" with her the experience that had profoundly affected both our lives, and all these years later—I hoped she didn't mind—I still wanted to unleash a raft of questions: Did she ever think about the bike trip we took? Did she ever tell the story? How had she dealt with her injury? Did she feel any bitterness about her fate? Any bitterness toward the man who attacked us? Did she ever think back to the way she was before it happened, when she had her complete vision?

While the thirty-seven-year-old was writing this letter, my adolescent self took over, my insecure twenty-year-old self recalled from the deep strata of my psyche where time existed in overlapping layers. This adolescent self still demanded to know: Why had she been angry at me during the bike trip? What had gone wrong? Was it because I left her behind on the road that one time? I even gave her the opportunity to admit that maybe she'd pulled away because she sensed my infatuation with her, although I still didn't dare speak so directly. Was it my "overbearing preoccupation with you at the time"? the twenty-year-old self wrote, more obliquely.

Then the mature letter writer took the reins again, and I reminded her of the night in Moscow when I tried to tell her the story. I remarked how young people can be extreme and polarized in their behaviors. Surely, I suggested, we would take a more moderate approach now. I fully assumed she would now be completely forthcoming, that all that was unspoken could now be expressed. Maybe it would take quite a few letters, then a few phone conversations, but it would all come out, the past combed over and compassionately understood with the wisdom and maturity developed over the last seventeen years.

It took her several months to write back. I ripped into the envelope and pulled out her letter, again with its tattered edge, the pages torn from a spiral notebook. Again she began with news of mutual friends. She had selected only a few of my questions to answer: The changes she had undergone in the aftermath of the attack were so much a part of her life now that it was hard for her to step back and see them. First of all, she didn't really associate the axe attack with a "person." Because she had retrograde amnesia—a medical term for loss of memory of events proceeding from head trauma—she had gone to sleep one night, waked the next morning, and found that her life was different. She wrote that the change in her sight had left her with formidable challenges. She was proud that she had been able to handle those challenges, and felt no bitterness at her fate. She was a wiser, better person, she felt, with a richer life. Being "vulnerable" herself—having to live life with a handicap—made her a better doctor. And she could do everything as a doctor except fine work, such as suturing. It was still hard for her to read a computer screen, to read music (and here, as she wrote, her handwritten words bounced irregularly over and under the lines of the notebook paper). She was especially frustrated that she couldn't drive, though she still rode a bike. (She still rode a bike!) She went on, giving heavy answers to my heavy questions, in simple words. If somehow she were offered her normal vision back in exchange for the lessons she'd learned with her disability, she'd take her eyesight back. But given the circumstances, she would continue her personal growth.

She concluded that the single luckiest thing to have happened that night—besides surviving—was that she lost her memory. She preferred to live and grow without terrifying, violent recollections haunting her. So while she certainly wanted to be sure the individual who attacked us would hurt no one else, she didn't feel there was any point to learning the "gory details" of the story, as that would do nothing to help her cope with the changes she had to live with. Her last paragraph was written in a conclusive, have-a-good-life kind of tone; then she signed off with "Love, Shayna."

I set aside the letter and decided I wouldn't write back. So that's how it would be, I thought, regressing to a familiar feeling of confusion and hurt. I would be the sole bearer of the "gory details" of our shared history. I would continue on, telling others every bloody detail until I was spent with telling the story, and after that no amount of prodding would make it issue from my lips.

Again my adult self stepped in and rescued the adolescent: I acknowledged that the letter I had written Shayna was not intended for the real Shayna but rather for the figure in those maddening dreams where both of us were stuck at the age of twenty. I knew she was present with me in those dreams, though I seldom recollected the exact narration the following day. Most mornings I didn't try to call up exactly how she had appeared because the dreams always left a residue of sadness, a mournful hangover that would linger and cling to me through most hours of the next day. Shayna was almost always a mysterious figure. Sometimes she was injured or sick. Sometimes she was vibrantly well. At times she beamed warmth toward me. Other times she was indifferent and aloof. Often we were exploring together landscapes of rare and surreal beauty. I recalled quite specifically one dream in which she gave me a contraption, an intricate backpack with lots of pockets that was also a kind of recording device, and I interpreted this symbol to mean that though she wouldn't hear the story, she was giving me her blessing to explore it more deeply. In at least one dream, I felt her rage that I had dared to make public our mutual tale.

If I could resolve whatever it was that kept Shayna in my dreams, wouldn't I lose the need to tell her the story in real life? All I could do, I decided, was to continue my ambiguous quest, to follow the emotional charge and let it sweep me to the next question.

My Little Buddy

"By the way, why are you so interested in Bud Godwin?" Godwin's former prosecutors from Lane County, Oregon, asked me, when I called from California. "Don't you have enough down your way in L.A.?" It was the summer of '94, and O. J. Simpson was the only news.

I told them the story of the Cline Falls axe attack, which they remembered quite well, and I speculated on whether or not Godwin's supposed jailhouse confession was true.

The reason for my call had taken them by surprise. None of the prosecutors involved in Richard Wayne Godwin's case in the late seventies was aware that he might be released in early 1995, a mere year away.

All of them vividly remembered Godwin. One former deputy DA told me he still kept a photo somewhere of five-year-old Andrea Tolentino's skull, the one found in Godwin's trailer more than two years after he murdered her. Peculiar thing was, the former DA told me in a slow Western drawl, the lower jawbone had been carefully glued into place with a thin line of adhesive. Then the former prosecutor shared with me that he remembered Godwin had used the skull as a candleholder in a sort of ritual.

I paused to absorb this fact, while he offered to dig out that old photo of the skull if I planned to pay a visit to Eugene. I made a mental note that I definitely wanted him to dig it out for me. Then I wondered why.

The prosecutors also filled me in on a little Oregon criminal justice history. That the parole board would dare release Godwin the following year wouldn't surprise them at all. The parole board of the seventies through the early nineties, along with the Department of Corrections, would essentially ignore the rulings of the sentencing judges and juries, who had given big sentences for heinous acts of violence. After the egregious event—whatever it was—had passed into history, and the public had forgotten it, the board would find ways of cutting time. They'd let felons quietly out the back door. The ostensible reason was not enough space in prisons.

The public wasn't generally aware of just how little time murderers were doing: in Oregon, as in many parts of the country, throughout the seventies and eighties, a "life sentence" actually meant around eight years. In the 1970s in California, no one with a first-degree murder charge could be sentenced to life in prison without parole. In Oregon, felons were doing an average of thirty-four months for various categories of homicide.

As time went on, the public demanded stiffer penalties. Oregonians voted for new sentencing guidelines, giving judges the power to determine real sentences, which eventually included a "true life" option, life in prison without the possibility of parole. But in this era still—the late eighties into the early nineties—a lenient philosophy about sentences still prevailed: the prison population was fit to the number of beds available.

Convicts such as Godwin were allowed to serve their sentences under the laws that stood at the time they committed their crimes. And under those laws, "life" never meant life but rather some number falling dramatically short of their final days on the planet.

The former Lane County district attorneys, judges, and cops—those who saw Godwin, talked to him, knew him—all considered his acts of depravity well beyond the pale for most child molesters. They all told me they believed he was a serious threat to the public. I pictured (we all did) his next victim: another young girl, name and place unknown.

AMERICANS IMBUED the Northwest of the continent with religious connotations. The settlers of the Oregon Territory were not gun-slinging adventurers in fringed buckskin, greedy for gold. Oregon was a "new Eden" for nineteenth-century pioneers, middle-class missionaries, and families. Gripped by "Oregon fever," they pulled their wagon trains for four to six months to the fertile valleys, mountain ranges, and high deserts at the end of the Oregon Trail, to a land they considered biblical in its scale and bounty, a land that would shelter the righteous from encroaching civilization. In the words of an early settler, Oregon was "the last reach of an enlightened emigration." The name of its capital, Salem, derived from *Jerusalem*.

Some vestige of that notion persisted well into the seventies, when Oregonians believed theirs was a land unsullied, particularly when compared with the state's neighbor to the south, iniquitous California. Governor Tom McCall announced on billboards, VISIT BUT DON'T STAY—an invitation I recalled from the bike trip—because he wanted to protect the pristine livability of his state. Oregonians took up the cause with relish, even printing Oregon "Ungreeting" cards. They wanted to keep out the teeming masses from elsewhere.

It seemed to me that the cast of miscreants who roamed Oregon in the late seventies was rather large, considering the state's small population and its culture of pristine livability. If I could take Eugene as an example: two five-year-old girls abducted and murdered in this bucolic college town in 1976? Even Ted Bundy left a body count in Eugene at that time.

One county judge told me that the late seventies—when Shayna and I were biking Oregon—was the beginning of an escalating crime rate that reached its peak in 1980, and had remained the same since. It was his opinion that in Oregon it was open season for criminals because the penitentiary system hadn't increased according to the population.

"It was a pristine state, but unless you keep up with the bad guys, your pristine state is going to be preyed upon, and you were one of them," he told me.

I wondered if the illusion that Oregon was a paradise wasn't also part of the problem.

IN A CRUSADING MOOD, I dialed a flurry of numbers from home. I warned the Oregon press, women's groups, and victims' groups about Godwin's release date. I was undergoing a process that later—after Polly Klaas and Megan Kanka became symbols of murdered children across America—was to become a ritual of American life: lobbying to save the public, particularly children, from dangerous predators. "We have to make a career out of it," I had been advised by the prosecutor who put Godwin away in 1979. "As long as the spotlight is on him, he won't get out. Like Manson. Like Sirhan Sirhan." Unknowingly, I had plugged into the zeitgeist: my phone calls yielded me news that the Oregon citizenry was already in an uproar because the Oregon parole board had just released a murderer named Russell Obremski into their midst, when supposedly he had been locked up "forever" for slaughtering two women in 1969.

In order to figure out how long a criminal should actually serve of his original "life" sentence, in 1977, Oregon cooked up what they called a "matrix" system, a kind of questionnaire that assigned scores to various factors regarding the severity of the crime and the criminal history of the perpetrator. Based on the overall score, the criminal would earn a minimum number of years in jail and the parole board could award him a fixed release date. Once that date had been established, only a negative psychological evaluation could keep the prisoner behind bars.

According to the calculus of this mysterious "matrix," Oregon's 1970 parole board deemed that Obremski's rape and murder of pregnant Laverna Lowe, while he was a guest in her house, followed by the murder of Betty Richie, whom he had kidnapped from a parking lot, qualified Obremski for fourteen years behind bars. That meant release in 1983. Public outrage managed to keep Obremski behind bars for another ten years. But finally, in 1993, one shrink examined Obremski, by now a model prisoner, and deemed conclusively that he was no longer a threat to the public. The 1993 Oregon parole board freed Russell Obremski, claiming that, legally, their hands were tied because one law on the books decreed that the state must a release an inmate if a single psychiatrist holds the opinion that he is no longer a danger.

At Obremski's exit interview, Laverna Lowe's daughter had the opportunity to ask the burly killer, "How does it feel to rape the twitching body of a pregnant woman?" Then the forty-nine-year-old felon walked out of the penitentiary. The public lashed the parole board for hiding behind the rule of a dubious law and for not bothering to ask a second psychiatrist whether Obremski was still a menace. Two weeks later, Obremski was arrested on charges of sexually abusing a four-year-old girl.

Just like Obremski, Godwin fell under the "matrix" rules. In Godwin's case, the matrix deemed sixteen years as adequate prison time for committing sex crimes against his five-year-old daughter (not to mention that he abused his daughter while on probation for sodomizing his five-year-old niece) and for the kidnap, rape, and murder of another five-year-old girl, a stranger to him, along with the abuse of her corpse.

What was the thinking behind this matrix? In my view, any formula on the likelihood of recidivism (that off-putting word, which means killing, raping, robbing again . . . and again and again) was wild guesswork. Even if it were provable that Godwin would never attack again (and it wasn't—not on this planet), society had been thrown off kilter by the murder of Andrea Tolentino, and the scales of justice had to be brought back in balance. Though an impossible goal, didn't the punishment need to reach for some equivalency to the harm done? Moreover, didn't punishment need to demonstrate symbolically that society was showing solidarity among decent people by embracing the victim and exiling the perpetrator?

I called the Oregon parole board and asked them to send me a copy of this matrix. I was curious to see if I could decipher how their odd formula was achieved. I knew it was outdated, but it still held the considerable power of releasing into the world a possibly dangerous killer. I tried to do the math on what I knew about Godwin and his crimes: two prior convictions for "sodomy in the first degree," a probation violation, "murder and kidnapping in the first degree." Surely the numbers were adding up, but how do we arrive at sixteen years, not fifteen, eighteen, twenty . . . ? I scanned the laundry list of evils and the scores assigned to them. A scale called a Crime Severity Rating assigned numbers to crimes from one to eight—the higher the score, the more years awarded in prison. Crimes as diverse as dog fighting, "paying for viewing child's sexual conduct," and bigamy were, for mysterious reasons, awarded the lowest score, a one, while the crime of "promoting prostitution" earned a two. Incest, "abuse of a corpse," and "trafficking in stolen vehicles" were presumed to have something in common: all scored a three. "Theft: $10,000+" earned a four. Crimes of murder, manslaughter, rape, and sodomy racked up scores of as little as three and as much as eight, depending on various factors.

This number-crunching exercise twisted my brain into knots, and I gave up. It was one society's sorry attempt to grapple with the Big Question—to delineate, draw strict boundaries around, control, rationalize, and liberate evil from being truly itself.

One psychiatrist, in 1979, had advocated for Godwin's rehabilitation in a public sex offender program instead of his imprisonment: "I would recommend that Mr. Godwin be given the utmost opportunity to be rid of these sexual impulses rather than merely assigned to incarceration," wrote this psychiatrist to Godwin's lawyers after examining him once. "I believe this is the least that we can do and offers a maximal chance for success so that he can once again become a functioning member of society without danger to the people around him. In other words, Mr. Godwin has many strengths," he wrote. The psychiatrist's evaluation is dated May 16, 1979. That a five-year-old girl's skull was found in Godwin's trailer had been public knowledge since mid-March.

ON AUGUST 3, 1994, a crime beat reporter I'd contacted at the *Register-Guard* broke news of Godwin's potential release: "A man who was sentenced to life in prison for the bizarre 1976 abduction, rape, and murder of a five-year-old girl in Blue River is tentatively scheduled to be freed next March, the state parole board said. Richard Wayne Godwin, who decapitated Andrea Tolentino and then lit candles in the girl's skull, is expected to return to Lane County after his release."

All hell broke loose. The parole board was deluged with angry phone calls from citizens, former prosecutors, and even the judge who had sent Godwin to prison. Honorable Judge James Hargreaves told the *Register-Guard* that he knew when he pronounced a sentence of life in prison that Godwin would someday be released. "It sounds really wonderful but you sat there knowing it was just a big fraud on everybody." No longer known only to a few DAs, Godwin's victims, and me, Godwin was now a household name in Oregon. The parole board hotfooted it over to the *Register-Guard* to assure the press that in the wake of the Obremski brouhaha, the 1993 Oregon legislature had passed a law now requiring *two* psychological evaluations for parole candidates convicted of crimes such as murder and rape.

Just after the news story broke, one of Godwin's victims contacted the newspaper under the pseudonym "Rose." The twenty-two-year-old was one of Godwin's several nieces, a girl he molested when she was between the ages of three and five. News of Uncle Bud's possible release had taken her completely by surprise. "There were many, many times. I can't remember all of them . . . He's sly. He's shrewd, he knows secret ways. He knew the ways, the ins and outs, how to get around everybody. He knew, real good." Rose told the *Register-Guard* that she had learned to deal with the abuse; it was a part of her now. But she absolutely couldn't cope with the idea of Uncle Bud coming back to town.

A pulse of sadness passed through me as I read about Rose. Two years before, I had seen her name on yellowed court papers I found in the Lane County courthouse archives—a five-year-old child, victim of "sodomy I." Now she had sprung to life, a grown woman with an open wound.

I GLANCED OUT the window of the airplane, spotted the icy Cascade Range down below, and my gut buckled up tight. In September 1994, I was approaching Oregon by air for the first time. It seemed almost too easy to fly there. Both prior trips had been long voyages—overland across America by Greyhound bus; two days up the freeway. But looking down on the terrain from forty thousand feet was a way of controlling it, diminishing its power to terrorize me.

I landed in Portland, alone this time. No one was following me around with a video camera. Portland was the place that, seventeen years before, had granted me a vision of paradise, when from atop Washington Park, I looked to the north to behold two volcanic cones in receding perspective as in a Renaissance painting, reigning over the coastal plain, above the cloud cover, as though suspended in some kind of fifth dimension.

But now, the view to the north wasn't the same. Mount Hood was still its magnificent self. But Mount St. Helens had blown its top. That perfect cone that rose to a point, the Mount Fuji of America, silent for 123 years, had unleashed the equivalent of twenty-seven thousand Hiroshima-size bombs on May 18, 1980— and, within seconds, incinerated forests of old-growth trees that girdled its flanks, stripped the giants of their bark until they lay like matchsticks. When Mount St. Helens erupted in the 1800s, it ushered in a volcanic awakening: seven cones in three states blazed to life in quick succession.

I rented a car, and even on the Portland streets, far from the crime scene, I felt an amorphous fear, as though I were driving behind enemy lines. This part of Oregon was the periphery, after all, of my deathscape. I drove erratically, anticipating menace around every corner, and headed south on Interstate 5, through the farmland of the Willamette Valley, toward Eugene and Springfield—Godwin country.

DID WHAT I knew of Godwin fit the profile of a man who would drive a truck over two girls in a local park, a man who would flaunt an audacious, brazen act in a public place? Was Godwin the Cline Falls attacker? Forsberg's allegations aside, I took an inventory of what fit and what didn't.

The timeline made sense. Godwin murdered Andrea Tolentino in the fall of 1976 but remained at large. By late summer 1977, he was arrested for molesting his young relatives. During that span of time he must have suffered from intense anxiety. The Cline Falls attack, in June '77, fell at a time when he was likely to have escalated his death-dealing ways.

I consulted FBI bulletins to find out what a profiler might think. I was given to understand that, based on extensive experience with murderers of every stripe, the FBI classified them into one of two categories: organized or disorganized, and their crime scenes were accordingly different. An organized murderer carefully planned his kill so he wouldn't get caught. He targeted a stranger, then tried to develop a kind of personal relationship with that person. His crime scene reflected overall control. He got rid of the evidence, especially the weapon and the body. If you could believe these theories, it seemed to me, the murder of Andrea Tolentino was the work of an organized killer in consummate control.

The disorganized offender, on the other hand, killed impulsively. He didn't try to build a relationship with the victim; in fact he depersonalized the victim, perpetrated sudden, brutal violence, often with excessive assault to the face. He left the crime scene in disarray, with no plan for getting away with the crime. He left the body and the weapon, making no effort to hide evidence.

Indeed, the Cline Falls perpetrator had left the body and, in a way, the weapon—because though he did not leave the axe, he left the memory of it. And he left physical evidence: fresh tire tracks in the ground. The Cline Falls axe attack seemed like spontaneous chaos that had erupted out of an unprovoked, private fury.

The organized offender has different traits from the disorganized offender. An organized type often has a higher-than-average IQ, prefers a skilled occupation, is socially adept, and usually lives with a partner. The disorganized type is likely to be of below-average intelligence, socially inadequate, and sexually incompetent; he has never married and lives alone or with a parent, close to the crime scene. He is fearful of people and may have developed a well-defined delusional system. He acts impulsively under stress, finding a victim usually within his own geographic area.

Godwin, in his careful abduction and murder of Andrea Tolentino, seemed to fit the characteristics of an "organized" offender, and yet I knew from the former Lane County DA that Godwin was capable of spontaneous violence: in 1976 he was arrested for running two girls in a car off the road. Though they were strangers to him, something had triggered his rage and he raced after them with his pickup, overtook them, and crashed their vehicle. A charge of reckless endangerment landed him in the Cottage Grove jail for four days. That he used his pickup as weapon was an uncanny resemblance to the Cline Falls attack. And more clues seemed to fit: when the skull was found in Godwin's trailer, a search of his property turned up that Godwin drove a maroon 1976 Chevrolet pickup with a white camper, licensed in Oregon.

Was he the guy in his twenties or thirties, wearing a T-shirt and jeans, seen with the maroon or red pickup with a white canopy—maybe a Chevy, maybe a Ford—that several witnesses saw parked near the tent site on the night of June 22, 1977? His niece Robin told investigators that the man she saw was driving a red *Ford* pickup. Did she change the model of the pickup to thinly disguise her uncle's identity? Police found in Godwin's maroon Chevrolet pickup two pink towels and a crocheted pillow covering a hole in the upholstery of the driver's side of the front seat, and they noted four dark red stains on the cab seat, two of which tested positive for blood. Had Godwin torn up the upholstery because his jeans had been drenched in blood? Godwin was a hunter. Had those bloodstains come from an animal? Or were they Andrea's? Mine? Shayna's? Someone else's altogether? Did these swatches of upholstery still exist in an evidence locker somewhere?

The police warrant stated that Godwin's truck was fitted with Falls Glacier King tires, size 78-15. The Cline Falls police report indicated that evidence of tire size and wheelbase were left in the dirt at the crime scene. Might there still be a record somewhere of the exact tire tread?

According to police reports, Godwin's pal at work said that Bud was fond of driving the McKenzie Highway. Was he fond of the McKenzie Highway because it led over the Cascades to Central Oregon, to Sisters and to Redmond—east to his obsession, his niece? We could assume he spent time in Central Oregon: in their search of his home, police found a Springfield rifle with a stock bearing the legend BOB'S SPORTING GOODS, BEND, OREGON. Did Godwin spot two girls on bicycles sweating up the switchbacks of the McKenzie Highway on June 22, 1977?

Then there was the matter of Godwin's modus operandi. Godwin molested children. He killed a child. Would this homicidal child molester have tried to kill two young women? Would a child killer cross over to an adult killer? Serial killer Arthur Shawcross slaughtered two children as a young man, spent ten years in prison, then went on to murder eleven prostitutes.

Finally, and most pertinent: Did anything in my memory match the physiognomy of Godwin as seen in photos from old records? In one picture taken in 1977, he looked a little like a certain infamous German tyrant: a thin brush mustache cropped at the sides of his mouth, hair swept down at a slant over his forehead. By 1979 he had taken a dive. His hair drooped down on his forehead. His eyebrows drooped over heavy-lidded eyes rimmed with dark pigmentation. His mustache drooped to a scraggly beard. His small mouth drooped at each corner. The missing hair under his lips mirrored his drooping mouth.

I tried to picture this sad sack atop the trim torso in cowboy dress that I remembered. The droop didn't match the meticulously tucked-in shirt. Still, with some imagination, I could place it there. I'd seen, among physical laborers of all sorts, from ditch diggers to fisherman, some droopy faces on tight bodies. I had thought the guy was around twenty. Godwin was thirty-five. Could I have so miscalculated? But how can you determine age from a clothed body in the dark? Also, I had told investigators that the guy I saw was five ten to five eleven. Godwin was five six.

Could Godwin have mustered the dark charisma I remembered? Maybe the sad sack from the police photo could, in the moment of the kill, have transmogrified into a psycho with a galvanizing, potent presence. The way he signed his name on court papers told me he was no weak little wimp. The way he inscribed the letter *W* in his middle name, Wayne: the bump in the middle was a sharp jab, like an upthrust knife. It was aggressive and scary. But could he have shapeshifted into a figure so meticulous he looked as if he were modeling Wrangler jeans?—as this was one of my unassailable memories. I had plenty of doubts. But I pushed them away. The guy had supposedly confessed. He had to be thoroughly checked out.

FORMER LANE COUNTY district attorney Pat Horton was supportive of my efforts to document more aspects of Godwin's deviance so that I could present the findings to the parole board. He introduced me to a former investigator on the Tolentino murder case, Howard Williams, now in private practice. I met Williams, a stylish man in his late fifties, with silver hair offset by all-black clothes, in Horton's office in the center of Eugene. Williams was the first private eye I had had occasion to meet.

I immediately hired him to assist me in re-interviewing the people in the old crime report. Though I wanted heartily to go off and investigate those names on the police report myself, it seemed risky to do so. Besides, it would probably take an ex-cop to prod the state police into flushing out any buried files on the case.

Williams was dubious about my pursuit of this ancient crime. He regarded my mission with a hint of amusement and a dash of condescension. But he seemed to enjoy reminiscing about this particular fiend. He had his theories: "Godwin was quiet and unassuming. He followed orders. Was very shy. Afraid of everything around him all the time. When you meet a murder suspect and he's very quiet—when they don't rant and rave, don't use profanity and are generally very polite—you know you're talking to a dangerous guy." Williams had been responsible for taking Godwin out to the site where Forsberg, using Godwin's map, had located Andrea's body.

"I got to the jail and said, 'Good morning, Bud, we're taking you for a ride.' I never spoke a word to him. Until he got there he didn't know where he was going. We walked him right up to the stump. He sat there in silence for eighteen hours and never confessed." The "stump" had been a marker on Godwin's map indicating Andrea's burial ground. According to Williams, Godwin had originally planned to murder the child at the Finn Rock dump, but he changed his mind and took a logging road deeper into the forest, where he put her behind a log and killed her.

"The interesting thing about Godwin. He carried the body *uphill* from where he parked the car to dispose of Andrea's body. Most killers throw a body downhill. He carried her up. That's really different."

In 1970, Williams was dispatched to drive Godwin from Oregon to the federal pen in El Reno, a bleak garrison commanding the prairie dating from the 1880s. "I left Godwin sitting in his cell. He was docile, in chains, like a trained dog. For a moment, I actually felt sorry for him."

WHEN INVESTIGATORS searched Godwin's possessions at the time of his arrest they found taxidermy paraphernalia: a book bound in leather and wood entitled *Taxidermy*, and a cardboard box similarly labeled containing borax, clay, glue, string, plaster of Paris, papier-mâché, artificial green leaves, one bird skin and bird head, feet and feathers, and ten pairs of glass eyes.

The passion of the taxidermist is the art of bringing a carcass to life, which grants him a godlike power over death. Ten glass eyes would produce five birds, which would cling to branches with artificial leaves, poised for flight—eternally. Is that why, according to these musty old police files, investigators found in Godwin's pink-and-white fifteen-foot 1957 Midway trailer—amid personal papers and Christian Family Institute appointment slips—a plastic bottle containing one bundle of blond hair wrapped in adhesive tape, one fawn in the freezer, and one round pin bearing the words I HELPED A CHILD IN '76? If I kill you I can resurrect you, he seems to have been saying. By keeping your skull and lighting a candle in it, I can animate and possess your soul forever.

I'd read enough profiles of serial killers to posit that such killers come alive in the death of another human being, that they prefer the dead to the living for their companions. Serial killer Henry Lee Lucas claimed that he drove in a car for three days with a decapitated head on the seat next to him. Jeffrey Dahmer's father, Lionel, struggled to figure out what made his freaky son tick: "In general, Jeff had simply wanted to 'keep' people permanently . . . It had begun with fantasies of unmoving bodies, to drugging men in bathhouses, to cannibalism, so that they would be a part of him forever."

I was gripped by the horrific image of Andrea's skull, its jaw held in place by a thin line of glue, stashed in a paper bag in the bedroom closet of a 1957 pink-and-white trailer. It brought to my mind the skull cults from the first known human settlement, Neolithic Jericho, in the Middle East, where ten-thousand-year-old skulls were found, plastered over to restore their human features, with shells inserted into their eye sockets. "From this treatment of the skulls," British archaeologist Dame Kathleen Kenyon writes in her book *Digging Up Jericho*, "it may be deduced that these early inhabitants . . . had already developed a conception of a spiritual life . . . They must have felt that some power, perhaps protective, perhaps of wisdom, would survive death, and somehow they must have realized that the seat of the skull secured the use of the power to succeeding generations, perhaps that it placated the spirit, perhaps controlled it."

Did the necrophiliac Godwin, this lover of death, imagine himself a kind of black magician who tried to preserve the power of this girl's spirit, to seize for himself the innocence of this small girl—when he himself had none? Was his ritual—imagined or real—of illuminating the skull an atavistic but corrupted impulse to acquire divinity?

People talk of "senseless," motiveless murders. They think there's no rational or conscious explanation for these acts. But I could not accept that the stranger who had tried to kill me lacked motivation. It had to be more complex than woman-hating in a culture that denigrates the feminine, though it was certainly that.

What if murderous acts are rooted in a craving for heightened reality, a quickening, a yearning to transcend banal existence? Perhaps everyday life is not adequate for some people's inner needs. Perhaps ecstasy—a rush of energy, intense feelings of potency, a release from inhibition—is a deep psychic need, one that was satisfied by ritual in archaic societies but for which prosaic modern life offers few outlets. Perhaps the willful taking of life is fueled by a psychic energy meant to serve a higher spiritual function, but one that has been perverted.

Holocaust survivor Jean Amery writes of his death camp experience:

> I saw it in their serious, tense faces, which were not swelling, let us say, with sexual-sadistic delight, but concentrated in murderous self-realization. With heart and soul they went about their business, and the name of it was power, dominion over spirit and flesh, orgy of unchecked self-expansion. I also have not forgotten that there were moments when I felt a kind of wretched admiration for the agonizing sovereignty they exercised over me. For is not the one who can reduce a person so entirely to a body and a whimpering prey of death a god or, at least, a demigod?

Perhaps there is an ecstatic enjoyment to be derived from having the ultimate power over others, a quasar of intense experience derived from the moment of the kill. One only has to read about the jubilation of the citizens of Jedwabne, Poland, who on July 10, 1941, massacred 1,500 of their Jewish neighbors, with axes and clubs and fire, while the Nazis stood by and took pictures. Or what about the scenes of gleeful merriment, the raucous village jamborees, as the Hutu killers in Rwanda in 1994 hacked to death a million of their Tutsi neighbors with machetes?

"Shedding of one's own blood or that of another—one is in touch with the life-force—this in itself can be an intoxicating experience on the archaic level," Erich Fromm writes in *The Anatomy of Human Destructiveness*.

It was a part of my story that left me deeply unsettled and would provoke a searching expression in those to whom I described it—and I seldom did, because people might misinterpret, might think it was some sadomasochistic fantasy come true, when in fact I harbored no such fantasies. Perhaps because I had no time to work up a feeling of fear, I felt I had a glimpse of the attacker's state of mind, some intimate understanding of murderous transgression. I can still remember the rush of that night—something about the radiation he emitted, the dark charisma during the explosion of power on the brink of murder. (Perhaps my observation of his power forced me back into my flesh, and tapped my will to survive.)

Perhaps a fascination with transgressive excess, our seduction by the spectacle of power, goes some distance in explaining why Americans are in a swoon, why the movies, books, and popular music dwell on criminals, particularly killers of the serial or mass-murdering variety. Isn't part of the allure (let's come clean) to be on the side of power, on the side of those who dare to tear the fabric of normal existence, to force their will on the world, in a culture that demands routine, the submergence of personality in the crowd? Henry David Thoreau said it a long time ago. Underneath the supposedly cheery optimism in America, "the mass of men lead lives of quiet desperation."

As recently as 1933, the *New York Herald-Tribune* contended that in no country during peacetime except the United States did lynching and mob violence form such an important part of the nation's roster of crimes. The paper had this analysis about the modern craving for violence, and the fierceness of usually peaceful people when aroused: they would do anything "which would contribute towards giving them a thrill and a sense of power. The lynching party and the man-hunt, the baying of the dogs in the dead of night, and the entire scene lit by the flaring of pine-knots or fuel-oil torches, affords a good road to emotional escape from the drab lives most lynchers usually lead."

John Steinbeck drove across America with a poodle named Charlie, in search of what Americans had on their minds. He was looking, among other things, for what people wanted to read and hear. He found a lot of comic books and a lot of novels about "sex, sadism and homicide." It was 1960. Hitchcock's *Psycho* probably hadn't even hit the drive-in theaters yet. Steinbeck surmised that Americans read those things to fill up their plastic, homogenized, bland, and empty lives.

You hear a lot about killers and little about victims. No one thinks about the victim, the one who loses the contest. Most people don't want to consider the aftermath of murder, or those whose dignity and identity have been stripped away. If attention is paid to victims, it runs to the other extreme: they are enshrined as ones who have glimpsed a deeper reality, touched the quick of life in a way that is impossible in the everyday. I found myself, briefly, such a shrine of devotion in college. In this case still, victims are anointed with the power of their attackers. They win their illustrious identity through the transgressive violence perpetrated against them, because ultimately this culture is fixated on the ultimate badass outlaw who knows no limits, the one who mesmerizes with violence—the one with the riveting aesthetic of evil.

You read in magazines about an actor described as having "serial killer charm" and you're supposed to find him seductive.

JEFFREY DAHMER'S father, Lionel, describes in his book how he was astounded at the enormity of his son's crimes because "all of his life he had seemed so small. There were times when he was so small that I scarcely saw him at all. Now he was gigantic, the public personality around which enormous forces swirled . . . How could so small and insignificant a man be blown up to such dimensions at such a blinding speed?" As he sat in the courtroom, Lionel Dahmer was astonished at the security forces arrayed—a garrison with armed guards positioned around the room—and his son Jeffrey seated behind an eight-foot barrier of bulletproof glass. Jeffrey's dad ruminated as he sat in the courtroom: "It was impossible for me to reconcile his passivity and facelessness, the monotone of his speech and the flatness of his personality, with the flurry of activity that surrounded me."

Dahmer's extreme transgression granted him power. And power garners a following.

Underneath our fantasies about ourselves—that we are a heroic culture—exists, too, a shadow culture of people of weak will ceding power to daring criminals.

Lionel Dahmer tells us that Jeffrey got 241 letters from people who thought he was capable of curing them.

IF GODWIN was docile with authority figures, I wondered how he behaved with the women and children he lorded over, bullied, and abused. I wanted to interview Godwin's ex-wife, Martha, who never remarried but changed her name and was living with her teenage daughter in Springfield. Though I knew she hadn't been in touch with Godwin in years, it spooked me to call her. I'd never before met a person intimately connected to someone who had committed sickening crimes.

From my Eugene motel room I distractedly watched Diane Sawyer interview Nicole Simpson's two sisters, who seemed unusually cheerful given their present circumstance . . . I was stalling. I turned off the tube, dialed the phone, and told Martha that I had heard about her through my connection at the Eugene *Register-Guard*. She didn't ask me what I was writing, or why I had contacted her, and I didn't offer that Godwin was a suspect in my case. She agreed to meet me the next day in a Springfield mall.

Martha had tight reddish curls and an armored stiffness in her demeanor until she laughed, and then her blue eyes twinkled and she softened a bit. She was wearing a sweatshirt with a drawing of a bear on it. I understood immediately that she wanted to talk to me in order to rectify an old injustice: When Godwin's murder case was in the public eye fifteen years before, all attention was riveted on her killer husband. She was dismissed as a negligent mother who had not protected her children, and the Department of Child Services took her son and daughter away from her for a period of time. "Everyone cared what happened to him. Nobody cared what happened to me. All I wanted was my children back. All I wanted was to be safe." After that, she was left with the stigma that her husband was a murderer. That association got her fired from a job. Now that Godwin was back in the news, she wanted her say, too.

Martha confirmed what I already knew: she had met Godwin as a child in Cottage Grove, Oregon, where his parents managed the dump. As it happened, the dump figured into her vivid childhood recollections. It was from the dump that some of her Christmas presents came: Godwin's dad would pick cast-off toys out of the trash, repair and paint them, and give them to Martha and her sister for Christmas.

When she was a teenage girl, she and her sister used to play with Bud Godwin, and when she grew up, she married this childhood neighbor. At first their courtship was formal. They never kissed or touched until they married. Afterward, Godwin changed. He controlled her every move: he wouldn't let her watch TV, made her put her dog down. He never wanted children, but then one day he saw someone with a baby and he said to her, "Let's have a baby." He missed anniversaries, missed her birthdays. Even her husband's rough-and-tumble mother, Audrey—who drove gravel trucks and Harleys and who seldom had a kind word for Martha—told her son, "You gotta give her something."

Later he started to do weird things. He'd take off and leave her home alone. He'd take her out camping in bizarre places in the dark woods by the side of logging roads, then take off in the truck, stranding her alone with the baby.

"I was scared," Martha recalled. "What if someone with a gun would come up?"

She wasn't attracted to him. His breath reeked of cigarette smoke. He was extremely tied to his parents and talked to them on the phone every night for several hours. "When he was born his dad called him 'My Little Buddy,'" Martha told me. Godwin confided in his father about everything.

When Godwin was first charged with child abuse, in 1977, Martha stuck with him, thinking he could be healed and the marriage would work. Released on probation, he told Martha, "I did it because it was done to me." She said to him, "If it was done to you, you should never have done it to anyone again."

When Godwin was arrested for probation violations after charges of molesting their daughter, Martha's children were taken away from her. She had no job, no training, and was saddled with Godwin's debts. But she hung on a bit longer, thinking she could still reconcile with him. Then, after counseling, she broke all contact, filed for divorce, changed her name, and went to school to be a nurse. Meanwhile, she fought to get her children back, and when she finally got them, a judge told her that he had never seen anyone fight so hard and come so far. After Godwin, Martha didn't want to get involved with anyone else. She went out with one guy, and when he left her she said, "The hell with it.

"There are times I wish I had the courage to remarry. But you can't tell anybody your husband is a murderer, because they run. It scares the bejesus out of them. They don't want to be associated with that. What if he gets out? What if he confronts us?"

Sitting in a coffee shop interviewing Martha was surreal. I was still getting into my role as investigator, reluctant to press too hard. We talked about the day she found the skull in her husband's trailer. "I didn't put two and two together," she said, and I understood. I didn't think most people would draw a link between a small skull—maybe a relic from an Indian burial ground?—and a murderous spouse.

Godwin had a high IQ, she told me. "He's got it upstairs."

"Did he dress cowboy?" I asked—my one pertinent question.

"Not cowboy," she said. "He mostly wore blue jeans. He was a straight guy. Straitlaced."

Not cowboy? When I tried to picture the man, I pictured a machinist seated at his workbench dressed in cowboy attire, keenly focused on drilling holes in pieces of metal with a sharp drill bit.

She added that Godwin liked country music.

I privately registered that fact as a clue and asked her if she remembered something that former Lane County DA Pat Horton had told me: that once, in 1976, Godwin chased two girls down the freeway, headed them off, and smashed into their car.

Yes, she remembered that he spent four days in the Cottage Grove jail. "It tore me up that he would do something like that. Scare those girls."

It was a brief meeting—just long enough to drain a cup of coffee. I didn't challenge Martha about letting her husband back in the house that January winter in 1979, when his pipes had frozen. The young Martha had been like so many women who don't leave their abominably abusive husbands—inured with biblical beliefs about the redemptive power of suffering, about the sacredness of marriage vows no matter what, about the need to forgive and help to heal, no matter how egregious the deeds—a creed I was coming to believe let perpetrators off the hook too easily.

I walked her out to her SUV under a drizzling sky, and she told me again about the day she decided to get a degree to become a nurse. It was the day the spaceship *Challenger* exploded. She said to herself, "Those people put themselves out there—and I will, too. I'll be more than just a welfare mother." She wanted to impress on me how much the role of protecting mother had meant to her. "I should have been likened to a mother bear, protecting her cubs," she told me, illuminating me about the significance of the bear pictured on her sweatshirt.

We parted after sharing opinions about whether O. J. Simpson was the killer or not. I told her I was sure he was. She was certain he wasn't.

Sisters and Cowboys

Every peak is a crater. This is the law of volcanoes,
Making them eternally and visibly female.
No height without depth, without a burning core

—ADRIENNE RICH, *DREAM OF A COMMON LANGUAGE*

I had driven from Eugene along the McKenzie River, climbed the precipitous McKenzie Pass, and now stood on the Cascade crest—the point where the trees disappeared and a havoc of jagged lava stretched to a horizon lined with a lavish display of volcanic cones. I'd been carrying a photo of this spectacular summit in my wallet for two years. It still had a fix on me.

My senses went on high alert, as though cued to unforeseen danger. This wasn't a place to linger. Harsh, cold, windy—it felt unnatural, unfit for human habitation. Small wonder NASA astronauts in space suits had prepared for the 1969 moonwalk here. I returned to my car and descended. I had by now undertaken this trek over the McKenzie Pass three times, by bicycle and by car, and each time I had the same peculiar sensation: a curious release from the burden of all that was earthly, a kind of dry weightlessness, then a descent into freefall with a tinge of vertigo, as though I had taken a crazy leap off a cliff, only to discover that wings were bearing me aloft. I was not imagining this. In photos taken from the air, you can see what in climatological terms might contribute to the sensation: cumulus clouds billow up on the western side of the Cascade peaks, trapped against the hard rock. The sky on the eastern side is expansive, free of clouds and moisture, free of anything that impedes you—urging you to slide down into the ponderosas and beyond. The effect on me all those years before, that day in 1977—I remembered it still—was as though I had entered a lucid dream and something remarkable was about to happen.

I popped a country-western tape into the deck, pulled out my Western prop (a cowboy hat), and thus outfitted, streaked down the mountain, falling. I was east of Eden now, and the road flattened as I passed the pure stands of ponderosa on the outskirts of Sisters.

Though the pine-forested hamlet that sits on the eastern base of the Cascades was most famous for its annual rodeo, "The Biggest Little Show in the World," the tiny town of Sisters, with its gentle name and associations of girlish intimacy, didn't conjure images of rough riders and lasso throwers. Its feminine name and green mountain freshness drew me to the place and made me feel secure enough to base myself there during my investigation of Redmond, further east into the desert.

Sisters had spruced itself up since my last trip, in 1992. By 1994, its boardwalks and Old West–style storefronts had proliferated in accordance with its thematically zoned ordinances, and were jammed with tourists. I was reassured to see that the old-fashioned Dairy Queen—where Shayna and I split from our fellow bikers Mark and Kathy in 1977—remained unaltered near the junction of Oregon Highway 126 and OR 243. At this junction, a simple sign read, '76 BIKE-CENTENNIAL TRAIL, one of the old signs, which brought a rueful smile to my lips. I knew the trail still existed, but it now ran through more congested byways across America, as the two lanes with tarred cracks had been replaced by four-lane slabs.

I spotted a fifties-vintage roadside motel across the street, Sisters Motor Lodge, and rang the bell on the counter of the saloon door, which produced the motel owner. Mary was a well-groomed woman in Ralph Lauren, a transplant from Vermont taking up the Western lifestyle. "The town of Sisters is very healing for women," she told me, out of nowhere. Maybe I looked strained and in need of comfort? She rattled off a list of female power brokers in Sisters, including lots of business owners, the forest ranger, and even the mayor.

"That's good. If you knew what I was doing here you'd know how much I appreciate that," I said without explaining.

I took a room with a view of the Three Sisters, the glacier-covered volcanoes after which the town was named. Pioneers called the three mountains Faith, Hope, and Charity, after those theological virtues that helped them survive the hardships of the frontier. "Although quiescent during the past century, the Three Sisters and Mt. Bachelor have been violently active within the recent geologic past. At some time in the not too distant future, it is possible that one of these mountains will be making headlines around the world," read the *Atlas of Deschutes County*.

These volcanoes filled me with considerable emotion; my psyche seized them as a metaphor for a hot inner life. Volcanoes were long ago conflated with my personal history—the shimmering cones outside my hospital window had mixed with my agony and opiate-induced ecstasy—and now, many years later, these channels for fires from the deepest layers of the earth reminded me of my turbo-charged state.

SHEER FAINTHEARTEDNESS ratcheted up my anxiety, and I had to sedate myself with sleep. I was unfamiliar with my role as investigator. Two days went by and I hardly moved from the bed, except to wander the boardwalk and browse in shops. Finally I could dawdle no more. I had to force myself forward, to call about the blood. Where was the T-shirt with the seven cut and torn holes? I felt sure my blood was on file somewhere up here in the juniper-scented mountain air.

I phoned Howard Williams, my private eye, to ask him if being part of the law enforcement brotherhood had helped him lay his hands on any of the physical evidence. Nothing, he told me in a jaded tone. His search had turned up no more than the crime report I already possessed. The state police told him that any physical evidence had been disposed of a while back. He wasn't surprised, and he didn't seem to care that I was disappointed.

Next, my investigation required me to leave my secure nest in Sisters and journey to Redmond, a place I dreaded. Redmond was the town closest to Cline Falls State Park, home of the kids listed in the crime report, the ones who had cruised the park road that night. I hadn't interviewed anyone from Redmond during my previous trip in 1992, just after I picked up the police report—except for a guy who worked in the motel where I was staying. I told him my story, and I told him I was looking for the attacker, who was a cowboy.

"What do you mean by *cowboy*?" he inquired, explaining that *cowboy* could describe a lot of folks, but he could narrow the category down. He knew of three types: there was the "drugstore cowboy" variety, we had them down in Los Angeles, too. Drugstore cowboys wore hats and cowboy boots and wanted to look like cool Western dudes, but they'd never been on a horse and wouldn't want to get their backsides sore riding one. These were tin men compared with real cowboys, the buckaroos who herded cattle and broke colts and roped horses, who were proud of their honorable work and of the way they lived on the range and came to town only for two-stepping at the 86 Corral in Redmond. There was a third kind of cowboy, another inauthentic cowboy like the drugstore type. This one might aspire to riding a horse but wasn't sober enough to stay on.

"Which kind of cowboy do you think you saw?" he asked. I said I didn't know.

I marshaled my energies to drive the nineteen miles down Highway 126, from the ponderosas that surrounded Sisters, past the llama and show horse farms, the trendy ranches of the new West, until the irrigated patches of mint and alfalfa mutated to brown desert lands of juniper and sage. I approached the sign to Cline Falls State Park. I tried my best to ignore the looming presence of this memory-laden place. But my pulse quickened and my heart gave a leap. I had formed such a peculiar relationship with this tiny patch of earth, this epicenter of psychic upheaval. Would the day ever arrive when I would feel neutral in this spot?

It occurred to me: the name "Cline Falls" couldn't have been better chosen to describe this place. Something about the *falls* lent a gothic aura to the name. Didn't Lizzie Borden hack up her parents in a town called Fall River?

According to the crime report, several teens canvassed by police in the summer of '77 talked about a swimming hole on the north side of the highway where young people congregated. Apparently Cline Falls, as a local hangout, encom-passed a larger area than the park itself.

On this, my second visit to Oregon after my original fateful journey, it seemed radical, even subversive, for me to depart from the itinerary of the original Bike-Centennial Trail. In an ideal world, this terrain should never have been part of my route in life. But exploring the perimeter of the park was an important step in my investigation, and might lead to a bigger picture of what happened the night of June 22, 1977.

I crossed to the north side of Highway 126, which spanned the river, and found a dirt lane that wound through juniper and sage down to the banks of the Deschutes River. Here, upstream, were the falls of the park's name: streams of silver sliding over jet black lava rocks. Pocks of dark water looked like deep swim-ming holes. A high light raked the junipers and lit the golden heads of autumn-blooming bitterbrush. A fresh deer carcass rotted on the ground. Its antlers were sawed off, its eyes pecked out, and flies were circling the decomposing tongue lolling from its mouth.

Here the Old West seemed untouched. History tells us that this site was a ghost town. More than a ghost town, it was the ghost of a ghost town. A bustling pio-neer hamlet named Cline Falls once stood here, a place with dreams for the fu-ture, with stores, two hotels, a school, fine homes, even a stone jail—but not a trace of it remained. When a life-giving irrigation canal was developed, flowing to Redmond, three miles east into the desert, Cline Falls was bypassed. The town died.

It occurred to me that here, in this haunted place, the true character of the place named Cline Falls was revealed. This was the shadow side of the pretty green park on the other side of the highway, the forbidding land I had conjured in my imagination. This, more than the park, seemed like the scene of an unexpi-ated crime.

I headed back up the rutted road and saw nestled under the canyon walls a sad little shack shaded by an ancient juniper. The ground was piled high with old bi-cycle parts and sacks of birdseed. Was this the home of the "Birdman" I had read about in the old newspaper accounts? Today the Birdman didn't appear to be home, so I followed the lane to the highway and drove the remaining ten minutes into Redmond.

Arriving in the center of town meant crossing its lifeline: its main water canal, a vein cut into the ragged black lava. At the turn of the twentieth century, when the U.S. government was hell-bent on opening the desert lands in the West to set-tlement, an irrigation outfit promised to cut arteries in the hard lava and bring water from the Deschutes River to transform this patch of desert into a garden. That promise drew the town's first residents, a man named Frank Redmond and his wife, Josephine. Redmond was a schoolteacher from North Dakota—I imag-ined that the intrepid couple was a lot like my own Dakota pioneer ancestors, only more restless still. The Redmonds sold their Dakota homestead and pushed even farther west along the same latitude, then pitched their tent on a patch of sagebrush and juniper that lay at three thousand feet above sea level. They lived in their tent alone on the desert, and walked several times a week to get water from Cline Falls, until more settlers arrived and a community of tents grew up. In 1906, the promised irrigation ditch bypassed Cline Falls and was finally dug through Redmond. While the established town of Cline Falls perished of drought, in Redmond buildings replaced tents. The desert dwellers made a big effort to green their raw little settlement. They planted fast-growing leafy trees wherever they could. In the 1920s, the Redmond chapter of Daughters of the American Revolution won a national prize for planting more trees per capita than any other chapter in the United States. But those green trees weren't enough, I'd guess, to take away the strong desert character of the place. In the Oregon Centennial in 1959, the town won the name Juniper Junction. And Juniper Junction earned another nickname: Flag City, U.S.A. Every legal holiday, Redmond showed off its civic pride and patriotism by displaying six hundred standard-size flags along its parallel thoroughfares. Six hundred flapping American flags. *There* was the image I had expected to encounter—not a torso of a meticulous cowboy wielding an axe—on my bicycle trip in '77.

Redmond tried hard to lay itself out on grids in a north–south, east–west axis, like most towns in the West, but the shattered landscape on its periphery made any rigid plan impossible to keep up. Squiggly roads radiated out from its symmetrical center, and these roads sprouted self-contained residential subdivisions, until, on a map, Redmond looked like an atom splitting apart.

At the end of the twentieth century it was clearly a town in transition away from its ranching and lumber milling economy. There was brand-new development everywhere: video stores, discount stores, real estate offices, industry. Roadside development clogged the highways heading into town. Two business establishments, one called Dick's Chain Saws and another a used car lot, stood side by side, and between them: a rushing mountain stream with a vista of volcanoes on the horizon. It struck me that even roadside sprawl couldn't suppress the vitality of the landscape here.

I drove up and down the streets, but didn't see it. The TRU-AX gas station had vanished from the earth! In its place was a national gas brand. I felt betrayed that this distinctive place had let a bland, corporate franchise pave over my personal myth.

A sign at the old rodeo and fairgrounds, located in the center of town, announced a shindig—an "Oktoberfest" during which the local population got to celebrate its strong German heritage. I figured it might give me an opportunity to observe the locals firsthand, so I ate a bratwurst alone among the boisterous families and watched the Redmonites dance in lederhosen. I wondered what it would take to get to know the people in this town of seven thousand souls—a number doubled since 1977. Truth to tell, the town scared me. Even the *red* in Redmond reminded me of blood.

Back in my Sisters lodging the next morning I lay in a fetal sleep until 11:00 a.m. The odor of horse dung wafting in the window roused me with the reminder that I wasn't at home. I pulled a blanket over my head to delay the scary work that awaited me, until the sun blazing over the pasture fired up the living rocks Faith, Hope, and Charity in the distance, and at last I sat up in bed and faced the inevitable.

My private investigator, the man with a gun, would be in the area the following week to interview the people listed in the crime report, locals who were joyriding in the park the night of June 22, 1977. Of course I wanted to interview them myself. I could hardly bear that their stories would be filtered through the investigator's brain before reaching me. But I had no way of knowing what manner of people they were.

Whether it was safe for me or not, the person I felt compelled to contact myself was Godwin's niece—the girl with whom I may have traded destinies.

I found her name easily in the Redmond phone book and hastily dialed her number. An older woman answered. Her husky, sandpaper voice struck me as menacing and finished off my courage. I hung up without saying a word. One can't always be brave. This task I would leave for another day.

Instead, I would look for Bill Penhollow, my rescuer. Surely I would place myself in no danger by seeking the company of one who had already saved me. I reviewed the digest of a cop's interview with Penhollow, which had taken place an oddly long four days after the attack.

At 6:05 PM 6-27-77 WILLIAM LYLE PENHOLLOW was interviewed regarding his actions and observations on the late evening of 6-22-77 when he found the injured girls at Cline Falls Park. As near as he could estimate it was about 11:30 PM 6-22-77 when he entered the park with his girl friend. As he was slowly driving through the one way entrance he saw a flashlight in the grassy area to his right. He could hear a female crying out for help stating something about being run over and attacked and she was afraid her friend might die. He later learned that this was Terri Jentz. He helped the other girl into the cab of his pickup. She was semi-conscious and both were bleeding badly. At the Jentz girl's insistence he took all of their property in the back of his pickup and Jentz rode to the hospital in the back of his vehicle. He was unsure but thought he delivered the girls to the Redmond Hospital between 11:30 PM and 11:45 PM. While he was in the park he did not observe any other vehicles except a pickup some distance away turning around near the restroom. He was occupied with the two injured girls and noted only that the vehicle was equipped with some kind of covering in the back similar to a canopy.

I'd been thinking about Bill for the last two years. Or, rather, I'd been fixated on the story of how he'd wake up screaming from nightmares a long time after that episode in Cline Falls. I pictured him sitting bolt upright in bed, in a fevered sweat—as you see in the movies. Two years had passed since I got the news from the woman at the DA's office that Bill didn't want to see me. Now I intended to force the issue. Two years was long enough.

What was he envisioning, anyway? That I would reappear smeared in red with long blood-clotted hair? By showing my updated self to him, perhaps I would flip the channel in his memory: my red-smeared visage would appear—*presto change-o*—normal, healthy, and smiling.

He had no telephone, so I had written him a letter two weeks earlier, assuring him I wasn't interested in reviving bad memories: *I know the last time I saw you I was a bloody mess, but I'm definitely looking very healthy now, so I don't think my presence will in any way remind you of what I looked like then.*

DESCHUTES COUNTY atlas in hand ("Never again become lost in Deschutes County!" was printed on the cover), I drove to the southwest quadrant of Redmond. At the outer limits of town, the atlas didn't match the landscape. A road might dead-end in a pile of lava rocks. You would have to take a detour around the rocks, in pursuit of the other half of the same road. But quite often your detour would lead to another road divided by another pile of lava rocks. I wasn't in the mood to play in a labyrinth, so I looked for Penhollow's parents, who resided on the easier street grid. Even that address wasn't easy to find.

Finally, I found myself standing on the porch of a tidy ranch house, where I took a few deep breaths to overcome my shyness. It seemed especially presumptuous of me to show up unannounced: two years before, these people wouldn't even agree to see me.

The door opened and a big man stood there. I launched into a rapid-fire rap about how "This is a little weird . . . but I was the girl in Cline Falls . . ."

"Cline Falls." The password had been spoken. He cut me off before I could finish and boomed, "Oh, it's so great to meet you! Billy told me he'd gotten your letter, and we've really been looking forward to your visit."

The exceedingly courtly Clyde Penhollow—silver hair, round nose, wide smile, wearing suspenders that curved around his barrel chest—bowed slightly as he held the door. He helped me off with my coat and introduced me to his wife, Carolann, a fastidious, classy woman with a tight hairdo and a smile as big as his. Within minutes, I was sitting in their comfortable living room, which was decorated with pictures of Western landscapes and awash in western hospitality, amazed I had been granted entry.

Yes, they were all expecting me, although Bill hadn't written back inviting me to come. He had read my letter aloud to his parents: *Last time you saw me I was a bloody mess!* Clyde repeated my own words back to me in baritone, adding that Bill said to his parents, "That was an understatement."

Bill worked construction, but he'd be back from his job site in a week, and they were sure he'd love to meet me. Meanwhile, Clyde and Carolann introduced me to their clan via a tour of the pictures lining the hallway. They talked affectionately about their brood of seven—their twin daughters, their buckaroo son, pictured with his mother in a photo all decked out in cowboy "glad rags." And there was Bill, who'd had his troubles but who was a "sweet boy," a kind, compassionate person who brought out the best in people and who wanted nothing of material things. They told me how Bill and Darlene, Bill's girlfriend at the time of the Cline Falls incident, weren't together anymore. Bill's parents always regretted their breakup and wished they'd get back together again because Darlene would have been better for Bill than the woman he was hitched to now—whom they delicately described as being on the rough side.

It was clear that no discussion with the Penhollows would have been complete without paying homage to their patriarch, Clyde's father, the guiding spiritual center in their family and a man greatly beloved by the whole community. Penny Penhollow had been a county judge and a preacher who presided over a parish in the nearby hamlet of Powell Butte. The parish was famous nationwide for its annual church sale called "Lord's Acre." In 1959, Jackie and Jack Kennedy even dropped by during the presidential campaign and bought a quilt.

"Penny befriended everyone in the world. He would always pick up hitchhikers and give them a ride," Clyde told me. One young hitchhiker Penny picked up was so inspired by his magnanimous host that he turned to the ministry himself. Another hitchhiker stole Penny's tiepin embedded with a gold nugget from the Alaskan gold rush and pummeled the preacher so badly he ended up in the hospital.

"Nobody was beyond or beneath him. And my kids have that to live up to," Clyde said. Bill did do something to live up to Penny and his legacy. He gave a lift to a girl in need who flagged him down in the summer of '77.

"My boy did the right thing at the right time," Carolann added.

Clyde was a trucker on night shift, and he now rose to leave for work. I stood up with him, but he said, "You sit here with Carolann." I looked her way, and she launched into another topic, so I settled back into the sofa—until the door opened and a tall, thin woman in her early thirties, with long legs and a cowboy belt buckle cinching her tiny waist, stood in the frame. She had dark blond, shoulder-length big hair, and when she took off her coat, I could see she had shapely arms.

Lureen was Bill's girlfriend. She looked, if not rough, glamorously tough.

"Terri is that girl Billy saved in Cline Falls. She came around, wantin' to see Bill. And Bill's out of town."

Lureen's large almond-shaped eyes, shadowed in mauve and carefully lined in black, shone bright over high cheekbones. She looked fixedly at me and after a pause said, "Oh my God."

"I was telling Terri, Billy'll be back at the end of the week . . ." Carolann went on.

"You know, Billy didn't want to meet you two years ago," Lureen cut in. Her shining eyes hadn't left me for a second. "It took him three whole years before he would even tell me the story."

"And now?" I asked.

"Now I think it'd be good for him," she said. So Bill's new girlfriend and I shared the same idea.

Lureen didn't have a phone where she lived and she was waiting to hear from Bill, so she and I continued to chat until Carolann disappeared into the kitchen. Then Lureen drew me aside and whispered, "So why did you come back to Redmond?"

I told her about Godwin—how he was a suspect in my attack, how I came back to Redmond to find the people mentioned in the police report from long ago, thinking they might help me make a case for Godwin's guilt that would keep him in jail longer.

Lureen turned serious and edgy. "I think I know who did it. And I don't think that's who did it."

Watch Your Back

I leaped on her with questions, but Lureen clammed up quickly when the door opened and one of the Penhollow daughters appeared. Now there were more introductions to be made, and the conversation moved on to other things. But when mother and daughter left the room, Lureen turned to me again, her demeanor hushed and conspiratorial.

"I was hoein' onions in Terrebonne—me and a bunch of kids—out on a seed ranch near Smith Rock. It was right after what happened out there at Cline Falls." Her voice fell into the cadence of a story. "And Janey Firestone was there, hoein' onions. And Dirk Duran showed up. He came runnin' up and he grabbed Janey, and I seen the look in his eye and it was *evil*." Lureen had a sharp, high-pitched voice that she modulated to a husky whisper. "And he said, 'Janey, we gotta get out of here. You don't know what I done.' And she started fightin' with him, and she ran in the pond, and he went after her and tried to drown her, right there in front of all of us. He kept pushing her face underwater and then he'd let her out and started beating her up again."

Dirk Duran? A description tumbled out: he was a high school kid, seventeen at the time. A good-looking cowboy with a great build, close to six feet tall, as Lureen remembered. Always dressed really neatly in Wranglers and cowboy shirts and cowboy belts and cowboy boots. He had blue eyes, startling eyes no one would forget. Everyone knew him as a kid with a violent temper who always beat up his girlfriend. Janey Firestone was often seen around town with black eyes.

Then Lureen related some vague, unspecific memories—she was only fourteen at the time: a week after the episode in Cline Falls, Lureen showed up for band practice and she was told by the guys in the band that Dirk Duran was there, and his presence had created such a stir that rehearsal was canceled for the night. But she could see Dirk some distance away, sitting on the tailgate of his pickup with a piece of wood in his hand and a pocketknife. She remembered how he was trying to get a bloodstain out of his initials carved on that piece of wood. And she remembered that piece of wood just might have been the handle of a hatchet, because everyone knew Dirk Duran had a hatchet with the initials D.D. carved on the handle, and that's probably what he had in his hand as he sat on the tailgate of his pickup, though she didn't see the wooden object up close. She also remembered something about there being blood on the tailgate of the pickup. And an excuse he made about the blood: that he had been out chopping coyotes.

If she didn't see the hatchet up close, how did she know there was blood on it? How did she know that initials were on it? I tried to pin down her sketchy vignettes, but she hushed up, as if she were holding something back.

"Where's he now?" I asked.

No one was sure of his whereabouts. He used to be seen around Redmond from to time to time, but as far as she knew, nobody had spotted him for a long time.

This was enervating information that I wanted to push away. It seemed too much for me to go off in this wholly new direction. Besides, the axeman being a local high school kid? It seemed preposterous. I took Lureen as a colorful character, full of tall tales and muddy rumors, someone who liked drama and knew how to varnish a story.

"It would take an especially depraved person to go after someone with an axe. Few people would do that," I said. "One thing I know for sure about my attacker, whoever did this wanted revenge against some woman," I added with conviction.

Lureen nodded. "You take revenge against a woman. Add drugs and alcohol, and you've got Dirk Duran. He always used to go around town saying, 'If I can't have her, nobody can' . . . And the pickup. Billy thought he saw a pickup down there that night. We're just guessing, but Billy could tell us. I think when he was loading your stuff, a pickup pulled down, shined the lights, and went away. Billy says, that's when he thought he recognized Dirk's pickup."

Carolann walked back in the room and caught the tail end of our conversation.

"Billy got that information from people around who said, 'Dirk Duran did this and that.' And they put the whole story together. Billy didn't see any of that did he?" Carolann put in. "That could have been just anyone coming down there for peace, just like anybody, and saw there was a car there. Could have been an innocent bystander."

The phone rang. Bill was calling for Lureen, who left to take the call in the kitchen. Carolann told me that she worked at Redmond High for twenty-five years, and she knew Dirk Duran from school. She'd heard the rumors around town ever since it happened—a lot of folks had been saying Dirk Duran was the one who attacked the girls in Cline Falls. "He had a real volatile temper and could fly off the handle, but I never thought he was capable of doing anything like that."

Lureen got off the phone and left as abruptly as she had arrived. She made eye contact with me as she headed for the door and said softly, "I wouldn't be telling too many people what you're doing around here. Watch your back."

Carolann was busy dialing a number. "Say, I wonder if Boo is in town," she said.

"Boo?"

Boo, I was delighted to learn, was Darlene Gervais, Bill's girlfriend in 1977 and my other rescuer, who had recently returned to the Redmond area, where she lived on a ranch with her mother. Carolann handed me the receiver, and I told Boo how much I wanted to meet her.

Boo's voice was warm, enthusiastic. "You would? Really?" and I wondered why she was surprised.

EN ROUTE BACK to Sisters, I defended against the possibility that my axeman might have been a seventeen-year-old schoolboy. If I had to suffer the outrage of a heinous crime, I needed to believe that it was committed by the most depraved killer imaginable—a Godwin type, a *serial* killer, a Green River or Zodiac Killer— not some teenage hothead.

Lureen's warning echoed in my mind. In this particular patch of black desert, it took little for paranoia to take root. I felt eyes on my back, though my rational self reminded me it was impossible that anyone could be trailing me now.

Five miles out of Redmond, the lights from ranches on either side of the road were fewer and the sky was a rich black. My headlights streaked across a sign up ahead, setting aglow luminescent letters that spelled out CLINE FALLS STATE PARK, and then I passed the park road, chained at night. I accelerated to eighty, reached the Sisters city limits ten miles later, and curbed my speed to forty. Not soon enough. My rearview mirror exploded in light and a siren blared. A startling intrusion into my night reverie. I braked to the curb, and a clean-cut cub patrol officer appeared in my window.

"Did you know you were speeding in a school zone?" He was polite. It was eleven o'clock at night. It struck me that being caught in a speed trap on this particular stretch of road added insult to injury.

"Officer, I was chopped up with an axe on this same road seventeen years ago and police never found my attacker and the only reason I'm driving this road at all is because all these years later I'm back investigating the crime myself . . ." What did I have to lose? ". . . so maybe you could let me go this time."

"Ma'am. People tell me stories all the time. I don't know if I can believe you. I'm afraid I'm going to have to give you this ticket." He whipped out his pad.

Nothing to lose: "I just wish you guys had been as effective catching the psychopath that chopped me up with the axe as you are at giving speeding tickets to people like me."

"Psychopaths are a lot harder to catch, ma'am," he said, still politely, handing me a ticket for $135.

Boo

If you save a life you are responsible for it.
—OLD CHINESE PROVERB

Her face in the window of the pickup truck: I recognized the large expressive eyes. She looked deeply familiar. Her face had lived inside me for seventeen years. Boo was doing the same—scrutinizing me, trying to match the woman in front of her with her memory.

"I was so nervous coming here, just because you wanted to talk to me. Nobody ever talked to me about this. There were several newspapers that didn't even mention my name."

We sat together in a red rolled-vinyl booth in Mrs. Beasley's, a seventies-era coffee shop amid the development on Highway 97 on the route between Redmond and Bend. I remembered that night she wore a bandanna and a hippie style of dress. Now she was outfitted for the ranch: plaid shirt under a vest, her slim body in tight blue jeans, straight dark hair falling simply down either side of a widow's peak on her forehead. She rocked back and forth as she talked, long turquoise earrings swaying, and looked at me steadily with gleaming eyes rimmed with liner.

"I have always wondered how you guys handled your life. I just always wondered about you. Were you getting those little mental drifts? You must have if you came back."

I didn't admit that although I remembered her from her visit to me in the hospital, I had focused on Bill when I returned to start my search. Bill's girlfriend—I knew her only as "Darlene"—was mentioned only once in the crime report because police never interviewed her. I'd looked her up in telephone registries, didn't find her name, and quit there. I had a vague plan to continue my search one day.

"I've often thought about how you feel being out at night . . . I always wondered if you have nightmares. I wondered if you can camp out. I can never camp in a tent, *no way!*"

I told Boo I wasn't afraid of camping, though—small wonder—I never found many willing to camp with me. Then I urged her on to tell more of her own tale.

"When your face came in that window I thought, Oh my God. You were so bloody, you looked like you'd been swimming in a pool of blood—your hair was dripping with blood, you had blood everywhere. It was just devastating. When I went home that night I was dripping from head to toe." That day in 1977, Boo wore the color most likely to stain. White shirt. White pants. All white. White like a nurse.

"I remember rinsing my clothes out and blood going in the drain."

"I owe you a new outfit," I quipped, adopting a flip tone to fend off the acute emotion now closing off my throat.

"It's just a good thing Billy and I were fighting that night. Because that's why we went into Cline Falls. Matter of fact, I broke up with him that night and I didn't want to talk about it, but he was crying and he wanted to settle it, so we drove into the park and as we were driving through slowly, right where the turn-around was, you started running from the side, then beside us for a while. Billy didn't want to stop. I made him stop and back up . . . you know how when you sense when somebody needs help? Your little figure that night in the dark against our headlights running to our car, the way you were waving the light, I saw asking for help in that, and he did not, and I said, 'Billy, that's somebody that needs help, damn it, stop!' And we backed up, and sure enough, your little face . . ."

Her story went straight to my heart. I lost my composure at this revelation of a moment of compassion from a stranger who had the sensitivity to pay attention and the courage to answer a need. Boo grasped my hands on the Formica table.

"I have cold hands," I said.

"That's okay."

I tried to reassemble my voice, struggled to put words to pure emotion, but to no avail. I quavered and stopped. Boo talked on. She had a story to tell.

"Billy thought it was just some punk, but I said, no, that person needs help because I could tell by the way you were running with the flashlight. I don't know, it was a sense—I could tell you needed help. And your first words were 'I was hatcheted up.' And we were going to take you to the hospital, but you said, 'No, no, you've got to pick up all my stuff'—so we're backing up as fast as we can."

To have my actions described back to me magnified them for the first time. Doubtless I wasted precious moments forcing my rescuers to pick up our camp-site, but I'd never once questioned my judgment. My stubborn will that refused death, then sought help, swept up absolutely everything in its wake. Our possessions had become our life support. I remembered the feeling: get *everything* out of this black hole, as though anything left behind might make us more deeply vulnerable.

"God, the destruction of your little camp was so tremendous. It looked like somebody had taken your stuff and pitched it out of the pickup and drove off. The tent was down. And Shayna was over by the edge of the water. She was laying there by the edge of the water, so still and not moving, and when we got everything all picked up and put everything in the back of the truck, we went to get her last . . . it was the weirdest feeling I have ever felt in my entire life. She was laying there. All three of us froze a second and we were standing over her, and it was like a thickness in the air. We didn't even touch her until she moved, and when she moved all three of us grabbed her . . . Do you remember that, when she was laying on the ground and we all stood back because we didn't want to touch her?"

No. I was certain my perception was entirely different. To me, Shayna was vitally alive, even as her wound throbbed into my fingers.

"I swear to this day—maybe not you—but Billy and I thought, that girl is dead. Then she moaned, and we just flew on her. But why would you feel that about a dead body? We both felt the same thing I'm sure, because it was like thick air . . . until she moved, and we just jumped on her, we grabbed her as fast as we could."

"I couldn't have helped you move her because I had no arms."

"Baloney. You were moving like nothing was wrong with you. That's why I was so shocked when I found out later the truck had driven over you. You were pitching things in that truck . . . you were running around a hundred miles an hour, like you were overdosed on speed, talking a mile a minute. You said you'd been hatcheted and we had to help you and we had to pick everything up that was out there—*we had to pick it up.* I didn't want to argue with you.

"You were moving like nothing happened to you," Boo repeated, and I transferred her memory to my mind's eye: this strange behavior wasn't familiar to me, and yet I now remembered it as mine. In proximity to death, swimming in the "thickness" of the air, extraordinary capacities became available to me.

"Isn't it amazing, the power of adrenaline? You could have probably lifted that truck up, I swear. It seemed like ten minutes but I knew it was only a half a second, and then she moaned and moved, and we grabbed her. I'm not sure if you helped lift her; I think it was Bill and I. We carried her to the front seat of the car and we put her in the front, and you just flew in the back of the truck. And I remember her being in the cab and holding her head and she woke up in spurts and she was moaning."

Was it possible Boo also bore witness to those sounds that seemed to fill all the desert—sounds I had never heard before and have never heard since?

"They were earth-shattering moans, a total pain moan. She was just hurtin', hurtin'. She'd be still, then she'd move and moan. Dreadful, dreadful moans."

She'd heard what I had heard.

"Course my brain was spinning so fast—I wanted to comfort her, but I didn't know how hurt she was. But I remember her just laying there, putting her hands on her head. She'd get up and go, 'Ohhhh.' And Shayna's head, her little head, her brains were exposed."

"What was that like for you, holding her?"

"It wasn't bad . . . I felt bad for her. I don't know how to describe it—the relief at her being alive, because I thought she was dead.

"But the thing that galled me that night . . ." Boo was seized by upswelling memories, eager to get to the end of her story. "We get to the emergency room and the door is locked, and I was beating on that door, and the nurse comes to the door and opens it up and says, 'What's wrong here?' I said, 'These girls have been hatcheted up, get a doctor!'—and I ran down the hall, screaming, 'Where's the doctor?' . . . There wasn't even a doctor on duty. What the hell was an emergency center for when the doors are locked?

"You were trying to get out of the back of the truck yourself, I think. But I remember helping you and seeing your little arm, and seeing the hack mark out of it—I mean it was just . . ." Boo imitated the sound of a hatchet chop. "It was a clean cut. Pie-shaped. An axe cut, chopped just like a tree. Right out of your forearm, where there's not much meat."

Chopped like a tree. I hadn't before considered the tree analogy. It was a raw comparison, especially disturbing here in logging country. If you were writing a novel and you were describing a body part chopped like a tree, you would want the reader to feel a special horror, to evoke how easily our bodies can be reduced to their thingness.

On cue, I rolled up my sleeve and showed her my old white scar, which snaked around my left forearm. Boo made a far more appropriate audience than most others, nearly all others, to whom I had shown it.

"God, you were so lucky. You coulda' had an ear cut off. Your fingers cut off. I'm surprised you didn't have your hands cut off."

In all the years in which I had told the story, never had it been like this. Never before had I discussed the memory with one who had been there. This was a remarkable experience, consoling to my psyche. And it made me remember another night, a wounding night on the other side of the Iron Curtain, when I tried to tell my story to another who had been there. But this day was undoing that long-ago night, the pain of the untold story. An image formed in my mind: pillows falling away from ears.

The perfect listener turned out to be a perfect stranger.

And now it was my turn to give my own account. Out tumbled my richly detailed story, and I watched the way Boo's eyes took it all in. When I finished, I asked her, though I felt shy about the request, if she would accompany me on a visit to Cline Falls, or if that seemed just too weird.

BOO WALKED right to the spot—to the patch of earth where I remembered lying on my back after the cowboy had left, looking up at the tree framing the sky, aware that I had experienced a most unthinkable thing, and had survived.

"The tent was right here," she said, and my heart swelled. I was not alone inside this white-hot memory any longer.

"And Shayna was laying way over there, by the river." Boo walked a few feet to a thicket of reeds obscuring the water. "It wasn't so dense then."

I remembered also that I found Shayna lying right next to the water. I paused to assimilate a fact I did not know until this moment: dragged by the truck, the tent (and me in it) had been situated a few feet away from where Shayna lay. That meant that while I was trapped under the wheels of the vehicle, she must have escaped the tangle of nylon and tried to get away before she was struck down. Shayna, too, had memory, before it was extinguished.

"What I remember so vividly is the smell of the blood," I told Boo. "Do you remember that, too?"

"No, I don't remember that." Boo took a long drag on her cigarette. "You know, after that happened, hardly anyone came down here."

We gazed around the park, as though that night were present again. Boo remembered something else. "While we were loading the truck, before we were picking up Shayna, a car came down. It pulled real slow in front of the bathrooms, scanned its lights, and went back up. My heart was out of my chest. I thought, Good Lord, he's coming back to finish the job. Then when the car turned around and left, we were back at it, throwing everything back in the pickup."

The only vehicle I remembered scanning its lights that night was the truck that turned out to contain Bill and Boo. A second vehicle coming into the park was never part of my memory. But I knew from the police report that Bill told investigators he remembered a *truck*, not a car, coming down into the park.

"No, it was a *car*, not a truck," Boo insisted. She didn't want to alter a single detail of the story she'd told for so long.

And speaking of the stories people tell, it just so happened that Boo recently ran into a guy from high school who suddenly, out of the clear blue, started talking to her about how he was the guy who'd found the bloody girls at Cline Falls.

" 'I don't think so!' I said to him. 'I kinda think I found 'em.' And he said, 'Are you *sure*?' I snapped back at him. 'No, I love to lie about things like that.' "

Boo had lightened her tone. "He kept saying 'Are you sure?' Then he changed his story. Now he's telling me he was there when the police were there." She let out a loud, hearty laugh.

We sat on the picnic table in the middle of the crime scene and tried to take the measure of each other. We were linked, for sure. But did we have anything in common beyond that one night? We were one year apart in age. We laughed at how our adolescent selves perceived time.

"Back then I thought you were so much older than me," she said.

"And I thought you were so much younger than me!"

Boo was sixteen when her mother married a man with a ranch, and she and three of four sisters moved to the sticks of Central Oregon from an urban part of Washington. She had always thought cowboys were a thing of the past until she moved to Redmond, where she felt as though she'd walked into a *Bonanza* episode. She left as soon as she could, after high school, and worked as a welder. She told me she was one of the first women to enter that profession. For years she welded pipe as far north as Alaska, but the hard labor took its toll, and she quit. She also quit her husband and put her drug-addicted lifestyle behind her. Two years ago she came back to Redmond to help her mother work a cattle ranch.

"How'd you get a name like Boo?"

Boo's older sisters had given this nickname to her when she was a baby. She'd never been called Darlene. Always Boo.

I suggested it was pretty ironic for her to have a name like that, given her connection to that dark night.

"Yeah . . . You know, I could be a hundred years old and I'll still remember every detail of that night—your face in the truck window, you running out with your little light. You had beautiful hair. When I saw you in the hospital with it all shaved off . . . what a shame."

Billy

A situation has not been satisfactorily liquidated, has not
been fully assimilated, until we have achieved, not merely
through our movements, but also an inward reaction
through the words we address to ourselves, through the
organization of the recital of the event to others and to
ourselves, and through the putting of this recital in its
place as one of the chapters in our personal history.
—PIERRE JANET, *PRINCIPLES OF PSYCHOTHERAPY*, 1924

Bill sat close to Lureen on the couch, his
veined, ropy arms folded in his lap. I remembered clearly his white-blond hair
from that long-ago night, how he wore it close to the shoulders and flipped in a
feminine curl at the ends. Now his hair was darker, cut short, and covered by a
cap. Deep lines crisscrossed his handsome face, and he looked older than his
thirty-six years.

"I wondered over the years how they both survived . . . where they'd gone." He
spoke of me in the third person. His soft blue eyes avoided me altogether, as
though I were not just now sitting in his parents' living room, directly across from
him.

Bill was back in town and had agreed finally to meet me. We were all assembled in the Penhollows' comfortable living room lit by warm lamplight—he and
Lureen, his parents, Boo and I—each to tell our own version of the tale, each offering a few narrative strands that would together weave themselves into a more
complete view of the story than any one of us possessed on our own.

Clyde's version of the tale had Bill calling him from the hospital almost inco-
herent. "They tried to kill 'em! They ran over them and tried to kill 'em, Dad!"
When Clyde finally saw his son that night, Bill told him that he'd flown down the
highway at top speed toward the hospital, unescorted by the police. Usually local
cops were trolling to pick up teens on a wild ride.

"Billy told me he couldn't find a cop when he wanted one that night," Clyde
said, and a smile broke out on Bill's solemn face.

The next day, it was Clyde who cleaned up Bill's pickup. There was so much blood in every corner of it—in the truck bed, against the door in the cab. He had to find a fire hose just to wash it out.

As we told our tales, each of us assembled in the room was poised on the threshold of a memory that was coming to life.

I'VE ALWAYS been blessed with a superb memory. When I was two, I found it nourishing to dwell on the day I turned one, engraving into my brain the moment of receiving my first birthday gift. Memory has always helped me to shape my life, forge it into a series of events, a narrative. When I was twenty, I experienced a memory of a different kind. A memory that burned.

The mind processes traumatic memories differently from normal memories. When the brain assimilates data from the five senses, it attaches emotional significance and then organizes it into narrative structures. Ordinary memory is how people make sense of what happens to them, stitching together events into a completed story of the past.

Traumatic experience overwhelms the brain. Because of its unexpectedness or horror, because the experience defies comprehension, the event itself is not integrated into one's consciousness. It imprints as free-floating fragments—sometimes terrifying—of image, sound, smell, and emotion, not as part of any narrative story. Or it imprints as a frozen story—static, emotionless, lacking depth. My repetitive tale, the original story, the cheerful beats of my narrow escape, was a version of this.

One Holocaust scholar who interviewed concentration camp survivors compared these memory fragments to "damaged mosaics" that can't yet be fitted into the larger mosaic design. Until these damaged tiles are integrated—if they ever are—they live on in a separate parallel reality, often obscured from conscious thought, but leaving an indelible mark that can intrude on the present.

For me, the white-hot memory wasn't just the static tale of how a mythic *Seven Brides for Seven Brothers* cowboy with an axe turned me into a "scarecrow." There were floating fragments, too: the sensation of the wind blowing through my veins, the smell of juniper commingled with blood. Otherwise insignificant details were charged with the power of explosive associations, became objects of numinous significance. The macaroni and tuna we ate that night, the mess kit we prepared it in, the yellow plastic flashlight—in a constellation, these prosaic things pulsed with an energy that lifted them out of the everyday, removed them from the contours of the rest of my life.

Here in this living room I was beginning to understand that I was not alone with this overwhelming memory of Cline Falls. This event, on the twenty-second of June 1977, had left an unassimilated imprint on a small collective. "It never leaves your mind, really," my mother told me. "It made a memory in me," Nola the librarian claimed; she who was not even present on the scene.

I began to recognize the outlines of a less obvious motivation compelling me to return to this western desert community. On some subterranean level, we were all waiting to reconnect, to bring together our searing memories, to imbue them with meaning and a historical context, to integrate them into a larger, shared narrative.

"REMEMBER, BILLY, you didn't want to stop?" Boo was talking matter-of-factly. She wasn't rocking back and forth like she had when we talked the day before. "I knew she needed help by the way she was waving the light."

"Yeah, I wasn't sure if I wanted to stop or not," Bill fessed up. "I think I rolled on by about ten or fifteen feet."

Clyde wanted to offer a reason for his son's reluctance. "I remember you saying you told your girlfriend to lock the door until you found out what was going on. You had thoughts it was going to be a setup deal, and you didn't want anything to do with that."

"I don't know if it was a setup, but you know . . ." Bill's deep voice had a halting cadence. "You see this in the movies, not in Redmond . . . It was right there— point blank. It was a shock." Bill's eyebrows had a life of their own. They leapt high onto his forehead until he looked like a scared child, while his eyes retreated deep under his browridges as though fleeing the sight even now. I studied him from across the room as carefully as I could without appearing to do so. He exuded a vulnerability I hadn't seen in any other young man with so ravaged a face, and I had the urge to comfort him with a hug.

"When I first could see it was a person, I could tell they were soaked in blood . . . I could see the redness in the light, from the side of my headlights. It was quite startling, really: 'I don't want to stop for this,' but then . . . You gotta stop. You took ahold of my arm . . . to show me where the problem was . . ." By now, Bill was addressing me, but still not looking my way.

"And you said, 'We need help. You've got to get us out of here and load up all our stuff.' And I did it without a second thought," he added quickly, with a hint of pride. "I think it took a very short period of time. We weren't there but five minutes at the most."

Lureen piped up in her sharp, high-pitched voice, "Billy told me you were running back and forth, following them as though if you didn't, they might run away. Somebody should have made you set down!"

"Then a vehicle pulled down when we were loading up," Bill drawled. "The adrenaline was pumping real good then. The headlights stopped right on us for a second, then they went up the hill. At that point I thought it was round two . . . I think normally a person would have drove through. But whoever it was didn't want to go through. They scanned their lights across and saw there was a vehicle there and turned around and went back up. You wouldn't just turn around and go back up; whenever we went down we made the full loop. But they stopped right in the lot in front of the bathrooms, and they swung real wide, real slow, and scanned the lights, to see who was in the park."

Bill said he thought it was a pickup and that's what he told the police. I knew that's what he told the police. I read his testimony in the crime report.

Boo was never interviewed by the police, but she insisted she saw "a big old heavy car like a Cadillac or Impala."

"Just the shape made me think it was a car, but it was too dark. I couldn't see your face ten feet away," Boo said to me. "You couldn't see the color of any cars . . . I could have sworn it was a car."

Then she asked Bill, "You remember when we went to pick up Shayna and there was that moment of dead air?"

Bill shook his head, no. That wasn't anything that fired up his memory.

"Yeah, and all three of us froze in our tracks until she moved, and we just grabbed her," Boo insisted. This was the moment that struck her, the one that had sifted itself out from the others, the one with the most explosive emotional charge.

"I don't see why they didn't make you lay down or sit down or something," Lureen offered up again. She was focused on her own most memorable moment, experienced secondhand through Bill's story.

"We didn't know she was hurt," Boo said. "She was running around like a madwoman."

"I saw the cut, and I knew that explained the blood," Bill added, "but after the headlights, all we had is that little flashlight you had—it was dark, we couldn't see."

"Did you have nightmares after that night?" I pressed Bill.

"Ahhhh . . . I didn't really have nightmares," he said at last, "but I had some problems out there in the dark alone at night, you know, some days were real bad. I kept looking behind me, from the house to the car."

"He still do not like the dark," Lureen interjected.

When everyone had told their piece of the story, I again told mine. When I observed their rapt attention, I knew we had rolled time back, as though the walls of the room had dissolved and that summer night was palpable, taking up space in the room as though it were corporeal.

My tale unwound with its incantatory power: "I heard seven blows . . ." Bill's eyes widened and his eyebrows were so high up on his forehead that they disappeared under his cap brim. When I shifted the story into high gear, I did what I had never done before. I stood in the middle of the Penhollows' living room and posed with an invisible axe suspended in the air.

"And he held the axe and came down with it. Slowly. Very slowly. And I folded my hands around the blade . . . and he gently withdrew it." I continued on with the beats of the story, then finally, in a momentary lapse into an earlier performance, I rolled up my shirtsleeve to show off the scar on my left forearm.

"A perfect axe cut," I said.

Finally, spent with the past, we settled into the lighter mood of the present. Clyde showed off his cowboy shirt collection, Carolann played the organ for us, and Bill got up to go home. It was after nightfall.

As Bill and Lureen stood up to say their goodbyes, Lureen shot me a meaningful glance. When no one was listening she said, "If you're not leavin', I can talk to you tomorrow."

I was planning to leave early the next morning.

"No, I'm not leaving," I answered as casually as I could.

CRUISING HIGHWAY 126 again, en route back to Sisters, I thought of the night, the images tumbling out in pace with the white road dashes my headlights lit up. It fascinated me to consider that when a number of people share a memory of an unusually intense single event, every individual will unconsciously choose one detail that blazes in bold relief, and that detail is as unique as that person's personality. For Boo, it was the moment she thought she breathed death in the air. For Bill, a figure glowing red in the headlights. For me, the scent of blood. Somehow, although she wasn't present, the story had stirred up Lureen's memory, too—and what she had picked out from the tale Bill told her was the sight of a woman with broken bones in a manic dance.

Billy Don't Do Dark

At first she said nothing. I waited for her. After all, she was the one who'd called me here. And then: "I have five hundred questions to ask you. But I'm going to start with one: *Why* did you come back here? What are you lookin' for?"

Lureen sat straight-backed in the tidy kitchen of Bill's parents' ranch-style home. She folded her long fingers with groomed long nails on the table in front of her. Her almond-shaped eyes gleamed over high cheekbones—she had told me she was part Cherokee and part German, but her magnificent Native American cheekbones flowing from a nose shaped like an arrowhead overwhelmed her Germanic features. She fixed me with those gleaming eyes as if she could see through me, right into my insides, until red splotches traveled up my neck and my eyes glistened with unexpected tears.

Another pause thickened the suspense. I could feel the weight of something in the silence between us. Her question had to be rhetorical. It was too large for an answer, and we both knew it.

"I've thought about this since two years ago," she said. "We were living right here with Billy's parents when the lady from the DA's office contacted Billy's mom that you wanted to see Billy. His mom mentioned it to him, and Billy said, 'Oh, I don't know.' After the lights went out that night. Silence. And I said, 'Not only for you, Billy, but I'd like to meet that girl.' He said, 'Whatever.' And he didn't respond the way I thought he would. That's why I kept questioning him, and I think he was afraid. That whoever did it knew he knew."

"Why would Billy be afraid, if a lot of people in town thought they knew who it was?"

"If you'd seen what Billy'd seen—what a man did to two women—don't you think you'd be afraid of that person? And so he goes back to: 'I don't know anything.' "

Then she told me again what she had revealed the previous evening: "Ever since that night, Billy don't do dark." Lureen remembered an especially romantic night when the moon was "shining on the pond, and shining on the bank"—and she couldn't get Bill to take a walk with her.

"People don't even notice anymore. No one says anything. But Billy don't go out to dinner or dancing. He goes to bed at sundown and gets up at sunrise. If it's dark, he leaves his truck lights on to get inside the door."

I had noticed that Bill had been the first to leave our gathering. While we were all talking, was he watching shades of night fall on the street outside?

"I've told Billy a hundred times, I've always wanted to talk to you," Lureen continued. "Maybe you're not alone."

Maybe I'm not alone? What did she mean?

"Maybe you're not the only one who thinks this is crazy. Someone can't come here and do what happened to you and get away with it. I don't have answers. But none of it makes sense. None of it does."

The other night I had shown Lureen the police report on the investigation of the Cline Falls case that mentioned Godwin as a suspect. Now she picked up the document from the table and read aloud Forsberg's account of Godwin's alleged confession: "In these conversations Godwin told Forsberg that he was responsible for running over Jentz and Weiss at a State Park over near Bend . . ."

She waved the thin stack of papers as if it were worthless piffle.

"This stuff to me is B.S.—a written hearsay confession? That was two years later. This guy is already doin' life for whatever he's already done. He could have got every detail of what happened from anywhere. He could have been promised cigarettes for the rest of the time, or someone on the outside says, 'I'm willing to put X amount of dollars on your books for X amount of time and all you have to do is say this.' I mean, you're a maniac anyway. It happens.

"And anyway," Lureen continued, "if this Godwin is gonna cut the head off and save the skull of the girl, why'd he leave *you* alive? That type of man should have got the pleasure out of watching you with your eyes open, begging, 'Please don't! Take what you want!' He liked the scare," she said with bitterness.

I shared with Lureen the theory I'd developed while studying Godwin. Someone told me that when Godwin was a child, people would drop stray cats at the dump where his father was a caretaker. One night every few months, his dad would round up his sons and they would club the cats and throw them on the dump heap, half dead. Later Godwin would lie awake in bed listening to their howls. If my attacker had indeed been Godwin, something in that anecdote had sunk into my brain and put down roots: he clubbed them until they were half dead and then threw them away to suffer. Maybe that childhood habit—leaving his kill to howl all night—had reached into adulthood. Maybe his intention all along was to take me to the *edge* of death, not all the way.

Lureen gave my theory some real consideration—as it flashed through my mind that there was a large element of the absurd in my attempts at forensic psychology—but she was dubious. "Why did the guy come back to you twice, then? Why didn't he leave you alone the first time?" It seemed that Lureen had retained the precise details of the story I told the night before.

"What I always thought back then was that he drove his truck back on the road so when he was finished he'd have a quick getaway."

"And then decided to come back?" She didn't subscribe to this theory at all.

True, I hadn't fully examined this especially strange moment in my story: that our attacker walked away, granting me a moment of reprieve that allowed me the presence of mind to yank myself back from the brink by the time he walked back. Why that moment of reprieve? Was it the obvious answer? He thought he'd finished me off when he walked away, then noticed I was stirring and came back?

That odd moment between attacks reminded Lureen of something else entirely: Dirk Duran would beat up his girlfriend Janey Firestone, then suddenly stop and comfort her. "After he beat her up, he always made sure she had a washrag. 'It's okay. It's better. I'm sorry,' he would always say."

Dirk Duran, it seemed, was in the habit of stopping short of annihilation. But that didn't explain what had happened to Shayna.

"Maybe I'm just stuck on Dirk Duran," Lureen said. "Maybe that's totally wrong. On the other hand, I would like to find out more than I know, because if I'm all these years so bitter against a person and if he's really not guilty, that's not fair."

If it was true, as she claimed, that just after the incident in Cline Falls, a hotheaded kid in the same community tried to beat and drown his girlfriend, I could imagine he ought to be looked at carefully. But I still had deep misgivings that my attacker was a seventeen-year-old boy; I defended against the possibility of even considering it. "What *exactly* did he look like?" I asked Lureen again.

She repeated what she'd told me before. He was a snappy dresser, an attractive cowboy.

"A well-built guy? Did he wear his jeans pretty tight?"

She confirmed that he wore his jeans tight, and so neat you could see the creases in the legs. Dark blue Wranglers. Boot cut, so the fabric fell down in neat folds over his Tony Llamas. That's how cowboys back then liked their pants to fall.

That detail resonated. I hadn't described jeans in folds around the boots in my own retellings. But, yes, I could almost say my memory recognized long pant legs breaking over cowboy boots.

"And he walked like this." Lureen stood in front of me and took a couple of paces with a cowboy swagger, exaggeratedly swinging her right shoulder forward with her right foot, then her left shoulder forward with her left foot. Tall and thin, her tight jeans cinched at the waist with a huge cowboy belt buckle, her shirt neatly tucked into a trim waistline—Lureen was, bizarrely, almost a female version of the attractive cowboy she was describing.

"What I remember was a guy with his shirt really neatly tucked in."

Oh, yeah, she assured me. He always dressed perfectly.

Before I had ever returned to Oregon, I recorded on videotape my description of the vivid cowboy torso that faded away above the neck. The image had made such an impression on me that an odd thought had even flitted through my awareness: this axeman was exceptionally attractive. My recollections were secure, documented. I wasn't about to revise them with every subsequent detail I heard about a suspect. But there was an alignment between the portrait Lureen had pantomimed and the image stirring in my mind. Her description, her imitation of a macho swagger, seemed to elaborate details of that meticulous torso frozen in time, seemed to revive some trace of an ancient memory that was now trickling in from the back of my skull.

"And he was wild and he was crazy." Lureen's voice turned shrill like an alarm. "I've heard lots of stories, yeah, but I've also heard that he was out to find her, and if he couldn't have her, nobody could, and he was looking for her, and in his rage—and the more whiskey and the more beer, and the way he was—if he thought he seen her, he would be the type to set up there above Cline Falls and watch."

She lowered her voice to a hoarse whisper. "I mean, he could have even thought it was Janey with another man from the view from the highway, because you could see down into the park at that time, and if he thought she was down there, and if he was in a rage to find her . . . He always said, 'If I can't have you, no one will.' If he thought he seen her, he might've waited till dark, then went back there. You said first he parked on you, then you heard seven whacks—he probably didn't even see you. He was whackin', then he seen that he's parked on somebody, and it's a girl. Well, now he's gotta finish it, but she's the wrong one."

I didn't believe it was possible that he had confused our identity. It's true, after we arrived in Cline Falls, we felt a sharp intuition that we were being watched. Maybe he was spying on us from the road. But he would have known that Janey didn't have a pup tent and a couple of ten-speeds.

"I always thought we were attacked by some man who was angry at a woman, and he couldn't get to her, so he took it out on us."

"See, that even fits the pattern of him."

"You mean, 'These friggin' women, I'm going to kill them all'?"

"That's what I mean. There's so many ways of looking at it, and he ties to every one, in my opinion. And also, Dirk Duran walked straight up to Billy's brother and said, 'You're sayin' I did it? You better stop talkin'. I'll shut you up.' Now why would you even threaten someone for tellin' a story if you're not guilty? I think a normal person would say, 'Look, I know I'm bein' accused. Here I am. Clear my name.' That's my opinion. If you're innocent, you don't change your tires and try to destroy them. You don't pick up and immediately leave town. People don't tell you, 'So-and-so is in the next room, get out of here.' "

Her story was getting more elaborate. Tires were changed and destroyed? I wanted to pin her down about this hint of a cover-up, but she rolled over me with the exaggerated vehemence of her delivery, and hushed her voice to a dramatic whisper, "I left a band practice because he was sitting in another room, and they said, 'That's Dirk Duran. Get out of here.' "

Who told her to leave band practice? And why?

Lureen had related these fragments when I saw her earlier in the week—that she had arrived at band practice to see Dirk Duran sitting on the tailgate of his pickup, digging dried blood out of the initials in his hatchet handle.

"And that was the next day after the Cline Falls attack?" I asked again.

"I'm not sure when Cline Falls happened. But I'm sure it was the following Wednesday—that's when I always practiced."

The Cline Falls attack took place on Wednesday night. The scene she described must have taken place a week later.

She went on, "You don't hatchet coyotes around here. Why was that accepted?"

My mind grabbed ahold of this picture: a meticulous young cowboy sitting on the bloody tailgate of his pickup, carving blood out of the initials in his hatchet, telling the guys in the band, hey, what's all the excitement about? I know two girls got chopped in Cline Falls. But it wasn't me who did it. I was out chopping coyotes!

I wanted to know: Why did the boys in the band cancel practice? Were they confronting Dirk while he was claiming he was innocent? Or did they know he was guilty, and they were conferring among themselves about keeping it secret out of some fraternal teen code, to protect one another from the authorities? One thing was for sure, if I could believe Lureen: this cabal of boys didn't want a fourteen-year-old girl to overhear their conversation.

Lureen swept on without allowing me to question her. I no longer bothered trying to make her be more specific.

"And you know, for such a popular troublemaking brat that he was, there was too much silence from him after that point. He chased Janey Firestone for I don't know how many years. Why all the sudden after he tried to drown her the day after the Cline Falls incident . . . then why did he leave her alone? They had to have separated." Lureen implied that maybe Dirk Duran went away somewhere, until the situation quieted down.

Then she reminded me of Bill's story again: Bill said that while he and Boo were rescuing us in Cline Falls, he saw a pickup pull down into the park, fan its lights, then drive back up to the highway.

"If you shined your lights on somebody and seen somebody helping somebody else, and movements and blood, wouldn't you have hightailed it to the cops?

Any normal person would have got to a pay phone and *anonymously* reported it. Whoever viewed in has got to be found. You could go on TV and say, 'I'm just asking if there's anybody out there, that on June twenty-second, 1977, happened to pull into a park and see something unusual, please contact me.' That person's got to still be around, *or they're the one who did it.* Did he think, 'Gosh, I left her alive, I could be prosecuted for murder?' You can't kill somebody and leave a witness. Or did he click and come back to help? To be the hero of Redmond: 'I didn't do it, I just seen them and brought them to you'—because he realized he left tire marks down there?

"Now there's a difference between being naïve and country, and just plain stupid. People aren't stupid here. But they're naïve enough to believe she's not ever going to come back here and pursue this? Why would you even come back here? Why would anybody come back to the place they were . . . you know . . .?"

"I should have done it a long time ago," I said, suddenly sure of my mission.

"But you weren't ready. You've got a lot to go through. I personally believe in God—Baptist and all—but the way you described it, no pain, the easy flow, and all of a sudden: no, I can't die. I can't die. I think in my way, there is a God, and you definitely passed on, and yet the will to live brought you back. And there is a God and there's got to be a purpose and a reason. And there's got to be a purpose and reason for the guy who attacked you, too—because He's not a mean, punishing God. And if He's going to make you live through this and tell it and come to redo it, there's got to be a reason to put you through this. God is not doing this for fun!"

Lureen sounded impressively like a TV evangelist, moderating her voice between impassioned tones and a low whisper. "Coming here is to help you accept it or justify it." Wind chimes sounded from the porch, like background music.

"See, Billy was driven to help you. Why didn't they just drive on? Billy and Boo have to be the kind of people to even get out and help. Back then, a lot of people wouldn't have. Somebody else would never have been able to handle it. So you've seen an incredible, unexplainable desire or need or want or will: to help. The person that helped you had to be driven to help you. So your answer is: same as this is where you were attacked, this is where your life was saved, too. And maybe that's what you feel you have got to pass that on. In the same degree.

"If I was you, I don't know if I would be able to come back. And I wouldn't— unless I was having trouble accepting it, putting it to rest. There's got to be a question for you that's still unanswered. *And it's not just the question of who the guy is.*"

This charismatic woman with her uncanny insight into my life really intimidated me. I could feel my face burning, a rash forming on my chest and creeping up my neck, which always betrayed my rattled nerves.

Yes, I was here for complex reasons. But I wouldn't talk to her about that just now. It's true, I wasn't here only because I was fixated on finding the perpetrator. He was, after all, only a lowly psycho who needed to be put out of commission.

Lureen agreed. "He's a dime a dozen. We just got to get rid of those dozen."

She and I were both on a roll. I told her my pet theory about why people are obsessed with serial killers: that they assume these weakest of people have awesome power because they're audacious enough to kill.

"They're weak," she agreed. "People think if we've got 'em behind bars we at least can study them. Study them? Heck! Study your dictionary. The definition of a serial killer is someone that will kill, kill, kill, kill, kill. If you're killin', what it tells me is you're stupid. Get rid of him. Why are we spending these thousands of dollars feeding someone who would do nothing but kill? Why? When you could drive through downtown Redmond and there should be thousands of dollars distributed in some of these poor homes. I don't have cable at my house; why should he be watching cable at his? You know?" Her voice lifted in indignation.

"This pisses me off," she continued. "People with degrees will sit and talk with him and write books about him. Come write my story. You want to write about a serial killer? Well, write about a serial killer that kills serial killers. Not the ones that kill innocent people. That pisses me off. That pisses me off!

"I think all abusers should be on an island together. They should be in a fenced area for the first thirty days. They should have to breathe each other's air for a while. There's always going to be someone bigger than the biggest one. I think they ought to feel that fear and terror . . ."

She was punching out her words stridently now. "Is bitterness eating you up?" she asked me.

"No," I said. It was the question I'd asked Shayna in my letter to her: I'd asked whether her fate had made her bitter. If I'd ever felt bitterness—unexpressed, festering rage—I couldn't access that feeling just now. I couldn't relate to the ferocity of her words. "No," I said.

"It will."

I'd known Lureen only since Monday. For all I knew, she got worked up about everything, but she certainly was talking at a fever pitch now. Her own bitterness spewed forth: about the confines of a woman's life, about what she could and couldn't do as a woman. A woman had less strength than a man. "I am walking proof that in arm-to-arm, one-to-one combat, I had no chance. You see. No chance," Lureen said. A woman had to carry an "equalizer," she said—her word for a gun. Or a woman had to learn self-defense. "We know it's not fair, but it's what we got to deal with right now.

"I feel the injustice," Lureen went on. "I live here, I've got two little girls here. I don't care if they're a homeboy or not. If they did wrong, get rid of them. Life's not been fair to me, whether it's because of the justice system, or whatever . . ."

I was struggling to follow her meaning. I asked, "Have men beaten you up?"

"Yeah. I've seen and had close encounters with psychopaths. I've seen and felt that look." She leapt into a story about getting beaten and left at death's door by a man she was seeing. But he came back and rescued her. And the only reason he came back was because he remembered that she had hidden money in her shoe. "He was so nice for the next three days, as usual. See? Money in my shoe. That's why he come back to save me. Not because he was sorry. Doesn't make sense, but that's the way it is.

"And you know what? I'm thankful for what I went through. I'm thankful I got a little taste of what you went through—and I call it a *taste* of what you went through—I'm really thankful, because after that, I have a concealed gun permit for a forty-four, and I can shoot it. Smith & Wesson four-and-a-half-inch barrel. And, Bud, you can whine and cry and complain that you're mentally insane and on drugs, but you take one step and I'm gonna blow you in half, and like it. That's my feeling. That's my hate. *I can ride my bike anywhere I want.*"

By now I was exploding with emotion, but I wanted to appear cool, so I squeezed back my tears.

"Just because I'm a girl, doesn't give you the upper hand," she said. "And I'm not a mean person; I just got an equalizer. There's so many things I wanted to do and couldn't do 'cause I was a girl, because I was scared, because I was this, because I was that. You got to take another class in life just because you are gifted as a girl? It's going to take a long process to get through to men.

"Now. Somebody messed up your investigation. I can even watch *Matlock* or *Perry Mason* and figure out how to do it myself. Back then, you were only here ten days? You should have been here until he was caught. They should have drug every farmboy from the Far West in here for identification. There's got to be an answer to each one of these questions. One step at a time."

Lureen launched into a plan of action for our investigation. She would begin to ask casual questions around town. She and I would write back and forth using code names—her nom de guerre would be "Egbert"—so not even the people at the post office would know we were in touch. Because everyone gossips in a small town.

She would find me a good photo of Dirk Duran, to see if I recognized him. "A high school picture isn't enough. You need a photo of just the body standing there—digging potatoes, you know? Right now the only reason we want to know who did it is so we can find him to prevent him from doing other things. If I can find out it's truly Dirk Duran, I'll do everything I can to get him stopped, because who knows what he's doing this moment?

"It might take a year. You're dealing with something that is non-average and non-ordinary, so you're going to have to do something non-average and non-ordinary to deal with it. But it all can make sense. There's got to be somebody that seen it. I would go talk to the Birdman if I was you."

I remembered the Birdman as the old character who lived in the shack on the upper run of the Deschutes River, across the highway from Cline Falls State Park.

"To witness something like that—isn't that going to affect a person's mind where you just want to feed the birds?" She let out a wry laugh. "And there's been a house overlooking the park at Cline Falls for too many years. And that woman who lives there doesn't miss a trick. Never has, never will. You know, it all can make sense. There's got to be somebody that seen it.

"But finding out isn't going to happen overnight. It's going to happen slow. It's even hard for me to back up seventeen years and think of who to talk to. And it's hard to admit something like that happened in your town. People were chicken. We're going to have to say to them: Why didn't you go to the police if you knew? I'd have you stand there, and me here . . ." Lureen was pantomiming our future interrogations. "And you say to this person, 'So you're coming clean and you're telling me Dirk Duran did this?' And he says, 'Yes.' And I say, 'Why didn't you go to the police when you knew he's the one who did this to her?' Because that person would be as guilty as the person who did it. Back then, if someone would have just told the truth, the town would have taken care of it."

"What do you mean?" I asked, wondering about Redmond's brand of frontier justice.

"They would have taken care of it. They knew the police wouldn't take care of it. But nobody knew sure enough that he did it. They are too good a people to actually kill him, but he was a lonely boy. He disappeared too much. I know he dropped in and out. Maybe he visited his mom and dad for a while. Or brought his girlfriend down here and told her it was all a hypothetical story. And she said, 'Bullshit, it is.' But he was banned basically, because no one could really prove in their hearts that he had done it. Yet we are just country people—anybody who'd do something like that, we don't want to get that close to provin' it anyway. Look, we have people comin' here; they come here on the run, because it is a quiet place. People stick to their own family. They take care of theirs. There's gossip goin' on constantly and the story floats around, and everyone can pawn it off that they were drunk or high or this or that. So just as it's a naïve, mellow country hick town, it's also hard-core—they take care of their own and they stay right here."

Was that why she'd told me to watch my back the other night?

"You don't know who he is, and if he's got friends and cousins in town, and you're tromping around Redmond saying, 'I'm the girl that got chopped,' they're all going to assume you're here to look for him, because we all know no one ever got caught. Everybody in this town has the possibility of snapping. Until we know the path of people that he comes from, I wouldn't be saying much of anything."

At Lureen's suggestion that a dark secret was stitched into the heart of this town, paranoia overtook me again, as though I were now trapped behind enemy lines. We left the kitchen table and continued our conversation on the front porch, under a pale October sky. I was feeling anxious to leave.

Lureen's rage had stirred me profoundly. This was sharp oratory from one who'd never read a feminist manifesto. Her politics were forged in the crucible of her own life experience. I'd guessed that she'd set up that rhetorical question, *Why did you come back here?* because she wanted to answer it herself.

"You want to know yourself who did it. You *really* want to know, do you?" I asked.

"I just want something to turn out, finally, halfway fair. I don't want my kids to have to worry about tomorrow in that way. I love to hunt and fish and camp and go and do, and it's not fair to look over your shoulder like that. You were done wrong, and I don't think we should let that happen. Someone like you would have such an influence. You can say, 'I'm here. I'm real. I'm all messed up. Do you want to see it? Do you want to feel it?' "

She turned my self-image inside out. I thought back to all those years I used my scars, my tale, as a colorful back story in my autobiography. But here in this place, I was entirely naked: "the girl that got chopped" returned like a specter, saying to all who would listen, *"I'm here. I'm real. I'm all messed up. Do you want to see it? Do you want to feel it?"*

"Even if you can't change it, maybe you can stand for something," Lureen said. "If you only save one person it will be worth it. Maybe your courage will give someone else enough guts at just the right time to put somebody away. If it's drilled in, heard about and talked about. That's what it's going to take. It's more than you and me."

I remembered her face from the night before—the electric glow in her eyes, her flushed cheeks, how she didn't take her eyes off me. I probed: "What was going through your mind last night when I was telling my story?"

"I seen a lot of hate and bitterness. It's eatin' you alive. You were almost evil lookin' when you stood up like him and were sayin', 'He brought the hatchet down.' And when you looked up, you had his look. You were there. It's real. And no one should ever experience that or look like that or see that."

I tried to picture my face as she described it. My passport photo from 1982 entered my mind: white heat radiating from my high forehead, peaked brows knit into a scowl, bulges between my eyes, flared nostrils.

"And you gave him too much credit when you said he brought the axe down gently. He was measuring you, measuring you to chop—like you were a piece of wood."

While we are living each phase of our life we rarely realize its true pathos. Now I can see that Lureen's sprawling vehemence compensated for my subdued response to the stark and disfiguring violence in my past. Her insight that he was measuring me to chop, like a piece of wood, evoked no more emotion in me that day—maybe less—than if someone told me my credit card had been refused.

I always described how slowly he brought the axe down, as though my words had tamed him. Lureen was trying to knock some sense into me: he was measuring me for a careful stroke. A careful stroke could have divided my heart in two.

" 'A perfect axe cut,' you said last night. 'A perfect axe cut.' "

She was making fun of me, of the way I had described how the doctor had inserted the plate in the original cut. It did occur to me in that instant how odd it was that I had always taken pride in that fact.

"You should be proud of that scar," Lureen said.

At last Lureen was showing signs of winding down. "I gotta go home. I haven't gotten any sleep since I met you Monday night."

My own sleep had been restless, too. In the motel in Sisters, I was visited by the dreams where I was stuck at the age of twenty, a relentless onslaught of them. I don't think I ever had as many in a single week.

Lureen walked me to the car and promised that when I returned on another trip she would take me to see the sights around Redmond. An intimate of this soil, she'd grown up on the edge of Smith Rock. She promised she'd show me the secret places, the caves, the trails only natives knew, and I said I'd take her up on that.

She closed my car door and leaned into the window. "I said to Billy last night, 'She really got to you, didn't she?' And he said to me, 'You gave her a hug?' I told him, 'Yeah.' And he said, 'I wish I'd given her a hug.'"

THERE WAS A buzzing pressure in my head. I sped out into the desert on a two-lane blacktop en route to Mitchell. Mitchell to the east, nestled in the Ochoco Mountains, was the next station on our journey across America seventeen years ago, the town where Shayna and I planned to meet up with Mark and Kathy after our one night alone in Cline Falls. Now I wanted to go where I would have gone had destiny not intervened. Something about driving to Mitchell felt at once illicit and liberating. To continue on to Mitchell felt like flaunting fate.

Lureen had emboldened me and scared me at the same time.

"*I can ride my bicycle wherever I want . . .*" Her shrill words sounded deep in my ears. I marveled that a stranger had had the intuitive genius to pull out threads of inchoate yearnings not even my conscious self could articulate. "*Why are you here? What are you looking for?*" Who would have thought to ask me that?

Behind me, the sun dropped westward over the violet-hued volcanoes. After Prineville, the atmosphere turned Wild West. The volcanoes were no longer in sight behind me. Llama ranches and show horse farms no longer lined the road. Only cattle grazed in patches of pasture carved out of the desert. In the gathering darkness, lights blinked in spots, dwarfed by the black shadows covering the hills.

I imagined two girls on bicycles. I imagined a journey that never happened—the two of us in a thirsty land day after day, feeling increasingly alone as the tension grew between us, until the open places ceased to give solace, until the expanse became a giant, claustrophobic dungeon of space. I could picture us pedaling into one town after another, drawn to the warm lights in the windows of houses that weren't ours, not our families', not our friends'.

Pre-Axe and Post-Axe

On June 22 the sun was at its zenith for the year 1977. At eight o'clock in the evening, light still drenched the juniper and sage surrounding the tiny town of Redmond. A young woman and young man in bike shorts and T-shirts sat at a table in front of a picture window in a Mexican restaurant on the edge of town. Though they were ravenous from the day's ride, they absently ate their beans and burritos, and kept an eye on the lonesome two-lane blacktop that slashed through the desert.

"We just kept looking down the road—this is all very clear—looking down the road thinking, maybe they'll come on in," Kathy Rentenbach told me eighteen years later. "And the road is nothing. It's just a ribbon. It's so clear because all you've got is desert and this one paved road. We kept saying, 'If they come by, we'll see them. Where are they? Where are they?'

"And you didn't come and you didn't come."

Finding fellow bikers Kathy and Mark Rentenbach was an obligatory part of my excavation of the larger story of the events of the summer of 1977. I'd lost touch with them long ago—in 1978, after I visited them in their home in Charlottesville, Virginia, one year after the bike trip. I remembered that Mark was from Grosse Pointe, Michigan, and had studied law at Michigan State, where he met Kathy.

Earlier in 1994, I called the Michigan Bar Association from my home in Los Angeles. Someone told me that the only Mark Rentenbach they had listed was deceased. In all likelihood, the vigorous Mark Rentenbach, marathon runner, would still be running marathons and biking mountain passes. This couldn't be the same guy. I searched the phone records for Rentenbachs in Grosse Pointe and wrote to a woman I guessed was Mark's mother.

Elizabeth Rentenbach wrote back quickly to say that she was sorry, but the information I had received about Mark was true. He had died in October 1983, from a choking accident. Mark and Kathy had divorced, and Mark was living alone. He choked to death while eating a meal. No one was there to rescue him.

Mark's mother was still in touch with her former daughter-in-law, who was living in Portland, Oregon, working as a nurse. She gave me the latest address she had for her.

Kathy in Oregon? Kathy was a Midwesterner who had moved to Virginia from Ann Arbor, Michigan, with Mark. At the time I knew her in the seventies, she had no connection to Oregon or the West other than that bike trip. Why would she be living in Portland now? It seemed a stretch, but I wondered if it was even remotely possible that Kathy might have been drawn back to that turf because it held an emotional charge for her. Then I dismissed that notion as absurd.

I let some time pass before I wrote to Kathy. I was waiting for just the right moment when I would be ready for what I considered a sacred occasion: a reunion with this woman whom I had met as a stranger and who had left me one week later as an intimate. In my letter to her, I described myself and my connection to her—just in case she'd forgotten. *I know it's probably weird and wild to hear from me out of the blue, but some events in life are so compelling, they bring people back together after 18 years . . .*

Three days later I arrived home to a message on my machine.

"Terri Jentz." She stated my name like a declaration. Her voice was sad. There was a long pause. "Hi, this is Kathy Rentenbach. And I have your letter in front of me. I just received it today. And of course I remember who you are. How could I forget?" she asked flatly, no rise at the end of her question. "I've told the hatchet story many times and I actually went back to the Deschutes state park for the very first time just three years ago and it, ahh, still sent chills through me, and I remember a lot about that summer. So certainly I would, of course, love to see you."

She said that she was still in touch with Mark's mother, at Christmastime. Although she and Mark divorced shortly after that bike trip, they stayed in close contact until his death in 1983. "So, yes. It is sad, and it was sad, and it still is," she said with a rueful laugh. "So, I would be very interested in talking to you. It would be a delight." Another pause. "And also quite sad."

She gave me her unlisted phone number and concluded abruptly, "See you later, bye." I popped the tape out of my answering machine and stored it away with important things. I wrote her back of my plans to be in Portland. I didn't want a phone conversation to defuse a face-to-face reunion.

KATHY AND I met at an Italian restaurant near her apartment in the fashionable northeast quadrant of the city, an area of renovated industrial buildings. She was already seated at a table covered by a red-and-white-checked tablecloth when I arrived, and when her eyes met mine, she looked quite sad. Now she wasn't the loose-limbed woman I remembered, with pigtails hanging from under a fishing hat and a delightfully silly sense of humor: She sat with a stiff, erect posture, accentuated by her very straight light brown hair, as though bracing herself for a burden. She was as lean and fit as she had been at twenty-seven, as though she'd cycled over a mountain only yesterday. Only the tiniest lines on her face hinted at the eighteen intervening years.

"You know I've told this story so many times and every time I tell it, I feel like I'm just so distraught, and I'm getting that way again. In fact I got your message yesterday and I hesitated to call you back—though I wanted to talk to you," Kathy said. I noticed she was wearing a sweatshirt that read CYCLE OREGON.

We spoke first of the one who was no longer with us. One year after the Bike-Centennial trip, after yet another summer bike tour, this time in Nova Scotia, Kathy packed her bags and headed back to Ann Arbor. I had visited them in Charlottesville only a month before. I had no idea their marriage was about to dissolve.

"But we were bonded. I never lost him." Now, in Portland, no one in her circle knew of the life she had led those many years ago with Mark. By reappearing in her life, I had revived the emotions of two ancient traumas. She hadn't let go of the memory of either.

"Actually that '77 trip I always counted as one of the most intense experiences of my life. The total bike trip. The axe thing. The pre-axe. The post-axe. Pre-Redmond and post-Redmond. It was one of the most incredible experiences I have ever had. And Mark and I were the best friends in the world then. But trying to get along as a couple—it was very hard. But we went through that whole summer just helping each other, very supportive of each other, more than we had ever been, especially after you guys had that big axe thing go on." Kathy's down-to-earth way of talking, and her gap-toothed smile, brought back memories of the merriment in our campsite, how she lifted the rest of us to gaiety.

"In the earlier years, I'd begin to shake when I told people the story. About how the police found us on the road, and how I collapsed by my bicycle. I get shivers every time I hear the word *Deschutes*."

In an odd synchronicity, she felt compelled, like I did, to make a pilgrimage to Cline Falls State Park in the very same year, 1992, to take a look at the site. She had never actually been to Cline Falls. She and Mark had only passed by it on the road.

I asked her to tell me her story of the "axe thing"—pre and post—and I would tell her mine. She remembered how just after our meeting on the bus, we'd stayed together in an old hotel in Astoria, on the coast, in adjoining rooms connected by a bathroom.

"You guys took off in the morning—like 'Nice to meet you. Bye!' And I thought, oh, where did they go? Aw, I'm never going to see them again! This was a good match, you know."

But they found us on the side of the road the very next day, waving excitedly at them. "I thought, ah-ha, they missed us. Now they know what it's like to bike alone. So I was very happy—we both were very happy—to team up with you. So we camped out in the rain, rode in rain, woke up in rain, then I remember thinking, I'm doing my first mountain pass. I remember thinking how hard it was to get that heavy bike over McKenzie Pass, then the lava beds on top. It was cold, the snow had just left, then coming off the mountain. Coming off the mountain was D day."

Then we went to the heart of my fateful decision: why Shayna and I had let the couple go on alone at Sisters.

"I remember when we left Sisters," Kathy said, "you were going to look at something, you were dawdling. And Mark was saying to me, 'Let's go, let's go. We need to go twenty miles more.' "

The dawdling was intentional. That was what we had agreed to do. That was the agreement I forced Shayna to live up to.

"We thought you might want to make love, and we didn't want to be hanging around!" I told Kathy.

"Oh, come on! It's not like we wanted to be screaming in the tent. It was the last thing on our minds!"

Kathy related how she and Mark left ahead of us, and when they reached Cline Falls, they asked someone how safe it was to camp overnight there. A park employee told them there was no overnight camping. In any event, the place was infested with rattlesnakes. They moved on.

"We got to Redmond and there was a Mexican restaurant. We waited at La Esperanza for you to show up because we had found there was no overnight camping in Cline Falls."

Could that restaurant really have been called La Esperanza? Hope. Expectancy. Hope, I thought, now in retrospect, that events might have a different outcome.

"The irony of that whole night was that we waited for you and watched for you. And you never came. *Why* did we sit there and watch for you guys?"

"But I didn't think we could find you," I said, reaching for the simplest rationalization for the road not taken.

"It wasn't such a big place," she said. "All you would have had to do was yell, and we would have heard you. We were camping! It wasn't like we were hiding behind buildings!

"We had found the fairgrounds and set up camp on this lush green grass with a water spigot. We were in heaven. We never had a water spigot. Life is perfect. We've eaten. It's beautiful. Sunny. We're out of the rain. And we'll overlap with you guys up in the morning. Somehow. We were sure. Then in the morning, we got out about seven-thirty, and as we leave Redmond, I see the little hospital there, which is where you guys were taken—because even then I was thinking of becoming a nurse, and Mark was saying, 'We don't have time to put you through nursing school because we have to put me through law school!' And as we went by the hospital, we commented, 'Look at this little hospital, look how tiny it is.

Who would ever think that could be a hospital?' Then we're on the road to Prineville, it's a beautiful sunny day, and an unmarked car pulls us over. It's a detective—he's unshaven and looks like he's been up all night. He says, 'Do you know Shayna Weiss and Terri Jentz?' I was bubbling, totally clueless. 'Why? Do they have a message for us?' Mark didn't say anything. Next, all I can remember is: 'Well, they were assaulted last night where they camped.' They knew our names. They got that from Shayna's journal. Oh my God, this still sends chills through me."

The recall caught Kathy short of breath. "My first thought was that you guys had been raped. To me at that point in time, *assault* meant rape. I think I was standing up over my bike, holding the handlebars, and leaning against my handlebar pad, and he goes, 'Well, they were assaulted by a man with a hatchet.' Oh my God, were you still alive? Assaulted with a hatchet? How can you live through that? 'Yeah, they're still alive.' And I started to cry. I put my head down on my front pack and I was just sobbing. Mark was blank, which was his form of hysteria. Then a police car pulled up and they said, 'Let's give her a place to sit down before she falls over.' And I remember putting my bike in the ditch on the side of the road and getting in the back of the car and just sobbing and sobbing and sobbing. And we're both asking questions, and I'm saying, 'Well, how bad is it?' They must not have told us much because my next question was 'Will they be able to bike?' Because I couldn't imagine you guys stopping the trip. We were just getting going—it's only day seven! I'm sure we were questioned by the detective. Where were we? Where did we stay? We had no idea we were suspects. Then the police put Mark's bike in the back and lashed mine to the front—and it wasn't until we got into Bend that we knew how bad it was.

"Then I remember walking back to an ICU and I remember it being very empty and very white—I wasn't a nurse yet then. I remember you, your black eyes, your shaved head, and the various suturing. And I remember having to sit down because I was going to faint. Then we started asking you questions. 'What happened?' And the nurse cut us off and said, 'She doesn't want to go through that again.'"

"And I probably wanted to tell you," I said.

"I don't think we spent much time with you. When we saw Shayna she was in the hospital room with her father. We were told she couldn't see us. She was wearing her turban and looked like a bunny rabbit. 'I'm fine,' she told us. Her father said, 'You're not fine, you're blind. Somebody tried to kill you.' We're thinking, this is odd. Is this just the way she is? 'You're not fine,' he kept saying. 'Quit saying that.'"

Kathy told me she and Mark stayed in a basement room in a hostel in Bend for five days, until one afternoon my father drove them back to the trail in Prineville, and they continued on. I tried to imagine how they must have felt in the pit of their stomachs as they left us behind in our hospital beds and pedaled off alone in the desert, toward what was their destiny to fulfill—those ninety-mile days riding across the sagebrush uplands in a heat wave, with burning backs and parched lips, through dust storms and hailstorms, across roads empty but for the reeking carcasses of decomposing antelope—and toward their own unknown destiny: their divorce and Mark's early death.

"Every hostel along the road clear across the BikeCentennial Trail, people would say, 'Beware of the Hatchet Man.' We never slept alone again."

I recounted to Kathy what I knew about Shayna—that we had exchanged letters recently and that Shayna had told me that Mark came to Boston to run the marathon in the early eighties, and when they met after the race, he wouldn't let her ride the subway alone that night. "I let something bad happen to you once and I won't again," he had said as he hobbled onto the train with sore feet and escorted her home.

Could Mark have felt he was somehow responsible for not protecting us from what happened that night?

"I can tell you about that—even though he liked you guys a lot, and especially felt close to Shayna. As we left you guys at Sisters, he said, 'I'm getting tired of herding women around. Let's go. We have to move faster.' And that was the way Mark was. There were a certain number of miles he wanted to do a day. So even though he said that, we still waited for you guys to come in. Even in the morning, when we left, we were saying, 'Now where are they?' "

Because of a badly timed honest remark, Mark, too, like me, had carried a burden of guilt that in truth belonged exclusively to the disappeared hatchet man.

And speaking of the disappeared hatchet man: I confided to Kathy that I was hot on his trail. I talked feverishly about the new leads I had uncovered. Lureen's warnings about watching my back had sent me into an exhilarated state of physical alertness. Kathy regarded me curiously, as though she couldn't wrap her mind around my reappearance in her life, let alone my outlandish and (to outward appearances) fearless zeal to hunt down my own would-be killer.

I showed her the artifact I'd been carrying around with me for two years—the original police crime report—though it was now useless, as my investigation had expanded way beyond its pages.

"Holy shit! My name and birth date!" she said. It's chilling to find one's name in the record of an ancient murder investigation. She made deep exhalations as she paged through the police version of our shared tale.

"Why *did* you come back to Oregon?" I finally asked her.

"The ocean. McKenzie Pass. Because of Bend and because of Redmond and because of you guys. My connection to Oregon was that bike trip."

So the improbable was actually true. She did share my hypermemory, which had drawn her into an emotional intimacy with that strange land of Oregon.

There she had experienced the highest and deepest extremes of emotion—rapture and grief. I wish there were a word in English to describe the experience. The Russian *umilenie* would have to do.

She told me she'd been biking Oregon ever since she moved here—taking long trips through the green valleys, across the Cascades, into the brown lands. She'd even traversed the same stretch of the BikeCentennial Trail—from Prineville to John Day—that she and Mark cycled after they left us at the hospital in Bend.

"Why *did* you stay in Cline Falls?" she asked me again, compelled to return to the pivotal question of fate. *"What could have enticed you to stay there?"* Kathy pleaded, incredulous still that the depressing hollow called Cline Falls State Park—that rattlesnake pit she and Mark had passed on the road to Redmond—could ever have lured us in. As they waited for us in the Mexican restaurant, they never guessed that we might haved stayed there. They knew that surely, at any minute, two dots would appear on the horizon, and in the undulating mirage at the end of the empty blacktop they would discern the outline of two girls on bicycles.

It moved me to think that on the night of June 22, 1977, safety was just up the road, if only I had not stubbornly fixated on my agenda. If only I had been capable of taking flight for that moment, as we stood at the top of the road staring into that parched underworld. If only I had been able to step back from myself and let my thoughts fly to Redmond, to imagine Kathy and Mark in the lush green grass with a water spigot. Maybe Shayna had taken that intuitive leap, and I had shut her down.

When I left Kathy, I was exhausted. We made promises to stay in touch and to exchange the mementos we had both hoarded for eighteen years, pieces of each other's lives that each of us was missing: She had a trip diary and photos of me I didn't have. I had detailed accounts of her trip—which she'd written to me along the road and sent to the hospital, and even to Moscow—which I had saved, improbably, through nine changes of residence in four cities.

When Kathy later mailed me her diary from the '77 bike trip, she wrote to warn me that I would find a line in one of the entries, on a day we were struggling up the mountain, indicating that they wanted to leave Shayna and me behind. "But that wasn't really true," Kathy wrote. "That's not how we felt at all."

I studied the diary. The writing was in Kathy's hand, but these were not her private thoughts. She told me it was her job to make the official record of the day for both herself and Mark. Sure enough, there was the line: *We want to leave the 2 girls we're with but don't know how to go about it politely.* Here was vindication that I hadn't made it up: though it was true I was shut down to any idea that Shayna and I should continue on and join them that particular night of June 22, my unwillingness had been based on something real. This investigation was yielding revelation: the part of me that felt culpable for our fate felt less so.

Kathy also sent along two photos of our foursome. The photos amazed me.

They were the only images I had ever seen of myself on that trip. After excavating, channeling, bringing up in trance the flow of thought and emotion that formed my consciousness at that time, it was strange indeed to have images of my twenty-year-old self. It was a startling face-to-face encounter: the biographer suddenly getting the chance to meet the long-dead subject.

A chubby, disheveled girl in aviator glasses, I'm wearing my father's International Harvester RED POWER windbreaker. One leg of my bike shorts is riding higher on my leg than the other. I'm half glowering. I didn't recognize myself in this picture. At thirty-eight, I no longer looked like her at all. Was there anything besides memory connecting us?

In the photo, Kathy, Mark, and Shayna, like me, have struck Napoleonic stances, with right arms held stiffly in front of their waists, hands tucked into their jackets. We're ready to head off into undiscovered country. They're all grinning broadly. I am frowning.

Like three girls in the same family, Kathy, Shayna, and I all wear the same scarves around our heads—patterned Western bandannas. Shayna's is red. Kathy's is turquoise. Mine is blue.

THE ACCIDENT of a bus ride. Ever since Kathy and Mark, I have considered the possibility of significance in any encounter with a stranger who crosses my path. After all, being a stranger is but a temporary condition.

Kathy finished her letter with a refrain of what she'd told me on the day we reconnected: "I will always remember waiting and watching on the edge of town that evening—expecting the two of you to come into town, and wondering the next morning why you didn't catch up with us."

Part Three

We take down into our depths whatever one casts into us—for we are deep; we do not forget.

—NIETZSCHE, *THE GAY SCIENCE*

Allies

My growing focus on a seventeen-year-old local Redmond boy had siphoned off some of my interest in Bud Godwin. I was having serious doubts that Godwin was *my* particular psychopath. But he was somebody else's, for sure—and regardless of his connection to my personal fate, I was committed to the crusade of keeping the public safe from him.

Actually, Godwin did have an effect on my fate. It was because of him that I met the people who would become central to my quest. It was a lovely irony that one so malevolent should bring me together with Bob and Dee Dee Kouns, as an unusually intense preoccupation with evil was something we three had in common. I believe you meet people who are vital to your transformation only when the conditions are right, when the tenacious concerns of the unconscious break through into awareness. Then such kindred spirits are drawn to each other like iron shavings to a magnet.

Earlier in the summer of 1994, when I was organizing people who might band together in outrage to keep Godwin in prison, an Oregon judge and an Oregon newspaper reporter both urged me to get in touch with a nervy husband-and-wife team of victims' advocates whose grassroots efforts had turned the Oregon criminal justice system—historically soft on criminals since the early seventies—into a safer haven for victims. In August, from Los Angeles, I decided to ring the Kounses in Portland. I found myself talking to Dee Dee, whose voice was most unusual—both husky and high-pitched at once. She told me that her only daughter, Valerie, had been murdered in 1980, and in the thirteen years since, she and her husband, Bob, had volunteered on behalf of people who had fallen prey to violent crime: they devoted all their time and their own money, getting by on a shoestring, while offering people a steady stream of advice and solace—"and unfortunately," Dee Dee said, "there's no shortage of victims."

I told Dee Dee about my singular interest in Godwin. We discussed the complex reasons for my search for my attacker, and how "justice" could never be my goal because the statute of limitations on attempted murder was only three years in the state of Oregon. We agreed that the fact that a crime in which two girls were run over by a truck and attacked with an axe could go unpunished indeed defied all rationality.

"We kind of reward you because you're not very good at what you do. The only difference between attempted murder and murder is that somebody was inadequate in what they tried to do. Their intent was the same. That person is as great a danger to society as the person who completed the murder. Maybe they're a bad shot. Why would you reward them?" Dee Dee said, serving up her insights with a wry twist that immediately drew me to her. Of course, Dee Dee pointed out, this outcome did have one silver lining. If the Cline Falls case had come to trial between 1977 and 1980, most assuredly, Shayna and I would have been depicted as the cause of the whole mess. We would have been discredited and slandered. In the way of our adversarial justice system, particularly at that time, the defense would surely have made us out to be rouged harlots in skimpy shorts on bicycles, soliciting in campgrounds, luring the likes of a handsome young cowboy into our pup tent brothel.

WHEN THEY started their group in early 1983, named forthrightly Crime Victims United, Dee Dee and Bob Kouns were pioneers. Today there are thousands of victims' advocacy groups in the country. The emergence of the victims' movement had its genesis in the women's movement of the early seventies, when impassioned, mostly twentysomething women protested violence against women and changed laws for rape, child abuse, and battery. The victims' movement soon sprang to life and gained momentum in the late seventies as random violence paralyzed the country.

It was an era when the criminal justice system was overwhelmingly focused on the rights and rehabilitation of the accused. "The crime is against the state. Butt out. Victims were just another piece of evidence. Difficult to deal with. A pain in the ass," as Dee Dee described the attitude of the time. Cutting-edge theory on criminal justice prescribed making arrests and convictions more difficult in order to safeguard defendants' rights. This was the accepted liberal thinking, ever since a series of important Warren court decisions in the 1960s. Defense attorneys had a field day in court, especially in an era when misguided sixties and seventies "sensitivity" devolved into breathtakingly naïve tolerance for outrageous criminal behavior.

Several high-profile cases showcased the ethos of the time: when Richard Herrin murdered my classmate Bonnie Garland in 1977, a supposedly moral community threw up a protective shield around the unrepentant killer, while the victim was relegated to the background. When Peace Corps volunteer Deborah Gardner was killed by a fellow volunteer in Tonga in 1976, Dennis Priven was convicted of murder by a Tongan court. The Peace Corps and members of the State Department arranged to bring him home, and immediately released him. The Tongans were appalled at the lack of compassion Americans felt for their dead girl.

The justice system rubbed salt in the wounds of victims, intensifying feelings of humiliation and loss of control that paralyze those who have been traumatized by crime. When the Kounses made the highly unusual decision to investigate their daughter's murder in California in 1980, they learned the hard way that crime victims desperately needed *rights*. They returned to Oregon to find violent crime raging out of control, and got involved in a string of gut-wrenching cases that highlighted the need to sign into law the most basic rights for victims. Early on, they lent their support to one young woman who was not allowed to be present at the trial of the men who had stabbed her husband to death because they wanted to break in a new hunting knife with "nigger blood." The defense used the dubious justification that they were going to recall the victim's loved one as a witness, when actually they feared that the sight of a grieving beloved would create undue sympathy in the courtroom.

I asked Dee Dee if she thought the current Oregon parole board would decide to free Godwin after his upcoming parole hearing.

"Not if we raise hell. But he will get out down the road a ways," she said.

"Every two years we've got to keep raising hell?" I asked.

"Yep. And they may release him anyway. Like Obremski. I've talked to that guy. This is a dangerous, god-awful monster, and they let him out." The Kounses backed a movement to keep Obremski and other deadly perpetrators out of circulation. "I am sick to death of having to put out the energy to keep people like that in prison; my patience has long ago run out." Among their efforts, she and Bob once found concrete proof that Oregon's parole board in the 1980s changed three aggravated murders down to murder. These so-called errors could have allowed extremely dangerous offenders to be released early. Dee Dee and Bob exposed the situation to the secretary of state, and an audit resulted in allowing victims to sit in on a newly formed committee that would now give advice on parole board policy.

Dee Dee told me that the justice system still used the excuse that there weren't enough prison beds in the state. From the late seventies through the eighties, the state stuck to an anti-incarceration policy even in the face of dramatically rising crime. Many in the Oregon criminal justice system fastened onto an underlying philosophy. In the ancient and ongoing quarrel over determinism versus free will, people in key positions settled on the far-left pole: society's shortcomings are the root cause of an individual's criminality, and so the criminal shouldn't be locked up for great lengths of time because incarceration with other criminals only makes his problems worse. Rather, if he were outside the penal system, society would have an opportunity to cure him.

After the blistering three-year ordeal of investigating their daughter's murder, Dee Dee and Bob sought to find out for themselves what made criminals tick. They didn't want to buy into received formulas on criminality, so they plunged into dark waters on their own. For over four years they showed up at the pen in Salem to mingle with criminals attending the Lifer's Club, an educational meeting of convicted murderers. And they spent time with young offenders who had committed serious crimes at MacLaren Youth Correctional Facility.

When they started their journey, these liberal-leaning Americans didn't believe in the existence of human evil. They were drenched in the thinking of the eighteenth-century Enlightenment: mankind is steadily progressing, and under the right conditions, humankind's original goodness will blossom automatically. All it takes is fixing the problems in the conditions of people's lives.

"Outside of the pain of Val's death, it was most painful to find out how wrong we were about criminality . . . thinking if people were aware of the right choices to make, they would make them," Dee Dee said. There's much we don't understand, she acknowledged, and there was no single cause for the complex and profound problem of crime, but rather an interweaving of elements that maybe no one was capable of listing. But she learned that one of the primary motivations driving a variety of crimes was the excitement, the high, the "rush" criminals get from executing their deeds. "I believe people do crime because they *like* to do it."

I sat up straight when I heard the voice over the phone raise a subject I'd already teased around in my mind for years. It's a difficult notion to face up to. But when I concentrate on the memory of that night in 1977, I know that the young cowboy *was* getting high off what he was doing; he was doing just what he wanted to do. His actions sprang from desire. These thoughts were on my mind as Dee Dee quoted one forensic psychologist who told her how one of his clients described the thrill of committing a rape-murder: "Imagine the best sexual experience you've ever had, Doc, *then multiply that by a billion.*"

And contrary to our cherished ideas about the root causes of crime—including the ready-made opinion that *all* criminals were abused as children—she and her husband learned that what most of the kids at MacLaren had in common was having grown up in settings where no boundaries were set. Some came from neglectful homes. But just as many came from indulgent homes.

"I know of case after case of people who were abused who didn't become abusers. If we truly thought as a society that abuse was the cause of criminal behavior, wouldn't it make sense to lock up every criminal and never let them see the light of day? To think that there were a hundred and forty-nine thousand personal victimizations in Oregon last year—if we truly believed these people were going to turn into offenders themselves as a result of being offended against, we are the stupidest people in the world not to stop the victimization."

Dee Dee insisted that society was trying to operate under two conflicting philosophies that could not coexist: We demand to be treated as individuals. And as individuals we have inherent rights that cannot be trampled by society, the state, the masses. A logical consequence of believing in the creed of the individual would be to make sure the individual took responsibility for his actions.

But that isn't how we operate. We also see ourselves as blank slates, written over by society, and mirroring its ills. Because we believe a person's problems are caused by society, individuals are not asked to assume responsibilities. Or as Dee Dee put it, "Society doesn't have any possible way of being responsible over these individuals who have all the rights over the rest of us."

IN THE FALL of 1994, I flew to Oregon for Godwin's parole hearing, only to learn that at the last minute the parole board had postponed until early 1995 what was shaping up to be a media event. I set out to meet Dee Dee anyway. It should have taken twenty minutes to drive to her house, but the journey turned into an hour and a half in the rain. I was off-kilter because my apprehensions about Oregon, even Portland, had planted an imaginary demon around every corner. When I finally pulled into the driveway of a large ranch home in southwest Portland, a woman in her sixties met me at the door. She had a full, strong face with high cheekbones, wore her white-blond hair with bangs and cut straight at the chin, and carried herself with a proud posture that brought my attention to the vivid colors she was wearing that day.

She settled me into a huge couch in a living room decorated in soothing earth tones, with carefully arranged native baskets and masks lining the walls. Dee Dee listened to my story with a meditative calm, scrutinizing me with up-slanted blue eyes behind tortoiseshell-rimmed glasses, slowing me down as I described what I saw of my attacker on the night of June 22, 1977. I was impressed by the extraordinary attention she was focusing on me, how seriously she was regarding every fine detail. She drew a crystalline recollection out of me and urged me to fix it in my mind, because just after this first meeting with her, I was heading to Central Oregon to carry out the investigation into my own near murder, and it was possible I could learn things that might taint my memory.

I imagined that surely this powerhouse would be hitched to a more subdued mate. But then the next day I met Bob, whose handshake was charged with energy and enthusiasm, imparting a great generosity of spirit. Tall and loose-limbed, curly-haired and boyish at sixty-four, Bob could probably command anyone's attention when he talked, as he had a booming voice and prominent facial features that changed expression dramatically as he moved from topic to topic—he was as likely to drill you with his exceptionally large eyes as let loose a distinct, raucous laugh.

I became an immediate audience to the couple's tale of their years of investigating the murder of their daughter, Valerie, which they poured forth in an unedited ramble. There was no end to the permutations of the stories—association leading to association. Dee Dee spoke in a slow, measured pace, sometimes laboring without pause to take a breath; Bob talked like a public speaker, with rises and falls conveying a great sense of drama. Each would interrupt the other, rescuing the other from inevitable digressions until, circuitously, all stories eventually converged and were clarified. I caught no signs of waffling, no contradictions in their accounts, no hypocrisy. Their unshakeable, nonnegotiable opinions had been forged in a crucible of atrocious hurt. They had tested their beliefs against the raw data of the world they were examining, and they validated those beliefs with intelligence, intuition, and heart.

Their combined energy—which at times overwhelmed me as much as it fascinated me—was a force that had propelled their search for what happened to Valerie. They hadn't told too many other people the detailed chronicle of their investigation into their daughter's murder. It was too convoluted, too complicated to fit into any smooth narrative, too dark for most audiences. But we three had struck fire. I wanted to hear whatever they cared to tell, and over time, I would become saturated with Valerie's fate.

I asked to see a picture of Valerie and detected a flash of pain cross Dee Dee's face. But she produced one for me. Strawberry blond hair. Up-slanted blue eyes. High cheekbones, a square jaw and pointed chin. Valerie bore a strong resemblance to her mother.

IN 1980, Valerie McDonald was a twenty-six-year-old aspiring filmmaker, a graduate of the San Francisco Art Institute, and lived alone in an apartment in the city's arty North Beach district. When the owner of her building hired two ex-convicts to manage the place, they started threatening tenants, and Valerie moved. On November 9, she and some friends were removing more of her belongings from her room when a man showed up who had managed the building earlier in the summer. Valerie had had a passing acquaintance with Michael Hennessey, a fit, well-dressed young man, who told her he was working on a Dino de Laurentiis film production shooting in town. Hennessey knew of Val's passion for movies, and that she'd taken bit parts before. This production starred Dustin Hoffman as a detective tracking a serial killer who was stalking beautiful blondes up the Pacific Coast. Val would be perfect to play one of the beautiful blondes, the one that got away. Her walk-on would take place that night in a warehouse location nearby. Val and her friends were leery of the story, but when Hennessey "phoned the set" several times, making the offer sound more authentic, Val left with him.

When Valerie didn't return, her best friend spent a week pleading with police to take action, and frantically trying to reach Valerie's parents in Oregon, who were out of town. Finally she was able to make contact with them, and Bob and Dee Dee immediately flew to San Francisco. On November 16, they met with the Missing Persons officer, who callously dismissed their concerns that Val had been a victim of foul play. Outraged by his response, the couple hired a pair of private investigators to learn about the management of Valerie's former apartment building. They turned up: Phillip Thompson, thirty-six years old, had a violent criminal history stretching back to 1965; John Abbott, twenty-six, was Thompson's longtime crime partner, and had been his San Quentin cellmate on two separate occasions; and Michael Hennessey, twenty-three, had a minor record for burglary.

As the Kounses learned from their P.I.s what the first steps were in investigating a crime, the mystery deepened. They began to track the ringleader, Phillip Thompson, who had a perverse criminal mind for inventing schemes and disguises, and who took delight in surrounding his shocking activities in clouds of mystification to throw off whoever might be on his trail.

Even though they believed Valerie was already dead, whenever Bob and Dee Dee saw a head of long strawberry blond hair somewhere on the streets of San Francisco, they'd drive around the block in the hope that their gut instincts were wrong—only to have the head turn, revealing a profile they didn't recognize.

On November 22, twelve days after Valerie disappeared, Abbott and Hennessey came to the attention of the Royal Canadian Mounties in the town of Trail, British Columbia, who were keeping an eye on the two men because Abbott was wanted in California. When they confronted the pair at a car repair shop on November 26, a wild melee ensued. A frenzied Abbott told Hennessey to shoot one of the Mounties, and the Mounties gunned down and killed Hennessey. Abbott was arrested.

Pieces of Valerie's identification and her black leather jacket were found among Abbott's and Hennessey's belongings. Strands of 21- and 22-inch-long strawberry blond hair were found by a Canadian crime lab in the trunk of the green Monte Carlo the men had brought to the shop for repairs.

In the last days of 1980, Bob and Dee Dee drove to Trail, British Columbia, to investigate every movement of Abbott and Hennessey from the day they arrived in Canada to the shootout on November 26.

In January 1981, presumably under pressure from the Kounses, their private investigators, and the news media, San Francisco police put Phillip Thompson under surveillance. They staked out a warehouse south of Candlestick Park, which turned out to be Thompson's and Abbott's operational headquarters. Criminals with affluent backgrounds, the two men were well educated and used their exceptional intellects to plot crimes as elaborate as their twisted imaginations could conjure—including, as Thompson claimed, trading guns to groups in Central America for drugs. When police searched the warehouse, they found it loaded with stolen property and maps pinpointing targets throughout the Bay Area. It was becoming apparent that Michael Hennessey, the one who lured Val to the warehouse, had been Thompson and Abbott's flunky.

Police took Bob and Dee Dee to the brick warehouse to look, in vain, for anything that might belong to Valerie. The natural setting had once been stunning: a sandbar washed with the ethereal light of the San Francisco Bay. Now it was a malevolent spot, a place filled with trash. In a dark, windowless upstairs room they found a mattress on the floor. Drilled into the ceiling above the mattress: a massive eyehook. "For chains," Dee Dee told me, then appeared to get disoriented. "I get confused when discussing this—even now. My mind goes off in a million directions."

Although long strawberry blond hair was found in the trunk of the green Monte Carlo Abbott and Hennessey had used in Canada—and receipts for a number three washtub, a hoe, and several bags of quick-dry cement were found in Abbott's pocket when he was arrested—the San Francisco Police Department paid scant attention to the physical evidence sent down from Canada. The Kounses put massive pressure on the police until they transferred Valerie's case out of Missing Persons and assigned it to Homicide. After a while, every time they contacted the San Francisco police, the Kounses were told police needed just one more piece of evidence. The couple soon believed that the police department willingly bungled the case because Thompson was valuable in some way, or because he had information no one wanted to come to light.

Shut out by law enforcement, Dee Dee and Bob pursued the case alone for more than two years—into the murky web of the criminal underground that spun off from the ex-cons. They tracked down two separate criminals who told them they later saw a bag sitting close to where Valerie had been held on the mattress that contained a syringe, potassium cyanide, and a tincture of mercury. The Kounses found others who described hearing screams from the upstairs warehouse room during the days Val was held captive there. They pushed on, driven by what Dee Dee described as a "cold anger" that kept them from normal faintheartedness.

Ultimately—by interviewing witnesses, obtaining records, and working with various law enforcement investigators in California and Canada—the Kounses pieced together what they believed happened to Valerie: she was abducted and held for ten days and then murdered in the San Francisco warehouse, where her feet and legs were anchored in a cement-filled metal washtub. Phillip Thompson loaded her body in the trunk of a green Monte Carlo and drove north up the coast. Wire cutters later found in his car pointed to his having entered Canada through farm fences. Thompson arrived in Trail, British Columbia, on November 22, and then immediately flew out—leaving the green Monte Carlo with Abbott and Hennessey. Thompson took the trunk key and gas cap key with him, and left the car with a dead battery. Valerie's body was in the trunk. Abbott and Hennessey got the Monte Carlo to a garage, bought a new gas cap, recharged the battery, and then found a lock shop. When the locksmith tried to test the new key in the trunk lock, Abbott put his hand on the trunk, flashed the man a threatening look with his intense blue eyes, and wouldn't let him open it.

The car's transmission failed the very next day. It appeared that Thompson was trying to stick Abbott and Hennessey with the body, presumably to frame them for her murder.

John Abbott was a prolific, even literary, diarist. From a notebook left in his belongings, the Kounses gleaned that the two men dumped the washtub of concrete anchoring Valerie's body in a river, possibly the Canadian Columbia. They also learned why Abbott did what he did: "the rush of crime," he wrote, fulfilled for him some "atavistic urge." He brimmed with delight when he described his appetite for the uniqueness of criminal activity: "I like, like it, yes I do."

Bob and Dee Dee found others to help them keep the heat on the ringleader, Phillip Thompson, until he was finally convicted of two unrelated charges of kidnapping and robbery. To date, neither suspect, Thompson or Abbott, has ever been charged with Valerie McDonald's disappearance or murder.

AS BOB AND Dee Dee told me their story, I thought about Valerie's last days, tried to live into the moment when the benign turned sinister, the moment when the door of the warehouse closed behind her and she saw no film crew inside, the moment she realized that her well-dressed friend, who had chatted amiably about career aspirations, was actually her captor. That moment of the startling eruption, when the world as she knew it was over, all trust betrayed, all love and support inaccessible, as she was trapped in a warehouse for the remainder of her short life, in a dominion of depravity where, on that mattress and chained to the ceiling, she may even have wanted to die—while just down the street, sailboats rocked in the ethereal light of San Francisco Bay. I imagined the fate of her parents, who had known intuitively of their daughter's plight but had been impotent to do anything to save her. I had willfully undergone a personal study of the affects of atrocity on the soul, and I had found these others—Valerie, Dee Dee, and Bob—who granted me a new angle of vision.

I STUDIED the San Francisco newspapers from the winter of 1980 and 1981, the winter John Lennon was slain, the winter Ronald Reagan was sworn in as president. The preponderance of murder and mayhem in the articles all through the papers which ran the series on the disappearance of Valerie McDonald surprised even me, an omnivorous collector of clippings on crime.

I read about Christina, a girl of sixteen, a "happy girl" with lots of friends, who liked picnics and parties but who didn't return from one. She was found beaten, raped, and murdered in a place called Lucky Alley, in San Francisco. I read about the I-5 bandit, wanted for a two-day crime spree along the Oregon/California border, which included a double murder, several rapes, and hotel stickups. I read about a twenty-three-year-old German girl named Inez who turned up dead a couple of months after Valerie was reported missing. Valerie's name, coincidentally, was found on a scrap of paper in Inez's wallet. It seemed their murders were not related. They had merely met and exchanged numbers. Two young women artists trying to make a go of it in the city would both wind up dead within weeks of their brief meeting, where perhaps they shared aspirations.

This was 1980, the year that America's murder rate, as of this writing, was at its peak. It was the same year—in fact on the very same week of Valerie's murder—that my college classmate Sarai Ribicoff, niece of the Connecticut senator, was murdered farther south, in Venice, California. One of the clippings in the tattered, yellowing VIOLENCE file I'd been keeping since 1980 printed a photo of Sarai, at twenty-three, sprawled on a sidewalk under a body blanket after a mugging turned to murder. Her image had been used, greedily, to illustrate a story—not about Sarai and the heartache her death would leave, but about America's newest trend, predatory violent crime: "the rise in unprovoked, random violence—the menace of any shadow at the street corner, any rustling in the shrubbery along a hiking trail, any squeak in the floorboard of a home. And always, the threat of a murderous psychopath."

Criminals were murdering, raping, robbing with impunity, and yet Valerie was blamed by the media as one who drew this dark fate to herself. More than one *San Francisco Examiner* reporter who followed the disappearance of Valerie McDonald knew well how to typecast her: evidently the beautiful blonde seeking a movie part triggered a play of associative pathways in their brains that had her wearing "stiletto-heeled boots and provocative dresses." In truth, Val dressed like other stylish young, educated San Francisco or New York women. That she was a beautiful young woman who thought she was getting a bit part in a movie was enough, in their view, to make a mockery of her by relegating her to the bimbo category. Many of the *San Francisco Chronicle* and *Examiner* stories were a case study in the intense biases the supposedly objective news reporter can harbor against female victims of crime.

"They tried to make Valerie the sick one," Dee Dee explained. "It's a societal sickness. A creeping, oozing mental sickness to excuse bad behavior and transfer the evil to an innocent. That's what society does. It happens with incredible regularity. In the Hillside Strangler case in Los Angeles, the media said the women were prostitutes. None were. One was twelve years old."

Dee Dee told me that over the years, when people would find out her daughter was murdered, they would ask her again and again, "What did she do?"—as if there were always some culpability on the part of the victim.

Dee Dee knotted her brows together, looked off to the side, then straight back at me. She told me she always responded with the same simple reply: "She died."

A Turn of the Screw

The tension in my body drained into the sofa of my new friends' large living room in Portland. It was October 1992, two weeks after I first met Bob and Dee Dee. I had just returned from my second investigative expedition to Central Oregon, and hadn't realized until I was on the ocean side of the mountains, away from that desert turf charged with memories, how edgy I'd felt there (particularly after being warned to *watch my back*). In Portland, where presumably nobody's eyes were on me, I confidently launched into a lengthy account of my investigation and the tantalizing clues it had unearthed. Bob interrupted before I was out of the gate: "The first thing you gotta do is learn how to say 'Oregon' properly. It's 'OR-Y-GUN.'" Could this still be happening? I wondered.

"Bob, let her talk!"

I did, and it struck me how serendipitous it was that I'd encountered two strangers with the largesse to assimilate the evolving back story of my personal drama as though it were their own.

I regaled them with the stories Bill's new girlfriend, Lureen, had told me: how a seventeen-year-old local bully tried to drown his girlfriend in front of a whole group of teens right after the Cline Falls attack. I recounted how Lureen described this ill-tempered boy with the piercing eyes as a cowboy who always dressed in fine duds. Immediately, Bob and Dee Dee were suspicious of Lureen's conspirational tone. It threw her reliability into doubt, as it seemed she was trying to make herself a more important source than she actually was. I told them I wasn't jumping to the conclusion that the intriguing tales told by this colorful woman were actually true—but no one by a long shot had ever described Richard Wayne Godwin as a dapper cowboy. That the cowboy who attacked me was meticulous was my unassailable memory.

"And I thought Godwin wasn't very big," Dee Dee said.

"He was five six."

"You said the person you saw back then was five ten." Dee Dee had retained every detail of my story.

I acknowledged that when a person is standing over you with a hatchet, it's hard to figure between five six and five ten.

"It's amazing you had any idea at all."

But now a suspect had surfaced who was described as standing between five foot ten and six feet back in those days. "I remember vividly the shirt tucked in— this was the detail that made me suspect that Godwin didn't fit my memory of my attacker. His wife described him as slovenly. The guy I saw was anything but slovenly."

"That convinces me more than anything I've heard," Dee Dee said.

"Yeah," Bob agreed.

Dee Dee believed I must surely have seen his face—but that trauma had obliterated my memory. How else would I have thought him attractive? How else would I have placed him in his twenties instead of his thirties? She believed that one day an odd remark or sight or event might be an unexpected trigger, and I would be visited with a full-blown flashback: face, head, the axeman.

I argued with her on this point. I was adamant that trauma hadn't obliterated a memory of his face. I felt certain that my vigilant consciousness of that night would not have recoiled from a fearsome sight. I had willfully taken him on. When I finally opened my eyes, I opened them to *see*. And if I couldn't see, I argued, it was because my eyesight was poor, or because his face was shadowed by a hat, or because his head was backlit and his face was thrown into darkness.

I would later revise this insistent belief that I'd never be capable of remembering more details of that night. The ur-memory of the attack—the young man standing over me, poised symmetrically with the axe—might have been an example of what psychologists call weapon focus, when the victim disregards details of the attacker's face because he is peripheral to what is causing the immediate threat. But that day, talking to Dee Dee and Bob, I needed to stick up for the authenticity of what I was certain of remembering.

The Kounses cautioned me not to be too quick to believe rumors circulating in Redmond that a kid who beat up his girlfriend might have perpetrated an attack such as the one I'd endured. "There are a lot of guys who slap girlfriends around. But they don't go run over someone and chop them up with an axe. I can't believe he would do just one attack like that. He's somebody who enjoys inflicting pain on others." The way they saw it, whoever committed the Cline Falls attack "is either dead, in prison, or he's still doing crime."

Bob added, "One of the biggest mysteries of this case is, why did he leave you alive? The guy that killed Valerie would have laughed."

By the way, I wondered, did they think there was any basis in Lureen's warning to "Watch my back" while snooping around Central Oregon?

"People like to be dramatic. When we were investigating Valerie's murder, people were always thinking we were in great danger. Because we heard so much of that kind of stuff, I got to the point where I could kick a lion and nothing would happen," Dee Dee advised. But I weighed her words against the other times I'd heard her say of the two of them, "It's a wonder we didn't get killed!"

I was drawing courage from the outlandishly bold moves they had taken in their investigation. Bob told a story about how, before they figured out how Valerie's body was disposed of, they got a tip that her body was to be smuggled out of the warehouse one night in a crushed car and sent to Japan as scrap metal. One cold summer night they dressed in old clothes and hats and sat up till dawn in a junkyard next to the warehouse, watching suspicious movements. A prostitute recognized that they weren't from the street and asked them, "How can I help you?"

"And not just to get money from us. She meant *'How can I help you?'* " Bob was frantically making phone calls on a pay phone and he ran out of money. The prostitute gave him a quarter. She told the street people that the Kounses' daughter had been murdered, and soon others came up to them and offered to help.

Then we segued seamlessly back to my case.

"I don't see how you could be in any danger. He can't be prosecuted because of the statute of limitations," Dee Dee told me.

"That's what I told Lureen, and she said, 'They don't know that!' So I plan to keep a low profile around town when I go back. Everyone will be talking."

"Especially on something like that. Everyone in town would know you're there, and who you talked to, what you said, how you looked, what they said, and how they looked," Bob put in. "You're used to a big town, where you have anonymity. One of the good and bad parts of little towns is everyone knows everyone's business."

One more thing: I told them I had looked up the Duran name in the phone book and had driven out to the address. Our new suspect's parents lived on a ranch outside of Redmond, and though the house wasn't visible from the road, a FOR SALE sign stood out front. Perhaps on my next trip to Central Oregon I'd find an excuse to pay Mom and Dad a little visit.

TWO AUTUMN months passed and I had resumed my life in California, taking a needed respite from this evolving mystery. I did manage to write former detective Bob Cooley to inquire if he remembered a suspect, one "Dirk Duran," as this name did not appear in the Oregon State Police crime report in my possession. I called him later, and we spoke briefly on the phone. No, Cooley had no memory whatsoever of the name Duran.

Then I wrote to Lureen, using her nom de guerre, Egbert. I could easily picture the tall, slim cowgirl with the flashing eyes luring locals into bars and wrestling, manipulating, flirting the truth out of drunken sods about what happened that long-ago summer.

I got no reply from her. When I sent her a more urgent missive through Federal Express, the company called to tell me their dispatcher couldn't find the address, the one Lureen had given me.

Dee Dee and Bob offered to step in and do some investigation in Central Oregon for me. They were planning a trip over the Cascades anyway, to attend a meeting in Bend. Afterward, they figured they could drop in on the local cops and "pump them for what we can. I don't think we'd hurt anything, and maybe we'd get information," Dee Dee told me.

I took the private investigator I had hired off the case entirely. His cynical tone had been betraying his true sentiments. When I had phoned him to say that I thought it likely my attacker was *not* Godwin after all, and I was refocusing my suspicions on a local schoolboy, he said, "You're taking swings and loops and dives. You switch around when you want to." Even if there were any truth to rumors I'd heard, he lectured, "the odds are against you."

THE FIRST WEEK of December, Bob and Dee Dee phoned me after a day of poking around Central Oregon with my crime report in hand, and I got a taste of their zest for sleuthing, their gift for shape-shifting, blending into whatever demimonde might hold a clue. Their first task had been to locate my mole, Lureen, on the slight chance that she might have unearthed some leads for me. They found her address through Bill Penhollow's father. Dee Dee related to me that when they got to the house, it appeared that the residents had just moved out.

"A woman in the driveway next door got the impression that Billy and Lureen had split. Billy's father told us they had fights. We knew you'd be upset to lose her, so we found out she worked at this tavern and went there, and it was filled with not the best sort of guys. There was this bartender lady who looked like she'd nibbled on nails for breakfast—she had this straight, chopped-off, totally bleached white hair—you know how some women put white makeup on and look like a spook? She looked like that, and she had these little slit eyes in the middle of all that white. Her face was scarred and she was a little twisted when she talked. We bought a beer because we wanted to see what we could find out about Lureen. We asked her and, boy, she turned tough. 'She doesn't work here anymore.' And her face was all twisted. Man, she didn't like Lureen. They must have had a big whoop-de-do there. She was really tough with us when she thought we were Lureen's friends. She sort of warmed up to us when she found out we didn't know Lureen, and went over and asked this guy how long it'd been since Lureen worked there. He said a month. And when we left, she was really nice and said, 'I hope you find her.' "

They didn't. Instead, they picked up where my private investigator had left off, setting out to interview the teens who cruised Cline Falls State Park the night of June 22, 1977. One of the them, a boy named Adolph Wende, seemed significant, as he contacted police more than one time, as described in the police report: At 6:50 a.m., June 23, the morning after the attack, an eighteen-year-old teen,

Adolph William Wende, heard about the assault over the radio and felt he should report what he knew. He said he was in the park around 11:30 p.m. with a friend Richard Sala, of Redmond. He recalled seeing the small tent in the park and observed a red pickup with a white camper bearing Washington license plates parked nearby.

On June 24, Wende approached the police again. He said that contrary to the information he had given police the night before, he had been in the park twice during the night of June 22, 1977. He and Richard Sala traveled through about 11:30 p.m. and observed a small two-man tent near the riverbank. A red pickup with a white camper was situated on the one-way entrance just a short distance from the tent. They then went over to the other side of the highway to where young people congregate, and returned to the park five minutes later. This time, Wende claimed, they noticed the tent was gone and the red pickup was in another location slightly farther into the park. A white male about twenty-seven years old, about five-eleven or six feet tall and wearing blue jeans and a white T-shirt, was getting into the pickup.

Bob and Dee Dee learned from police that Adolph Wende was a petty criminal with a record for burglary, and they got a tip as to his whereabouts. Then they journeyed through the first blizzard of the season thirty miles south of Bend to La Pine, a town hidden in a pine forest, street after street tucked away in the big trees.

"We found his house, a god-awful trailer with three gigantic Airedales in it," Dee Dee related to me. "He wasn't there, so we talked to a woman in front who said she thought he went into town with her son, who drove a faded green '69 Plymouth, so we decided to try to find him, and you know something, we did! We found them in this parking lot—Adolph almost had a coronary because someone knew him. He looked real leery, didn't want to go with us. But he got in our car, and talked and talked and talked—we thought maybe we'd have to keep him forever. At first he was scared. He kept saying, 'I didn't have anything to do with it. I was just a witness!' When we told him the statute of limitations ran out—we thought it would relieve him to think the person who did it wouldn't come and get him—but instead it made him mad. Here's this petty criminal and he kept saying, 'He can get away with it?'

"He told us he and a friend bought a six-pack that night and went to the park to drink it. He left his car on the other side of the highway from the park because the cops always showed up and hassled him. They were sitting with a view of the tent, and saw what he remembered to be a van with two guys—he said several times he wasn't sure whether it was a truck or van, but was exactly sure where it happened. We made him go through it—two guys, he thinks, ran over the tent, backed up, and did it again and again. Is that true?" Dee Dee asked me.

"He backed off me and came back on foot. He didn't run over me two or three times," I said with certainty.

"He said one guy drove the truck back and forth over you and backed up and ran over again, and the other guy on the passenger side got out and started hitting the girls with a hatchet-type weapon. He says he and his friends started screaming and throwing full cans of beer at him—this has to be bull, of course. He says they were scared out of their wits, then Adolph went to his sister's because he was so upset. They were terrified that they'd seen this, and they didn't know what to do. Terrified if they reported it they'd get blamed, and they thought you were both dead—they didn't think there was any possible way you would not be dead."

"And he made a point of repeating that three or four times," Bob added.

"Like it was bothering him that he didn't do anything about it?" I asked.

"Yeah."

Bob said, "The cops know him as a liar, so now he has given *three* different stories about events of that night. He may be telling you the truth for the first time because now he's not dealing with the cops. Or maybe his story is truth and lies."

"If he was such a pathological liar, you'd think he would have made himself look better," Dee Dee added.

Then Bob interjected. "This was a genuine-seeming part of his statement—he brought up several times how ashamed they were. If Adolph and the other guy witnessed this incredible act, they were watching pure evil at work. That just tears you apart." Then Dee Dee: "Adolph was trying so hard to be somebody; then he reacted in the most cowardly way. It must have affected his manliness. The fact that he acted poorly has been a problem all these years. He said it took him two years to get over it enough to even function."

I remonstrated, "In spite of what Adolph said, I just don't think there were two guys—I didn't sense the presence of more than one person. There was no conversation, no words. Shayna was knocked out. I was under the wheel. You wouldn't think they'd suppress their conversation for fear that I would overhear them."

"I wouldn't think so," Bob said.

"I had a profound sense there was only one person there," I insisted.

"The other guy might have been stunned speechless," Bob said.

The Kounses had convinced me that Adolph Wende was someone I had to interview myself. "Will he talk to me?" I asked.

"He said hell, he'd put on a barbecue and you can bring cameras. He absolutely would talk to you," Bob assured me.

"Yeah. It's vitally important that you find the guy he was with. And Adolph's sister, to whom he supposedly told the whole story."

But would it be prudent for me to interview Adolph alone, given his reputation as a petty criminal? Yes, he seemed benign, they both agreed. "And this old lady has been around some scary folks," Dee Dee added.

NEXT EVENING I got another call from my new moles. They'd taken it upon themselves to venture up the dirt driveway beyond the FOR SALE sign to talk to my supposed suspect's parents, on the pretext of being interested in buying their ranch. Lou and Lou Ellen Duran were, as described by Dee Dee, "cowboy folks," and at first they were reticent with these two strangers barging in on them, but Bob and Dee Dee's overwhelming friendliness overcame early suspicions. Soon they were invited into the tidy double-wide, where the four carried on a warm conversation. Dee Dee spotted a collage of photos on the wall and asked, "Is that your son?" Lou Ellen answered yes, and added only that he lived in Washington and the photo showed him with his wife and two kids. Dee Dee thought it was curious that they never mentioned their son's name. "What was odd—they talked about their daughter, their grandchildren, their cattle, and her teapot collection, but they wouldn't talk about Dirk, other than depicting him as a family man in the photo."

Dee Dee, and Bob, too, still had a hunch that Lureen and her folktales had led me astray. "I just don't think he did it. It's not because of his parents. A lot of nice people have grisly kids." Dee Dee repeated her main point. "I just think that whoever did that to you and Shayna is either dead, in prison, or still doing crime. But this guy has a wife and kids and is living up in Washington!"

I felt my heart sink.

"You think I'm wrong, don't you?"

I had a hunch that her hunch was wrong.

"Maybe you got some kind of hit on this guy when you were talking to Lureen," Dee Dee said. "There could be something special about that."

Dee Dee described the day she first saw the suspect they believed murdered Valerie. It was a couple of months after Val's disappearance. Dee Dee had heard that Phillip Thompson was in court after police picked him up in the warehouse on a gun charge. She showed up to get a look at him. It was the first time she'd ever been in a courthouse for a criminal proceeding. When a well-built, tall man with square shoulders and no neck—"his head looked like a bowling ball perched on a curb," as Bob described him—walked down the courthouse steps, Dee Dee was sure who it was: "I felt like the mother tiger out in the forest and I had this great urge to attack him. I could feel my claws, and that's not anything I've ever felt before."

"That's him," she whispered to her private investigator, who had talked to Thompson on a previous occasion. "No, that's not him," her investigator answered back. "I said, 'It is too.' We go to the courtroom and he'd cleaned up and had on a suit and looked like a businessman. My guts recognized him, and I'd never seen him before."

SINCE THE KOUNSES were exhilarated from their productive day of sleuthing, I asked them to spend the next one trying to find Robin, Godwin's niece and the girl, according to Forsberg, whom Godwin wanted to "teach a lesson to" when he allegedly attacked two female bikers camping in Cline Falls State Park. When I imagined myself finding and interviewing Robin, I still felt as fainthearted as I had when I made a cold call to her residence from my motel in Sisters earlier that same autumn.

The next night I got a call from my new detectives; their voices were bursting at the seams. They had found Robin with little effort. Now in her early thirties, she lived in a little travel trailer behind her mother's neat double-wide, on the outskirts of Redmond. Along with her lovely, gracious mother, Sue—so much for impressions gathered from a voice saying hello on the phone—Robin was more than willing to talk about Cline Falls. She told the Kounses she'd retained a clear memory of what she saw in the park that long-ago night—and she insisted that her uncle Bud Godwin had not been there.

The Kounses had reason to believe her. Robin had vivid recall of details near our tent site; she relayed the very same account she had given police eighteen years before, as recorded in the crime report, without a single revision, and her recall was instant. Both Robin and her mother were offended that this outrageous crime had happened, and no arrest had ever occurred.

That meant that "Frosty" Forsberg might have known from Godwin that his niece was in Cline Falls the night of the attack, and he might have spun a tale using that fact. The Kounses urged me to seek Robin out and listen to her story, and I breathed a sigh of relief that it would require little courage on my part to approach her now.

Finally, Bob and Dee Dee dropped by the police station in Redmond, Oregon, and asked a few pointed questions about the old unsolved Cline Falls case. It so happened that the officers sitting around the Redmond station house that day had been in service way back in '77, and they remembered the case well. The Redmond cops told the Kounses that of the three police agencies that might have had jurisdiction over the area in and around Cline Falls in those days, the case belonged to the Oregon State Police.

Since Cline Falls fell outside the Redmond city limits, the Redmond Police Department didn't have anything to do with it. The Deschutes County Sheriff's Office did cover the rural areas of Deschutes County, but a major case like Cline Falls fell to the state police to investigate, and they were the only ones responsible for its outcome.

Then one of the officers who had worked the same beat way back in the seventies, a Corporal Richard Little, casually admitted to the Kounses that though the Redmond P.D. had had nothing whatsoever to do with the Cline Falls case— nothing at all—all these years they'd privately suspected a local kid, seventeen years old at the time: one Dirk Duran.

Bob and Dee Dee catapulted out of their seats when the name that originated with Lureen filled the air in the Redmond station house: What were the reasons for their private hunches? Suddenly an emergency call came in. The troopers rushed out the door without answering their question.

"We were hugging in the car after we heard that name mentioned. Because it was the first official person to link him to the crime," Dee Dee said.

Bob and Dee Dee now apologized to me for dismissing my intuition.

"This thing is wearing my head out. I don't think of anything else," Dee Dee said. "We got so into it, last night I dreamed there was an axeman at the back door. It was almost like I crawled into your skin or something. It's crazy that I've been affected this way." In fact, she'd been seeing and hearing about axes everywhere. "Before I met you the only axe I heard about was Lizzie Borden," she said and let out one of her hoarse, high-pitched laughs.

THE KOUNSES had powered this investigation with an irreversible momentum. But with this decided turn in the case away from Godwin, whom I'd studied, to this unknown local schoolboy, I actually felt a little deflated because I no longer had a fix on a concrete person whom I could contemplate. I found myself *between* psychopaths—a rather peculiar intermezzo.

An acquaintance had recently criticized me for referring to the axeman as *my* attacker, as *my* axeman. "You are *not* connected to this guy," she had insisted bluntly, tossing off a casual comment.

I had done an about-face on the stance I held when I was younger, when I didn't care to know the identity of the young cowboy who had ambushed me and Shayna—or about whether he was apprehended, charged, and convicted of the crime. By now I believed I was *intimately* connected to him—and there was great urgency to finding out who he was and why he tried to kill that night. This knowledge would, I thought, help me recover my will. Everything now was at stake.

"I can tell you that being mutilated by a man with an axe is a very intimate encounter," I wrote in a letter I fired off to this acquaintance who had unwittingly stepped into a minefield. "He changed the course of my life. He blinded my friend. He is '*my axeman.*'" But, no: I was not infected with affection and gratitude for one who had been lord over life and death and who had spared me. I was not in the clutches of the Stockholm syndrome, when a victim comes to identify with her captors, comes to see them as protectors, and cooperates with them in the crime against her. I told my acquaintance that if I didn't want to know about "my attacker," if I didn't want to find him, study him, shout out his name, how would he be stopped? *One particular* man committed *this specific* act.

Human evil may be a murky blight that inhabits particular individuals to different degrees at different times, or it may occur across societies whose particular cultural values are the product of a diseased consciousness (like the mass psychosis in humankind everywhere that devalues women), but the malefic cannot be dealt with as a vague, unspecific force. It is the baneful details that must be confronted.

I FLEW to Oregon and sat, one overcast January morning in 1995, in the hearing room of the Oregon parole board in Salem, noting that I was not pulsing with jittery passion as I had been when I was tracing Godwin's footsteps over mossy logging roads.

No members of the victim Andrea Tolentino's family were present, and no members of Godwin's family—only a line of reporters and television cameras, a district attorney from Lane County, Bob and Dee Dee sporting PUBLIC SAFETY #1 buttons.

Godwin himself was not present. He would be represented only by his voice, on speakerphone from the federal pen in Colorado, and it was his voice that I was most eager to hear. The parole board had indeed obtained not one but *two* evaluations by different psychiatrists to determine whether Godwin would still pose a threat to public safety, and the chairperson excerpted them for the record: the findings of the first indicated that "although there is evidence of improved psychological stability in this individual, the data suggests a personality profile compatible with continued erratic, impulsive behavior such as pedophilic activity." And the second report: "Inmate Godwin is currently seen as having a condition that would predispose him to the commission of future criminal activity to a degree that would render him dangerous to the health and safety of the community. The Board should postpone scheduled parole until a specific future date to allow Godwin to participate in and complete a sexual offender program at a secure institution."

"Mr. Godwin, do you have any comments about these psychological reports?"

"No." He cleared his throat. "No, I have no comments at this time." The voice was deep and raspy.

Another board member asked, "Mr. Godwin, could you tell us what programs you've been involved in at the institution that might give us reason for your release?"

"The programs that I've been involved in?" The voice sounded so ominous it took me off guard. "I've been involved in very few programs . . . the programs have been mostly tool-and-die apprenticeship programs and church involvement and that's about it. There really has been nothing much else available."

You could feel the collective awe in the room: tool-and-die training?

"What have you done to address your pedophilic problems, your sexual offender problems in particular, the problems that led to the murder of this child?"

Godwin cleared his throat again. "As I said before, there wasn't much available here in that regard where I've been incarcerated," he rasped. "So I haven't been involved in any programs that way."

"Have you made personal changes you can discuss that would assist us in making your decision?"

"Personal changes. What I can say on that is I've been involved with the Church of Christ for thirteen years now . . . As far as the benefit in your lives, I couldn't really say, but I believe it's benefited me to have personal involvement, to be able to learn more Scripture, and I've taught Sunday school over the years. That's the most I can say about my personal involvement."

Dee Dee looked down and shook her head.

The board asked a couple of perfunctory questions about Godwin's plans for living in a free society, what support system he might have—questions he answered cheerfully. Then the assistant DA from Lane County read a statement insisting that "the nature of the crime committed by Mr. Godwin was one of the most horrific the community could experience . . . suffice it to say that the acts of Mr. Godwin cause me to wonder how such an evil person could actually exist."

"You are allowed to respond to the DA's comments," the chair said.

There was a long pause. "No, I don't wish to make a comment."

"Do you have anything else to say on why the board should grant release at this time?"

"I really have no extenuating circumstances whatever that I can bring out at this point. I have been incarcerated for nearly sixteen years. I would hope to have an opportunity to become established in a community and work toward my retirement at least, you know."

The notion of a guy who had committed a crime considered as "one of the most horrific the community could experience" working toward his retirement was creating cognitive dissonance in my head.

The board sent us out of the room and then quickly reconvened: they would defer release another twenty-four months because, although Godwin was involved with religion, he had sought out absolutely no rehabilitation programs in prison to address his criminality.

"Almost all criminals find the Lord in prison," Dee Dee commented as we left the room. "I don't see why everyone thinks prison is such a bad place. Prisons have got a better track record than all the churches for getting people to find the Lord! We never go to a parole hearing or a trial but that these guys haven't found the Lord . . . Maybe they think they can con God. I know they con parole boards and psychiatrists."

ANOTHER FEW months passed before I launched another campaign north. This time my plan was to drive to Oregon alone and stay awhile, really sink roots into the place, cool my heels long enough to let secrets bubble to the surface. I scheduled a trip for the first week of spring 1995. When March came, I developed the flu. My skin broke out. My stomach clenched at even the thought of leaving home. And Lureen's words—*Watch your back!*—still echoed in my thoughts.

Boo sent me a card, inviting me to stay on the ranch with her and her mother, Vee. "We're calving right now—up to 38 babies with more to come. Wish you could see them. They are so adorable. We lost one first-year heifer because the calf was too big—and two more calves we had to pull out, and that's convinced me I'll *never* have kids," she wrote in her bold handwriting, all caps. A month passed until I could no longer delay the inevitable. I packed my '79 Volvo, filled the trunk with my totemic collection of five hatchets—my mojo—and headed up Interstate 5.

The brown, plain-lettered WELCOME TO OREGON sign in the Siskiyou Mountains brought a curious emotion. Behind me was the teeming anonymity of California, and I crossed with a curious relief into the intimacy of Oregon. I noted the irony of that shift in attitude, and how different it was from my jittery passage in 1992, when the landscape stretching ahead, in that place called Oregon, had seemed filled with shadows.

Hot Rocks

It had been like dying, that sliding down the mountain pass.
It had been like the death of someone, irrational, that sliding
down the mountain pass and into the region of dread. It
was like slipping into fever, or falling down that hole in
sleep from which you wake yourself whimpering.

—ANNIE DILLARD,
　on crossing the Cascade Mountains
　from west to east, *Teaching a Stone to Talk*

It was a whiteout. Through the wind-
shield of my Volvo, swirls of fog fluttered like a curtain, parting occasionally, affording me a glimpse of an icy fang, a piece of volcano. I had turned eastward and
was crossing the Cascade Mountains on the Santiam Pass. As on the higher
McKenzie Pass, which Shayna and I had crossed, there was a moment on this descent when the moisture-loving firs disappeared, the ponderosas took their place,
and the sweet pine scent drifting on dry air filled my nostrils. I felt the same fris-
son that passed through me every time I experienced this shift in the landscape.

　I was in free fall: my ears popped and I fell into the desert again. Soon the ponderosas lay behind me and I headed farther east, into junipers and sage. With
one-hundred-mile visibility, settling into the desert was like entering a clear-eyed
dream. The scent of juniper had a hypnotic effect on me—transmuting a hazy
anxiety into a sensory intensity, an acutely alert calm.

　These native junipers held me in their thrall. Their shaggy shreds of bark
twisting up the trunk made the trees look like they were spiraling up from the
earth because the bedrock wouldn't let their roots grow down. Their limbs jutted
out from the main trunk and contorted haphazardly as though in response to
some unmentionable trauma. More than one person in this country had recited
to me a cherished local phrase: "Central Oregon is God's country." They claimed
these junipers bestowed upon the land a special honor because they grew only in
two places, Central Oregon and the Holy Land. In fact, *Juniperus occidentalis*
doesn't grow in the Middle East at all. But what "God's country" did have in com-

mon with a part of the Holy Land was a landscape littered with somber black basalt chunks from ancient volcanic eruptions. Residents who lived on streets called Volcano, Obsidian, Pumice, Quartz, Lava, and Rock Crest rimmed their gardens with rocks, piled them in wooden bins called rock cribs to substitute for fence posts, stacked them in their front yards, one stack with a sign reading FREE ROCKS. HELP YOURSELF.

In that stony landscape along a country road that formed part of the '76 Bike-Centennial Trail, which I would have traversed seven miles after Cline Falls State Park, Boo lived with her mother on a ranch that painted one hundred acres of desert floor a brilliant green.

On the periphery of the fenced ranch, the black rocks had been cleared, and long Bermuda grass surrounded the trunks of tortured junipers, as though these tragic beings had been brought here and given a good home to rest from their torment. Amid the junipers lolled 120 head of sublimely content red-and-white Hereford and spotted shorthorn cattle, with little numbered tags hanging from their ears (though each had her own name). Their lowing was the bass line to the cacophony that issued from the nucleus of the ranch. In the yard, four conceited peacocks gave off ear-splitting whistles as they folded and unfolded their fans. Exotic frizzle chickens clucked, tall strutting Chinese geese honked, a couple of roosters crowed and scratched, nine cats prowled the barn and yowled, and two guard dogs ran around warning any intruders with gruff, intimidating barks. Considerable yowling and yapping also came from the two-story cedar ranch house itself—from those animals invited into the inner sanctum: two white cats and four miniature dachshunds.

Boo and her mother, Vee, and her stepfather, Jim, invited me to live under their roof as I launched the next phase of my investigation. They assured me I would be safe with them: no one could trespass without the peacocks emitting their shrill alarms, which in turn alerted the barking dogs. They were ranch people. Ranch people had guns and knew how to use them.

Vee Sanders was a small, fast-talking dynamo in her mid-sixties who alternated her active ranch chores—speeding around the pastures on trucks and tractors—with retiring in the kitchen on a rocking chair in front of a cast-iron stove, dachshunds on her lap.

She, too, shared with me her own experience of that ill-begotten night eighteen years before, when her eighteen-year-old daughter came home, her white clothes dyed crimson. Not only had Boo visited me in the hospital, but also Vee had tried to. Against her strong-willed protests, hospital officials barred her from entering my room. This struck me as a mishap of fate, because in an uncanny coincidence, Vee and my own mother might have discovered that they had both lived in the same exceedingly remote farmtown in the early 1940s, Fairview, on the border of Montana and North Dakota. Though they never met, they probably worked in the beet fields down the road from each other, as all farm kids did. Vee was the same age and of the same descent as my mother—German stock that inhabited the Russian steppes for centuries—and with her bright blue eyes and square jaw, she looked like one of my mother's siblings. The discovery of this geographic linkage between our families, and our shared bloodlines, was a resonance that further bonded me to Boo.

How to describe my feelings for this woman, this perfect stranger, whose eyes I met through a truck window one night in the summer of '77? I pondered how odd it was to find myself on this ranch, reunited with her, that our bond could sustain more than one meeting in a coffee shop, that she had turned out to be someone I felt comfortable hanging out with, which meant someone whose company I could share with contentment, without feeling pressure to talk. Boo told me many times that had I sought her out at any period earlier in her life, she wouldn't have wanted to meet me. She was in a bad marriage and absent on drugs then. Our fellowship could have formed only now, at this specific time.

I'd get up late and Boo would tease me that she'd been working for four hours already, laying irrigation pipe in the pasture, and jumping on and off trucks and tractors and backhoes, followed by a herd of barking dogs. She wore a vest and jeans, rubber boots splattered with mud, and a cap pulled down over her striking eyes, always rimmed with liner. She stopped now and then to comfort a duckling or yell at a cat bullying a chick. She'd pause to light a cigarette and, with a feminine tilt of her hips, take a long draw. As I watched her, calmness spread over me. I imagined that just being in her presence was surrounding me with an invisible protective halo.

When her chores were done, Boo and I talked upstairs in her wing of the ranch house, where I was installed. In a living room decorated with Boo's sculptures carved out of soapstone and enlivened by little plants she was always propagating, we sat on sofas arranged around a TV and compulsively reran our common oral history, to get all the details straight—because *all* remembered details had to be shared.

"Were you standing or lying on the ground when you struggled with him?" she asked.

"Lying on the ground," I answered. That's not what she imagined all these years. She pictured me standing as I battled him.

"Did you see flesh hanging out of my arm?" I wanted to know. I was hungrier than ever for these concrete details.

It was a clean axe cut, she remembered. "Right on your forearm where there's not much meat."

Boo still mulled over that moment when she thought she breathed death in the air. "I swear to this day, maybe not you, but Billy and I thought, that girl is dead. Then when she moaned, we just flew on her. I could never understand why

I would feel that horrified over a dead body. You get a queer feeling. Ice goes through your bones. I was disgusted that I reacted like that. I don't think I'd feel that way now."

I shared with Boo the unexpected turn in my investigation towards a local kid. It turned out the name Dirk Duran wasn't confined to Lureen's conspiratorial imagination or to the suspicions of a few cops. Back in the summer of '77, Boo had also heard talk in the community that Duran was a suspect.

"Everyone in this whole town suspected him."

Everyone in the whole town? This validated my quest that the range of rumor was expanding from the whispered suspicions of people I didn't know into the ken of one I trusted. *But everyone in this whole town?*

"Didn't he beat his girlfriend up real bad and put her in the hospital that same week? I heard the cops investigated him, too," Boo added.

I was having a hard time understanding how a whole town could suspect him, including local police—and nothing of that knowledge had found its way to the police agency in charge of the investigation. There was a gap in logic here. Or something was amiss.

"And I heard they found an axe in the river with the initials *D.D.* carved on it."

A story had circulated that the weapon was found in the river? This contradicted Lureen's scenario of Dirk Duran digging blood out of his initials in the axe. Besides, would an attacker throw his weapon in the river *with his initials carved into it?* My instinct was to dismiss this rumor as a folktale, a rural legend. I questioned Boo about whether she had ever had occasion to meet Dirk Duran, or seen him around.

Sure, she remembered him. A cowboy in Wranglers with a great physique, but not "heavy-duty muscular." She recalled he was around five foot eleven. Clean-shaven.

I remembered thinking my attacker had the build of someone who was at least twenty years old. Dirk Duran would have been seventeen at the time. Boo reminded me that kids who worked the ranches had bodies that were well developed. All that pitching hay worked wonders on the physique.

"Back then there were cowboys and hippies," she said, running down for me the social strata of the three to four hundred kids who attended Redmond High School in the late seventies—which included the usual jocks and straights. I'd taken my own tour of the sprawling early-seventies-vintage building with a lava rock foundation located in the treeless western end of town, which would have stood alone in the desert back then. It looked remarkably like my own suburban Chicago high school, with one difference: the trophy case at Redmond High was filled with shiny rodeo statues.

Boo pulled out her high school yearbook and located a tiny black-and-white photo of a freshman boy: Dirk Duran, at fourteen. It was hard to make out the face in this tiny mug shot, but I could see that he was a dark-haired boy with choppy bangs and extra-wide seventies-style shirt lapels. He looked handsome among his other goofy-looking peers.

"There were no long-haired cowboys like you see today. Cowboys were the dominant group in town; they hated hippies and used to beat them up and cut off their hair. But Dirk became one of the transitioning cowboys who started growing their hair longer, stopped wearing their ten-gallon hats to school, and started smoking dope and blending in with everyone else. He somehow got into the hippie-drugger crowd and was still a cowboy."

I supposed this impulse wasn't terribly original. It was the seventies. The Eagles were the number one band. Every teen boy west of the Mississippi probably wanted to be a cowboy-hippie-outlaw-drugger-rocker. A desperado.

I asked Boo if she remembered what vehicle Dirk drove. What came to her mind was an image of a "cool van," green in color, that she learned he lost to drugs. "I asked the local drug dealer, 'What are you doing driving Dirk Duran's van?' He said, 'It's my van now.' "

Boo didn't know if the innuendo about Duran's guilt held any water. It's in the nature of rumors that the hearer holds them at a distance and tries not to let them sink in. But she recalled the peculiar voltage that passed between her and Dirk Duran years later when she ran into him. She wondered whether it was because she was famous around town for having rescued the girls in Cline Falls.

"It was the eeriest feeling seeing that guy. I went to a twelve-step meeting in the late eighties, and he came in there with this girl, and he wouldn't look me in the face—an electrical current was in the air between us. I believe people feel that stuff." The encounter left her shaking. She hadn't seen him around since that day.

Now that I had arrived to test the veracity of these suspicions, the real possibility that her schoolmate might have committed this concealed crime was finally penetrating. As Boo invited me to jump into her yellow pickup for a tour of her mom's acreage, she described the feeling: "It's stirring to my mind and soul." It was surely stirring to mine.

FOR SALE still marked the entrance to the Duran ranch. Boo was eager to go on a fishing expedition with me. We wanted to see for ourselves the kind of place where our suspect had been raised—what kind of stock he came from—and we figured we might flush out a clue as to exactly where in Washington he was living now. We turned off the main road and headed into the ranch along a long dirt lane. The place had a bleak, forsaken feeling. The neighbors' property on either side was irrigated. Not the Duran ranch. The green stopped abruptly at its borders, and the raw desert strewn with lava rocks reasserted itself. This field of black rubble barely concealed by weeds reminded me distinctly of the bleak terrain on McKenzie Pass. Was it just my associations with the boy who grew up here, or did this place seem like the hideout in a Western movie for cowboys in black hats?

The road seemed to wind on forever, past weathered buildings, telephone poles hewn from crooked pines, a small abandoned feedlot, dead junipers—until we spotted a tidy double-wide trailer on a rise, with a glorious view of volcanoes spread out to the west. Tidy flower beds surrounded the trailer. A steer's head was perched in a tree. An old rancher in his seventies, a small man wearing a ten-gallon hat out of proportion to his size, sauntered to our car. His face was shaped like an anvil; his nose had been broken some time in the past, and a cleft split his chin. Boo rambled on about how I was her friend from New York City looking to buy a Western ranch, and the man answered tersely that his property was already in escrow. "Oh, darn," Boo said. Well, it's a nice piece of property. And oh, by the way, was he Dirk Duran's dad? She went to high school with Dirk. And how was he doing now?

The poker-faced old man looked suspicious and didn't give news of his son. Just then his wife drove up. A plain woman with mouse-colored hair, younger than her husband, she smiled, but gave us no excuse to stay and chat.

Boo said, "Okay, well, you tell Dirk someone from high school said hello."

We got in the car and drove away, and I wondered: Could this unassuming ranch couple have spawned an axeman?

I SET OUT to track down Lureen, but I didn't have a clue about where to look. So I followed a whim and headed into the old Redmond fair and rodeo grounds in the center of town, where an auction was taking place. This hallowed turf—with its charming, antiquated rodeo ring and bull chutes, with its Buckaroo Breakfast Shack and pastoral fields—had been a kind of spiritual center for generations of Central Oregonians who congregated for seasonal festivities, particularly the Deschutes County Fair, which had taken place each August for decades. This place was also the utopian oasis with green grass and a water spigot that might have altered Shayna's and my destiny on June 22, 1977. It was here where Kathy and Mark set up their camp while we remained in the rattlesnake pit of Cline Falls.

I took my seat among the cowboys and looked over my shoulder at a couple of broncobusters who'd come to town from a working cattle ranch. These cowboys had survived the evolutionary trends in Central Oregon with no other influences, hippie or otherwise, thrown in. But these were no Marlboro men with unfettered freedom to gallop into a boundless horizon. One imperturbably solemn buckaroo rested his cowboy hat on his lap—its tight grip had smashed his short hair into a ring around his head like a sweaty jelly mold; a red kerchief choked his neck in the heat; the snaps of his long sleeves encased his forearms. Another specimen strutted unsteadily in high heels and pointy toes, his jeans improbably tight. In their cowboy vestments these men's men seemed pinched and stuffed in, as uncomfortable and restricted as any Victorian woman in corsets and bustles. I could understand why the hippie influence might have been a refreshing option.

It strained credibility that I might have any use for the old spurs and coils of barbed wire on sale, so I left the fairgrounds and drove back to Boo's ranch, where Boo announced proudly that she'd sighted Lureen: my lanky, elusive sleuth had turned up working as a waitress at the Sunspot, a hamburger joint in Terrebonne, on Highway 97.

The tiny burg of Terrebonne—an epicenter in my mind ever since Lureen told me her inciting tale about "hoein' onions in Terrebonne"—was a Western idyll four miles north of Redmond along Highway 97. It was tucked in gently rolling desert hills at the foot of Smith Rock, a stunning escarpment more ancient than the Cascade Range, a little piece of Monument Valley in Central Oregon.

I flew over to the greasy spoon, and the minute I walked in, I found myself looking into Lureen's gleaming wide-set eyes. She held out her hand to me and, picking up right where she'd left off, cast me another of her conspiratorial glances—without explaining why, instead of sending me clandestine letters and encrypted communication, she'd just disappeared. Not giving me the chance to ask, she instructed me to meet her and Bill at the Sunspot the next day at noon.

BILL'S HAND had gotten chewed up pretty badly when a chain saw ran amok and ripped through it. The sight of him there, his young face crisscrossed with age lines, though boyish fuzz lined his lip, his wounded hand all bound up, only increased the protective instinct I'd felt for him the year before. As for Lureen—how odd, I thought, to find this oracle of my mission in life in a white polyester waitress's uniform sliding two plates of hot dogs on the Formica in front of us. Bill had been pretty closemouthed about what he knew regarding a suspect in the Cline Falls case the last time I saw him. But at that time he was in the presence of his parents. I wondered if he'd be more forthcoming this time around. I pressed him about the rumors of Dirk Duran's involvement: What exactly had he seen that night, or subsequently heard?

"Just rumors," he answered as vaguely as before. "Then seeing that pickup in Cline Falls shining the lights and leaving. Seems like I saw a two-toned paint job that I thought was blue on top and white on the bottom and that was the kind of pickup he drove." I looked down at the crime report in my hands. Bill had told investigators that while he was rescuing the two girls, he saw a pickup some distance away turning around near the restrooms—but he hadn't described a color.

I pressed Lureen to clarify her loose memories of the night she went to band practice—around a week after the Cline Falls incident—and practice was canceled because Dirk Duran was there and he said something about chopping coyotes. I did believe that Lureen saw Dirk Duran assault his girlfriend at the pond around the time of the Cline Falls incident. But was this fourteen-year-old girl so terrified by this assault that she'd embroidered a memory to make Duran responsible for Cline Falls, too? Had she really seen Dirk Duran sitting on the tailgate of his pickup carving blood out of the initials in his hatchet handle?

"Did you actually *see* that?"

"Sitting on the tailgate. Blood on the tailgate," she responded as elliptically as she did every time she spoke of this particular recollection.

"You *saw* blood on the tailgate?"

"I saw wood in his hands."

"You saw wood in his hands?" I was getting more aggressive, trying to winnow truth from fantasy.

Lureen told me just what she'd told me before. She was a drummer in a band at the time, and when she showed up for practice at the home of one of the guys in the band, she was told they weren't practicing because Dirk Duran was there.

Why did Dirk's presence make the band cancel practice? Were they making an excuse to get rid of her so she wouldn't overhear something? "What *exactly* did you see?" Out of desperation for a kernel of truth, I acted like a prosecutor turning up the heat.

"Just the pickup, and they were talking about tires. Looking for tires to change. Talking about the blood. Got to get the blood off the tailgate and stuff. And the wood in his hands." Someone told her—she thought it was the guy whose house it was, Ken—that they had to get the stains out of his initials carved into his hatchet.

"They told you that. You didn't see it." I tried to focus Lureen on what she'd actually seen with her own eyeballs, not what she remembered having been told.

"I seen the piece of wood. Dirk Duran. Wood in his hand and pocketknife sitting on the tailgate."

"You saw that," I challenged.

"I seen that."

"You didn't know if it was a hatchet or not."

"Right. Because I said, 'You guys, what are you doing?' 'He's got to get the stains out of his initials and the tires have to be changed or they can match the tires.' "

She still hadn't admitted actually laying eyes on a piece of wood attached to a blade. Every time I saw Lureen, her story got slightly more elaborate, verging on the realm of real conspiracy. Had this fourteen-year-old girl really overheard a fraternity of boys advising Duran on how to destroy evidence?

I knew that few kids were courageous enough to step out of the crowd to rat on one of their own to authorities. But taking action to help conceal a crime was of another magnitude of wrongdoing. I grilled her about the guy who had the band practice at his home.

His name was Ken Block and he still lived in the area. She pulled a tiny phone book out of her purse and gave me his address. I eyed her little book, wondering, was it a passport to the past? I waited anxiously as she paged through it and pulled up one name: Doris, the local bus driver and town gossip. "She knew everything that was goin' on," Lureen said, flipping through a few more pages. She copied down only one other name and handed it over: a woman who could help me track down Janey Firestone, Dirk Duran's girlfriend whom he beat up and tried to drown in the pond, according to Lureen's memory, close on the heels of the Cline Falls event. After waiting this long for Lureen to come through, I had expected more.

I'd apparently extracted everything I could from Bill and Lureen in this meeting, and conversation mellowed into small talk. I told them that what really struck me, after all these years, was that people around here still recalled the Cline Falls incident so vividly.

"Yeah. A guy I was working for was introducing me to somebody," Bill related in his halting baritone. " 'Oh, his name sounds familiar.' 'Yeah, well, his granddaddy was a preacher for fifty years, and he's the one who picked up those girls in Cline Falls.' 'Oh, you're the one?' Then they automatically know. It was eighteen years ago."

Lureen added, "They don't know who he is—the man on the moon—but he mentions Cline Falls, everybody knows him. 'Oh, yeah.' " Lureen had even told the woman she worked with at the Sunspot that the girl from Cline Falls was coming in today, and the woman knew right away who I was.

"You guys are no longer strangers."

I wondered whom she was referring to when she said "you guys," then realized she must be referring to me *and Shayna*. It had been a long time, an age, since anyone had lumped me together with Shayna. Her invisible presence here at the Sunspot caused my heart to feel a pinch.

From the police crime report on the Cline Falls axe attack, June 22, 1977:

> At 7:00 P.M. 6-27-77 contact was made with Robin Dawn Williams and her brother, James Emerson Williams. Miss Williams had called the Redmond Police Department reporting that she had been in the park the night of the attack. She reported that she was a passenger in their family car driven by her brother when they went through the park at about 10:55 P.M. to 11:00 P.M. the night of 6-22-77. They were accompanied by Adolph Wende, Richard Sala, and William Jonas. At the beginning of the interview James Williams could not recall being in the park that evening. As his sister recounted the event his memory improved and both were able to describe a vehicle and individual they observed at the park. They noticed an orange pup tent and two bicycles leaning against the picnic table near the river. Parked nearby was a red newer model Ford pickup with a white canopy. With the narrowness of the roadway they had to pass close to the parked pickup. The driver was standing by the door waiting for them to go by. He appeared to be 34 to 35 years, 5'9" or 5'10", wearing a light shirt and faded blue jeans. They recalled that the man was wearing metal rimmed sun-

glasses, his hair was combed back over his ears and was relatively long in back. After passing the pickup and driver they heard the vehicle start. James Williams described the pickup as having a smooth-operating 8 cylinder engine.

I drove to the double-wide where Robin lived, in a treeless residential subdivision southwest of Redmond, and pulled into a driveway decorated by a wagon wheel. The woman whose sandpaper voice I had hung up on the previous fall turned out to belong to Sue Williams, Robin's mother, a wiry, physically fit woman exuding a warmth beyond what you might reasonably expect from a stranger. Robin's mother wrapped me in a big hug at the doorstep of her house and told me how glad she was to see me well, and how the Cline Falls attack had "devastated" the community at the time.

Sue called her daughter in from a small trailer out back, where she lived with her husband. Robin was exactly as described: sharp features and long dark straight hair in braids, an intense presence emanating from behind sunglasses that she hadn't taken off. She looked straight at me and said, "Glad to meet you. I've often wondered—"

"—we've talked about this. What do you suppose ever happened—" Sue broke in. Her pace of talking betrayed her East Coast origins, more rapid than her daughter's Western cadence.

"—or what you looked like, you know, and how bad you were hurt—" Robin continued.

"—putting a face with the name—" Her mother cut in.

"—right and—" Robin picked up from Sue.

"—knowing that you're okay and now you're healing—"

"—and wondering if anything had ever come about it, and you know—"

"—and if anyone was ever caught . . ."

"—yeah." Robin pulled off her sunglasses.

I told them about my search to retrace the events of that night, and they offered enthusiastically to help in any way they could.

I knew from the Kounses that Robin's memory of the night of June 22, 1977, was clear and factual (though she was only fourteen at the time), that her account to them matched what she told police in 1977, and that she was convinced that the perpetrator of the Cline Falls attack was a guy in a red pickup she had seen near the tent shortly before the attack, whose presence had scared her.

I wanted to know if her testimony would remain consistent.

Robin told me she was out with her brother, Jim, that night. They borrowed their mother's car and cruised down into Cline Falls State Park to look for friends they were supposed to meet.

"When we drove down, past the restrooms—your tent was off in the grass there—and I thought, wow, somebody's camping down here. And I saw your bikes parked right by the tent, and there's a pump house up further and there was this pickup parked there. And I didn't see anybody, and then all of a sudden, this man is at the back of his pickup—it startled me because he came from nowhere, and it was like he was right there at my window. And he was wearin' sunglasses, you know, and it was dark. I thought that was really weird. Then we drove really slow past this pickup truck, and he got in his truck and started it, and he came up behind us like he was gonna come out of the park also. And he never did. Because we stopped up there at the road for a good three, four minutes and he never did come up."

"So you got a really bad feeling from this person," I asked.

"Oh, yeah. Yeah. Way hard." Robin got intense as she summoned the memory. She sat with her arms and legs crossed and her dark eyes rolled in their sockets. She remembered that the man had had dark hair and a mustache. He wore blue jeans and a long-sleeved flannel shirt, and a baseball or cowboy hat. He was short for a man. Around five foot eight. Stocky but not muscular.

"And it was nobody you recognized," I asked.

"Not at all."

The next day she was at work when she heard on the radio about the Cline Falls attack. "I flipped out. I thought, oh my God, and I told one of the girls at work that we were down there." She hesitated to call the police because she wasn't supposed to be cruising that night, and she was afraid she'd get in trouble with her mother. But a woman she worked with told her it was the right thing to do.

Robin told the Redmond Police about the man in the red pickup, and she claimed she had remembered all but the last three digits of his license plate. Redmond police told her that detectives would return to hypnotize her in case she might remember the remaining digits. The family waited for a whole week, eager to help the investigation in any way they could. The detectives never turned up. The whole family was upset because law enforcement didn't come back even to show them a composite drawing. For years they were offended that this horrible crime had happened, that they were there with information to give, but that they hadn't been asked for further assistance, and the crime had never been solved.

A long period passed before detectives finally came to talk to Robin. She said she didn't recognize them; they weren't local Redmond cops.

"They tried to tell me it was my uncle. That he thought it was me down there, and he had wanted to hurt me or something. And I said, 'No, it's not.' And they said, 'How do you know?' I said, 'Because I saw the man.' "

"You would recognize your uncle," Sue added.

"Right."

I knew Robin was describing the time in 1979 when Detectives Durr and Cooley followed up on convict Floyd Forsberg's lead.

Robin confessed a fondness for her uncle Bud Godwin, her father's half brother through their mother. "Don't get me wrong, he belongs where he is; until

I was in the fourth grade, he really scared me bad." She said that on one occasion, during one of their many family get-togethers, he made a move on her and she ran away. After that, she kept her distance from Uncle Buddy and kept the incident to herself.

Sue said, "It was kind of devastating on everybody—especially because we're so family-oriented and we wouldn't hurt a fly; then you find somebody like that in the family . . . putting the candles in the skull . . . oh my God." I had no trouble believing that the Williams clan was family-oriented, as it seemed that extended family was buzzing everywhere around the house while we talked privately on the closed-in back porch.

Counting on the clarity of Robin's memory, I asked her if she recollected whether the guy she saw was particularly neat, messy, or average in his appearance. In spite of my suspicions about Dirk Duran, I had to fully explore the possibility that the man (and there may have been more than one) seen by so many in the park driving a red pickup with a white canopy might really have been my attacker.

"I'd say average. He wasn't neat, I know that. But he wasn't like, gross-yucky."

I jotted Robin's words in my notebook, highlighting with three big stars. The guy wasn't neat.

I described for Robin what I saw that night—shirt tucked in, not a single wrinkle, thin body, nice physique, an "advertisement for Wrangler jeans."

"So was what I described the man you saw?" I asked her pointedly.

"Not at all."

So the guy in the red pickup wasn't even neat, let alone meticulous.

Now Robin and Sue wanted to hear my story. "The scar on your arm is from . . . ?" they asked. "How long did it take to recover from your wounds?"

My account led to the speculation on what might have been the "motive" behind the crime.

"You girls were camping. Back then it was still kind of a no-no for girls to be doing things . . ." Robin didn't want to sound judgmental.

I urged her on, "Doing things like . . ."

"Like comin' across the United States by yourselves. So he's probably thinking you're hookers . . ."

"Where I come from it would never be perceived that way," I said.

"Oh, but from here, I'm sure. Back then women weren't thumbing," Robin said.

"So if two women were alone, we'd be considered prostitutes."

"Or fast women, or—that's why we always sheltered Robin a lot. 'You don't go out by yourself,' " Sue added.

"So that was the culture here?" I asked.

"Yes. Yes." Sue knew that women were protesting for equal rights back East. "Here they didn't do that type of thing. They were behind the times."

Even though it was the Bicentennial era, I said, and the locals were exposed to great numbers of women coming through on the BikeCentennial Trail in skimpy bike shorts?

"But they weren't alone. You were two women alone. It was different from being in a group," Sue said.

"See, we didn't have the freedom then," Robin said.

"It wasn't seen a lot. Maybe in California. Maybe back East. But not in Redmond, Oregon."

"So we were just passing through, looking at the pretty scenery, and we had no idea we had entered a time warp," I said, and an image arose in my mind: Kaye Turner, from the progressive town of Eugene, Oregon, taking a vacation on the nether side of the Cascades, speeding through a time-warped tunnel of ponderosas, alone, in her bright yellow jogging shorts.

"You did. Right," Robin responded.

I asked Robin if she was aware, when she passed by that night, that two women were in the tent.

"I knew there were two people because there were two bikes."

"If you had known we were two women what would you have thought?"

"I would have thought, oh, you're so brave."

"Brave or stupid?"

"Brave. Brave. Really."

"Why? Because something might happen to us?"

"Yeah. I could never see myself doing that. Not with another female."

I wondered if Robin had ever heard rumors that a local named Dirk Duran was a suspect in the Cline Falls attack.

"No. Dirk Duran was an alcoholic. I don't want to say weirdo, because he never was weird when I was around him. But he was just a dumb, drunk cowboy."

"You have trouble imagining him doing something like this?" I asked.

"Well, yeah. I've never seen him so violent. So, yeah, I have problems."

But Robin's husband knew Dirk Duran, she said, and didn't like him because he was violent. Robin's brother, Jimmy, had brought him around the house a few times. Sue remembered him, too. "Oh, yeah. Real arrogant. Snobbish," she recalled.

"For a cowboy, yeah, he was," Robin said.

"Cowboys aren't usually?" I asked.

"No, they're not."

"He was good-looking but, 'I am the Almighty.' He was above everyone," Sue recalled.

Almost on cue, Robin's husband, Leroy, walked in, home from work, covered in mud.

"Come 'ere. Remember those girls hatcheted in Cline Falls that time?"

"Yeah."

"This is one of them."

"Oh, really?"

Leroy had gone to school with Dirk Duran. "I didn't think much of him," he said. "I fought with him. All I know is that he hung around with the drugstore cowboys, and him and I didn't get along. He thought he was tough, but only around his cowboy friends. Otherwise he was timid. He was always strange . . . if he was with his cowboy friends he'd be mouthing off to you, but if he was alone, it was a different story."

Leroy remembered one day when Dirk and a real cowboy got into a pissin' match inside the high school gym.

" 'I've got cow manure on my boots, I'm a cowboy,' said the real cowboy. Of course Dirk showed his boots and there wouldn't be anything on them. People were saying he was 'drugstore.' He hung out with other drugstore cowboys who decided they didn't want to be drugstore cowboys anymore, then they grew their hair long . . . They never did find the guy who did that, did they? I can remember for the longest period of time afterward everyone thought Dirk Duran was the one who did. Really. *Everybody* thought Dirk Duran did it."

But not Leroy's wife, Robin. As this was rumor, I guess I wasn't meant to take that *everybody* literally.

"You remember specifics?" I pumped him.

"Not really. Just that nobody would put it past him. It's just something he would do."

WHAT ABOUT the others mentioned in the police report who saw a suspicious man in a red pickup in Cline Falls on the night of June 22, 1977? If someone could corroborate Robin's memory—*"He wasn't neat, I know that"*—I could eliminate the guy in the red or maroon pickup as the immaculate axe-wielding cowboy I saw.

I wanted to speak to a girl named Dana, who had reported to police that she observed a suspicious character driving a "red newer Chevrolet pickup" who watched her at a swimming hole across Highway 126 from Cline Falls State Park. The police report described him as "about 25 years, maybe a beard, curly dark hair just below the ears, wearing a white T-shirt and blue jeans."

I found Dana's family name in the Redmond phone book and dialed the number. Her father picked up the phone, and I figured I'd plow his own memory of that historic event.

"Send your mind back eighteen years . . . in 1977 two women were chopped up with an axe in Cline Falls State Park. I was one of them . . ." I said to him.

"Okay, let me stop and think a second." I could hear him take a deep breath. "I should shut up, but everyone in Redmond thinks they know who did that and they never proved it, you know," he said.

"Uh-huh." I downplayed my excitement, but I felt my blood starting to move faster. Was a consensus forming around one suspect?

"I even had the kid in school, and he's psycho as a pet goat. And I'm going to leave it at that. But he's the type who'd throw a fit like that. The rumors been all over, they knew who it was but couldn't prove it. Just one of those technical things."

I asked this longtime Redmond resident whether the person he was referring to was perhaps named Dirk Duran.

"Yes. He drove a big black truck all over town. I know nothing but hearsay, nothing but rumors, okay? But he drove a big black truck like you ladies talked about; plus they said the tire marks fit."

They said the tire marks fit. As he didn't say who "they" was, I assumed this matching of the tire marks was another of the rural legends about the Cline Falls attack floating around town, source unknown.

He went on: "And Dirk Duran, if you even talked two words crooked to him, he'd come unglued and throw a fit at school like you won't believe." Dana's father talked so fast I could scarcely keep up.

"Why didn't people in Redmond call the police and demand to know what was happening with the investigation?" I challenged him.

"I have no idea."

"Didn't you fear for your daughter?" A local axe murderer running amok wouldn't have struck fear in every parent, particularly those with daughters?

"Oh, I can't answer that." This struck me as odd; then he quickly segued into: "I was fully under the assumption by rumors that they had investigated him. I was told through rumors that they knew Dirk Duran did it, but they couldn't prove it. His name was mentioned all over the place, but they couldn't prove he did it. That's what I was told . . . but back up." His memory was improving. "We were told the police thought they knew who it was, in fact, it seems like I talked to a detective . . . seems like . . . but it's been so far I can't remember, but I'm sortin' this out in my mind because you surprised me with a phone call . . . Seems to me there was two factors. The police said: 'We know who did it, but we can't prove it because we can't put the evidence together.' Then in another conversation later, I was told that person was Dirk Duran. It wasn't the same person who told me that. It was two different people. You follow what I'm saying? Then I never heard a word since then."

This was the first I'd heard of a thwarted investigation. Which police department thought they knew who it was but couldn't put the evidence together?

Without hesitation, he gave me his daughter's phone number. "Hey, good luck on this, kiddo."

"MY GIRLFRIEND and I went down there to swim, and there was just some guy that was kind of mean or suspicious-looking, and he had that look on his face, and it kind of bugged us enough that we left," Dana told me on the phone.

I asked pointedly: "On the scale of things, do you remember if he was a messy kind of person, or really neat, or something in between?"

"He wasn't neat at all. He seemed to me kind of rough—not rough, I don't know what the word is—not like a biker, but kind of scrungy."

"So you remember him being scrungy," I repeated.

"He wasn't clean-cut but he wasn't the real dirtbag look. It was in-between." She thought she might remember him if she saw a picture.

By all available evidence—two eyewitnesses so far—the guy in the red pickup described in the police report did not match my specific memory.

"Good luck to you," Dana said as I thanked her for helping me reconstruct this unsolved crime. "Lots of anger to resolve, huh?"

The Hatchet-in-the-River Hoax
and Other Rumors

This Adolph Wende seemed to have a great need to talk about the Cline Falls attack. He contacted the police three different times and gave them different stories. First he said he was in the park around 11:30 p.m. the night of the attack with a friend, Richard Sala. He recalled seeing the small tent and observed a red pickup with a white camper parked nearby. Two days after the attack, Adolph called police again and told them that he had been in the park twice, not once. On his second visit, the tent was gone, and the pickup had moved to another location, where "a white male about 27 years old, about 5'11" or 6' tall wearing blue jeans and a white T-shirt was getting into the pickup."

Three days after the attack, Wende reappeared, and "turned into the Redmond police a small collapsible hatchet. Wende reported that he received the item from a Terry Wilson at Mountain Charley's Restaurant in Redmond that day." The crimed report indicated that police bothered to follow up on his lead:

At 12:05 AM 6-26-77 contact was made with Terry Dean Wilson. Wilson confirmed that he had found the hatchet while he was swimming in the river during the afternoon of June 23, 1977. He reported that he was alone diving off the old Highway 126 bridge when he found the hatchet approximately 10 to 15 feet upstream from the bridge. The blade was stained when he found the small axe. He later cleaned it at home with boiling water. The hatchet was later shown to Terri Jentz at the hospital. She was certain the instrument was not the same one she had glimpsed during the assault.

Now, eighteen years later, he'd given the Kounses an entirely different account—in which he claimed he'd witnessed the crime and had seen two perpetrators. As dubious as his veracity was, he was someone who was present in Cline Falls at the crucial moments—and who now, these many years later, was claiming that he had seen *two* attackers, a potentially significant clue.

So on a tip from a cop who told me Adolph had pulled his trailer from La Pine, a village in the pines, to a considerably less sylvan setting in Bend, a tiny trailer park on a sliver of bare dirt just off the commercial strip on Highway 97, I set off to find him. He wasn't home, so I returned the next day. When I identified myself as one of the girls in Cline Falls, the enormous man stuffed into a tiny Airstream trailer with three Airedale dogs boomed at me in a sleepy baritone as though he'd just been napping, "You're *kidding!*"

He didn't seem threatening—redheaded Adolph was handsome in a Teutonic way, with a name that suited him—so I ducked into his crowded Airstream.

"That experience—when you see something like that happen—it kinda ruined my life. Stunted my growth. Did it ruin your life?" he asked, as though, compared with him, I had somehow been on the periphery of the event. "I didn't know who you guys were—all we knew is reading about it later, two girls doing their own thing. We knew you guys were from out of town, from way out of town, and everybody was thinking: these girls rode their bikes that far? . . . But who in their sick mind would run over ladies in a tent, and back up and do it again?"

"Is that what you remember they did? They backed up and did it again?"

"Three times."

I remembered only one time, I thought to myself. But I guess three times made a better story.

"You want to hear something scary?" he inquired.

"What?" I asked gamely.

"I haven't been back there since . . . I haven't been back there since," he repeated, then segued seamlessly to the subject of himself. "I've got this high-pitched ringing in my ears, driving me up a wall," he bellowed, explaining that his skull was housing a nonmalignant tumor that wasn't going to kill him but "my whole life is kind of ruined. I wish the damn thing would just give me a rest." He described every detail of his treatment for this brain tumor and much of his life story as well: how he was married twenty years ago but a drunk driver killed his wife on their first anniversary; how these days he was on disability and couldn't work at his profession of selling sports memorabilia; how he'd put on weight and, believe it or not, he'd once run the Boston Marathon; how he once had a near-death experience during surgery and the angels told him he'd have to come back to earth—and how, no, angels don't have wings.

A big sweaty man and three Airedales packed tightly into a tiny trailer jammed with belongings, and now me, also sweating, meant oxygen was in short supply. Adolph swung open the trailer door. I inhaled and gently coaxed him back to the subject at hand.

"I was up on a ridge, drinking beer with my friend, having a good old time, when we heard ERRRRrrrrrrrr." He made the noise of a peeling vehicle. "And we saw this light. It was a clear evening and you could see down, and we seen this man; everybody says a truck, but it was a dark van."

"You really remember a van, huh?"

"Oh, yeah, 'cause afterwards for years I had massive nightmares. You know I came from a big family in Redmond—there's nine of us—and violence was never a big thing. Everyone says, Adolph, as big as you are—six four and three hundred and fifty pounds—people crap in their pants when they see you walking around. I'm sorry, man. God made me this way. I'm not a violent person. I don't go around beating on people like you think. I haven't fought in years."

I reminded him that, according to his testimony in the police report, he told police he'd seen a red pickup. "You didn't say anything about a van."

Adolph asked to see the document. "If that's the statement I made, I guess that's what I did . . . do you remember what you did on a day seventeen, eighteen years ago?"

"Do you remember a guy named Terry Wilson giving you a hatchet he found in the river?"

"I don't remember . . . see, I didn't think it was a hatchet. I always thought it was a baseball bat."

"It was a hatchet. I saw it. So you don't remember getting a hatchet from Terry Wilson?"

"Nope . . . I didn't do it . . . I hope you don't think I did it! Oh my God, I'm thinking, after eighteen years, she's coming after me! I'm not that kind of person!"

"Not in a million years."

"Where do you live now?" He changed the subject. "And you came all the way up here to talk to me? You gotta be kidding."

I assured him of what he wanted to hear—though others were on my list, he was among the most important.

"That town just shut down," he went on. "They died. That town. There were prayers and hope. Nobody would go down to that park for a long time afterwards. It was really spooky. Spooky stuff."

I led him back to the moment when he was on the ridge, drinking beer with his friend.

"He came from the park entrance," he said, speaking of the assailant. "He stopped for a moment. I don't know what he stopped for. Probably looking around. Jumped the curb, goes over the tent, backs up, then goes over the tent again, then turns around and takes off. One sick individual."

"But there was some time in there when he got out of the truck," I said.

Adolph disagreed with my version of events. "No. He might have got out further back. We were up on the ridge where I could look down on the park. We could see him coming to a certain point, with the lights and all, but there was one section where we didn't know anything. Why? Did they say he came out over by your tent?"

I didn't know what "they" he was referring to. I was present and conscious, and I knew that he got out of the truck. "He had to come out," I said. "He started chopping me up with an axe."

"Ohhhhhhhh. Ohhhhh," Adolph groaned.

"You didn't see that part?"

"I don't want to talk about it," he said almost inaudibly. " 'Cause I know you guys were sleeping. It's funny because after that happened my friend started screamin' and yellin' and throwing beer cans down the ridge. And that's when we heard ERRRRrrrr tearing out of there. You know it's been so long. You can re-member everything because you were there. Sure, I was up on a ridge and seen it, but it takes a lot to refresh my memory."

I grilled him, "So did you see the guy chopping with an axe?"

"I thought it was a baseball bat."

"You did see something then?"

Adolph hung his big red head and mumbled under his breath. "That's some-thing I don't ever talk about."

I prodded him to continue, and he pulled out a piece of paper and drew a di-agram of the crime scene, suddenly happy to continue.

"Okay. Before it pulled forward and run over the tent, he stopped for a long period of time. You could see these big beamer lights from the ridge . . . he comes in and he stopped again, then he just flew right over that curb, big curb—those mothers are monsters—and went toward the tent. BOOM, BOOM, BOOM. Then he went forward again for the third time and that's when he got out here." He was pointing to his map, his tone more subdued. "It's something I just really don't like to talk about. Sorry."

"Please talk about it. It will help me," I egged him on, then realized I sounded ridiculous even to myself.

"I seen a bunch of pounding." Adolph suddenly came forward with new pieces of story, now that I had supplied him with the second part of the murderous equation: the chopping of the occupants.

"There was someone else in the truck. You could see another head."

"Did you see anyone clearly?" I asked.

"I seen one."

"Do you remember him?"

"Yeah. Twenties. Thirties. Scrabbly beard. Dark. Tan. Rude . . . He was just WHAM, WHAM, WHAM. We were up there honking the horns, screaming with our beer cans, 'Hey, you son of bitch!' He heard us. We were loud. My friend had one of those psychedelic horns. That sucker heard us. He chucked it, whatever he had, in the river. That's when he jumped in his rig and burned out of there, and we freaked out. I said to my friend, 'If there's anybody in there, they're dead.' "

"So when you saw that happen, did you think about coming down and seeing what was going on, or did you just leave right then?"

"After throwing up and crying our hearts out?" Adolph let out another big sigh. "We went and reported it to the police. We made some phone calls."

I reminded Adolph that he had told my friends Bob and Dee Dee that he told his sister everything he saw that night.

"Yeah, I don't talk to her anymore. I have another sister I haven't seen in ten years." When I pressed for more information about the sister he talked to that night, he said she was weird and druggy and a "hard one to talk to," but he eventually came up with an address.

"Well, I wish the very best for you," he said as we burst out of the Airstream and into the fresh outdoors. "I just want you to be happy. What you guys went through. You have to thank God for the gift of life. What kind of penalties did you face getting hacked up and run over." A rumination, not a question.

Adolph regarded his environs with disgust. "This place is a dump. I'm getting out of here. They throw their cigarette butts. The older I get, the less excited I get about other people." Adolph was planning to sell his Airstream and head deep into the "tulies" with his dogs.

"These damn trucks are driving me up the wall. If you have a brain tumor and a near-death experience, trust me—fast cars, booze, that doesn't interest me at all."

I headed to my Volvo, and Adolph made me a gift of a football card carefully encased in plastic, featuring some football hero with a neck like a cork. "A rare card," he assured me, and I thanked him.

In my conversation with Adolph, the shame he reported to the Kounses—the shame he'd felt because he hadn't been heroic, the bawling, the sobbing—had never come up.

NOW I WAS the one calling in enthralling updates on the investigation to Bob and Dee Dee in Portland, and they were dispensing advice back to me: "You always want to show up without warning. You don't want them thinking about Cline Falls until you're right there watching and listening." Pretty soon they were in the car and heading my way, to join me on the eastern side of the Cascades.

Sleuthing together for the first time, we arrived unannounced at Adolph's sister's modest home in a hilly neighborhood of Bend, where people were not well off but managed to live a rustic good life. Kathy was as Teutonic as Adolph, hugely tall with long white-blond hair and bangs cut straight across her forehead.

Bob told Kathy right from the start, as he would throughout the investigation, "We're trying to eliminate rumor from fact."

Kathy was dubious about any claims her brother had made. She had no memory of talking to him that night. "I want to hear his story. What was he saying?" she asked in a tone dripping with disbelief.

Dee Dee recounted the story he had told her. "He told a different story to us now than he told police eighteen years ago. But he knew details that weren't common knowledge. That's why we gave some credence to his story. He said he was scared, was ashamed he hadn't acted better, was scared authorities would think it was him."

"He was a troublemaker. He was in prison two years later," Kathy said.

"He told stuff to Terri he didn't tell us; he said he was married and his wife was killed," Dee Dee added.

"Yeah, and he always says Danielle was killed and she wasn't, and he said he has kids and he doesn't."

"Yeah, he told us he had twin kids," Dee Dee said.

Doubtless, the truth was a malleable thing for Adolph.

"He told us he went to his sister's house and sat up all night talking about what he saw."

"It had to be me. We were the only ones that talked. No one else really talked to him. I lived with Mary Ann. We did sit up all night a lot—it'd be Mary Ann's house; she still lives there. Mary Ann would know. She has a great memory. She'd be a fountain of knowledge."

I jotted in my notebook that "Mary Ann" was "a fountain of knowledge" and got details from Kathy on how to find her. At our request, Kathy reached into her memory—which she admitted was full of holes—about the summer of '77.

"Dirk Duran the Hatchet Man!" This rhyming, alliterative name, like the title of some gruesome folk ballad, came crashing through the barriers to the past.

" 'Dirk Duran the Hatchet Man.' That's what we called him from that day on, and we knew he did it and we didn't know why. He was crazy. We didn't hang out with him. We were scared of him." She added, "I think he even showed the hatchet to a few people afterward—serious."

Of the two versions of the rumor—that someone had thrown the hatchet in the river or that Dirk Duran had kept it with him and showed the weapon to his peers—I put another check next to the second one.

"You remember more about that?" I asked.

"I don't. Everything is just bits and pieces from back then." Kathy was exercising synapses that hadn't seen much attention. "Did anybody ever get arrested in connection with that?" she asked. "The cops never had any leads or nothing? Please. We all in Redmond had it figured out, and we were just teenagers."

"But none of you guys ever went to the cops. Everybody must have been scared to death of this. Nobody ever went to the cops and said, 'Have you looked at this guy?' Nobody ever did that, that we know about," Bob said.

There was a long pause.

"I wonder why," Kathy said finally, and Bob speculated that "the kids were all doing drugs and booze and not stepping up to the plate."

Kathy sent us out with good wishes for finding what we were looking for, and assurances that whatever she lacked in memory, Mary Ann would make up for in spades. But I couldn't drink from the fountain of knowledge just yet, as my next move was to find Richard Sala, the boy who accompanied Adolph to Cline Falls on the night of June 22, 1977.

THE WOMAN I was speaking to on the phone could hardly believe it. "Here I am talking to the person in the town ghost story!"

The town ghost story was a grisly little tale of "girls being cut up down at the river. Bill Penhollow and his girlfriend found them. There was a Cline Falls mad guy. A creepy person out in the woods . . ."

And now, in the eyes of the woman I was speaking to, I was the original ghost of her childhood. I suggested to her that I didn't think I was old enough—or dead enough—to be the subject of a ghost story, a figure of myth and legend.

"Are you scarred up?" she asked me. I tried to divine what she might be seeing in her mind's eye: a white vapor with red gashes, a bandage bound around my head and under my jaw?

I happened to find myself talking ghosts with this woman on the phone because I was hunting for Richard Sala. I left word and eventually got a call from an especially soft voice.

Sala's memory was vague about the Cline Falls incident, though he recalled talking to police. He didn't remember whether or not he was cruising Cline Falls with Adolph Wende that night, but he knew for certain he hadn't seen an attack take place.

He hadn't participated in any screaming or yelling or throwing beer cans down from the ridge. He hadn't honked his psychedelic horn, thrown up, or cried his heart out. He hadn't seen anything—let alone two attackers in a dark van.

I asked him if he had ever known a guy named Dirk Duran.

"I remember Dirk Duran. In fact, I still have a scar on my face from a fight I had with that guy. I have a scar on my lip from Dirk Duran," he said with disgust, as though he were amazed that this punk had managed to scarify him for a lifetime. "He was a real violent guy and would always start fights in school. I remember he was a drummer in town. Never really liked the guy. We auditioned Dirk for the band just to tell him we didn't want him. Everyone thought he was a wimp. A crybaby." He told me, with what struck me as fine memory, "He cried a lot."

CLEARLY, IN THE midsummer of 1977, there was a lot of bad news in Redmond. Televisions and radios blared bulletins from faraway New York City, where Son of Sam was on the loose, the lights had blacked out, making the city seethe and burn—and rumors about the Cline Falls incident swirled through this country town, in and out of the shops and restaurants and drive-throughs that lined the two parallel main streets running north and south, from bar stool to bar stool, from bungalow to bungalow; I imagined whispered insinuations in the hallways of the sprawling high school and confided through the party lines connecting the ranch houses on the desert periphery.

The rumors I was hearing were hazy and contradictory. But there was so much intensity behind the innuendos that a local boy named Dirk Duran was involved, I was hooked on finding out whether the source of the smoke was a real fire.

My agenda now was to sort out two versions of the hatchet story: that Dirk Duran threw his hatchet carved with his initials into the river. Or that he kept his weapon and showed it to friends.

I found an Erma Wilson in the Redmond phone book and called her number, hoping she might be the mother of Terry Wilson, the man who, the crime report claimed, had found a hatchet in the Deschutes River. She was, and she did remember the Cline Falls incident. I asked her what she remembered about the hatchet her son found.

"He was down there swimming," she recounted. "He found a hatchet in the river. He came into Redmond and was at Mountain Charley's playing games. He had the hatchet in his hip pocket. It was a little kid's hatchet. Some redheaded guy saw it in his pocket. Then cops came down to talk to Terry and 'bout scared me to death."

I wondered about the toy hatchet Terry Wilson found in the river. Was it a coincidence that a hatchet was found in the river, even a toy, just after an axe attack at that location?

Just after the attack, the police paid a visit to me in my hospital room and displayed a collection of hatchets. "Are you sure it wasn't this one?" they asked, selecting from the sharp tools displayed in a box a tiny one with a plastic handle that looked like a toy. I later read in the *Chicago Daily News* that Lieutenant Lamkin of the Oregon State Police told the press that a hatchet was found in the Deschutes River, but they had figured out it was a hoax.

But word had already gotten around town that a hatchet was found in the river.

I would hazard a guess that Adolph Wende himself had set this rumor loose.

Then the town added on to the story. A number of people must have known that Dirk Duran possessed a hatchet with his initials carved into it. Since "everyone in town" suspected Dirk Duran, they assumed the hatchet found in the river had the initials D.D. on it.

That's how rumors get started. I decided to put to rest the hatchet-in-the-river story.

"FOR SOMEONE to come out in the middle of the night and drive over two girls, when he didn't have any idea who they were, and then in a very personal way take a hatchet to them, it's very, very hard to understand . . . It cries out for resolution. Everyone in Redmond remembers, like the day President Kennedy was shot." Bob was leaning forward in his chair and, accompanied by dramatic hand gestures, was mustering once again his outrage that such a thing as the Cline Falls attack could have happened and remained unsolved.

Former detective Clayton Durr looked just as wary as he did three years before when I interviewed him. Once again his wife sat primly on the couch turning pages of a large women's magazine without saying a word, as her reluctant husband fielded questions from three out-of-towners who had virtually invited themselves into their house to once again run down the former cop's involvement in a case he hadn't solved eighteen years before. Durr recounted in his gruff tenor precisely the same story he had told me three years before.

We asked him if he remembered the name *Dirk Duran* ever coming up in the investigation.

"No, I don't. I don't remember. It could well be, but I don't remember. Up until the time Godwin entered the picture, I had no idea who had done it."

So neither Bob Cooley nor Clayton Durr remembered the name Dirk Duran.

I wanted to know where Durr stood in the hierarchy of the investigation at that time. Durr answered that he and Bob Cooley were both senior troopers, the only officers assigned to the Cline Falls case. They took their orders from a Lieutenant Lamkin, who was in charge of traffic, criminal, and even game violations for the state police.

And Bob Cooley shared with Durr everything he learned about the case?

"Oh, yeah, we worked together on it. But some things he did I wasn't there—they'd pull you off one thing and put you on another, and you do it. It may not have been right, but Bob and I, we covered everything in them days, from a dog-barking complaint to a homicide. Things have changed so bad in the last six years since I retired, I go back to the state police office—I'm walking into another world."

"Cooley said you were busier than hell in that era, with several cases going on," Bob said, feigning sympathy.

"We had Kaye Turner, Mary Jo Templeton . . ."

The Kounses and I knew that the three famous crimes in Central Oregon of that era, which fell in Cooley and Durr's jurisdiction—Cline Falls in '77, the murder of Kaye Turner at the end of '78, and the murder of Mary Jo Templeton in the summer of 1980—were separated by substantial gaps. All three were "motiveless" crimes, attacks by strangers. All had remained unsolved under Cooley and Durr's watch.

Durr's wife dropped her church mouse pose, looked up from her magazine, and piped up, "We're just glad it's all in the past, aren't we, Clay?"

Serious talk wound down, and the Kounses segued into their down-home

Oregon small-town talk. Turned out Bob and Durr had gone to the same high school in Albany (just as, in a peculiar twist, Dee Dee had gone to high school with the other investigator on the Cline Falls case, Bob Cooley). Durr even remembered Bob was a baseball pitcher.

"Was he a good pitcher?" I asked.

"Yeah, he was. As I remember he had a good fastball." In fact, I knew that Bob played pro ball as a teenager and still kept a newspaper clipping saying he was the hardest-throwing pitcher the professional scouts had seen since Hall of Fame pitcher Walter Johnson. I complimented Durr on his superb memory, and Durr seemed to soak in the compliment. "I can remember things. Then sometimes I can't remember," he added quickly.

"WHAT NEXT?" Bob asked enthusiastically. Where next to turn for leads to reconstruct the events of June 22, 1977? I pictured Lureen's long painted fingernails paging through her magical little phone book. That little book, because it belonged to such an orphic source, must surely contain names of people who held the secrets to my past. The high school bus driver, Doris, whose ears had overheard decades of gossip from the mouths of noisy teenagers, gave me special hope. At Doris's place, unlike at most rural homes in the area, a high gate sealed the driveway. I walked to the gate alone. A thick older woman emerged from her house and padded toward me. I expected her to swing open the bars, but she stopped short, requiring me to spin my "do you remember Cline Falls?" patter through the iron. She eyed me suspiciously as I spat out what had generally worked to elicit sympathy, that I happened to be one of those unfortunate girls.

"I don't remember anything!" she barked and showed me her thick back.

We were not cops, we were not engaged in a criminal investigation per se. Rather, we were on a mission to resurrect a moment of time, to tap into an emotional reservoir, to uncover pieces of a larger story. Returning to the scene of the crime to find memory alive, almost a breathing entity in this community, to find that I had an affiliation with strangers in a place where I was, in Lureen's words, "done wrong," and that they shared the weight of memory with me—this discovery was buoying me, was beginning to restore something vital in my core. And the Kounses, after their defeat in Valerie's investigation, were living a little through me.

In light of our reception so far, even this little rejection felt like a deep downer.

"What's next?" Bob asked me flatly.

I pulled out the crime report. No impasse would impede this inquiry. Back to the names on the list. I figured that something might come of just turning up, without warning, on the doorsteps of the people interviewed by police who were in the Cline Falls park that night. I remembered reading about one guy who had seen a green van pass through the park. Boo remembered that Dirk owned a green van at one point.

On 6-25-77 at 1:25 PM Thomas Weaver was interviewed regarding his being in Cline Falls State Park on the evening of 6-22-77. Weaver related that he had a beef with his wife that evening so went to town and had a drink. He then purchased a six pack of beer and drove to Cline Falls State Park in his yellow 1964 Chevrolet. When he arrived at 8:00 PM he parked just east of the pump house, got out of his vehicle and went to the river bank to drink his beer. He observed the girls talking to other people and the tent was not pitched at that time. He observed a blue Ford pickup about middle 1960's parked near the girls. It had a steer on both doors but no canopy. There were also two compact cars there but he could not recall the colors or makes. A metallic green van drove through the park several times.

"What is this guy who's drinking a six-pack after having a beef with his wife going to remember?" Bob asked me cynically. "He's probably a crud."

OUTFITTED IN crisp red-and-white-pinstriped baseball uniforms, a fit, handsome man around forty and his tall young son sat in the tidy living room of their Redmond home on the grids near the center of town. Their eyes were wide, hardly believing the person they found in their living room when they got back from Little League.

Tom Weaver was a solid citizen if there ever was one.

"I'm trying to think back, trying to remember—did they ever find him? I never saw anything in the paper about anyone being apprehended, or anything. It's so bizarre."

Perhaps there was something, a tiny remembrance, that might help me piece together the chronology of events?

No. Nothing. "But I thought about that for a long time—what a terrible thing—I know I mentioned that incident two or three dozen times to people. 'You know, they never caught whoever it was who did that.' It's always given me a creepy, eerie feeling. I've traced it through my mind, somebody out there did this and never got caught."

"Did you ever hear any speculation about who might have done it?" Bob asked.

"No, and I've kind of been aware of that, too. Never heard anyone make even a remark."

I thought to myself, clearly the rumors I'd been hearing around town hadn't penetrated every social strata.

Tom's wife, Deni, spoke up. She had a friendly, upbeat demeanor. "I think it was most people's opinion it was somebody passing through who would do something like that, probably because we didn't want to believe it was someone in our midst." The phone rang and Deni left the room to answer it.

"When something like this happens in your community, it's fundamental to our nature to ask: How could this happen? Who could possibly do a thing like that?" Bob intoned, something I had heard him say again and again, but it was from the heart every single time. "It cries out that this is something that ought to be put to right . . ." Bob went on as Dee Dee and I were trading glances, making signals to leave. Clearly Tom didn't know anything.

Deni reappeared. "In the police report, of all the people who were interviewed, do you have a gentleman in there by the name of Duran?"

"No, coincidentally I don't. Why do you ask?" I tried to sound deadpan.

"The phone call I just received was from a friend of mine. I said to Jean, 'Did you remember what happened in 1977?' She said, 'Yeah, I do.' 'Well, I have one of them in my living room.' Jean said, 'That's really weird,' because her husband, Duane, had been in a Bible study group right after the Cline Falls episode, and in that group was a weird kid, with piercing scary eyes, who made some suspicious remarks."

First Murder in a Little Town

Not ten minutes later, we all listened—the Kounses and I, and the Weaver family, arranged on the sofas in the Weavers' living room—as Duane Francis offered up his piece of the tale.

"I was a disc jockey back then at a local station. I was on the next morning after the attack happened. It was a big deal—it was close to me; it was such a little town. And I was scurrying around trying to get the news," Duane told us. Three details struck me about Duane: his broad smile and huge cowboy belt buckle—both of which looked almost outsize on his lean body—and his earnest, bright eyes.

"I remember how tragic it was," he went on. "Remember seeing a picture in the newspaper, and one of the fathers said he was taking his girl home because it was safer on the streets of Chicago—was that your dad? I never forgot that."

Yep. My dad letting off steam.

"Now that you say that, I remember that," Deni added.

"And I thought, gosh, that's not true. But we didn't blame him. You guys were on a trip, clear across America. It was 1977. I was nineteen or twenty. And I was singing in a group with this kid, and his folks were Catholics and had this Bible study, so I went to that Bible study, and this kid started coming. And he was really kinda mixed up, kinda weird, kinda strange. And we were talking about forgiveness, and he kept making comments. He said, 'Well, some things can't be forgiven.' And I said, 'I don't think that's true,' and he said, 'Well, I've done some things and you've read about them recently in the paper that are unforgivable.' He kept alluding to this thing—and of course, this attack is in all our minds, and we're thinking, my goodness. We didn't really pry, but we kept trying to talk to him, and I said, 'Gosh if you really did this thing, you need to go get this straight, it will haunt you until you die.' Our conversation went on like that—and he came three, four times, and I remember he alluded that the police had been investigating him, too, things like that. Then he stopped coming after that."

"How do you know the police interviewed Dirk Duran?" I pressed Duane, the interview with Durr fresh in my mind.

"All I know is that he said it, at one of the services, he had mentioned that the police were on him, or something like that. He kept saying, 'I've done something really awful and can't be forgiven for what I've done, and you've read about it.' What it reminded me of was someone who really wanted to get caught at something; you've seen kids do that—they do something wrong and they don't want to tell you but they want to give you enough information."

"Did you think, I wonder if he did those girls in Cline Falls?"

"Exactly."

"But nobody called the police," I challenged.

"At the time I don't remember how far after it was—I know it was right on our minds. My personality at the time—if I wasn't convinced it wasn't just a ploy, I would have called the police. That's the way I am. At the time I really thought he was just trying to get attention. We just wrote it off to that end. If he'd been under investigation and if I'd a known it, I'd been thinking, hey, this guy here is confessing this. But I don't remember hearing it again. Never seeing it in the paper . . . In a small town, there was so much speculation. People talk like crazy. We were all concerned about it. The guys at the radio station and I, we sat around and said, how could things like that happen in a town like this? We're going to find out who that guy is, who did that? Was it a transient going through or one of us? Some of the guys were trying to be detectives about it and figure out things. We never saw it in the papers. It was real intense for a couple of weeks. Then nothin'."

Bob lowered his already deep voice, imbuing his statement with urgency. "One of the things that is very weird is this name Duran keeps showing up from some really good sources, but this guy's name never shows up on the police reports," he said. "And the two main investigators of this case claim to know zip about him."

Duane was emphatic. "I *know* this kid said that he was being investigated, that they were on him or something like that, otherwise I wouldn't have remembered it. I don't know why I wouldn't have remembered it if it hadn't happened. I saw him not that long ago, a year or so ago, and the minute I saw him, that incident is what I thought of. The weird thing is I never heard it from anybody that anyone was thinking of him in eighteen years until tonight."

"You remember what the guy you saw looked like?" Duane asked me, and I described the meticulous cowboy torso.

"Oh, man. He was cowboy, too. Used to wear Lee boot-cut jeans, and used to wear country shirts, with the little snaps and all the little preciseness. A cowboy hat."

"Did his boot-cut jeans wrinkle down around his boots?" I asked. That detail, one that Lureen had mentioned, stuck with me, because from the moment I heard it, the image gelled with the memory trying to break through from my past.

"That was the style then. We used to wear Lee boot-cut jeans and they'd be kind of tight and slick and they'd crinkle up around your boots. It was pretty typical. If you were a thirty-four you wore a thirty-six. That's what we did in school back then."

So this detail I half remembered would have fit a lot of boys in Redmond, I thought to myself.

"We've had some tragedies the last few years in our town as it gets bigger," Duane went on. "It's inevitable, I think. But for me that was the biggest that I remember: what happened to our little town. We all, the whole community was devastated. I don't know of anyone that doesn't remember the event. I know no one I've ever talked to over the years who doesn't remember it, unless they didn't live here. I don't know anybody," Duane said, lifting his eyes toward me.

"It was the first murder in a little town," he said.

NEWS SPREAD fast in Redmond. Next day we were invited to the Redmond Chamber of Commerce in the center of town, where Deni Weaver worked. Bob, Dee Dee, Boo, and I arranged ourselves on metal chairs around a circle, as chamber head Linda Swearingen said, "I just talked to someone who talked about this a week ago. It's just like it happened yesterday."

When Deni had come to work that morning she immediately asked Linda what she remembered about the 1977 Cline Falls attack. Linda slapped the table. Only one name came to mind, a kid she'd gone to high school with in Redmond.

Linda said in a bright, confident voice, "Within a couple days of the accident, I remember my brother said, 'You know Dirk Duran did this.' We knew him from school. Nobody cared for him. He was violent. A cowboy. Why would his name keep coming up? Over and over again? For years? He must have told somebody."

"We were sitting there last night in your good friends' home and we're hearing Duane say that he heard something like a confession," Bob interjected.

"And why didn't they say something?" Linda asked in a tone of outrage.

"It's just incredible that all of this information is flowing out here and it never shows up where it could do some good," Bob added.

The Redmond natives tossed around some hasty speculation as to why this might be. The story terrified people. That terror led to a few responses: It was such a heinous crime that no one wanted to finger an innocent guy. Then, too, since it was such a heinous crime, the community assumed the experts were on top of it. How could an average, nonprofessional citizen offer any clues the police didn't already have? Finally, if you did know who did this heinous crime, and you snitched on him, wasn't he likely to come after you?

"I have no problem believing that people are hesitant to do that type of thing," Dee Dee said. "Or kids into drugs wouldn't want to be involved. But I can't understand how it wasn't investigated more thoroughly! And I know it wasn't. Because we've talked to people who were not even questioned, as they should have been."

"I wasn't even questioned," Boo put in. "I picked up all her stuff from the ground and I wasn't even questioned!" Then she added under her breath, "The nurses in the hospital didn't even ask my name." No matter how many times I introduced Boo as the woman who saved my life, she always deflected praise or acknowledgment by saying, "She rescued herself." Or "I don't feel deserving. I thought it was destiny." Now I wondered whether it bothered Boo more than she'd ever let on, the little recognition she got for her courage and generosity of spirit.

The folks at the Redmond chamber had speedily done their own research on the Cline Falls case. That very morning they tracked down the very same black-and-white yearbook photo of Dirk Duran that Boo had shown me, and had been busy with their photocopy machine, enlarging the tiny mug shot bigger and bigger—so big that his face was but a pattern of grainy dots. They were looking, deeper and deeper, closer and closer, searching for evil in his eyes. Could you see, they wondered, the malefic in the pupils of this high school freshman? I studied the enlargements. Yes, the eyes seemed especially beady. But no. I shuddered to imagine what my own yearbook photo would reveal under such scrutiny.

They also spent the morning combing local newspaper clippings from the summer of '77—only to come up with nothing more than I'd found: one tiny article about the Cline Falls attack appeared in *The Redmond Spokesman*, and that article had been stuffed into the bottom quadrant of the page under a story about the Birdman, who lived in his shack by the Deschutes River, upstream from Cline Falls State Park.

"The Birdman got bigger billing than you," said a young woman named Danni, who had not lived in the community in '77 but who, by now, was in the grip of the story.

THE CURIOUS behavior of the teen with the piercing blue eyes present at a Bible study group sometime after the Cline Falls attack needed corroboration. Had others overheard the same oblique confession?

Duane Francis insisted that a man named Tom, son of the Bible study leader, had brought Dirk Duran to the group. In an attempt to cross-check Duane's story, Dee Dee, Bob, and I sat at a table in a Salem restaurant with Tom, a small man with an altar-boy face disturbed by an expression of distress. He looked as though he'd seen a bloody accident on the road just minutes before meeting us. I knew his shock came from the trigger (my call to him the night before) that detonated a buried memory, and that the intervening eighteen years had done nothing to dilute the sickening stab of emotion that surrounded it.

"It was amazing all the emotion that came back . . . After your call last night I started talking to my wife. I was so horrified at the time I heard about it, and last night that same horrified feeling came back. To think that in our community, something like that would happen. And right away there was speculation about who would have done such a thing, and I recall hearing—and I have no idea where that information came from—that there was an axe found in the river with initials *D.D.* carved in it. I don't know whether that was true or not. But Dirk was a person, from my earliest memory, to be avoided, by anyone and everyone. He had a mean streak. When I first moved to Redmond in the fifth grade he tried to pick a fight with me, and somebody said, 'Stay away from that guy,' and I did. He was well known for being in trouble: the joke was, if something went wrong, teachers automatically thought it was him. So it was real early I heard about him.

"So the speculation was, well, yeah, he could have been the person. I wouldn't have had anything to do with the guy, but a friend of mine, we were in a little band together doing some gospel music, and a guy named John knew him well enough to invite him to Bible study. John was trying to get him to straighten out his life at the time. The impression I got from John was that Dirk was trying to figure out the meaning in life, struggling to figure out all kinds of things, and John spent a lot of time talking with him, was busy trying to convert him. So here we had this guy coming into Bible study two, three times, and it felt real creepy and strange to have him there, wondering, not knowing."

I asked Tom if he recalled how long it was after the Cline Falls attack that Dirk Duran attended Bible study.

"It had to be six months to a year and a half after that. It must have been recent enough that everyone was still nervous. We were aware here was a potential suspect and here he was in the living room, and I remember my mom making a comment, 'Gee, should we have this person in our home? I have two young daughters here, yet I don't want to exclude him based on a speculation.' Another lady who led the group—she was a crusty old character, and she said, 'Hey, this is a person who needs help. We don't know what happened.' And as I recall, Dirk sat quietly at the meetings—he was probably terrified—as we were sharing prayer concerns and talking about Bible verses. There was a lot of singing. He just sort of sat there, taking it all in, looking uncomfortable. I can't remember him ever speaking out, other than 'What does that mean?' About something in the Bible."

"Knowing the rumors about Dirk, the hatchet found in the river—were you looking for clues, or behavior to validate those rumors?" I asked.

"Probably in the back of my mind." Tom admitted that he had had a "naïve upbringing." He was shocked that something like Cline Falls could even have happened, let alone that the person who was rumored to have been involved was in the very same room with him. If Dirk had said anything suspicious, Tom was sure it would have stuck with him.

But Tom also admitted he wasn't a person who would ask Dirk any direct questions. He was taught to mind his own business and not delve into what was going on with people. He also remembered that John told him about his conversations with Dirk. Apparently John had asked Dirk about Cline Falls. Dirk had told John he had no idea where he was or what he was doing that night because he was so messed up on drugs. Tom recalled that John believed Dirk was innocent. But he added that John was the sort of person who believed the best about everyone, no matter what. "I have a tendency to be that way myself," he added. "But the older I get, the less I am. I'm not nearly as naïve as I used to be."

Bob let out a knowing laugh.

Tom insisted that he had no direct memory of Dirk making suspicious remarks. Only a memory of talking with John about his conversation with Dirk about Cline Falls.

"Sometimes your mind throws out something so shocking to you," Dee Dee suggested, taking her cue from Tom himself.

But no, Tom insisted he couldn't picture himself blocking his own direct memory of suspicious remarks, while remembering John's conversation with Dirk. And yet John believed the best about Dirk. Tom probably wanted to believe the best about Dirk as well. Did he remember only what fit the patterns in his mind? That people are basically good?

When Bob asked Tom what he remembered generally about the Cline Falls attack, Tom said he'd never known if the two girls had lived or died. And he was haunted by the idea that he didn't know whether there was an investigation or not, or what the result was. Cline Falls State Park was a place where he used to play as a child. But from that time on he never went back. "It cast a dark shadow," he said.

After we left Tom, I found that Dee Dee had read my mind. She said she didn't entirely believe Tom's teen memories either. She felt sure that, as a young man, he had been one of those people who, if they saw, heard, or felt something that outraged their sense of what should be, quickly brushed the thing away, suppressed it, made it disappear. Tom, as a teenager, was a "denier," Dee Dee insisted, of which there was an abundance in the world. Tom didn't do dark. He admitted it himself. But he hadn't filtered out the horror of the attack. Cline Falls had left him deeply affected. That he had allowed the full sensory memory to revisit him felt like grace to me.

I CALLED DUANE FRANCIS and reported to him that I'd met with Tom, who'd remembered Dirk Duran in Bible study but couldn't corroborate Duane's story. I'd also tracked down John. John responded with certainty that he hadn't been the one to invite Duran there: "I can't imagine Dirk Duran going to no Bible study!" he'd exclaimed.

I stated the facts on record so far: Tom said that Dirk had attended Bible study but that he hadn't invited him, John had. John said he hadn't invited Dirk, and that Dirk hadn't even been there. Neither recalled the "confession" described by Duane.

Duane was really "irked." "I told my wife, is it possible I just embellished this over the years and it's grown into something that's not true?" He thought that because he worked at the radio station and he himself spoke the news into a microphone in the early morning of June 23, 1977, and because the event touched him so deeply, he might have been more attuned to a clue. Duane was ripping through memory banks trying to nail down an image to validate his memory. "I can *remember* sitting there. They've got a fireplace. I *remember* their house, and I remember where we were standing, where we were praying for people that night. I just remember it. And I can't obviously go word for word, but I know what I got out of the conversation. He never said, 'I was down in Cline Falls and stabbed those girls,' but to me he made it pretty plain that that was the thing he was talking about."

Duane's honesty—that he would even consider the possibility that he might have embellished his story until it became an untruth—made me trust some kernel of his memory. I guessed that his antennae, a combination of his heart and his mind, plucked out and gave meaning to what seemed insignificant to others. Duane was looking for a design that might explain Cline Falls. I assured him that I would continue to try to corroborate his story. There was truth in the living past, and I would sift through rumor to find it as best I could.

"Okay, kid. Good luck to you."

I CALLED another name listed in the crime report: a Mrs. Gilbert, who had been picnicking in the park next to our tent in Cline Falls the night of June 22, 1977. "You remember the Cline Falls incident where two girls where chopped up with an axe?"

Mrs. Gilbert didn't skip a beat. "You know, it's so funny. Going to work the other morning I was thinking about you girls. It just come to me so clear and I wondered whatever happened."

After eighteen years. *It just come to me so clear.*

It would happen only in a peripatetic culture such as America's, that two girls pedal through a town on bicycles, nearly get murdered, spend a few days in the hospital, then fly away from the community that had grieved for them—never to be seen again.

In traditional societies, primitive societies throughout time, when violence was done, the community would rally around the victim and banish the perpetrator. It was vital to human psychology, vital to the commonwealth, to do so. In the modern era, crimes are considered to be against the state, leaving a deep disconnect between the crime and its effects on the society in which it took place. In my case, when the criminal justice system failed me, at least some members of the community tried to compensate.

I reread the cards and letters I received in the hospital in June 1977. One woman wrote, "I just wanted you to know there are people who care and wish you a rapid recovery." She'd written again, six months later, when I was in the Soviet Union. "I don't expect you to write. I just wanted you to know you are in my thoughts." Somebody else wrote that he felt a "special closeness" to me. "We're sorry we didn't get to know you personally." Though their cards and letters touched me at the time, I didn't feel a part of this Central Oregon community.

Now, eighteen years later, improbably, I had been pulled back into this society. Just as improbably, the umbilical connection that I denied then was still waiting for me. Just that week, one Redmond resident told me, "We would have loved to have known you. There was so much sorrow. It would really have been good for us if we could have seen you."

The Other Woman

Perhaps the seeds of detective work had always resided in me. I devoured Nancy Drew as a girl. What inspired me about tales of the "titian blond" sleuthing for clues in the hidden staircase or in the brass-bound trunk or at the Shadow Ranch: the chapters always ended in an exclamation mark and often in *italics that gave you goosebumps!* Now I was living life in italics. I had been taken over by that bug that settles in your brain and makes you obsessive to uncover some secret or clue or deception, some missing piece of a mystery, concealed and waiting, pressing to be revealed. My investigation had become not only a mission of repair, a quest for justice, but an intellectual mystery I yearned to solve.

Lureen's little phone book finally yielded gold. The name she gave me, through which I might find Janey Firestone, Dirk Duran's girlfriend in '77, led to a trail of names until eventually I received a call back from a high-spirited voice. The sudden, out-of-the-blue appearance of one of the girls attacked in Cline Falls rendered Janey short of breath. We would meet, and she would tell all. But for now, I should know that directly after the Cline Falls attack, she went down into the park, to the crime scene, and found what she was looking for: there in the dirt, she recognized the distinct tire marks of her boyfriend's truck.

I was staying at Boo's ranch when I heard this galvanizing news. I put Boo on the phone. When we hung up with Janey, we were both shaking.

Suddenly, my surroundings exploded with sensory intensity. The fragrance of juniper wafting through the windows lightened my spirits like incense burning in a temple. When I looked at the shimmering green-gold peacocks strutting around the ranch yard, their tails were full of suns.

"*The tire marks fit!*" Janey had told me. "*They were his tire marks!*"

. . .

CLINE FALLS was in a benign mood. On a summer day in May 1995, the desert was coated with deep green and sunlight scattered into sparkles on the Deschutes. Anglers cast their lines for rainbow trout and children splashed joyously in the white water—when a pretty woman with a mane of auburn hair tumbling on her shoulders roared around the curve of the park drive in an immaculate vintage pickup, a 1974 Ford four-wheel-drive model with a long, wide box and shiny chrome grill and trim and hubcaps.

Janey hopped out of her blue rig and announced that it was the *very same model* her old boyfriend Dirk Duran had driven that June of 1977. She happened to own one herself and brought it along for show-and-tell, a good visual prop for the tale she had come to tell.

I'd heard many accounts of the color of a pickup Dirk Duran drove. Folks around these parts kept track of the color of their neighbors' rigs. I'd heard from Bill that it was white and blue. I'd heard elsewhere that it was silver and blue. I'd even heard it was big and black. According to Janey, it looked like this: only Dirk's had two tones of blue, with silver trim.

Janey and I hugged in acknowledgment of our unparalleled connection: we were here to discuss whether we both had been assaulted by the very same young man and whether perhaps he had substituted two girls camping in Cline Falls for revenge against her.

I studied Janey carefully. She was an attractive person with deep violet eyes who exuded an effervescent warmth. I sensed in her an open, passionate nature.

"I hope I can help you link everything together," she said forthrightly, and I flushed with anticipation. Janey's two young boys trotted off to skip stones on the river. As we took our places around a picnic table at the crime scene, she made it clear to us—I was with Boo, Dee Dee, Bob, and the crime reporter from Eugene who broke the story about Godwin and was now following my ongoing investigation—that she was happily married, a good mother, and leading a religious life. She told us tales of her days as a wild young girl, when she cavorted with the likes of a Dirk Duran—but she'd wised up since then.

Janey was a high school sophomore when she started dating Dirk, whom she found irresistible, although his bad-boy reputation was already well known around town. He always looked really good in his Lee jeans, she said, and in long-sleeved cowboy shirts that his mother made for him, and sometimes cowboy hats. He was a really neat and clean type of guy. And he had courtly ways. He had even impressed her parents by asking permission to date her.

But a relentless jealousy surfaced shortly after they began dating. "If we were driving down the road and I looked at a nice-looking car, he'd think I was looking at the guy in the car," she said, insisting that it really was the *car* she was looking at. As a girl who worked alongside her boyfriend in a body shop and knew how to change her own spark plugs, Janey had an eye for a good-looking rig. But if she even glanced sideways at one, Dirk would unleash a fast whack with the back of his hand.

Dirk knew she had dated other guys before him. "He always told me I was a slut. I was fifteen years old when I started dating him, so I kind of believed him. I felt really trashy about myself . . . oh, man," she said, remembering how Dirk's constant derision ground down her self-esteem.

"I could have easily committed suicide if it weren't for my parents. At that time I thought about it. But no way could I do that to my mom and dad."

"What did they think about you going out with him?" Dee Dee asked.

"They didn't know about all the abuse going on. But when they did find out, they hated it. But if they would have said, 'No, you can't be with him,' I'd a went off and married him. So they had to handle it carefully."

Dirk and Janey dated through high school, and at the end of their senior year, May of 1977, they attended the senior prom. Janey laid a large photograph on the table.

And now here he was in Technicolor, as he looked at the time of the Cline Falls attack! My eyes devoured this prom picture, taken in May 1977: he looked like a handsome red-blooded all-American boy, with light blue eyes, a perfect nose, and a crooked mouth that tried a cocky smile that didn't come off as friendly, not quite. His short dark hair was swept forward slightly over the temples and matted down, as though he'd just tipped his cowboy hat. He was wearing a white tuxedo coat with wide lapels, seventies style, rimmed in black, a red ruffled shirt, and a big black bow tie. His black pants fell long over shiny black cowboy boots. He stood just a bit taller than Janey, whose elbow he touched with his right four fingers.

Her auburn hair swept into a bouffant and tied behind in back and a ribbon tight around her neck, a slightly plump Janey smiles brightly and meets the camera with a direct gaze. She wears a lacy red-and-white dress with a lace-up bustier front. Her two hands clasp in an insecure gesture.

The prom couple stands on what looks like a parade float stuffed with white tissue and made to look like a corral, against a backdrop of blue with white stars. The picture looks overwhelmingly red-white-and-blue, stars-and-stripes-forever patriotic. (How does it go? Red for hardiness and valor. White for innocence and purity. Blue for vigilance, perseverance, and justice?) More Fourth of July than high school prom.

Here was my chance to fill in the black hole above the neck of that meticulous cowboy torso: I reached into my memory and tried to imagine whether this young man in the Liberace-type tuxedo was someone I recognized. But no. I could not make that stretch. And because I could not, I trusted myself not to embellish memory. My sharp remembrance of the headless torso remained unadulterated.

I thanked Janey for bringing this photo and silently blessed her for her keen insight that I would want her to bring the past alive with visual aids—first the pickup, now this. She let me keep the photo for myself—her original.

After school was out in late June 1977, Janey had a summer job working in a crew of local kids who hoed and weeded rows of vegetables cultivated for seed on a ranch in the shadow of Smith Rock, near Terrebonne. Janey related that the evening of June 22 the kids had quit work and cooled off in a pond on the ranch. Her boyfriend, Dirk, was there, too.

"It was pretty late because it was starting to get dark and it was summertime. It was really hot. I remember the sun being down—it was still kind of light out— and we were diving off the toolbox on Dirk's pickup, because it was a really deep pond. Gosh, I don't remember where we went then or what we did that night. Fighting was an all-the-time thing, so if we had a fight that day, who knows, we could have, but I know at that point, when he dropped me off, everything was great. Everything seemed hunky-dory. I think he dropped me off at ten-thirty, quarter to eleven. Then of course I didn't see or hear from him until the next day."

At six o'clock the next morning, Janey was driving her car to work and heard on the radio—I could imagine Duane Francis's voice sounding the alarm—that two girls on bicycles had been attacked by a man with a hatchet in Cline Falls.

"I had a sick feeling. This is our little neighborhood. I couldn't believe something like this could happen here. I used to ride my bicycle down there alone." She got to the ranch, and the crew was buzzing with the news.

It was late morning, near lunch hour, when Dirk arrived, wasted on vodka. Janey didn't like the way her boyfriend was behaving, so she slipped into his truck, found the half-empty gallon bottle of vodka, poured it out, and filled it with water up to the same level. While she was removing the bottle from his truck, she noticed that the wooden toolbox in his truck bed was missing, the toolbox the kids had used as a diving board just the evening before. One of the boys ratted on Janey to Dirk about the vodka. Dirk came barreling after her. *"I'm going to kill you, bitch!"*

"He started chasin' after me, and I can't run from somebody if they're chasing me like that. I've got to turn around and face them and take whatever I get, I guess. So he was hitting me and had me down on the ground kicking me, and I remember him over me, hitting me, my head was going back and forth, and he chewed Copenhagen and he was spitting it on me. I remember him kicking me on the side and calling me names. Then I managed to get away from him and tried to kick him in the balls and couldn't reach with my foot, and that just made him madder. Somehow I crawled up and got away from him and I ran around the side of the pond, and I thought, well, I'll dive and swim away from him to the other side—there's people over there and they'd help me. So I did that and he came in after me—and it was in slow motion, swimming, and he's saying, 'I'm going to kill you, bitch!' And I could feel his hand on the back of my neck and my head's under and I thought, it's all over. And I look up and I could see the light filtering through the water."

"People were watching?"

"Everybody was around the side."

"And nobody did anything to help you?"

"There was a little fourteen-year-old girl, and she picked up a big rock and said, 'If you don't let go of her I'm going to hit you in the head with this rock,' and he let go of me and went after her, and that's when the owner of the ranch came, Mr. Shepherd, who was yelling at him and grabbed his arm. And his daughter Linda, who was the foreman, came, too.

"Then Dirk said, 'I just want to talk to you, I just want to talk to you for a minute.' Mr. Shepherd let him because he seemed to have calmed down. He was talking, got mad, and went WHAM. He got me in the nose with his ring."

Janey was giggling a little as she related this last little indignity she suffered, and it occurred to me how odd it was for her to laugh off this particular point in her tale. Then I realized that she reminded me of myself, years before, when I would relate my own story with similar inappropriate affect. It was for her, as it was for me, a distancing technique.

"They put me in a car and drove off," Janey went on. "And Dirk was hanging off the window saying, 'I love you, don't leave me!' He was dragging, and finally he fell off. The cops were there when we got back to the house."

The seed ranch was on or near the border of Deschutes County and Crook County, but Janey was certain that it was officers from the Deschutes County Sheriff's Office who showed up at the ranch, subdued Dirk, took him away in a squad car to Prineville in Crook County, and put him in jail there.

While Dirk was behind bars, it wouldn't leave Janey's head that the toolbox was missing from his pickup, the one she'd noticed was gone when she poured out the vodka. It had been a homemade white wooden box with a slanted top that stretched the width of his truck bed.

"Of course we had heard what happened at Cline Falls that morning on the news. I heard there was a hatchet."

Janey knew Dirk kept a hatchet in his toolbox. It had a wooden handle with his initials carved in it. She remembered seeing that hatchet frequently when she and Dirk would go four-wheeling—he'd use it to cut branches to put under the tires for traction when they'd get stuck.

"You remember distinctly seeing the hatchet in the toolbox?" I asked.

"Oh, yeah, it was definitely in there."

"When you first noticed the box was gone, what did you think?"

"Could he or couldn't he? He was definitely a scary guy and it took nothing to set him off."

"Did you ever see the toolbox again?"

"No. It was gone."

"Did you ask him about it?"

"I think I did. He always had good responses. I might have asked him if he did it, but he was kind of a scary guy, you know." She laughed nervously. "You didn't want to push it too far."

"What else was in the box?"

"Tire chains. Even rope for ropin' cows."

"Did the axe have a sheath?"

"No, it was just in there."

"What did the hatchet look like?"

"It was a small one. Not a great big axe or anything. Had the blade on one side."

I asked Janey to draw the hatchet in my notebook, as she remembered it.

"It had a wood handle. It looked weathered. Not a new wood handle—if we could have gotten together ten years before or if they'd showed it to me at that time I could have told them beyond a shadow of a doubt if it was the same one. Ten years ago I probably could have drawn the Ds on the hatchet exactly how they were, but now I can't even remember exactly where they were at. The thing I do remember is the ends of the Ds kind of tailed—like knife marks going back. I think it was done with a knife, because you know it was kind of choppy lookin'."

She drew two Ds as though they were inscribed with a knife, and explained

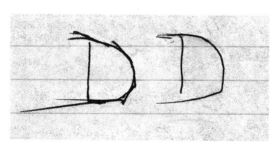

that Dirk carved his initials in everything. He even had his name branded into the back of his belt.

She said she never laid eyes on that hatchet again.

I wanted to get something straight. I told Janey about Lureen, one of the young girls hired to hoe the seed fields, and what Lureen had so vividly remembered: Dirk came running up to Janey in the fields, grabbed her, and said, "Janey, we gotta get outa here. You don't know what I done!"

"No. No. That was not it," Janey insisted. "He was angry at me for dumping out the vodka."

I could see Lureen's designing mind at work. What she had witnessed terrified her: it was of a magnitude that had meaning beyond the ordinary. Her creative memory, conflating violent events, had invented a narrative that explained what she saw. That I was unable to authenticate her precise account of the event didn't matter. What did matter was that some over-the-limit, transgressive energy had made her remember the way he acted: *"I seen the look in his eyes, and it was evil."*

As Janey remembered it, if the Cline Falls attack took place on June 22, Wednesday night, it was the very next day, Thursday, when Dirk beat her up and was hauled off to jail. She thought it must have been Friday when she went down to Cline Falls State Park—it was a place where she and Dirk had spent much time together. There she looked for Dirk's tire tracks. She felt safe because she knew he was behind bars.

"I just had my own suspicions. Because the box and the axe were gone, I just wanted to see. So I came down and saw the tire marks—and they were his tire marks."

We'd known this news already, but everyone at the table went on high alert again. *They were his tire marks!*

"I knew that pickup. It had mismatched tires. They were totally different tires on the front. They were mismatched tires on the front, and they were them. I thought it was so weird that he would keep them on his pickup like that," Janey said, adding that she used to kid Dirk about his mongrel tires.

Janey told us she had a knack for tracking tires like other people tracked footprints. "I've always been a person to read tire tracks. I still do it. 'Oh, gee, who's been up my driveway?' I know people's tires. I just really remember those tire marks."

"That's cute," Boo said. And I thought it was astonishing that such a peculiar talent would lead to providing what could be a key clue in the investigation of this case.

"Do you remember that those tires were standard road tires?" Bob asked.

"Yeah. They weren't real fat. In those days they weren't."

I asked Janey, not out of investigative thoroughness, but out of the zeal of my preoccupations, if she remembered any blood at the crime scene.

"I remember it being muddy like maybe it had been washed down."

"But the tire marks had made deep grooves that were still there?" someone asked.

"There were deep tire marks, yeah," Janey confirmed.

Then she recollected that she and her mother were phoned by the police. She didn't recall which of the three police agencies they had gone to talk to—the Deschutes County Sheriff or Oregon State Police or the Redmond Police Department. Her mother certainly would have remembered everything, but she had died just a couple of years before. Janey remembered sitting at a table telling the police the story she'd just told me. She and her mother were there for a half hour to forty-five minutes. She thought she remembered that two cops were present throughout the interview and others walked in and out.

"We talked about what time he left me that night, and it would have been just the right amount of time for him to arrive down there at Cline Falls to do that."

"And you told them about the tire tracks."

"Yeah."

"And there was no question in your mind those were his tire tracks?"

"No question in my mind at all. I knew then, and I know now. There's no question in my mind now." Janey told us that the police in the room that day didn't get especially excited about the story she was reciting, but she understood that cops tended to give nothing away. She didn't remember whether, at a later time, she and Dirk ever discussed that she had gone to the police with her suspicions.

There was a persistent and unsettling gap here. The state police crime report made no mention of Janey Firestone and her mother giving an interview to the police. It made no mention of the name of Dirk Duran.

Although I had been told on many occasions that the Oregon State Police alone were responsible for investigating the Cline Falls case, officers from the Deschutes County Sheriff and the Redmond Police Department were mentioned in passing in the crime report. Was it possible that the investigation was so inept or corrupt that Janey's information never made it to the investigating agency, the state police?

I asked Janey to describe more specifically the building and the room where she met the police. She remembered it was an old building. She thought it might have been the old state police building in Bend, along Highway 97, which now housed the Department of Motor Vehicles. She felt sure she had not gone to the headquarters of the Redmond police. And she felt sure she hadn't gone to the Deschutes County courthouse in Bend, which housed the sheriff's office. She recalled going through the front entrance of the building, turning to the left, and walking down a hallway. She and her mother entered a big conference room at the end of the hall.

"I remember the table. I remember the room like it was yesterday. I sat there. It was kind of a long table. With some high windows. I remember the light coming through the windows," she said as she sketched the layout of the room in my notebook.

The week following her attack, Janey was scared when she found out that Dirk had been released. But he was laying low. She didn't see him for a long time. At the Deschutes County Fair, in Redmond, the first weekend of August, a posse of Janey's cowboy friends got ahold of Dirk at the Hammer ride. One of the guys knocked him over the fence underneath the Hammer, and they had to stop the ride. The tale was told that the carnival guy came over to break it up, and one of the young cowboys said, "This guy likes to beat up women." The carney guy apparently turned around and went back to his job. Another cowboy clocked Dirk, and he went flying back across the fence, and the Hammer started back up again.

By the next summer, Janey and Dirk crossed paths again, and Dirk sweet-talked Janey into believing he'd changed. "And I had changed, too. I wasn't going to take crap from anybody anymore. So we dated for a while, and I had the upper hand. I could fight back."

Then an episode occurred that gave Janey more insight into the heart of her on-again, off-again beau. They were attending the annual picnic of the Moon Country Snowmobilers Club in the Cascades when they heard about a bad motorcycle accident. They rushed to the scene and found one rider suffering from compound fractures and a girl on the road with her breast scraped off. The sight incited Dirk to scream at the wounded, "Serves you right, you filthy bikers and hippies!"

Janey had witnessed smaller acts of sadism toward others. He'd been mean to his younger sister and his sister's cat and had kicked Janey's dog and forced Janey to watch a cow get slaughtered, an animal that she had developed an affection for. The implications of those acts had never penetrated her awareness completely, until she witnessed firsthand how he took delight in deriding those who suffered. Then she left him for good. But he wouldn't leave her alone. He hounded her after work, lay in wait for her in the parking lot, shouted at her that she was a whore who slept with dogs and the whole football team.

Janey went on to tell us that both Dirk and his sister, Betty, had been adopted. By her account, Dirk confided in Janey that his dad told him his biological mother was a loose woman and that Dirk's adoptive parents had saved Dirk from a life with the likes of his real mother, leading to, Janey insisted, Dirk's obsession with whether or not women were sluts.

I wondered: Could a childhood complex that led to women-hating in adulthood be more textbook than this?

As Janey spoke, my mind drifted back to Robin and Sue Williams limning the geographic boundary line, somewhere at the base of the Cascade Mountains, where the high desert began—a line that divided old-fashioned versus modern attitudes toward women. It probably wasn't a straight line—it meandered around the desert and included some communities and not others—but in some places, women traveling alone were perceived as strong and independent, and in other places, they were perceived as loose. Apparently Cline Falls was situated squarely in the land of Old West attitudes that played hell on women. It resonated in my mind that perhaps Shayna and I took the blade for another shadow woman even further back than Janey.

ONE DAY IN the summer of 1978, Dirk found Janey at work and asked her to smoke pot with him. By that time he'd sold his two-tone blue Ford pickup and was driving a green van. Bewitched by his dangerous charisma again, Janey stepped into the van. Dirk took off for a remote area near the railroad tracks, stripped off her clothing, and threw it on the tracks. He forced her out of the van and drove off. Janey moved all the way to Portland to get away from him and didn't see him again until she was living in Central Oregon in the early eighties and married to her first husband, who happened to be one of Dirk's associates. One day Dirk and his new wife, Ruby, came to visit. When the men had stepped out, Janey noticed bruises on Ruby's arms. At first Ruby told Janey she'd fallen down the stairs, then finally admitted that Dirk had grabbed her. When Dirk came back "that poor girl was petrified, literally sitting there shaking."

"I bet she's got some stories to tell," I suggested, anticipating that one day I might seek her out.

"She was really nice. Pretty. Outgoing. Probably a lot like me. Only blond."

"You're a very warm, alive, appealing person, very attractive," Bob said. "What is it about a guy like Duran that pulls a woman like you?"

"He was very charming. Sweeps you off your feet. Ruby will probably say the same thing when you talk to her. Very sweet, nice words. You'll have a fight, but the making-up part is so good. He can call you all kinds of names, but then turn around and tell you how wonderful you are, and you just go for it. You love it."

Janey asked me if I remembered my assailant wearing a cowboy hat, and I repeated that his face disappeared in darkness. She guessed that's why I couldn't see his face—it was shadowed by a brim. Her point was significant. She had seen him that night: it's likely that he was wearing a hat.

Finally, we all turned to the blue '74 Ford pickup truck—that boxy chrome-laden relic of the seventies, the look-alike of what might have been the offending vehicle. How macabre to see it parked here next to the six-and-a-half-inch curb in Cline Falls State Park.

"Can I get in?" I asked her.

"Yeah! Crawl in it!" she said enthusiastically. Knowing my investigation had a psychological component, she suggested intuitively, "Crawl under it!"

A Deep Breath in a Dark Place

The fragrant juniper barely reached this dark place, which was stuffy and smelled of oil. But I took a deep breath anyway. Then I asked Janey to climb into the cab of the rig.

"Does it seem like that truck is the right height?" she called down, referring to the moment in my story when I surmised, based on the sounds coming from high above, that it was a truck with a high undercarriage, not a car, that had come to a dead stop on my chest. I reconstructed sounds from above, and I guessed that, yes, the linear distance seemed right, if I could say so at a temporal distance of eighteen years.

It was oddly gratifying to lie under this pickup. There were many levels to this bizarre activity. First, this was a reenactment—a ritualized focus on having the power to take a breath under a truck that had held me in bondage. It was a ceremonial replaying of the events of 1977, imposing the present, with its freedom of self-will, upon the helpless past. Then, too, there was a real search for a clue. Based on my memory of sounds, was this the truck I remembered resting on top of me? Black humor was effecting a cure as well. That eighteen years later I was happy to lie underneath this alleged replica of one of the weapons used against me, at the crime scene itself, was plainly funny. But then, I was finding out as I went along that humor of the gallows variety was a vital part of this quest.

I wanted to remain a bit longer, but the ritual was weird, and people were waiting.

As we said goodbye, Janey insisted I talk to her father, and to others as well. I might try to find Linda and Robin, two sisters who had helped her the day Dirk pummeled her at the seed farm. And there was another good friend of both hers and Dirk's. His name was Ken Block and he had had a band that she and Dirk had played in. I should definitely talk to Ken.

Ken Block was the very same bandleader Lureen had mentioned to me. And

Lureen's sketchy account indicated that it seemed possible that this same Ken was helping Dirk erase evidence after the Cline Falls attack, or at least had looked the other way.

No, Janey insisted. Ken was a close friend of hers. She couldn't imagine that he'd have covered up for Dirk.

JANEY'S YOUTHFUL father, Bart, still burned with outrage that Dirk Duran had never been held accountable for his actions. A natural storyteller, Bart spewed tale after tale about his contrary teenage daughter's unfortunate entanglement with the young cowboy. "We'd say, 'Janey, he's mean. He's going to hurt you.' 'Oh, no, he would never hurt me.' She wanted to prove to us that she was right, that she would help him and he would stop doing these things and we were wrong about him. Until she finally proved to herself she couldn't."

Bart distinctly remembered his daughter telling him her suspicions that her boyfriend was responsible for the Cline Falls attack. He remembered her saying, "Dad, he let me off fifteen minutes before the attack." In their view the timeline worked: the Firestones lived four miles from Cline Falls. Dirk himself lived less than three miles from the park.

Bart recalled Janey and her mother talking to the police: he remembered it was the sheriff. I asked him why, of all the local law enforcement agencies, they had brought their suspicions to the Deschutes County Sheriff's Office?

When Dirk beat up Janey on the seed ranch, the Deschutes county sheriff took him to the jail in Prineville, in neighboring Crook County. He was never arrested, charged, or tried for the assault. He was simply detained in the city jail in Prineville. For a long time, Prineville had the only facility in Central Oregon that would jail juveniles. Dirk was kept in jail over a weekend, and Bart remembered that Monday he was released to the boss of Dirk's father, Bob Mackey, a successful rancher who ran a large feedlot operation, one of the more influential citizens in the community at that time. I asked Bart: How did he know that Dirk was released to his dad's boss, and not to his own dad?

"It was one of those things: 'Why did they give him to Mackey? Why wasn't he in his dad's custody?' " Bart and I both wondered the same thing: Had influence been brought to make the police turn away from a more careful look at this kid regarding Cline Falls?

Bart reasoned that because sheriff's deputies picked him up, it was the Deschutes County Sheriff's Office whom Janey's mother called. She wanted Dirk to be officially arrested. The sheriff told Janey's parents to consult their own attorney. When they asked an attorney how Dirk could be held accountable for beating Janey, they learned that if Dirk had killed Janey, he would have been arrested and treated as an adult with the court's permission. But because he had only beaten her up, they couldn't do anything because he was under eighteen. All the Firestones could do was to get the Durans to pay Janey's medical bills. Bart sent

Janey's doctor's bills to Dirk's parents, and he was amazed to find a check from them in the mail two days later.

After Janey told her father about her suspicions regarding Dirk and the Cline Falls attack, Bart phoned a friend who was a deputy in the Search and Rescue Division of the Sheriff's Office. He remembered Deputy Williams telling him, "The police know who did it. They just don't have any evidence." Bart told Williams that Dirk had a toolbox the day before the attack, in which he kept a hatchet, and suddenly after the Cline Falls incident, the toolbox was no longer in his truck. Bart remembered the deputy saying, "Well, that's something for them to look for."

This corroborated something I myself had heard before: a Redmond resident told me he'd heard police say they knew who was responsible for Cline Falls but they couldn't prove it.

Bart also believed it was possible that if Dirk were ever investigated, his father might have offered up an alibi for his son's whereabouts on the night of June 22, 1977. Their attitude was: my son, right or wrong.

"The thought of their little boy being convicted of some hideous murder or attack . . . if they were able somehow, they'd fight it; even if they knew for sure their kid did the deed, they'd try to protect him and keep his name clean, so it doesn't reflect on them. And he can go out and do this stuff, and they'll cover it up, just because they're so ashamed that they would have a son who would do something like that." Bart described a day not long after Dirk attacked Janey when he and his wife paid a visit to Dirk's parents to insist that their son seriously needed help. Dirk's mother said, " 'Oh, no, it's not Dirk. There's nothing wrong with Dirk. It's Janey that's causing all of his problems.' I said, 'Janey isn't doing anything. She went to work in the morning and he drove out and beat her up. How did she cause him to do that?' Dirk's mom would reply, 'Oh, it's not him. She's making him nervous.' "

Bart remembered that Dirk himself would rewrite history in such a way that his own wrongdoings would magically disappear from the record. A few months after the beating, Bart and his wife ran into Dirk at a bar. When Bart told a waitress to throw out this underage boy, Dirk got up and confronted Janey's parents: "I don't know what I've ever done to make you angry with me. Why do you dislike me so much?" Janey's mother said, "Do you want us to show you the pictures of what you did to Janey?" Dirk said, "I never did anything to Janey. I never did that."

Janey went back to Dirk for a while, but finally soured on him for good. Bart remembered the last time she went out with him. She'd gotten off work, and he was sitting in his pickup calling her a whore. When she told him to leave her alone, he slammed his pickup door into the side of her car. Seeing her Firebird convertible with a dent and a smashed mirror, Janey jerked Dirk's pickup door open, grabbed him by the hair, and started smashing him. She scratched him and punched him and broke his lip and blackened his eye.

I thought about Janey with her flashing eyes and sparkly vitality—a girl, I'd learned, who loved thrills and loved to flout authority; who liked to fix her own cars and chew Copenhagen in front of the campus cops; who could throw a punch when she needed to; who defied the conventions of female behavior; a girl who seemed to me to live from passion—this was the type of girl whom the young cowboy chose to degrade.

Bart was stroking two tiny dogs on his lap. "Well, it sounds like you're getting a tremendous amount of information—what I say, and somebody else says—and all these things fit together, and pretty quick the right piece is going to fall in there.

"Every now and then the subject came up with Janey, just in passing: 'I wonder if they'll ever catch Dirk.' And we talked in passing about the toolbox, but over the years I've always kind of wondered what happened, what you went through, and the last we heard was that you were released from the hospital and went back East, and we never really heard anything more at all. When Janey called and said, do you remember Cline Falls, and the girls Dirk worked over, and said that you would like to talk to me . . . it was like, wow, where did this come from? That hole out of the past that you wonder about sometimes." Bart ruminated on the way the news tells you a tragic turning point in people's lives without telling you the end. "The media drops you as soon as you're no longer front-page headlines. There was a teacher in Bend in a bad car accident—hit a wooden guardrail, a splinter went through his chest, into the backseat. Ambulance took him to the hospital. Eighteen operations later he was down to seventy pounds. Never have heard whether he lived or died."

I checked in with Janey later—to ask her to repeat facets of her own story, and to check her father's story against hers. She told me she had had a bizarre dream: "Dirk was in my dreams and he was saying what he used to say when we got back together: 'I didn't do that. People said I did that, but I didn't do that thing in Cline Falls.' It was really weird."

THERE WAS a taint on this investigation. What had happened? Carelessness? Ineptitude? Cover-up? A payoff to local law enforcement so they wouldn't look carefully at a local boy known for hair-trigger violence? Did the police make a deal with him so that they could nail another criminal? The minutiae of what had happened to the police investigation had started to obsess me. Because somewhere underlying the treatment of the case, I suspected an—unconscious perhaps, but operative nonetheless—business-as-usual attitude toward the maiming of women. As long as they didn't wind up dead (and even if they did), couldn't a lot be overlooked? Thinking about it made me grit my teeth and approach the mystery with renewed vehemence.

Janey didn't remember precisely which police agency she had talked to, though she recalled talking to police in a building that seemed like it might have been the old state police headquarters. Janey's father thought he remembered that she and her mother had talked to the Deschutes County Sheriff's Office.

And which agency she talked to was of vital importance. (It added to my confusion, and maybe everyone else's as well, that there were three police agencies hovering around the Cline Falls area at that time.) I had been told that without question, Oregon State Police detectives had been in charge of investigating the Cline Falls case. But the state police crime report made no mention of Dirk Duran, and the two lead investigators, now retired, claimed they didn't remember ever hearing the name.

The two rival branches of law enforcement operating in the vicinity at that time, the Sheriff's Office, the boys in tan uniforms, and the Redmond Police Department, the boys in blue, were both listed in the crime report as having assisted the state police.

If there was no record anywhere of Janey Firestone and her mother telling police about a good suspect in the Cline Falls incident, the following might have happened: Janey talked to one of the police agencies *not* in charge of the case, and they for some reason, intentional or unintentional, had not passed the information to the state police.

But that led to another question: Had some influence been brought to bear that had caused the information to vanish before it even reached the Oregon State Police, who might have investigated it further? Or had the information gotten stuck at one police agency because of rivalry among agencies and no free flow of information? (The bane of crime solving throughout the country is that there are different police jurisdictions city to county to state, and across state lines, and these agencies often don't share crime data, either because of power games or because no channels of communication exist.)

But if Janey's information did get to the state police, either passed on by one of the other agencies or if Janey and her mother had actually talked to them directly, why had records of that meeting disappeared entirely?

I SET OUT to find the former deputy who had headed up the Search and Rescue Division for the Deschutes County Sheriff's Office. In the seventies, he was the man who had allegedly told Janey's father, "We know who did it. But we don't have enough evidence."

"I was the one involved in that Cline Falls incident," I said over the phone to Chris Williams, now retired and living in Alaska. I expected that the mere uttering of the place name would bring forth neon memories from him, but he didn't remember anything at all.

Two girls on bicycles? A guy in a pickup running over a tent? Chopping with an axe?

"Nope."

I said that his old friend Bart Firestone remembered discussing the case with him.

"He was probably right. It might have slipped my memory."

What the ex-cop did remember from his police work in that era was the chilly atmosphere that existed between the Oregon State Police and the Sheriff's Office. "We did some cooperative work with the state police—but the state was hard to work with. They were prima donnas. Thought they could do it and nobody else could. Management was the problem in those days. The guys in the field we could work with real good. But Lieutenant Lamkin was political hierarchy tied in with Salem. I won't say we had bad ties with him, but there was a lot of politics between him and the Sheriff's Office. We were able to do our job, but sometimes we had to be a little stern about it," he said, and continued to comb his past for any relevant detail. "There must be something that would spark my memory, but what that is I don't know."

"A white toolbox?" I suggested.

No. Nothing there.

I DROVE NORTH of Redmond, behind Cinder Butte, the long-dead core of a volcano, now a heap of red scoria, a powder that at one time was used to build the gorgeous red two-lane roads that crisscrossed Central Oregon. I remembered the red roads from my bike trip in '77, and I loved the idea that Oregonians used the guts of dead volcanoes to build their roads. But those red highways were history now. They didn't hold up and Oregon began to use that same bituminous black stuff everyone else made highways with.

After I'd studied the Cline Falls crime report even more thoroughly, I noted a detail I'd not given much consideration earlier. Two deputies from the Deschutes County Sheriff's Office were the first officers to arrive at the Cline Falls crime scene in 1977, before the case was assigned to the Oregon State Police.

I found former deputy sheriff Leonard Kirby's bungalow, and laid out the odd anomalies of the case to a big man in a wheelchair. But he had no memory of Sheriff's Office deputies arresting a young man who beat his girlfriend the day after Cline Falls. And he didn't know which deputies might have hauled the boy off to jail. He had no memory of a meeting with a teen girl, Janey Firestone, and her mother, in which they laid out reasons the young man might have been involved in the Cline Falls attack.

"If any evidence came into the sheriff, it would have been turned over to the state police," Kirby insisted, yet acknowledged there was indeed tension between the two police agencies at the time.

I asked Kirby if he'd visited the old state police building often enough to remember what it looked like inside. He drew me a layout. "You go in the front door that's facing Highway 97. You come down the hallway here, and there was a conference room and a big table."

I asked him if there would have been windows in that room.

"A lot of windows."

I showed him the layout Janey had drawn me of the building where she remembered telling police of her suspicions about her boyfriend's involvement in Cline Falls.

"She's got it the wrong way," Kirby said, and put the finishing touches on his own layout of the former state police building.

It was the exact mirror image of the map Janey had drawn. As Kirby drew it, you enter the building from Highway 97 and turn to the right: a big conference room is situated at the end of the hall.

The spotlight had been moving around the stage, but now it focused again on the Oregon State Police.

CORPORAL RICHARD LITTLE of the Redmond Police Department was a cop who seemed to enjoy amassing archives of information about members of his community, collected from over two decades of service. Little had a round genial face and wore his red hair in a comb-over. He greeted Bob, Dee Dee, and me in the humble police headquarters in downtown Redmond. He was the Redmond policeman who had first dared tell Bob and Dee Dee that their department had always suspected a local kid named Dirk Duran in connection with Cline Falls—a case that had always "haunted" him—and now he was going to tell us why.

He remembered Dirk's name surfacing as a suspect, and he remembered talk that there was not enough evidence to indict him. But only the investigating agency of record, the Oregon State Police, would have been able to determine that. "If we got information, we passed it on to them. What they did with it—it'd be up to them."

He did think it was exceedingly peculiar that a high-profile case like the Cline Falls attack (which took place just after the Bicentennial year, when loads of people from out of town were passing through, and which attracted national media attention) was documented in an investigative file as puny and paltry as the file we had before us.

Little remembered Dirk well. He remembered that he drove a high-rider four-by-four pickup, two-tone blue in color. The pickup was Dirk's pride and joy. "Dirk was the type of guy . . . one minute he was a tough guy, and the next minute he was a crier."

"He was a crier?" I asked.

"Oh, yes. Oh, when you arrest him: 'I didn't mean to do that.' But up until that time he's having a hell of a good time."

Little picked through a primitive-looking index card file in a small metal box, hunting for any record of arrests our suspect might have racked up over the years, but he turned up nothing. Duran hadn't lived in the area for a while, and Little wasn't sure why, but apparently any old file cards with his name on them weren't in the box anymore.

But Little did have a good memory of an incident that should have been on record somewhere: In the spring of 1979, he was involved in an undercover drug surveillance. One night he pulled his police car up to a residence where a party was taking place and he observed the resident, another local bad actor named Chris Peterson, wielding a loaded shotgun outside his house. Little arrested Peterson for furnishing alcoholic beverages to minors.

"And Chris was wanting to do a deal, and he came to me and said, 'Hey, I know who did the crime down at Cline Falls.' I said, 'Okay, that's out of my jurisdiction; the state police is handling that, so I'll get the appropriate people.' Which was at that time Cooley and Durr. Durr wasn't available, so Cooley came and we met up with Chris and had Chris take us to Cline Falls. We had Chris direct us; we didn't say nothing to him. And we had Chris point out the camp area. We said, 'You tell us what occurred.' We went down to the grassy area toward the river— can't remember if there was a fire pit or not. Then he said the truck—he used the word *truck*—came down and came over . . . What did he say then? Anyway, the assault occurred, the truck took off, and it was Dirk Duran."

Little said he remembered Peterson mentioning something about Dirk being angry at his girlfriend or some other girl, and he remembered Bob Cooley taking notes on the interview.

We told Little that no mention of Dirk Duran as a suspect had made it into the crime report, and former detective Bob Cooley had no memory of Dirk's name. Little promised he'd check his police notebooks for the specific notation of that meeting.

"Everyone says, 'Yeah it was Dirk.' But because they say something, doesn't mean it occurred. And you know probably in your heart it's true that possibly Dirk did do it. But you try to put the physical with the circumstantial, and you can't quite do it."

Bob queried him, "Was Dirk a suspect in this in the beginning?"

"If he was a suspect from the beginning I don't know. But I know his name came up more than one time prior to Peterson trying to make a deal."

If we wanted to talk to Peterson, we'd find him in the pen. Corporal Little took credit for putting him there. Little spun tale after tale about the felon he referred to as a sexual sadist. For years he'd been pursuing him—Peterson was apparently Little's career nemesis—and had finally gotten him put away for raping his girlfriend.

THE DATA-GATHERING on my suspect was unearthing a list of villainies: we knew, at least, he beat his girlfriends, laughed at the injured, was cruel to animals, and denied his misdeeds with a straight face. Even without accusing him of the attack on Shayna and me, a dark portrait was emerging. It raised the question: What were his early brushes with the law? I headed to the somber black-lava-rock Deschutes County courthouse in downtown Bend and rifled through a primitive card catalogue in the Records Department. I unearthed just a single record of malfeasance: in 1989 the suspect was convicted of "criminal mischief in the first degree" for breaking the windshield of a car owned by a woman named Marie, "against the peace and dignity of the State of Oregon."

With that, I dropped in on the Deschutes County district attorney, Mike Dugan, and found him just as willing to meet me without an appointment as the last time I came knocking. I told the affable Dugan that I'd worked up a suspect on the 1977 Cline Falls case, and I laid out my evolving investigation. Dugan obligingly called up Duran's "rap sheet" on a computer and had a look himself. In Oregon, as in most states, criminal histories—the master list of arrests and adjudication of the charges—were kept from the public based on the presumption that a full disclosure of misdeeds would invade the miscreant's privacy. (Individual court records were public, if you were willing to visit every county where a criminal had perpetrated a crime. But court records were often not well organized or complete.) Dugan scanned the file and read off to me a 1987 charge of "assault in the fourth degree" on Duran's wife (a record that I should have found in the court records department, though clearly it was missing) along with a series of "driving while suspended" and "driving under the influence" charges dating back to 1979. That was the sum total of Duran's criminal record in Oregon—and the 1989 "criminal mischief" charge was the last entry. Dugan admitted that he was familiar with my suspect, having acted as his court-appointed defense attorney earlier in his career, and he knew him as a wife beater. He couldn't make it fit that Duran had been implicated in an attempted double axe murder.

"Forget about Dirk Duran," Dugan said to me cordially, and sent me out the door with a reminder that it was a non-prosecutable case anyway, but that he'd be happy to tell a local crime reporter about the old case so that it might get solved.

By now I had fully comprehended that it was a non-prosecutable crime because the statute of limitations on attempted murder ran out after three years. I could have wound up a head and torso with no arms and legs—but after June 22, 1980, as long as I was a living, breathing head and torso with no arms and legs, the perpetrator could have shouted to the rooftops "I did it!" and he still would have remained a free man.

Dugan's well-meaning response reminded me of the people whom I interviewed who invariably wanted me to get the media to solve my crime. "Why don't you call *Unsolved Mysteries? America's Most Wanted?*" they'd ask me. No way, I always said. I couldn't allow my internal processes to become fodder for the endless pursuit of lurid stories to fill endlessly multiplying channels. It was okay that the patriarch of the airwaves in quaint 1977 had made mention of the attack on the *CBS Evening News*. His was an antique version of the modern media tempest, way before carnivals of mobile units camped out on lawns wherever an outbreak of depravity rippled American society's bland surfaces. This investigation was more than a crime-fighting exercise: it was a voyage of discovery, a ritual of imposing the present on the past to regain my will, an odyssey to find the truth of the living past. Since it was a non-prosecutable crime, the quest for the heart of my story was mine to do with as I wished.

Bibles, Blades, and Blood

It was firmly believed by all ancients, that some malignant
influence darted from the eyes of envious or angry persons,
and so infected the air as to penetrate and corrupt the
bodies of both living creatures and inanimate objects.

—FREDERICK THOMAS ELWORTHY, *THE EVIL EYE*, 1892

I couldn't fit the pieces together: the
Cline Falls story had been told in banner headlines in big-city newspapers, broadcast by Walter Cronkite himself. The state of Oregon had been stunned. The local Deschutes County had been "devastated." And in the small community of Redmond, Oregon, a seventeen-year-old boy had beaten and tried to drown his girlfriend in front of witnesses allegedly the very next day after the assault on two girls in a nearby park. *In his toolbox he kept a hatchet with his initials D.D. carved on it. The next day the toolbox was missing!* While he was in jail, this girlfriend went to the park and recognized the tread of her boyfriend's tires. *They were his tire marks!* In an area where homicide was nearly nonexistent, why hadn't police investigators paid attention to a possible link?

It was the late spring of 1995, and I'd been in Central Oregon for several weeks. By now I was possessed by no less than a mania to re-create the story of what happened that night of June 22, 1977. As I was undergoing my metamorphosis into a private eye, I developed my own quirky technique to strengthen my exploratory powers. I believed that if I could keep the past alive in myself, I might better evoke remembrance in others, so I made myself into a time machine, performing rituals for reviving memory. I lay on my bed in a darkened room and submerged myself in the past—sometimes with a 1970s Fleetwood Mac CD playing as a trigger—until my heart beat fast and I summoned what flashes of that night would return.

Then, as I got into my car and set off, I tried to hold the memory stable, certain that if it were present in the air, it would attract and retrieve those lost fragments of the past alive in others. I put fear aside and, fueled by "lava javas"—triple shots of espresso from the kiosk in the gas station parking lot—I drove, alone or with my team of crime-solvers, Bob and Dee Dee, or Boo, depending on who was available. I didn't know where my next revelation was coming from, but I was sure the story was alive somewhere, fresh and green—maybe behind the next stand of junipers, behind a cinder cone, under the shadow of a red rock, at the end of a rutted driveway, maybe beyond the fence surrounding that double-wide trailer, where a Rottweiler strained at its chain. I would dawdle in the car and suss out the energy of the place. Cats on porches were good omens, and contrary to expectations, a museum of vehicles rusting in the yard did not mean a brusque send-off. I would ring the bell almost always unannounced, as I didn't want to dilute memory with a warning, or allow people to compare stories with one another. When the door opened I had but a moment to state my case. "This is kind of strange . . ." I would say right off, or "I was one of those girls in Cline Falls . . ." or "Think back to 1977, when two girls were attacked by the river . . ." Variations on the theme. But the principle was: Cut to the quick. Rope them in with the story. I was a stranger on the doorstep, with no more status than someone hawking religion or politics or widgets or a scam. Does anybody show up unannounced on a doorstep anymore? Even in small-town America?

I noticed a pattern emerging. Their first images arose spontaneously, inspired by the shock of my unexpected presence. They would tell me, "All I can remember is . . ." until they came to an apparent end, and a "Sorry I can't help more." Then the barriers to the past tore open, and more traces spilled out. Some memories were held back consciously—they didn't trust me yet, or they didn't think it appropriate to tell some long-held, charged secret. Some were held back unconsciously—too brutal to bear? If I stayed long enough, usually both the consciously and unconsciously withheld would spring forth.

I composed lists in my notebook: names in the crime report, cops, my suspect's childhood friends, his bosses, coworkers, neighbors, former teachers. I had ambitions to get to each one eventually. I arranged the list around certain themes: the guys at band practice who may or may not have helped Dirk Duran cover up a crime; buddies to whom he might have told something; those in the community who observed his behavior; those who were present at the seed ranch when he attacked Janey; others in the Bible study group.

One friend counseled me, "Who would have thought to run over girls in a tent? It takes *crazy guts* to do that. It's *crazy guts* you have to look for. Sense it with your instincts."

FOLLOWING UP on Janey Firestone's leads, Boo and I set out to find two sisters, Linda and Robin, who tried to rescue Janey from Dirk's rage in the seed fields in Terrebonne, allegedly the day after the Cline Falls incident.

"The saddest thing about this whole thing is, I thought you guys died. Isn't that terrible? I always thought you were killed. And I don't know why. After you guys left the area, everything was left unsaid," Robin told me on the phone from

Idaho. She had a quality of extraordinary openness that made the phone like an intimate room.

"It was so shocking. It was such a small town. I was pretty young at the time. Thirteen or fourteen." She told the story just as Janey had. She was among the kids who worked the seed fields. Dirk arrived in the middle of the day, high on a cocktail of vodka and Valium, then suddenly started beating Janey. He had her on the ground by the pond, kicking her in the head. Robin and her sister Linda were the smallest kids there, and while the others, including all the boys, stood by in terror, the two girls picked up sticks and climbed barefoot over a barbed-wire fence to rescue Janey.

"And I was halfway up that fence in my bare feet and I remember, he was probably twenty-five feet from the fence, down on the ground, and he was kicking her, and she was just down there in a ball, trying to keep him from kicking her anymore in the head, and I just remember thinking he was going to kill her." I could hear Robin, out of breath, swallowing on the phone.

"And he looked at me and Linda with *the coldest, weirdest eyes* I've ever seen and—I'll never forget it—he said, 'If you come over that fence, *I will kill you.*' And we both stopped. He meant it, you know. He looked at us and said that, and we froze and got back down."

"Was he trying to hit her on the head?"

"He was kicking her in the head."

"He was aiming for the head specifically?"

"Yeah! Oh, yeah, I remember seeing her elbows over her head."

I could hear Robin swallow again, breathless, as though she were relating an event happening before her eyes. Janey got away from Dirk, but he kept grabbing her by the hair and throwing her down, until he threw her in the water, held a rock above her head, and tried to drown her. Then Linda Shepherd, the field boss, showed up with a gun.

"We were all so scared. Everyone was scared for their lives at that point—and somehow they got Janey in this great big brown car. They got the doors locked, and Dirk was freaking out; he's jumping on the car. My sister Linda had this little Vega hatchback, and we opened up the back of it and all the kids that could fit piled in the car—in the backseat, in the hatchback, in the front, and then there were kids on top of it, holding on up by the windshield, to get out of there."

"To get away from him?"

"Yes. And I remember the brown car taking off, and Janey was in it. And the window was rolled up four inches, and Dirk was hanging on the side of that car as they took off, with his feet curled up, holding on that window, just trying to keep her from going. Linda took off so fast—I remember rocks flying, and she was spinning out, to take off out of there. And Dirk fell off. Dirk got in his truck then and chased us. They got us to the ranch house. And he chased us there. He took the distributor wires off some of the cars so that no one could leave. Then the cops got there. I remember we were all inside the house and Dirk was pacing around outside the house. The cops evidently knew he was on drugs. They didn't try to physically take him. I remember them trying to work with him, walking around, trying to talk with him. It was like he was crazy. I don't remember them ever getting physical with him to take him away. I don't remember them throwing him down, putting handcuffs on him or anything like that. Seemed like we were out there in that house a very long time. Everybody was in such a frantic state. The kids. You know, I just remember us all . . . when I look back on it . . . To see something that frightening and to be so afraid of someone."

A picture of one young girl arose in my mind: Lureen ("*I seen the look in his eyes and it was evil . . .*").

"Do you think he would have killed her had nobody intervened?" I asked.

"Ohhhh, yeah. Ohh, yeah. He had all the intention in the world of killing her. He was kicking her in the head, he had her in the water and was trying to drown her, and had a rock in his hand and was going to hit her in the head."

"What shape was Janey in at this point?"

"Oh my God. She was black and blue and swollen. Her eyes. Her face. She had marks everywhere. She had black eyes for a long time. Then Janey started saying things about the toolbox and axe and stuff. The only facts I had were the things that happened that day out in the field. The only other thing I know is what Janey told us. The story that I remember is that he came to her house that night that happened to you guys, and she thought he was on something, and that's where the Valium thing came up again. Because I didn't know people took drugs like that—I think that was a real shock to me, so it stuck in my mind. That he would take stuff like that. That he was upset and really acting weird."

"The night of my attack?"

"Yeah. That he came to her house in the middle of the night. Or late that night."

"You remember Janey telling you this?"

"Uh-huh. Now this is probably what she would have told us. That he came there. And was acting really strange and weird and they got in a fight. What time did the attack happen?"

"About eleven-thirty," I said.

"So he had plenty of time to go to Janey's after that. I remember her saying he was there really late."

I told Robin that Janey had related to me that Dirk had dropped her off at home around eleven, quarter past eleven.

"But he never came back?"

"She never told me that. Is that what you remember?"

"I remember her saying that. Did she say he was acting weird?" Robin paused, then got insistent. "*I remember her saying* he was on drugs that night. That's why I thought he went over there afterward. He stopped by and wanted to fight with her . . . But maybe that's all a memory. And it seemed like I was so young then."

"You said he was doing other weird things after that incident?"

"Yeah! Yeah. The main things that sticks in my mind was with his damn truck, trying to run over people or trying to run people off the road, groups of kids in cars. It was always the kids who were there when he beat up Janey. He tried to run Linda off the road. Like he was mad at all of us. Then of course word got around that he did this. Then he kind of ran scared. He didn't hang out in town anymore because there were guys looking for him, looking to get ahold of him. Then Dirk kind of disappeared for a while. He didn't dare pull into the local parking lot and try to talk to people."

He disappeared for a while: that's what Lureen had remembered.

"Then the next thing I knew, he had found a religion and was all saved. That he had found God and was a new person, and everything was fine. He was all healed. That's all I remember."

I thanked Robin for her astonishing memory—her almost total recall of sight and sound and emotion that took place when she was a girl—and she said she was sorry she couldn't remember more.

"The main thing I remember is him threatening us out there—saying I will kill you—and I remember *really* believing him. If I didn't I would never have backed down. Ever. If I didn't believe that he was going to kill me, I would have kept going. Because I was *determined* to help her. That's why I believed him. And in my mind all these years that whole part went through my mind, how true I thought that was."

I was profoundly impressed by Robin's and her sister Linda's courage. These girls, the tiniest kids there, had been determined to save their friend, and had only stopped because the stakes were death.

The intensity of the scene as Lureen had described it was matched by the vividness of Robin's memory: the surreal unexpectedness of the danger; kids grasping onto the car to escape from Dirk after witnessing this spectacle of malevolence, a spastic rage to the tune of murder.

Janey remembered seeing light filtering through the water as Dirk held her head, a long time, under the surface of the pond. She was describing nothing short of death by drowning, an intimate form of killing.

He specifically hit Janey's head. I imagined her thrashing from side to side, "elbows over her head," to avoid the blows, just as I had done the night before. Had the cowboy's euphoria of wrath simmered overnight only to erupt again the next day?

Janey had described to me the photos the police took of her just after Dirk beat her up. She was bloody, filthy. With black eyes. I asked her to try to find those photos for me. I wondered if she and I looked similar on June 23, 1977.

· · ·

TO CLEAR UP this matter of what went on with the guys at band practice, Boo and I went in search of Ken Block, friend of Janey and Dirk at the time of the Cline Falls incident, the guy who held band practice at his house, the guy both Janey and Lureen had directed me to talk to. We drove past a line of tiny bungalows in Redmond and stopped at one even tinier than the rest, surrounded by a sculpture garden of junk and several children playing in the yard. A sturdy sweet-faced man built close to the ground, with a mop of curly red hair, came out to greet us.

Did he remember anything about suspicions that Dirk Duran was involved in that Cline Falls attack?

Ken looked blank. He said he was really sorry but he didn't remember anything at all.

Did he remember Janey telling him about how Dirk had a toolbox containing a hatchet, and the toolbox was missing the day after the Cline Falls attack, and Janey went down into the park and thought she recognized Dirk's truck's tire marks?

No, he didn't remember.

Didn't he used to have a band, and Dirk Duran showed up for band practice a week after the Cline Falls incident, and because he had blood on him there was some suspicion that he was connected to the Cline Falls attack, but maybe he made some excuse about chopping coyotes?

No, he didn't remember that either. It seemed that Ken had been in a fugue state eighteen years before. He said he was really sorry he couldn't help us. I studied his face and, indeed, it embodied blankness. If he was acting, he possessed talent.

BUT I would not lose heart. I remembered jotting in my notebook a reminder to look for a Mary Ann, who was, according to Adolph's sister, a veritable "fountain of knowledge" about the past. After my experience with Ken, I needed such a breakthrough.

In a tiny bungalow in the center of town, through a door hung with orange beads, we found Mary Ann, a small redhead in a flared miniskirt, who delivered on her reputation only in the sense that she delivered a fountain of words in a high-speed patter, punctuated by manic laughter, about her personal history as a tour singer who imitated everyone from Patsy Cline to Janis Joplin.

"Can you sing us a few bars?" I expected her to decline. Instead she opened her mouth and belted, *"Oh, Lorrrd, won't you buy me a Mercedes-Benz . . ."*

The hair on my arms stood straight up. Janis was in the room.

"That's killer!" Boo said—*killer* being her version of *cool* or *awesome*, and which, like her nickname Boo, I found ironic given the history she shared with me.

More to the point, back in the late seventies, Mary Ann had had a band—a different band from the one Lureen had performed in—and Dirk Duran had auditioned to be a drummer. He was driving a van at the time.

"I really don't know Dirk Duran personally. He came in like he was God. We went to help him unload his van of the drums. And hanging there is this hatchet with a really awesome hand-braided strap." Mary Ann let out a gallows-humor type of laugh.

"It's got its own hook on the wall inside of the van—like, who has a braided strap on a hatchet, for God's sake?" Mary Ann said that the axe handle looked like a billy club and was designed so that you could stick your wrist through the strap and swing.

"Anybody that could go that far on an axe was beyond me." When she looked in the van, she thought she remembered seeing other regular axes, as well as one double-ended axe sheath sitting empty.

"It scared me. I just felt horrible all of the sudden. I wouldn't stay in the garage with him. It spooked the shit out of me."

Mary Ann said that people talked about Dirk Duran for years after the Cline Falls incident. "It got so bad that teenagers who would have been just little kids when Cline Falls happened knew the name Dirk Duran."

JANEY FIRESTONE'S younger brother, Curt, lived in a trailer just down the highway from his big sister. Curt was a trim man with Janey's violet blue eyes, but his fastidiously blow-dried hair and careful, considered manner of speaking gave him a sober demeanor compared with that of his effervescent sister. Curt told me he was too young to remember much about Cline Falls, except that it seemed like Janey and Dirk had "had a falling out before the Cline Falls incident." And he did remember hearing Janey talking about Dirk's axe.

Curt had seen the axe himself, which he described as a tool with a short handle and a head with two blades on it. Curt and Dirk were out in a four-wheel-drive one day and got stuck. Curt used the double-blade axe to cut tree limbs to put under the tires to get the rig out of the sand.

"So you remember this axe as having blades on both sides?"

"Oh, yeah, because I was real impressed. That was the kind of axe I wanted. My dad had a double-blade axe he used in his wood splitting. This one was just like dad's except it had a short handle so I could use it."

I told Curt that I'd heard that Dirk had a D.D. carved into the handle of the axe.

"This D.D. wasn't carved. It was stamped, like with a metal stamp."

"Did he happen to keep that double-blade axe in the toolbox?" I asked.

"Yeah . . . Isn't it funny?" he said, referring to his elder sister's story that she knew Dirk kept an axe in his toolbox.

Curt heard more from Dirk himself about Dirk's association with Cline Falls—on two separate occasions. Once, years later, Curt was jamming at a bar in Redmond. Dirk happened to show up, and he sat in on Curt's drum set.

"He just brought it up—something to the effect of: 'You know a lot of people think I was involved in that Cline Falls incident, axing those girls, but I didn't do it. I wasn't there.' It was just out of the blue. Later, in a bar, it was basically the same thing. This would have been several months later."

"He brought it up again out of the clear blue sky?" I asked. Folks in Central Oregon were always describing things as happening "out of the clear blue sky," and I had gotten into the habit myself: it didn't seem like a cliché here in this land of eternally blue, cloudless skies. One had only to glance overhead.

"Yeah, so I don't know if he was trying to convince me or himself about that." Curt asked me if I'd talked to a guy named Ken Block.

Oh, no. Not Ken Block again. The redheaded guy with the nonexistent memory. Indeed I had talked to Ken. "What do you think Ken would know?" I asked.

"I don't know. Because he was pretty wild at that time himself. So he probably didn't have a whole lot of memory of specific things. And he might be puttin' some things aside, too."

"What would his motivation for that be?"

"I don't know. Maybe not wanting to be involved. Maybe not wanting to be close to it again." Ken was a good person, Curt insisted, an important mentor when he was growing up, and now Ken was going into the ministry. "I don't think he's trying to hide anything."

BOO AND I found John, another of Dirk's old chums, at the Big R, a large store on the outskirts of Redmond—the repository of all those dark blue, boot-cut Wrangler and Lee jeans the cowboys wore. When we told John we wanted to talk to him about Dirk Duran and Duran's possible involvement in the Cline Falls incident, he unfolded his large frame from behind the counter and led us outside to the back of the store. I was ready for a juicy tale. When I pulled out a tape recorder, I detected a jolt as he eyed the little plastic machine as though it were dangerous. No one I'd interviewed had responded this way. I regretted producing it, but it was too late. I'd spooked him.

"The only thing I heard that connected anything with your situation was barroom rumor—the hatchet and the blood and him saying something about a nosebleed, and that was it."

"Nosebleed? What did you hear about that?"

"God, it's been years ago, remember, but somebody told me that somebody had found blood in his toolbox in the back of his pickup and a hatchet or something, and they questioned him on it, and he said something about a nosebleed, and he was getting tools out of the toolbox."

I wanted to know who the "somebodys" were.

"You mean who questioned him? I have no idea. I have no idea." He paused more than a beat, then said again, "No idea."

It struck me that John protested too many times. Boo had an intuition that John was holding out on us. She reminded him again that no one could be prosecuted for Cline Falls anymore—he had nothing to worry about if he told us everything he remembered.

"Oh, no, I don't have anything to worry about at all," he repeated, and Boo gave him her phone number just in case his memory should happen to improve.

DONNY, ANOTHER of Dirk's high school peers, happened to be Boo's stepbrother. She sent me over the Cascades to see what he'd have to tell me. She herself didn't know.

"Can I ask you a few questions?" Donny asked me. His studied redneck appearance and way of talking was at odds with his well-appointed, prosperous farm in the Willamette Valley, populated with well-behaved children and a lovely wife, Valinda. "What were you guys doing? Honestly. Two good-looking chicks bicycling across country mysteriously get chopped up in Redmond. And this is what happened. Honestly?" Donny spoke with an exaggerated twang, more Grand Ole Opry than local dialect.

"Right," I responded. It was Valinda's sympathetic presence that kept me from getting prickly.

"One of my questions is, what did Dirk do? He just walk in your camp and start choppin'?" The identity of the Cline Falls axeman was not up for debate in Donny's mind. "Did he walk in and try to rape you?"

That question drew the story out of me, including a description of the axeman I saw that night, at which point Donny interrupted and said, "Dirk Duran. Did you see his eyes?"

It was Donny's turn to flesh out the historical record. "I never liked him. Ever. Far back as I can remember. Dirk Duran. Never liked him. He had a horrible glass jaw. Every time me and him fought, all I had to do was just hit him in the jaw—he's a lot bigger than I am physically, but just hit him in the jaw, fight's over, and I could go ahead and thump him and beat him. We'd thump Dirk just for the fun of it. If I seriously made him bleed at least, *at least* twenty times, where I had him on the ground and got him up by his pretty little cute face—we always told him, 'You're going to be a movie star'—WHACK."

It struck me that Donny was trying to impress me with the fact that he used to dominate the guy whom he believed had dominated me.

"So they never found the person that did this," said Valinda, keeping open the question of identity.

"I've seen the axe," Donny cut in.

"You've seen the axe?"

"I've seen the axe. After the cops gave it back to him. Actually it was a hatchet, not what you'd call a boy scout hatchet, but it had an eighteen- to twenty-inch handle on it, and on this axe . . . I can tell you about this axe . . ."

"You saw the axe after the Cline Falls attack?" I coaxed him on, noting that he was alternating his terminology between "axe" and "hatchet" just as I always had.

"Souvenir."

"Were his initials still carved in it?"

"Oh, absolutely. Once you carve something in wood they're carved there forever."

"So he showed it to you."

"No, he never volunteered it, no. But I seen it and picked it up. 'You asshole. This what you thumped them girls with, huh, Dirk? How does it feel to be a big man, huh? Feel good?' Stuff like that. By this time it was hanging in his van. By this time he had a van. Ask anyone who knew Dirk Duran he had a van."

"So he had this axe hanging in the van?"

"Uh-huh. Which was not that abnormal for growing up in Redmond. I seen that axe several times."

"He have any other axes in that van?"

"No. Not that I know of anyway. That's the only one I picked up and questioned. It had a hole drilled through the middle, had a little piece of leather through the hole, so you can wrap it around your wrist."

I instantly thought of Mary Ann. Fountain of Knowledge.

"So what makes you think the police had the axe?" I asked.

"Because Dirk told me."

"What did he say?"

" 'I just got my axe back from them. They were trying to bust me for something,' blah, blah, blah—and the first conversation with him went: 'Yeah, you asshole, you did it—and you got off.' 'Well, how do you know that?' 'Well, I'm not stupid. Who else is crazy in this town besides you?' 'You can't prove it.' "

Donny was noodling on a guitar. I pressed him to tell me more about this conversation, and he admitted he was high at the time—they both were—but it went something like this: "I accused him, right at him: 'Did you do it?' I said, 'You've got Satan in your eyes, asshole.' Because if you ever looked square in Dirk Duran's eyes, you'll never see that again. Anywhere. I am, what, thirty-seven? I've never seen eyes like that before, and I taunted him about it and taunted him about it, and this was a sore subject: his eyes. I said, 'Your eyes are telling me, Dirk. It was you. You chopped 'em up, didn't you?' He said, 'Well, you can't prove it.' "

"He said that?"

"Oh, yeah. He said, 'You can't prove it.' I said, 'No, I can't prove it. I don't want to prove it. I don't care. But you're the one who did it, didn't you?' He said, 'You can't prove it. And neither can the cops. They can't prove it.'

"As far as him coming right out and saying, 'Yes, I did it'—he never physically said that. But more than physically, he said that."

"By?"

"His eyes. 'You can't prove it. You can beat me up. You can't prove it. You can go to anyone you want to. You can't prove it.' So."

We took a break from the storytelling so Donny and his son could play a John Cougar Mellencamp song. "I was born in a small town . . ." Donny called out chords to the little boy, yelling "Hammer it!" at chord changes, as the tot struggled to wrap his hand around the guitar stem.

When the song ended, the kids went to bed.

Valinda's eyes had been moist the entire time we were discussing the attack. "Why would somebody do something like that? He didn't rape you guys or anything? That's weird. I can't fathom why someone would deliberately do something like that."

"Well, I can't fathom it either," Donny said. "But the guy's eyes, even in sixth and seventh grade, they were Satan—a sixth grader looking into a friend's eyes makes his hair stand up on his neck? There's something wrong with this guy—and you ask anybody who knows Dirk Duran about his eyes, anybody. The prettiest blue eyes—oh, they were so pretty—goddang. If a guy had the tools this guy had to work with, we'd all be rich, but obviously he was chaptered the wrong way. My belief in God . . . this guy was Satan possessed from birth."

Since Dirk was such "easy pickin's," I figured that Donny never feared Dirk.

"Oh, yes, I feared Dirk highly," he said, explaining that "the fear was more inside, internal, spiritual."

I asked Donny why—if belief in Dirk Duran's guilt was so widespread in the community, if word around town was that he was being investigated for Cline Falls—why did he think Dirk Duran's name hadn't made it into the files of the investigating agency?

"Two reasons. Number one: he was a minor. Number two: at this period of time, Central Oregon was down. Had nothing going for it. Yet they knew they had these resources, mountains and rivers. Maybe they covered up because they didn't want to bring anything negative to it.

"I'm trying to put my mind to fix on this . . . the way these country-boy, hokey backwoods people are thinkin'. These pretty little girls pedaling their little bikes all the way across the country, they stop off in Redmond, they get hacked up. Now, without a great big scene of bringing everything down on a nice little ole redneck community—you got a little group here, the po-lice, you get two little girls here, chopped up. We just whitewash it. Send 'em on down the road. This never happened. Why they covered up, I don't know. Could that be a possibility?"

But how could they get away with whitewashing what had become a national news story?

"So maybe Walter covered it," Donny said. "He said two, three sentences about it on national TV—somebody was cut up in Central Oregon, we can't find him, crime is everywhere. End of conversation. But this was not a great big national

e-chopper-in-Central-Oregon-everyone-beware type of thing, happened. Because if he's gonna chop you, he's gonna chop some-
lat's the way I see it. Because if there's a random murderer out
, ...y uo not stop. Now if I get pissed off at somebody and go out and kill them, that's one thing. But someone just out of the clear blue sky, for no reason at all . . . during the bicycle ride, didn't anybody go up and ask you to do anything? Nothing like that? Zero?"

"Nothing."

"Okay. This is just a fruitcake. And once a fruitcake does it—Son of Sam, Charlie Manson, any of the rest of them, on down to the queers stuffing bodies in the icebox—they don't stop doin' it."

Donny told me it was just too bad that Shayna and I had chosen the wrong side of Cline Falls to camp. We should have pitched our tent on the other side— in the raw desert that hadn't been tamed into a docile park, that forbidding-looking place where the Birdman lived, where the Old West looked untouched. That very night, Donny and his buddies were down there burning a juniper in a bonfire. We'd have been safe with them.

I NEVER turned up anyone who could corroborate that Dirk had confessed to the attack in a Bible study group. But hearing Robin tell me that six months after the axe attack, Dirk supposedly "found religion and was all saved," meant that I could put into the equation that Dirk's behavior had been highly suspicious. He was looking for some kind of conversion experience. Why all of a sudden after Cline Falls did he need to find God?

I also turned up descriptions of Dirk you'd find only in literature—say, Milton's *Paradise Lost*. And they weren't descriptions of the angels: Tom's younger sister, who also attended their mother's Bible study group, didn't remember Dirk Duran saying anything suspicious. But she was pierced by the memory of his eyes: "I have to say, they're beautiful. But it just gives you the eeriest feeling to look into his eyes. You can just glance, and they'll penetrate. Ohhh . . ." I could hear her shudder on the phone. Her mother, the leader of the gathering, didn't remember a confession either, but she remembered a physicality she would never forget: "I wasn't afraid of him. But it was the strangest thing in the world to hug him. I've never felt anything like that. I don't know how to explain it. I can't even think of anything to liken it to. He was so icy cold. It was just like he was almost devoid of life. It made my heart hurt, it was so empty. Even thinking of it now makes me hurt."

She told me that she felt the group was protected from any danger Dirk might have brought because of their prayers, but then she caught herself. "But that doesn't help you! I would think: Where was God when that happened to you? And that's not one of these things any of us can explain . . . boy, it's sure not, is it?"

. . .

ONE DAY, Boo and I stood on the doorstep of a modest house in the older part of Redmond. Randy, a stocky man with a pleasant round face, stood barefoot outside his screen door. He was willing to answer questions about his old school buddy: they'd had a falling-out in high school when Dirk took a path toward drugs and alcohol. Randy had no contact with Dirk after early high school, in the mid-seventies. Then one day in the late eighties, Randy, married and the father of a newborn, had a visitor on his doorstep: Dirk Duran, looking stoned and haggard, and wanting to talk.

"One thing I remember, he said that he had a parasite in him and he was smoking pot to kill this thing. It was weird. I'd never heard of a parasite in anybody."

"He said that out of the clear blue sky?" I asked.

"Yeah, just setting there talking."

I asked Randy if he had any idea what he meant by "parasite."

He didn't know, but there was something about his eyes. "You look that guy in the eyes and you just see evil in his eyes . . . almost like he was possessed.

"Is he still alive?" he added. "If he's still alive, that really surprises me, that really does. He's screwed with a lot of people. He was in a fight every day. Sooner or later somebody was going to catch up with him, somebody was going to get him."

Randy's description of the suspect in the late eighties made me profoundly uneasy. This sourceless wickedness felt to me like touching evil. Like an opportunistic parasite, it colonizes and metastasizes. The vibration of evil registers on the primitive part of the brain. You don't so much understand it with your brain as feel it with your body. Your hair stands up on end. Your skin crawls.

What spooked me more was that Randy had placed Dirk closer to the present. When my image of him was the clean-cut boy in the prom photo, even if his presence was described as "icy cold," he seemed less malign. But now that he appeared older, haggard, and possessed by a parasite, I felt a jolt of fear.

The stories were working on me. I slept alone in a huge upper bedroom of Boo's ranch house. The sounds of the night—cats prancing on the roof like burglars, the creaking of cedar planks, the caterwauling of cows in heat—were enough to wake the dead. I slept fitfully.

I'd been talking about Dirk Duran around town for weeks now. He currently lived in Washington, although people reported a local sighting here and there. Apparently he came and went. Did he know I was going around asking questions about him—cementing his reputation as Dirk Duran the Hatchet Man?

I wondered if my preoccupation with him could somehow conjure him from wherever he was, like when you think of people intensely and they call, or you round the corner and there they are.

I SPENT SIX spring weeks in 1995 racing around the countryside on many blue-sky days, playing country music on my car radio, passing the hours on an electric edge, in a state of fearful pleasure, tracing every lead I had the time or courage to follow.

Central Oregon was loaded with the past. It no longer looked like it did in the seventies. The Californians with their llamas and emus and vitamin companies had moved in and dramatically changed the face of the place. But there was still a hologram left of what the place was like during the summer of '77, because the natives had not left. If someone mentioned names I should look up, key players in the events of Cline Falls, chances were good that I'd find them still there, somewhere, within ten miles of where they lived back then.

I could now perceive gathering patterns: the town was bristling with bad news about Dirk Duran. He unnerved many who had crossed his path. The community had excommunicated him after the Cline Falls incident: "He'd come to parties, and people wouldn't let him in. He was blackballed. I just remember. 'Dirk Duran's here,' " someone told me.

This local Redmond boy was sneaky, someone who ambushed when he attacked, sometimes with his rig: "Dirk was a backstabber type. Never did anything to your face. Never a full-on fight. But he'd run someone over in his car—would use it as a weapon if he could"; "He tried to run over someone in his van. If it hadn't been for the cement blocks, he would have run over this kid."

He was obsessed with his reputation as the one who had committed the Cline Falls attack. "It was something that was eating him up . . . He brought it up constantly."

He had a cartoonish idea of masculinity: "He had a certain element of macho vanity about him all the time. Cocky, tough-guy stuff"; "Dirk walked around with a strut, with his chest puffed out. 'No one mess with me.' "

And he was a crybaby. That evicted him from the pantheon of real cowboys. Even when they're black and blue, cowboys don't cry.

He was especially fond of axes: if I could believe the rumors, he owned quite a few. A single-bladed one with his initials carved in the handle. It had a hole at the end and a string through the hole so he could use it as a club. He probably had a double-bladed axe, too, with his initials stamped on it. It's likely that he had kept an axe in a white toolbox when he had his pickup. Later, when he drove a green van, it seems he had one or more hanging in the back. It appeared to me that Dirk wanted all the axes he could get: "Me and a few people were down there below Mary Kay Falls, five miles down from Cline Falls, way downriver. Dirk Duran was there. We were walking down to go swimming. This is going to be hard to believe, but somebody found—I think I found it—an old, old axe. It had an old wooden handle and it was all rusty. And Dirk wanted to have that. And he got it. I'll tell you why he got it—because I wasn't going to argue him for it."

"So how did he come up and ask you for it?"

"Everyone said—'Hey, that's cool. That's neat.' And Dirk said, 'Can I have that? Can I have that?' I was so much younger and he was bigger. He could intimidate you by the fact that he wanted that hatchet. He might have known everybody thought he did it—and he's an evil kind of a guy."

Did the cowboy of Cline Falls, that night marauder who blindsided us by running over our tent with his pickup, simply seize on the most readily available weapon in his truck? As one who always looked for the deeper meaning of things, I thought not.

It wasn't a gun he used. Not even a knife. Not his bare hands. A pillow over the mouth. Not a wire garrote slicing through the neck like the Mafia likes to use. But, precisely, an axe.

It seemed to me the axe had the whiff of the ancient about it. To use an axe to murder had much in common with other primeval ways of killing. Axes—like stones, wooden clubs or sabers or iron bars—were an ancient form of weaponry. Fire and water, too. Murder by burning and drowning. All ancient. All involved a profoundly intimate participation in the death process.

In Redmond, Oregon, there was a myth that had gone the rounds: "An axe was found in the river with a *D.D.* on it." Such lore would not have grown up around a gun.

The axe elevated those who used it as a weapon to the world of mythic archetypes. It was meant to impress with a show of might: a triumph of the will. To smite with an axe planted precise imagery of mutilation in the imagination: its distinctive cuts, its capacity to dismember in a single stroke, the archaic spilling of blood in a modern world where clean, efficient death-dealing from a distance with a bullet was the order of the day.

OFTEN A MURDER investigation runs dry after twenty-four hours. Even after seven days, the trail might run cold. This investigation was 160,000 hours old and still alive. The Cline Falls incident had broken into a hundred shards of memory lodged in many minds. Stories were begging to be told, almost like they wanted, like tiles, to be inserted into a big, complicated mosaic.

Some stories converged, and others were contradictory and hazy. Memory is by nature constructive. We take away particular elements from our experiences and store them away. When we recall the memory, it isn't a precise piece of film on the cutting-room floor that we pick up, dust off, and put on the light box. We re-create our experiences, and while doing so, we elaborate with emotions, beliefs, even with information we obtain after the experience. When we relate a narrative of remembered events, we further distort them because we must fill in the blanks in order to bring order to the story. All of this I know.

But I had not returned to Central Oregon to prove the futility of recovering what happened in the past. For fifteen years I had allowed the elusiveness of truth to sap my will, and now I needed something more. After all, it wasn't a magic act. A specific man had committed a specific act of evil.

These converging stories, even the conflicting ones, were spreading sunshine on my psyche. I was making a movie in my mind of the events of 1977. When stories overlapped, when they corroborated one another, I would lay in an image.

Two girls with bikes, sleeping in a tent in Cline Falls. A red pickup parked nearby. A two-toned blue pickup. A hatchet in a white toolbox in a two-toned blue pickup. Right after Cline Falls, a meticulous young cowboy with white-hot rage on a cocktail of drugs and alcohol trying to drown his girlfriend in a pond. His girlfriend studying her boyfriend's tire tracks in the dirt at Cline Falls. An axe with a leather strap hanging in a green van. Kids singing gospel, holding hands. One looks uncomfortable, the kid with piercing blue eyes.

Blood on File

They [Americans] may be said not to perceive the mighty forests that surround them till they fall beneath the hatchet.
—ALEXIS DE TOCQUEVILLE, *DEMOCRACY IN AMERICA*

The Broad Axe: "Goes to the Quick Every Lick"
—NAME OF NINETEENTH-CENTURY NEWSPAPER
  FROM EUGENE, OREGON

The first time I saw Salem was in the fall of 1992. At the very outset of my quest, the city was shrouded in a murky light. In May 1995, the rays of the sun struck me full in the face as my allies, Bob and Dee Dee, and I walked past Oregon's state capital building. We were en route to the Oregon State Police headquarters to request an inquiry into the 1977 case of a double attempted murder in Cline Falls State Park.

The "Golden Pioneer," with his seven-foot-long gold axe, glittered and glowed atop the cylindrical rotunda of the statehouse, but its distance was such that I could not fully appreciate his figure.

Though I wanted to climb the 121 steps of the tower crowning the capital dome to get an intimate eyeful of the Golden Pioneer in his glory, the tower was closed for repairs due to damage from a 1993 earthquake. Had the shaking lasted even a few seconds longer (I read), the stalwart frontiersman would have toppled altogether.

Through a stroke of luck, I had a chanced upon a replica of the Pioneer in miniature a few weeks before, in an Oregon antique shop. It is a small but weighty bronze mold of the axeman in the form of a coin bank with THE COMMERCIAL BANK, SALEM, OREGON inscribed on its base under a slot that would accommodate quarters. It is a fine piece of American kitsch, as fine as the original. This miniature is so very specific that I can say with some expertise exactly what the axeman looks like.

Designed during the Art Deco period of the thirties, the statue hinted at totalitarian art, with its heroic idealization of a supermasculine figure, and reminded

me of a few statues I'd seen in the Soviet Union glorifying the industrious prole-
tarian workers. The Golden Pioneer stands in a rigid pose, with a perfectly erect
posture and a puffed-out chest. His boots straddle a tree stump, which he presumably has just cut with his axe. A washboard stomach is visible under the Pioneer's shirt, the fabric of which clings to his skin, and is meticulously tucked into
his breeches. His shirtsleeves are rolled up above his elbows so you can appreciate
the sinewy muscles of his forearms. One arm slings a cape over his left shoulder.
The other grasps the axe at his side. His bearded face, with a sweep of hair over
the brow, turns to look over his left shoulder, perhaps at the horizon now visible
through the clear-cut. He will build towns in the clear-cuts that will grow into
cities, advancing Western civilization. The Golden Pioneer is the archetypal Western hero. The Golden Pioneer is Manifest Destiny.

SEVEN COPS in plain clothes were arranged around a conference table at the Ore-
gon State Police general headquarters. I sat at the head of the table with Bob and
Dee Dee on either side of me. Four of the seven men regarded me pleasantly.
Three glowered.

"Do you mind if I tape this conversation?" I asked. They all shifted in their
seats. Cleared their throats. Looked down at the table. No, they didn't mind. The
police stenographer tapped away busily in the corner of the room. Neither the
cops nor I were sure whether we were among friends or foes.

The police superintendent was not in attendance. But he had sent his right-
hand man, Captain Bob Schmidt, who made introductions all around, then asked

me, "What, if I might ask, are you looking for, out of your search and your need
to come back and revisit this crime that you've been living with, obviously, since
it occurred? What do you need?"

"What, *if I might ask*" betrayed the policeman's true feelings. He himself probably couldn't believe that he was present at such a meeting. Indeed it was no ordinary occurrence that someone whose victimization dated back so many years had
managed to gather an audience of the best criminal investigators in the state. Two
years before, I had sent my private eye, a former cop himself, to request old files
from this very same man, and that investigator came back with the answer that all
files on the Cline Falls case had been purged. But now the Kounses had brought
their considerable influence to bear on reopening the 1977 Cline Falls case. The
supreme powers of the state police had decreed that it was good policy to bond
with "victims" and, astonishingly, had granted us an invitation to meet with the
brass.

The brass were staring at me now. From my seat at the head of the table, I
filled my lungs and stated my case into the charged air: "Two and a half years ago,
I was having trouble moving on in some basic areas of my life." I told them that I
had never set foot in the state of Oregon prior to 1977, and hadn't been back
since, and therefore, my whole experience of Oregon was that event, "a bloody
mess." By that I meant, Oregon to me "equaled mutilation, blood, axe attack." I
laughed uncomfortably and gazed off at the Oregon state seal, emblazoned on the
navy blue wall.

"Because I left on a stretcher in a million pieces"—I heard myself say "a million pieces" and realized my hyper-emotional second self had taken charge—
"because there was never any resolution and my attacker was never found, I felt
that this state, in a way, had taken away my power." I was breathing rapidly. I let
out another uncomfortable laugh and said something about how "I had to come
back here to solve this crime myself, in order to feel some recovery. Does that
make sense?"

There was no response.

Why on earth did I feel compelled to tell a roomful of cops some watered-
down version of the underpinnings of my quest? But wait, these men were not
one brain, one set of emotions, one web of nerve endings. Perhaps there was a
man in this room who got my meaning?

If so, he didn't say a word. None did. They all looked at me. I continued on, explaining that, naturally, apart from wanting to know who "essentially murdered
two girls," I wanted to know why he'd done it—and moreover, why he had never
been caught.

In sum, I told them that we had called them here because we believed that our
labors had turned up a good suspect. And we had a hunch that this malefactor
was still in circulation in the Central Oregon community. We had been told that
he lived in Washington but would show up on his home turf from time to time,

and given his violent propensities—which by now had possibly, even likely, escalated since his tender teens—we worried for those who might cross his path.

One of the smilers, Sergeant Marlen Hein, began to speak. Hein was a man in
his fifties with a pleasant face and plump cheeks. He was wearing aviator glasses
and a bowling-style shirt.

"We all know the statute of limitations is gone in this case," he said. "None of
us here today were around in '77. Methods of working today are entirely different
than back then. So we aren't going to be able to give you the answer to why it
didn't get solved; but what we want to do today is hear what information you've
gained." Sergeant Hein was exceedingly conciliatory.

One of the dour cops spoke for the first time. Sergeant Mike Ramsby was the
head of the Homicide Investigation Tracking System, which collected Pacific
Northwest crimes in a computer database so that agencies across state and county
lines could share crime data.

"One of the things we'd like to do is profile this case, and identify any other
cases that might potentially have been done by the same suspect," he said.

I said that given our information that this clearly dangerous suspect was a free
man, with a minimal criminal record, we might find out he'd been leading a
charmed life.

"There's nothing more frustrating. It was the same in the Kaye Turner case; it
went for years before we got a break," the amiable Sergeant Hein said. He didn't
need to give background on Kaye Turner. That her assailants were convicted in
the early nineties for her 1978 murder made it one of the most celebrated cases of
the era.

"The only difference between Kaye Turner and you two gals was that Kaye
died. That's the *only* difference between the two cases." Sergeant Hein said it
again: "That's the *only* difference between the two cases."

Sure enough: when I described that Shayna and I had been "essentially murdered," someone in the room had been listening—this man. Perhaps he, who
stood while the others sat, as though he were too kinetic to be confined to a chair,
understood the deeper currents of my mission. I looked around the table. Those
who had been glowering before were still glowering.

"A crime like this is so outrageous and so heinous in nature, it has great implications not just for the victim," boomed Bob Kouns, turning on his oratorical
skills. "We really resonate to Terri's case because some of the same things happened in our own case—it was an unsolved situation. But worse, gentleman, is
that the Redmond community needs closure almost as much as the victim. It's an
outrage to them. It has this great unsettling effect on a community, that we never
got to the bottom of this thing."

Dee Dee made the point that it wasn't good for law enforcement to have this
unsolved case floating in limbo. "People think you are corrupt and stupid and all
kinds of things automatically, whether there's any basis or isn't."

"Well, you can't put it to sleep. It's a stigma," Sergeant Hein said agreeably.

"People are haunted by it," I added. "I can't tell you how many people have said to me, you know, Cline Falls has come up four times in the last month. It's as alive as it was eighteen years ago. And there's this sense that the person who did it is still among them. He comes and he goes. And they all have this profound feeling of unease." I wanted to make plain: our suspect was no ordinary misfit but rather someone who had managed to dominate the town's consciousness by scaring the living daylights out of lots of people for a long time.

Captain Schmidt jumped in, "I think what you have here is a group that's ready to sit and listen and learn what you three have learned through searching out who's responsible and why."

I continued, telling how I had returned to Oregon two years before to pick up the crime report, which had set me on a path after my first suspect, Richard Godwin.

"Lynn Fredrickson went back to Oklahoma on the Kaye Turner case and interviewed Floyd Forsberg and Bud Godwin," Marlen Hein cut in, referring to the tall detective from the Bend office.

"I did ask them about your case," Fredrickson piped up. His slumped posture and jutting jaw betrayed his attitude toward me. "I spoke to Forsberg first in the federal pen in Sheridan about Kaye Turner, and I thought I might as well do a clearinghouse here so I talked to him about your case also. Frosty said it was a bunch of bull."

Fredrickson spoke in Frosty's supposed words: " 'I was having a good time getting all this notoriety, so I tried to make a deal. Anything I could make up. This guy was weak, would go along with anything. I offered him protection. I'd watch the news and read different articles about crimes, filled in the pieces of what I thought fit. I even wrote up one of the notes and had him sign. It was lies. It was not true. The only one he killed was the Tolentino girl down in Eugene. That's the truth; the rest I made up. I got nothing to win or lose on this. I've spent all these years in prison. You're asking me, I'm telling you.' "

I asked Fredrickson what year he talked to "Frosty."

"I'm guessing it's '91, '92. So then I go to El Reno to talk to Godwin. I had to go into the middle of a large room with all the other inmates around me to interview the guy. I got a really good feeling from talking to him he had nothing to do with it. I asked him about Kaye Turner, and he told me everything Frosty told me independently, because they had no communication all those years—how Frosty had conned him into writing all this stuff for protection. Everything meshed exactly right. Then I went to your case. He said, 'Absolutely not, I wasn't over there. You can check with my wife. I had nothing to do with that, mister. I didn't do that.' "

For me, the Godwin trail had turned cold more than a year ago. And this laid to rest any suspicions I had that the face of Bud Godwin, the droopy sad sack, would ever fit on top of the meticulous torso. I wondered now how I had ever thought it possible.

I continued my story: With Godwin on my mind, I had interviewed folks in the Redmond community until I heard about a scary seventeen-year-old whose description—a meticulous cowboy—matched my memory. "I remember saying to people all through the years, 'You wouldn't believe how neatly this guy tucked in his shirt. Now witness how I tuck in my shirt . . .'"

I gave a demonstration of the misshapen bulges at my waist, asserting that, as a constitutionally disheveled sort, it had made a whopping impression on me that the guy who was chopping me up with an axe had his shirt tucked in so neatly; he looked like he had walked off a movie set. The men arranged around the table looked at me quizzically, as though they couldn't quite believe they were witness to such a demonstration.

I went on to describe the puzzling aspects of what we'd learned. "It was a crime that got national attention in the media. Over the weekend, a seventeen-year-old cowboy is in jail in Prineville for nearly murdering his girlfriend. His girlfriend then tells police: 'I saw his tire tracks in the park. He had a toolbox with an axe. I think he did it.' He's known to be a violent character in this community. Police are looking at him. The whole nation is thinking, When are they going to find the axeman? He's released on Monday. And there's nothing in the police report."

"It's a very serious problem in this case, and there has got to be an answer to it," Bob Kouns chimed in. "We spent a lot of time on our case looking at police reports. We know what a police report looks like. And this is the worst damn police report I've ever seen. We've got just a few pages here."

"Including three pages from a psychic in Boston," I added.

Sergeant Marlen Hein wanted us to understand that modern police procedures were light-years from the dark ages of the seventies. At that time they had detectives Cooley and Durr playing Lone Ranger trying to solve crimes. And they had a commander above them named Lieutenant Lamkin calling the shots, and he wasn't skilled in criminal investigations. Moreover, record-keeping systems were antiquated in those days.

We said that we had spoken to the retired investigators on the case, Cooley and Durr, and they had no memory of the name Dirk Duran coming up in the investigation. Coincidentally, that name had come up among the Redmond police, and in fact Corporal Little remembered accompanying Cooley and a local in the drug circles named Chris Peterson down to Cline Falls. Peterson was trying to trade information about Dirk Duran's involvement in Cline Falls in return for clemency in his own case.

"The only assumption I can make is not a good one—that the reports are lost," Hein said. Officers had personal notebooks, wrote up reports, then sent them to headquarters in Salem. The "crime report" I had received was a copy of those reports written up from police notes. Officers were supposed to turn in their notebooks when they retired.

Hein promised me that every attempt would be made to scour the archives to find the personal notebooks of the two lead investigators.

"I'm not going to defend any of the actions of the officers involved in this. But your comment that Cooley didn't remember anything could be quite possible. Cooley was involved when the Kaye Turner case came to trial in '92, and if he didn't have the reports in front of him, written down, he couldn't remember."

"Clayton Durr also has zero memory of Dirk Duran. And he supposedly was a co-equal," Bob countered.

"Clayton Durr has the memory of an elephant." It was Lynn Fredrickson, the one with the jutting jaw. "If the man has no memory, he didn't know about it. I'd base my life on the guy. I worked for him for years. He was my Rock of Gibraltar in the Kaye Turner case. If somebody didn't remember something, he did. If there was a dispute, he kept digging, and we finally found out he knew what he was talking about."

"We know there's no criminal action possible on your case," Marlen Hein said. "But there's no question we'll be dedicating Lynn's time and resources to investigate."

Detective Lynn Fredrickson's mouth dropped at word of this grunt work assignment.

The meeting was winding down.

When I suggested to the room that I had every intention of continuing my own search, the scowlers among the group expressed grave concern that I might foul up their investigations—especially if I contacted the suspect.

Dee Dee needled them: "Now, after eighteen years, you've suddenly got a big hot case?"

I assured them that a meeting with the suspect wasn't currently on my dance card.

Marlen Hein stepped in genially: "As far as your involvement in investigations, I would hope the communication lines would be open. It can be a shoulder-to-shoulder type of thing."

Captain Rich Hein, head of Criminal Investigations, spoke up. "I think both sides have an interest in '77—what may have occurred recently and what could occur in the future if we don't take appropriate action." Captain Hein was Marlen's brother, and just as cordial. "I think we need to have a coordinated effort between what Terri is trying to accomplish and what we are trying to accomplish."

Yes, I would keep right on investigating. My agenda was moral, psychological, spiritual. I had a story to reconstruct. No, I wasn't going to stop. "Shoulder to shoulder" it would be, then. Besides, wasn't that how it should always have been? If the community had done its part a long time ago, and not assumed that the police would automatically take care of rooting out those who had sown fear in their midst, perhaps we wouldn't be sitting here. On that point, we all agreed.

The meeting adjourned. A long-ago case was reopened. And then the unexpected occurred: one of the smilers laid a stack of four-by-five prints on the table in front of me.

Crime scene photos.

I'd known it all along: my blood was still on file. Though I had been told the physical evidence had been purged, I had suspected that physical traces of the attack and its aftermath had not disappeared entirely; I imagined that I was feeling their phantom presence. Here they were: images of Cline Falls, June 23, 1977.

A self-satisfied smile crossed my lips.

I flipped through the photos, and a remembered place, the Cline Falls of 1977, came alive in yellowed Kodachrome, that bleak and lonely place on a hot summer day. It was as though a memory had been pulled from my brain and transferred to emulsion—no longer behind my eyes, but now in front of my eyes.

There were various establishing shots of the crime scene: on a thin crescent of desert soil and crabgrass between the river and the curb of a road, two picnic tables are cemented to the ground. A third green picnic table is freestanding between them. A fire grate is set up next to the green picnic table. Part of the riverbank is obscured by thick brush, but then gives way to a view of moving waters congested with reeds and boulders. A juniper tree with dying branches and a young black locust tree grow near the picnic tables.

Then details of the crime scene:

Forensic lab personnel squatting in the picnic area

Various shots of desert soil and crabgrass, nothing discernible from the detail

A green picnic table with a fresh chip of wood broken off the bench

A tape measure wrapped around the curb, marking six and a half inches

Parallel boards lying on the curb to mark the two spots where the truck jumped the curb, then returned to the road

A large brown house on the rimrock rising from the bank across the river

Desert dust. A tape measure marking the width of a set of tire tracks; grooves from tires have left depressions in the dirt

Desert dust. Many prints formed by wide soles typical of work boots with a heavy tread, running in frantic motion

Desert dust. What appears to be the imprint of a tire and the imprint of the sinuous lines of the sole of a cowboy boot

Various shots of tape measures lying in crabgrass. A darkened area appears to be a large swatch of dried blood soaking the soil

Desert Dust

The cop who had scowled throughout the state police meeting was a tall lanky detective wearing a candy-colored shirt and tie. His leather gun holster, which crossed under his armpits, was an incongruous martial twist on an outfit that was more suited to a dandy than a cop.

Detective Lynn Fredrickson was charged with the responsibility of recording my version of the Cline Falls attack. We took our places on opposite sides of a conference table in the patrol office in Bend. He leaned forward and drilled me with his bulging blue eyes. It was all too apparent that he considered me a neurotic victim, appearing about fifteen years too late, wasting his time. As I tried to figure out a way to build rapport, I noted that Fredrickson had two mysterious scars, one on the front of his neck and one on the back, suggesting that at some time during his long career a bullet had passed through him. But surely his presence here meant that that scenario was impossible.

I asked him anyway: Battle scars from the line of duty? No, a car accident and a separate surgical procedure. Fredrickson wasn't loosening up. I would try another tack. I knew cops loved to rehash the high-profile cases they'd helped crack, so I asked him about his part in solving the Kaye Turner case in the early nineties. It was the magic question. Fredrickson told me that when he first joined the force in the eighties, former state police detective Clayton Durr was his partner. Durr kept a few old unresolved cases in a file, which he turned over to his partner when he retired, hoping Fredrickson would eventually find time to dust them off.

"Durr took me down to Cline Falls and told me what happened to you," Fredrickson said. Durr also brought him up to date on the 1980 Mary Jo Templeton case, the woman in her forties whose body parts were found floating in Mirror Pond in downtown Bend.

"The suspect was a dentist in town," he went on about the Templeton case.

"They suspected someone with surgical background because the body was surgically dismembered. They felt the injuries were done by a scalpel. They did a search warrant on his office in the downtown area, went through the drains. The dentist relocated to Eastern Oregon and a short time after that killed himself. They have not been able to get conclusive proof that he's the one that did that."

The murder of Kaye Turner was the third famous unsolved violent case of the late seventies in Central Oregon. As soon as I learned about Kaye, I had carefully studied the details of her murder: The thirty-five-year-old marathon runner from Eugene, Oregon, had vanished the day before Christmas 1978. She had been renting a cabin with her husband on the eastern slopes of the Cascades, in the village of Camp Sherman. At 8:00 a.m. she left for a six-mile run and never returned from the woods.

A twenty-six-year-old highway worker named John Ackroyd reported seeing Kaye Turner the morning she disappeared. He told the state police that he had seen her jogging and had spoken to her briefly. Then he'd gone to his friend Roger Beck's home near Camp Sherman to pick him up for a hunting trip. This story was backed up by Beck's wife. Nine months later, the same John Ackroyd gave police a break in the case. He called them to say he was walking in the woods when his dog sniffed out some human remains. Ackroyd led investigators to a pair of weathered yellow shorts, a blue sweatshirt, one running shoe, underwear, a watch, and a human jawbone. These items were located close to a road that was part of Kaye's running course. Kaye's Timex had stopped at 9:05 on December 24.

When Fredrickson started working with Durr in the early eighties, Durr took him to meet the primary suspect. "He said, 'I want you to meet John Arthur Ackroyd. He's the one as far as I'm concerned killed Kaye Turner, but we can't prove it.' He took me up to the scene of the murder and said, 'People might not remember, but this is where it happened.' "

In 1990, John Ackroyd came under suspicion for the disappearance of his girlfriend's young daughter, Rachanda Pickle. When Fredrickson was assigned to the task force to search for the missing girl, John Ackroyd volunteered to be involved in the search.

"He didn't know I knew past stuff about the case. He'd start talking about Kaye Turner. I'd change the subject, and he'd bring it right back. He thought I wasn't interested. But he wanted to talk about Kaye Turner."

As a cloud of suspicion gathered around Ackroyd, FBI agents in charge of serial killings looked back into the 1978 murder. They tracked down Beck's ex-wife, divorced from him since '81. This time she recanted the alibi she had given for Beck and Ackroyd eleven years before. She told police her ex-husband had threatened a number of times that, as the Eugene *Register-Guard* reported, "he was going to do to me exactly what they did to Kaye Turner. And he told me that they raped her, and they shot her, and they cut her with a knife." Faced with Beck's ex-wife's testimony, Ackroyd tried to lay all the blame on Beck: he told police that after he dropped Beck off the day Kaye disappeared, Beck left his home again—and tied Kaye Turner to a tree, raped her, and killed her. In 1992, the very same year I returned to Oregon to investigate the '77 Cline Falls attack, the Kaye Turner case of 1978—which had also stymied the detective duo of Durr and Cooley—was finally brought to a close. Ackroyd and Beck were convicted for the rape and murder of Kaye Turner and sentenced to life without parole. The disappearance of Rachanda Pickle was never solved.

Fredrickson unleashed an avalanche of details about this old case, delivered in a breakneck patter, like a thirty-three record speeded up to forty-five. He told me he had been assigned the task of rounding up all evidence that had been dispersed among various agencies. He tracked down Kaye's skull and a bag of bones seized at the murder site in the ponderosa forest near the town of Camp Sherman and brought them to the medical examiner, who identified only one as a human bone. All the rest were deer bones. Then someone gave Fredrickson the idea to go down to a remarkable place, the National Fish and Wildlife Forensics Laboratory, in Ashland, Oregon, where they have an expert at identifying bones, second only to those at the Smithsonian. When Fredrickson laid out the bones for this expert, named Bonnie, she quickly went through them and identified a whole human arm out of what for years other people had identified as animal bones.

"This is just a sideline, but this is something I'll never forget: We're in there and I got the skull there, and Bonnie's lookin' at that, and says, 'Well, isn't that curious. Look at that right there. There's a single hair in a human tooth.' I says, 'Yeah?'" Bonnie put the hair under a microscope, then pulled a slide out of a tray of boxes categorized into types of animals. She compared the slide with the hair and then turned the microscope over to Fredrickson. "This is a Western Oregon pocket gopher hair, stuck in the tooth of the skull."

Fredrickson asked the other forensics experts at the lab to examine Kaye Turner's clothing, because there was never any evidence of exactly how she had died. They unleashed the power of their high-tech microscopes on a few tatters of her clothing and determined that Beck's ex-wife had indeed known exactly what had happened to Kaye: she was shot; she was stabbed; she was raped. Their science was so precise that "they were able to articulate that the panties have been cut off her body with a knife."

As Fredrickson conjured the wonders of a fancy forensics lab, as he went on about how science could prove the events of crime, I listened to the specifics of the atrocity: a woman reduced to lead particles, knife cuts, semen, and a strand of fur from a woodland creature that happened to mingle with her remains.

I possessed a grainy black-and-white picture of Kaye, from a newspaper article about her killer's trial in 1992. The photo pared her face down to its salient features, and these told me that she had been a woman in motion. A muscle bulged in her neck. Her blond hair was carried by the breeze. She was biting her lower lip in determination. The picture announced that Kaye was at home in her body, at home in the woods.

Like a detective reviewing an old case, I developed an attachment to this victim, this woman I never knew. Unlike a detective reviewing an old case, I paid special attention to her because she was a woman murdered on the same soil at roughly the same time as my close shave. I suspected that she, like me, had heard the call of freedom and spiritual renewal in the American woods from our mythmakers. But as women, in reality, we were not permitted that freedom without exposing ourselves to substantial risks.

The previous fall, I had visited the town near where she was murdered, an enchanted place tucked into the forest under the volcanoes. I tried to imagine Kaye's invigorating last run, her lungs filled with cool piney air, on that winter day as she sought the restorative power of the forest—and I wondered if she had read the headlines in June 1977. I wondered if she had tried to imagine two girls flying down the Cascades on bicycles, and what met them at the bottom of the road—as I tried to imagine the instant for her when the sun-splashed ponderosa heaven turned into an ineffable hell.

I imagined the desert dust subsuming the dead. All things you leave in the wilderness lose their own identity. Distilled by nature's chemistry, one thing becomes another. A human skull and a Western Oregon pocket gopher become part of the wilderness, submerged into the fluid natural world.

At least Kaye was free in the earth, if not on the earth.

IT BECAME CLEAR to me that all this talk about Ackroyd was not idle reminiscence on the part of Fredrickson. "When you were telling your story, I wrote in my notebook, 'John Ackroyd.' This was the thought that came to me," Fredrickson said.

"Ackroyd drove a pickup at the time, blue-and-white in color. I know at some point in his life, close to the Kaye Turner thing, he lived up on the mountain in the winter, and in summertime he'd drive to Bend during the day to work on trucks for the highway department. So he was back and forth. He also used to frequent the Redmond area, because I documented he bought firearms there in the early eighties."

This gave me pause. I knew much about Kaye Turner's fate. Could I have been so dense as to have overlooked such an obvious suspect? I asked quickly, "What did he look like?"

"Six foot. A little bit overweight, I'd put him a little over two hundred pounds at that time. Dark hair. Wore a sort of beard. Bulky face. Bulky features."

Bulky, no. I did not see an overweight man that night. I saw a lean, streamlined torso. I was certain of my memory.

Fredrickson bored into me with his popping eyes and cautioned me against drawing hasty assumptions of guilt. He illustrated with a parable about a man falsely accused: "Many years ago, we had three girls that came over the top of the Santiam Pass, and they stopped at a place called Sahali Falls. It's a beautiful water-fall. They got out of the car, walked down the path. They're looking at the falls, turn around, and there's a man standing behind them, he's got a knife and de-mands their panties from them."

Fredrickson developed a suspect. The victims identified him from a picture, but the accused claimed he hadn't done it. Fredrickson went to the man's wife's house and found a ski mask—dark green with eye and mouth holes, just as the girls had described. But one tiny detail didn't fit: the girls remembered a nose hole. And one other detail didn't fit: the girls described a guy pulling off white Jockeys, but the suspect's wife insisted that her husband wore *psychedelic* under-wear all the time. Still, the guy wound up in prison, and Fredrickson was ap-plauded for a brilliant investigation, but he was haunted by the case. A year later, the same thing happened again at Sahali Falls. When Fredrickson heard about the new incident, he called the prison. No, the man convicted of the first incident at Sahali Falls hadn't escaped. Three weeks later, police found a man hiding in the brush who confessed to both incidents.

"I could have turned away from that case—it bothered me; it may have satis-fied other people's level of expectation but it didn't solve mine. I wanted every piece."

I had listened irritably to Fredrickson's sermon and its obvious moral: some-times things aren't what they appear to be, and I better hold my horses before rushing to judgment.

"I want to know the truth," I said bluntly. "So don't think I have preconceived notions."

"I just want to make sure everybody gets a fair chance. I would like to evaluate the evidence objectively," he said with an adversarial tone.

"I'm with you on that. I'm not your adversary."

Fredrickson was turning out to be a veritable generator of suspects—anyone other than the one I'd presented to him. Indeed he appeared to be wedded to the belief that any suspect I came up with could not conceivably be guilty. "There was a guy that committed suicide in Drake Park in Bend during that same time pe-riod. Less than a week after you guys were attacked he put a gun in his mouth and shot the top of his head off. He was a younger man driving a red pickup with a white canopy. And the license plates on it were from Alberta—Washington and Alberta both had white-background plates. The continuous thread I find in every one of these is the red pickup. All these people saw this red pickup parked in Cline Falls. Maybe that's why he shot himself in the head. I have a picture, but you wouldn't want to see it. They knew who he was. He had a traveling compan-ion that reported him missing right before he shot himself. He was despondent or something."

Fredrickson picked up a police report and read from it, " 'Head above his eyes is blown away' . . . I don't know. May not have any connection whatsoever. But I'd like to explore every possibility."

Fredrickson managed to snag me with this tale. What had sent the guy in the red pickup over the top? For certain there was a guy in Cline Falls that distant summer night who drove a red pickup. Setting aside for a moment the possibility that he committed the crime, what if he had only been a witness to the crime? What if he had seen a pickup slam into a tent, and he fled the scene out of terror? Had the horror of what he had seen, and the shame he might have felt at not having helped us, contributed to pushing him over the edge?

Maybe the plot was thickening, I admitted, and I asked Fredrickson to keep me informed if that lead happened to develop. Then I spun the conversation back to Godwin. Supposedly, according to the information Lieutenant Lamkin or Detective Cooley had given my and Shayna's parents, Godwin took a polygraph for the Cline Falls incident, and the results pointed to his innocence. Why, I asked, had the police insisted he was the likely perpetrator?

"Lamkin was the fly in the ointment. He was the station commander in charge of the office. Back then we had gods. They said, 'That's the way it is,' and no one questioned it. We don't have that situation anymore. We don't have someone in charge of something they know nothing about. But he was the commander, so he could call you and say, 'Don't worry about it, we've got the guy, even though he took the polygraph and passed it, but don't worry about it'—to make you feel good.

"I talked to Clayton Durr two or three times, and he said, 'There's no doubt in my mind things weren't done as they should have been, because we had the boss telling us what you will and won't do.' "

My eyes drifted to the wall behind the conference table. There, displayed with other photos of dearly departed state police, was Lieutenant Kenneth Lamkin. His was the only face I specifically remembered from the '77 law enforcement crew—a tall, jovial manly man with a long dimple in a square jaw. He'd visited my hospital room more than once.

"I'm absolutely diametrically opposed to the idea that there was a good old boy system and some massive cover-up for some local boy who may have been involved," Fredrickson went on. "They didn't do everything right that they should of. I'm with you one hundred percent. People shouldn't have been trying to direct the investigation that knew nothing about it.

"If Janey Firestone had come to the state police we would have gotten Detectives Cooley and Durr immediately." Fredrickson told me that he personally asked Clayton Durr whether Janey Firestone ever came to the state police for an interview, and Durr had no memory whatsoever of an interview with her. Fredrickson reminded me again that former detective Cooley no longer had a good memory like he used to. In the early nineties, when Cooley was called in to give testimony in the Kaye Turner trial, he couldn't remember anything without his police notebooks. But Clayton Durr could.

Fredrickson had another illustrative tale at the ready to prove the perfection of Clayton Durr's memory. In the early nineties, Fredrickson was looking for the precise location of Kaye Turner's murder on that Christmas Eve day in 1978, but he couldn't find it. Durr had once taken Fredrickson to that very spot deep in the unaxed woods, but by then the forest had been logged and Fredrickson lost his bearings, so he asked Durr to help him find the site. Durr walked right to the place and got into an argument with a young detective about whether the spot was accurate, because a photo taken in 1979 didn't appear to correspond.

"Clayton says, 'Yeah, but the picture was developed backward. Come over here, son. Remember the tree in the picture with the scar on the side of it? Look, there's the tree.' We did another search thirteen years later and found another human bone. Buried. After they logged it off we still ended up finding a human femur sticking up."

A human femur sticking up from the clear-cut?—the thigh bone, the longest, largest, and strongest bone in the human body, particularly in a female body, the bone that enables a woman to unleash her maximum self-defensive power with a kick, the bone that carried Kaye all twenty-six miles of the marathons she ran. Thirteen years after her bones were collected from her murder site, Kaye's thigh bone would work its way out of the ground, unburied at last.

Fredrickson was undeniably good at planting pictures in my mind. And he was trying to impart a lesson, which I got clearly enough: if Durr didn't remember Janey Firestone, then he'd never met her. If Durr didn't remember Dirk Duran, then Duran wasn't investigated by Durr or his partner, Cooley, at the state police.

Fredrickson softened a little toward me—for what reason I hadn't a clue. "There's a lot of goddamn terrible things that never get solved, Terri, but I'll do the best to find out for you."

And how was he going to do that?

"My goal would be to see if Mr. Duran would take a polygraph. It's a tool that can substantiate or non-substantiate someone." It was Fredrickson's belief that accuracy wouldn't be 100 percent, but in the high nineties. "And I'd tell him, if you did this crime, don't take the polygraph and expect to beat it. I'd tell him, if I did it, there's no way in hell I'd take the polygraph. But if I didn't do it, I'd take it in a heartbeat.

"Some people are good cons. I've been conned before and I'll be conned again. No doubt about that. But a lot of times you can pick up really easy from talking to somebody whether they're lying to you. Used to say if they're lying to you they can't make eye contact. That's B.S. I've had some hell of good liars look me straight in the eye and swear to God this and that. Law of averages is, I'm going to pick up something really quick if that person did it or not."

We didn't know suspect Dirk Duran's whereabouts, but Fredrickson insisted he would flush him out.

The thought of locating a real person suspected of being the axeman jarred me with a dull shock.

A FEW DAYS LATER Fredrickson called me. I could forget about the guy in the red-and-white pickup who'd blown his own head off. Fredrickson had gotten the dates wrong. That incident took place in an entirely different time frame from the Cline Falls episode, and besides, law enforcement had determined that the guy was part of a suicide pact. The news disappointed me. A guy in a red pickup who witnessed a truck roll over a tent, had fled the scene, then driven to another park and shot his head off because he was derailed by the radical evil he had seen and because he failed to act in the face of it: I wanted someone to tell me a story like that.

What the Birdman Saw

Boo pulled me away from my reading, led me outside, and instructed me to hold a spotlight on the distant pasture. Forty-four babies had been born to the herd during the spring calving season. Molina's baby, the forty-fifth, needed help. Boo tied chains to two hooves erupting from the fleshy orifice of the bellowing cow.

"Okay, honey, push . . ." Boo gave a little pull on the hooves with each contraction until a wet mass of gangly legs dropped to the ground. Back in the warm ranch kitchen she said, "I didn't want you to miss that."

It wasn't typical to find Boo out alone in the deep darkness. One thing I had learned from living with her for several weeks now: Boo didn't "do dark" any more than Bill did. She hadn't been forthcoming about this little quirk at our first meeting, but she later admitted that ever since a long-ago night in June, she never wanted to find herself exposed and vulnerable under a cover of darkness. She would zigzag to her destination guided by a trail of whatever lights she could find, however far off her path.

I remembered asking her that first morning in the coffee shop how Cline Falls had changed her life. She didn't tell me about her fear of the dark. What she did tell me was that Cline Falls had planted in her a fear that somebody could just kill her out of the blue—that "anytime, anywhere, shit could happen."

One dark morning in June 1987, shit did happen. Asleep alone in her mother's ranch house, she was awakened by prowlers outside spraying a beam of light into her window. She had the instinct to shout "I've got a gun and I'm not afraid to use it!" She woke to the news that her neighbors just a few miles away in Terrebonne had been robbed and murdered in their ranch home. A local boy named Randy Guzek was convicted of the murders of Rod and Lois Hauser and sentenced to die.

"You may not have fears like that," she reasoned, because how many times can something so violent happen to one person in a single lifetime?

"I WOULD GO talk to the Birdman if I was you . . . To witness something like that— isn't that going to affect a person's mind where you just want to feed the birds?" Lureen's words had a habit of ringing in my skull.

Talk around town was that the Birdman had come to the Redmond area after World War II and set up his shack by a small waterfall just next to the tiny one-lane bridge that crossed the Deschutes River, before Highway 126 was built.

Some thought he came from Chicago originally. No one knew why he ended up in Central Oregon, and he wouldn't tell anyone exactly why. The rumors were that something happened to Abe Johnson in the war, that he'd come back from the service shell-shocked, and as far back as the 1940s, he could be seen running past the Penhollows' farm, terrifying Clyde's mother into sweeping her children into the house. Eventually Abe became the region's own St. Francis of Assisi, with birds perched on his big black coat and floppy hat. There was no stretch of highway cleaner than the four miles between Cline Falls and Redmond because Abe would stop to pick up litter as he trundled along on his three-wheeled bicycle to get birdseed.

What could the Birdman of Cline Falls know about what happened in the park that long-ago night in June? Might he have heard something in the course of eighteen years? At the very least, I had some notion that over the decades, as he fed birds, drew water from the river, and absorbed every detail of the land he inhabited, he'd undergone a metamorphosis and become the soul incarnate of Cline Falls. Some knowledge of that violating event might reside in him.

I had been down the dirt road that snaked through sagebrush until it reached the river where the water boiled and eddied against the bank. This was where Cline Falls was—not the pretty state park but the ghost of a ghost town. I had seen the Birdman's little shack—set among giant junipers and littered with bicycle parts, cans and bottles, and bags of birdseed—and had knocked on the door, but not long enough to lure the shy man out of his hovel. Now I had Boo along, and she was doing what she knew would produce him, calling out in her penetrating voice, "Birdman! Birdman! Come down and pull down some birds for us, Birdman!"

Five minutes passed, and a tiny man with a head of shaggy white locks, shaggy white eyebrows over watery cornflower-blue eyes, and a glowing nimbus of white beard appeared at the door. The sight of him filled me with sadness—as though I'd finally found Santa Claus, and how anachronistic he seemed, how poorly he had fared. Too full of simple goodness to fit into our times, he was consigned to squalor.

He immediately began the Evocation of the Birds.

C'mere. Fi Fi! he trilled in a peculiar falsetto. *Pew! Pew! Rrrrrrr!* It took a few trills, but eventually a black-capped chickadee perched on his hand, and the Bird-man's face filled with wonder, as though this were a miracle that was occurring for the first time. His mouth spread wide, like a jack-o'-lantern's, revealing a tooth on either side of his mouth.

Great spiritual lessons could be learned from this man's simple joy.

The Evocation of the Birds continued until Boo got around to asking the Bird-man whether he remembered the night long ago when two girls were attacked on the other side of Cline Falls.

His face lit up again in glee. "Yeah! I remember! That guy that did it . . ." I drew in my breath, waited through his pause. Then he continued, "I went down there to look myself. And the guy that did that . . ." He broke off again. "There was a lot of blood there, too. That was shocking."

The Birdman's voice had the timbre of a dwarf's. "And going out he went clear over the top of a knee-high cement thing and I said to the cop, did you notice that? The way the truck circled around? And he said, yes. And some blood. I never did know. They never did catch up with that guy, did they?"

"Never did."

"Uh-huh," said the Birdman.

"Were there a lot of kids hanging out that night, by the falls here?" I asked.

"I can't remember . . . I wish you could catch up with whoever did it. There was one guy . . . ummmmm . . ." I drew in my breath again. The Birdman looked at the ground, trying to summon a working brain. He was silent a long time, like a man praying.

Boo rescued him. "That was a long time ago."

"Yes, it was quite a while back." He craned his neck to the sky. "Did a bird come?"

Then to me, "I'm deeply sorry. It's my age. *C'mere. Pee Pee! Pee! Pee! Pee!* . . . I was harassed a lot. Out here. They fired a shotgun at my head. Round over here. That's been some years ago. One time a drug addict tried to rob me. Rode my bi-cycle. Got my bike over here, but I can't ride it anymore."

He pointed to the three-wheeled contraption rusting in a junk pile. Over it, a rusty horseshoe hung by a string from a juniper branch. "Went down to get some water up and out of the river there. Car came right behind me. Figured I must have money on me. I did a lot of prayin' there. Boy, I was scared . . . Here, little baby. There's that little baby. Red-winged blackbirds I like so much . . . just about out of walnuts here." The birds snatched what was left in the bag and flew into the juniper branches.

THE NEXT DAY, I headed home, back to California. On my way out of town I pulled off the road on the north side of Cline Falls, bearing a bag of walnuts.

"Birdman! Birdman! It's me from yesterday." The door opened after a time. "I brought you some walnuts!"

"Oh, didja? That's wonderful. I appreciate it. We talked about it, but I didn't believe ya," he said in his dwarf's voice, with his toothless grin.

"See, some things really do come true," I said, reversing roles with Santa Claus.

"Yeah. I'm amazed."

The day before, it had seemed he was on the verge of arriving at a memory about the Cline Falls attack, so I asked him if by now it had come to him.

"I've been thinking about it this morning, trying to remember . . . Let's see, yeah, let me see . . . I've got a poor memory." He looked down at the earth again. "Uh-huh. I was deeply concerned, I know."

"You said you went down to the park the next day and there was blood all over."

"Yeah, uh-huh. I remember I said to the cop, 'Did you notice this?' I said to the cop, 'You noticed that blood?' He said yes . . . I did some scoutin' there."

I formed an image in my mind of the fat loops of his bicycle tires making tracks in the desert dust of the crime scene.

"When you went down there the next day were you very upset about it?" I asked, figuring if I fished for emotion, I might pull up a fact.

"Yeah, was I! Yeah, I was." He giggled uncomfortably. "I was horribly upset about it . . . Then there was this gal, too—real young, pretty youthful like—had a little kid out of wedlock, I guess . . ."

His memory of upset had pulled up another association, a recollection of another girl he'd seen around Cline Falls. Instead of steering him back to my own story, I followed his drift. This teen mother and her child lived nearby and she had once helped Birdman get a bucket of water out of the river. One day she vanished.

"Do you think she was murdered?" I asked.

"Yeah. That was my idea about it," he said, on no greater evidence than that he never saw her again. His conclusion told me a lot about how the Birdman understood the world. "It bothered me all these years since then."

Something about him compelled me to state the obvious. "Terrible things happen in this world," I said, maybe because he struck me as an American West version of a Russian holy fool—a prophet, a miracle worker, a voice for the wretched of the earth—with flowing hair and a luminous beard, wandering the countryside denouncing injustice wherever he saw it.

I regretfully told him I had to go but would visit him on my next trip.

"Want a bird in the hand?" he asked as I headed for my car.

"Next time I'll have a bird in the hand."

He lingered at the door, not wanting me to leave. "Uh-huh. Thinking about it, I'll try to remember. I wish I could remember . . ." A lifetime of heavy concern was

carved in deep grooves between his worried eyes. "I deeply appreciate the walnuts you brought. I deeply appreciate that. Okay, goodbye. I deeply appreciate it. I'm not kidding you."

I was glad to get in my car and drive away, so forbidding did this side of Cline Falls look to me in its outward appearance, where streams of silver slid over jet black lava rock and pooled and fizzled in the rock's pockmarks and fissures. Yet, on this side of Cline Falls, Shayna and I would have been safe on the night of June 22, eighteen years ago, safe with Donny and the boys standing around their juniper campfire. Safe with the Birdman.

ONE HUNDRED and sixty thousand hours later, the trail of this double attempted murder investigation was not cold. Nor was it easily giving up its secrets.

I had managed to turn up a story that had passed into local myth, embroidered here and there, encased in amber—a rural legend with these elements: two girls were chopped in Cline Falls. Maybe one or both died. A hatchet was found in the river, with the initials *D.D.* on it. A local teen was investigated. But they didn't have enough evidence to convict him. People didn't know for sure if they could attach his name to this dark mystery, but a lot of folks believed it in their hearts, and they called him Dirk Duran the Hatchet Man until this turned into an old jingle.

It occurred to me that the rural legend served a function. If the psycho kid known for his hair-trigger temper who nearly killed his girlfriend in front of an audience the very next day after the Cline Falls attack—if this raging homeboy was *not* the perpetrator of this attack on two girls passing through their community (a community with little or no history of murder), wasn't that even more unsettling?

It was an odd paradox. This community where people were intertwined and no one could be anonymous; where lots of folks remembered a decade later the models, years, and colors of the cars or trucks half the town had once driven—this community also had a stubborn, hardheaded western streak of go-it-alone independence. It had a reputation for attracting people who wanted to be left alone. And they got left alone.

In the end, with regard to the community's efforts to resolve the hideous assault on two girls in a local park: the folk will was running in different directions. This was not a place of vigilante justice or lynch mobs. Mad dogs might be informally banished from the social scene—they were shunned—but there was no noose hung from a tree and there were no cowboy boots swinging three feet off the ground. The community had progressed that far, beyond these heinous American traditions.

And yet it wasn't a community looking to eradicate problems before they reached criminality. There were a lot of red flares the town ignored—a violent boy with ignited eyes who performed deeds way beyond homegrown waywardness. In this community with large pockets of decency and goodwill, there was a disconnect between people's good intentions and the fact that most of them had done nothing to put a stop to the boy's ravening. No amount of emotional devastation had translated into action toward finding out whether their own seedling had committed the Cline Falls attack.

I told the story to a business acquaintance from the East Coast. "It's bizarre. I can't believe what you're telling me," Helen said. "An entire community covering up for a man who could chop anybody at any moment? It's just bizarre."

"But they weren't really covering up."

"But they were! Policemen who were sworn to protect the public. A community who wasn't helping to find out who did this. The police and the community. It's incredible. Can you imagine living there? Let's say you lived there, and it happened to someone else. What would you do? Wouldn't you call up and say, 'Who did it?' "

I explained to Helen that members of the local community in Central Oregon described the episode as "the first murder in a little town," and many used the word *devastated* to describe the event's effect on them and their fellow citizens, and a lot of them no longer returned to the park where it happened because they found the place disturbing.

"There was no fear?" she asked.

"Yes, there was fear."

"But no one wanted to find out if he was still there?"

"No one seems to have done that. It was kind of dropped."

"Wow. Wow." Helen kept making deeper and deeper "wows."

MY TRUNK filled with five hatchets, my notebooks brimming with hatchet drawings, I headed south on a radiant June day, toward the California border, toward home, on Highway 97. Then I abruptly turned onto back roads toward the Cascades—*Seven Brides for Seven Brothers* land, fantastic high country—and set out on an impulse to climb the mother of all volcanoes, Mount Mazuma, which had exploded seven thousand years before, sending ash so far around the globe that conditions for brilliant sunsets were produced throughout the Northern Hemisphere.

My senses were reeling from the drama of the landscape. I pushed my old red Volvo beyond its capacity, heading for the unruffled blue Crater Lake of so many calendar photographs, imagining that the tranquil depths would symbolize for me that place of calm after violence.

I pressed the accelerator pedal to the floor, labored up the switchbacks. The June sun disappeared into the clouds, and a full-out blizzard enveloped the car. Chugging on, I reached the summit—but the view of that serene blue lake was completely obscured. No crater. No lake. Nothing but white. I inched to the very edge of the precipice. The veil was so thick my eyes could not see through it.

I ARRIVED HOME to find a letter. A few months before, I had fired off a note to the town of Sisters, petitioning for leniency with regard to the traffic ticket I had been given in September 1994, for speeding in a school zone near midnight. I laid out in rather grim detail the sole reason I was in Sisters in the first place, and suggested that being caught in a speed trap on the same road where I was nearly "chopped to bits" added insult to injury—and I sent along 1977 newspaper clippings as proof.

The letter to me was from the Sisters Municipal Court, on stationery illustrated with the three sibling volcanoes, Faith, Hope, and Charity, and a refund of my check for $134.

I knew I liked any town named "Sisters."

A Trip Back to the Midwest

It is with compassion and fond memories that we remember
our classmates.

—"IN MEMORIAM," LYONS TOWNSHIP HIGH SCHOOL
    TEN-YEAR REUNION PROGRAM

Back home, I was eager to shrug off my
girl-from-Cline-Falls identity. It was hard to wear for long periods of time. And
yet, I was growing ever more confused about who my more normal self was.

The notion of identity is a slippery idea for anyone. The ways in which I defined myself in my usual environment seemed a great deal more confining than
what I had experienced in the community where I had launched my investigation. Back home, as I re-installed myself into old roles, I felt a shrinkage. I didn't
feel as authentic to myself as when I was crunching the gravel of the unpaved
back roads of Central Oregon.

Once, I had dreams where I was stepping on ice and sliding through life, making no headway. On Oregon back roads, every roll of wheel over gravel had
seemed freighted with will, determination, intent. Something about crunching up
and down driveways had made me solid inside. That assertive search had given
me a feeling of equilibrium.

Since I'd been thrown into motion, I'd transformed fear into vitality. A turbulent wave had disturbed the sediment; the unconscious was rising to the surface.
I was seeing a deeper echo of myself as my past was integrating with my present.
If one of the basic drives of life is to become real to ourselves, I was making
progress.

I remember, as a teenager, I was young and naïve enough to believe that I
could generate some eternal sense of self that would remain consistent throughout my lifetime. Even if there had been no bloodstained sleeping bag in the closet,
I doubt that I could have done so.

And yet I still had homesickness for this "before" self whose life veered in another direction in June 1977. I knew that a fossil record of me lay undisturbed in
the western Chicago suburbs. I hadn't been back to my childhood home since I
was airlifted out of my green, leafy neighborhood—with my shaved head and

Frankenstein sutures—and whisked behind the Iron Curtain in July 1977. The grim newspaper headlines evidently left my classmates at Lyons Township High School assuming the worst, because when the tenth reunion program for the Lyons Township High School Class of '75 was printed in 1985, my name appeared on the "In Memoriam" page, along with a handful of others doomed to die young.

The summer of '95 brought the twentieth reunion celebration. Expanding on my ghost-of-Cline-Falls identity, I would fly back as a ghost of Lyons Township High School. When I signed in with the twentieth reunion organizers, the same who had organized the tenth, they looked at me sheepishly and said nothing—not even a "Glad you're still among us." Earlier I had sent them a postcard informing them that I would attend the upcoming function, and not from the grave.

When my old friend Maryann laid eyes on me, she stood stock-still, rooted to the ground. Could it be? Just before she came to the reunion she had reminisced with her old yearbook, looked up my picture, conjured memories of me, and mourned. She knew I had survived the attack, so when she read my name in the "In Memoriam" section, she assumed I had later died of complications, somewhere along life's path to the tenth reunion.

Over the crowd of faces, many of whom looked as if they'd had too much sun and drink since their tender teens (affording me a certain smugness about my own aging process, especially considering I was supposed to be dead), I caught sight of my old best friend Kathy, who had been well aware of my aliveness all these years. She yelled, "Jentz!" (summoning me the way she had when we were kids) and motioned me over to where a woman with an appalled visage was standing. I studied the woman's face, and a name associated with her features leaked into my brain—she was a junior high school acquaintance I had not thought of, literally, since the last time I'd laid eyes on her an age ago.

"You remember Carol?" Kathy asked with a grin, and I nodded. Carol stood there looking at me, a peculiar expression on her face.

"Carol comes up to me and says, 'Do you know what happened to Terri Jentz?' I said, 'You know she's *not dead*, don't you?' And Carol says, 'I know that! But did you hear she had a *sex-change operation*?' "

There was a rumor going around that I had had a sex-change operation?

Kathy broke into laughter, then I did. Carol did not laugh.

It's true that I had always been in tension with culturally prescribed female roles. Here was an example from my own life about how rumors get constructed.

MY CHILDHOOD suburb struck me as supernaturally green. The canopies of hardwood trees that arched over the quiet streets were denser still, and seemed to hold the town's residents in a secure and loving embrace. Though at nineteen I considered Western Springs a tame prison, at thirty-seven, I silently blessed these streets for the sanctuary granted me when I was a developing girl, for helping me grow up with self-confidence and the solid sense that nothing would daunt me.

That I was dauntless as a teen wasn't just a memory I had touched up. My classmates at the twentieth reunion told me how they remembered me— "courageous," one woman said—another reason why I had revisited this place, to spade up the turf and find the buried time capsule of who I was then, this repository of a deeper layer of essential self, one I needed to draw on in these times.

Most things had not changed in Western Springs since my leave-taking. The big old houses lined streets where no RVs or pickups were allowed to mar the suburban perfection. Freight trains and commuter trains still cut through the village center several times a day and kept the traffic from moving too fast.

But nowadays kids didn't ride their bikes just anywhere without fear of lurking danger. Parents didn't let their children out of their sight anymore. According to my friend Kathy's mother, Western Springs even had a rapist "who got two girls," as she put it, a few years ago.

Kathy's parents hadn't seen me in ages, but through the years they'd thought a lot about what happened to me that summer of '77. They told me about the "violation" they felt (they curiously used the same word as people in Central Oregon). They were affected for many years, especially because I had asked their daughter Kathy to join us on that BikeCentennial trip, and she had seriously considered my offer.

But if Kathy had been with us, wouldn't the sequence of events have differed? Like flipping a deck of cards, I replayed in my mind the series of minute decisions we made over the course of our seven-day trip, driving us toward the night of June 22, 1977: a solid group that vowed to take a bicycle trip across America, one which dwindled to two; meeting up with a pair of convivial bikers who gave us safety in numbers and whose pace quickened our own; a drought that caused a punishing mountain pass to open early; a decision to leave our biking companions because they were stronger than we; tension on the road that broke down the friendship between Shayna and me, never restored to this day; the vow to always stay in campgrounds, which trumped my intuition and led me to insist on staying in Cline Falls State Park, where it turned out we found ourselves camping alone after all.

Surely, a third person would have influenced the sequence of decisions, altered the ill-omened set of circumstances—and thus the twists of fate that landed us precisely in that place at that time.

God Is My Witness

"What was he like?" I inquired of the detective, noting what a loaded question I was asking.

He had long silver hair tied back in a ponytail, the detective told me.

Striking, I thought, and noted with still greater irony that I myself had prematurely silver hair tied back in a ponytail, one of my more arresting features. The first dramatic shock of silver appeared in my twenties—sprung from a former battlefield, a scar in my scalp just above my forehead. This coincidence was a detail you might expect in a novel. Other than that, I told myself the fact had no meaning.

In July of 1995, I had received a phone call at home from Detective Lynn Fredrickson from the Oregon State Police. He had tracked down Dirk Duran in Washington and interviewed him, just as he promised he would.

This news shook me. Yes, I really did want to know the identity of my attacker, and yet I had been engaged in what sometimes seemed like a sort of literary investigation, reconstructing a story from many fragments. In spite of my attempts to pare away the scar tissue of denial, maybe I hadn't fully considered that this phantom axeman was anything but a myth. The oral transmissions told and retold—of a scary young cowboy who brandished axes—were phantasmagoric, like something out of *Beowulf*, the monster Grendel rising from his lair to unleash murderous rampages throughout the kingdom. Now I was being told that the suspect existed in current time and space. Detective Fredrickson's phone calls to Dirk's father had flushed him out from under some rock somewhere. Dirk Duran returned Fredrickson's call, and they met in Washington. Fredrickson approached him by saying that the victim of the Cline Falls attack wanted answers. Dirk was willing to cooperate. He wanted to clear his name.

"Don't take this the wrong way or anything, but I thought he was a very good-looking guy," the detective confessed to me over the phone, which I thought a bit strange coming from a cop, "except his teeth were all rotten." Fredrickson promised to show me a photo the next time we met. He assured me that later on in the summer there would be a meeting with the state police, where I would learn the findings of his investigative review. So far, he had found no record indicating that Dirk Duran was ever investigated by *any* police agency whatsoever, contrary to the rumors circulating around the Redmond community at the time. He himself had interviewed Janey Firestone and heard her version of the events of the summer of 1977. That Janey Firestone was interviewed by any policemen, that she told police that Dirk's toolbox was missing, that she told them she'd found Dirk's tracks in the park—all of this was still completely unsubstantiated. Furthermore, there was nothing to substantiate Janey's claim that it was *the very next morning* after the Cline Falls attack when Dirk Duran beat her up in the seed field. Since the juxtaposition of the two violent incidents was one reason Dirk Duran's name got linked to the Cline Falls attack, the timing was crucial.

Finally, Fredrickson had found Durr's and Cooley's police notebooks for the year 1977 in a storeroom. Both detectives had made notations and drawn pictures of the tire tracks they saw, and in Fredrickson's personal opinion, these did not fit Janey Firestone's description. Fredrickson claimed that Janey told him the tread on Dirk's two front tires was mismatched, while the rear tires had matching tread. Her statements, in his opinion, contradicted descriptions of the tires in Durr's and Cooley's notes.

But the biggest news of all was that Dirk Duran had agreed to take a polygraph regarding the Cline Falls attack, so that he might have an opportunity once and for all to clear himself of the stigma.

"Before he took it, he told me he wanted me to clear the family name," Fredrickson told me. "He said, 'Only way I'll take it is if you publish the results in the newspaper.' I told him, 'I can't do that, but I'll spread it around the community.'"

Dirk took this first polygraph near his home in Washington. According to Fredrickson, the examiner's report pointed to Dirk's innocence, but the results were deemed inconclusive because Dirk had consumed muscle relaxants and alcohol before the test. Dirk had agreed to take another test to make the results conclusive.

Fredrickson suggested that I start disabusing myself of the notion that Dirk might have been my attacker.

I could feel the blood in my body rush to my head and flush my face. I jumped in to remonstrate against Fredrickson's hasty conclusion. The detective saw fit to lecture me.

"Hearsay can get really out of hand," he said, referring to the rumors flying around Redmond for two decades.

"I agree with you, hearsay can get out of hand." I knew all about how vague speculation and hastily formed impressions get turned into concrete facts in the process of being passed from one person to another, as in: "They found a hatchet in the river with *D.D.* on it." That tale I knew to be apocryphal, but it was by now encased under a hundred coats of shellac.

"One thing that is not hearsay is my memory," I snapped back at him. I had seen a young cowboy who looked like he stepped off a movie set, and Dirk Duran fit that description to a tee. I had a powerful hunch about him. At first I couldn't believe that a local hothead, whom everyone in the community knew, could possibly have been my attacker. Through rigorous investigation tempered by a healthy dose of skepticism, I had arrived at my present intuition. I felt a deep sense of ethical responsibility with regard to my belief in his guilt. I would have abhorred accusing the wrong guy, and if new information emerged that pointed away from him, I would be the first to pay attention.

Something Dee Dee said to me had stuck. In her fifteen-odd years working with hundreds of victims of violent crime, she had yet to meet one who wanted someone other than the guilty party convicted. She never met anyone who didn't anguish over whether the accused had actually done the deed. The psyche of the outraged victim seeking resolution and justice did not abhor a vacuum to the extent that filling it with just anyone would do.

A FEW DAYS LATER, Fredrickson mailed me copies of Durr's and Cooley's notebooks, just as he had promised. As a recap of what he had told me on the telephone, he'd attached a yellow Post-it to the copies, with a notation in his neat hand: "Terri. Please call me. I have contacted Dirk Duran, interviewed and polygraphed. (He isn't your attacker.)—Lynn Fredrickson."

Pain shot through my skull. *He isn't your attacker.* I looked at the scar winding around my left forearm. *He isn't your attacker.* But surely somebody was. (Surely this sinister scar hadn't arrived on my arm like a spontaneously erupting stigmata.)

I burned with thwarted energy. The police had dropped the investigation of this crime. The woman who had experienced the attack with me never wanted to speak of it again. I hadn't seen his face.

The tendency to suppress, to deny, to leave it alone—to disappear the whole thing—was like the relentless dominance of gravity, invisible yet all-powerful. That denying energy had always been, and still was, stronger by far than the will to assign these specific acts of human moral evil to a specific identity. I felt a miasma start to take me over, to drain me.

I WILLED MYSELF to continue my quest, to take another step, which I hoped would, as it had now for three years, lead to another and another. That step would mean leafing through these notebooks, the hour-by-hour, day-by-day records of Detectives Cooley's and Durr's movements following June 22, 1977.

Unlike the "crime report," which was a compilation of digested interviews that were once and sometimes twice removed from the source, and written days later, these notes had been recorded by the detectives spontaneously.

At 1:25 a.m., on June 23, 1977, in Cline Falls State Park, they pointed their flashlights at the ground where the vehicle first left the paved roadway, studied patterns in the dirt, then jotted their impressions on their pads.

Cooley scrawled: "assault vehicle has 2 bald tires 6″ in width" and "R.F. 4 groove Hwy." By this I assumed he meant that the right front tire was a highway tire, with four grooves. He even sketched the pattern: four squiggly lines indicating tread grooves. He noted nothing about the left front tire.

Durr jotted: "2 Tires Back Bald possible" and "2 tires have tread. Right front has 4 groove. Better tread than other." He drew a sketch of four straight lines (not squiggly), indicating tire grooves. I made the assumption that Durr had drawn the same right front tire as Cooley had—that he was taking a shortcut when he chose to draw the tread grooves with straight rather than squiggly lines.

Neither cop indicated that the front two tires had matching tread, but they also didn't note that the tread was different. Only Durr said that both front tires had tread. It did seem odd that neither detective noted whether the front tires were different or the same. It was curious, too, that they had both sketched only the right tire, and not the left.

Could it be that they could gather only enough information about the left front tire to note that it had some amount of tread?

Both detectives were clear that the rear tires were bald. But we couldn't know if the rear tires matched each other or whether either or both matched either or both front tires.

I studied the crime scene photos of grooves in the dirt, but I could make out only a single squiggly groove of tread. I remembered Janey telling me earlier in the summer: *Those were totally different tires on the front . . . I thought it was so weird that he would keep them on his pickup like that.* By my own assessment of the police notes, it was inconclusive whether the two front tires had the same

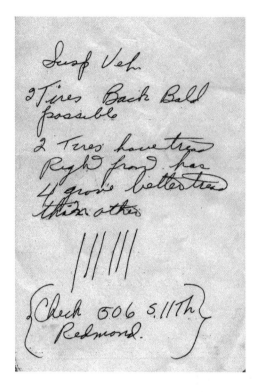

tread or whether they had a different tread. It was also inconclusive whether either tire in the rear matched either tire in the front.

Fredrickson did not have the evidence to conclude that Janey's claims were invalid. It was certainly true that the four tires were different enough that they hadn't made four matching prints on the ground. What was clear was that Janey Firestone knew that her boyfriend's tires had made a distinctive, irregular pattern on the ground. Janey had a talent for reading tire tracks! And she bothered to go to the crime scene to look for the template she had memorized from her own driveway.

On the third page of notes for the morning of June 23, 1977, Cooley wrote in his small notebook: "At blood site: 1 black felt pen. 6 tent pegs. 1 white sweat sock. 2 tent straps or pack straps." I pictured this scenario in my mind—*the blood site*—illumined by the beams of two flashlights. The spare language of police reports—reducing a scene of atrocity to its stark thingness—seemed to elevate it to a tragic sublime.

Continuing on: Cooley went to the hospital; Cooley interviewed the girls; Cooley canvassed the area, talking to people about what they knew. As the days went on, he listed name after name of those he spoke to at specific hours of the day. He interviewed far more people than those he had entered in the crime report, the official document that was sent to headquarters in Salem. Often he did not describe what information they told him. Other times, however, he noted events with great specificity, including one I distinctly remembered.

On June 29, 1977:

2:35 Bimart to borrow three hatchets
2:50 Hospital. Display Hatchets to Jentz
4:45 Bimart Return Hatchets

Only one notation mentioned "Dirk Duran." On August 11, Cooley noted that the Redmond Police Department suggested he make contact with a resident of

Redmond, a woman who "advised her sons have heard that Dirk Duran is number 1 suspect." There is no mention of follow-up.

Durr's notes were half the quantity of Cooley's, and roughly followed the outline of the interviews listed in the crime report. He, too, dutifully documented the borrowing, displaying, and returning of hatchets. One other notation, made in early July, caught my interest: "Call from Mr. Weiss re. Cline Falls attack. Stated to throw away sleeping bag and foam mattress."

I thought about how Shayna's and my differing responses to the same event—that dialectic between amnesia and remembrance—was no better symbolized than this: Shayna's father ordered that her bloody sleeping bag be tossed in the garbage, while I instructed my father to toss mine in the washing machine.

By now scores of locals had told me, "Dirk Duran was investigated," but the record of an investigation was still in hiding, if one existed at all. The mystery of the origins of this oft-repeated tale haunted me.

It was late and I was zonked, but I pulled from my office closet boxes of old newspaper articles from 1977. Was there any clue I had overlooked earlier? My eyes were bleary as I reread each one, then paused on one yellowed clipping from the Bend *Bulletin*, dated Monday, June 27, 1977:

Meanwhile Cooley said little progress was made over the weekend in the search for clues in the Cline Falls attack.

"We'd like to think it's a local person who assaulted the Yale coeds," he said. "But that's only a gut feeling."

He said he is not ruling out a possibility there may have been more than one person involved in the assault.

Cooley talked with Jentz Saturday at the hospital. But he said the young woman was "heavily sedated" and unable to help much with descriptions of the suspect or the vehicle.

Cooley said he plans to talk today with a 17-year-old youth charged Friday with assault in connection with a beating incident involving his girlfriend but doesn't expect to tie the youth to the Cline Falls attack.

The youth was charged by Deschutes County sheriff's deputies and detained over the weekend at the Prineville City Jail. He was released to his parents today, according to Deschutes County juvenile authorities.

Here was proof that Dirk Duran was a person of interest! It also helped establish a time frame. The Cline Falls attack took place Wednesday night. If Dirk was charged on Friday for his assault on Janey, that assault may have taken place on either Thursday or Friday. But it was patently evident that Dirk couldn't use as an alibi that he was sitting in a jail cell Wednesday night.

Cooley doesn't expect to tie the youth to the Cline Falls attack? Why not?

I went back to Cooley's notebooks for Monday, June 27. At 7:30 a.m. he made a notation that he had had contact with the press regarding the assault. (I assume that this "contact with the press" was when he gave the information quoted in the newspaper.) At 4:25 in the afternoon he left for the Redmond area, and noted that he interviewed William Penhollow and Robin and James Williams before returning to Bend. By 8:30 p.m. he was off duty. Durr was off duty all that day.

What happened to his talk with the seventeen-year-old youth just released from jail? Was Cooley turned away? Dissuaded from conducting the interview? What information did he know in advance that led him to expect not to tie the youth to the Cline Falls attack?

WHEN I MADE an appointment for the next meeting with the state police, Sergeant Marlen Hein tipped me off that Dirk Duran had recently taken a second polygraph, and its findings had made the police considerably more appreciative of our focus on him. When the Kounses and I walked into the meeting room in August 1995, we found that the officers' tone of voice, body language, and pre-meeting patter had changed dramatically since our last meeting. Only Detective Lynn Fredrickson continued to glower.

The genial Sergeant Marlen Hein said that he himself would take charge of the next stage of the investigation. He reiterated why their organization was maintaining involvement in a non-prosecutable case like Cline Falls. He could justify this investigation only to try to prevent some new crime from erupting from this same suspect.

Also, the state police could use this case as an example of how the statute of limitations on attempted murder was outdated. This was an emblematic case that might sway lawmakers to change that statute to an unlimited period of time. If it were provable beyond a reasonable doubt who the perpetrator of the Cline Falls incident was, why shouldn't he, even after these eighteen years, be held accountable?

Finally, there were deeper reasons. Captain Rich Hein, Marlen's amiable brother, spoke up: "We can't correct what happened in '77. If we could, we would. But if a case like this is never solved, it never dies. It never dies for the victims and never dies for the community, and what you instill in the community is fear. The only way to lessen the fear is to resolve the incident."

Marlen (we were on a first-name basis now) pointed out that he believed that members of the community did feel personal responsibility for the Cline Falls crime having happened: they felt it was a negative reflection on the whole population.

These were my talking points in my first police meeting, and now these men had adopted the themes as their own. Remarkable, I thought privately, that they were willing even to consider the psychic ramifications of a crime that could never be prosecuted.

Detective Lynn Fredrickson had concluded his initial investigation a few weeks before, and he personally found no concrete evidence to link suspect Dirk Duran to the crime—no physical evidence to indicate that he was there, no statements he had made to someone else that he was there, no eyewitnesses. What Fredrickson discovered was this: Duran was no longer living in Washington. In fact, just in the last month he had moved back to Redmond and was living on the ranch with his mom and dad.

He was back?

Mild nausea passed through me. Before now, Duran was a rumor seen here and there. I was relieved when someone once told me that they thought he was working as a long-haul trucker. That meant he was on the road somewhere, not near me. Although I'd made progress in being able to imagine that the "meticulous cowboy" was a real flesh-and-blood person, I wasn't yet prepared to picture his flesh and blood in proximity to me.

But why had he come back now to the scene of the crime he was suspected of having committed? What had made him want to migrate home precisely when I had put into motion a massive effort to find out who was responsible for Cline Falls?

Now he was in my orbit.

Before asking Duran to take the first polygraph test, Fredrickson interviewed him at least twice, formally and informally, regarding his memories of 1977.

I thought to myself: Something about such an interview didn't seem real. A plain old interview with Dirk Duran to get his version of events didn't seem quite phantasmagoric enough. It seemed as preposterous as sitting the monster Grendel down in a plastic chair and asking him to describe his version of the rampages throughout the kingdom.

Though on some level I felt it unlikely that words could even issue from the mouth of the headless, speechless cowboy torso I saw in the summer of '77—if this were he, what did he have to say for himself?

During the course of two interviews, Dirk Duran told Detective Fredrickson that he was working at Skyview Mobile Homes in Terrebonne, Oregon, during the summer of '77. During that time he was going out with Janey Firestone, and she was working at the Shepherds' onion fields. He used to go out and see her during his breaks. When he visited, they would use the tailgate of his pickup for a diving board to swim in the irrigation pond. At that time he owned a 1974 Ford, three-quarter-ton, four-by-four pickup. One day he went out to visit Janey; he had been drinking vodka and had taken ten milligrams of Valium. They had both been cheating on each other and got into a big argument. Dirk totally lost his cool and struck Janey. He didn't remember pursuing her into the water but could remember getting arrested for hurting her.

Dirk related that the sheriff took him to the courthouse in Bend and interviewed him for a while in an upstairs room; then police took him to the Prineville jail. He appeared before a Judge Edmonds and received a *four-day* [italics are mine] jail sentence and was put on probation to the court.

Dirk said that the night before he hurt Janey they had been at his house. It was late and they had gotten into a big argument. He woke his father, and his dad took Janey home. Dirk said he never left the house until the next day. When he hurt Janey the next day, it was just a continuation of their argument. Dirk told Fredrickson that he always had a problem with his temper and used to get in fights all the time. He also told him that he did have access to a hatchet that belonged to his father. It was a regular type of hatchet and had a leather sheath on it. He told Fredrickson that he thought his father still had the hatchet he used. He said he did carry a white utility box in the back of his pickup, but he doesn't know what happened to it. He told Fredrickson that he had to deal with rumors all his life that he was responsible for injuring the two girls at Cline Falls. He didn't know how the rumors got started, but he swore he had nothing to do with the incident. They even used to call him "Dirk Duran the Hatchet Man." He thought that whoever it was who injured the girls was a sick person and should be punished for what they did. He admitted he slammed every type of dope you could think of, had a history of violent outbreaks, and used to say things to perpetuate his reputation for being a bad dude, but he told Fredrickson he would take any test he could to prove his innocence and clear his family name.

I noted that in Fredrickson's digest of his two interviews with Dirk Duran, Dirk never actually answered the question of what he was doing the night of June 22, 1977. He did say he had been fighting with Janey the night before his assault on her (though he never specifically said his assault on Janey took place the day after the Cline Falls attack). It was, ironically, his story I believed over hers when it came to how well they got along the night of the Cline Falls attack. Janey told me that when he dropped her off that night (which she identified as Wednesday, the night of Cline Falls), everything was "hunky-dory." In fact, I had called Janey after I spoke to the sisters, Linda and Robin, who, along with Janey's brother Curt, both remembered Janey telling them she had had a fight with Dirk the night the Cline Falls incident took place.

"No, it was a really good night," Janey had told me. "We fought so much, but I remember that night was pleasant. A happy day. A good ride home. And the next day, it was the opposite."

Why did Janey remember that she and Dirk were getting along hunky-dory?

With Dee Dee's dead-eye perception, she homed in on a point that made sense: If Janey and Dirk had fought on the night of June 22, might she feel culpable for my fate and Shayna's? The moment she saw that the toolbox was missing from her violent boyfriend's pickup, did she feel a shiver of guilt that two girls passing through on bicycles had taken blows for her?

Apparently Dirk Duran had produced no airtight alibi or alibi witness to account for his whereabouts on the night of the Cline Falls attack. When Detective Fredrickson asked Lou Duran about the events of that night—whether he remembered his son having had a fight with Janey and whether his son had awakened him to drive her home—the elder Duran said he didn't remember.

Fredrickson found no remaining police or government record of Dirk Duran's assault on Janey Firestone. Because he was under eighteen, he technically was never arrested, as it was illegal to arrest a juvenile in that era. Juveniles could only be taken into temporary custody. They could be "detained." At that time, anyone under eighteen could not even be fingerprinted. Without fingerprints, there would be no mention in the criminal history of the period of temporary custody. Fredrickson had searched the Deschutes County Sheriff's Office for a record of the detainment, and had searched the Crook County jail archives for a record that Dirk Duran was signed into the jail. The Deschutes County Juvenile Department told Fredrickson that any juvenile records that existed would have been expunged by now. In short, Fredrickson said, it was common in the late seventies to hold a juvenile over the weekend with no record for arrest or incarceration. Bob, Dee Dee, and I all muttered to ourselves how misguided those beliefs were: that children weren't capable of bad deeds; those confused little souls would surely grow into law-abiding solid citizens the minute they turned eighteen, wouldn't they?

Evidence for the exact date of the assault on Janey remained elusive. But I did the mental calculations. The newspaper said that Dirk was released on Monday, June 27. I had to rely on the suspect's own memory of how many days he was in jail, because Fredrickson never managed to turn up records of Dirk's appearance before the judge who sentenced him. If Dirk's sentence truly was four days, counting back from Monday, that meant he was jailed on Thursday—the day after the Cline Falls attack on Wednesday night. Just as Janey and her friend Robin had insisted.

Once Fredrickson finished the recital of his supposedly dead-end investigation, Marlen took the floor again, speaking with breathless enthusiasm. He said that because the results of the polygraph examination taken in Washington had been inconclusive, Dirk had agreed to take a second polygraph, on July 14. This second polygraph had quite a different outcome. The examiner scored the results as "deceptive." Because it was determined that Dirk had drugs in his system during both polygraph examinations, he himself requested to take a third. When he didn't show up on the morning the test was scheduled, Marlen himself paid Dirk a visit at his parent's ranch to find out why. A verbal confrontation took place in front of Dirk's father, and as the conversation spiraled rapidly out of control, Dirk made an obscene gesture to Marlen and ordered him off the property, while his father stood silently by.

"He was threatening, but I wasn't worried about it. I'm no John Wayne. I just don't have that syndrome," Marlen told us cheerfully.

The following day the police got a call from one of Dirk's associates with a warning: the next patrol car that came up that driveway asking about Cline Falls would meet a bullet through its windshield.

Marlen put out an "officer safety alert" warning all law enforcement agencies in Central Oregon to use extreme caution if they deemed it necessary to make contact with Dirk Duran. Marlen said he wasn't trying to scare us, but he just wanted us to know what we were getting into. It seemed Dirk was gunning for anyone asking questions about his connection to Cline Falls, particularly those who had bothered his parents.

I thought to myself that Marlen, this man of breathless demeanor, who said "Jeez Almighty!" a lot, and who had witnessed a demonstration of Dirk's fabled rage, was now invested in my case. I knew I could ask no more from a cop than his emotional involvement.

MARLEN SWORE up and down there was no indication of an informal police cover-up back in '77, and if there was one, he strenuously insisted, the current regime of the state police would come clean. He reiterated that investigative methods were primitive in those days. There were three red flags that Cooley and Durr should have followed up on.

The first was inexplicable: that Cooley told the press on Monday, June 27, that he was on his way to interview a seventeen-year-old youth held in jail in Prineville for beating his girlfriend, but he didn't expect to link the youth to the attack. There was nothing in Cooley's notebooks for that day, or for the surrounding days, saying anything about the seventeen-year-old, an interview with him, or why the interview had been canceled.

The second red flag was a call on August 11 from a resident of Redmond, a mother who said that her son had claimed Dirk Duran was the number one suspect in the Cline Falls attack. I told the officers assembled in the room that recently I followed up on that lead myself. I found this woman in the phone book and knocked on the front door of her neat home in Redmond. She told me simply that during the time of Cline Falls she called the police because her son came home saying that talk around school had Dirk Duran as the likely suspect. She had no inside scoop other than that. She heard rumors, and she wanted to make sure the police knew about them.

Unlike some others whom I'd spoken to—who seemed to have the same visceral reaction to the memory as I did—this woman felt no particular charge from the Cline Falls incident. (I thought it peculiar that the only *woman* on record as having called the police department seemed all these years later to have been rather unaffected by the incident.) She then sent me over to the home of her son, in Redmond.

"All I heard is they were investigating him," her son told me. "They tried to trace his tire tracks. We went to school with Dirk Duran and he was known to have a temper—but you can't frame him for that."

"So all you heard was rumor."

"Yeah . . . eighteen years is a long time. I'd done forgot about that," he said.

Red flag number three was the incident described by Corporal Richard Little of the Redmond Police Department: Little's 1979 arrest of local man Chris Peterson for furnishing alcoholic beverages to minors, and Peterson's subsequent desire to make a deal by fingering Duran as the suspect in the Cline Falls attack.

As part of his investigative review, Fredrickson interviewed Cooley, who said he had no recollection of ever talking to Dirk Duran in connection with the Cline Falls investigation—nor did he remember talking to Chris Peterson about the Cline Falls assault. When Fredrickson asked Cooley if he could check his notebook for March 17, 1979, the date of Peterson's arrest, he found this notation:

2:40 Leave for Redmond

3:05 Redmond PD

   Chris M. Peterson

3:35 Interview Chris Peterson with Redmond PD Little. Peterson has no positive information regarding Cline Falls assault. Has lived Redmond since summer of 78. Has heard other tales with Dirk Duran re. being suspect. Duran has vicious temper. Has seen his conduct toward older woman—appeared that he might attack her physically with little provocation.

Cooley's notes, it seemed to me, downplayed Corporal Little's memory of Peterson's accusation against Duran; his very first notation was that "Peterson has no positive information" about the Cline Falls assault. Had Cooley automatically dismissed Peterson's account because Peterson could only have heard the information secondhand?

Fredrickson didn't find it surprising that Cooley hadn't remembered this encounter. He reminded us again that Cooley had a poor memory, although Cooley's partner Clayton Durr's memory was flawless. Fredrickson also re-interviewed Durr. He, like Cooley, still had no recollection of the name Dirk Duran surfacing as a suspect in the Cline Falls case.

Bob Kouns broke in on Fredrickson's recitation of his investigation. "You have said Durr had an impeccable memory in the Kaye Turner case. It seems incredible to me that this guy has this lapse about all of the stuff that has happened. Here's a newspaper article where Durr's partner Cooley is saying 'We've got this person of interest, but we don't think he's connected.' "

Bob pointed out that if Cooley didn't expect to link the seventeen-year-old to the attack in advance of talking to him, he had to have been privy to some piece of information, and probably Durr was, too. Didn't they discuss their mutual case?

"Everyone we've talked to involved in law enforcement all over Oregon at that period of time remembered Cline Falls rather vividly," Bob continued. "I can't believe that Durr didn't have enough interest in that case that he wouldn't have questioned Cooley. If I were a police officer in this current investigation, I'd put Durr in a corner and say, 'What the hell is happening?' "

One of the officers in the room reiterated that Durr and Cooley took orders from their supervisor, Lieutenant Lamkin, who had little experience in criminal investigations. "They were told to answer phones sometimes. It wasn't an ideal situation for the detectives."

Fredrickson said that when he interviewed Cooley, Cooley told him that it was Lamkin who had directed him to call the parents of Jentz and Weiss to tell them that Bud Godwin was responsible for the Cline Falls attack. (Lamkin. The "fly in the ointment" again, the boss who had made Fredrickson really prickly. I remember Fredrickson telling me, "Back then we had gods. They said, 'That's the way it is,' and no one questioned it.")

"Be diplomatic when talking to Durr," Fredrickson lectured. "He's been approached several times and is starting to get his feathers ruffled. He talked to me because we were partners for a long time."

"I talked to Durr two times in three years," I said.

"The fact that this pisses him off is tough shit as far as I'm concerned," Bob said. I'd seen Bob Kouns before when he was really angry and it wasn't a pretty sight. His soft eyes turned reptilian, his heavy lids lowered; he gazed off to the side as he formulated his point, then turned his eyes back to his victim and reamed him straight on.

Bob and Dee Dee were both furious at Fredrickson because the detective had acted unprofessionally by blowing their cover, telling Dirk's father, Lou, that agents for the victim had been out to the Duran ranch, asking questions about Dirk under the guise of looking for real estate. Lou Duran remembered the Kounses well, as "a pretty nosey pair."

"We're talking about a very serious lapse in an investigation that as of right now is inexplicable, and is central to the case," Bob boomed. "Durr and Cooley were co-equals—they were the people in charge of this thing and they made a major screw-up. I don't care whether they're angry!"

Of course it wouldn't be the first time that small-town cops in an unsophisticated place during an innocent era had botched an attempted murder investigation. But we would keep searching for answers as to whether this particular investigation had somehow gotten willfully swept under the carpet.

Fred Ackom, introduced as the coordinator of Polygraph Unity and Quality Control, rose from his seat. He was a big man, tall with a square jaw, a mustache trimmed to the edges of his mouth, long dimples in his cheeks, and a cleft in his chin. He told the assembled group that the polygraph examiner in Washington who had given the original polygraph to Dirk Duran claimed that there were no consistent deceptive results to the questions administered. But prior to taking the

test, Duran had taken a prescription drug called Soma and had consumed beer—
and in fact, according to Ackom's own reading of the Washington polygraph examiner's charts, the instruments recorded little response at all to any of the
questions on the test.

On July 14, Ackom himself administered a second polygraph to Duran.
Though Ackom had admonished Duran not to take drugs or alcohol, the examinee admitted in the pre-test interview that he had taken methamphetamines the
night before, and the night before that. "But I got what I consider very conclusive
charts. I had our examiner Lorin Weilacher in the Bend office blind-score them.
He scored them deceptive. I since had the charts quality-controlled by another
examiner, in Salem. He scored it even higher, more deceptive, than either Lorin or
myself. There's no question the charts are deceptive.

"In addition to that, Mr. Duran sits there for five hours. I felt he wanted to
confess, has a need to confess. He has a *piercing* stare. He can stare right through
you. And you talk about eye contact—there's no blink of the eye or anything. But
after his failed test, and I confront him about not being truthful with me, he cowers. He will not look at me. I'm right up there invading his space—and here's an
intimidating guy—and he's just a broken man. He will not look at me. He looks
down and away from me. He breaks down. He's down to zero state. He weeps
openly. Reaches out and grasps my hands. He's saying things like, 'Fred, I know I
didn't do this, but maybe I don't believe that. God is my witness—may He strike
me dead if I did this.' He goes on and on about how this thing has haunted him:
'There isn't a day gone by that I haven't thought about this. That I haven't
thought about that car running over those girls' tent. That I haven't thought
about those girls being hacked at.' The interesting thing about that: he never ex-
cludes himself. He doesn't say, 'Someone else is running over the tent.' He words
it in such a way that . . . 'I can picture that happening.' Why is he picturing that
happening, over and over again?"

I felt my chest tighten. Perhaps this was one of the more remarkable events in
this meandering quest—to realize that the prime suspect shared my everyday
preoccupation with the events of June 22, 1977. It was an unsettling intimacy, as
though he occupied the same fluorescent memory I had imagined was only mine.

I felt a spasm of sympathy for him, taken in especially by this touching little
detail of him reaching for his interrogator's hands. Then I watched my feeling
heart, noticed how quickly the compassion response was invoked. Wasn't I being
manipulated? Weren't these crocodile tears? Simply a performance?

"I figure, he's ready to confess," Ackom continued. "I press the issue. I give him
a scenario and even tell him what I think happened. He had a fight with his girlfriend. Then he had to go and contemplate life. He's there. And I try to give him
an out: 'It wasn't that you intended to hurt these girls but you ran over their tent,
and you didn't know what to do . . .' And he quickly withdrew. It was a tug-of-war
there for a minute. I wanted to hang on to him. He actually pulled away from my

grasp, began to regroup, then systematically tried to deny he had anything to do with this.

"After all that time he said, I want to go call my dad. He goes through it with his dad over the phone about the failed polygraph. 'They think I did this, Dad. Could you come and get me?' I'm in the room until the cows come home because I want this guy to confess. He's looking at his watch, 'Dad's coming to get me,' and he eventually gets up and walks out of the room, never even mentioning wanting to talk to an attorney. In fact, he asked to take another polygraph, which is also indicative of a deceptive person. He said, 'Well, I'll see you next Monday on my polygraph.' And I said, 'I'm not interested in that. Because this shows us what really happened.' It went right over his head. He just didn't want to hear it. He said, 'And I'll be clean this time. It was probably the drugs that affected this.' According to his boss, he was clean most of that week, then all of the sudden when the polygraph comes up Monday, he doesn't show up to work.

"So, behaviorally, I'm convinced that he did it. Unfortunately I don't have any concrete proof. Just a series of excuses. Anybody that stays there for five hours trying to justify their innocence is not typical of an innocent person."

I could feel a charge building in my blood. I looked over at Bob and Dee Dee. They were expressive souls to begin with. Now they were radiating a mood of elation. Our hunches, fragile because they were based on stories from the past, had now landed on terra firma, present-day fact.

Even among the cops, there was a palpable thickening of the emotional atmosphere. I had a feeling that the polygraph examiner, especially, was invested in this eighteen-year-old non-prosecutable case. By happenstance of his job he had been plunked down inside the story of something tragic that happened one long ago night involving two girls in a tent and a young cowboy fueled with rage.

I scanned the room. The only dissenter was Lynn Fredrickson, frowning in the corner. I remembered his words to me, *"I've been conned before and I'll be conned again."* At least this odd detective knew he had a blind spot.

One of the officers passed out a color mug shot taken of Dirk Duran by Washington police. It was a frontal view, chilling in the way all police mug shots are. His silver hair is pulled straight back in a ponytail. His forehead protrudes over his eyes, which are widely spaced, each pupil like the bull's-eye of a doughnut frosted baby blue. Finally, here was the man, as he looked today. I stared at the image in fascination.

Ackom passed out the written reports of both polygraph examinations that Dirk had taken. In the first polygraph, I noted that when asked in the pre-test interview what he was doing the night of the Cline Falls attack, he said that the first time he heard about this incident he was serving time in the jail in Prineville.

In the second polygraph, the one conducted by Ackom, when asked what he was doing the night of the Cline Falls assault, Dirk said something entirely different: he said he had a fight with his girlfriend—"it may have even been on the day of the incident or the day before or the day after, he cannot remember."

As I read the report, I imagined myself in the room with Dirk and the examiner.

"When confronted about his deceptiveness to the relevant questions in these two tests, Mr. Duran stated that he knows he didn't do it but maybe he doesn't believe that. This thing has haunted him all these years. He has thought about this every day since it happened in 1977. He has pictured this in his mind almost every day since it happened . . . He pictures a vehicle driving over the tent. He pictures those girls being hacked by a hatchet or hatchet type instrument. This interviewer asked Mr. Duran if he saw himself in the picture, and Duran stated no . . . Mr. Duran stated I swear to God I didn't do it may God strike me dead right now if I did this. He then began to weep openly and reached down—and grabbed this examiner's hands and started sobbing with tears streaming down his face."

I put myself into this scenario. I imagined myself disembodied, a seeing eye floating above the two men, as my suspect brought a curse down upon his own head.

ONE OF MY favorite pastimes as a child in the sixties was playing a board game called Lie Detector. You had a whole pile of bizarre suspects pictured on cards, and you wanted to find out who was guilty. So you stuck a card into a plastic machine, then you punched a plastic pen into a grid above the drawing, and if the machine rang a bell, you knew your suspect was lying. Whodunit? The maharaja wearing the funny turban or the tennis star in the white sweater with the tanned leathery skin?

I couldn't even picture what it looked like when someone took a polygraph examination—so I read up. It's based on the theory that the body tells the truth even if the head wants to lie. Sensors that read physiological changes are attached to the examinee. A rubber bellows stretches across the chest and abdomen, and is connected to a pen that traces a graphic representation of the respiration rate. A blood pressure cuff is held against the brachial artery of the upper arm and is linked up with a pen that measures blood pumping through the veins. Electrodes on the tips of fingers measure sweat emitting from the hands, connected to a third pen.

The underlying theory of a polygraph is that when people lie, they get measurably nervous about lying. Their heartbeat speeds up. Blood pressure rises. They breathe in a different rhythm. Their hands sweat.

The ability of these measurements to discern a lie has been a subject of intense debate. The American Polygraph Association has a list of research studies on the validity and reliability of polygraph testing—and claims that those studies averaged an accuracy rate of between 80 and 98 percent. Law enforcement agencies all over the country, federal and state, have polygraph departments.

There are serious detractors of polygraph testing, though in smaller numbers, who consider it junk science. Whole books have been written on how to beat the exam. Techniques abound. Hold your breath. Bite the inside of your mouth. Take sedatives to depress the heart rate. Some claim anyone can be coached. Aldrich Ames, the Soviet mole who masqueraded during the 1980s as a CIA operative, easily passed a polygraph, which indicated he was lily white innocent of espionage.

Regardless of the question of its ultimate validity, personally, I liked the idea. The body has a mind of its own, and the polygraph gives it a chance to talk. The pens scratching lines on moving graph paper were the body's voice box. No matter what the brain tells the tongue to say, those skittering pens bear their own message from deep within. That to me was pure poetry.

One thing all sides of the debate seemed to agree on was that polygraph exams were a good interrogation tool. They induced fear of being found out, and fear leads to confessions.

What interested me was not only that the tracings of Dirk Duran's second polygraph had been read by three licensed polygraph examiners as deceptive, but that this man, when told that the charts read deceptive, admitted a lifelong obsession with the crime. It struck me as preposterous that a seventeen-year-old kid who was innocent of a crime—even if others thought he was guilty—would dwell on the specifics of that crime *every single day of his life,* on into his late thirties.

It didn't take much to push me over the edge on this; I was almost there. My powerful hunch that Duran was my attacker had now hardened into conviction.

It frustrated me that an event of this significance, these admissions, had taken place offstage in my life. I would have given anything to have been a fly on the wall during that second examination. I wondered if perhaps some part of me could be present at the next polygraph. Could I make a tape of my voice, to be played to him in the event that he agreed to take another one? I phoned Fred Ackom to ask if he felt it was likely that the suspect would agree to take another exam, and if so, might I be present in voice? Perhaps my voice might cajole a full confession.

Fred (we were on a first-name basis now) immediately sparked to the idea. "Hearing your voice would be powerful stuff."

He seemed to want to revisit again what he considered a most unusual encounter with my suspect. "During the pre-test, I got an eerie feeling—his eyes made the hair stand up on my head. I got goose bumps. But after the test, when he was told the results read deceptive, he was a changed man. And what does he do? Does he lash out at me? No. He cowers. He holds his head down. Won't look at me. Starts bawling, tears streaming down his face. I've never had anybody do that."

"Never?"

"I've never had anybody reach out and grab my hand like that. It startled me. And I just grabbed his hands and held on to them."

I supposed that Fred's gentle, fatherly approach had softened Dirk, who let down his guard, only to find the polygraph examiner hardening when the exam results came back guilty. He seemed hardly capable of turning into a third-degree interrogator, but it was when he raised his voice like a punitive father that Dirk had voluntarily spilled his admission.

Fred plotted with me: if Dirk agreed to another polygraph, he would try to bring him to the same state of complete remorse, then he would push a button on a tape recorder, and my disembodied voice would issue forth, bringing the suspect back to the night of June 22, 1977. He advised me to think of some little detail that had never been publicized, something that only he, the suspect, and I, the victim, would know.

I thought of two things: when I told the young cowboy to go away, he gently pulled the axe out of my hand. The motion was peculiar; he didn't grab it back. He softened and removed it. Also: he said absolutely nothing. Nothing to Shayna. Nothing to me. Nothing at all.

I asked Fred if he thought Dirk would remember those details.

"I think he remembers every detail. When I think of other major cases, the guilty remember the details. It's a vivid picture in their minds. Like he said, 'Hasn't a day gone by I haven't thought about this. It's haunted me.' "

I asked him if he thought Duran truly felt guilt about this crime?

"He has remorse. The crying. The reaching out. That's his way of saying, 'I'm sorry this happened.' There are forces out there that won't allow him to tell us that. Dad has bailed him out all these years, and they live in the community, and they've been expressing his innocence all these years. He doesn't want to hurt them. If Dad wasn't there, this guy would give it up. He wants to talk about it. I would think he would have had to talk to somebody somewhere, some lowlife doper buddy of his."

If such a buddy existed, I would flush that person out eventually.

"I get into cases, and I want to solve them, too. I want to get to the bottom of it." Fred admitted to me in his slow, gentle voice that he was personally touched by my story. "We just need to keep plugging away and not get discouraged, and eventually we're going to get the information."

I'd started from zero, and it was a miracle I'd come even this far, I told him.

"You can't do it alone. It's just too overwhelming. No cases are solved by one super-sleuth. And just because we can't prosecute, it still needs to be solved for your sake."

The Ditchdigger's Bosses

Never, never be alone. Keep on the move. Stay in different places. Make sure you have enough gas. Check your tires. Don't go into any room alone. Don't wear lipstick. Just drab, drab, drab," a friend counseled me when I told her the suspect had reappeared in town just when I planned to infiltrate his inner circle. "I don't mean to scare you," she added helpfully.

When I began my investigation nobody knew precisely where Dirk Duran was residing. Then I started asking questions, and somehow after I'd asked enough questions to resuscitate the past . . . the suspect reappears! If I continued to study him, might I unknowingly end up in his crosshairs?

Though it may have weakened my knees, the prospect of investigating under the suspect's nose did not diminish my zeal. From my home in California in late July 1995, I strategized my next trip to Central Oregon as a guerrilla attack. I would pass quickly through town to conduct a few interviews with Duran's current employers, two guys Boo had lined up for me, and then I would slip out by the time word had spread.

The question of whether it was now safe for me to conduct my investigation produced in me a kind of cognitive dissonance. Part of me said of course it is safe. Another part said, it most definitely is not. On balance, I ended up assuming the dangers were more psychic than physical. In any case, that's what Bob and Dee Dee tried to argue while I sat at a picnic table in Cline Falls State Park on a hot day in August.

"I wouldn't put it past him to pick us off with a long-range rifle," I said. "If we hang around here a few days, eventually he'll catch up with us. Anybody could watch my comings and goings. It's not that hard to stalk someone in Redmond. People could say, 'There she is.' I think now is an especially dangerous time to be walking around. Right now, he's rabid." My unadorned fear had shown up. It was as though I had been wearing a blindfold that had suddenly fallen off, and I found myself teetering on the edge of a precipice.

Bob bore down on me. He didn't suffer timorous souls gladly. "Sure there's some danger. But I think you can manage the danger. The fact that somebody is dangerous doesn't mean you can't *manage* the danger. All the time we were on the Valerie investigation, there were an awful lot of people trying to scare us off."

Dee Dee added, "Month after month they would try to scare us off, and it would get us in a twit. Then we'd go someplace and reflect on it, and we'd go, 'God, they are just twisting us around.' "

I plucked up my courage and thickened my skin. The Kounses had continued on with their investigation, and so would I. Whenever I succumbed to faintheartedness, I pictured Bob and Dee Dee dressed like the homeless and sitting in a junkyard at night, watching for their daughter's body.

I kept to a minimum updates about my plans to worried family and friends on the home front. My parents in particular had no inkling of what I was doing during these vast stretches of time spent in Oregon.

A GUY NAMED MIKE owned the earth-moving construction company where Dirk Duran was employed. On the day Detective Lynn Fredrickson was scheduled to pick Dirk up from his job to take him to his third scheduled polygraph, Mike told Fredrickson that Dirk hadn't shown up for work at all. And he didn't show up the entire next week. Mike told us he was an ex-cop himself, a former homicide detective, and he was genuinely hooked on figuring out whether the backhoe operator he employed on and off for years was the Cline Falls hatchet man. While Dirk was presumably hard at work burrowing in a ditch at one of Mike's job sites, Mike sat with me and Boo and Bob and Dee Dee for a quick lunch in Bend. It was beginning to dawn on him that there was some possibility his loyal employee had done something all those years ago that defied comprehension, and had gotten away with it. He wanted to talk to me about what I remembered about the night of June 22, 1977, and he listened to my story with his mouth open and his thick dark eyebrows arching high on his forehead, an expression I read as rapt attention and astonishment.

"Well, you know, I gotta say it—that what you described is exactly the way he was back then. He's always been an immaculate dresser all his life. And a very good-lookin' guy." Then he added, apropos of nothing: "The most striking thing about Dirk is his eyes. If you ever saw his eyes, you'd never forget him. It looks like he's lookin' a hole right through you. Very piercing. They're almost scary."

Mike related that the day after Dirk took the second polygraph and flunked it, Mike and his brother Pat sat down with Dirk to talk, thinking that if he were the attacker, they and only they could persuade him to come clean. If he didn't do it, surely they would know he was telling the truth.

"He was agitated that he flunked the test and he was upset with me. He said, 'You told me it was accurate.' 'It is,' I said. He said, 'Something's wrong. I didn't do it.' He totally denied it.

"After my brother and I got through talking to him—I even called Detective Fredrickson and said, 'Even with all my police experience and background, you know, if this was the first time I'd talked to the guy, I probably would have walked away thinking he didn't have anything to do with it. He can look at you without ever blinking and tell you something. Straight in the eye. That's why Dirk is so convincing.' I told Fredrickson the impression I got, and he had gotten the same impression. He said, 'You know I had the same feeling—after Dirk answered the questions, he looked me right in the eye—I walked out of there thinking he had nothing to do with it.' "

I marveled at the gullibility of both cop and ex-cop, and told Mike flat out, "I would read that behavior as the opposite of innocence. If I were questioning a guy who was staring straight at me, I'd suspect he was trying to control me."

Since my crisis of will at the picnic table the day before, I'd calmed down considerably. In fact, now I was feeling quite bold. I leaned across the table, summoned sparks into my eyes, and stared at Dirk's boss.

"Mike, I'm going to make you believe me. I'm going to hold your gaze so steady that you're going to believe what I say."

Under my stare, Mike pulled away a little from the table. His thick eyebrows arched higher on his forehead.

"When somebody stares at me, I'm going to read that as intimidation," I said. I was still staring. I'd played this game many times before. But only with members of the canine species.

Mike let out a nervous, goofy laugh and admitted that the fellow whom he'd employed off and on for seventeen years was, indeed, a scary guy. He also admitted that as a former cop, he felt that most of the time the results of polygraphs were accurate.

"You've got to look at it this way," Mike said, finally fessing up to his growing belief in Dirk's guilt. "He's been denying it for eighteen years, and I'm a firm believer that he will never, ever admit it. I'll tell you why. He is so close to his mother and father, if he were to admit this, it will kill them. I really believe if he's guilty, that's the number one reason he won't admit it."

I asked Mike whether he was inclined now, with his new suspicions, to keep Dirk in his employ, to hire this ditchdigger again and again.

"I'm not sure whether I'm going to have him back. I just don't know that I will. But if I need somebody and he's clean, I'll probably call him." Mike seemed genuinely conflicted. "I don't know. As I told my wife, I don't want to *not hire* him, because that might upset him. He knows where I live. I don't want him in a wild rage and looking at me as the guy that fired him."

A couple of hours after lunch, Mike called me on my cell phone. He'd thought of another pertinent question for me.

"The guy you saw that night . . . did he smell like garlic?"

"Why?"

Mike told me that Dirk ate a lot of garlic and always reeked of it.

No, I told him. Garlic was not my petite madeleine, dipped in lime-blossom tea.

MIKE'S BROTHER Pat was a Marlboro classic, tall and lanky with chiseled features, salt-and-pepper hair, a sway in his back, and a drawl in his delivery. He ran a lo-cal tourist attraction, an old train that ran a scenic route along a canyon where diners could watch a train get robbed or, on alternate nights, witness a murder on the train and figure out whodunit—just like in the Old West. In the lobby of a restored frontier hotel, Pat laid out for Boo and me his relationship with my suspect.

"He's worked for me since he was seventeen years old. He's always been a dif-ferent kind of a person. But Mike and I are both the kind of guys that—hell, if nobody will give someone a job, or nobody likes 'em, if they treat us good, we'll help 'em out and give 'em a job. And he does good work. He's the kind of guy that if you ask him to go shovel shit, he just goes and shovels it.

"And he's always insinuated that I'm one of the best friends he's ever had. Don't get the idea I did a lot for this kid. I didn't go out of my way to do anything for him—when I needed him I used him and paid him for it; somebody else needed him, they wouldn't touch him. That's the only difference. Dirk, when he comes back to town he usually calls me first. I need just a five-dollar-an-hour hand and he come along just the right time."

While Pat was drawling on about "poor old Dirk" doing menial tasks that wouldn't even earn him a living wage, I felt a distinct pluck on my heartstrings and I joked to myself that, listening to enough talk like this, I might offer him a job myself, at six an hour.

" 'Bout that time, Dirk did tell me that this thing come up again about the Cline Falls deal, and I'm still thinkin', I can't imagine him doin' that, and he said he took a lie detector test and passed it. I said, 'That's good, you get it behind you.' Next thing I know, that's when Mike finds out this thing is serious. These people are going to try to find out who done this again after all these years. So Dirk tells me he's going to take another lie detector test. I'm still thinking, well, that'd be good. We can get this out of the way and poor old Dirk can get on his way."

Pat had heard the rumors about Dirk being involved in Cline Falls way back a year or two after it happened, and it was from the horse's mouth, Dirk himself.

"He's the one who brought it up . . . a long time ago during the time it happened. That people were saying that about him and he was terribly distressed about it and it caused him a lot of problems. It was always something he would bring up different times. But to tell you the truth, when I did hear that, I passed it off as, nah, he wouldn't do it—he's not a crazy idiot like that.

"So I'm out there working on the train, and Mike comes out. And Mike's sayin', 'He flunked that test.' Pretty quick Mike got around and said, 'I think he did it, Pat.' I said, 'What?' He said, 'I mean I think he did.'

"Mike is talking to me like the old investigator I used to know. And I'm thinking, that son of a gun, all these years, maybe he did do this. This was the first time I even considered him doing that. I set down at the dinner train out there and said, 'Why'd he take the test then, Mike?' He said, 'Lots of them do. He thinks he can beat it.' So then I said, 'I'll be damned. Do you suppose that son of a bitch did that thing?' So we all met in the office. He was just ranting and raving, blaming Mike: 'Goddamn, Mike, I trusted you. You said if I was innocent I should take that lie detector test . . . this guy had his head that close, and I just wanted to up-end him, and I don't know why I didn't.' I said, 'This guy is doing his job, Dirk. You flunked that test. That's his job.'

"After the talk, I didn't feel as strong as Mike that he was guilty. But I did have a feeling that I would like to pursue something. It really dawned on me that this is very possible, just by the way he was talking about being very violent towards those guys that give him the test and towards the investigators hassling him. But Mike's right. As long as his parents are alive he won't ever admit it. After all these years of denying it and believing in him. If he had to tell his dad all these years he'd been lying. I don't think there's any way in the world. We could even torture him."

Pat confided that he wanted to investigate the deal himself—prove one way or another whether Dirk did it or not. The first step in his investigation was to find out the original story, from the victim's point of view. That meant he would interview me.

"Well, here I am," I said.

"What I'd be curious about—if you don't mind, I'd like to know exactly what happened. You's just camped there?"

I began my tale, and Pat leaned back in his chair, with arms crossed over his chest. Then I got to the description of the cowboy I saw: "He had tight jeans on, his body was thin and sinewy—"

Pat interjected: "Small waist?"

Yes, I said. His body was "muscular but not beefy."

"Shapely," Pat said.

"Trim and in good shape," I said.

"When he was seventeen years old that would fit him to a tee," Pat declared.

"Real neat. Proud of his appearance," I added.

"Proud of his appearance," Pat repeated.

In fact, before I ever returned to Oregon on this investigation I had started writing about the attack and described him as a "decent sort of a cowboy."

"Maybe you didn't look into his eyes. Have you ever wanted to see him?" Pat asked.

"Yes!" Oh, I wanted to see him. I'd been rehearsing such an encounter in my mind for some time. "I don't want him to see me."

"I can arrange it. He doesn't have to know."

Boo asked Pat what Duran looked like nowadays.

"I'll tell you, he's a pretty good-looking guy. In fact if you didn't know him as a weird guy, you'd look at him as a very handsome guy. Now he runs around with a big ol' salt-and-pepper beard with his hair pulled back in a big ol' ponytail, but when he's cleaned up who would he look like . . . ?" Pat cast about for a famous person Dirk resembled, then pulled us over to a rack of videotapes and pointed to a heartthrob with good cheekbones and blazing eyes on the jacket of an action video. It always amazed me when a heterosexual manly type described alluring masculine attributes in another. Women were supposed to look at one another. That men did was their secret vanity.

As step two in Pat's investigation, he wanted me to meet another of his employees, Bill, a guy who had driven trucks with Dirk for twenty years—the guy, in fact, who'd taught Dirk how to drive a truck. Within minutes, Bill, a stout man with a drooping face, shambled into the Redmond Hotel.

When Bill settled in for a talk with Boo and me, Pat said, "It just keeps adding up. I'm very much leaning towards the fact that that son of a bitch probably did do that. Just like you always said, Bill, you know damn well he's capable of it. I never really thought about that. But I damn well do now."

"Oh, yeah," Bill said in a gravelly growl.

I asked Bill why he thought so. He didn't have any direct knowledge. "But I heard from several people from Redmond who ran in his particular crowd that he did it."

Confession to a buddy, probably on a bar stool somewhere? This was what I was after. I knew somewhere in that town was a guy who knew something concrete. "Do you remember who these people were?" I quickly asked.

"Uh-huh."

Bill was holding back. "I'll talk to them, then I'll tell you."

"Okay."

He reconsidered. "I'll tell you his name." Clearly, the gratification of giving me the information I was hungry for was too tempting to pass up.

"His name is Ken Block."

Not Ken Block again! The guy who supposedly knew everything was just about the only guy in town who claimed to remember absolutely nothing.

"We've talked to him already. He doesn't remember."

"You're kidding me."

"No."

"Huh."

I asked Bill why he thought Ken Block would know something.

"He was one of the first ones . . . that's when I first ever heard of Dirk Duran. This is just what I heard, now," he qualified, and insisted that he didn't remember *exactly* who told him. "But he'd been by Cline Falls earlier in the day, for what reason I don't know. I heard he came back, that he ran up on the tent with a pickup—"

I interrupted him. "What was significant about the fact that he was there earlier in the day?"

"It gives him a motive."

"That he'd seen us."

"Right. Maybe it was just an incidental 'hi' or whatever. Dirk is very vindictive, I'll tell you that—if he was rebuffed or anything like that."

How had a guy in Dirk's circle learned that he had been in the park earlier in the afternoon? Had he said something to his friends about getting back at a couple of stuck-up women? I spun back, replayed for the umpteenth time the memory of that depressing sun-beaten hollow along the Deschutes River in 1977: Shayna and I setting up our tent, chatting with the groups of people clustered around picnic tables. No young cowboy approached me during that early evening, I was sure of it. There were no casual "hi"s that I repelled—and I certainly would have.

"How about the other girl. A chance meeting? 'Hi.' Nothing?" Bill asked.

I recalled that the bathrooms were situated close to the entrance of the park, just as they were now, some walking distance from our campsite. Shayna had surely walked that route alone. Had a young cowboy with burning eyes said, 'Hey!'? He might have reminded her of the weirdo who had harassed us in the Connecticut campground just one month before. I could picture her chilly rebuke. But Shayna had told investigators she remembered no one.

Or was he just watching us from an overlook behind some junipers? I remembered with undiminished clarity our presentiments: our inexplicable uneasiness, our feral perceptiveness—in retrospect I could call it our atavistic instincts that felt the evil eye, a malevolent glance that could blight—that late afternoon in Cline Falls State Park.

"I've talked to Dirk a lot about it, too," Bill went on. "Dirk was always talking about that incident. He's the one that would always bring it up. Because it gets old after a while." Bill's gruff features rearranged themselves into a look of embarrassment. Who was he to tell a victim of an axe attack looking for her attacker eighteen years later that "it gets old after a while"? He corrected himself. "I'm not trying to make it any smaller . . ."

No offense taken.

"But to this day when he's at the house, if he's there for over five minutes, somehow or other he brings that up. I'm not kidding one little bit. Ever since I've known him. He's been doing it for almost twenty years now. That's the truth. My wife will tell you the same thing. And she didn't even know him then."

"How does it come up?"

"We'll start talking about something. He'll say something about somebody: 'then maybe they'll forget that I'm the one who's supposed to have done it.' He was always talking about taking the lie detector test. He was going to get on that show of F. Lee Bailey's, the one that had the lie detector."

I wondered at the uncanny fate that I would arrive so many years later to grant him his wish.

"You probably heard about him breaking the window," Bill added. I had. In 1989, Dirk Duran used a bottle to smash the windshield of a girl named Marie, earning himself a conviction for "criminal mischief." It was the suspect's one and only malfeasance filed in hard copy in Deschutes County's Public Records Department.

Bill told me that that tantrum also involved the topic of—what else? *Cline Falls.* By Dirk's own account, Dirk and this Marie were arguing on a bar stool about Cline Falls. The question of Dirk's innocence or guilt arose, and so derailed Dirk that he sent a bottle through Marie's window in the parking lot. After venting his spleen in this way, he dropped the same bottle off at his buddy Bill's house, trying to plant evidence on him, but the bottle was smeared with Dirk's fingerprints.

"Have you talked to Ruby? Ruby'd be a real good person to talk to." Ruby was Dirk's ex-wife. Bill had spent time with Ruby and Dirk when they were married and when they were breaking up. "I don't know how much actual physical abuse there was in the house, but I know there was a lot of mental anguish going on in there. I thought Ruby was a neat lady. She was always smiling. But such a different person when she was around Dirk. It was a shock. Hot and cold."

I told Bill I was still fearful of contacting anyone intimately connected to my suspect. I wondered how Ruby might respond to me.

"I'd guess there's no love whatsoever between the two. I think she'd be honest to you. Oh, yeah. She was that type of person when I knew her."

Bill didn't want to paint a 100 percent bad picture of Dirk. "I like Dirk as far as the way I have known him. But there is something about him that will make you really uncomfortable. A little bit of him goes a long way." Of course, Bill admitted, he wouldn't want to leave his wife or daughter with him. "I'm not saying anything would be wrong. But I know what Dirk is capable of."

BEFORE BOO and I left the Redmond Hotel, Bill took me aside and whispered: just after Ruby left Dirk for good, she took off to the Southwest with a boyfriend named Robert Lee. "He's a little worm junkie. But he might have some insight," Bill growled.

Pat assured me he would keep trying to find out what had happened in Cline Falls. His face darkened. It really bothered him that someone could do something like that and get away with it. That Dirk might have beaten the rap just didn't square with Pat's notions of justice in the Old West. I bet the bad guys got theirs on Pat's murder mystery train.

Axe Choppin' Program

Something stuck in my mind about that little piece of evidence I had found printed in the Bend *Bulletin* on June 27, 1977. On that day, Monday, investigator Bob Cooley told a reporter that he was en route to speak to a seventeen-year-old who was in the Prineville jail for assaulting his girlfriend, but he didn't expect to tie the youth to the Cline Falls attack.

I hadn't been able to find any record or memory existing that Cooley ever interviewed the youth at all. Although the *Bulletin* stated that the boy was released to his parents on Monday, June 27, Janey's father insisted that it was a prosperous rancher, a bigwig in the community named Mackey, who had taken custody of Dirk Duran on Monday and put him to work that very same day. The question nagged me, whether influence was brought to bear to dissuade the state police from interviewing the volatile seventeen-year-old.

From the highway—if you shield the view with your left hand—Mackey's ranch looks like a movie version of the Old West: an abandoned feedlot tumbles across a rolling hillside, fences lean to and fro, organically following the natural contours of the landscape. The feedlot is ghostly in atmosphere. No animals feed among the artfully leaning fences. Take your left hand away and suddenly you see that the hillside is shaved off. Several yards above the feedlot, separated by a retaining wall, begins the relentlessly flat asphalt parking lot of a brand-new cell-block motel.

The motel slipped from view as the Kounses and I turned into Mackey's drive. A tangle of antlers hung from the walls of the ranch house and outer buildings, their points heading every which way. If animals were absent in the feedlot, their ghosts were everywhere here.

Shadows moved inside the house, its occupants wondering why strangers were pulling up their drive. We were greeted at the door by the rancher and hunter himself, a large man in cowboy attire, and his well-coiffed wife. Our presence made them suspicious, understandably, but Bob spun out his Cline Falls rap fast enough to secure an invite, and soon we were lounging on a sofa in the cedar-paneled living room.

The cattleman leaned back in his easy chair. He was going to listen to our story before he gave up anything himself. Bob started in about the "Cline Falls incident" without describing what the Cline Falls incident entailed, as its meaning was clear in the Redmond area. He explained that we were here to talk to the rancher because the main suspect in the Cline Falls case, one Dirk Duran, was the very same who assaulted his girlfriend the very next day and was jailed. And we had heard around town from folks who remembered those long-ago events that it was Mr. Mackey himself who had picked Duran up from jail on Monday and placed him in his employ—although the Bend *Bulletin* reported that Duran was released to his parents.

"Now, slow down. Now, this deal—that was a hatchet deal?" the cattleman asked.

Yes, yes, it was. We described the incident.

"You never did know him?" the cattleman asked, meaning had we made the acquaintance of our attacker before?

"No, no." I said. "My friend and I had never been to Redmond before that night."

"And he attacked you with a hatchet?"

"Yeah."

"Chopped you?"

"Yeah."

Dee Dee asked the rancher innocently, "Do you remember when that happened?"

"Oh, yeah."

Mackey's wife cut in. "All I remember hearing about was hearsay."

The rancher sat back in his chair and took a breath. "As it happened, it had just come up the other day. Dirk was down here from Washington, I was told. They said they'd seen him over at his folks and they mentioned that he's the one that supposedly run over those girls out at the park. That person didn't say nothin' about the choppin'. But I remembered the hatchet business. At that time, I didn't know about being run over.

"They never did solve that deal. He was always fingered as the one who did it. It's common. I've heard it down through. A lot of people have thought that. I always wondered." Mackey was sitting under a large painting of a horse. A tiny Pomeranian rested on his lap. "I don't know. I never got into it," he said, stroking the toy dog's tail. "All I know is that when he 'bout drowned that girl down there, they put him in jail in Prineville. *And I didn't get him out.* See, his dad worked for me for twenty years. A partnership. I financed him in buying and selling cattle. And I worked Dirk here when he was younger. He was a real good worker, but af-

ter he did that to that girl, and they threw him in jail, of course his dad come—
Friday, as I recall, or maybe Saturday—and he wanted to get him out. He didn't
think he should be locked up." Dirk was like a caged animal in jail, Mackey said.

"So I talked to our attorney. Bodie was a real good attorney in Prineville. He
checked it out. And he said, 'Well, if you want to spend the money—but probably
the best thing for the kid is to stay in there for a few days.' So I told Lou, the kid's
on dope. He said, 'Well, no, he's taking some stuff for nerves.' I said the best thing
for him would be to be right there. So they left him there a few days and then he
got out. So I put him on the ranch and worked him. He was a good worker."

"So you didn't go and pick him up from jail."

"Where'd you hear that now?"

We told him our sources.

"Dadgumit. I didn't get him out of jail. In fact I had an attorney talk me into
not getting him out of jail." Mackey explained that he owned a ranch sixty-five
miles east into the desert from Redmond. Lou asked if Dirk could work out there,
and Mackey said yes, he'd put him on the payroll. "But it wasn't put to me, 'If he
gets the job he gets off the deal,'" Mackey said. "So I imagined Lou went back and
said, 'Hey, I got him a job.'"

"That's one of your good guesses, then," Bob said, giving Mackey an opportunity to come up with a more specific memory of whether Lou might have turned
the heat off his son. Bob, Dee Dee, and I were all alert for self-justification and
denial.

"We weren't even told how serious it was to begin with," Mackey's wife piped up.

"I didn't know. I just know that he got the girl—he'd been drinkin' some
vodka. It wasn't until two, three weeks later somebody said, 'Hey, down there,
they'd been doing carrots or something, and if it hadn't been for somebody, he'd
a killed that gal.' I hear that later, see. I didn't know it was such a serious deal. I
didn't think nothing of it when he got out three days or a week—or however long
he was in there. Then later we got to hearing more about it, that he 'bout killed
that gal."

My bullshit meter was running, and it seemed to me that Mackey really didn't
know anything more.

"We were told that Dirk's parents blamed his girlfriend rather than him," Dee
Dee said.

"I would buy that," Mackey said.

"Do you think his parents would have denied or protected him if they'd
thought he'd done a crime like the hatchet crime?" Dee Dee asked.

Mackey gave a long pause. "I think so."

"I think they might ignore it," his wife said.

"Just put it aside," Mackey added. "Lou's attitude in the girl deal as I remember
was she caused it, see. Egged it on."

The Mackeys remembered Dirk as a kid with a mean streak from way back.

And his dad wouldn't make him behave. "He'd get into trouble with the teachers in school and his dad would stick up for him—instead of saying, 'I'll give you a beatin' when you get home,' he said, 'I'll go down there with you and we'll beat up the teachers,' " Mackey said.

"They're wonderful people. They're very loving people themselves," Mrs. Mackey insisted.

But Mr. Mackey wanted to make plain: Lou Duran always had a weak hand with his son. "They just wouldn't make him mind. He worked for me, I got along with him good. He could run equipment. He had a lot of ability. He was a really sharp kid. Really energetic. I don't know. You tell me."

I already knew that Dirk chopped hay for Mackey when he was a teen. A guy he worked with told me he got so pissed off at Dirk one day that he put him on the conveyor belt of the hay chopper and tried to send him through: this story struck me as Dirk's karma working in advance.

Feelings in the room had gotten cozy. Mackey wanted to hear my story, and in particular: "What got him stopped from killing you?" He sat back and listened as I spun my tale, and then he had something to offer.

"Another funny thing about Dirk. Deer hunting. He'd shoot a deer. He'd knock it down and it wasn't dead. He wouldn't finish it off."

He'd knock it down and it wasn't dead. He wouldn't finish it off.

I burst out in spontaneous laughter. My body did—as though it wasn't at all under my conscious control. Dee Dee and I reached for each other's hands.

"He wouldn't kill it. His dad would have to come finish it off and kill it. Shoot it in the head or neck and kill it."

I thought of the antlers displayed everywhere on the walls of Mackey's ranch house and suddenly felt a great kinship with these fallen animals.

"It's kind of a coincidence you guys come in," Mackey went on. "Just two, three days ago, someone said, 'Well, guess they never did figure out nothing on that—supposedly he was involved in that axe choppin' program.' I always wondered, you know, 'cause if a guy would have known, had an idea, he coulda got to his pickup. Because there had to be blood in that pickup."

As we were leaving, Mackey said, "I hope you find out your deal . . . and I hope it rests your mind—"

"Helps you in some way . . ." his wife cut in.

"And sorry we couldn't help you more."

I remembered something I'd heard once about hunters. Some hunters have a nervous response when they raise their rifles to kill their prey. Their nerves cause them to miss their shot. When that happens, it's called buck fever. Maybe it was buck fever that saved me that night, June 22, 1977?

Cowboy Movie Star

Pat stood in a tall slump, his back swayed, cowboy boots in a wide stance, arms folded across his chest, a scowl on his face. He'd been thinking about it and had decided that his longtime employee couldn't have committed that Cline Falls deal after all. "I don't see how you could have been run over by a three-quarter-ton pickup and survived," he drawled.

That I couldn't answer. I couldn't surmise how I had survived the weight of any vehicle. I couldn't surmise how I had survived death blows from the business end of an axe without dying. None of it made sense.

And another thing: Pat had spent a lot of time thinking about the description I'd given him the other day. I told him I had seen someone around five ten or five eleven. Dirk stands around six three.

I had already figured out how that could have been so: Dirk was a growing boy. I'd spent a lot of time looking at the prom photo Janey had given me. I estimated Dirk's index finger at about three inches long. Using his index finger as a scale, that meant he stood three inches higher than Janey. Janey was no doubt wearing high heels, but Dirk's cowboy boots would also have had a heel. My estimation put him four inches taller than Janey. She had probably reached her full adult height, five-six, by age eighteen. So on the evidence of the photograph, Dirk, a boy of seventeen, stood at around five-ten, or thereabouts—exactly as I described him to the cops at the time.

Pat listened and shrugged. He was having a hard time imagining the kid he'd known for so long involved in the Cline Falls attack. "I've heard some bad things about him, but I never personally got to see the bad side of Dirk."

Pat admitted to us that since Dirk had been working for him lately, he didn't feel comfortable sneaking around behind his back. He'd told Dirk straight up that he'd been talking to the Cline Falls victim.

I winced.

"I made it out like I found you, and not the other way around," Pat said. " 'I'm going to prove you didn't do it,' I told him. He said, 'I appreciate that.' I told him, 'Dirk, this woman wants to know who done this to her, and she has a right to know.' "

"What did he say?" I asked, frustrated again that pivotal events were taking place that I wasn't a part of.

"He said, 'I understand that.' Then he asked me, 'What was she like?' 'She seemed nice,' I told him."

The flesh on my whole body erupted in goose pimples like a prairie catching fire in the wind.

"So I said to him, 'Where were you that night, Dirk?' He didn't have much memory, then it started to come back. He had a fight with his girlfriend." Pat still held his arms across his chest in a defensive posture. "I'm more of an authority figure than his dad. I'm a godfather to him. Give him work. Pay him some money. I'm the only guy that's gonna prove he did or didn't do it. And I'm going to do it. I'm intense. This has been bothering me ever since we talked."

Great, I said. I could always use another sleuth. But what I really wanted from Pat was a chance to lay eyes on Dirk without giving Dirk the chance to lay eyes on me.

Pat could do that easily enough, but he asked, "Why don't you two just set down across the table and talk this thing out?"

Just talk it out. As though we were on equal moral ground. As though we'd quibbled long ago, had some unfinished business to clean up, and it was time to let bygones be bygones. I'd just set down and shoot the breeze with ol' Dirk.

No. There was a great chasm between Dirk and me; it was as though the physical laws of the universe made it impossible for me to sit across a table from him. It would be like, say, flying to the moon. Yes, it was physically possible for me to fly to the moon. But utterly impossible. Did he understand?

Okay, then, Pat agreed, he'd round him up and bring him to a restaurant where Boo and I had planted ourselves. But one more thing: we could expect Dirk to bring along his new girlfriend, who worked with him now and then. Her name was Scotty. She worked construction, and she and her small boy lived with Dirk in a trailer park outside of Redmond.

"Okay, Pat. Are you a good enough actor?" I asked him. "Are you gonna be able to pull this off, or are you gonna blow it and get us all killed?"

This was an obligatory scene, and I knew it. I was the heroine in one of those narratives about female fear—where the woman comes face-to-face with her suspected attacker. I would recall that flashbulb memory. I would look to see if any part of the man fit that template.

What would happen to me viscerally? Might an instinctual recognition kick in, an animal's innate knowledge in the presence of its predator? Would I remember his face? Would he remember mine?

It was a brisk overcast October day in 1995. I had flown back to Central Oregon once again. This would be a short trip. I sped down the road from my motel in Bend. It had been arranged that Boo and I should arrive first, set ourselves up in the restaurant, and then Pat would bring Dirk before us.

My hair was tucked into a red cap, my lips free of lipstick, my nerve endings raw but finely tuned. At the appointed time—precisely twelve noon—I waited for Boo in the parking lot behind Sully's, a modest Italian eatery in Redmond.

A head of silver hair is what I saw first. Then I saw Boo in her pickup on the other side of him. We'd missed each other and ended up on opposite sides of a wide parking lot, with him in between. We looked at each other helplessly.

Dirk was in the company of Pat, a tall redheaded woman, and a young boy. Dirk walked with an exaggerated swagger, sending his left shoulder jutting forward aggressively with his left haunch, his right shoulder with his right haunch.

Pat spotted me, surprised that I wasn't yet in the restaurant, then jerked his head back fast. They stepped into the back entrance, and Boo and I waited for them to get settled. Then we pulled our caps low over our eyes and entered by the same door. The four were seated at the first booth, directly in front of the back entrance. I could hear blood rushing loudly in my head.

Dirk looked up, cocked his head, and his light blue eyes met mine for a space of a second.

In that space of a second I took him in. He wore a plaid shirt and red bandanna tied neatly across a prominent brow. He was handsome, with even features and a perfect nose, a trim beard. His skin had a glow, as though lit from inside. His light blue eyes looked mean. He looked radiantly mean.

No one prepared me for how much his prematurely silver hair, tied in a ponytail, resembled my own prematurely silver hair tied in a ponytail—thankfully now hidden from view by my red cap.

He removed his eyes from mine.

I wanted to stand and stare. I wanted to be invisible and stand and stare. Instead, Boo and I hurried to the other side of the restaurant and took the first open booth we saw. We ate our lunch and glanced over our shoulders at the booth on the other side of the room, unfortunately obscured from view. We bided our time. Finally, playing it cool, sending not even a flicker of acknowledgment our way, Pat led his little group past us. The prize moment had arrived.

I sat sideways in my booth. I had a box seat now. He was only five feet from me. I felt my heart race, but not from fear. I felt not a quiver of terror.

I waited for a sensation arising from my past. I studied the bend of his legs, the sinew of his muscles. I could not say that I'd seen them before.

What was unmistakable: this was a fastidious man. There was perfection in the way his red bandanna was rolled across his high forehead. I observed distinct teeth marks from a comb in his freshly washed hair. This tall man with broad shoulders, long legs, and narrow hips, wearing a plaid shirt and jeans without a belt, exuded a kind of charisma—the magnetism that emits from certain people, like some movie stars whose talents may be slim, whose intelligence may be nil, but who can trade, in a big way, on just the stuff they ooze.

Had instinct or preternatural knowing helped me identify my attacker? I could say only that this man possessed the qualities of meticulousness and radiant charisma I remembered.

As though he felt my eyes on him, Dirk turned around briefly, and then they all left the restaurant. Through the slatted Venetian blinds I could see them on the street. Scotty, with a freckled face and a riot of red curls spilling from under a Confederate cap, clearly enraptured by her new boyfriend, reached up to kiss him on the corner of his mouth. Dirk's glowing face wore a haughty, vain expression: a self-adoring man accepting worship.

Such a voyeur I had become. Poor Scotty had no idea that she, too, by association with him, was being spied on. Boo and I wondered what we could do to warn her of what we knew about her new beau, whom I stared at until he disappeared from view, this man with whom I shared a hairstyle, and a long preoccupation with hands chopping up two girls.

The Other Women

machacar—to crush, pound

machado—hatchet

machar—to crush

machete—machete, chopper

macho—male, masculine, robust, stupid

—*CASSELL'S COMPACT SPANISH DICTIONARY*

What stayed with me was the memory of his haughty airs, as the woman known as Scotty reached up to kiss his glowing cheek. Was there a woman in his past that meant more to him than Scotty did? I heard stories about his ex-wife, Ruby, the one Janey had met, whom she remembered as a pretty blonde with bruises on her arms—whom several others described as a lively, likable woman. I wanted to find her, she was the mother of his child and the most likely one to hold information about his past—but I was leery of how she'd receive me.

Earlier in the summer I did my research and turned up an earlier husband, a man named Todd. We met in a mall for a few minutes over coffee. Todd was a small man with a boyish face and vaguely Elvis-style hair, protectively sheltering an arm that ended in a stump. Speaking candidly, he told me (with a notably compulsive drive) about his ex-wife. Yes, Ruby was a piece of work. She had already married several times before they wed, on impulse. Todd didn't want children, and she said she couldn't give birth. That was the first of what Todd considered her exaggerations of the truth. She got pregnant with a son, and their marriage lasted one year. Then Ruby fell in with Dirk Duran and the two slid into heavy drug use that drained her trust fund.

After their disastrous marriage fell apart, Todd didn't see Ruby much. In Todd's view, she led a "typical biker lifestyle." She changed apartments every few months. She would have phone service one month, and none the next. There was always a big party at the house, people coming and going.

One thing was certain: Ruby desperately wanted nothing to do with her ex-husband. But the child they shared linked them forever.

When I asked him what he knew about Dirk, Todd described him as having a split personality. He was a "silver-tongued devil" until he went berserk. "I've seen him full-tilt-berserk, and it's not a pleasant place to be . . . It's like another presence comes over him, his whole face starts to change . . . like it's some kind of possession or something.

"As far as Dirk Duran goes," Todd added, "the police didn't want to deal with Dirk Duran either."

"How do you know that?"

"General observations. I called them to get him out of my house—he was chasing me around with a board with a nail in it. He pulled a gun on me. They don't want to deal with that."

I asked him what agency he called.

"Redmond police. There's probably a file on him in the Redmond Police Department."

There were no files on Dirk, I told him. For one who was preceded by his reputation for violence, he'd left very little paper trail in law enforcement records.

"Well, that's really crazy. Police know him very well. When I worked at the mill, I knew people who grew up with him and he was always in trouble with the police."

Maybe Todd observed my eyes drift toward his missing arm—as so many eyes had drifted towards my scarred one. "When I lost my hand in the mill, I went into a bad state: posttraumatic stress syndrome. It got ground off in a mill in '85. It took fifteen surgeries and three years of my life. My hand was ground down to a perfect half inch, and I watched it just be ripped apart, and everybody passed out when they came, and it took me an hour to take the machine apart—it took me so long my forearm was melting on the head as I was taking the machine apart."

"I didn't feel anything when my arm was chopped," I said.

"I didn't feel any pain either. After I got the machine apart, and the ambulance showed up, that's when I started feeling a lot of pain."

I had found a point of connection with this man. I fit in here in logging country, where people lost a lot of limbs. Someone told me a story about a woman at a bank who was astounded at the number of chopped-off stubs she observed pushing bills under her teller's window.

"I have had phantom dreams," Todd said. "You feel like your hand is there, and your fingers itch. People don't understand phantom pains."

Hearing what happened to Todd made me think of a parallel destiny—the amputation that never occurred, how I might have had to coexist not only with a second self but also with a phantom limb.

BOO HAD BEEN bitten by the investigative bug. In the course of revisiting June 22, 1977, while helping me to unravel the puzzle surrounding that night, she'd gotten hooked on the true-crime genre. She hadn't been much of a reader before, but now she devoured true-crime paperbacks—with a special passion for forensics. She decided to take time out from her ranch duties to accompany me on a visit to my suspect's ex-wife.

When the day arrived for us to depart for Washington, I balked. But Boo coaxed and pushed and reassured me, and soon we were in my car traveling eastward along the Columbia River. We arrived in the early evening in the Tri-Cities, three towns on the flat high plains of southeastern Washington arranged along the bend of the Columbia River as it changes course. We cruised the two-story prefab apartment building on a cul-de-sac where Ruby was presumed to be living, and sat in our car to watch. Just as Todd had warned, children, teens, and adults were revolving in and out of what we thought was her second-story apartment, tromping up and down metal stairs that shook.

We needed to be more circumspect than to announce our mission to a crowd. We would return in the morning and, we hoped, find Ruby alone. We found a motel and made our shared room into a cocoon. Boo's miniature dachshund licked her bare feet until she fell asleep. I watched her peaceful exhalations. Boo rarely could sleep well. Though I generally had no trouble sleeping, I lay awake with apprehension.

It was a cool, overcast Sunday morning as we watched Ruby's apartment from inside the car. Everything was quiet until a woman appeared from a ground-floor apartment. I jumped out and asked her if Ruby lived in the apartment above hers just as a blond woman in her forties appeared on the upper balcony.

"Are you Ruby?"

She eyed us suspiciously as we approached. Outfitted in a bright red fleece sweater, my hair tied back off my face, I beamed at her as openly and forthrightly as I could. She stepped backward toward her apartment door, excusing herself because she was sick with the flu, but I sprang forth, explaining as fast as I could that we'd just arrived from Redmond, Oregon.

"My ex-husband lives in Redmond," she said, still more suspiciously.

Before she could slip away from us, I reeled out my identity as the figure in an old hatchet tale that she might have heard, "and I have the scars to prove it."

The scars won us our invitation into her home.

Ruby's living room was down-at-the-heels clean and comfortable—old sofas arranged around a TV, a picture of Jesus on the wall: not what I expected of a "typical biker" pad. Ruby played gracious hostess, and invited Boo and me to settle in for what I had a hunch would be some good talk. She was a zaftig blonde wearing a baggy turtleneck, with the wide-set blue eyes and sensual face of a classic Scandinavian model, but one who'd put on a few years, a few pounds, and a load of life experience that hadn't been good for her health. Her voice resonated in the lower registers, throaty and rich. If I'd spoken to her on the phone, I might have taken her for a black blues singer.

She sat close enough that I could touch her knee for reassurance and connection, and when I began to set forth why I had sought her out, she answered straightaway. Though I suspected she didn't trust easily, she had made an intuitive decision to trust me just then. My presence was not completely unexpected. Todd had tipped her off that I might come calling, and she had learned, to her surprise, that both girls survived the Cline Falls attack, and therefore the statute of limitations on that case had expired long ago.

"I got married to him in '82. It had to be late that summer, in the back room at Danny's Den in Redmond. I was sitting there drinking pop. Dirk was drinking. And a girl kept goin', 'Come 'ere.' But with Dirk's temper, you had to be careful, so I just said, 'I have to go to the bathroom.' So I met her in there and she quickly told the story that he had been suspected of chopping up two girls at Cline Falls. I said, 'What?' I said, 'Who are you?' 'I went to school with him, I know him. I went to bed with him. Who hasn't? And we all know what he's all about.'

"I was scared because I had seen his temper. I was pregnant. I didn't know how involved he was in drugs. I ran into her again one day. She came over to the house with her sister to see my baby daughter. That was her excuse. Dirk and her talked pleasantries, then he went out and she said, 'Are you going to leave now?' I said, 'I just can't believe this story.' And she said, 'Am I the only one that's told you this?' And I said, 'Yes.' I didn't know who to bring it up to, since everyone's afraid of Dirk, and they're going to say to him, 'Hey, your old lady's checking up on you . . .' "

It was a couple of years into their relationship before Dirk warned her, "I'm going to tell you a story and this is how it went."

"He had been up for a couple of days. He scared me, he'd been beating me, and then he told me, 'I'm going to tell you a story,' and he made me sit there in a corner while he started telling me the story. I'm so scared. And I'm trying to listen, and he's hitting me: 'Pay attention!'

"He was in jail in Prineville for beating up his girlfriend when apparently this happened to you. This was what he was telling me. 'She'd screwed around, and I went to a pond and drank vodka and I beat her up and I was in Prineville.' It was even in the paper—a seventeen-year-old is in Prineville jail for assault and battery on his girlfriend. And that was supposed to be Dirk. He said, 'I was in the Prineville jail then.' He said, 'That's why I was covered and people were going around saying it was me. I was sitting in jail, Ruby, I was not out. And if people don't believe me, they can look it up.' "

Ruby was playing both parts of her dialogue with her ex-husband. She lowered her voice into a deep masculine growl to imitate Dirk. " 'That fucking paper. It was in the paper.' "

She went on, "I think he said he sold his tires—I don't quite remember . . . my mind . . . I think I've tried to forget that part of my life—and that there was an investigation, but they discovered he sold these tires to a guy he knew apparently before he beat Janey—I don't remember quite which way it went. Everyone was thinking they were his tires, because someone matched the tire marks to these tires. These tires were supposed to be Dirk's, but Dirk sold these. They were on this guy's pickup. So this guy must have done it. And Dirk was cleared. But at the time he was sitting in Prineville jail, because he beat up his girlfriend very badly. This was the only time he's ever, ever talked to me about this."

"That one time?" I asked.

"That one time."

I was skeptical as I listened to Ruby. Todd had warned me that I couldn't believe everything she said, but these were real facts she was presenting: if she knew about an article in the newspaper about a seventeen-year-old in jail in Prineville for beating up his girlfriend, she likely knew it from the suspect himself. Only someone preoccupied with the Cline Falls case would have remembered the single line that appeared in the Bend *Bulletin* on June 27, 1977.

I asked Ruby if Dirk told her that he was investigated by the police for his involvement in the Cline Falls incident.

"Yes, he was. Then when he finally got out of jail, it was going all around the frigging town, it was 'Dirk Duran the Hatchet Man.' Then this was why he became even more angry and more involved in drugs because, again, he was accused of doing something he did not do. He's mad at the whole damn world because he was sitting in the Prineville jail the time this happened. He said he really threw himself into drugs and drinking and was going to screw everybody and anybody because he was accused of something he did not do. And I'm sitting there, 'Oh, yes, that would be terrible.' What else do you say when he's beating you in a corner? 'I would do the same thing, Dirk.' He's telling you a story, and you don't dare blink, you don't ask why, you don't ask nothin'. I will not forget the rage in him that night. There were lots of nights—but I will never forget that rage. Uh-huh. And I didn't go correlate the story. I was just too scared."

"You probably wanted to believe him."

"I didn't know what to believe. Looking at a man who could kill you right there, you think, you know he did it or he's capable of doing something like that, but you don't even want to question the story. Right now, you're just thinking of your children and your life."

Ruby emphasized the singular nature of the episode. "That was the one time he ever said anything about that—the *only* time."

I asked her if he kept any hatchets around the house.

"When I bought my house, I had a wood-burning stove. He'd chop wood . . ." She paused.

I asked her if she remembered that he had a fixation on his hatchet.

"It was not in the house. It was kept out in the garage . . ." She paused again. "Then he would help his father do the wood out on the ranch. No."

A sense of frustration started to rise in me. I felt sure there had to be more to this incongruous tale about how her ex-husband beat her in order to convince her he wasn't the Cline Falls hatchet man. I was thinking about how Kaye Turner's killer threatened his wife that he was going to do to her exactly what he'd done to Kaye. I knew an interrogator should never do it, but I couldn't help myself: I leaped at Ruby with a leading question.

"Did he ever say, 'If you don't do as I say, you're going to end up like those girls in Cline Falls?' "

"No. But I dug my own grave. I've had to dig my own grave," she said.

"What?" Boo interjected. She was nearly screaming.

"Oh, yes. Oh, yes. In the backyard. Because he was going to kill me. Oh, yes, I'd have to dig, in my backyard, my own grave. Uh-huh. Nice and deep. This was a ritual with him. You dig your own grave, oh, yes. Then he'd put the dirt back in. Do it in the middle of the night so no one would see."

Boo said, "What?" even louder this time. I could feel a charge building in my blood, rushing to my face, pulsing everywhere in my body—the kind of reaction I get from an overload of stimuli. I quickly recovered my analytical mind, which was busy drawing a portrait of this man. I asked fairly calmly how many times this grave-digging ritual had taken place.

"Fifteen, twenty times. I'd have to start digging. A lot of torture. A lot of beatings. Oh, it just does not stop."

"What other tortures?" I dared ask, filled with a peculiar intensity that came from the ultimate confirmation that the seventeen-year-old boy suspected of having attacked me was turning out to be as depraved, as ghoulish, as Bud Godwin after all.

"Being tied up. Being raped. Being put in a nightgown when you're eight months pregnant in the garage, freezing cold out. He's laughing. Won't let you come in. Taking your kitty and putting it in the snow and making you watch while it freezes to death. It does not stop. Dirk and his Copenhagen—chewing, then spitting in your eyes. Breaking both arms. Ribs. Nose. Eardrum."

"He broke both your arms!" This was Boo. I was thinking the same thing. The tortures were tumbling out of Ruby's mouth so fast we could only freeze-frame one at a time.

"Oh, yes. It just does not stop. I was in Central Oregon Hospital, St. Charles Hospital, a shelter for battered women, about ten times. I'm telling you, that movie on TV, *The Burning Bed*, with Farrah Fawcett, looks almost like a fairy tale. You know, as terrible as it is, I watched that movie and thought, my God, someone's peeking in my window.

"You watch people on Oprah . . . 'Why don't you just leave? Pick up, get those kids, and leave.' You don't; it's not that way. Psychologically . . . every fiber of you is brainwashed, is under his control. They have got you so you're so scared to leave, and it's unreal. Because I was strong. Smart. From a well-to-do family. I don't know. I kept saying, 'What did I do in my life? Why me?' But then, why not me? I guess. I guess God knew I would survive. But this was something that I never knew. I knew women got hurt and beat. I knew there was domestic violence. But this was beyond belief. The tortures. The way he would talk to me about things he was going to do to me. Taking me out in the woods. Leaving me where no one will find me. He was always going to torture me, rape me, slowly let me die. Or want me to beg him to kill me. Everything has got to be slow. Because he enjoys watching."

I understood why they stayed. Just that autumn I was volunteering for a domestic violence hotline in California, where I learned that the dynamics of coercion and entrapment are not well understood. People are bewildered when a victim won't leave her abuser, not even when she has an opportunity to escape. It seems to the outsider that she is submitting to the abuse voluntarily.

A process of debasement erases a woman's earlier stronger self, until the point where her sense of self is drastically altered. Her will is entirely reconfigured. There's a systematic process involved, a dizzying progression of absolutely deliberate intimidation intended to coerce the victim to do the will of the victimizer.

Abusers are clever. They take possession of their victims gradually. The process builds by degree. It starts with isolation, depriving her of social supports. It proceeds to monopolization of the victim's world, then induces exhaustion, which weakens her mental and physical ability to resist. The captor proceeds with threats, which cultivate anxiety and despair in the victim. And verbal degradation, like name-calling, which makes it seem that resistance is more damaging to self-esteem than capitulation. Then the captor enforces trivial demands, which develops the habit of compliance. The abuser then escalates to accomplish the total annihilation of the will, until the victim is convinced that she cannot escape and survive. This means assaults on her body—slaps, shoves, hair pulling, and sexual sadism. In the extreme, physical violence passes into torture: sleep deprivation, bondage, semi-starvation, exposure, near drowning, rape.

Mind you, the total destruction of the will of another cannot be accomplished without a few perks and rewards for the victim. Occasional indulgences motivate the prisoner to comply. The perpetrator is seductive, assuring the victim he's very sorry for what he's done, and he promises never to do it again. The battered partner mistakes these apologies for empathy or love, and she is convinced he will never do it again. But actually these indulgences, kindnesses, acts of contrition, are a charade; they are but a part of the process of coercion.

"When was the last time you saw him?" Boo asked. Ruby had let us know that Dirk moved back to Redmond, Oregon, earlier in the year, because things had gotten too hot for him in Washington.

"About two weeks ago he called here for my daughter. I've got a daughter with him. He'll always have a gateway to me. Always. Always will be in my life until he's put away."

This was a high-octane moment, to learn that my suspect had called Ruby just two weeks before, that her connection to him was still a hot wire. To be sitting in my suspect's ex-wife's living room—on whom he was perhaps still fixated—made me feel I had the drop on him. I felt reassured that I knew where he was. We were a full four hours' driving time away. So I settled deeper into the couch and asked Ruby to regale me with the history of her marriage to Dirk from the beginning.

She had divorced Todd, her fifth husband ("crazy, isn't it?") and was working as a nurse. She was planning to leave Redmond to go back to her hometown of Portland when she met Dirk Duran at a bar. Soon he started calling her constantly. Instead of putting her house up for sale, she let him move in. Inside of three months they were married, and she was lavishing expensive gifts on her handsome new husband with the coal black brilliantined hair and mustache and the sky blue eyes.

"Dirk has a way about him. He can put on. He's charismatic. Extremely handsome. And the women just fall. My prince charming just drove up on a white horse. This good-looking meticulous man . . . loves me, adores my son . . . really, you think you have stepped off earth and gone to heaven."

In her telling, within a few months the beatings started, for no special reason—slapping, hitting, kicking—and he pressured her to withdraw money from her trust fund for drugs.

The couch under me started to sway and I was wondering, with the 1994 Southern California earthquake so fresh in my mind, whether the ground was shifting, when the door burst open and Ruby's daughter, Shasta, stomped in, demanding that her mother take her fishing. When the beautiful blond child wearing boyish attire saw two women she'd never seen before sitting in her living room, she stared at us with striking light blue eyes. Ruby introduced us to her eleven-year-old as friends from Portland who'd come visiting. Satisfied with that explanation, Shasta tore out the door and the apartment shook again. Then a fifteen-year-old with dark hair and wide-set velvet brown eyes walked in and folded his lithe, androgynous frame on the couch. Dylan, Ruby's son by Todd, was a teen heartthrob, and he knew it. Ruby told her son forthrightly why Boo and I were sitting in their living room. Dylan's voice was breathy and soft, and he told us his own tales.

"He was beating my mom one day. My mom called my sister in the room and he had a .357 and he shot it at my mom. He was so high on drugs."

"Yeah, he was going to kill me and Shasta," Ruby said.

Boo wanted to know how Dylan handled that situation.

"I was only a little kid—five, six years old. What could I really do? But one time I tried to do something. I remember that."

"You pulled the gun on him," Ruby said. "I don't know guns that well, we had a small gun in our hall closet. He had been beating me, and Dylan climbed up on a chair and got it. Dirk was dragging me by my hair, and when he got me down to the dining room, Dylan was on the chair with the gun. I begged Dylan, 'Don't shoot him!' 'You're not going to hit my mommy no more. You're not going to beat her.'"

Dylan finished the story. "So I pulled the trigger anyway. Dirk actually had an unloaded gun for once."

"He liked to hold guns a lot, between my legs—excuse me—or on my head . . . Mostly it was fists, against the wall, throwing things at me, heavy things, against the furniture, getting me in a corner where you can't get out. And by then the intimidation is so bad—he could look at me and I would start falling apart. He checked the odometer on my car. Put tape on my screen door. He'd see if I let anybody in or out when he was gone. I couldn't have friends."

Ruby riled herself into a frenzy disgorging her tales—strings of white-hot memories were leaping forward without segue, and I coaxed her on. I wanted to hear them all. I knew that I might never again have an opportunity, that revelations such as these—revelations doused with shame—often surface only once, when you're still a stranger to someone.

Dirk smashed Dylan's favorite guitars over Ruby's head. They went through at least ten. Dirk hated Cheerios, and once Ruby smuggled some to her son because he loved them. Dirk found out and smashed them into the carpet. "And my tongue licked up every bit of that box of Cheerios. *That's how they were picked up that day.*" Ruby was spitting out her words in her husky alto. Her voice started to quaver and tears sprouted in her eyes.

I was still skeptical. Ruby's sudden modulations between anger, toughness, vulnerability, and tears seemed so expert. I had a feeling I was watching a performance. But it would have taken the most active imagination to invent all this.

"Dirk loves to see something sick. He loves to see something squirm. To see someone in real pain is a turn-on to him. Where we would cry if we watch a movie and something sad happened, he laughs."

There was a long silence.

This discovery of his depredations bewildered me until I reminded myself I had started with the endpoint of investigating the type of soul who would run over and take a hatchet to two girls asleep in a tent. That I should find myself immersed in the present subject matter really shouldn't have taken me by surprise.

Then it was my turn to give an account of a piece of my history, while Boo jumped in with her own startling tale of that June night. As we gained liftoff, a lean, ponytailed man walked in, Ruby's boyfriend, Don, who settled into the couch, took Ruby's hand, and signaled disdain that we would even be discussing Ruby's ex-husband.

Ruby pointed to Boo. "She rescued her, by the way," she told Don, referring to the Cline Falls tale, which he apparently had some prior knowledge of.

"I'm responsible for her for the rest of my damn life," Boo said.

"You're an angel, yes you are," Ruby said to Boo.

I told the tale about the meticulous cowboy I saw—the impression it had made on me that his shirt was so neatly tucked into his pants, that I'd always told people he looked like a movie star or a model in a jeans commercial.

Ruby didn't skip a beat. "There's a certain way he does it. He used to be very methodical about that. The way he lays his pants over, and the way he puts his shirts in." She described how he'd zip his pants partway up, then he'd start to carefully place his shirttail inside. "Everything is flat, never is it wrinkly. No, uh-uh. Usually he will put it inside his long johns." She mimed the motion of laying the left, then the right shirt flap inside his long underwear. Long johns, Ruby explained, were a signature item of clothing for Dirk, one or two pairs. Even if it was 110 degrees, Dirk liked the way the extra layer of clothing made him look like a bigger guy.

"And everything is straightened. There is *not* a crease. Everything is lined up. Buttoned. His shirts are perfect. You know, some people are like . . ." Ruby made a gesture of having a shirt rumpled up around the waist. Chills rippled through my body. It was the very same gesture I myself had made so many times in demonstration of the opposite approach to tucking in a shirt to the one favored by the axeman I had seen the night of June 22, 1977.

"He will make sure there was not a hair out of line. That mustache was trimmed. We never left that house without looking like a million bucks. He could go out and chop wood, and he looked like he'd just stepped out of the shower. Everything's got to be just perfect. That's all he does. Everyone does everything for him. Dirk has only his personal hygiene to worry about. His shirt and pants have to be ironed a certain way. His nails. Perfect. His nails are never even cracked. He's got the baby powder in his boots. That goes in a certain way. A certain deodorant. That's all he's got to do is sit and tell this world how lucky we all are that he's here and we're even around him."

Don had gotten up to pick up the phone. He came back into the room. "That was Dirk on the phone."

All went quiet. Taut as a tightrope. Then all at once we roared with laughter.

"What did he want?" Ruby asked.

"Talk to Shasta."

I guessed Dirk's ears were burning. The fellow had gifts of intuition? I thought about the way he looked at me in the restaurant earlier in the week: his quick dark glance. I was picturing the road between Redmond and Washington, and reassured myself that even flying down that highway would take a matter of hours.

"There's a girl up here, Kelly, a girl that lived with him, too. She wanted me to help her out. She called me and said, 'Ruby, please talk to me,' she said. 'What did he do to you?'

"The women will just fall. Then once they get to know him they say, 'What am I in?' It becomes this funnel. This whirlwind of evilness.

"There is such a darkness in his eyes, and a darkness in his soul and heart. We started to go back to church, and even the people at church didn't want to be around him, because of his evilness. Yes. The devil is really, really working. One of the churchwomen would say to me privately, 'Something's not right, there's a darkness around him.' If you look in his eyes, there's a hole that goes right to the core—they're very black, they're crystal eyes—but if you look right into his eyes, there's a very dark hole."

I looked at my watch. Five hours had passed since we first settled into the crushed-velvet couch. I asked Ruby if she could give me leads for my investigation, and she had an idea that I might squeeze something out of Dirk's best friend, Wayne.

"Wayne would talk to you as long as Dirk would never know. Wayne has no respect for him. He doesn't really like Dirk, but he's scared of him. If Dirk was passed out, Wayne and I could talk through a window, 'Hey, get away from Dirk, he's dangerous.' Then Dirk would come. Many times, Wayne would sit and watch while Dirk would beat me mercilessly. In all these beatings, Wayne never once stood up to him, and he'd sit at my table—and I had a beautiful table—and he'd sit there and smoke a cigarette and watch him beat me."

Ruby told me that Dirk's uncertain origins convinced him, at one point, that he was Italian, and his ancestry gave him pull with the Cosa Nostra. And at another point, he was sure that his father was Elvis Presley. "For about a year anything with Elvis on it—he'd be fascinated, he'd sit and watch, 'Look at the way he walks. I walk like that.' I would say, 'Yeah, there's a resemblance,' because you don't want to ruffle him."

I asked her if she knew how he felt about his biological mother having given him up for adoption, and she answered immediately: "He hates women. I know he does. The only woman that is pure and good is his mother, Lou Ellen. The rest of us are tramps, only good for one thing and that's beating. He hates us. I felt so sorry for his sister, Betty.

"He came from a damn good home. This is what people couldn't understand. Lou and Lou Ellen were good people. Where did he learn the abuse? He has his parents so scared."

"Does Dirk ever feel guilty about what he's done?" I asked the question without expecting a real answer.

"I think a lot of times he beat me even more because he felt guilty. Because he knew he did so wrong, and he wanted me to love him and he'd think: How could she ever love me—look what I just did to her? And it would make him so mad at himself and hate himself more for what a lowlife he is, then he'd beat me some more. He would hit me for hours. If I would say, I love you, he would quit hitting me."

As Ruby described this scenario, I imagined his state of mind: as he beat her, as he asserted power over her, the energy of wrath began to build inside himself, and that charge made him feel alive, a euphoria of rage that he equated with love—because the beatings resulted in his victim uttering the words "I love you."

"Last couple months before the final separation, my mind was getting so bad I was thinking how to kill him. I would pray that he would get in an accident. Someone would take him out . . . he just wouldn't come home. Then I'd hear the Monte Carlo or the pickups or the Bronco pulling up. 'Oh, no, he's home again.' " Her voice trembled. Tears slid from her eyes. "He made it home another night. Why? You just couldn't understand why."

Ruby had the date etched in her mind when she finally got away from Dirk: on July 14, 1987, she fled to an isolated community named Crooked River that stretched inside canyon walls north of Redmond.

I told Ruby that Dirk had been seen around Redmond these days with a new girlfriend named Scotty.

"I just hope there's someone to catch her when he starts hitting on her," Ruby said. "Hopefully something will happen between him and Scotty—once she starts saying, 'God, he's sick' . . . just like with Kelly . . . And who's the next one? And there will be another one."

I was carrying in my mind an image of Dirk's high school girlfriend, Janey Firestone. Something of Ruby reminded me of her—Janey had said so herself— and I marveled at what good taste this man had, that he would choose these warm women with zest and sparkle, women whose company I had begun to crave. These were the women he wanted to control and torture.

Kelly lived nearby and she would talk to us in a heartbeat, Ruby insisted, and sent us out the door with a scrawled note, asking Kelly to open her door to Boo and me. *"They are soulmates,"* she wrote, reminding Kelly of the investigation having to do with the women and the hatchet. She asked Kelly to share with us as Ruby herself had done. *"We need to bond together regarding Dirk and getting him put away. Love ya, Ruby."*

THE CAT'S CLEAR eyes, discs of celestial blue, had a weird gaze. A cat lover by nature, I was especially drawn to this one. As Kelly wasn't home, Boo and I lingered with the creature on the front stoop of Kelly's manufactured home—until Kelly and her latest boyfriend, both with flowing black hair and both outfitted in black leather and boots and dangling Native American jewelry, rolled up on a single motorcycle.

What a sweet kitty, Boo and I said to Kelly after explaining to her why we were on her doorstep in the dusk of an October evening. That sweet kitty was retarded, Kelly told us—brain damaged ever since her former boyfriend, Dirk, squeezed its head until it couldn't cry any longer. It was the only one of Kelly's animals that remained alive in the one year and six hours that Dirk was in her life.

Kelly looked tough, even forbidding, when she didn't smile. And she didn't smile at all at first, shaken to find in her living room one of the characters in the old hatchet tale she'd heard many times from Dirk.

Kelly was a genuine butch woman. She stood in a mannish pose, her solid frame in a masculine-cut shirt with sleeves rolled up her forearms. A slight stomach rolled over a Native American belt buckle. The thumb of her tattooed left hand hooked on the pocket of her jeans.

But when she smiled, her close-set dark eyes, which peeked out from under a fringe of long bangs, turned downward to meet a broad and unbridled upturned grin framed by plump cheeks. The features of her smiling face were almost a cartoonist's rendering of what struck me as a deep sweetness. As always, I was intensely interested in the type of woman my suspect singled out.

Arrows and feathers—American Indians everywhere, in drawing and photos, statues and dolls—were arranged with genuine artistry from floor to ceiling in the home Kelly owned herself. When she wasn't a handyman, repairing subsidized low-income apartment buildings, she was fashioning dream catchers out of beads and skins, drawing inspiration from her Native heritage, encouraged by her boyfriend, Jimmy, who himself dressed like a giant chieftain with creative flair, with NEZ PERCE tattooed across his back.

Boo and I sank into the sofa, decompressing after the harrowing hours of Ruby's revelations. Kelly disappeared into the hallway, only to return bearing a gopher. Boo cooed, "Hi, baby," in her characteristic talking-to-animals falsetto.

"It should be in hibernation now, but we keep waking it up," Jimmy said, producing from the kitchen a cat with too many toes, which Kelly had rescued. "You don't know Kelly. She comes home on Monday with a seagull, on Tuesday with a bat, on Wednesday she comes home with this cat."

"So Dirk really knew how to get to you," I said to Kelly.

"All he had to do was kill one of my animals. When he first started killing 'em, he didn't want me to know, he wanted me to cry on his shoulder about it. So I cried on his shoulder. Until I figured it out."

Kelly's year of bedlam lasted from New Year's Eve of 1993 to New Year's Eve, 1994. She met Dirk at a time when life had flattened her. First she lost her two kids in a custody battle. Then, as a single mother, she gave birth to another child, Sam. On Sam's third birthday Kelly took her three children camping. They settled into bed. When Kelly woke to rouse her family for an early start, she found her three-year-old dead. The coroner couldn't clearly determine how her son had died, other than perhaps from a mystery ailment such as SIDS. When the newspapers got a hold of the story they implied that Kelly's negligence had caused Sam's death.

I looked around Kelly's living room: framed photos of a little boy hung in a couple places. He had Kelly's grin, so broad that it curved up to meet his downward-sloping eyes.

She told us she had been alone and not ready to hook up with another man, but her coworker convinced her that this fellow he knew by the name of Dirk Duran was just the sort she needed. Kelly assumed her friend had known the guy awhile, so she agreed to meet Dirk. "Dirk said he was a Christian man, was very polite, seemed to be very generous, very kind and a simple sort of a person. And I thought I'd died and gone to heaven."

By the next day he began to spread over her life, inexorable as a late-afternoon shadow. He started coming every day to her home, though she never invited him. He moved in, a few possessions at a time, though she never said he could. He talked about how he was working in construction and making a lot of money. In fact, he was unemployed—which gave him the time to move in more junk, day by day, until finally he had moved in everything he owned and had annexed her home.

After three months, the polite, simple, Christian Dirk disappeared—the day Kelly walked into the bathroom and spotted him on the toilet with a hypodermic needle jabbed in a vein, and dope tracks in his arm. Kelly grabbed his things and told him to get out.

Dirk bawled and pleaded with her, "I wanted to get rid of this before you found out, but I know now that I can't do it without your help."

She believed his excuses. "I'd never seen anything like that in my life. I didn't know anything about that drug world. I was heartbroken. It hurt really a lot. And I didn't want to believe that he had a problem that couldn't be dealt with. I had no idea what I was in for, to try to save that Christian person. It was right after that, though, the evil came out instantly. Instantly."

Kelly had a dog, a wolf hybrid with a golden coat. One day Dirk kicked the dog and said he was going to get his gun and use the dog for target practice. A couple of days later, the dog disappeared and never came back. She had a rare white-faced cockatiel, who snapped at Dirk. Kelly got up one morning, and the bird was bloody, dead on the bottom of its cage. Dirk was jealous of her pet gophers because Kelly fussed over the decoration of their cages and showered them with attention. One morning she found the most energetic gopher with a hole in the middle of its head.

"And when he squeezed the cat's neck?" I asked, picturing the moment the cat's eyes changed from feline wisdom and canny wariness to a queer, dumb gaze.

"I didn't witness it. My son Allen told me."

The acts accrued. Quarrels broke out regularly between them. He busted a hardwood kitchen chair over her back. He arched brown streams of Copenhagen chew into her face. He cadged thousands of dollars from her to supply his drug habit. He looted her jewelry. Hocked his own daughter's bike, and her son's bike—three times. Once she came home from work and caught him cleaning up her TV, which was headed for the pawnshop. Another time he took Kelly's possessions next door and tried to sell them to her neighbor Shorty. Shorty recognized the items as Kelly's and wouldn't buy. After that, Dirk would stand in a window overlooking Shorty's house, laugh like a witch, and call Shorty a schizophrenic and a "retard." One morning Shorty woke up to find six pig hooves planted in a row in his front yard.

"It wigged me out. Whoa. This can't be real," Kelly recalled. But every time she told Dirk to leave her home, he'd plead, "Don't you love me anymore?" and she would relent and let him stay.

"I didn't want to believe anybody was that evil. It must be me." Because she couldn't help him, she believed that she had to be doing something wrong.

He ratcheted up the terror tactics. He deprived her of sleep by screaming and yelling all night. When she was beaten down to a weak point, he'd wait until she was in a dead sleep, then stick a needle in her arm. "After a certain point, after you haven't had any sleep at all . . . you don't wake up." She'd wake up with points of blood on her body where he had stuck needles into her veins. He wanted her to get hooked on heroin, too, so she'd know how it felt to be an addict deprived of junk.

Kelly got three or four restraining orders against her tormentor—he'd violate the order every time, but she wouldn't call the police.

"Because I didn't want to fight with him. I didn't want a big deal to happen. Because I was so tired. Because in between kicking him out and fighting with him, all I wanted to do was sleep. It was a total depression, too, on top of it all. Being depressed and being deprived of sleep is a combination, and it breaks the body down, and that's what he was doing to me. He was breaking me down. Not only mentally but physically." She took a long pause. "And I never believed that anybody could do anything like that to me."

It was time to call attention to the theme that had brought me here: So what did he say about that hatchet business?

"He talked about that all the time," she said.

As it happened, it was the subject of Sam's death that gave Dirk his opening lines about Cline Falls. Early in their relationship, Dirk was curious about the details surrounding the tragedy. When Kelly told Dirk that the local newspapers had trashed her and accused her of negligence, Dirk empathized with his new girlfriend. They had something in common, he said. "I know what that's like," he said. "Because I've been accused of doing something I didn't do."

"This is what he told me about Cline Falls. He said he was in jail being investigated. He told me he was 'held as a suspect.' The reason was because he had slapped his girlfriend the day before. That's all he did to her; he slapped her. They put him in jail, held him as a suspect—for a couple of days, or a week—then let him go because they found out they didn't have proof. And then he'd cry, 'They called me Dirk Duran the Hatchet Man.' " Kelly imitated him, lowering her voice to a deep masculine register with a whiny tone.

"Then he'd start bawling and screaming and crying and telling me that he thought I believed that he did it. He said that was the reason he had to leave Oregon, because they blamed him for this. That's why he's got so many problems, because they didn't apologize to him. But he swore up and down he didn't have anything to do with it, but somebody stole his hatchet out of his truck, put his initials on it. Somebody was trying to frame him. And he also told me they caught the guy that did it. He actually told me that they had caught the guy that did it. I asked him, 'If they caught the guy, why are you still crying about it?'

"I think that was the biggest thing that bothered him—that he was worried I would believe he really did it—because I got mad at him one night and told him that I felt he was capable of it. And he just completely come unglued. I flat out told him he did it. And he denied it. He said, 'God is my witness.' "

God is my witness. Dirk Duran said the same thing after he was told he failed the second polygraph regarding his involvement in Cline Falls.

Kelly went on, "I said, 'You're a liar. I've been with you long enough to know—you are a liar.' Because why would he cry constantly about something he didn't do? It doesn't make any sense. It's, like, duh. I told him flat out, 'You did it. And I know you did. This God-is-my-witness shit. You're going to burn in hell for that statement.' "

"Did you get a beating then?" I asked her.

"Oh, yeah. But I never hit him back until right up at the end. Then I beat the shit out of him."

They hadn't had sex in a long while, and on New Year's Eve, Dirk told Kelly she was obviously getting it bigger and better elsewhere, and finally Kelly had had enough smut and told him to either shut up or she was going to get the duct tape and wrap it across his face. So he started to slam things around and throw plants and trash the place. One of her kids ran next door and called the cops, and when they arrived Kelly told them the situation was under control. The cops left, and Dirk started jabbing Kelly in the ribs and backhanding her. "And I was not ready for it. I spun around and fell back, and landed on the couch. And then he lunged at me, and I had cowboy boots on. And he was in mid-lunge, and I kicked my foot, and the heel of my boot caught the top of his nose and it put him in shock for a second. Because he got up and kind of shook and he saw his blood and then he gave me the evil eye. He put his hands behind his back and said, 'I dare you to hit me again.' I said, 'Oh, really?' I jumped off that couch and plowed my fist in his face as hard as I could and he went flying across and hit his head on the front door. And then he ran into the bedroom, and I ran after him and I said, 'You're not going anywhere.' And he started crying and whining about 'How come you hit me?' And 'You started it.' "

Kelly was grimacing. "And I said, 'Motherfucker, it's a good day to die.' I was insane with anger. He had knocked me up against the door, and I fell forward, landed on my knees. And he grabbed my hair and was going to stuff his knee into my face. And I could see it all happening in slow motion. So it's like, think fast. I got enough room to get my elbow back behind me and I swung forward and I slugged him, a straight shot right between the legs. And I saw his feet come up off the ground. He was climbing over the top of me trying to get away from me. And when he got over the top of me, I wrapped his leg and he started dragging me down the hall with his foot. He was trying to get away from me that bad. For some reason it was the first time I saw fear in his face. I saw fear."

Kelly's eleven-year-old daughter, Jennifer, and Dirk's ten-year-old daughter,

Shasta, had been playing in the other room when the fight broke out. For Shasta's benefit, Kelly told the cops not to take Dirk to jail. But according to Kelly, Shasta said, "No, take him away. He started it all. We were having a good time until he started trying to beat her up."

Kelly took out a restraining order against him. A few days later he broke into her house. She called the police while Dirk hid in a box in the garage. The police searched the house with a dog, and when they found him they chased him around—in the process pulling out a wad of his hair—cuffed him, and brought him out. At his trial in April for criminal trespass in the first degree and violation of the no-contact order, he might have gotten at least a year of jail time if convicted of criminal trespass, but "he stood up there and told the court I'd kicked him out and called him back later and told him to come back home. Then when he showed up, and I called the cops, he told them I set him up." Kelly took the stand and told the jury her side of story, and they didn't believe her. Dirk was acquitted. "Because I had taken him back all those times before. So he was believed, and I wasn't. They made me look like a fool. I finally had had enough, and they didn't believe me. That was what was so bizarre. I got no satisfaction at all. That's how he gets away with stuff."

After her bedlam year with Dirk, Kelly removed every last thing from her house—before he could hock, steal, or destroy it. By the time she broke his chokehold, her home was drained of all warmth, broken and bare.

"You know, I feel I was lucky that I actually had the strength, just in a moment, to get rid of him. I'll tell you there would not be more satisfaction in my heart to find out that he was put away in prison forever. I tell you what, I would literally want to kill him if I saw him, on sight, because I thought about the people he could do harm to after me."

The toughness of Kelly's talk could hardly change the impression of sweetness I got from her. If Ruby had a reputation for stretching the truth, nothing about Kelly excited my skepticism. I didn't think she could dissemble if she tried, and the two women had told me much the same tale.

I had laid eyes on my suspected attacker for the first time just the week before. At first I wasn't sure what effect that encounter would have on me. Now I could say that there was something fortifying in filling in an abstraction with a specific form, attaching a face to a heretofore faceless threat in my unconscious. Knowing him better made me less phobic. I had lifted the generalized fear, which arose from my past, out of the deep psyche, brought it to the surface, attached it to the threat of a specific man in the present day. I no longer felt as though I were facing the menace of a sheer drop into terror. And this was ironic, given that my understanding of this man had deepened by several fathoms, and I now found myself looking into a profound moral abyss.

Evil Equals *Live* Spelled Backward

Boo and I sped into the night. A radioactive box sat between us. I looked at it and wondered whether the devil was in the box. Would it spell trouble for us? Would it cause us to crack up on the road?

The box belonged to Dirk Duran. As we were leaving, Kelly had appeared bearing a cardboard shirt box. It contained a trove of Dirk's precious writing, letters, scraps of memorabilia—in other words, the contents of my suspect's brain. She explained that when Dirk moved out the previous winter, he tore up her garage looking for this box. She motioned me toward the garage door. The place looked like an unclean force had blown through—upended furniture, boxes with their contents strewn everywhere. In ten months Kelly hadn't been able to find the strength to clean it up. I asked her how Dirk, in hot pursuit of the box, had managed not to find it. Kelly related that when he was packing to leave, her neighbor Shorty came by and placed a shirt in the box, on top of Dirk's pile of writings, so the box went unnoticed. He panicked when he couldn't find it. *"My whole life is in that box!"* he had cried. The box disappeared right from under his nose. He actually had nightmares that the box was taken mysteriously from him.

"I'd love to give you that box," Kelly said to me gleefully. "Now that you have the box, you have his 'whole life.' " With that, Kelly let out a tremendous chortle. We all enjoyed the irony that I, chopped-up specter from the past come back to haunt him, might now possess what he regarded as his "whole life."

Boo and I made a restrained decision to wait until we'd gotten back to the ranch, but at Bigg's Junction, along the Columbia River, we abruptly veered off the highway. Sitting in a booth at a truck stop, we hungrily pulled the contents out of the treasure trove and read them aloud to each other.

A folder with newspaper clippings about drugs. A 1986 issue of *The Marijuana Report*, published by the Oregon Marijuana Initiative. A series from the Bend

Bulletin, vintage late eighties, covering the drug scene in Central Oregon and various methamphetamine busts (through which I learned that Central Oregon was an attractive place for dealers, as it was relatively remote, with plenty of isolated places to cook meth, the drug of choice for rural whites).

The third edition of *Alcoholics Anonymous* inscribed with many names of previous owners and peace signs scribbled in ink on its blue fabric cover.

An otherwise empty scrap of paper with the words *Birds* and *Ocean* scribbled in the corner. A Post-it with "She couldn't ride but mounted with great authority." Another with "Grow a penis."

Several different pages filled with lists of words with no theme or organizing principle I could make out. A couple of specific dates broken down into numerological components. Acrostics I deemed not worth the effort to unravel because they looked like gibberish.

Poems of the most amateurish nature—sentimental and garbled—on such subjects as the solitary wanderer in a forest pondering that he may be the first to walk this path, and a tree standing alone in the forest, with strong roots but no family.

Various spiritual manifestos. Jottings about consciousness. Rituals to conjure strength and a higher power under a full moon. Quasi-mystic ramblings, joining words that looked impressive into sentences that had no meaning.

Song lyrics on homiletic themes: about how the passage can be long or short but, either way, what we gain is important to all of us in our own way—the refrain "Baby, Oh Baby" punctuating the stanzas. Photocopies of crude sayings and jokes and cartoons: "Wood and paper products no longer available—wipe your ass with a spotted owl." A crude drawing of a flying saucer. A couple of references to the Cosa Nostra. Jotted on the back of a photocopy of a Christian poem that obviously came from some sort of Bible study class: "*Devil* = *lived* backwards. *Evil* = *live* backwards."

On a scrap of paper. "I hear no evil, I see no evil, I speak no evil."

A religious booklet on caring. A photocopied magazine article on "How to Love Another Person"—as though he needed a paint-by-number description of the behavior appropriate to love. A six-page letter to Ruby infused with the gibberish contained in all his poems, songs, and prayers, but magnified to a fever pitch to try to win her back.

Growing bored with the contents of this box, I longed for some intelligence to shine through in one of these scrawled ravings, something like the compulsively readable diary of John Abbott, one of the suspects in Valerie McDonald's disappearance and murder, who wrote clear-eyed descriptions of his own malfeasance. But there was nothing. I was reminded of how it had shocked Hitler's architect, Albert Speer, to find the Führer unproductively lazing away his days, screening Hollywood fluff like *Snow White and the Seven Dwarfs* in his private quarters.

I'm not speaking of the by-now-well-worn concept of the banality of evil. As

Austrian-Belgian intellectual and Holocaust survivor Jean Amery points out: "When an event places the most extreme demands on us, we ought not to speak of banality." But those who adore the drama of destruction, who can effect vast change with startlingly little effort, don't do well with the subtler pursuits of building, creating something positive and enduring, because those pursuits require daily process, daily patience—faith and humility.

I CALLED RUBY a week later. She had warned me that the phone company was on the verge of disconnecting her, so I was grateful to hear her throaty voice when she picked up. To have found a community of similarly suffering souls was intoxicating to me. I didn't care if I slipped over into sentimentality; I wanted to push our relationship to a new register, so I confessed that I'd been thinking about her all week, to which she responded, "I couldn't get you out of my mind. When you guys walked out the door, you took something with me. You took a part of my heart with you. We all bonded so hard."

Yes, we bonded hard. I told her that I guessed it was a good thing we dropped by and caught her by surprise. Ruby told me she was glad we came. It was good for her. But she hadn't slept for two nights after Boo and I showed up and tampered with her past.

I wondered how traumatic it was for her to dredge up corrosive memories a second time in a week. On my recommendation, Sergeant Marlen Hein had shot up to Washington to plumb Ruby's memory while she was in the remembering mood. She told me that the sergeant had asked her to tell him about her life with her ex-husband in chronological order, and as he listened to her tales he held back tears a couple of times.

"Yes, he took his glasses off and wiped his eyes. He couldn't look at me. I think he would have lost control. I think he thought if he looked at me, he couldn't be the professional pushing me on—instead of breaking down, he's saying, 'Now what happened in May 1984?' He just kept trying to keep it going so there wouldn't be a total breakdown. The next time he was typing, and I was talking, and I didn't hear the clicking, I looked over and again, he was wiping his eyes . . . I just kind of went into a trance talking. I didn't leave my body by far, but I was thinking okay, I gotta do this. We're going to be strong. I'm just going to stay and say this happened, and this happened . . . I'm scared to drum up other memories, I don't know how I'm going to react."

So there were more I hadn't heard?

"I was able to tell him about the crawl space, though."

Crawl space?

"In our bedroom, you opened the closet, and there was a small space underneath the house. I could barely fit in it. He would put me in it, then put something heavy on it or stomp on it—and I was in it a day and a half. Spiders. No water. Darkness. Oh, yeah. His crawl space. Oh, that was his favorite when I was really, really bad. On Glacier Avenue."

Favorite? He did it more than once?

"At the most seven, eight times. It was terrible. I was out of my body."

I wanted to get this straight: It was like a coffin?

"It was horizontal."

Now I understood. This narrow prison (I didn't think to ask her what circumstances had led to the fabrication of such a space) reminded me of what I'd read of the "isolator" in the Soviet gulag. It was as though Dirk was constitutionally possessed of the genetic memory of a gulag prison guard—much like the memories a hunting dog has in him innately. Point by point, Dirk's control tactics exactly matched those that had been documented by psychologists, based on accounts of American POWs, political prisoners, hostages, and concentration camp survivors. These strikingly similar techniques were codified in a chart of coercion published by Amnesty International in 1973. This handy reference guide is often reproduced and handed out at support groups for battered women.

Is the basic grammar of terror intuitive? I knew from my own frontline work on a violence-against-women crisis hotline in Southern California that women—regardless of race, class or ethnicity—were telling the same stories. It's as though they were all describing the very same guy, recounting stories of violence drawn from an identical arsenal of tortures.

"You should have seen my body after that," Ruby went on. "Bites. You're hungry. No water. Air. You go crazy. I'm surprised I don't have a multiple personality . . . your mind leaves your body. That's the only way you can handle it. I would go other places. Oh, I would sing . . ." she said in a singsong voice.

I wanted to share yet another bond with Ruby, wanted to find all common causes between us—so I told her, "That's what happened to me that night—the night of the attack—I left my body and it has taken me fifteen years and more to get back into it." I told Ruby I became a different girl after that night. Originally I was a tough young girl who had the will to save myself and the life of another.

"You were gung-ho, and what you set out to do, you did, didn't ya?"

"Then all that changed, and for a while I became someone who couldn't defend myself—"

"How could you have been a victim of anything? You would have been the one to save victims."

That's what violence does. It severs you from yourself. You are not the person you once were. From then on, you have to remake yourself from a different place. Ruby knew what I meant.

"Wounded bird can't even fly. I'm not in flight anymore. I'm a wounded bird," she said.

Severed

My conversation with Ruby brought to mind a talk I'd recently had with Dave, my friend from high school. He was telling me, eighteen years later, how he perceived me in early July, summer of '77, back from the Oregon desert, as I sat propped on my parents' couch.

"Your parents had left to go someplace, so they wanted me to stay there with you, and I was glad to do that. But it was difficult, because there was nothing to talk about."

Nothing to talk about. He meant: what had happened fit no familiar places in the mind, belonged to no shared stories we knew. This was an experience beyond what was circumscribable. So there was nothing to talk about.

"I also remember the cut on your arm looked like an axe cut! That's exactly what I thought. I use an axe every day. The skin was folded back, but there it was. It was just like a chop of wood. And of course your head was shaved. There was an anger, a terrible anger bordering on hatred that I felt you might be taking out on me at any minute. Terri, if I hadn't known you, I wouldn't have stayed there. I would have been afraid of you. Like if you could kill, you would have.

"The last time I had seen you we loaded up my truck, and we said goodbye to your parents and I took you down to the Greyhound bus on Randolph Street. You were like two little kids going on a sandbox adventure. I thought all along it was unrealistic to think that two people could take on a course they'd never been on before, from coast to coast. The risks were unbelievable. Two people on bicycles were targets for anybody."

I asked Dave if he thought the trip was more dangerous for two women.

"No, because I always thought you were tough as nails. You could beat the shit out of anybody. You had a presence about you. I wouldn't fool with you, you know what I mean. You had a toughness about you."

· · ·

THE NATURAL extrapolation of the girl I once was—the girl with the inviolable sense of self, a solid sense of physical boundaries, the sense that my unconscious desires were at least reasonably in sync with my conscious will—that natural extrapolation wasn't possible because I had taken a turn, gone into exile.

After June 1977, I had changed without being aware of it, although now I can see it clearly, in my passport photo from 1982. I was twenty-four. You get a little blurry looking into the eyes of the young woman in the photo, because they follow different sight lines. Then, too, if you cover up different parts of the portrait you see different things: Focus on the forehead and eyebrows and you see the inarticulate rage that gives me the air of a mental patient. Cover the forehead and eyebrows and you see grief and resignation. Here was tangible evidence of a split, a fractured self. This was damage that couldn't be X-rayed, but it showed up all the same.

By the winter of 1986 I was twenty-nine. I scrawled my thoughts on the neat grids of my graph paper notebook, unofficially my "journal": *My problem now. Spirit is not in the body. Because it is afraid of the issues it has to face now. But lack of unity between spirit and body is causing lack of power. When absorbed in exercising or work, spirit unites with the body. Can tell when spirit isn't in the body—when I exercise, I get weak.*

That same year, 1986, a friend described my physicality as "doelike." No longer "tough as nails," I was fragile and quick to frighten. I had a fawnlike appearance, with delicate stick arms and no upper-body strength—an opposite body type from the broad-shouldered girl I was at the age of twenty.

The years began to wear on me badly. Life's rough moments were accruing, as New York in the late 1980s got ever more dangerous. There came a point when I became convinced that my life was a script in which unspeakable things would *absolutely* have to happen, and regularly, as though something lethal inside me were drawing them in. It began to seem that cataclysm could come from everything, everywhere. There were myriad, multiplying sources of danger: the night, the subway, car accidents, disease, attacks by strangers, apocalyptic fires, earthquakes—a hundred fears in one converging threat could at any moment create the destructive eruption that would drag me out of my comfortable routine and into the region of dread.

Compulsive thoughts about the many sources of fear gathered velocity. My default setting was hysteria. I felt the kind of fright where the wind rushes through your skull and erases all thoughts, where breath ceases, the rib cage sucks up, and the body crumples forward. As fate would have it, my body was perfect for that posture. The weight of a truck still carved into my chest created a natural concave curve where my right shoulder dipped down and forward. When overcome with panic, I would continue the curling motion and naturally fold in on myself like a dry autumn leaf. During those years, routine visits to doctors' offices triggered intense phobias. I would cry for no apparent reason, because I expected dreadful news of my impending death. One doctor said he felt that my body was still torqued in the direction of a truck running up my chest. Another queried me about my jutting rib cage. When I gave her a two-line recitation of my history, she said, "Your body is an encyclopedia of terror." How I hated to hear articulated what I implicitly knew to be true.

By then I had no choice but to begin a mission of repair. I made the rounds of therapy and bodywork and self-development seminars. (In one, the lecturer wanted to make the point that most human beings suppress and deny fear in order to life sanely. When he asked, "How many of you are afraid to cross the street?" only my arm shot up.)

All of it added up to some restoration, so that by 1992 I was somewhat becalmed. I left New York City. Its canyons of tall buildings that glittered in the day and turned black and mysterious by night had turned into a mise-en-scène for my urban nightmare. I fled to California, to a tree house on stilts hanging over a cliff, with a view of snowcapped mountains that let me pretend I was a character in a children's story. In my crow's nest, I communed with the treetops, above the earth and all its sordid concerns. There I let in some light, ceased the obsessive stream-of-consciousness scrawls in my journal detailing my dark thoughts. For the first time in years I walked with an airy bounce in my step. Had fun in the sun, with less fear and more faith. It was only in the safe haven of this sunny place that I dared drag out the memorabilia from the axe attack, the radioactive box, and think about returning north.

Since then, much had happened to bring me to where I was at this moment, at Ruby's door.

A woman once called me on the hotline where I was counseling women who had been abused, raped, battered. "My spirit is broken. I want to get back to the way I was," she told me. But there's a trick. The self can't be reconstituted in just the same way. The pieces fit back together differently. And the reparation is hard work. The way to overcome paralysis, the way to recover the will, is to take action. Even little steps. Day by day. Action had been my salvation.

Bonding Hard

Now Ruby was telling me how she turned the tables on her ex-husband the last time he threatened her not quite a year before. She has a real gift for storytelling. She would convincingly play all the characters in a scene, sweeping me into her tale as though it were a play unfolding before my eyes.

"What happened is: he went to jail for domestic violence on Kelly. My daughter, Shasta, went to the mall with her friends. Dirk gets out of jail, goes to the mall, and has some drinks. My daughter is walking around the mall. He grabs her from her friends, walks my daughter four miles, the whole time yelling at her, 'You little bitch!'—because Kelly had said, 'Go call the cops,' and Shasta and Kelly's daughter ran out to the neighbors and called the cops."

I'd heard this story before. I knew from Kelly that it was Shasta herself, a girl of ten, who boldly made the decision to call the cops so they would haul away the abuser in their midst, the man who was her father. So I knew that at least part of Ruby's story was true, and I could easily picture Ruby as she described herself in this aftermath of Shasta's decision.

"I'm in there cleaning the house. I hear this sobbing and this terrible screaming, and the door opens. It's my little girl, oh, God, shaking, crying, 'I have to go to jail now.' And Dirk's drunk. I said, 'What? What did you do to her?'" Ruby mimicked Dirk, as though his was the deep voice of a snotty adolescent. " 'That little fucking bitch. She's the one that called the police and put me in jail. I don't care what I'm doing, you don't call the cops on me. I'm your blood.'

"I said, 'You get the hell out now. You leave her alone.' 'Who do you think you're talking to?' 'Get out, Dirk.' Shasta was shaking. 'I have to go to jail now, Mommy.'

"Dirk said, 'She's goin' in. You're going into juvenile detention, Shasta.' I said,

'You better get out of here. I'll cap your ass.' 'What did you say to me?' And I screamed, 'Get the fuck out now.' My nose was almost touching his, and I've never done that to him.

"He was in shock . . . I said, 'Get out!' *I was hot.* I said, 'I'll cap your ass.' My whole face and everything changed. I guess he'd never seen me like this. I remember him backing up. I thought, Okay, we're dancing and I'm leadin'. And he looked at me and turned around. I said, 'Come on, motherfucker.' I was going to go back and get a gun. I said, 'You know, I'm going to take you on, Dirk.' Shasta was crying hysterically. He looked in my eyes, and literally backed up away from me slowly, then he turned . . . and he started running, asses and elbows . . ."

Ruby broke into one of her infectious giggles. "The neighbors came up and asked, 'Is there a little confrontation going on?'"

Ruby told me that what Dirk had done to torment her she put in one category, but when she thought of how he had psychologically tormented her daughter, it put her in a killing mood. She'd already told the police, on the record, she was going to go kill the son of a bitch. "I'm going to say, 'Before I kill you, you're going to confess to whatever you've done in your life. Remember when you put me in a corner? That Dirk-Duran-Hatchet-Man crap?' I'm going to make him confess."

I suggested she might not want to go behind bars for Dirk. Exacting other tortures might be more suitable.

"I'd make him dig his own grave." She giggled girlishly. " 'Faster, faster!' 'Not deep enough! Start another one.' I've got him digging . . . oh, yeah."

I egged her on, conjuring Dirk's spirit of perverseness to cook up tortures. Ruby had something theatrical in mind: an ordinary restaurant visit that turns into a nasty surprise. We rent the place for the night. The diners are cops in disguise. He sits down. He gets a special menu with the crime scene photos of the bloody grass pasted inside. "You know, we have a Cline Falls Special. Would you like your steak *rare?*"

"Or would you like the Hatchet Burger?" We played off one another.

" 'Cut in half! We'll even do it for you!' And here's this little mini hatchet right in front of him. 'We can slice and dice!' "

Like a playwriting team we orchestrated the whole charade: A map of Cline Falls for table napkins. Salt and pepper shakers shaped like little pup tents. A little toy pickup as a centerpiece. Cocktails with little hatchets.

"It would send him over the edge. Oh, we could do it. 'Yes, I did it! Release me from this hell! I confess!' . . . Oh, Ruby has a wicked mind. Well, I learned from the best! Oh, yeah, screw with him. Dirk yells, 'I'm in hell!' 'Oh, no, you've just stepped in!' Okay, Terri, I'm enjoying this way too much."

I felt desperate to connect to Ruby. By bonding with someone who had been tortured by the very same man who I believed had tortured me, something had gelled in my psyche, fit just right, filled a hole. Omissions of the past, stories never shared, were being compensated for. I would listen to her every tale of torment, take in the uprush of her memories: the hours she was trapped in the crawl space, the nights she spent digging her own grave, turning up a few spades of earth with her weak arms before collapsing. I would commiserate with her dreadful ordeals until all her shame-drenched secrets came out. Most of all I wanted to piece her back together. The savior fantasies I had had in my childhood, of rescuing a girl in trouble, a girl trapped in a deep pit in flames, had taken hold of me once again.

Not two months later, I returned to Washington specifically to rescue Ruby from her fear of Dirk popping in on her at any time. "He's wearing me down. I get up at night and think Dirk is around. You can't live like that." The day I accompanied Ruby to the Benton County Courthouse to make a bid for a restraining order against Dirk, she told me about the last time she'd gone to court to get a restraining order against him. Dirk strode into the courtroom, passed behind her, and whispered, "You just wait, bitch."

"Those eyes, those eyes," Ruby remembered his intimidating stare. This time, if she could find the power within herself, she would play the same game of primate dominance and shoot him an unblinking stare. Ruby demonstrated to me, bulging her wide-set blue eyes, now rimmed with black eyeliner, her lashes lacquered with mascara. In the end, both she and Dirk called in medical excuses, so no contest ever took place, but Ruby won the law's support for keeping her ex-husband off her doorstep for one year's duration.

IT WASN'T LONG before I got a letter from Kelly, that other kindred soul. "Our roads have crossed in the strangest way," she said. "So it was fate. One of those meant-to-be kind of things. I suppose I find a common place where our roads cross, you give me strength where I could only find weakness and fear, and therefore I look up to you and feel the need to protect you."

She added that, after I'd left, she had second thoughts about a plan we'd cooked up to torture Dirk: by sending his "stupid" poems back to him, his originals, with postmarks from Sicily, Japan, Moscow, as though the contents of his precious box were now possessed by a crime syndicate with tentacles everywhere. "Not 'cause I was worried he could do anything to you. What worried me is how it would affect you mentally. I'm sorry I was being selfish! All I had on my mind was revenge, and that really isn't like me at all (even though it would be cool), but neither one of us is a fly on the wall to see his reactions so it really wouldn't have that satisfaction (as imagined). Sucks, huh!"

Conjuring these outlandish fantasies together with Ruby and Kelly had been part of our cure—with humor as an active ingredient.

Kelly had added a couple of mementos to her letter. One was an old restraining order she'd found from October 1994, stating that "The above defendant has been arrested on Monday, 10-03-94, for a crime of domestic violence, to wit: 'Dirk did assault girlfriend by grabbing her hair and hitting her face.' "

The other memento was a torn-up picture of Dirk she'd found while cleaning out a junk drawer. The laminated color snapshot was from a Photomat. A corner was torn out of the lower-right quadrant—tearing a gash out of Dirk's cheek. I imagined Kelly had taken scissors and cut her cheek away from his. I gathered that the photo was a product of an incident Kelly had described to me—when Dirk insisted they drive to the mall Photomat to have a portrait taken together, as a happy couple. Dirk had even ordered copies made. I imagined that the image of perfect coupledom was something he desired in theory (he had said as much in his love letter to Ruby), perhaps because it contributed to the vain image of perfection he liked the world to see.

In my examination of him, I noted a theme emerging rather consistently: that he wanted to hold up an image of perfection, apparently to mask his deeds, which in their shameful, incredulous aspect for the most part remained untold.

I studied the man in the picture before me: an older version of the boy in the prom photo, a younger version of the man in the police mug shot. This torturer did not have the face you'd imagine—one with pockmarks, knife scars, and a broken nose—but rather he was all spruced up, a handsome man with that perfect nose and pretty, light blue eyes. Though he wore a beard that was not especially coiffed, he was a bit of a dandy. The costume he'd chosen for himself was a peach-and-white plaid shirt, and the bandanna folded across his forehead had a pink-and-red floral motif.

The man in his thirties regarded the camera in precisely the same fashion as the boy at seventeen—his head turned away slightly, so that his clear blue eyes under thick eyebrows shifted to the right and did not quite meet the lens. And in just the same way as in the earlier picture, his mouth turned up at the right, as though he were attempting to manufacture a smile. I would say, at first glance, the photo showed a very attractive man. His face had qualities of beauty that registered automatic pleasure in some part of the brain. A closer look revealed something distasteful underlying the beauty of external form. His smile was shifty, really more of a sneer; his teeth, barely visible, were stained dark, from a lifetime of soaking wads of chew under his lips.

Something about my sudden revulsion to this face brought to mind a folktale from Chicano Texas. A young good-looking cowboy, tall, immaculately dressed, with a light complexion and light eyes, is known to frequent the cantinas of Texas and the Southwest. He's irresistible to the young women who flock to the bars, often waitresses or taxi dancers, and he lures them into a dance. When they get up close, they're shocked to get a glimpse of his one flaw—a scarred or twisted hand, or a foot shaped like a goat's or chicken's. In these folktales, these urban legends that have been circulating through the Southwest for decades, the light-skinned, blue-eyed, immaculately dressed stranger is a demon. And if a young woman leaves the cantina with him, she's never seen alive again.

Western Trees Bear Strange Fruit

The question of ear is vital. Only the writer whose ear is reliable is in a position to use bad grammar deliberately; only he knows for sure when a colloquialism is better than formal phrasing; only he is able to sustain his work at the level of good taste. So cock your ear. Years ago, students were warned not to end a sentence with a preposition: time, of course, has softened that rigid decree. Not only is the preposition acceptable at the end, sometimes it is more effective in that spot than anywhere else. "A claw hammer, not an ax, was the tool he murdered her with." This is preferable to "A claw hammer, not an ax, was the tool with which he murdered her." Why? Because it sounds more violent, more like murder. A matter of ear.

—WILLIAM STRUNK, JR., AND E. B. WHITE,
THE ELEMENTS OF STYLE, FOURTH EDITION

It wasn't long after we'd seen the infatuated Scotty, the latest woman in our prime suspect's life, kiss the self-adoring Dirk's cheek that Boo called me to tell me that she had had a nightmare or two about something violent happening to Scotty. Not long after that, I received a phone call from Fred Ackom of the Oregon State Police. In early December 1995, Dirk Duran was arrested and charged with two counts of assault IV on his girlfriend. Dirk had invited Scotty to shack up with him in the snug travel trailer in which he was domiciled by his dad. One December afternoon, Dirk woke from a nap and caught Scotty moving out. He whacked her around until several neighbors came to her rescue, and one guy pummeled him with a heavy metal flashlight.

I immediately felt the weight of responsibility: I had had an instinct to warn Scotty, but I had never followed through. I phoned Sergeant Marlen Hein in the Bend office, who told me he had just interviewed her about the incident. She told Marlen that she'd exited Dirk's trailer with a set of "finely matched luggage"— three green plastic garbage bags—and fled into hiding with friends. Fortunately she intended to leave Dirk Duran for good, and was willing to cooperate in his prosecution.

I wanted to talk to Scotty myself, to get news from the trenches, so I flew to Oregon in the winter of 1996. Marlen clued me in that I could find her through a guy named Herby, the wielder of the flashlight. Herby was easy to find. He parked his tiny turquoise vintage trailer in the Green Acres RV park.

THE KOUNSES and I pulled up next to the turquoise hovel on wheels, its curtained windows festooned with Christmas decorations though the holiday had long passed. The trailer's tiny door opened and a huge man with a black hat shadowing the top third of his black aviator sunglasses ducked out into the bright desert light. His fierce demeanor softened to a simple grin when he learned that we had sought him out for the tale of his rescue of a damsel in distress. He delightedly related to us how he had grabbed Scotty's abuser "by a piece of the neck and tapped him a few times." He produced the weapon itself from within his trailer. I took the heavy twelve-inch flashlight-cum–billy club in my hand as Herby told us that he only quit whaling on Dirk because Scotty called him off. Herby recounted that Dirk allegedly said to him, "Why don't we go fist to fist?" to which Herby apparently responded, "Sorry, I only do that with men. You're not a man. You're beating on a woman."

HER RED CURLY hair escaping from under a genuine Confederate army cap, a tall freckle-faced woman was heaving junk into a Chevy Silverado on the corner of Seventh and Birch. When we pulled up and told her we wanted to talk to her about Dirk Duran, she reared back and rasped in a loud, throaty voice, "Whose side are you on?"

She was expecting us, though we had left Herby's only ten minutes before. Surely Herby had no phone—but I supposed that people who live without phones figured out other ingenious ways to stay in touch. "People find it hard to find me. You're lucky you didn't have to go three or four places." When we referred to Herby as her "rescuer," she sniffed, "I didn't need Herby," plainly annoyed that he had assumed a savior role in her story.

Scotty obligingly let us take her to a nearby bar where she held forth on her no-good boyfriend. She'd met Dirk at the Fireside Pub in Redmond. "My mom says I like my men and my horses the same. Long-legged with a nice butt. And his *was* nice. And I was lookin' at it. Then he turned around—and he is very good-looking. And I walked by him and I said, 'I don't usually go for long-haired guys, but you're sure good-looking.' And I just kept on walking to the bathroom; later he started talking to me. And then he walked with me over to the school and talked my son out of a temper tantrum. He didn't get uptight about Jack acting up. He worked with him, talked calmly to him. Which impressed me."

It impressed her so much that she said to him, "The way my luck has been runnin,' I'm amazed I met a nice guy." And he said to her, "Oh, yeah, I'm a nice guy. Ask my mom." Scotty's mom had also counseled her: "Find a guy that's good to his mom, and he'll be good to you."

Unnerving behavior began soon enough. "Like we'd be sitting somewhere and he'd say, 'See that guy over there? He's sittin' there looking at me. I should go over there and kick his face in.' That's when I knew he had personality traits I didn't need, because I'm usually a very sunny person. I do have red hair and green eyes, and you don't want to piss me off, but I don't walk in and say, 'That guy should have a bad day, and here I am.'

"Then he hinted he might be an off-duty hit man. But he's on vacation. Like they're just letting him cool off with Mom and Pop in Oregon. He'd say, 'I know a lot of things that happened, and how they happened.' He was trying to make everything a mystery. Trying to make you wonder. He was always saying, 'I can make a phone call and have somebody killed.' "

Then, about six weeks before he beat Scotty, a "switch flipped all of a sudden." He started spitting Copenhagen in her eyes. (When I informed her that spitting chewed Copenhagen into women's eyes was one of the favorite tortures in Dirk's kit bag, Scotty suggested other uses to which stinging Copenhagen might be put, should she ever get her hands on Dirk again.) Then one day Dirk actually popped her with his hand, and he called his dad to come over and take her away to one of her girlfriend's homes. "So I packed my perfectly matching luggage. Within an hour he was calling back, saying, 'I'm sorry I lost my temper.' "

Scotty went back to him, only to have him backhand her and split her lip on another occasion. She never called the cops. Then, one afternoon, "My girlfriend Rachel brought Dirk back to the trailer. I'd been home cleaning and waiting for him to get back. So when he came in, he said, 'That Rachel is really nice, but that daughter of hers—she likes law and order, and I think she'd snitch me off for smoking pot, and she sure doesn't like us drinking around there, and I should have one of my friends from Washington come down and butt-fuck her so bad she never wants to see a man again, then tie her up to a tree near your place so you can find her.' "

Tied to a tree. Tied to a tree. Tied to a tree . . . my file of associations led me to the image of Kaye Turner's murderers tying her to a tree while they raped and killed her.

Scotty rasped on that her friend Rachel's daughter was only seventeen years old and was like a daughter to Scotty—and the tree Dirk was referring to, the tree he threatened to tie the girl to, was on a property Scotty owned, a place where she kept a trailer way off the grid in the desert north of Alfalfa, Oregon.

"I started shaking and going, 'Wow, you've really gone off the deep end.' He was slamming beers and shoving shit all over the trailer and being verbally abusive. And I looked him in the eye and said, 'So what made your switch flip this time?' He backhanded me and split my lip, which he'd split three days before, so it split easy. And I'm going, okay, keep calm and keep your mouth shut and let him pass out. I waited. I tried to extinguish the situation. If you talk to a psychologist about people like him—you need to be calm to defuse it as you can, especially when they've had as much alcohol as he had. I was in a twenty-three-foot travel trailer with him—that was the confines. It was a terrorization."

She recounted to us the details of her escape from the trailer. Then she said, "After I left him I pulled a restraining order on him and he called my girlfriend and said the reason he beat me up and kicked me out was because I beat up my son in front of him. My girlfriend said he was a fucking liar and hung up on him." Scotty was leaning forward on the table, picking scabs off her hands until they bled, really worked up, eager to pour forth everything she knew.

"You obviously can take care of yourself, but I spent some time worrying about you," I told Scotty, and filled her in about the day Boo and I spied on her from the restaurant.

"You just didn't know me yet." She told us that once she'd whacked her ex-husband with a cast-iron skillet when he got drunk and abusive. And she worked as a bouncer at the '86 Corral. "I used to grab cowboys by the earlobes and pull them out—usually they don't fight too bad. I do defend myself."

Confident that we truly were all on the same side, I asked Scotty the obligatory question: What, if anything, had Dirk told her about his involvement in the Cline Falls incident?

"Somebody warned me about how violent he was. That he'd been in that Cline Falls thing and I'd better watch my back. Dirk always swore he didn't do it."

"Did you believe him?"

"I wasn't sure. But with him denying it, it's always in the back of your mind."

It was Scotty's opinion that the cops and the DAs in Deschutes County were not "scratching the same set of nuts," and if they had been, Dirk might have been in jail a long time ago. She knew about injustice in Deschutes County because once when she was performing a stunt in a horse training ring, an unknown guy from the audience attacked her in the ring because he thought she was too tough on her horse. Scotty's injuries were serious: the man broke her jaw in two places, broke her nose and her rear molar. Her jaw was wired shut for two months. Her attacker was arrested on an assault II charge, a felony, but maneuvered to get off on a harassment charge, a minor misdemeanor. "Now you explain the DA to me," Scotty said. "We all know how Dirk gets away with it."

Dee Dee asked Scotty: Why else did she think Dirk had the magic all these years to escape responsibility for his deeds?

Scotty answered right away: "Because he sweet-talks his way out of things. And because his parents protect him, especially his dad." His dad bought the trailer for him and paid the rent at the trailer park. Both parents kept him supplied in groceries, chewing tobacco, beer, and lunches with garlic and toothpicks, just the way he liked them. He had his parents well trained, Scotty said.

"His mom does his hair for him, if he's over there. He tried to get me to do it whenever he could. He wants it perfectly back, just the right tightness everywhere. He takes handfuls of conditioner. It goes on so it's perfect. He's a very meticulous dresser," she said, and I noted she used the word *meticulous* as I always had when describing my attacker, although it seemed an odd word for Scotty to use.

"His mom does his laundry for him. He's a king. He was raised that way. He expects to be treated that way. Likes to be massaged, pampered. I'm sure if you talked to any of the other victims, they're probably saying pretty close to the same thing.

"One lady his parent's age, she knew I was with Dirk, and she came up to me and asked if he was still as strange as he was when he was a child, and were his parents still protecting him? And I thought, wow, the neighbors even know."

After she got away from Dirk, Scotty called his mother to try to tell her that there was something wrong with her son. "She denied it totally and told me never to call again."

I asked Scotty if Dirk's mom blamed her son's behavior on her. "No. She said I shouldn't have gone back, that I knew what he was capable of, so why did I even go back? I said, 'I tried to love him and give him the love you do.' She said, 'Well, we give him enough love. Just stay away from him and we'll all be better off.'"

THOUGH SCOTTY camped out on her friends' couches most of the time, she was in fact a landowner. She'd managed to scare up enough cash to buy a patch of juniper and sage out in the backcountry. I was curious to see the full portrait of the kind of woman Dirk was attracted to, so I asked to see her digs. She gave me directions in the local way, drawing me a crude map, and I drove alone out to Alfalfa. I turned into the desert on a paved road until it turned to dirt, then miles more on a bumpy meander through matted sagebrush; then veered onto an even ruttier road, which obscured my windshield with dust. About the time I was sure I'd never see another human being again, I spotted a tiny sign that miraculously matched my map: EGGS, 1 CENT. I drove up to the chained gate and honked.

Hulking Herby was there, his black hat pulled over his eyes. While Herby blasted tin cans with Scotty's towheaded son, Jack, Scotty led me on a walking tour of her spread (its boundary marked with a handpainted sign on a battered board nailed to a juniper that read HORSE POWER UNLIMITED). We strolled past two dilapidated trailers, an old engine from a submarine rigged up as a generator—stuff everywhere that Scotty had picked up in case it might come in handy one day. All four corners of her parcel were marked with distinct piles; an old plastic shower stall anchored the southwest corner. Tour finished, she led me inside the main trailer, so cluttered there was scarcely room to press through.

"Well, sit down!" she offered, and I sought out a patch of sofa and looked out the window. Scotty sure had a pretty view. One thing I'd learned about Central Oregon: the quality of life is out of the ordinary. From the humblest abode, you can have a view of pristine landscape, and room for every vehicle you have ever owned in your whole life to lie fallow under your nostalgic eye.

Shots were blasting in the distance. Scotty was busying herself with her possessions. I guessed it was time to get back. Scotty wanted to hitch a ride to the store. We headed down the rutted road, and at one point she cracked a joke and let out a horselaugh, and whacked my right arm holding the gearshift with such high-spirited bonhomie that she nearly dislocated my elbow. It would be months before the pain would subside. It was another indication of the sort of woman this spiritless man I was studying wanted to dominate and beat and control—the sort of woman who would name her acreage Horse Power Unlimited.

DIRK DIDN'T own land, like Scotty did. I imagined he might have been envious. After all, he hadn't been able to cobble anything together for himself. Maybe his envy was one reason he got the idea to tie Scotty's friend's daughter to one of Scotty's trees.

The tree image. I couldn't shake it. Tied to a tree. I thought back to Kaye Turner tied to a ponderosa. It reminded me of a corollary malignancy, lynching, one that Billie Holiday sang about: Southern trees bearing strange fruit, "Blood on the leaves, and blood at the root."

The image brought to mind a story that was going around in my head, told to me by an old woman I knew. Monica was on vacation alone, this woman of eighty, rambling through the woods on marked forest trails. She rounded the bend, and there before her was a woman, naked, murdered, tied to a tree. Monica had the beginning stages of Alzheimer's. She hadn't remembered telling me the story before, and she told me again, in a plummy British accent, about her vacation in America, how she set out by foot into the dark wood, and when she rounded the bend, there was a woman, naked, murdered, tied to a tree. She told me still another time. And I followed Monica as she strolled and rounded the leafy bend, and before she said it, I saw the woman there:

Tied to a tree. Tied to a tree. Tied to a tree.

Monica's repetition of this single image reminded me of how we were being told the same tales of heinous violence day after day. And for every story recounted, thousands more were taking place in secret, and (considering the degree of carnage) you hear very few cries of resistance coming from humankind.

By investigating the story of my own near murder, I had wandered into the borderlands, into the margins of society's denial—denial of the fact that with regard to this issue of men dominating and controlling women through fear and force, molesting, raping, murdering—humanity has absolutely taken leave of its senses.

There is inexhaustible inventory of evil against women in the world. And there is, too, another kind of evil: that of callous indifference and passive complicity, an evil kind of innocence, an ignorant naïveté.

These stories I found myself in the midst of seemed at first far from my own life experience. My behind-the-scenes look at "domestic violence" of the darkest hue, finding my own life interwoven with the lives of these battered women, had laid bare an unsettling discovery. Categories of male violence against women and children are not distinct: beating a wife or girlfriend is not distinct from raping or murdering strangers, not distinct from molesting a niece or nephew. A guy who slaps his wife around is along the same continuum as rape and incest and murder, which are merely situated farther along the spectrum. Street harassment is on this same continuum. Pioneering feminists in the early seventies had a name for such hectoring as wolf whistles and animals noises. They called them "little rapes." My body knew this all along, the atavistic fear I felt in my early twenties when I heard hissing on the street—like a rattlesnake in the grass.

I found myself in the middle of this degree of male violence quite by accident. I had grown up in an atmosphere of decency; violence of any sort was never a feature of my childhood. I never lived a "lifestyle" where I might have expected to find myself among such brutal goings-on. If I, of all people, had found myself linked to these battered women through one violent man, a stranger to me, how prevalent this male violence against women must be—and what a long shadow it surely casts on the lives of all women.

From this perspective, it wasn't surprising that my axe murderer hadn't turned out to be a ghoulish serial killer. From this perspective, it made sense that my axe murderer might have been a local schoolboy who beat his girlfriend.

Some Words with an Axeman

No animal could ever be as cruel as a man,
so artfully, so artistically cruel.

—DOSTOYEVSKY, *THE BROTHERS KARAMAZOV*

"This was a sneaking, sadistic calculating kind of attack with two ladies who were asleep in the tent, where he runs over them and tries to pin them with a truck and tries to attack. There's only one kind of creature that does that kind of thing, and that's a sadist. He's delighting in this power and control and making other people suffer."

Dr. John Cochran didn't look anything like the image I had of a forensic psychologist. Rotund and ruddy-faced, wearing a dapper light blue suit, he looked more like an Irish politician in a big city back East—but he knew something about psychopaths.

We were gathered, the Kounses and I, at the offices of the state police. The investigation had proceeded to its next stage: police were still looking to learn what had happened to the '77 investigation, although the inquiry into the whereabouts of the report on Janey Firestone's interview with the police had gone nowhere, even after Marlen Hein had re-interviewed Janey and all of the other key witnesses in Fredrickson's report. Police were in the process of making a timeline of the activities of our prime suspect from 1977 to the present, in order to ascertain whether he had committed any prosecutable crimes. Finally, it was agreed by all that the perpetrator's confession to the Cline Falls crime was vital for the community, and would possibly lead to confessions of other crimes. If Dirk Duran were convicted of any other criminal act, and if the opportunity arose while he was in custody, it was important to see if he was willing to take a third polygraph. Fred Ackom, in particular, wanted to finish the conversation that had been left dangling when Duran walked away from that second polygraph test.

Dr. Cochran was called in to provide a profile of the sort of person who would have committed an attack such as that in Cline Falls. Cochran also weighed in on the particular characteristics of our focal suspect, and the likelihood of his having committed this particular act. In Cochran's expert opinion, the likelihood was great. Duran fit the profile precisely.

"He feels he's special, one of a kind, an extremely narcissistic individual. He's above rules, above regulations. He doesn't have a conscience. This little foreign thing he's got isn't worth a hill of beans. The usual kind of love and respect for others—and shame, guilt, and remorse—are lacking in his character. Consequently he can do anything because there are no internal kinds of controls that are there, and from his patterns we can tell he doesn't learn to profit from his past mistakes. He's a drug-abusing, alcohol-swilling, very arrogant, aggressive, sneaky, sadistic individual.

"His parents, his father in particular, are very enabling. There were never proper boundaries. He's constantly running interference for the boy, ever since the boy was very small. For example, when the boy had problems with his teacher, he would suggest going back to the school and fighting the teachers together. And of course, every time the boy would get into trouble, the father would buy him off. He just simply cannot see what this kid has become in his life.

"In this instance we have a failed polygraph regarding the Cline Falls attempted murders. It was only by grace that they were not effective murders. He's seventeen years old and he's enraged. Remember the world is his oyster, and he's got a right, or entitlement, a special mission here, where he can do anything he wants without reprisal. He's never had significant consequences for anything he's done. And it's just more of the same. He can do these sorts of things, and he's not expecting to be incarcerated.

"This guy used enormous amounts of displaced rage and aggression, worked up because of problems with girls, Janey, or others in the past—if, for example, his father told him his biological mother was a prostitute. This guy is packing an enormous amount of rage toward females, getting acted out in Cline Falls."

From the interviews conducted with Dirk's associates, Cochran surmised that Dirk had an "overly close, symbiotic relationship" with his mother, one in which she didn't abide by the customary parent-child boundaries. She helped build the narcissistic props for Dirk. And she couldn't tolerate competition with other women for Dirk's affection, thereby unconsciously vilifying all other women. The result, Cochran explained, was a "wild split" in regard to Dirk's understanding of women: they were either wonderful, like his adoptive mother, the model of an "all-giving Mom," or sluts like his biological mother. When women displeased him or denied him anything, they were "sluts," and he would respond with rage.

"In Cline Falls, very probably the trigger was that Ms. Weiss got up and was aggressive, and began to talk in his face. This is very well known in the FBI literature. With a certain type of individual, if you get in their face, they go into a rage. But when Terri used a firm tone of voice, he left. It was almost more appealing, supplicant, it was not that she was being dominant. From what I understand, Ms.

Weiss was angry, confrontational. A guy like this can't stand that. He has to have dominant authority over women. If they reject him, he will take it as far as he can."

I piped in to say—this was, after all, my story—that, make no mistake, I hadn't acted the supplicant with this axeman. My tone had been firm, even conversational. And I recalled further that Shayna hadn't been shrill, she wasn't getting in his face. She had been startled and was frightened.

"What made the difference," Cochran said, "is that Shayna threatened his masculinity with her tone of voice. It was a stark threat to his kind of masculinity. He was dominant. He was in control. For whatever reasons, Ms. Weiss came across as threatening, and he retaliated. What you did wasn't threatening. It was an appeal. You said, 'Take anything, please leave us alone.' What you were able to do was come across in a non-threatening way. You gave him some options. With you, there was an immediate understanding, and he was able to back off. He was able to see some kind of humanity in you. You weren't totally demonized. You were not a total prostitute or devil. Whatever you did out there, it had to be done in a way—if it wasn't supplicating or beseeching, it was done in a non-threatening manner that was effective, that got through to him and saved your life."

I sent myself back to that distant summer night: the piercing memory, from under the truck, my eyes closed. I had heard Shayna's scream—sharp, high-pitched, and absolute. *Leave us alone!* I heard the blows. When I came face-to-face with him myself, I remembered some change of tack on my part, no doubt instinctual, something I had learned from Shayna's response: screams would not work here. Let him have something, I remembered thinking. Don't ask him to go away empty-handed. Give some ground. *Take anything.* Even our bikes, our magic carpets across America. *But leave us alone.* My tone was both submissive and self-assured.

I marveled that sweet Shayna, who would admonish me, the more aggressive adolescent, to stop pushing my camera into people's faces, had ended up the one, in an ironic reversal of roles, to lace into our attacker. I paused to recalibrate the story I'd told myself for nineteen years: Before, I had seen Shayna as a passive victim by circumstance. But now I saw that tough and willful action on her part had contributed to the inexorable chain of events. Boo told me she found Shayna several feet from the tent. That space of time while I was under the truck implied a story—one that only Shayna and her attacker knew.

Dee Dee questioned the notion that Shayna could have escalated Dirk's rage: "He was in a pretty bad mood already. He had his truck settin' on Terri's chin," was how Dee Dee put it, her brand of baseline logic.

"What about his mother?" Bob asked. "One of the things puzzling to me—here's a mom that made this guy's shirts, did the washing, very neatly. He had to have come home with blood everywhere. You can't be whaling away at somebody with a damn axe and not have this stuff splashing around! If I had come home with blood all over me, my mother would have said, 'What the hell happened?' My mother would have wanted to know everything about those blood spots."

"I had three sons. None of them would have gotten away with anything," Dee Dee said, and I believed her.

"If he didn't wash it out in a stream close by there before he got home—yeah, she probably would have had to know," Cochran said.

Dee Dee wanted to make the point that, even if he did wash his own clothes in a stream, a mother accustomed to attending to his every need ought to have found that behavior suspicious.

"The thing is, she is sitting with the knowledge of a huge crime," Cochran went on. "And the way they do it is through this kind of enablement pattern— when they put him on a pedestal and he can do no wrong. They refuse to look at this. He wouldn't come right out and say what he did. But there are hints, suggestions—enough to know he did it. If you have to view your world as perfect, without troubles, then what do you do? You have to discount certain things, and have to take these perceptions and rob them of affect, dull yourself to them, dissociate. You don't come to the conclusions that a normal, rational person would come to. 'No, my boy wouldn't have done it. He told me he wouldn't. He wouldn't be a bad boy like that.' We see it all the time. An ostrich approach to life. Louise Bundy never accepted what her son had become. That people would go to this extent— this system of enablement is worthy of a book in itself. It might seem shocking, but we have seen many extraordinarily violent people come from permissive family systems." He had observed that abusive parenting and overindulgent parenting—both extremes—could lead to criminal behavior.

I asked Cochran how our suspect might regard me right now: What would he think if he knew the degree to which I had infiltrated his life, sought out his ex-girlfriends, his ex-wife, even to the extent of going to another state to track them down?

"He will respond with rage, and also fear. You're not just a passive victim now. You're out there. You're not going to take any crap. This is the very thing these guys fear more than anything else. You're taking control over your life. You're becoming a survivor. They can't stand that. He would rather have you a passive little thing that he can kick around and terrify. When you become this other kind of person, he can't get the drop on you. Can't get you in some vulnerable area. Cline Falls. Where he can run over you with a pickup, then proceed to try to dispatch you with a hatchet. He's scared. There's anger. But also a lot of fear. The more you stand tall, the smaller he gets. It doesn't give him a chance to build up his power. He becomes weak and vulnerable."

Would he be the type to try to take us all out with him? The Kounses and I had discussed at length the dangerous aspects of our investigation, and we reassured ourselves on many occasions that he wasn't the sort to go after us openly—but we were sure eager to know what the doctor thought.

No. Cochran didn't view Dirk as a mass murderer who crops up in the headlines on a regular basis—the type who sprays bullets into his classmates or co-workers or shoppers in a convenience store, then blows his own head off. Dirk was too narcissistic to kill himself. He was the sort who wanted to escape severe consequences, and that characteristic would act as a check on his behavior. Cochran cautioned me against finding myself isolated again with this sneaky, sadistic individual. "But he will just hope you will go away. You're turning the tables on this guy. And there's going to be some rage, but a hell of a lot of fear."

COCHRAN'S ANALYSIS had convinced all officers present that Dirk Duran was our major suspect. The doctor had a lot of enthusiasm behind his convictions. He even stopped the Kounses and me in the hall to tell us that he'd rated Dirk Duran on the "Psychopathy Checklist," a list of twenty characteristics put together by Dr. Robert Hare, a world-renowned expert on psychopaths, also known as sociopaths. Duran had scored highly psychopathic.

The psychopath is glib and superficial. He is egocentric and grandiose. He lacks empathy. He is deceitful and manipulative. He has shallow emotions. He is impulsive. He has poor behavior controls. He has a need for constant excitement. He doesn't take responsibility for his actions. He uses his eyes in a predatory stare. He's not crazy or delusional, but fully aware of the choices he's making. He's not necessarily a criminal, though he usually operates on the shady side of the law and certainly has left wrecked lives in his wake. Some psychopaths come from troubled backgrounds, but just as many grow up in warm and nurturing families, with normal siblings who have the capacity to care deeply for others.

For what are commonly known as sociopaths or psychopaths, the closest diagnosis in the canon of approved diagnoses of mental illnesses is antisocial personality disorder, which includes elements of Hare's list, but the *DSM-IV* definition is not precisely the same as Hare's. Its central feature: "a pervasive pattern of disregard for, and violation of, the rights of others that begins in childhood or early adolescence and continues into adulthood." In other words, those with this disorder believe that things or people in the outer world have no dignity or integrity. They experience others as objects, being useful or dangerous to themselves, no more. They are incapable of loving identification with others. They have no reverence for anything.

I've read lots of books on psychopaths. I've read that, for your own good, you should learn to recognize them and keep them at bay. One book had a tear-out page describing their characteristics, a list that you could keep in your pocket, and presumably take along to meetings with potential business partners or new dates.

No one can adequately explain the mystery of psychopathy's origins. Scientific studies show that it is 50 percent nature. But nurture accounts for the other half. There is a cultural context, and America has a lot of the soil in which psychopathy grows. Bad parenting can encourage the demon seed to flourish, but even more influential: bad culture. A culture that makes a cult out of admiring the badass outlaw. A thrill-seeking culture that promotes the wrong thrills. A culture that does little to teach respect or empathy for others, or respect for their dignity. A culture that doesn't teach accountability. A culture that values self-gratification, impulsivity, and irresponsibility, and rewards preening narcissism. A culture that promotes the cult of the individual way above social concerns and responsibility for others. A culture that diminishes the idea that the individual must be responsible for the well-being of others. A culture that devalues the feminine.

No, one cannot generalize, but doesn't one face of the many-faceted America fit this profile? As Dee Dee Kouns likes to say, "America is a Garden of Eden for psychopaths. They don't tell you in society to watch out for them. Nobody says, Drive safe and watch out for psychopaths. Don't catch a cold, and watch out for psychopaths."

But ultimately these clinical or medical definitions have a staleness to them. They merely restate the mystery of human evil. It's fundamentally inexplicable, but in some percentage of humanity, something is missing; there is a drought in their souls. It's preposterous that for years the criminal justice system in Oregon imagined that a single psychologist, or even two, was capable of making a life-and-death judgment on whether to release into society one as beyond the pale as a Richard Wayne Godwin. As social critic Lance Morrow writes in *Evil*, "A lively awareness of evil, once a part of any healthy mind, must be re-installed in the consciousness of the West. Without an awareness of evil, people become confused, fail to anticipate its ruthless possibilities."

I CONCENTRATED on the nether recesses of my suspect's psyche, tried to saturate myself with his presence, as his pickup hit the tent and it crumpled, like a wounded thing, to the ground. My consciousness leapt into his eyes as he delivered his blows: I pulled out the photo of my chubby face that Kathy Rentenbach had sent to me. I imagined the face from the picture lying on the grass at a distance of a few feet—my hazel eyes looking blearily skyward, my skin marbled with blood, the gold ORYGUN T-shirt, now red and gold, the wetness of it clinging to my body like skin.

It was in this frame of mind that I set out to wrest a confession from him. If during some other business the police had with him Duran took a polygraph, a tape of my voice would be on hand to pop into a tape recorder. I hoped that my voice, in calm soothing tones, firm but not rebuking, might transport him back to a night long ago.

Both Dr. Cochran and polygraph examiner Fred Ackom believed Dirk truly wanted to confess. He only needed a reason to do so. My scheme was to inspire some kind of repentance in him. I would feign that, if only he would spill the whole story to me, I would grant him absolution. Cochran told me that, though such types have no conscience, they have little islands of sentimentality we can appeal to. I knew that sentimentality was often a quality that could be found in brutal people. I wanted to appeal to this separate chamber of his psyche where he stored the faux empathy.

I meditated long and hard on what I might say, tried to feel my way into this uncanny imaginary contact with him. I did a mental inventory of everything I knew about him: his preoccupation with insisting to others that he hadn't done the Cline Falls deed, his Bible study affiliations, his habit of crying in supposed remorse after his oft-repeated villainies. I read and reread the writings in his precious box. I tried to dream up what would move him.

First I tried to establish rapport: "I know you've thought about this thing every day for nineteen years. You and me both, Dirk. We're the only two who've been thinking about this every day for nineteen years.

"I've been really interested in finding your side of the story, and maybe you're a little interested in mine . . ." Surely, I thought, one so self-adoring would be interested in someone wanting to know *his* side of the story.

I proceeded to tell him my side of the story, the sequence of events before the moment he put pedal to metal and went flying over that six-and-a-half-inch curb. (I even planned to provide photos of me and Shayna on our bikes on the road, in case an opportunity presented itself for show-and-tell.) I tried to humanize myself to him, present myself as more than just a mere *woman*. I told him the reason my friend and I were in Cline Falls State Park that night of June 22, 1977: we were under the impression that it was a campground, and when we found it wasn't, we were too tired to move on (an appeal to his love of camping; an appeal to him to understand that we were not tramps hooking in the park).

Moment by moment, I led him through the sequence: "I heard my friend scream out, 'Leave us alone!' Then I heard a thud. And another . . ."

Fred Ackom told me it was important to include some little thing that hadn't been publicized—something only Dirk and I would know—so the polygraph examiner could look for peak attention, the polygraph term meaning the hot spots the scribbling pens record if the examinee hears a truthful detail come to the surface. What he knew: He uttered not a word to me that night—"You said nothing to me. Not a word. You were completely silent."

I tried to trigger his memory: "You remember me lying there—in that gold T-shirt that said 'ORYGUN' on it? Soaked in blood? Do you remember that?" I complimented his appearance: "I remember your neat Wranglers. I remember your shirt that your mother probably made for you was tucked so neatly into your jeans. I remember thinking, this is a really attractive cowboy. I'm being murdered by this guy who doesn't even look like a scumbag murderer. Dirk, you looked like a decent guy." I gave him credit for sparing my life: "You brought the axe down really slowly. Was that because my eyes were open and you were looking into them? Was that because I had suddenly turned into a real person for you? And then you did something really incredible—you withdrew the hatchet, really gently, like maybe you were feeling bad about what you had done. You spared my life, Dirk. I give you credit for that."

I knew Dirk was a coward when it came to experiencing physical pain. I let him know, quite frankly, that if he put himself in my shoes—though it was probably fantasy to think he could—he wouldn't like being there: "Try to imagine the worst time somebody beat the shit out of you—and multiply that by a million. Imagine being sound asleep in a tent. You aren't expecting anything. You're having great dreams. And suddenly you're under a truck, gasping for air, and somebody who has somehow decided that you should die is chopping you up with a hatchet, just because he feels like it. You're lying there, dying, totally under his control. Try to imagine that."

After laying some guilt on him, I gave him the opportunity to justify and minimize his actions: "So what was your side of the story that night?" I suggested he got a little carried away in anger at his girlfriend: "I know you were young then. It was a crazy thing you did when you were really young and stupid." I let him know that I, wise and receptive to his inner anguish, knew he was still troubled by what he had done. And he might have had reasons—a hard childhood, perhaps?

Playing the adoption card was my way of getting under his skin. According to the "experts" at extracting confessions, there's always a way to get under someone's skin. I surmised that being adopted was Dirk's hot button, and I deeply sympathized that the mystery of his origins must have haunted him.

I gave him a chance to wash away his sins and confess. To deserve forgiveness, I made clear, he must forfeit his pose of innocence. I used the protectiveness he felt about his family's reputation. "An awful lot of people in the community think you did the Cline Falls thing, Dirk. And every time they see your parents, they think, it's really terrible that their kid did that and then lied to them about it. It's a lot worse that you're lying to them, saying that you didn't do it. Think about your parents, Dirk. They must know that you're lying to them, on some level. And it's really painful to them. I know it must be horrible for you that your dad has told the whole community that you're innocent when you're guilty."

I used the religiosity of his writings from the box, his pseudocosmic lingo and his quasi-spiritual prayers for expanding energy—to appeal to his need for freedom: "You're not free now, Dirk. Your soul is in bondage, and you know it. You can feel it. You've been walled off with this secret for nineteen years. It must have been very lonely." I appealed to his need for a "fresh start," brazenly appealed to his need to "plant the seed of a brand-new positive beginning"—subtly I used his very own words, not so that he would recognize them, but rather so that he might relate to them and think to himself, "Now *that's* a good idea. That makes sense."

I rambled on, just as he himself might have done. "For your own heart and soul. You need to come clean and admit it. You've been haunted by this every day for nineteen years. And now you can put it all behind you. You have a couple of choices now. Take this terrible crime with you into eternity, or let it go now and be free. It's going to feel so good to do it. You'll feel your energy expand, you'll feel your power increase when you release this. You'll take a ton of bricks off yourself. It can be like a spiritual experience. Your passage can be long or short. Choose the short way, Dirk.

"Since you spared my life," I concluded, "I hope and pray for you that you can be free from this once and for all."

Amen.

Such was my bid for a confession. I recorded it using a low tone of voice: calm, nonconfrontational, showing concern, maintaining an atmosphere of respect, yet firm. It had worked that night. It would work again.

A lousy actress, I recorded the recitation a second time, then a third. In the end, it sounded more or less sincere. I had put a lot of energy into this exercise. I was certain this tape had sorcerous powers.

Suffocating in Juniper

Outside relationships and contact were solely limited to
subject's mother and father, who continued to excuse,
condone, and indulge their son without end.

—OREGON STATE CORRECTIONAL INSTITUTION COUNSELOR ON
TWENTY-YEAR-OLD GARY GILMORE'S PRISON BEHAVIOR, FROM
MIKAL GILMORE'S *SHOT IN THE HEART*

One blustery late-winter day in 1996,
the Kounses and I headed deeper into the Eastern Oregon desert on a mission to
penetrate the suspect's inner circle—to talk to his parents' best friends, whom we
had identified from talk around the community.

Though now I was hard on Dirk Duran's heels, I feared nothing. I felt no
wrenching in my stomach, no thwarting of energy. That day or two of panic I had
felt the summer before was a distant memory. At that stage, before I'd ever laid
eyes on him, the vague suggestion that he might suddenly appear in my vicinity
inspired a raw, chest-clutching terror. Now I had reached into the dark void and
pulled out a shape and form. Now I knew a thing or two about the man I supposed was my attacker. I knew where he was. I knew what his vulnerabilities were.
I knew whom he had hurt. And I was game to find out what those closest to him
knew.

In spite of the immunity from fear, after we'd turned off the main highway
and started down a washboard gravel road toward a seemingly empty horizon,
thirsty yellow lands without a tree in sight, I found my body feeling queasy. With
mounting unease, I slipped down in the backseat of the car and scrawled out my
last will and testament on a page of my Day Runner. If these folks didn't like our
faces, we were sure a long way from someone who might.

We pulled into the orderly ranch yard and stated forthrightly who we were and
what our mission was. Roy was a baby-faced former rodeo rider—he used to ride
rodeo with Dirk's dad—whose photo taking a noble dive off a bull, circa 1950s,
was displayed in the living room. He said to me kindly, "I'm surprised to see
you," and my trepidation let up. The Duran's best friends, Roy and May, it turned

out, were the Durans' only good friends. And they were none too enamored of their friends' son.

May was a tall and lithe woman in her sixties. And she remembered the summer of '77. "He was going with that gal at the time. And he was insanely jealous of her. And I don't know what set him off, but we had heard the talk was around in Redmond, playing bridge and golf . . . But for me to say he did it . . ." May's voice trailed off. "You know ever since they got him—he was adopted—the kid always had a look in his eye."

When I asked May if she'd ever seen one of his infamous rages, she segued into a story that she had at the ready, a vivid account that had stuck in her mind all these years, and which came to the surface now that we were here discussing Cline Falls. At four years of age, little Dirk, her friends' child, was walking in the pea row of May's garden, and he stepped on one of the plants pushing out of the soil. "Don't step on the plants, Dirk. They're trying to grow." Next time May turned around, she saw that four-year-old Dirk had gone up and down the row and pulled up every single plant.

At first, May wouldn't answer directly whether she had a hunch Dirk Duran was the assailant in the Cline Falls case.

"It was so horrible, we didn't want to think it was a local."

Her talk went around in loops. She told us how violent crime had shadowed her own life—her adult brother had been murdered a few years back by a thirteen-year-old—and that she understood why the victim or victim's family would have a compulsive fixation to know the perpetrator's identity.

I asked May if she ever thought of calling police and putting pressure on them to find this strange axe murderer who had turned up in town. Wasn't she worried for the safety of her family?

"No we weren't worried. We were young and busy. And we kind of thought it was Dirk . . . Then we thought the cops couldn't solve it anyway, even if they'd pressured them . . ." She wavered, probably knowing how preposterous her logic was sounding. "It was another world back then . . ." She trailed off again.

Another world? This world.

Hers was a curious case of doublethink. The Cline Falls perpetrator was both a psycho drifter—a highwayman who came into town from elsewhere—and at the same time, he was the ill-tempered local kid who wasn't going to take an axe to his parents' best friends. In either case there was nothing to worry about.

If he did do it, Roy and May both put forward, he'd never admit it as long as his parents were alive.

May felt sorry for her best friends, Lou and Lou Ellen, whom she described as having hearts of gold. The kind of people who brought food to the sick.

"They're always walking on eggshells trying to keep Dirk happy. Lou Ellen is sick with love for that boy," was how May phrased it.

We five talked until the light was nearly extinguished over the desert and we ended up deciding that May would talk to Lou Ellen, and Roy would try to broach the topic with Lou, just to let them have a say on what they thought about the accusations against their son regarding Cline Falls. It wouldn't be easy with Lou, Roy admitted. "Lou thinks World War Two was fought for his privacy." May proposed that I talk to Betty, Dirk's younger sibling, also adopted.

Both May and Roy took note that their friends Lou and Lou Ellen raised their daughter differently from their son. They were very strict with their girl, while they were permissive with their boy. One time, they remembered, Betty even got into trouble for not preventing her older teen brother from drinking. "Betty's a real good kid," Mary said.

On the lonesome stretch of road from the remote ranch back to the main highway, Bob was teaching me how to drive fast over a gravel road. Tensions in the car were running high. A full moon loomed over the desert wastes as we drove west toward Bend and Redmond. It was a night of a full moon, Dee Dee believed, when Val's body was disposed of. Full moons triggered Dee Dee's sore heart.

I HAD DARED make incursions on his ex-wife, his parents' best friends—and now I was ready to quiz his sister. With stealth, I would get to know this tyrant. I heard from his last girlfriend, Scotty, that our suspect stayed with his sister occasionally; apparently they still maintained a relationship. Since I knew from police that he had obliquely threatened anyone who tried to talk to his parents, naturally I wondered whether he was as touchy about his sibling.

Betty worked at a furniture manufacturer on the outskirts of Bend. I entered the company's lobby and asked for her. The receptionist immediately pointed me toward the lobby phone. I rang Betty's extension, told her my name, and explained that I was in Redmond exploring something that had happened to me nineteen years before. I told her I had been interviewing dozens of people, and her name had come up among others.

"What incident?"

"The Cline Falls incident in 1977."

"I don't want to talk to you," she said abruptly, as though she didn't have to shift back at all, as though Cline Falls were alive and kicking in her brain. Then she changed her tone: "At least not here." I could detect a quaver in her voice.

"Wherever you want I can meet you."

"I'll call you," she said.

"Well, I'm kind of floating around, kind of hard to reach. Can I just come by your place tonight?"

"I don't know how long I'll be working."

I assured her that I would be discreet about our meeting, that I wouldn't do anything to get us both in trouble—assuming she knew full well why a lack of discretion might place us in jeopardy.

"Could you call in a couple of days?" She was giving me a little opening; then she gave me some information.

"This is a real sore spot . . . I don't want to get involved."

"What if I came over?"

She paused, and finally said, "I'd listen."

I'd listen? Did she mean: She'd say nothing in return? But why would she even deign to listen? Could she want details from me to fill in a picture? To add to her own incomplete tale?

I got aggressive. "What if I came over tonight?"

"*No.*" Suddenly she took a stand, shaky but firm. "I don't want you coming over."

It was time to back off.

"Okay. I'll call in a couple of days." I put down the phone and my heart was hammering.

When I got back in the car I jotted down notes from the conversation. Then I was gripped with a case of nervous shock. Sweat poured from my forehead and scalp, dripped under my shirt, and mingled with the scent of juniper, with its pervasive odiferous resin running through the timber and drifting on the winds.

I had kept fear mostly at bay. But fear was seated in the body. It sprang up and ambushed me unawares. Now, the smell of the juniper brought a descent into memory, and harrowing feelings awakened.

It was peculiar. When I actually laid eyes on the suspect I found the experience hair-raising and a little thrilling. But I wasn't scared. No memories were triggered. Mysteriously, it was not the mean blue eyes he cast on me that invoked visceral memories of that night. It was talking to his sister that brought fear back. Was that because I was in the presence of *her* fear, one rooted in buried childhood experiences, and therefore so immense that it activated mine?

Was I also sensing that Betty held the answers to my questions? That what she knew haunted her? That behind the biggest terrors usually lie the biggest unspoken truths? That a lagoon of shame surrounded those secrets that she knew?

Betty had a lot at stake. In a family that values secrecy, the one who dares give up a secret can be cast out. Dee Dee said to me, "If he wasn't guilty, wouldn't she welcome the opportunity to tell you? A call from you has been one she's been dreading, unconsciously, for years."

Or did this astonishing fright arise from pure common sense? By now I had broken into his inner ring. By contacting someone who could have an unqualified loyalty to him, I truly might have gone past the point of no return.

From that hour on, for four days, inhabiting Central Oregon was like being trapped in an alternate universe—an extraterrestrial hothouse. Everywhere in that landscape (which I could not escape without taking a plane or driving for hours), smells crowded in, assailed me. I was trapped in a gigantic claustrophobic bell jar reeking of juniper breath. I couldn't keep the landscape out of my body. I wanted to close down my senses, but it got inside me. Juniper-scented air invaded my veins.

Four days later, the spell broke.

After a clear-eyed, levelheaded assessment of the true dangers, I recovered my cool. In the parking lot of Betty's workplace, Boo and I waited in our car from two-thirty to six, next to Betty's immaculate little Japanese model. Sergeant Marlen Hein, in an unmarked car parked on the other side of the road, waited along with us. He would make sure we were safe in this adventure. (In case she pulled out a cell phone, and five minutes later we looked up to see her brother, one beady blue eye squinting down a gun's sight?) I felt the need for prudence. Maybe Marlen felt the same, and wanted to wrap us in psychological security at least.

People disgorged from inside the building and disappeared into their cars. Apparently Betty was working late. Finally, a woman appeared in the doorway: early thirties, slightly plump, with a mop of curly dark hair half covering her face, and a tendency to look at the ground as she walked. I had an idea I knew who she was. She wore a tank top, bright orange in color—a bold fashion choice, in contrast to the hair hiding her face—and as she walked out with a friend, she did a playful little jig. I figured the jig fit with the side of her personality that went with the orange tank top. As she said goodbye to her friend and walked toward what I knew was her car, she threw a towel over her shoulder, as one would after a hard day, feeling a swell of pride at a job well done. I jumped out of my car.

"Betty."

"I don't want to talk to you."

Yes, she was ready for me; she'd been expecting this; she'd been deciding how she should respond to me when my voice returned with a face attached, as she knew that it would, inevitably—and she had decided she would be pissed as hell.

She marched away from me and opened her car door, refusing to look my way.

I thought fast about what to say to her and came up with: "You seem really upset."

She paused. Softened. Leaned on her open car door.

"People have been persecuting my family for twenty years. Why are you after me? I didn't do it."

I tried to soften her. I told her that finding out the identity of my attacker was something I just had to do for my own state of mind. Nobody could be prosecuted anyway, I told her. The statute of limitations had run out a long time ago.

"There's no statute of limitations on murder," she said blackly and with authority, as though she thought I was trying to trick her.

"It wasn't murder. We both lived."

Betty registered surprise, but said nothing. I tried to intuit the right moves, tried another tack.

"Are you close to your brother?"

She nodded.

"That's really nice. In fact, I'm really jealous. I wish I had that kind of relationship with my brother."

She looked a little pleased with herself. Because she had been able to preserve a relationship with her brother, difficult as it might have been? Forgiveness and familial loyalty had sustained her? Maybe so. The only evidence I had was that she was smiling slightly as she hung on the door, a timorous soul looking at the ground and not at me, true to her word, "listening."

Boo stood quietly by as I came up with still another approach. This was a blunt one.

"You know your brother flunked a polygraph about Cline Falls?"

Hanging on the door, she registered surprise—as though she had heard from him the opposite?—then decided to get aggressive.

"We're about ready to do something about the people harassing us."

"You can't sue someone for asking questions," I said gamely.

"If the cops are going to do something to him, I wish they'd just do it," she said suddenly, as if to say it was the tension in the family causing her pain, not fear that her brother would be put away.

"I don't know if you've ever had something in your life that was a mystery you needed to resolve . . ." I contrived to lure her with an emotional appeal to the yawning need I thought she might feel, as an adopted child, to solve the mystery of her parentage. I told her that I was overcome with the need to learn what happened that long-ago June night, because I sought rest for my psyche. As I was speaking, I got myself so worked up that tears welled up in my eyes, because of course it was true, even if it was a ploy in this instance. I described how I wanted to be really sure who had attacked me that night, because the last thing I wanted to do was persecute her brother if he was the wrong guy. I let her know that "No victim ever wants to persecute the wrong guy. If Dirk isn't guilty, I'd love to know. I'd just walk away—no matter what else he's done in his life."

Betty didn't tell me he was the wrong guy. She didn't tell me anything at all. I pressed forward.

"You know, the community thinks you and your parents are great people." At that, she smiled more perceptibly than before and said shyly, "Well, no one really knows me." I felt an opening and I quickly shifted my inquiry, sprang a question on her that might entice her into storytelling.

"Did Janey and Dirk have a fight that night?"

"I'm not talking about it." She bit her lip.

Boo took my lead and blurted out, eager to cut to the quick, "Do you know if he was ever investigated by the cops?"

"I'm not talking about it" was the cordon she put up.

"Let me tell you what happened to me that night . . ." And then I would hold my peace.

She didn't get into her Japanese compact and slam the door. She was caught in the glare of my story. When I got to the part about what I saw that night, I really played up the "handsome cowboy" part, describing how he was dressed, and how impressed I was by his immaculate appearance—and I noted her lips formed a smile, and I read into it that it was a smile of family pride. I told her honestly, although I had seen his body clearly, I had not gotten a look at his face. When I got to the grittier details—and I spared none—she bit her lip again.

Betty's lips were expressive. She was surely listening, and she was responding, silently.

When I finished my story, I said, "So I've just been babbling and you're not talking, so I'd better let you go." I walked to my car. "Have a good life," I called back to her, and meant it.

"You, too," she said as her lips formed a smile, and I thought she meant it, too. She bore me no ill will. I supposed it was really hard for her to play the antagonist with me.

Betty got into her car and drove the wrong way—into a cul-de-sac, where she stopped for a moment. Boo and I watched her curious behavior. After a minute the car lurched into reverse and she pulled past us, her face awash with emotion.

She was a speck on the road when Marlen swung his car toward mine and lined up, driver's side to driver's side. Marlen always had a breathlessness to his voice, and now he was even perspiring a little. He'd gotten a close-up look at Dirk's sister as she pulled past him down the highway.

"She had tears in her eyes," he told us excitedly, and I knew how poignant he understood this detail to be.

This man was yet another model of masculine gentleness—of which I had found many in my quest—in hopeful contrast to the feminine-hating male depravity I was studying. I remember when I first met Marlen, the year before, I told him how moved I was by how personally he regarded his participation in this investigation. He confided in me (as Fred Ackom also had done) that he had suggested that Detective Fredrickson leave the Cline Falls case partly because Fredrickson lacked compassion for the victims.

"Basically, where I'm coming from is, if I were the victim or if it were my daughter that was the victim in this case, the police would have felt *real* aggression from me. And I mean it."

He said to me another time, about the life of a cop, "We get hardened, maybe even to the point where we laugh at situations so we can survive mentally. But you can't lose the sensitivity."

LATER I CHECKED in with May by phone and she told me that she had had an opportunity to talk to her friend Lou Ellen about her son's possible connection to the Cline Falls attack (though not to Lou, because "he's very closemouthed about everything").

"She swore up and down he didn't do it. She's very emphatic, and I seriously believe that if they thought for one minute that he did it, they would be the first to chastise him, but neither one of them think he did, so what was I to say? Lou Ellen said, to do something that heinous, he'd have to have blood all over him. She said he did not. He had on the same clothes he left in."

"He had on the same clothes he left in?"

At least, I thought to myself, our suspect's mom admitted remembering that her son left her house that summer night in '77—and she provided no alibi for his whereabouts.

"So that's how it was," May said, a touch of resignation in her voice, which I read as sympathy for me. When I asked her if she and Lou Ellen discussed the fact that Dirk had recently flunked a polygraph for the Cline Falls attack, May said, yes, they talked about that polygraph, but Lou Ellen believed police have methods of coercing the results they want.

"I don't want to get too involved. They're old and they're tired and they've done the very best they can. I feel bad for them. Somewhere along the line they need a rest."

I remembered an item I found in my suspect's box. It was a Rudyard Kipling motivational poem about self-development, inscribed in Dirk's mother's perfect cursive (which I had identified from her cards to him signed "Mom"). The poem was written to a son.

If you can keep your head when all about you
Are losing theirs and blaming it on you;
If you can trust yourself when all men doubt you,
But make allowance for their doubting too:
If you can wait and not be tired of waiting,
Or, being lied about, don't deal in lies;
Or being hated don't give way to hating,
And yet don't look too good, nor talk too wise . . .

The poem goes on for three stanzas—if, if, if—and then:

Yours is the Earth and everything that's on it,
And—which is more—you'll be a Man, my son!

MY MOTHER'S father was a nineteenth-century man, a farmer all his life who settled the lower Yellowstone River Valley. The last time I saw him before he died he was ninety. This fine-boned man wore frayed suspenders, his skin translucent as the skin of an insect, and when I unfocused my eyes I thought I saw a spectral mist surrounding him. He tapped his cane on the ground and spoke in a gentle German accent. He was always gentle in old age, though I knew he could be hard in his younger days.

"Mama and I," he said to me, one of his thirty-two grandchildren, offspring of his ten children, "we lived on the land. And we lived off the land. But I did it with a good woman. And my children who helped me. All my children were good. If there'd been a bad one, I would have had to fight him." He spoke out of context. I never knew why he told me this.

Moans at Okinawa

The stretcher bearer . . . listens with a different part of
himself to the voices of the wounded and dying as they cry
for help . . . This singing near the edge of death travels far
beyond even the capability of celebrated singers, and at the
same time passes outside the limits circumscribed by
gender. In the moment of crisis, social sanction dissolves.
Men sing like women. And to hear this truly is to pass into
an undiscovered country.

—SUSAN GRIFFIN, *A CHORUS OF STONES*

" 'Bout all they saw of him were his legs
when he attacked them," said the heavy-lidded, slow-talking retired detective
about the Cline Falls attack. He was being interviewed in the late fall of 1995 by a
Bend TV station for a segment on Central Oregon's own homegrown unsolved
mysteries.

" *'Bout all they saw of him were his legs*" was how the detective's mind had reduced my brightly illumined 3-D frame of a meticulous cowboy torso, a recollection vivid enough to include details of his grooming.

The very existence of this TV segment made me cross. One of my contacts in
Redmond tipped me off that the show was being produced, and I asked her to request of the producers that they cancel their Cline Falls feature for now, since I
had revisited the area to conduct my own investigation of this unsolved crime.
They aired it anyway to the Central Oregon public, and worse yet, they aired my
high school graduation picture—peaked eyebrows and thick lips framed by long
hair parted straight down the middle. I supposed it was possible that my focal
suspect was watching TV in his travel trailer on just that night, and might refresh
his memory of my visage.

The news anchor, bundled up against desert winds, doing his stand-up from
on location in Cline Falls: "The crime was very hard to solve. They never saw
anyone coming or saw who was driving—which means that by the time they
got their first glimpse of their attacker, they had already been run over by a

car and they were in no condition to get a good look or a description of their attacker."

A talking head of former state police investigator Cooley: "We thought perhaps at first, in bicycling over the coast, they'd become involved with some traffic over the coast—got someone upset with them—but there was nothing to indicate they had a run-in with anyone."

The news anchor continued: "The search would continue for years—rumors about who committed the crime circulated among the Central Oregon community. Bob Cooley said investigators followed every serious lead in depth and each ended with nothing."

Talking head Cooley again: "You run down leads, you get tips here and there. Or some other agencies might come up with some information that somebody might give them, and you run that down—and of course all the time you're working on this, you've got five or six or ten cases you're working on. Some leads look good and then they turn out to be nothing."

I wanted to reach into the TV screen and open the investigator's half-closed eyelids with my thumb.

THE PUZZLE of what happened to the police investigation of the Cline Falls double attempted murder case vexed me still.

The inconsistencies of the case went like this: Two Deschutes County Sheriff's Office deputies were the very first officers to arrive at the crime scene the night of the Cline Falls attack, but the investigation wound up with the Oregon State Police. According to the police notebooks of investigators Cooley and Durr, in the weeks following, the state police accepted leads with regard to the Cline Falls incident from both the Deschutes County sheriff's office and the Redmond Police Department. (Although Cooley and Durr were in charge, they operated out of the Bend patrol office, twenty miles from the Redmond and Cline Falls area. Therefore they would not have known the local community as well as the sheriffs or the Redmond police.)

It was the Deschutes County Sheriff's Office that apprehended Dirk Duran and jailed him for beating up his girlfriend, Janey Firestone, the day following the Cline Falls attack—a Thursday, June 23, 1977.

Though I never managed to locate those officers who apprehended, interviewed, and jailed Dirk Duran for assault on his girlfriend, I talked briefly to two members of the current sheriff's office who worked for the same agency in 1977, and they admitted to me: they remembered the name Dirk Duran in connection with Cline Falls, and they heard—word of mouth, they insisted, nothing direct—that he was being investigated for that crime. One of the deputies even repeated to me the *I heard he was investigated but there wasn't enough evidence* line, the very same recounted to me time and again by locals.

The following Monday after the attack, June 27, 1977, the investigator for the

Oregon State Police, Bob Cooley, told a newspaper reporter that he was on his way to interview a seventeen-year-old youth incarcerated for beating up his girlfriend, but didn't "expect to tie him to the crime."

And no record existed to indicate specifically which police agency Janey Firestone spoke to about the fresh tire tracks in the park that she believed belonged to her boyfriend Dirk Duran, and the missing toolbox in his truck that contained a hatchet. Janey vaguely remembered entering a building something like the Oregon State Police headquarters, although her father insisted that Janey and her mother gave their story to the Deschutes County Sheriff's Office.

Lead investigators Bob Cooley and Clayton Durr had no memory of a Dirk Duran in connection with Cline Falls, in spite of the fact that Cooley scrawled in his notebook in 1980 that Dirk Duran had been accused of the crime by another local troublemaker, Chris Peterson. Cooley, accompanied by both Peterson and Richard Little of the Redmond Police Department, actually made a trip to Cline Falls, where Peterson explained his allegations.

These, again, were the anomalies of the case.

I'd heard enough about historic turf battles between the Deschutes County Sheriff's Office and the Oregon State Police to think that maybe the rivalry had roots as deep as in the famous rivalry between the Los Angeles Sheriff's Department and the LAPD, or between the FBI and the CIA. Rivalries among law enforcement agencies, causing crimes to slip through the cracks, seemed the order of the day.

If evidence got suppressed in some secret corner of the Deschutes County Sheriff's Office or the Redmond Police Department, or even by someone in the state police, I thought it possible that investigator Cooley got turned away before he talked to the seventeen-year-old schoolboy who beat up his girlfriend, dissuaded by someone with an interest in protecting the loony kid. Had Cooley knowingly or unknowingly allowed the investigation to be pushed aside?

If so, would the former elected sheriff have been privy to any illuminating detail?

I learned that F. C. "Poe" Sholes, who served seven terms as sheriff of Deschutes County, from the fifties through the seventies, was living outside Bend. One night, in heavy winds and under threatening purple skies, I drove a few miles east to look for his ranch house. I drove back and forth down the highway until I spotted a sign, AGATES FOR SALE. This was the place.

As usual, I showed up unannounced and took a reading on how the old sheriff and his wife might react to a stranger on their doorstep. Immediately they settled me warmly in their living room for storytelling.

It was the first time I'd met a real old-fashioned sheriff. Poe, a man in his midseventies, had a posture so erect and a chest so proudly rounded you could almost see a badge in the shape of a star glittering on his breast. Poe grew up in

Bend, and remembered the town when it was nothing but a straight line of old Western storefronts along a dusty road. Some years after the war, in 1952, he ran for sheriff in a popular election and was voted in the "same day Ike was." The sheriff's office, located in the old courthouse built of somber black lava rock, was so small he shared one secretary, "the amazing Ruth," with Deschutes County's first full-time district attorney (the same DA who held the post in 1977), whom Poe described as often inebriated.

"I loved it! I really loved it. There was always something going on!" said the sheriff with his china blue eyes glittering. As I was in my Nancy Drew phase of life, I knew just what he meant.

Poe and Doris both listened attentively to my tale as I laid out the oddities of the unsolved Cline Falls case.

Poe jabbed at his old rivals: "If the state worked on it, I didn't find out about it until it was too late . . . The head of the state police was a director of a social club," he said of Lieutenant Lamkin, for whom it was evident he didn't have the highest regard, though he wouldn't come right out and say it.

Of the two investigators from the Oregon State Police assigned to the Cline Falls case, Poe wouldn't comment on Senior Trooper Clay Durr, except to remind me that he "had his ear shot off with a long-range rifle," but he described Bob Cooley as "a hell of an investigator."

Poe leaned into me conspiratorially as he talked, his eyes bugging out under gold aviator glasses, and I leaned into him, unable to resist his magnetic pull. It was easy to understand how Poe had remained the popularly elected sheriff for three decades.

"Beans! Cooley doesn't have a memory problem," he said in a low voice.

Poe made a proposal to me. Retired law enforcement guys from all the local agencies met every second Wednesday of the month. There the elders put away their yesteryear differences and broke coffee cake together. Poe admitted that at this coffee klatch, he even liked his old rivals, the state police.

There he would get Cooley in a corner and ask him just exactly what happened back then.

"I'll do it for you, kiddo," Poe assured me. "I'm going to say: 'Get it out. It'll hurt a little, but . . .'"

"Truth is the best thing," I finished his words.

"Yep. Be a straight arrow—except when it comes to lying to your wife," he joked, and I suspected nothing had ever gotten past Doris, and he knew it.

Just as I was making motions to leave, the old sheriff said, "I want to ask you one last question: How did you get away from him?"

I sat back down on the hassock and told a detailed rendition of my tale, unleashed a flow of picture and sound: catching the axe in my hands, hearing the harrowing moans that Boo had heard, too, "earth-shattering moans," as Boo described them—that lament from an unconscious girl.

Poe's mouth dropped open. He was sunk in thought, his gaze fixed on something I couldn't see. Then he interrupted me.

"Like during the war . . . when the guys were dying . . . they made a strange moan . . . horrible." He was feeling the heat of direct memory, hearing the concussive effects of exploding shells. He was back in the moment when, as a young marine during the campaign on Okinawa, he watched bullets erupt into the bodies of two young soldiers.

"You know, I've never told my wife that." Poe paused. We fell silent. Doris was in the other room on the phone.

The campaign on Okinawa, the last great land battle of World War II, took eighty-three days. More than 12,000 American soldiers, sailors, marines, and airmen were killed, on land, sea, and in the air. Never before had so much American blood been shed in so short a time, on such a tiny patch of land, along with 70,000 Japanese troops and somewhere between 62,000 and 150,000 Japanese civilians.

A new soldier's average time in combat before death or wounding was only a few hours—but F. C. Poe Sholes returned home to his new bride Doris without a single wound.

"I remember . . . at Okinawa," Poe went on, staring off into the middle distance, in sort of a glazed trance recall. "There was a Japanese baby sitting alone in the field. Bullets were flying everywhere . . . nothing ever hit that baby."

Long before 1980, when the *Diagnostic Manual of Psychiatric Disorders III* defined posttraumatic stress disorder into existence, that displacement of the soul had gone by other, more poetic, names. In World War I they called it shell shock. Before that, during the American Civil War, it was soldier's heart.

I guessed Poe and I both suffered from a case of it—that soldier's heart.

WHEN A FEW days later I checked back with Poe, I noticed stacks of agates piled in the zigzags of his split-rail fence. Many things about Central Oregon reminded me of northern latitudes farther east, North Dakota on the Montana border, where I played out my fondest childhood days on my grandparents' farm. The agates I collected and polished in my rock tumbler littered Central Oregon as well—traces of a volcanic past.

The sheriff was out back by his rock tumbler fiddling with his "thunder eggs." He showed me the inside of one, how he tenderly cut it in half with his machine. The thunder egg is Oregon's state rock. It has a rough brown rind on the outside. Sliced in half, a picture emerged on each opposing face, made from silica and agate: miniature landscapes of pine forests, glaciers, and canyons.

This was surely an odd landscape where you could find tiny replicas of the vast gorgeous scenery reproduced inside its stones.

Though Poe had been described by many as a "good ole boy," I liked this version of the breed. I tried to focus him on whether he'd had a chance to talk to Cooley about the Cline Falls case at their retired cop coffee klatch.

"Cooley said that the case was kind of a dud. It didn't go anywhere." According to Poe, Cooley also said he didn't remember anything about a local kid named Dirk Duran. But Poe mentioned to Cooley that this same fellow, Duran, now an adult, had recently taken a polygraph about his complicity in the Cline Falls case and flunked it. That got Cooley's attention.

"A polygraph. Oh, is that right?" he apparently responded.

Poe digressed back to the subject of rocks. It was hard keeping him on course. As an inveterate cop, he was more comfortable in the role of acquiring information than divulging it.

"Cooley's 'Mr. Reliable,' " Poe said obliquely, as he turned over a thunder egg. He lowered his voice. "But I was spooked about Lamkin." Back in the era when Poe ran the sheriff's office and Lieutenant Lamkin ran the Oregon State Police, Poe brought some problems to the attention of Lamkin. "And he didn't do anything about it."

"Like he looked the other way?" I asked.

Poe nodded and his blue eyes were especially bugged out.

Unfortunately, Lieutenant Lamkin, the strong-jawed, handsome cop, the only one I specifically remembered from 1977, was not around to tell me his version of the events of that summer.

The Antichrist Asks for an Attorney

Fred Ackom called me from Oregon
with the news: the case against Dirk Duran for assaulting Scotty never got to
court. In a plea agreement, Dirk's two assault IV charges and a menacing charge
were reduced to a single conviction for menacing (commonly known as "harassment"). That meant he would get minimal punishment. And his criminal history
would continue to make him look a whole lot sweeter than he really was. He was
sentenced to twenty-four months supervised probation, including fifteen days in
the county jail. Probation required him to perform alcohol rehab, pass an anger-
management program, and do 120 days of community service. Should he fail at
any time to live up to the conditions of his probation, he could be sentenced to
up to three months in jail.

I wanted to check on whether there was some truth to the theory that the cops
and the district attorneys indeed were "not scratching the same set of nuts," as
Scotty had put it. The next time I was in Oregon, in the spring of 1996, the
Kounses and I sought out the Deschutes County deputy DA who had arranged
the plea agreement, to ask him why it was that Dirk Duran's two charges had
been minimized, given his long history of arrests for domestic assault in two
states. Perhaps I could clear up some of the mystery of Duran's magic, why he
consistently managed to beat the rap.

I knew that every court in every county in America had its native customs, a
different way of doing business. Arriving at an understanding of criminal justice
in the Promised Land of America was a piecemeal undertaking.

The deputy prosecutor, a short man with a crew cut and a resolutely unflap-
pable manner, told me that he had accepted a guilty plea to menacing because the
victim had stated that her injury had caused her no pain. "You have to have injury," he told me, and then asked a rhetorical question: "What constitutes injury?"

My eyes narrowed until they crossed. "*What constitutes injury?*" I repeated back his rhetorical question. "What about a lip that's been smacked open? It could have been a lot worse if her friends hadn't intervened!"

In point of fact, according to the report from the Deschutes County Sheriff's Office, Dirk attacked Scotty by repeatedly hitting and pushing her. Officers at the scene recorded that the victim suffered a laceration of the lip and an injury to her foot.

"No, no, no. There's a specific definition of injury," the prosecutor droned with a maddening evenness. "And one of the things is—obviously if there's broken skin, blood and cuts, and things like that—that's injury. But there must be substantial pain. And the minute you say to the jury, you play the macho and say, 'That didn't hurt,' you've got a harassment. You don't have an assault."

I was dumbstruck by the inane logic of this impassive deputy prosecutor. I knew Scotty was a butch girl and proud of it. It would have been just like her to admit to the prosecutor that Dirk split her lip open but it didn't hurt. It probably didn't hurt nearly as much as having her jaw wired shut.

Bob was mad as hell and had to leave the room so he wouldn't unload on the deputy DA, leaving Dee Dee to knock some sense into him. I could always count on the Kounses to question the impoverished and wrongheaded ways in which society conducted itself, when others would simply shake their heads.

"Are you saying, on an assault in the fourth degree there has to be lingering pain?" she asked.

"Substantial pain. All she would have had to say was 'It hurt like hell, thank you, ma'am. Let's go to trial!' All she had to say."

"But there were witnesses!" Dee Dee all but shrieked. "People all around her! A guy took a flashlight to him!"

"The difference between harassment and assault is just the level of pain. That's the only difference. That's the case law."

But what about Dirk Duran's history? His six prior arrests for domestic violence or assault or menacing? What about his four priors for drug and alcohol offenses? What about the fact that most violence in the home or in dating relationships isn't even brought to the attention of police? How about the notion that smaller acts of violence are often stepping-stones to bigger crimes? Shouldn't heavier penalties be handed down for repeat offenders?

He went on, "Unfortunately in domestic violence it's not uncommon—one of the things that upsets me, you get down to trial and here comes the guy and girl and they're hand in hand, and you sit there. 'Let me guess, you're the victim, and you're the defendant, and love's in bloom again. He's promised you he won't beat you again.' And frankly I think that's what happened here."

"It didn't. IT DID NOT." Smoke was behind Dee Dee's words.

The deputy DA was skirting the real issue, and the real issue, he admitted, was that "The system dealing with misdemeanors is broke and does not work." There were way too many people in this fast-growing community committing those smallish nasties labeled "misdemeanors" for the system to deal with. The system didn't want them in the courts. Didn't have room for them in the jails. Didn't have time to supervise them on probation. The prosecutor told us that he'd seen the system go from overload to broke in the last ten years.

"Last year we filed thirty-five hundred misdemeanor crimes. I've got myself and three deputies. The system's broke. I sentenced a guy who since '91 has been convicted of nine felonies and that sucker hasn't spent thirty days in jail. I bought him ten days on a picky misdemeanor. Why is he out? Why isn't he in jail?"

Dee Dee made the point that if he knew so well that the system was broken, what was he personally doing to change the system to make it work?

The deputy DA didn't have much to say for himself in that regard. He turned to me again. He wanted to hammer home his point. "Look up the difference between menacing and assault. It's the level of pain. Check the statute. Has to be substantial pain."

When I checked the 1996 *Criminal Code of Oregon*, the statutes said no such thing. The statute clearly stated that when a person commits assault in the fourth degree, the person "intentionally, knowingly, or recklessly causes physical injury to another." The crime of menacing meant that one intentionally places another person "in fear of imminent serious physical injury." This charge implied that no physical injury occurred.

Instead of mustering some political will to make the system responsible, this public servant had cooked up his own definitions—all in the interest of perpetuating what wasn't working. With the crime of menacing in his criminal history, Dirk Duran would heretofore look like the kind of guy who might threaten a few bad things but wouldn't really be so bad as to actually do them.

SINCE THE MELEE at Desert Terrace Trailer Park over Scotty, Dirk's mom and dad had domiciled him in a new location—in a trailer on an elderly couple's ranch near Terrebonne, north of Redmond.

He didn't bother to report to his probation officer monthly, as required, and he didn't inform the officer that he was moving. He was caught stinking drunk in a car pulled over by the cops. He didn't complete an anger-management course or an evaluation for alcohol treatment. In short, on several counts, he was in violation of probation for even the minor menacing conviction he ended up with for battering Scotty.

There was a likelihood that in Deschutes County, this flouting of the rules would pass without as much as a slap on the hand. Dirk knew the ropes, the boundaries of what he could get away with, and that was just about anything that fell in the arena of a misdemeanor.

In the spring of 1996, the Kounses and I had put the members of the justice system in Deschutes County on alert about Dirk Duran's violent history, so it would work as it should this time around. One of their district attorney contacts in another Oregon county steered us toward the chief deputy of the Deschutes County District Attorney's Office, Pat Flaherty. By reputation, Pat felt he had a moral obligation to keep his community safe, even while dealing with a crushing caseload in a county skyrocketing with a population that wasn't getting anymore law-abiding with the passing years.

Flaherty was a man of around my age, with an especially serious demeanor at odds with his fresh-faced, boyish looks. When I filled him in on why I had returned to Deschutes County, he told me that he heard about the unsolved Cline Falls case when he first came to the county.

"I felt sick about it. It's an outrage," Flaherty said to me, which framed him in my view as a man of compassion. He explained that he had a long memory about unsolved cases, and was trying even now to tie a man who was still at large to the rape and murder of a girl twenty-five years ago.

When I brought him up to date on a local bad actor, he listened up. He was conscious of the need to survey his caseload in order to pay attention to the individual stories behind each offender—to identify the truly dangerous repeat offenders, as needing extra attention. He leaned back in his chair on the second floor of the Deschutes County District Attorney's Office and told us he'd see to it that Mr. Duran would actually get supervision on parole, which, in an ideal world, the system was supposed to provide. Flaherty would work with Parole and Probation to bridge the usually disjointed interface between the departments of the justice system.

One day, not long after this meeting, Dirk Duran was wrested from his job site for a probation violation and brought to the new Deschutes County Correctional Facility in Bend. He was arraigned, let out of jail, then picked up again from his travel trailer on the ranch owned by his parents' acquaintances. They found that he was in possession of a controlled substance. He was jailed a second time and sent before a judge.

In court, Flaherty wanted to establish Duran's belligerence with regard to his probation supervision. I listened to an official court recording of the proceeding as he questioned the probation officer about Duran's conduct during his first meeting with him.

"Mr. Duran showed up at my office just as he was instructed to," answered officer Terry Chubb. "I have a very small desk. He cleared it off and just leaned forward in a threatening, intimidating motion. I went through the conditions of his probation. Mr. Duran was very adamant about he was going to win his appeal, which had not been filed yet, and he was not going to do any conditions of his probation . . . As we were wrapping up our conversation, he just informed me he was going to go on a three-day heroin binge and set his head straight. I continued to talk to Mr. Duran about the thinking error involved with tripping on heroin to set his head straight, and he can't lie to me but he can lie to himself. And that's pretty much where it ended."

Both Flaherty and Chubb requested that Dirk's probation be amended to require polygraphs when requested—a reasonable requirement, they argued, considering his dubious compliance with the conditions of his probation.

The judge agreed that Dirk Duran had shirked his responsibilities for completing the conditions of his probation. She extended his probation to two years, insisted that he stay out of any establishment where alcohol was sold, required him to complete an anger and alcohol evaluation, gave him thirty days in jail with work release, so he could work at a job during the day—and she accepted the state's recommendation that he submit to a polygraph examination to encourage compliance with the conditions of probation.

BY LAW, Dirk Duran was now obliged to hook himself up to the skittering pens, which would determine his truthfulness in adhering to the conditions of his probation. Fred Ackom was hoping for a meltdown in which Dirk would disburden himself of at least one other, and maybe more, undetected criminal acts.

The day arrived in June 1996, when Dirk was brought from the jail to fulfill his obligation. The Oregon State Police and the sheriff's office allowed me to sit with Marlen Hein behind the one-way glass of an interrogation room to watch.

As the door to the room opened, my heart was hammering.

He looked nothing like he had that day in the restaurant. He had released his long hair to flow over his shoulders and halfway down his back, so that he looked like a cross between Charles Manson and one of those European renditions of a blue-eyed Christ. He sat in a chair, closed his eyes, and waited in the brightly lit space. I watched, with only a dark glass shielding me from him. I could feel his wrath. He emanated a frequency so intense that I imagined it could shatter the glass. The door opened again. Fred Ackom walked in.

"Hey, Dirk. You remember me?" Fred's edgy tone worried me. It wasn't the gentle, fatherly approach that had worked before.

Dirk took one look at Fred, stood up, and strode out of the room without a word. I could hear muffled angry noises in the hall as his jailers took him away.

Another day, they tried again. Not in the talking mood, he continually insisted that it was his right to have a lawyer present during such questioning, even though his probation officer, Terry Chubb, firmly and unequivocally explained to him that the right to have a lawyer present was a pre-trial privilege available to the accused, not to the convicted.

They let me watch a videotape of these proceedings. I observed the way his long hair fell in wavy strands down his broad, square shoulders wrapped in prison attire, a smock that suited him well. He held his manacled hands prayerfully and leaned to the side in a kind of long-suffering agony. The tortured blue-eyed "messiah" closed his eyes, and I thought I detected under his eyelids a white slit of eyeball that lent a menacing cast to the pseudosacred image. All of a sudden, his tongue flicked out of his mouth and he licked his lips, reptile-like. He'd turned into some kind of gargoyle. While I watched, I thought the vision might be a figment of my literary imagination. But I replayed the tape. It was real. He was posturing, as though consciously trying to summon the devil. Before, I had found him handsome. Now I'd never seen anyone so ugly.

He was soundless that summer night in '77. This was the first time his voice echoed in my inner ear. It was a deep voice, which he modulated as an actor would—first he sounded like a cowboy: then he sounded a little effeminate; then he was taunting and arrogant. An actor playing roles. He kept muttering about his attorney. "You bring my attorney, and we'll do 'er."

His court-appointed attorney never came. They tried another time, but Dirk wouldn't take the polygraph. They took him back to jail, and the judge would hear of his refusal to comply.

He never had an opportunity to hear my carefully taped recitation, my calm, understanding voice, calling for his contrition. I still believed it had magical powers to pull a full-out confession from him. But the genie never had the opportunity to get out of the bottle.

DIRK WAS hauled back into court, in violation of the terms of his probation once again. This time Pat Flaherty was away on vacation. There was no DA present in the courtroom who would have been committed to seeing that Dirk got proper supervision.

I listened to a recording of the proceedings as the judge asked his defense attorney: "Does he wish to be continued on probation?" (Does anybody enjoy being on probation? I wondered, staring in disbelief at the tape deck.)

His defense attorney responded, naturally, that no, his client did not wish to be continued on probation. Then he continued to sketch a portrait of Dirk's relationship to the parole and probation department. "I don't think the probation department likes him, and I don't think there's a good working relationship there." (Are they supposed to get along like one big happy family? I wondered.) The defense continued, "I think the best thing to do is revoke his probation, let him do his time. He's got a good job. He's been going out on work release. He could do his time free and clear of probation and be able to move on with his life."

The state's representative clicked into automatic and agreed with the defense: letting a perpetrator get off lightly was standard policy for misdemeanors. So the judge assigned Duran an extra month in jail, and erased his twenty-four-month probation altogether. That meant he would not have to do an anger and alcohol evaluation, and after another month of using the jail as a motel from which he would go to work each day, he could hang out in all the bars he wanted to. And he wouldn't be compelled to take the polygraph.

Complete belligerence, in other words, earned him a bit more jail time, but dropped him out of two years of probation, free and clear—this completely without regard for his seven prior arrests in Oregon for crimes of domestic violence, assault, and menacing and four prior arrests for drug and alcohol offenses.

This was a supermarket system of justice. Cases were prosecuted in a cookie-cutter fashion without regard for the stories behind each individual. One of the biggest flaws in American criminal justice, as I understood it, was its inability to intervene early in cases of violent deviant behavior. Minor crimes that disrupted communities very often escalated to serious violent crimes committed by repeat offenders like Duran.

I called Flaherty and asked him to explain the logic behind this absurdity. Flaherty admitted that what had happened was breathtakingly illogical. He was sorry it had happened this way. I called Dirk's probation officer, Terry Chubb. He was surprised that he hadn't even been notified of the court hearing. He never had the opportunity to make a statement in protest of allowing Dirk's probation to be revoked.

As for Dirk's movements as a free man (by now I always had good sources to inform me of his whereabouts): the elderly couple who owned the trailer he was renting weren't happy about law enforcement having come out and busted him for probation violations, so his parents moved him to a converted motel north of Redmond, a place fondly referred to by the local crooks as "Felony Flats."

I KNEW JUST where Dirk was working in Bend. He was on a construction site, busy tearing up this desert idyll to build a foundation for a conglomerate discount chain store. I did a drive-by of that site, parked on a strip of new pavement that slashed through the trampled dirt, and watched him from afar.

The man with the tidy silver ponytail wearing jeans and a plaid shirt approached my car, never looking my way. Then he crossed the road right in front of my windshield. I was delighted to think of the power I had over him at that moment. In spite of his infamous paranoia, he had no clue I was lowering in his path. Needless to say, I did not give into the temptation—only an imagined temptation—but just for fun I savored my moment of prepotency. If this were a movie, surely the one playing me would have put her foot to the accelerator, chased him to some wall, and smashed him until he lay across my bloody windshield, blue eyes occluded with death.

But this was no movie.

Clues from Two Felons

My first thought when I spotted the minimum-security federal penitentiary nestled in the rolling hills of the Willamette Valley outside Sheridan, Oregon, was that the clean gray building and pert red roof exuded a quality of serenity that belied the nature of the population it held.

It had been a year since Dirk's old construction partner, Bill, had whispered a clue into my ear in his gruff voice, telling me to talk to one of Ruby's ex-boyfriends. I gave Detective Fred Ackom this tip, and he interviewed Robert Lee, who was incarcerated at the penitentiary on drug charges.

Fred reported in to me that Robert indeed had an astonishing story to tell.

I wrote Robert myself, asking if he would be willing to talk to me about anything he knew regarding the Cline Falls attack and my prime suspect, Dirk Duran. In the late summer of 1996, the Kounses and I passed through several security gates until we finally filed into a private conference room with the hushed quiet of a library. A slightly pudgy man, handsome with salt-and-pepper short hair, in a prison-issue khaki shirt and pants smiled sweetly at us as guards brought him in. His gentle voice and mild demeanor matched the library silence, and his pleasant face turned sorrowful when we brought up the topic at hand. Robert had found Jesus, he told us, and he exuded the energy of a convert.

He confirmed to us that he was Ruby's boyfriend after she escaped her husband in the summer of 1987 and went into hiding in the Crooked River Ranch. Robert told us that during his brief alliance with Ruby, Ruby told him about Dirk's capacity for violence.

More specifically, she told Robert that *Dirk had confessed the Cline Falls hatchet attack to her.*

I felt a flood of relief to hear this breakthrough piece of news confirmed. I had no reason to think Robert's story was made up. He had no agenda that I knew of. He would have no reason to lie to both a police investigator and to us.

"Ruby told me that Dirk confessed over and over. He would go through days of depression and he would cry, and that's when he would confess," Robert said gently.

I told Robert that Ruby had confided in me something altogether different: Dirk cornered her once and regaled her with the Cline Falls story, but only to insist that he hadn't done the deed. She claimed that he never confessed directly. Ruby emphasized that Cline Falls came up only one time in the five years she spent with Dirk. One time, and one time only.

Robert looked straight at me, eyes wide. "She never talked about the days of depression?"

"No."

"Wow . . ." He let that sink in. "She talked about it to me two or three times. She was telling the truth. She'd have no reason to lie—she wanted to warn me about getting involved with Dirk. How dangerous it was. Ruby said Dirk told her 'over and over' that he had kept the hatchet behind the seat of his truck. He wanted her to be afraid. Dirk was good at saying little and being threatening."

No indeed, Ruby had not shared with me the story of Dirk's confessions and the days of depression that followed. She had not shared the detail about his *hatchet kept behind the seat of his pickup*. The only axe she had spoken of was one Dirk kept in the garage to chop wood. If Ruby had withheld this detail, she was capable of withholding more. Why? Because she was not willing to take responsibility for the confession I wanted?

My face burned when I thought of Ruby withholding from me the information I most wanted. How "hard" had Ruby and I really bonded?

Our time with Robert was short, but what he told us echoed the other stories I had heard repeated about Dirk Duran: he had made some alterations on his pickup after the attack—he changed his tires and had body work done. Before we left, Robert seemed worried about what he'd told us—not that he'd "snitched off" Dirk but that his wife and family in Redmond could be in jeopardy.

"You ever seen Dirk's eyes? He's got demons in him. I've seen 'em. He ain't the type who would confront you; he's the type who'd stick you in the back."

There in the serene prison—which I later learned had once been a monastery—I think I came as close to a hearsay confession as I thought I would ever get.

I WAS ON the road, en route to visit a felon in another prison on Oregon turf, on the far eastern side of the state, nearly on the Idaho line.

I had always had an appetite for road trips. But my zeal to strike out on the roads of Oregon was exceptional—to tool along at full throttle, in my old but fleet BMW, which had replaced my cautious old Volvo. The mile-consuming roads worked like a sedative on my overheated brain, while my emotions were charged by the falsettos and tortured passion of country-western singers on the radio: Rivers of tears. Lonely nights and broken hearts. Sickness, toil, and, trouble. These were songs not of the American dream but of the American wound.

Driving a desolate highway, free of human presence, was a heartrending experience. There was a power in the great emptiness to bring forth bereavement, sadness, and exhilaration all at once. And this desert landscape east of the Cascades particularly had an erogenous appeal—it exerted a power of attraction on me, its very beauty was lacerating. The high-elevation light. Pungent juniper and sage. Driving through this land was both a slow-burning rapture and an elegiac lament.

The hours of open road loosed the unconscious—whatever sores were trapped in the throbbing heart surfaced, unspooling with the white dotted lines in the center of the highway, along with the weeping songs.

These road trips across Oregon were my rituals for regaining mastery of my destiny. Driving Oregon was controllable. Crossing the state from west to east, and from north to south, took just six hours.

In her letters to me, Shayna mentioned twice her frustration that she couldn't drive. This woman had wanted to ride her bike 4,200 miles across America. The end result of her desire to travel became an inability to travel in the most basic way Americans do. In this American culture, driving is self-determining. If Shayna cannot drive, I will drive Oregon for her. A wild longing took possession of me to rove every single road in this state (though I knew I never would), highways and byways.

The Snake River Correctional Institution came into view, a sand-colored complex sprawled on a patch of brown high plains. I turned off the freeway and onto a quiet rural lane.

A FELON BY the name of Chris Peterson had tried to deal away a charge of delivering alcohol to minors in 1979 by accompanying Detective Little of the Redmond Police Department and Trooper Bob Cooley of the state police to Cline Falls State Park to finger a local Redmond boy by the name of Dirk Duran. They ignored what he had to tell them—disregarded what I suppose they thought was hearsay testimony from a snitch.

But what did he actually know? Specifically, who had told him? I meant to get access to this cabal of boys with whom Dirk conferred shortly after the Cline Falls attack. I had written to Peterson at the pen and appealed to him to help me clear up stubborn mysteries and heal my troubled psyche.

Bob, Dee Dee, and I had already done our research on Peterson by interviewing his ex-girlfriend in a coffee shop south of Portland. First off, she made it clear that anything Peterson knew about Cline Falls was secondhand, because he moved to Redmond from California a year or two after the crime. Then she took the opportunity to bend the ears of a couple of compassionate victims' advocates about her own tenure as a victim of domestic violence—though that term was far too pale (as it usually is) for what went on in their household. She candidly laid out for us her years with this sexual sadist who kept her in a kind of psychic bondage. She told us that Peterson could be incredibly charming when he wanted to be, but would morph into a demon when lit by drugs and alcohol. He'd almost bitten off a guy's nose, then got some Tabasco sauce to put on it, and he wasn't fooling around. Another time he'd taken a chain saw and buzzed through an entire bar in La Pine.

"Chris loved to drive people clear to the edge to see just how far he could push 'em," his ex-girlfriend said. Finally he pushed her too far, and she pressed charges for rape, sodomy, and "penetration with a foreign object in the first degree." The record states that the foreign object in question was a Carolann's Irish Liquor bottle. Peterson was convicted in 1986 and sentenced to twenty years, eligible for parole in nine.

Thanks to the good offices of the Oregon Department of Corrections, the rocker-biker-demon of legend was brought before me—a man of medium height in convict clothes, stocky but not huge, with strawberry red hair and a goatee. He was smiling at me bashfully.

We were immediately on a first-name basis. In a conference room alone with Chris, I basked in his warmth. He rested big forearms covered with reddish fuzz on the table and leaned toward me. His baby blues twinkled. His sweet demeanor so took me off guard, I felt as though I were having a reunion with an old friend. His charm seemed completely natural, not manipulative, like types who drill you with their blazing eyes and bulldoze you with their charisma—no, I'd learned to be on the lookout for that type of psychopath. Chris was not bullying or intimidating. He was the kind of guy you think you want as a brother. For the duration of this hour, within the secure walls of the Snake River Correctional Institution, I would let myself be wooed. This would be an object lesson in how normal people like me get lured into perilous webs.

"I'll tell you everything you want to know," he reassured me.

Since we two were acting out a charade of friendship, Chris digressed to tell me a bit about himself, as his residency here in Snake River merited explanation.

"I'm not a rapist," he said. "It's just that my sexual practices are illegal," he confided, explaining that he had a tendency to get involved with women who had been wounded in their lives, and as a result these women liked to get it hard and rough from their men. He agreed that there was a dysfunctional aspect to that type of relationship.

Chris was jolly and articulate as he talked, telling me that officer Richard Little of the Redmond Police Department had accused him of raping a woman once, but Chris insisted that the woman had actually told Little, "I'd be glad to be raped by Chris Peterson!"

At that, I let out a big laugh, completely going along with Chris's program, which, given my personal biography, struck my mind with ironic force even as my body was letting out a few more hearty laughs. Segueing to the purpose of my visit, I asked Chris about the incident when Richard Little of the Redmond PD and another detective had taken him down to Cline Falls State Park in the spring of 1979.

"It's funny," he said to me. "This is such a coincidence because I was just talking about the Cline Falls thing the other night."

A ring of Central Oregon druggers had been busted and sent to Snake River, and caught Chris up on the local buzz. The Cline Falls incident came up, and the guys wondered: Was the guy who supposedly did that still around?

So the Cline Falls incident came up *just the other night*? I was by now accustomed to the currency of the Cline Falls case. But to imagine jailbirds sitting around the cellblock at Snake River chitchatting about Cline Falls was reaching the realm of the seriously absurd.

Chris first heard of Dirk Duran when he moved to Central Oregon from California in 1978, and quickly got up to speed on the scene in Central Oregon. He'd been told how two girls were hatcheted in Cline Falls, supposedly by one of the bullyboys in town, a cowboy named Dirk Duran. Chris also heard that this badass cowboy's attitude was: " 'We run bikers out of town here, cut your hair and send you back where you came from.' Back then I ran a biker scenario against a cowboy scenario, and I thought this might be a challenge. I can pit with him."

The locals let Chris know that because he was the kingpin from Los Angeles, they were putting him up to the task of circling the drain with Dirk Duran.

"He was almost dead because of what he did to you," Chris said, setting himself up as one who settles scores for the weaker.

In the spring of '79, he threw a birthday party at his house for a guy named Pat. "I'd been drinking the whole day. Had a bonfire and was about ready to call it a night. Pat comes in, 'That guy's here that hurt those women.' So I got my double-aught barrel and walked out onto the porch. The dust of the muraled-up green van was settling, and it came to a full-blown stop. I pulled the double-sawed up—my intention was to shoot in front of the van. I had both hammers back. When I looked to my left, three, four cops came over."

Chris was busted for supplying liquor to minors and got hauled into the Redmond police station. "They seemed to have known there was a problem with this Dirk Duran." They wanted to talk to Chris about him.

I asked why the cops wanted to talk to him about Duran.

"I might have indicated that I wanted to put him out."

Soon after that night, Officer Little and a couple of plainclothes cops picked Chris up and drove him to Cline Falls and asked him if he knew what happened out there in '77.

"What did you tell them?" I asked.

"I told them that you were camped, Dirk was hitting on you, you tactfully declined his offer, then he ran over your tent, then came back with the weapons he used."

Chris apparently had asked the cops, "What are you going to do if you find out for sure?" and offered to take Dirk Duran out for them. The cop in plain clothes apparently said, "Oh my God, no, don't do that. Let us deal with this."

Chris told me, "I was thinking: How could somebody not deal with this guy? How can police not deal with this?"

I marveled at this criminal's selective code of ethics.

That was as much as Chris knew about Dirk Duran. He couldn't give me a specific name where he got the information about just what happened down in Cline Falls. But there was a woman named Justine who'd kept company with Dirk for a while in the eighties. Chris gave me a strong signal to talk to Justine, though she might not be easy to find.

Now it was my turn. Chris wanted to hear the whole story of Cline Falls. As I recounted the part about being under the hatchet, I noted that he looked genuinely horrified. I continued, ever vigilant about how I described the meticulous, attractive cowboy to a guy like Chris. (I wondered, in fact, whether I should describe my attacker's physical attributes at all, but I was hoping that something in my description would trigger a memory in him.)

Taking it the wrong way, Chris interjected, "Sounds like you're trauma-bonded with Dirk."

"Trauma-bonded?"

Chris explained that he was in a prison program for sex offenders and he'd been learning about trauma-bonding: how victimization changes a person so profoundly that they come to develop a kind of bond with their attacker, how they become obsessed in a way with their attacker, he explained, and that fixation can last a long time.

A chilling creepiness set in, and I remembered for a moment a famous Italian movie I had once liked and later learned to detest, in which a Holocaust survivor finds her Nazi tormenter years after the war, and cavorts with him in exciting sexual escapades—an erotic fascist ethos that I deplored.

Is it really wise, I wondered, to teach perpetrators about trauma-bonding? I could understand that victims might need to get clued in—but teaching perpetrators about trauma-bonding presupposed you could teach a base of moral values to everyone. The supposition is that the default setting for humanity is goodness. But what if the thrill of abusing someone were an end in itself? Wouldn't understanding the dynamic of hooking a wounded person so as to continue the drama of the wounding only increase a perpetrator's power to create spontaneous thrills?

The burly felon told me he understood trauma-bonding from personal experience. "In every motorcycle accident I had, I trauma-bonded with that motorcycle." And speaking of motorcycles, Chris was now a member of the Christian Crusaders, a drug-free religious biker group. When he'd done his time, he intended to organize a parade of "bikers for victims," to take place at the famous annual biker rendezvous in Sturgis, South Dakota. He described a scenario where victims would parade through town on their Harleys. It was "going to be this big healing thing." I pictured a lot of engines gunning for empowerment. When I was ready to leave, Chris asked me to stay in touch. "Write me a letter," he pleaded with his most shy and ingratiating facial expression, and I felt his manipulative tug on my heart. I almost said, "Sure."

I got back on the road and headed westward across the John Day Desert, toward Bend. I thought: for all my love of covering miles with speed, I'd sworn off motorcycles a long time ago as too dangerous. I'd had enough trauma in my adult life; I didn't need to bond with crashed motorcycles, too. Anyway, wasn't it Jack Nicholson, after an easy ride across the desert in that classic American road movie from the sixties, who ended up chopped with an axe in a campground at night?

Immediate Family

Bob was telling a story about his aunt Blanche, his mother's sister. Blanche was a woman in her seventies who lived with her husband on a farm on the prairie of eastern Kansas. One November day in 1959, Aunt Blanche, who was nearly blind, was summoned from the house by the vicious yapping of her little fox terrier. Outside the white picket fence stood a young man, blond with a face shaped like a narrow wedge and a stray eye. He looked fastidiously scrubbed and combed. His friend, a short, stocky, darkly handsome young man, waited in a black Chevrolet. The terrier jumped as high as the fence in a frenzy of barking. The blond man asked, "Is this dog dangerous? I need to use your phone." Aunt Blanche replied, "Well, he looks pretty dangerous to me. If I were you, I'd head on down the road." They moved on to her neighbors and ransacked their guns. Hundreds of miles down the road, on the high plains near the western Kansas town of Holcolm, they broke into another neat farmhouse in the wheat fields. The family's name was Clutter, and the parents and two teen children wound up shot point-blank in their home. Perry Smith and Dick Hickock went to the gallows in Kansas, and Truman Capote spawned a genre chronicling their deeds and demise. I relished the irony that Bob Kouns, with his life devoted to fighting crime, had a relative named, of all names, Aunt Blanche, who had managed to escape two of the most infamous killers in the era of the American fifties.

Bob loved to tell stories, and over the years since I'd known him, I'd heard a lot of them. I was hearing this one in a restaurant in a hidden canyon. Bob and Dee Dee had joined me in Central Oregon, to keep me company again in what was beginning to seem like a perpetual quest. They pulled their RV into Crooked River, a self-contained, remote community nestled under the rimrock.

Since the day when a woman from out of town turned up on Bob and Dee Dee's doorstep with an unsolved crime on her mind—a woman who was close to Valerie's age and who had been attacked in a way that seemed unsurvivable, but who had survived—the connections between the three of us had been uncanny. By now this inspiring relationship had blossomed, and we three had formed a tribe, with an intimacy that went way beyond the world of crime.

Bob was a man in constant motion, pacing, wiggling, gesturing with his large hands, as he talked about everything from the natural splendor of the Oregon landscape—and he seemed to know every detail of its splendid flora and fauna—to how the criminal justice system was a perfect mirror of the ever-shifting beliefs Americans held about themselves. He was the most civic-minded man I'd ever met: it impressed me that he framed nearly every issue in terms of how it impacted society.

In the mid-eighties, Bob realized that the idealistic 136-year-old thinking behind the Oregon constitution was underlying many of the problems of the justice system there. It read, "Laws for the punishment of crime shall be founded on the principles of reformation, and not of vindictive justice." That meant, reforming the criminal's behavior was the guiding principle for criminal laws. By the late twentieth century the sad truth was clear: many well-meaning rehabilitation and treatment programs had little or no lasting effect on crime. Society hadn't settled upon truly effective strategies to cure criminals. The promise of rehabilitation remained unfulfilled, putting society at risk. For twelve years, the Kounses had worked to change the hearts and minds in the system, and were finally proposing a culmination of their work: a ballot measure in the upcoming election that would reword the Oregon constitution. The measure would win by wide margins, and would read that the laws for the punishment of crime would be founded on "protection of society, personal responsibility, accountability for one's actions and reformation." In other words, public safety should be the first priority of sentencing. In keeping with this philosophy, programs of rehabilitation were to be vigorously monitored, to determine if they really worked, before inmates were released into the public.

By 1996, Oregon criminal justice, as was true in other parts of the nation, had undergone quite a few changes, even since the start of my investigation. The state had adopted predetermined minimum mandatory sentences for the most violent crimes and serious sex offenses, assuring that the next generation of murderers would spend at least twenty-five years in jail. However, the entire evolution of Oregon's past thinking about how to punish criminals would continue to operate: an offender's sentence would depend on the laws that were in place at the time the crime was committed. That meant that even Bud Godwin would forever remain eligible for release into society.

Soon, the Kounses and I would have another date with Godwin, on Halloween of 1996, his biannual parole hearing.

I HAD LISTENED to the Kounses' arguments over the years, fueled by an inexhaustible sense of justice, and though at times I felt overpowered by their strong opinions, I had come to agree with their broad vision. They were, as they tried to be, mostly untainted by the ideologies of right and left. They had tested their beliefs against their own experience. Behind the list of changes they were seeking were two beating hearts, not ideologues. Theirs was a rage born of compassion, so others wouldn't have to endure what they had.

It's easier to forget than to travel through the dark tunnel and face injustice—which requires the unleashing of love *and* rage. The cocktail of love and rage isn't a comfortable mix for most. In fact most people think they should not be mingled. But it is rage that powers the will and finds a way out of impotence. Sympathy and compassion alone often lead to nothing. As Susan Sontag writes, "Compassion is an unstable emotion. It needs to be translated into action, or it withers."

A good example of compassion without rage is the way members of the community of my alma mater, Yale University, behaved in the face of the murder of my classmate Bonnie Garland, in 1977, at the hands of her boyfriend, Yale student Richard Herrin. With their feeling hearts, members of Yale's Catholic community and others decided that one soul was already lost, Bonnie's—so why lose another soul, Richard's? They rallied around Bonnie's killer. Their intervention allowed him to walk free, to take classes, and they mounted a defense fund that won him the best counsel. As Willard Gaylin, M.D., points out in *The Killing of Bonnie Garland*, compassion due to the victim was granted instead to the criminal. "Compassion is an alternative to and protection against facing the revulsion." The Catholic pastoral community in particular did an end run around feeling the revulsion of the crime, and misplaced their mercy on Herrin.

And then there's the notion—a vacuous one—that we're all capable of heinous crimes, the notion that we in the family of humanity have the seeds of cruelty in us all, so let's not neglect the one who acts them out. If any individual perpetrator is just an expression of collective sin, then isn't individual guilt excused? If the individual is subsumed into the general—be it articulated as original sin, societal sin, or bad social conditions—aren't these ways of evading the horror of the singular act of violence?

The Kounses, with their rage born of compassion, forced society to recognize that a flawed criminal justice system left casualties—loss of property, body, life, soul. A criminal justice system such as ours often resulted in social injustice and indifference to suffering, as surely as any other violation of civil rights.

They were unrelenting. Their moral system and capacity for outrage never shut down. It was in part their "cold anger" that kept them going. Aside from the circumstances of Valerie's abduction and death, the murderers controlled even the disposal of her body. Having been denied the ritual of burying their daughter, Bob and Dee Dee suffered ever deeper degrees of loss of control.

Dee Dee's first husband, Valerie's father, had died in a diving accident when Dee Dee was only twenty-six, a mother of three. "But you can rise above an accident in a different way. When an evil is involved and you haven't received justice—that we were lied to, didn't receive any sense of fairness we should have been able to expect—all of that has kept us in the victim's mode," she once railed at me, pausing to cry a little. She then asked in a small voice, "Have I frozen you with my outrage?"

No. Never frozen. Only impassioned.

Dee Dee and Bob made changes in the system as a way of overcoming impotence. Their gift to others similarly bereaved, it seemed to me, was that they had not allowed their beleaguered lives to grind them down; they could walk in and out of the region of grief at will, and this was the source of their vision. They had the energy and courage to give a damn. They could give inspiration to the passive or to the nihilistic or to the compromisers looking out for their own skin—and their lives had proven that individuals could make a difference.

For me, they were a warming fire. Whenever I needed an infusion, I sought out Bob and Dee Dee. Bob had been diagnosed with cancer years before, and he seemed to sense his days on this earth might be limited. I was ever honored to know that he had chosen to devote so much of his time to my cause.

So, too, by 1996, my relationship with the community in Central Oregon had blossomed. I had two sides to my character, one introverted and one extroverted. At home, I enjoyed the pleasure of my own company, my primary relationship, and a handful of close friends. I sent the extroverted version of myself to Oregon, pitched higher than usual. The social bonds I formed in Oregon, forged by trauma and memory, had exhilarated me. It felt like the community had given me a transfusion. It had enlarged the circumference of myself. The very way I moved through the world had changed. To pursue my agenda for so many years had stretched my capacity for intimacy, connection, and persuasion—skills that might otherwise have lain dormant. And I believed that those people I had touched had found their worlds enlarged as well. At times I felt like connective tissue—bringing souls together who might never have met.

THE YEARS WERE dissolving away, with questions still unanswered. Although Robert Lee's claims about Dirk Duran having confessed to Ruby were ringing in our ears, we hadn't gotten a confession from Dirk. There was no shortcut to the truth. We'd have to piece the story together the hard way. The three of us sat in the Crooked River restaurant and lamented that no tantalizing clues had been unearthed for a while. "Bringing alive this investigation is like bringing alive a dead dog," Dee Dee said flatly. We'd made significant advances from the time we convinced the police to reopen the case—increasing the cooperation of various departments, first the police, then the DA's office, then Parole and Probation. But I was really irked because I felt sure a few people in the community were still not talking. We had every reason to believe that Robert Lee was telling us the truth. And if Dirk Duran had spilled his guts to Ruby, maybe he spilled them to someone else close to him. I seriously considered sending a copy of the 1977 Bend *Bulletin* editorial to Betty Duran: "Someone knows . . ."

Then I caught a glimpse through the revolving door of the restaurant: "Lureen!" I called out, my energy suddenly revived. It was my elusive sleuth, code name Egbert, who had disappeared on me a year and a half before. How strange, a coincidence, to run into her again, in this hidden canyon.

A Sleuth Reappears

Lureen threw her arms around me. Though she appeared more relaxed than in our first charged encounter, the shine in her eyes was the same, and she flashed me another conspiratorial glance. She was on her way to a waitressing job but let me know she was eager to pick up where she had left off, helping me to unravel the mystery of Cline Falls, as though the fifteen months since I'd last seen her had never transpired. I introduced her to my comrades-in-arms, and although she didn't know that her reputation had preceded her, she lived up to the colorful description of her they had heard. She invited the three of us to join her the following morning in her home in Crooked River, where she lived with a new boyfriend.

Lureen applied mascara to her long lashes, rimmed her large eyes, lined her eyebrows, blued her lids, and dabbed her cheeks with rouge, letting us in on the magic of her compelling face—and we three watched, like fans in a star's dressing room. I thought it a tad unusual that she hadn't put on her face *before* we arrived, but when I noted the guitar and amps standing in a corner nearby, I figured she was playing at country-western theater. Outfitted in a sleeveless pink cowboy shirt with white ruffles on the bib—tucked neatly into her slim waist and tight jeans and cinched by a belt with an oval buckle the size of a solar disc—Lureen was finally ready to talk about Cline Falls, and the era of the seventies, those bygone days when cowboy culture was still alive, before it retreated by inches each year in an increasingly homogenized Central Oregon.

"Back then, Redmond was a redneck country town. Cowboys didn't have any insight for longhairs. My first husband truly believed that longhairs bring drugs. And I will give you a dollar, and you will be one thousand dollars rich for every longhair they waited outside the bar for, and took right down to the river and sheared 'em like sheep." Lureen imitated the deep baritone of a big ole cowboy,

" 'You got long hair, you get out of here.' Now that's changed, but seventeen years ago, longhairs were not wanted."

Lureen understood the culture of the cowboy West, because she still embodied it. In fact, she claimed she was the last of her female friends who still dressed the part. It struck me as perfect that Lureen was the first person I met who re-invoked the memory of the attractive, meticulous cowboy I'd seen the night of June 22, 1977. To be lean and fit and dressed to kill in cowboy finery was what she herself valued. Naturally, she had eyes for the good-looking cowboys of her day, and she ticked off a list of them, which included her ex-husband—the healthy, strapping lads who tossed the hay, who wore dark blue Wranglers, boot-cut, down over their boots but not so far that they dragged on the ground, who fes-tooned themselves in shirts with pearl buttons and silk kerchiefs and cowboy hats, and who drove the nice four-by-four rigs.

She was the perfect female consort to these young Marlboro men with whom she'd go two-stepping at the 86 Corral. She probably would have had eyes even for Dirk Duran, but for the fact that he scared her so bad that day in the seed fields that he seared a memory in her which burned in her brain to this day.

"We were all out in a hundred-acre field, hoein' green onions." Once again she began recounting the tale that had resonated in my ears now for two years. "That was our job from five in the morning till one in the afternoon. We hoed weeds on our hands and knees. We were the Terrebonne hoers!" she joked, pronouncing the word like *whores*.

"Dirk knew that Janey was leaving him. She was so scared to tell him, you know."

Now here was a fact I had not heard before. Pieces of a puzzle were tumbling into a pattern. A motive for his rage was showing up.

"So you remember that Janey was going to leave him?"

"Yeah, she was wanting to break up and get away from him."

"Did Janey confide in the girlfriends she worked with about wanting to leave?"

"Yeah, see the way I know about that conversation is my girlfriend Elaine—she was the best girlfriend Janey could have. I also remember Elaine goin', 'She's not even allowed to come talk to me at school or go have lunch. She was under his thumb.' "

On a tip from Lureen, I had spoken to Elaine the year before, and she had had nothing to say about that long-ago day in the fields, but she had helped me track down Janey Firestone.

Lureen was back in my life, and I could still use her help.

I believed it was a law of human nature to spill the beans to at least two peo-ple. Shortly after Cline Falls, Dirk Duran had made admissions to Boo's step-brother Donny, while eating mushrooms one night. When Donny accused him over and over, Dirk looked back at Donny with evil eyes and responded with only one answer: "You can't prove it." There had to be others; otherwise, how had Chris Peterson gotten his information?

Maybe there was something I could get by squeezing more out of Dirk's boyhood chum John, the man I interviewed at the Big R the year before, who remembered hearing something about blood in Dirk's toolbox, but wouldn't say more into my tape recorder. I had a hunch that if John had "heard about" blood in Dirk's toolbox, he had *seen* blood in the toolbox—and probably a great deal more.

This brought up the issue: where did Dirk keep the hatchet in the summer of 1977? I knew an axe was hanging in his van by 1978. But in '77, when he drove a pickup, was it in the toolbox, as Janey had said? Behind the seat of his rig, as he had allegedly told Ruby? Both places?

If he kept his hatchet behind the seat of his pickup, after whaling on two girls with it, I surmised, he couldn't have put it back without trailing blood into his cab. I told Lureen, "When he finished with the hatchet he probably put it in the toolbox. He's too smart to throw the hatchet in the river. So he put it in the toolbox. It gets blood all over the other tools. Now he's got to get rid of the whole toolbox. And maybe he's going to get help. It's a big box."

Lureen cut in (always eager to return to the graphic details of my original story), "And you said—you stopped him. He stepped over you, and he walked off with it. Everyone—even I do it—as you're walking up to get in your rig, you throw the tool in the toolbox. It's a habit. The pitch. The toss."

As she spoke, in my mind's eye I pictured it—the pitch, the toss. Of course. He threw it in the toolbox. Where else? There's blood in the toolbox, all over the tools, on the wooden box itself. So he has to get rid of the toolbox—with or without the hatchet. He approaches one or more of his friends. And maybe they help him—what? Burn it? Bury it? Dump it in nearby Billy Chinook Reservoir? I was just guessing. Maybe John knew.

Lureen was acquainted with John, sure enough. They frequented the same bar. She was willing and eager to interrogate him. She knew his schedule. She'd meet him at the bar, throw back a few beers, have a heart-to-heart. No problem.

I BROUGHT LUREEN back, yet again—for the fourth time since I'd met her—to the night of band practice during the summer of '77, when she claimed she saw Dirk Duran carving blood out of his initials on his hatchet.

What color was the wooden handle? I thought to ask her for the first time. I never had pinned her down to remembering a blade attached to a handle.

"Blond wood. A pine, light-colored handle."

I still wanted to find out if her memory of this possible cover-up by some of Dirk's friends held validity.

"For some reason, when I was telling you about him carving his initials, for some reason, and I don't know why, I remember the end being cut off?"

Bob tried to pin down her new memory: "So now we see a whole new cut on the end of the axe and we see Dirk Duran carving on this thing?"

"Right. I'm seeing the *D.D.* and I'm seeing the end of it. Maybe he cut the end off and was carving his initials back in. I wouldn't run on that, just for some reason something sticks in my mind."

He cut the end off the axe because his initials, *D.D.*, were carved in the end of the axe, and blood had soaked into the carving? But one such as Dirk Duran couldn't have an axe without his initials, so he carved them again? I was endlessly fascinated by people's attempts to offer me up any little detail about the "murder" weapon—as though they knew it was important for me to reconstitute it.

Days later I phoned Lureen to ask what had happened when she met with John. He hadn't turned up at the bar that night as expected, she said. She never talked to him. "There's nothin' new, but everything's goin' great," she told me in false voice: "But call me tomorrow."

I called at the appointed hour. She didn't answer the phone. The slippery sleuth had bailed on me again. I guess I could finally let Lureen go. She'd participated in my story with a great deal more gusto and insight than I had any right to expect.

THIS DETECTIVE business was not always a straightforward process of clue A leading to clue B, then clue C. Sometimes, when the channel between my unconscious and conscious mind was widening, I could dredge up a hunch. This time my hunch was that I should return to someone whom I'd already interviewed, one of Dirk's high school pals, on whose doorstep I'd shown up the year before.

Wind chimes tinkled above my head on a warm midsummer night as I knocked on the door of his small-frame home in an old residential part of Redmond—once again unannounced. Randy was pleased enough to see me again; he had nothing more to add to what he'd told me the year before, but through some grace stayed chatting with me on the porch until a stout man with a boyish face happened to wander across the street barefoot. Randy said that Rex was someone I might want to talk to because he was around in '77. When Randy introduced me as the "woman from Cline Falls," Rex took a beat to look me up and down—matching me up with the idea in his mind of what a chopped-up person would look like.

Rex knew Dirk, all right. Rex worked with Dirk. In fact, Rex had worked with Dirk in the summer of '77 at Skyview Mobile Homes. I perked up. Intuition had guided me well this time.

And Rex remembered Dirk's pickup. One time Dirk was going out to lunch with a bunch of the guys and he rolled his pickup in a ditch on Eleventh Street in Redmond and couldn't roll it back out. Dirk did all kinds of stupid stuff like that at work. Dirk damaged enough equipment that summer that Tom, the owner of the business, finally had to fire him and . . . Rex paused.

"Something always bothered me . . . The implement that he used—what was it?"

I thought he knew. "Axe," I said.

"How big was it?"

I pointed to the scar on my arm.

"He carried one behind the seat of his pickup," Rex went on.

He carried one behind the seat of his pickup. I could feel that tingly feeling I'd get when a piece of the story had come up out of hiding.

"When he dropped in the ditch he got tangled in the brush. Out of anger, he jerked it from the back of his seat and started chopping at the brush and weeds around his truck. He just pulled it out from behind the seat and went after it. 'Something is keeping my truck in the ditch!' and he's out there CHOP, CHOP, CHOP. And everybody's going, *'Give me a break!'* Finally somebody said, 'Put it in four-wheel drive, Dirk!' And he turned his hubs in, put it in reverse, backed out of the ditch, and went squealing out of there, all upset. It embarrassed him."

My skin erupted in goose bumps and my mind froze around one detail: the psychic who wrote to the Weisses after seeing Shayna on television the summer of 1977—the psychic who claimed she had had a vision of a man who jumped out of a truck and was chopping down brush or a small tree that had hung him up, the psychic who was willing to excuse the behavior of a man she felt "strongly" was a habitual drunk and a wife or child beater already known to police. Had this Boston psychic picked up on a real image after all, a vignette captured from another point in time, instead of on the day of the attack?

Rex asked me to describe the axe I'd seen.

"I thought the handle was this long wooden—"

He interrupted. "It was light-colored wood. Axe handle is light," he said with certainty.

"Blond wood?"

"Yeah."

Bingo. That's exactly how Lureen had described it.

"It was something between an axe and a hatchet," I said, in keeping with my original memory of an implement too small for an axe, too big for a hatchet.

"If it was Dirk's, it was a boy's axe. A boy's axe has a small handle."

"So it's a miniature axe for younger kids?" A toy?

"It's just a glorified hatchet with an axe handle. And the axe like his came standard, with a twenty-inch handle."

"Twenty-inch handle." I thought of the times I'd described the tool as sort of a hatchet, but Bob Kouns always insisted that if a hatchet with a twelve-inch handle had been used on me, the perpetrator's face would have been close enough for me to see it clearly. Still, Boo claimed that when I ran to the window of her truck that night, I said something about a "hatchet." The newspaper accounts of the time, perhaps echoing my various versions of the tale, used both "axe" and "hatchet" interchangeably.

"Twenty-inch handle. Standard boy's axe is a twenty-inch handle," Rex repeated.

"It's what the Boy Scouts used so we could cut our wood," Randy put in. Boo's stepbrother, Donny, had described a twenty-inch handle—a miniature compared with the standard twenty-six-inch axe handle. When Marlen Hein interviewed Janey Firestone, she described to him a hatchet, but with a longer-than-normal handle.

"Actually the old Boy Scout pack used to have a hole in the pack, and you slip it in the back there, and it hangs down to here. If you watch the old Disney shows, and you see the Boy Scouts walking along, and you see the handle hanging down; that's the boy's axe. A glorified hatchet. It was big enough so you could chop wood but small enough so a little boy could carry it."

I told Rex that I still retained a tactile memory of a curved pounding end of the metal on the other side of the hatchet head. Rex had a boy's axe himself at the time.

"Here's the way mine was—it was kind of like this . . ." Rex drew a round curve in my notebook. "This part here is theoretically flat, but when it came to the ends here, it curved out. Try Coast to Coast. They still sell 'em."

"When that incident happened—Dirk getting stuck in the ditch and pulling out his axe—when was it in relation to the Cline Falls event on June 22?" I asked him.

"Datewise . . . day before or day after. A week before, a week after—but it was close." He remembered Dirk's chopping his way out of a ditch taking place just after Rex moved into the house he still lived in—and he moved on the fifteenth of June, 1977.

"When you heard about the attack in Cline Falls, what went through your mind?" I asked, hoping to better fix his memory in time by calling up an association.

"I'm thinking the hatchet incident was just before the Cline Falls incident. We're talking days back then."

"Did you think about the connection immediately? You see that hatchet swinging in your mind?"

"Somewhat. That's one of the things that clinched it for me—because I saw the axe, then I saw the news reports, and I'm like, I seen that little axe come out from behind that seat! That was it! And that was no hatchet. That was a boy's axe." It occurred to me that Dirk's axes or hatchets had a family resemblance: Janey's brother had told me that the double-bladed axe Dirk owned had a short handle, so a boy could use it. Seems that Lou Duran had made sure his boy could handle his tools.

"And me and a lot of people around here didn't appreciate what the police did on it. Back then, KPRB, that's what we all listened to, or the *Spokesman*—none of them gave much of an account of what was actually going on. We heard the stories flying around, and nobody was very happy with it because, because my God, two girls were chopped up." Rex stopped himself and looked at me. "Excuse me. I didn't mean to say that."

"It's okay. That's what happened."

"And a lot of people were pretty upset about it because, you know, if this happened to you, it can happen to her, him, or me."

"There was one article in the paper, and that's all we heard more about it," Randy added.

"Everybody was so up in arms and running off at the mouth at the time about this whole thing, because it was a big thing—this kind of thing didn't happen."

"Not around here," Randy said.

I asked the two men if either one of them had considered calling the police and asking about the progress of the investigation.

"You do *know* he was investigated for it?" Rex asked me.

No, I told him. There was no record of any investigation of Dirk Duran.

Rex remembered times at the Skyview Mobile Homes when Dirk was away from work. "My service manager told me flat-out, Dirk was being investigated for it and Dirk had a day or two off work for it. I remember Dirk being let off work for two days.

"And I cannot believe how the whole thing back then was kind of just blown under the covers, and I didn't appreciate it. That was my personal feeling."

I let his comments wash through my brain: maybe small Western or midwestern towns were built to behave this way—indeed, this was just how I was raised, that *someone else* was responsible for speaking up, even though it was logical to assume that if *everyone else* was responsible for doing the talking, and the town wasn't very big, not much was going to get said.

"Lord knows, maybe Dirk never did that and he's been accused all these years of something. Because most of the people back then still wonder about Dirk. Did he do that?" Rex said as he headed back across the street. "I'm really sorry that happened to you. I'm sorry it happened here. You look at somebody like that and ask: Did he do it? Didn't he do it? I can't blame you for following it. If somebody did something like that to me, I'll tell you what—I'd spend my time looking."

IT WAS EDGING toward 10:00 p.m., and I was stalking the aisles of the Coast to Coast store in Bend, Oregon. Under eerie fluorescent light, a row of axes hung from a Peg-Board. Narrowing in on the display: a small axe, blond wood, twenty-inch handle, and sure enough, on the opposite side of the blade, a gently rounded metal pounding surface. I wrapped my hand around this rounded metal. This, I think, is what I saw with my eyes, felt with my hands. At least it was the closest I'd ever come to what my senses remembered of the weapon of destruction: a Boy Scout's trusty tool.

Missing Muscle

The small pack ax is about the best for camp chores . . .
the 1¼ pound head has real authority in expert hands—
correction *hand*. It's a *one*-hand tool, clumsy and
dangerous otherwise . . . the *three-quarter ax*—cruiser,
Super Scout, or Explorer—is a *two*-hand ax. The greater
weight and longer helve requires the control only possible
using both hands and a free swing. It is designed for
medium-duty work.

—BOY SCOUTS OF AMERICA,
  FIELD GUIDE FOR BOYS AND MEN, 1967

I had to unlock my psyche from the hunt. My fixation on finding out beyond a reasonable doubt the identity of the perpetrator, and how and why he became a hatchet man one June night, had crowded out my other quest—to spring myself from the dreams that held me captive at the age of twenty.

When I began collecting all existing documents regarding the events of the summer of 1977, I requested a copy of my case file from the hospital, but when the thick stack arrived I didn't have the appetite to study it thoroughly. Now, at home in the fall of 1996, I was overdue to turn my focus back to myself. I grabbed the pile and began to read:

> She presented with multiple lacerations, chiefly about the head, scalp and upper extremities. She had no fractures involving the skull or neck. There was a displaced overlapping fracture of the right clavicle, an undisplaced fracture line going through the right proximal humerus, a pulmonary contusion on the right with fractures involving probably the right third and fourth ribs without pneumo nor hemothorax. There was a 5 inch laceration in oblique fashion across the ulnar aspect of the mid left forearm, with laceration partially through muscle bellies of some of the common extensor muscle mass, and with an oblique sharp laceration of the midshaft of

the left ulna. She also had a nasal glabellar laceration with a left bony lamina fracture . . .

So went the narrative of Dr. Robert Corrigan, who treated me at St. Charles
Hospital in Bend the final week of June. Here was my story again, told in the
words of another professional observer. This doctor's language differed, naturally,
from the police version of the tale, but it engrossed me just as much. It struck me
as curious that he described how I "presented" with multiple lacerations—as
though I had worked up an exhibition, some version of myself put forth for the
world, like an outfit.

I continued to read the doctor's notes: "I treated the fracture with a 6 hole
Richard's compression plate on the ulna . . ."

I remembered the kindly older gentleman in the white coat holding a plate a
few inches long in front of my eyes and telling me he wouldn't make any new in-
cisions in my arm because he would manage to slip this plate into the existing
cut—neat and clean (that the good doctor tried not to inflict any new scars on
me was the sole reason that my scar had preserved so precisely the impression of
the weapon).

The doctor hadn't called this "6 hole Richard's compression plate" by name,
but who was this Richard anyway, that such a plate had been named for him?
Probably I should thank Richard for allowing me the nearly complete rotation of
my left forearm, but in truth, now I suddenly felt that some man named Richard
was compressing me, was holding down my life force, keeping me shackled.

Because that's how the plate had started to feel of late. For nearly all the years
in which I'd harbored the prosthesis in my body, I hadn't felt it—I'd completely forgotten it was sewn into me (by now grown into my bone), except when
I bumped my arm into something hard and felt skin pinch between the two
hard places, when I lifted something heavy or I tried a golf swing, which I had
done maybe twice. Only recently had I begun to detect the aching and itching
inside me. At first I wondered if it weren't just arthritis, like an old football injury that complains when it's damp. Then I began to feel it inside me all the
time, and soon there wasn't a moment when my body didn't want to be free of it.
My left arm, this part of the body designed to reach out and take action in the
world, felt like the three-inch-long "lotus hook" foot of an oppressed Chinese
woman.

I read on—yet another doctor's notations of my face wounds:

FINDINGS: Exploration of a nasal glabellar laceration delineated a left bony
lamina fracture. There is a depression and fragmentation of that lamina . . .
The left rim had a 1 cm. Flap avulsion horizontal laceration. The depths of
this were bony fragments but after exploration it was felt that the fragments
were from the orbital rim area . . .

This notation pertained to the miraculous fact that though I had been struck about the face with an axe or hatchet, no visible scars remained, with the exception of a most delicate, barely perceptible line tracing the bridge of my nose.

On I read, still another doctor's notes: "There is a ½ inch open wound over the right deltoid with protrusion of a small amount of deltoid muscle fibers through the wound. This muscle was trimmed off, the wound was irrigated, prepped and loosely closed with 2 sutures." Here was something I hadn't known: a piece of my muscle had been cut out of my right shoulder. It was missing. I took off my shirt and understood for the first time the mystery of the indentation in the deltoid flesh where arm meets shoulder, understood why for the first several years I hadn't been capable of raising this arm above my head. *A muscle was missing!*

I got myself all worked up with this thought. I touched this indentation with the fingers of my left hand, felt into the gnarled muscle tissue, then the hole where barely any tissue covered bone. It felt sore. I focused on the place of the missing muscle, on activating sparks of consciousness in this wound. And suddenly I felt a surge of grief arising from inside me, but soon the grief morphed into another emotion that filled my body with heat, compressed my skull, and sent blood to my face: rage.

Rage about a missing muscle? People have surgical procedures all the time where bits of muscle are clipped here and there. But because the muscle was taken by a man in the night—cut out of my body at the end of the day of my greatest physical feat, climbing a mountain on a bicycle—it made me want to gnash my teeth.

There was a time—it felt like an age ago, although it wasn't—when I believed that because I felt no anger at my attacker, I was humming on a higher spiritual plane. By the outset of my quest in 1992, I knew I had disguised my avoidance and my denial as spiritually vacuous notions. As time went on, as I began to imagine myself in proximity to my real attacker, I yearned to arouse this living rage at the events of the past. Now, as though I'd taken a time-release pill, here it was.

How far I had come, in these four years, since the earliest days of my inquiry: from a day when I wasn't interested in who my attacker might be, to this day of rage when I'd learned that he'd stolen a muscle from me. What better metaphor for the strangulation of my will than this?

I read on. Several pages of the hospital file were devoted to descriptions of the X-rays taken of my injuries. I had seen them once, and now tried to recall them—numinous white bones against a black field: pieces of severed rib floating in the rib cage; the right collarbone overlapping by an inch and a half; the Richard's compression plate bridging the ulna.

These descriptions brought to mind a Buddhist meditation meant to be practiced in days of health, while one is living life in the fullest. The meditation prepares the practitioner for her death, calling on her to conjure a mental picture of her skeleton in the days after mortal life, when the flesh has dissolved away. I brought to my mind's eye a picture of my own quirky skeleton, unique among skeletons, a lovely patchwork of bones stitched together here and there, bones wandering in unique directions, not as my DNA had originally prescribed. The contemplation somehow calmed me, and didn't fire my blood like the fact of a missing muscle.

Next in the file were notes from several nurses, jotted in various hands, throughout the duration of my hospital stay, June 23–July 3, 1977. Here was another tale about my post-assault condition. I extracted a short, objective narrative from the reams of nurses' scribblings on their clipboards. These were the highlights:

June 23. Alert. Oriented. Able to move all extremities. Vital signs stable.

June 24. Patient tearful. Complains of pain . . . Talks freely about bike trip and accident. Alert. Responsive. No apparent confusion. Left pupil remains moderately dilated and reaction to light very questionable . . . Tends to be a little uncooperative. Has remained cranky and irritable all shift . . . Awake. Complains of pain and worried about cosmetic appearance . . . Has continued to be very demanding but is more cooperative and patient when explanations are given. Family and friends visited—patient laughing and enjoying visit. Has stated several times she doesn't "want to sleep all the time—I want to talk." Has awakened crying with a nightmare—does not wish to discuss details of the accident.

June 25. Considerable pain, which she doesn't handle real well—and is very depressed . . . Awakened for vital signs. Immediately is angry with us for not turning her, not brushing her teeth, not having "eaten" all day, not giving her pain medication . . . She is very irritable, demanding. She issues 4 or 5 orders at once, becomes angry because the order in which nursing staff proceeds is not her priority. While proceeding with her #1 priority, she again becomes angry that 2 or 3 more requests have not yet been met. Cries frequently. Medicated for pain and rest. Wanted teeth brushed, then refused to allow it . . . Continues very uncomfortable and demanding. 2–3 nurses in attendance much of the time . . . parents visiting. Appears more comfortable and less depressed.

June 26. Continues to be cranky and irritable but more amenable to suggestions . . . Moans and wants to be left alone.

June 27. Left pupil remained dilated. Does not appear to react to light. Parents here. Patient in good spirits. Visiting with friends. Detectives here. Patient appears to tolerate this fairly well . . . Very demanding. States she is depressed . . . talking about mishap.

June 28. Alert. Oriented. Very particular about positioning. Refused to turn to side at present.

June 29. Cheerful . . . Sleeping soundly . . . Talkative and cheerful . . . Sleeping soundly . . . resting quietly with family in most of the evening.

June 30. Left pupil remains fixed and dilated. Awake and alert. Up to bathroom with arm in sling. Tolerated well. Resting and visiting with family.

July 1. Awake and alert. Left pupil dilated and fixed . . . Scalp lacerations clean and healing well . . . Upset about Shayna's leaving. Ambulated to Room 510 . . . Stated, "just wanted to be let alone." Refused bath when offered. Sleeping most of this afternoon . . . Talking on phone . . . Up ambulatory. Moves very well.

July 2. Awake. No pain or discomfort now. Left pupil remains fixed and dilated . . . Sleeping well. Head and shoulder lacerations appear to be healing well . . . Complete bath. Does not want to move. Has seemed irritated since doctor here. States home is boring . . . talked on phone several times. Cheerful since phone call. Mother in frequently . . . Awakened for vital signs. Patient cheerful and talkative.

July 3. Awakened. Made ready for discharge. Left pupil remains the same.

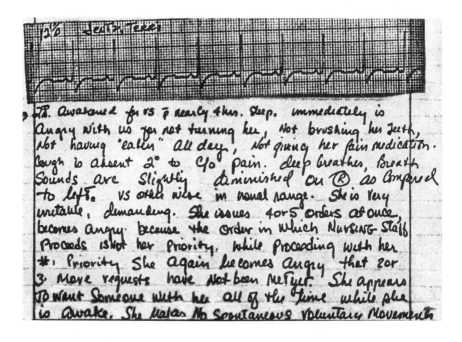

I noted one motif that ran through the entire ten days of jottings: the fixed and dilated left pupil that did not respond to light, the left eye that remained jammed in its wide-open position from June 23 to July 3, and probably after the record keeping stopped.

I read in a medical text that eyes dilate to allow more light in—a process that happens all the time in fight-or-flight situations, allowing you to see more clearly.

That my eye had jammed in its all-seeing position for ten days or more struck me as just one of the possible responses an eye might have after seeing what it had seen. Shayna's eyes—seeing what they had seen—had had another response, and one just as appropriate.

I winced as I read the nurses' descriptions of the tyrant issuing demands from her hospital bed. I had an idea that one nurse, the one who jotted notes on June 25, did not like me. "She issues 4 or 5 orders at once, becomes angry because the order in which nursing staff proceeds is not her priority." I pictured her, this angry nurse with her angry young patient. I wondered if she was one of the nurses my mother had told me about—the one who preferred attending to Shayna, sweet Shayna who felt little pain.

I wanted to be mad at the young tyrant, my twenty-year-old self. But if I listened closely to her, I could muster compassion. Her demands spoke for a torn body in fiery clouds of pain.

This ritual reading of the hospital records put me in a rare mood. I was immersed in body consciousness, dredging up levels astoundingly deep. I felt enveloped in my own viscera. And that was not unpleasant. On the night of June 22, 1977, when I was "bathed in blood," as Boo described me, I had an interesting experience of what it meant to be alive. Blood—viscous and dense, of the material world—is in the realm of nature. Fluids are the prime matter of human existence. We all enter the world bathed in blood. We don't often get that baptismal immersion a second time. I was now edging toward an insight about my early ritual of searching a sleeping bag for dark stains. After the night of the attack, I didn't focus on the violent image of blood, the superficial pornography of "gore." It was never "gore" to me. *Gore*: an Old English word meaning dirt, or filth of any kind. Blood should not be sullied by or confused with—as it is in our culture—the malevolence that causes violent bloodshed. It was a peculiar state of mind I conjured during this ritual reading of the hospital records, a twilight place on the edges, one I had experienced rarely, and not in a very long time. I found myself as close as I had ever been to a full multisensory memory of that distant summer night.

I had never stopped longing for that multisensory, eidetic memory. I wanted to refresh the story with what I suspected lay beneath layers of resistance. I had gotten close during my first revisitation of Cline Falls, but there was more to resuscitate. Perhaps now it would come: I pulled out the fluorescent-orange handlebar pack and its contents, the few items of camping gear left from the trip—aluminum mess kit, Sterno camp stove, bicycle lock, and the flashlight with which I'd saved my life. This small yellow flashlight, four inches in length, with the word *Durabeam* stamped on its side, was wrapped in a plastic bag, along with the original batteries, now leaking acid. Though it had been stored in a dry place, the plastic flashlight felt moist inside the bag, as though sweat had condensed on it. It bore the unmistakable odor of blood. Much DNA could be taken from this flashlight even now.

And much psychic energy. I fitted my hand around the flashlight and gripped it; what came to me was a body memory, reminiscence embedded in the cells of flesh—a recall not of fear, but of focus, an enduring beam of explosive emotion. I put the flashlight back into the plastic bag and tied it up tight. I wanted the air of that night at the campsite preserved.

Sisters of Mercy

Oh the sisters of mercy, they are not departed or gone
They were waiting for me when I thought I just can't go on
And they brought me their comfort and later they brought
   me this song
Oh I hope you run into to them, you, who've been traveling
   so long
—LEONARD COHEN

The compulsion to excavate the past had not been slaked after four whole years. In fact this stream of psychic energy had picked up velocity. I found myself again, in the autumn of 1996, three months after my last trip north, checking into a humble motel room on the commercial strip in Bend, preparing myself to piece together still more bits of the story.

Preparing for these interviews had never gotten easier, although I'd finally perfected the technique of bringing the past alive in myself so I might better evoke memories in others. Once again, I made myself into a time machine, lay on my bed in a darkened room and went deep-sea diving with seventies-vintage Fleetwood Mac. Throaty notes of sorrow, screams of anguish, a driving beat—I let the band work me over until my heart beat fast, and I summoned what flashes of the past would return.

Then as I left the motel and got into my car, I tried to hold the memories stable so they would activate lost fragments of the past lying dormant in those who answered my knock at their doors. By now I'd mastered my own quirky interviewing technique; I learned more about the laws of remembrance. If I stayed long enough, usually both the consciously and unconsciously withheld recollections would spring forth, and these interviews would turn into infused encounters, lifted out of the ordinary—as though by virtue of daring to inhabit those damaged mosaics of memory, we were graced for those hours with sacred time. When I knew I had created a sacral space for the story outside the chronology of time, when others were present with me in the past, my stomach unknotted and a kind of euphoria spread over me, and my scalp would tingle and sweat poured out of the crown of my head.

As I drove the roads of Central Oregon the autumn of 1996, I felt sure that this time my investigative task would be harder. Only the week before, I had activated the sparks of consciousness of the wounded body by reading the hospital reports, and now my body was fearful. It feared the Oregon desert landscape, and now I was back in it, and the comfort of the warm, dry skies was gone. It was a chill November, and darkness came early in these high parallels. And the landscape transformed. The rabbitbrush that had gleamed golden in October now paled to silver in late autumn. The native grasses silvered, too. The land lost its color and the junipers looked stark against fields of bleached-out vegetation. I felt like I was looking at the negative of someone's spooky but beautiful black-and-white film of the desert.

One part of me wanted to call it quits. How long could I keep up this rare pursuit, so far afield from my ordinary life in California? Another part of me surged on. Like a hungry unsettled ghost I headed to Rexall Drug. Retired sheriff Poe Sholes hadn't turned up much information about the failed police investigation—but he gave me an important tip that I should seek out a woman, the wife of the pharmacist at a Bend drugstore who had worked as a nurse at St. Charles Hospital in 1977.

TUCKED IN a shopping mall on Greenwood Avenue in Bend, the Rexall looked like other small-town drugstores, with cozy aisles and a Hallmark card shop leading to the pharmacy section lining the back. The tall, lean pharmacist behind the counter had an especially sober demeanor. "I'm sure Kathy would like to talk to you . . ."

He did not change his inscrutable expression but emerged from behind the counter. "Kathy, there's someone here I'm sure you'll want to see."

A woman threaded her way down one aisle toward me. Small in stature and attractive, with good bones and long straight blond hair, she looked up into my eyes inquisitively.

"Were you one of my nurses?" I asked without giving her the context. No Cline Falls. No "unsolved crime nineteen years ago."

She took both my hands. There was silence. A current traveled from hand to hand.

"Yes. I was."

We both acknowledged that we were talking about the same long-ago event.

"Oh my God, Bruce, how many years have I been talking about this?"

Bruce, the pharmacist, nodded. Just the week before, Kathy told me, by coincidence she had asked her husband to probe Poe Sholes about any recent developments in that long-ago Cline Falls incident.

"I often wondered what happened to those women. Where they are. How it affected their lives. Are they happy? Because I can just remember . . ."

So Kathy had beamed me in, I thought to myself. She sent me "mental drifts," just as Boo had. Along with flying TV pictures and radio waves, something else that connected us was vibrating in the air, as though our minds had reached out in a field beyond ourselves, pulling us with invisible rubber bands toward those who shared our preoccupations.

Kathy was a nursing student called to duty in the early hours of the morning of June 23, when extra help was needed. Light dawned early that summer solstice day in high latitudes when Kathy walked into Shayna's operating room.

The scene was "macabre." Kathy was short of breath as she recalled the hours of that day. "The head wound . . . her surgery . . ." She was talking about Shayna. She let out a black laugh. "I do remember . . . real well. It was real tense. And we were working so frantically and intensely."

"They didn't think they could keep her alive?"

"We weren't sure what her status would be. We knew what had happened. But heads bleed like crazy. You can have a very small cut and lots and lots of blood, so I remember the concern: Let's get this cleaned up. Let's see what we've got. We talked about the topography of the brain itself, that part of her anatomy that had been assaulted. We were worried about what might remain or what might not remain. We were very worried about her eyesight, I do remember.

"You, as I recall, were awake, alert, cooperative, of course in shock. And wondering about what was going on with your friend. I remember that distinctly. You were very worried about her. I kept trying to reassure. But it was very hard being in that situation, because we really didn't know about her yet.

"You provided us with the text for as much as we knew. Because Shayna never could. Though we could certainly look and see a story," Kathy said, and I was struck with her notion of reading a "story" in a wound.

"We knew so little—these were two young women from the East Coast and here they come to Oregon, and we find Bend to be this real small wonderful nature community, and this happens, and we were just devastated. We couldn't imagine this happening here. We felt so violated ourselves."

Devastated. Violated. These same words used again—as though some town hall meeting had taken place after the Cline Falls attack and these words were used in public dialogue, and repeated in newspapers, although I knew they had not been.

Devastated and *violated* were the words that language provided, with its limitations. *Devastate*: To lay waste. Render desolate. To overwhelm. *Violate*: To treat irreverently. Desecrate. Profane. Rape. The poignancy of the devastating feelings had waned, Kathy said, but not the immediacy of the memory. She continued, in vivid recall.

"And I remember the remark being made: boy, wait until we call the families. We were so concerned about getting hold of the families and how we were going to present this to the families. They're going to think we're just a bunch of hicks with a little first aid station. They're going to be out of their minds. They're going to look us up on the map and we're not going to be there. So how do we relay to the family that we really did have a real hospital that had been open only two years and was state of the art. That a neurologist had moved here in seventy-four and really knew his way around anatomy."

I shared with Kathy something I had learned from Shayna's parents. When they brought their daughter to the hospital in Boston in the same condition, they were told that a big-city Boston hospital would likely have considered her condition fatal. Apparently only doctors in this remote outpost would think a miracle possible.

Kathy acknowledged that the kind of medical care lavished on us in the summer of '77 in Bend, Oregon, had vanished in today's world, even in this same post. Back in those faraway days, everyone was called in to help, regardless of his position—doctor, nurse, or student. And occasionally, they would all be called on to vote their conscience when someone's life was in the balance.

Kathy's closest circle was a trio of young nurses. Marcie was the one who attended to me when I first arrived at the hospital, while Kathy attended to Shayna.

"You'll probably remember Marcie. She's the one that got you on the table. She's the one that kept you warm." And there was a third nurse in their inner circle, Lisa, whom Kathy described as "a great humanitarian woman who brought a dimension of consciousness to us."

"The three of us practically had the same mind, we were so close—we were the youngest nurses on the OR—we were 'the kids.' And we were so gung ho and our knowledge was so fresh. And our compassion . . . you would be like our sister coming in." Kathy said that because the three nurses were barely older than we were, they had felt tremendous emotional ties to us—as though they were looking at themselves.

"There's never a time when the three of us get together that we don't talk about this situation, what happened, and how it's so unsettling to all of us. It was a time when most of us were riding bikes—we were a pretty healthy crew at that point—so it was not unusual for us to think: two young women would do this, be extremely pooped, find this little park, and just drop in."

She turned back to her husband, behind the pharmacy counter. "Bruce, how long have I been talking about this? How many times have I just cried at night, 'Oh, I just wonder . . .' Twenty years? This is hitting me now . . . who you are . . .'"

Kathy was laughing, but I could detect tears in her eyes. "That this person lived. That both of you lived. You're alive. We did good. We did good."

As I stood in the aisle, bombarded by drugstore fragrances, I narrowed my range of attention to the soothing stream of words from Kathy's measured voice, as she told me her young son had once asked her, "Mom, what was the most terrible thing you ever had to do?"

"So I told him about this situation, and it really bothered him. He knows about how these two young women decided to camp here and were assaulted and how awful that was—and he had a lot of great questions: How did you call their parents? Did their parents come right away? Who took care of them? Where did they go when they were well? Even at the age of eight he was really concerned about those issues."

"Closure" to this event had eluded Kathy all these years. "For two reasons: It was like you were part of our community. You lived so far away. So when you were well enough to leave, you did. I think, from my standpoint, you did leave a part of yourself with us." And our departure, she explained, was a deep loss to our caregivers.

"I became you. I became Shayna. There is a time when you're such a part of the patient and the patient is such a part of you. We're the same person. You are at your most vulnerable, and you will give me anything. You will be anything I want you to be at that moment. I'm your lifeline. I'm your lifesaver. If you can reach out and touch me, everything is okay. What would I want done for me? I'd want to be safe. I'd want to be warm. I'd want someone to think of me in those terms. How would we have wanted to be treated? That is the way I was taught, and I know few nurses who were taught any differently, at least in my era.

"And secondly, when a perpetrator isn't caught, and there's no closure that way, it's always open, and since you still are a portion of that patient—and gosh, how would you feel? You are still a portion of that patient, and you don't know who did it, and nothing's being done . . ."

The words from this sage woman, this gentle intelligence, were stirring something deep. I thought she was speaking metaphysically—that's what my ears heard, and in fact, this moment of conversation seemed to exist out of time, and yet, how could so extraordinary a conversation be taking place with this perfect stranger in the aisles of Rexall Drug? I wanted to be sure I got her meaning right.

"You became part of us, so there was no closure for you—"

"No closure for me."

"You retain the same psychic unease that we have, in a way."

"Absolutely. There's no doubt in my mind that even when this is resolved, it won't be resolved . . . I don't know . . ." She broke off, searching for other words.

"Working in the operating room—you see it, you fix it, and it gets well. But this is a situation that has gone on now for twenty years. And that is almost my entire nursing career. So it was very different. We had nothing of this caliber where it seemed to us an assault *on purpose* . . ." She laughed nervously. "On purpose. You know this guy did this on purpose. And I can remember lots of nights after it happened just not feeling quite as safe in my community, and thinking how frightened you must have been. I think it will never be resolved because it was the first time, for me, it was the first what I would consider a brutal act of violence that I had ever experienced in my medical profession. I'd had hunting accidents that involved the same types of injuries. But I'd never had an assault like this. And haven't since, really. So I think this will always stick out in my mind, because it was such an isolated incident and because it really just touched this community quite a bit.

"And Cline Falls is a place where we would go on a Sunday drive—it was a wonderful place to drive down to. And then it became such a macabre sign on the road after that. You'd look at it and that's what I would think: these two women struggling for their lives. It was unsettling. Tremendously unsettling.

"I will share with you something that has haunted me all these years. At the time this happened I was in nursing school, and the director of my school lived on Cline Falls Road—and this was a huge topic of discussion and I thought she'd be incredibly upset because she lives on Cline Falls Road. She indicated to us something along the lines of—that everyone knew who it was, and because of who his family is, or because of his family's station in the community, this would be taken care of."

I tried to fix her meaning: "This would be taken care of by the community, in other words."

"That was my read on it. It bothered me so greatly, having been on this end of it."

I felt an old feeling. That same unease spread over me that I felt at the beginning of my investigation. I seized on this clue and asked her nursing teacher's name. Kathy lost touch long ago, but thought she might still be teaching at the Central Oregon School of Nursing.

I could see Kathy was eyeing the hospital records I held in my hand, so I handed the stack to her and she read passages aloud.

Why, I wondered aloud, didn't the truck do more damage to me than break a few ribs and collapse my lung? Why hadn't it flattened me dead? And how could I have remained conscious? Was there a medical explanation? Kathy had a guess.

"That was a day when you had just ridden your bike and your muscles were really pumped up, really engorged, like when you exercise and your fingers are filled with blood—because that's where the blood goes, to the muscles, to make them work—and so my feeling at that time was, you were really bulked up . . ."

I imagined pumped-up muscles holding aloft a truck and a thought sailed through my head that there could be no better metaphor than this for how the will and the heart and the blood strengthen flesh, so the flesh can perpetuate the soul.

Kathy was thumbing pages, captivated by the reminiscences these medical reports triggered. "I remember Dr. Lee coming in and looking at your face. He was desperate to get pictures of you. He always liked to get pictures of a patient so he would know what they looked like before. He would just say, 'Do we have any pictures? Do you know if we have any pictures?' " Dr. Lee, Kathy explained, was an ear, nose and throat doctor whose skills extended to reconstructive surgery, and he had an eye for beautification.

As Kathy was inspecting my nose, a thought occurred to me. "That's funny . . . my nose is not as wide as it used to be . . ." As a younger girl, I had had a pug nose. I always figured that my adult nose, the one that had garnered so many compliments (a so-called perfect nose), had fortuitously revealed itself when baby fat melted away.

Kathy perused the records again. "He just went in and took out bony fragments. You already had a fracture, so he's going to close it anyway . . ."

"He narrowed the bulbous part of my nose?"

"He went ahead and did a septorhinoplasty—it straightens your nose and narrows it down. As long as he's there he's going to make a good-looking nose. He's going to take care of whatever trauma is there."

She glanced down at the paperwork. "It doesn't come out that you had your nose operated on, but I can tell you from looking at it . . ." She looked back at my nose. "That's his nose. It's a classic Lee nose."

"This is the wildest thing." I was overawed. "Just the wildest thing!"

"Yeah, you would want that nose now. You would go to somebody and say, 'Can I have this nose?' It's a great nose. He's good."

The conversation had taken a turn to a lighter vein, and I was agog.

"So there's no genetics at work here? Can you see how wild it is for me that suddenly, at the age of thirty-nine, I find out there's a Dr. Lee, whom I never knew existed, but who nineteen years before had taken it upon himself to improve my nose?"

"Yes! But aren't you just glad? It suits you very well. He operated on my nose, too. Same year. And he did Marcie's, too. So when you see Marcie, we can talk about our noses."

Bruce reappeared from behind the counter. "Bruce, doesn't she look great? She has a Lee nose."

"I've come to find out I have a Lee nose."

"So does Kathy."

"And so does Marcie."

So the delicate scar on the bridge of my nose was all that told of the sculpting that had taken place—according to the laws of harmony and proportion and balance, those universal elements of beauty.

So this was how it was: a young cowboy narrowed my shoulder span and a male doctor narrowed my nose—lending to this big-boned girl a more delicately feminine appearance from that day forth. This was certainly a new twist on the Pygmalion myth.

Just for fun, I later drove to the clinic where Dr. Lee, these many years later, still plied his profession, and I managed to catch him rushing between surgeries. I asked the tall, burly man dressed in blue scrubs what he remembered of the Cline Falls incident and what he remembered of the surgery he did on my nose.

He studied my face with the eyes of an expert, and said sorry, no, he didn't remember me or the incident at all. Not at all.

WHEN MARCIE first laid eyes on me, outside a trendy Bend restaurant where Kathy, she, and I had arranged to meet, she looked slightly trepidatious. Her eyes were expectant—shades of Bill, afraid that I might appear as a searing sight. It was odd to go about my life, to look in the mirror and see myself as "normal," while, to select people—like Bill and Marcie and Kathy—I would always be a figure that conjured a memory of trauma.

This second sister of mercy was at first somewhat reserved, not as immediately accessible as Kathy, and they were opposites physically: Marcie was as slim and dark as Kathy was zaftig and blond. She was wearing a black leather jacket. I might have taken her for a New York City artist rather than a nurse in Bend, Oregon.

I studied their Dr. Lee noses and decided that, much as I liked the notion of sharing a nose with these kind spirits who had attended to me in my hours of need, my Dr. Lee model looked nothing like either of theirs.

Early one June morning in 1977, Marcie was driving to her regular shift at work when she heard the shocking news. With dread she pulled up to the brand-new hospital, the sand-colored modern building topped by a Christian cross commanding the desert on the east side of Bend. When she walked into emergency, a nurse at the desk said, "Marcie, get into room number four *now*."

"You have one of those girls in there?"

"We do."

"I didn't ask any other questions, I just went in," Marcie said. "You were agitated, you wanted to know how your friend was—one of your biggest concerns was for her because I believe you knew how seriously injured she was. And I was trying to comfort you. 'Let's take care of you; your friend's being cared for by other people and I'll keep you informed how she is doing, but right now we just need to take care of you—because to me, you're the most important thing right now.' "

"Did I go along with that?" I asked Marcie. The notion that not just Shayna, but I, too, had been seriously injured was far from my way of thinking, and it remained so for many years afterward, until, in fact, my current quest. It was hitting home only now, as I conjured the living rage at my missing muscle.

"A little bit. Trying to keep you concentrating on you was not possible. Your concern was for your friend. And you were agitated."

As Marcie, Kathy, and I talked in the restaurant, Marcie's initial reserve with me dissolved and I found her deeper voice as comforting as Kathy's. I thought my way back to those faraway days and tried to recall that voice, Marcie's vocal signature, floating somewhere over my head in the operating room.

"You were complaining about pain in your hip and I looked down at your right side, and for the first time I looked at your hip and saw the bruising and the impression of the tire tracks."

Tire tracks on my hip?

"The flesh didn't rebound right away," Kathy added, helpfully.

This was a detail I had not known. At one time my leg held the imprint of a tire. So the young cowboy left his tracks not only in the grass and dirt, but also on my limbs. This revelation, coming so late in my mission, was the closest I'd edged toward dissolving my denial of precisely what had happened to me. It was a lovely irony: hearing that my leg had once held the imprint of a tire was helping some exiled part of me, in a metaphoric sense at least, and maybe more, climb back into my flesh.

Marcie continued, "It was like, my God, I just couldn't get out of my mind that someone—"

Kathy finished her sentence. "—did this on purpose."

"It was horrifying to look at that and to see your shoulder and to think that someone drove over you—purposely went after you, for no reason we could figure out."

"And what amazed us was the *violence* of this, it wasn't a sexual violent act—this was just pure evil."

"I don't know why we got this impression, but we thought this person had followed you and seen that you set up your camp at Cline Falls, then waited to come back . . . with just the intent of murder. Or mutilation. His intention was only to hurt you guys . . . Just to see you lying there with those kinds of injuries was very traumatic for me, yet I was trying to give you the protection I felt you really were asking for and couldn't find. I don't think you ever felt safe while you were there. I don't remember ever leaving your side, and if I did leave your side, you were instantly aware that I was gone. You may not remember that at all."

I had vivid recall of the presence of the voice over my shoulder, but no, I didn't remember specifically (but I could imagine it) the void I must have sensed when the voice left my side.

"I can remember, I just pulled my little desk up to you and kept reassuring you, and whatever updates we had about your friend I would pass on to you because I told you I would do that."

I distinctly recalled that the voices of the nurses speaking to me had not cosseted me with denials. They had delivered bad tidings, and allowed me the possibility of deep loss. They were nearly as young as I—it was their initiation, too, that quantum leap into experiencing firsthand what until that night none of us knew life included.

"On some underlying level you needed the guarding while you were in the operating room—you needed that sensitivity. Because you allowed me to hold your hand that whole time."

I remembered these hours as the pinnacle of pain in my life to date. Now I came to find out that this stranger, this sister, was holding my hand, an act of succor previously unknown to me until this day. I could picture from a more mature perspective now, two young women holding hands: the one trying to give solace, the other unable to place her faith in the comfort of a stranger.

"On another level, you didn't want too much—it was almost like you wanted to be protected but you didn't want to *admit* you wanted to be protected. 'Here, I'll let you hold my hand and comfort me, but I'm still going to maintain control by setting limits in other places.' "

There was a long pause. Sometimes when several hearts open wide all at once, you can feel their fleshy substance in the room. This was one of those moments. No, I hadn't learned then the power of surrender, of vulnerability, the sinking from vigor to fragility, and the lessons it teaches—indeed, I was still trying to learn.

"Did you feel unsettled about the fact that, even with your best efforts, I wouldn't feel safe?"

"A little bit," she said. My heart gave a twitch. I knew Marcie felt a great deal more than a little bit.

Marcie needed to reach into metaphysical explanation, just as Kathy had, to describe what happened to her that night: that she had become one with me, her patient. And since she had become one with me, in the same way, she lacked closure from this long-ago episode.

"There are some things that you know you're never going to find closure to. You were people from the Midwest and East Coast, and we were never going to know what happened to you—we'll take care of you, we'll do what we can do here, and you move on, and you wonder. There probably hasn't been a year when I haven't wondered how you were, what was going on, what you ever did.

"I don't think people understand that when you take care of traumatized people, that we come away traumatized also. That we have to get over it somehow to some degree to be able to go home."

Talk turned again to Shayna.

"We were just ever so happy to see a piece of bone in there," Kathy said. "When you see someone with a head injury and they're bleeding and bleeding, you don't know what you're dealing with until you get them cleaned up—and were we ever glad to see that Band-Aid, that piece of bone."

"It saved her life," Marcie said. "It was the only thing that saved her life. Besides you."

It was remarkable to me that the jagged piece of bone that I had felt with my fingers like Braille was remembered in kind by these two women. We three in our bloodied innocence had connected, in this place of traumatized tissue.

WHEN I LEFT Kathy and Marcie, I was depleted of every ounce of adrenaline. I went back to my room. Still drenched in sweat, I lay on the bed and reflected on these extraordinary encounters, replayed the moment when Kathy said to me: *"I became you."*

Lying there with damp hair, I had a revelation: about those letters I wrote long ago, in Moscow, in the autumn of 1977, to Shayna, at home in Boston. Bursting with adolescent ardor, I wrote that as far as I was concerned, we had a "lifelong friendship sealed in blood," and that "being at one point so close to your life had a powerful psychological effect on me."

At last I understood the state of consciousness out of which that letter came, why I felt something had locked into my psyche in the desert air that night and rearranged me, why some part of me had merged boundaries and wouldn't let go, until I felt like her injuries were mine, pictured myself blind, until my mother had to say to me, *"Terri, it's Shayna who lost her sight, not you."*

The sisters of mercy helped me make sense of that liminal, threshold experience—alone in the desert with a dying Shayna—those moments that forged in my psyche such an intimacy with Shayna that she still ghosted through my dreams. The night's essence was: The commingled scent of juniper and blood. The wind blowing through my veins. The rush of adrenaline. The jagged edge of bone in Shayna's skull. The soft tissue of her brain. A kiss on her bled-white cheek. The amassing of strength to move body parts that had been severed. My ignited consciousness, a dedication to her living.

Next, the drama had come indoors and these young nurses were there with us.

In the midst of crisis we had traveled to a larger plane, experienced something mysterious that you couldn't explain with your rational mind, a breakthrough into self-transcending love. We did not stop at the edges of our bodies. Though separate skins contain our nerves, we felt separate only because of the way we experienced life, bound by the conditions of time and space.

And I understood for the first time: Shayna had been unconscious. She was left out of this merging. When she finally awakened, she was alone. Alone with her rational mind, with no sensory memory of that night. She could only imagine the horror. What I remembered of that night was myself as a field of awareness with my senses on fire, while my body and its pain retired into invisibility. I was conscious of my heart growing larger until it burst the bounds of my smaller self. I remembered all this, and Shayna could only imagine gore.

Back in the summer of '77, in July, Shayna and I, and the sisters of mercy, parted from one another, falling back into our separate skins. But for those of us with the memory of the traumatized tissue, who found ourselves running wet with lifeblood—it was as though we had met in the infinite waterways of one pumping heart. We, the sisters of mercy and I, who had experienced this mysterious breakthrough, were left with longing for that fluid state of living without finite contours, for this form of love we had discovered—as though, when confined to our separate skins again, a part of ourselves had gone missing.

Out of my compulsion to tell my story to as many who would hear it, I had found these nurses, strangers but intimates, ties of flesh and blood—like so many other women I had met during my quest—whose loving-kindness helped me understand something fundamental about my own core experience, about the fate that had cast a spell on me.

In a Rexall drugstore I found what I considered *data* proving the interconnectedness of all beings. I found a source of vision.

How Long Till You're Innocent?

It was the fall of '96 when my phone started ringing from Central Oregon: Dirk Duran had finally gotten caught red-handed. And this time, the nature of his acts, though no one was injured, could mean serious consequences for him.

Multiple sources filled me in on this cheerful news, including members of law enforcement, who by now enjoyed giving me this gratification. Even the kindly ex-sheriff Poe Sholes and his wife, Doris, mailed me a news clip from the Bend *Bulletin*. "We knew this article would interest you," Doris wrote in her neat hand.

The article recounted that sheriff's deputies had arrested Dirk Duran on a kidnapping charge, among others, after he allegedly fired two rounds from a handgun and pointed the weapon at his hunting partner. Duran and eighteen-year-old Timothy Bidwell were returning from a hunting trip at around 8:30 p.m. when Duran fired two rounds from a .357 Magnum revolver as the pair whipped into the driveway of a ranch where Bidwell was residing, then Duran held the gun to the young man's midsection. Duran reportedly was intoxicated. Shortly afterward, Duran allegedly ordered Bidwell to drive to another location. Meanwhile, others called the police, who stopped the car and arrested Duran without incident.

Chief Deputy DA Pat Flaherty assured me that he would not dispose of this case. He would bring together a grand jury to consider the evidence on three charges against Duran: kidnapping in the second degree, unlawful use of a dangerous weapon with a firearm, and coercion.

IN APRIL 1997, I found myself in the Oregon statehouse to do my bit as an activist. To stoke myself up for an oration before a senatorial audience, I headed downstairs to grab some coffee. It was an ordinary institutional coffee shop, except that an intriguing series of historical photographs lined the walls. One especially caught my attention: the axeman.

The twenty-foot-high Golden Pioneer. He was not yet perched on the cupola of the capitol, nor was he yet gold-leafed. He was lying on the ground, his axe beside him, covered from head to toe with scaffolding, chains, and ropes. He looked trussed up, captive. He reminded me of Swift's Gulliver, the giant tied down with ropes by the six-inch-tall Lilliputians—immobilized.

With that image of hope for the future, I found the testimony room and nodded to my friends at the state police who were present to support legislation to change the statute of limitations so that the clock would never run out on attempted murder. The room was disconcertingly small. What was I expecting? That I would be like Mr. Smith going to Washington and that my voice would ring off the marble walls?

When my turn came, I delivered my speech from a squeaky place in the back of my throat. I had boiled my story down into shocking slug lines, the likes of "I heard seven thuds, then silence," and "I heard ghastly death cries from my friend," and "Everyone I've talked to across America has been as shocked as I that this heinous crime cannot be prosecuted . . ." I found such neon lines difficult to deliver basso profundo, but nonetheless I elicited much shaking of heads from the senatorial audience seated on a platform in front of the room. The defense attorney whose job it was to oppose this change in legislation stood and acknowledged the difficulty of arguing his case in the face of such a story as mine, but: "Assume that a man is charged. Assume he is innocent. How is that person going to put together a defense? Memories are faulty after the passing of years . . . evidence deteriorates . . ."

Dee Dee whispered, "His claim is bogus; we're asking them to change the statute of limitations, not the burden of proof." A prosecutor stood to lend his support for the changing of the statute. He had a good tale to tell, of a prostitute in Washington State. She was found on a road one night, stabbed in the chest with such force that the ripped flesh of her bosom exposed her beating heart. But her heart never did stop beating. It beat until she recovered; it beat until she joined the Green River Task Force (as it was suspected that her predator was none other than the Green River Killer); it beat so strongly that her attacker could only be held accountable for a scant three years.

PAT FLAHERTY had shown me a document called *The Oregon Criminal Procedure Code*. Drafted in the early seventies by a commission that set out to modernize Oregon's century-old criminal laws and procedures, it was still the foundation in 1997 for the Oregon criminal justice system. I looked at the commentary that justified setting time limitations for all crimes other than murder or manslaughter. Oregon had borrowed its reasoning from the American Law Institute's *Model Penal Code*, drafted in 1962.

Point 1. *Foremost is the desirability of requiring that prosecutions be based on reasonably fresh evidence.* This first point struck me as practical-minded.

Point 2. *If the person refrains from further criminal activity, the likelihood increases with the passage of time that he has reformed, diminishing pro tanto the necessity for imposition of this criminal sanction.* This second point, based on the notion that even among criminals, human nature tends to be regenerate, struck me as wildly optimistic.

Point 3. *As time goes by the retributive impulse which may have existed in the community is likely to yield place to a sense of compassion for the person prosecuted for an offense long forgotten.* Based on my own collection of evidence, this third point struck me as baldly untrue, idealism veiling the facts.

And Point 4. *Finally, it is desirable to lessen the possibility of blackmail based on a threat to prosecute or to disclose evidence to enforcement. After a period of time, a person ought to be able to live without fear of prosecution.*

So, after three years, the axeman ought to be able to lead tours through Cline Falls, a tour guide to his own bloody inferno ("This is where I felt the left wheel of my rig riding up a body . . .") for which he could even charge admission—and the law couldn't lay a hand on him? Let bygones be bygones?

These arguments were similar to those made in Germany just after World War II, when officials debated the statute of limitations for crimes committed during the Nazi era. According to Holocaust survivor and philosopher Jean Amery, one French trial lawyer said, "And we, too, regard the remoteness through time as the principle of the statute of limitations. A crime causes disquiet in society, but as soon as public consciousness loses the memory of the crime, the disquiet also disappears. The punishment that is temporally far removed from the crime, becomes senseless."

I HAD NO SOONER left the testimony room when a small plump woman of about my age approached me, all riled up. She introduced herself as a denizen of Central Oregon. Donna had been present in the room when I spoke. Once I said the words *tent* and *run over* her memory had ripped open and she whispered to her friend, "Hatchet Man!" She was astonished to find me alive, as what she remembered was "You were chopped up in small, small pieces, and you guys were scattered all over."

I caught myself envisioning chunks of flesh landing helter-skelter among the juniper and sagebrush.

She remembered going down into Cline Falls after the attack and looking at the spots in the grass, wondering, "Did it happen here? Did it happen here?" She remembered talk: "That they never found the guy. But he got sneakier and sneakier. He did this to other people, but he didn't leave evidence around no more."

After that incident, Donna told me, terror descended on her crowd of friends and relatives. Every unfamiliar pickup was suspect. No girl was safe. No kid was safe, as long as the hatchet man was loose. "We all thought it was a local. The area was not well traveled except by locals. Years later we heard it was a prominent citizen. We truly believed the hatchet man was *after us all.*"

Once, a big pickup was closing in on her sister and mother as her sister was driving the highway in a smaller pickup. Seeing the ominous rig in the rearview mirror, her sister was certain it was the Cline Falls bogeyman. ("He's coming!" she said to her mother. "It's the hatchet man!") Donna's sister gunned her own vehicle, careened onto the rocks, and crashed it.

Donna told me the community was "devastated" for years after that Cline Falls calamity. *Devastated!* "Your legend lives on! I have friends who still talk about it . . . I can't believe it! I'm going to call everyone tonight!"

NOT LONG AFTER the day I testified, Oregon Senate Bill 614, which included a change in the statute of limitations for attempted murder, was signed into law by the governor. The updated ruling read, "A prosecution for aggravated murder, attempted aggravated murder, murder or attempted murder or manslaughter may be commenced at any time after the attempt to kill."

The legislation would not be retroactive, I was told. Shayna and I would never have our day in court. But those victims-waiting-to-happen wouldn't have to watch, as I did, while their suspect became innocent in the eyes of the law.

Red Lipstick on a White Scar

Chief Deputy District Attorney for Deschutes County Patrick Flaherty locked his hands behind his head, leaned way back in his chair, and described to me the night of terror caused by Dirk Duran. As he spoke I could hear the two loud cracks with magnum force shattering the peaceful quiet of a desert ranch bedding down for the night. I could feel the heart-pounding fear of an eighteen-year-old kid as a gun pregnant with a bullet jabbed him in the ribs. I could picture Dirk's piercing light blue eyes fixed on the boy as he said portentously. "You don't know the half of it. Yet." The boy told police that Dirk had stretched out the word: "Yeeeet."

Flaherty planned to prosecute to the full extent of the law. Of course I knew that a charge such as this would likely go unprosecuted in busy Deschutes County. But thanks to the attention law enforcement was giving to this dangerous character, Flaherty had already convened a grand jury to indict Dirk Duran.

There was one big problem: the victim was scared. Scared of Dirk. Scared of retaliation. So scared, he was embarrassed and didn't admit his terror in front of the grand jury. So scared he might just skip out on the trial and take off, going so far away that he couldn't be dragged into court, in which case Dirk would manage to bedevil the system another time.

Flaherty had just filed another charge against Duran. After Tim Bidwell testified in front of the grand jury, Dirk came out to the job site where Bidwell was working, got out of his dad's Ford, walked to where Bidwell was operating a backhoe, and stared at him, his arms crossed over his chest. The eighteen-year-old was loading a dump truck when he looked up into Dirk's burning eyes. Bidwell told police and the DA that this stare shook him up so much, he slammed the bucket of the backhoe against the side of the truck he was loading. According to his report, Dirk held the stare for several minutes from fifty to seventy feet away; then Bidwell got the boss's attention. The boss made Duran get back into the car that had brought him. It was Dirk's father who had chauffeured his son to the site of what appeared to be an act of intentional intimidation.

Flaherty found probable cause to have Dirk arrested, and he was booked into jail on the charge of tampering with a witness.

Dirk contended that he was standing, innocuously, a full two hundred yards away. At the hearing, Judge Michael Sullivan was not impressed with the evidence in the case and threw out the charge.

A trial on the three felony charges against Dirk would go forward, scheduled for May, but there were no assurances that Tim Bidwell would show up. The boy was still terrified. Even if he did show, based on his performance in front of the grand jury, Flaherty didn't have much confidence in him as a witness.

I WANTED TO meet this eighteen-year-old boy. Most of all I wanted to suggest to him that Dirk Duran had met with success all his life because his intimidation tactics had worked. I knew Tim was a macho kid, embarrassed to admit that a guy like Dirk could scare the shit out of him. I wanted to tell Tim: telling the public the truth, that he was scared for his life, was the most courageous action he could take.

With Bob and Dee Dee in tow, I showed up at a trailer park not far from Cline Falls, where Tim was staying with his girlfriend and her mother. I stood alone on the porch as the girlfriend's mother opened the door. She had a hard face. The kind of face that makes you want a time dissolve to before life had taken its toll, to when you could see her as pretty. She growled at me that Tim wasn't home.

When I tried another time I found her in a softer frame of mind, though I'd missed Tim again. I decided to include her in the mission, to share with her my interest in her daughter's boyfriend's participation in the upcoming trial of one Dirk Duran.

Dropping this name won Dee Dee and Bob and me an immediate invitation into her trailer. Roxy pretended to know nothing whatsoever about the trial. She let us ramble on until she added a couple of facts that clued us in that Tim had indeed spoken to her about it. I asked her if she knew Dirk Duran. She thought about it a second as I roughed out a description.

"Oh, I know him!" She knew him from the saloon where she tended bar. She said she'd gotten a hinky feeling from him right off the bat. "When he first came in I thought how good-looking he was. He looks like Jesus. Then he gets ugly . . . he's really scary. I wouldn't want to be alone with him. He's really evil. He could be sweet-talkin', but then he gets drunk and he gets ugly." On the subject of Dirk, Roxy's memory was getting ever more specific. She said to him in the barroom one night, "You're a nasty, nasty man. What's with you? Too bad a guy so good-looking can be so nasty." She turned saucy as she related that once Dirk even asked her out on a date. "Not in a million years," she shot back. He asked her where she lived. "Why? You writing a book? Because when you get it done, use it for toilet paper, because that's what it'll be—a piece of shit." He borrowed five dollars from her. She asked him to pay her back. When he refused, she refused to serve him. When she told him to leave the saloon, "Smoke was coming out of his ears and eyes. 'Get your ass outta here.' 'Who's going to make me?' 'I am. I'll throw you in the street and I hope a truck squashes you. We don't need people like you in here.' "

A long time ago Roxy drew the line on abusive men. She was married to a lout who beat her from 1969 to 1984. "Had my bottom teeth knocked out. Nose broken. Gravel in my face." Then she got mixed up with another lowlife, the father of her daughter, who beat her for two years, until she'd had it and wasn't going to take it from any guy ever again. She told us that her son, Wes, grew up witnessing men thumping on his mother, so now he throws himself on any man pummeling a woman. Coincidentally, her son lived in the Desert Terrace Trailer Park, and was one of the brave who had came to Scotty's rescue the night she escaped Dirk.

Roxy got pretty worked up on the subject of men beating women, and we won her promise to talk to Tim about stepping up to the plate and testifying against this known terrorizer and woman beater in the upcoming trial. "If he wants to marry my daughter, he'd better."

In the car, Dee Dee reminded me of the way Roxy decorated her trailer: pictures of lions and tigers and a poster of John Wayne on her wall, a figurine of a leopard on the coffee table. Dee Dee observed that Roxy surrounded herself with images of strength. "That woman has muscles in her urine."

WITH A RED lipstick pencil, I filled in the white scar that wrapped around my left forearm and held my work in front of the looking glass. Satisfied that it resembled a Frankenstein gash once again, I left the bathroom. I was wearing jeans, a denim shirt, and cowboy boots because I wanted Dirk to perceive me, in this, his first view of his stalker, as a Central Oregon kind of gal, not some city slicker, but someone he could identify with, in case at some future point in time he surrendered to me a straight confession. As I paced toward the courtroom, my mind filled with Nancy Sinatra's voice: *"One of these days these boots are gonna walk all over you . . . ."* I strode into the clean, modern courtroom with a large octagonal skylight showering light from above and took a seat next to Dee Dee, Bob, and Boo, in the blond-wood spectator benches on the right side of the courtroom, one row behind the prosecutor's table. It was a zestful beginning to a day I had anticipated for a long time. I had practiced my encounter with him. I decided that I must not convey fear or he would smell it. I must assert dominance.

When I looked up, he was already seated at the defense table. I hadn't seen him enter. I was just behind him, to his right. He was wearing the usual. Ever the man of denim and plaid, though he was missing traces of his old cowboy self. No cowboy belt or cowboy boots were in evidence that day. His silver hair was combed straight back from his high forehead and temples, tight into a high ponytail. His lashes were long, his nose aquiline, his beard coifed with picture-perfect swirls and whorls, as aesthetically manicured as an actor's. The skin on his face and arms was luminous. His shoulders broad and square. The muscle tone of his fore-arms altogether model-perfect. His fingernails manicured. His self-regard and vanity were abundant. He exuded high wattage.

Meticulous. The word derives from the Latin *meticulosus*—meaning full of fear.

I savored the leisure to watch him for hours, drill holes into the back of his head with my eyes. I thought, I'm feeling good here in my boots observing my prey. Strong and calm.

All rose for the Honorable Judge Michael Sullivan, a pleasant-looking man with a square jaw and close-cropped steel-gray hair, and jury selection began.

I cried three times during this trial. This was the first: when the citizens shuf-fled into the courtroom. My eyes teared up with gratitude toward these people who might bring me some version of justice. They were men and women of all ages. A middle-age elementary school teacher. A frumpy retired secretary. A trim, athletic technician in the semiconductor business. A couple of grizzled older guys. Then a recess was called. Everyone left the room except Bob, Dee Dee, Boo, and me. And, notably, Dirk, who got up from the defense table. Instead of exiting, he strategically positioned himself one row behind us. It was his turn now to drill into our backs.

This was his first sight of me, and I felt it was with full awareness of my iden-tity. He would know who I was because my presence in this particular courtroom was an oddity. I surely had nothing whatsoever to do with the crime in question. He would know because surely a description of me had made its way to him in the last year. He knew because I was present with Boo, whom he recognized from high school. He knew because I was accompanied by Bob and Dee Dee, that un-mistakable and easily described "nosy pair" who had pestered his parents awhile back.

I felt his eyes. I rolled up the left sleeve of my denim shirt and reached my arm around the back of Boo's chair, landing my scarlet scar just in front of his eyes. A few pregnant minutes passed in this pose. I willed my scar to show its savagery. I imagined it springing to life, into a fresh cut.

Boo whispered to me, "He's looking right at you." I felt a warm thrill in the center of my back.

Recess was over. The defendant returned to the defense table. The left side of the courtroom behind the defendant's table was empty. No one had come to sup-port him. Not even his mom and dad.

He closed his eyes, tilted his head in a saintly downward pose, pretending to meditate. But I knew he wasn't meditating. I could see blood rising in his cheeks.

He opened his eyes, and I thought I could see panic. He appeared to break into a sweat. He popped a pill.

Jury selection resumed, and then a moment came—I knew it would—when he looked back over his shoulder and we locked eyes.

I had been prepared for this moment, and I stared back at him with confidence and an attitude of dominance. And I studied these "windows into the soul." I knew his irises were blue, but I couldn't see a hint of that celestial color. His eyes were like two empty holes in a mask, with an inquiring blankness—trying to figure out if there was anything in my features that he recognized. Calmness increasingly stole over me as I held his gaze steady. He looked away.

I didn't remove my eyes from the defendant, separated from me by only a partition of blond wood. My attention to him was all-consuming, and I only half listened as Flaherty presented the state's case to the jury of seven women and five men. The victim, Tim Bidwell, was an eighteen-year-old local Redmond boy who met the defendant on a construction site. Tim and the defendant went deer hunting together one night late in September 1996, in the Cascades. On their way home, the defendant was passed out and Tim was driving the defendant's van. Tim pulled into the Johnson property, where he lived in one of three trailers on the small ranch. A short driveway led to the house where Johnny Johnson lived with his wife Marcella, and there was another stretch of road to where the three trailers sat. Tim Bidwell lived there, along with Johnson's grandchildren Brandon and Brian. This tiny trailer park on Johnson's property was also where the defendant Dirk Duran had resided earlier in the summer, before Johnson asked him to leave because the older man was tired of the police coming out to pay probation visits on Duran.

Tim turned off the highway into the Johnson ranch, intending to get his roommate, Brandon, to follow him to Duran's and then drive him back home. The defendant woke up and, finding himself in the Johnsons' driveway, started to rant and rave about Johnson. He drew his Colt King Cobra .357 Magnum revolver from the holster on his hip and fired two loud blasts out the window. Tim was scared. He drove fast down the ranch road toward his residence and said to the defendant, "You're crazy. I live here. What are you doing?" The defendant leveled his revolver at Tim's midsection, looked him in the eye, jammed the gun in his ribs, and said, "You don't know the half of it. Yet."

Tim hopped out of the van and made a beeline for his trailer. Mr. and Mrs. Johnson heard the shots and went outside to investigate. Johnson found the defendant and confronted him. Duran admitted he was the one who had done the shooting. Then an argument ensued concerning Johnson's having kicked Duran off his property. Johnson yelled at Tim to come out of the trailer and take Duran away, but Tim didn't want to come out because he was frightened. When Johnson asked Duran, "What were you shooting at?" Duran answered, "I was shooting at a tree." Meanwhile Tim sneaked out the back of the trailer to find Mrs. Johnson. Looking very scared, he asked her to call 911, which she did. The police were on the way.

Tim returned to his trailer and hid in the bathroom. Duran yelled for Tim to come out, until finally he strode into the trailer and grabbed hold of Tim and ordered him to drive him home. Tim was frightened, but he felt he had no choice. He thought if he didn't, Duran would hurt him. The defendant told Tim to drive the van. Unbeknownst to Duran, a deputy sheriff was waiting at the end of the driveway with his lights out. The deputy cuffed Duran and Tim, found the .357 in the back of the van, and asked Duran what he was shooting at. Duran replied that he was "shooting at a skunk."

Dee Dee watched the jury listening to the prosecutor. And I was in my world of two. Every now and then Dirk stole a glance at me.

What kind of life-form was this? On close inspection, his conduct was a résumé of anti-moral forces, an outrage of human decency. He had no praiseworthy deeds to his credit that I was aware of, except, arguably, his willingness to shovel shit. Nor was there anything in him to engage our sympathies, nothing pitiable. He judged his success in life by his ability to make others suffer. I never found anyone so universally disliked, even among the criminal underground.

His life themes were clear and consistent—his capricious thuggery, his cruel appetites, the tortures he crafted for recreation, his intrigues and dirty tricks, techniques to acquire status by scaring and intimidating, his phony acts of contrition, the way he could twist the truth of a story into a bald-faced lie. He performed the same stunts so repeatedly that they had become character traits, such as shooting brown streams of chewing tobacco into the eyes of his girlfriends. His compulsion for repetition was fascinating to me (in this sense I found his derangements stimulating. I had a compulsion to know every vile deed on his résumé). Dirk Duran brought recidivism to a whole new level. I know that if his hometown—old teachers, casual acquaintances, bystanders, bartenders, the many people I had talked to along with those I hadn't—were to get together and take an inventory of his misdeeds, it would make up a voluminous chronicle. The memories he created were the stuff of legend, deeds so intense they left a grip on the present.

It wasn't childhood abuse that had brought about his psychopathology. How much abuse could he have suffered? And it wasn't alcohol or drugs that had caused his malefactions. Alcohol gave him liquid courage to act on what was already inside him.

As one who believed he was the favored child of the gods, he was the incarnation of narcissism. He embodied the belief that anything, anyone outside him had no reality but was experienced only as being *useful* or *dangerous* to him.

This man was an object lesson in intentional wickedness, an object lesson for those who believed such a type—a human being of fundamental malevolence, roaming the world seeking the ruination of souls—didn't exist among humankind.

But what a sporting enemy he was in this sense. He was interesting to watch.

Meanwhile, the court-appointed defense counsel Jacques DeKalb, a big white-haired man with an easygoing, gentlemanly manner, outlined his competing narrative: Mr. Duran and Mr. Bidwell had enjoyed a leisurely, amiable hunting trip together. DeKalb stated the important fact that the Ford van belonged to Mr. Duran, and because his driving privileges had been revoked, Mr. Bidwell had to drive. On the way back, Mr. Duran wasn't intoxicated to any extreme degree, but he fell asleep. According to DeKalb, Mr. Duran planned to have Mr. Bidwell drive him to his own residence and then have Mr. Bidwell take the van to where he needed to go—home. "Obviously the evidence will be Mr. Duran didn't want to be stranded five miles from his home that evening after the hunting trip." But when Mr. Duran woke up and realized he was going to the Johnson property instead of home, he was naturally upset. He didn't want to be stuck there and forced to drive home in violation of the law. So he took the .357 and shot it out the window. That's how he showed his upset. And Mr. Duran was also upset because Mr. Johnson had asked Mr. Duran's father to remove him from the Johnson property earlier in the summer. Not only that, Mr. Bidwell cussed at Mr. Duran, calling him stupid and crazy. Mr. Duran was quite mad, understandably.

So Mr. Johnson ordered Mr. Duran off the property. But Mr. Duran couldn't drive without breaking the law—and he sure didn't want to break the law—so he told Mr. Bidwell to get out of the trailer and take him home. Finally, Mr. Bidwell agreed to come out and drive him home. "Maybe the least he could do in those circumstances." They drove out. The policeman was there. He demanded everyone get out of the van and he found the gun. No big deal.

Judge Sullivan banged the gavel for the noon recess.

At lunch, I sipped infusions of an herbal sedative as Dee Dee asked me, "What was it like to be in the same room with him?" I answered right off, acting tough, "He's just another piece of shit." The long shadow that had fallen on my life seemed separate from the criminal in this courtroom. I fully believed that he was guilty of the attack against Shayna and me. But I couldn't connect the dots between this man and the fingerprints he had left in my psyche. His presence had not triggered a seismic reaction in me.

Just before the afternoon session, before the jury filed in, the judge called the two attorneys to his bench and asked why Bob and Dee Dee Kouns had come to this county to attend a trial such as this? Flaherty frankly told the judge that the defendant in this case was a suspect in the unsolved Cline Falls attack from 1977. From then on, I noticed, the judge spent more time watching the suspect's reactions to the trial proceedings.

Flaherty called Mr. Johnson to the stand. Tall and lanky, in jeans and a jean vest, the sixty-five-year-old Johnson had a voice as twangy and slow-cadenced as they get in the West. From Johnson we learned that, on the night in question, he heard two shots in the driveway, shortly after dark. He went outside and asked Duran what he was doing. Duran, whose attitude was "quite hostile," told Johnson he was shooting at a tree. Johnson shouted at Bidwell to come out and drive the van and Duran away. But Bidwell was "fairly excited and reluctant to go outside."

During cross-examination, the defense elicited from Johnson that the .357 Magnum revolver was in a holster on Duran's hip the whole time, and he never made any threats of physical harm to Johnson.

The prosecution called Tim Bidwell to the stand.

I'd never laid eyes on him before, this small, stocky boy with a round, fresh face. Against expectations, he had shown up, all cleaned up for the jury. Today he was a regular choirboy. The bailiff asked, "Do you solemnly swear to tell the truth, the whole truth, and nothing but the truth?" "I do," he said, and told us he had gotten acquainted with Duran when he worked construction with him. Bidwell testified that while they were hunting, Duran did indeed drive his own van on the back roads, and even a bit on the main roads. When they returned to Redmond, Bidwell took the wheel and Duran passed out from drinking. Flaherty made Bidwell explain the plan: Bidwell didn't have a vehicle of his own, so he had to go home first to pick up his roommate, who would follow him back to Duran's, then take him home. At no time did Duran suggest that he wanted to be taken home first and then give Bidwell his van to drive home.

Driving into Johnson's driveway, Duran pulled his pistol out and shot out of the passenger's side two times, saying, "Johnny, come on out, I'll kill you, you SOB." Bidwell said, "Man, you're crazy." Duran leaned over toward Bidwell with his gun.

"When you said he leaned over with the gun, tell us what he did with the gun," Flaherty said.

"It was right there at my side. He leaned over and he knew I was scared. He was all mad and everything and I didn't know what he was going to do. He just kind of leaned over and said, 'You don't know the half of it, yet.' "

As Bidwell began his testimony, he stole glances at the defendant sitting at the defense table. As he proceeded, he gathered courage and looked straight at Duran as he testified. As he described the beats of his story, he kept describing how "scared he was."

Out of seemingly nowhere, emotion sped to the surface. I cried for the second time. This macho eighteen-year-old boy was, in the end, willing to say in public that he was scared of Dirk.

Flaherty tried to elicit from Bidwell all the reasons why he was so very scared.

"Because when I worked construction with him, some of the stories I heard about him."

Dirk shot up from his seat. His lawyer shouted, "Objection!" The judge sent the jury out of the room.

Now it was really getting interesting. Now the true, true story of this man was seeping into the courtroom, beyond the narrow confines of this particular crime.

The judge instructed Flaherty to ask Bidwell his question, and the prosecutor continued: "In addition to the fact that he pointed the gun at you and fired the gun and is angry, is there another reason you were afraid of the defendant?" Bidwell made reference to having heard "stories" about him. Dirk shot up from his seat again, as though ejected by a spring mechanism. Flaherty directed Bidwell to focus on what the defendant told him, not stories he heard from others.

"Like we were out after work, and he'd get halfway drunk, and then he'd go into his little phase where he'd close his eyes and just kind of start mumbling something." Playing it to the hilt, enjoying that Dirk had to watch his victim dramatize Dirk's own spooky, intimidating behavior in public, Bidwell threw back his head and let his eyes flutter back. "He told me to keep it confident between me and him. I guess he used to ride bikes. Harleys or whatever. So they went out into the desert once and urinated on a guy and stuff. And drove off and left him."

Flaherty asked, "Did he say anything to you about shooting somebody?"

"When they were out in the desert, that's what they did apparently. He didn't come right out and say it, but you kind of put two and two together."

Flaherty explained to the judge that it was relevant to bring into the courtroom the defendant's past statements because they would make Bidwell believe he might shoot him. The judge disagreed. He sustained the defense's objection, and the twelve citizens filed back in.

The prosecutor continued describing the coercion part of the event, when Duran came in the bathroom, grabbed Bidwell's shirt, and said, "Let's get the hell out of here."

Flaherty asked Bidwell, "What did you say to him?"

"I didn't say nothin'. I was scared. I didn't know if he had a pistol on him still or what, so of course I went with him."

DeKalb turned up the heat on his cross-examination of Bidwell. He made Mr. Bidwell out to be irresponsible for not wanting to take Mr. Duran home, when Mr. Duran clearly didn't want to be stuck on the Johnson property. DeKalb also emphasized that when Mr. Duran fired the shots, Mr. Bidwell responded by telling him that he was crazy. Of course that's why Mr. Duran responded as he did. And besides, DeKalb pointed to Bidwell, "You'd just been hunting. You're not afraid of guns, are you?" Bidwell said no.

The defense counsel concluded his cross—never managing once to intimidate the young man. Bidwell stuck to his story, kept his cool, and was brave enough to hold his gaze steady on Dirk, who was by now averting his eyes from Bidwell.

A sturdy young deputy sheriff took the stand, and Flaherty elicited from him that when he stopped Bidwell and Duran from leaving the ranch property in the van, he was concerned about his own safety in the presence of the defendant, whose reputation he was familiar with. He finally got the defendant to comply with his orders to stretch out on the ground with both hands at his sides. When the sheriff asked him what he had been shooting at, he told him he was shooting at a skunk. He also denied that he ever pointed the gun at Bidwell.

The state rested, and closing arguments were set for the following morning.

DAY TWO, the previously empty defendant's side of the courtroom was now filled with high school students on a field trip to see justice at work. I prayed there was a chance they might really see it.

I was seated at my post when Dirk arrived wearing the usual, jeans and a plaid shirt. Today it was red, white, and blue—which gave him a *Seven Brides for Seven Brothers* look, and I could well imagine him performing a dance, 1950s-musical-theater-style, while twirling an axe. Dee Dee, who never missed a trick, whispered to me that she thought his mother had made the shirt he wore today, but not the one from yesterday.

Flaherty summarized the well-recited history about how the two men went deer hunting and by the time they got back, ". . . as they're returning in the driveway, what occurs? The defendant becomes angry. You've got an intoxicated man, and now you've got an angry man. You've got an angry, intoxicated man that has a .357 Magnum on his hip, and he begins to rant and rave about Johnny Johnson." He was angry because Johnson had asked his dad to take him off Johnson's property. Flaherty yelled out (in imitation of a growling, drunk voice), *"Come 'on out, Johnny, I'm going to kill ya!"*

"How would you have felt?" Flaherty asked the jury. "He's frightened and he's a little angry, too, and he has a right to be. He turns to the defendant and says, 'You're crazy.' And what does he do? The defendant takes the .357 Magnum and points it in Timothy's side and he says, 'You don't know the half of it, yet.' "

I watched Dirk as he stroked his temples with his thumbs, and then he stroked his mustache and eyebrows. He seemed to be consoling himself with physical caresses. He was shaking his head back and forth, signaling to the jury, *No, it's not true!* He looked imploringly at the twelve. Dee Dee nudged me. She was worried about one elderly woman and one well-dressed woman in her forties. They both looked like they were sympathizing with him.

For a moment, I let it slip. My heart felt sorry for him. He seemed to be in such a tight spot. Not a single character witness had been asked to testify on his behalf.

Then I caught myself letting my compassion do an end run around justifiable anger at this man whose deeds I knew so well.

Flaherty wanted the jury to understand that this intimidation was vital to justifying the three felony charges. "What was Tim feeling? Tremendous fear. He was *terrified.* You've got an intoxicated, violent, angry man that's demonstrated a willingness to use a firearm . . ."

Dee Dee elbowed me. "He's doing that ghoul thing." I looked at the defendant. His handsomeness had disappeared as he performed a weird tic with his mouth, the slithering lip-licking again—the habit quite at odds with his movie-star looks.

Flaherty deftly brought the jury back into the double-wide when Duran strode in, grabbed Tim, and ordered him to go with him. He reminded the jury again, "He's intoxicated. He's very angry. The one time Tim confronted him about something—what happened?"

Flaherty picked up the cold shining thing, the gleaming black King Cobra .357 Magnum in all its badass beauty, and in an adroit move, placed it on the ledge in front of the jury box. A pretty young woman was seated there, stylishly dressed. As the King Cobra materialized in front of her, her eyes widened and her suspenders stretched over her chest, rounding with a deep intake of breath.

"What else could he do? What else could you expect an eighteen-year-old in that situation to do—except go with the crazy man with the gun?" Flaherty asked the twelve citizens. I noticed a zigzag vein, his fighting Irish blood, throbbing on Flaherty's right temple.

He let a long pause drop to the floor.

Flaherty summed up with that singular point of terror: "Keep in mind what happened when Timothy confronted him—the one and only time he confronted him that evening. Duran had the gun pointed at him. When he accuses the defendant of being crazy, he's told, 'You don't know the half of it.' What does that communicate? That felt to me, boy: This guy's not just a crazy man. He's beyond that. That's telling me I'm underestimating him if I think he's just crazy. He's not just crazy, he's extremely violent."

The spirit of Shakespeare must have been on hand. Timed precisely to the line, *"He's not just crazy, he's extremely violent,"* a thundercloud burst and hail pelted the octagonal skylight above the courtroom.

"In other words, don't think I won't use this gun on you," Flaherty ended with a flourish. "What other conclusion can you draw?"

I watched Dirk as he vigorously wagged his head from side to side—no! no! no! He looked at the jury as if to say, No, it's not true!

Dirk's counsel was up to bat, and he spent much time assuring the jury that they should draw no conclusion from the fact that Mr. Duran hadn't testified on his own behalf, which naturally planted in everyone's mind: Why hadn't he? Of course *we* knew why he hadn't. Because he would have flashed his volcanic temper under cross-examination. The gentlemanly DeKalb did a yeoman's job of mounting a defense, minimizing and rationalizing, making the point that none of the foaming and raving had been directed at Mr. Bidwell. The "you don't know the half of it" remark was merely a response to Mr. Bidwell's chewing him out for firing out the window.

Throughout his attorney's recitation, Dirk vigorously nodded his head up and down. Yes. Yes. Yes! From my post behind and to the right of him, I decoded his brow ridges doing this feint of innocence. I made drawings of his expressions in my notebook. Bad acting: the brow ridges and long-lashed, wide-open eyes were cartoonish in their depiction of innocence, boyishness—appealing, pleading, ingratiating.

"And, yes, maybe Mr. Duran was a wild man that night . . ."

A wild man that night? My eyes did a zoom from Dirk to the jury. All were listening intently.

"And I think if you and I have been close to events, close to people who get us excited, scared of what might happen . . ." The defendant's counsel had made a mistake in admitting Dirk was a wild man that night, but he was reading the jury. Now he was as much as admitting to the lesser charge, to get his client off the charges where he'd do the big time: coercion and kidnapping. DeKalb summarized: ". . . but you've also been in those situations and know that it wasn't kidnapping and it wasn't coercion against you." Then the defense counsel sort of fizzled out.

We all left for the deliberation and sat outside the courtroom—the concerned citizens, the Kounses, Boo, and I. The defendant stood with his dad, who had turned up. The victim was surrounded by the women in his life—girlfriend, mother, and grandmother, who had taken a day off work to support their brave boy. Tim's young mother, Connie, had known Dirk Duran's reputation since her school days, and she'd warned her son to stay away from him. She whispered to me that I might now have an opportunity to saunter past Dirk, my lipsticked scar at his blue-eyed level. I rose, and at that instant, as though he had radar, so did the tall blue-eyed man, then his tiny dad along with him.

He and his dad walked into an anteroom of the courthouse that had been cordoned off. He stood silhouetted in the shadows, motionless, looking out the window, held his arm above him against the glass, posed like an actor. I took my place under a skylight, light flooding me, volcanoes stretching across the horizon behind me. I crossed my legs, crossed my cowboy boots, crossed my arms, and watched him. He turned around and from the shadows I could see he was looking back at me. He crossed his arms and crossed his legs, mirroring my stance.

I was in the light and he in the shadow. A sign stood between us, marking the area behind where he stood, which read, improbably, DANGER. KEEP OUT. CAUTION. TEMPORARILY CLOSED.

There was an uncanny synchronicity here: I remembered a premonitory poem I had written twenty years before:

So we'll meet again. Only
This time (if you don't mind)
I'll stand.
I want to be

More dignified than previously
When you came like a flash and
Tried to abscond with my life.

How true my words had turned out to be:

Society sure enough will keep
You around (we're civilized in most
States). Life clings even to its blunders.
I survived in spite of you.
And you'll survive in spite of yourself.

It was surely remarkable that I had bent destiny to my will so that I could play out this poetic showdown. But other than that, this was no Hollywood cinematic climax. In the Hollywood version, the punishment would fit the crime. Justice would prevail. Society would return to balance.

Not this time. A substantial gap still separated June 22, 1977, from this day. These charges were but a minor comeuppance, this trial but a token.

We were called in. I took a step toward the courtroom. The tall defendant and his little dad moved in my direction, as though they wanted to talk to me or look at me or possess the space by the window where I had just stood, although that space was not on the way into the courtroom. I walked right past him, and sure enough, he took the space right under the skylight I had just occupied.

I walked into the courtroom and lost sight of him. We were asked to "All rise." We were asked to sit. I missed the bench and fell to the floor. Hands from either side of me pulled me up.

It had taken the jury an hour to deliberate. They filed in, and the foreman stood to recite the verdict. "We the jury . . . do find the defendant NOT GUILTY of the offense of kidnapping two. GUILTY of the offense of unlawful use of a dangerous weapon with a firearm. And GUILTY of the offense of coercion."

That outcome loosed in me a relief so deep that my menses started to flow.

Flaherty insisted that the defendant was a flight risk, and that witnesses were terrified of him, so he should be remanded to jail until sentencing. The judge agreed. We, sitting behind the prosecutor, all decompressed with relief. I could read disbelief in the defendant's countenance. This was the first time he had not succeeded in escaping judgment. These were his very first felony convictions.

With dramatic flair, he lowered his hands and in slow motion brought them around his back as they manacled him.

The man likes slow motion, I thought, remembering the axe lowering over me, remembering what his ex-wife had told me: "Everything's got to be slow, because he enjoys watching."

He trudged slowly, as if he were in a chain gang, to the back of the courtroom;

then he turned and fixed his gaze on me for a moment, and then trudged out the door.

Wholly unexpectedly, a rush of emotion charged through me. I burst into tears, leaned over, and covered my face. I could feel hands, many sets of hands, on my back. They came from every direction, from people sitting in the benches near me, some I knew, some who knew me.

When I looked up, I caught the judge's eye at the front of the courtroom as he was clearing papers from the bench. He had watched me cry.

As we filed out of the courtroom, one of the county commissioners who had dropped by the trial said, "This community really needs this. We've needed this for twenty years." That was Linda Swearingen, formerly of the Redmond Chamber of Commerce.

I ran for shelter in a bathroom stall. Euphoric. Sweaty. My heart racing.

NO, I NEVER got a confession. But the cumulative testimony that I had gathered—both conflicting and converging stories—had ultimately tumbled into a coherent picture. Dirk Duran fit the crime: A guy who tucked his shirt in his pants with ritual meticulousness. A guy who had a fetish for axes and hatchets. A guy who had told a number of people over the years why he hadn't done it, was obsessed with not having done it, and who varied the details of why he hadn't done it in such a way that his story was never consistent. A guy who was well known to have reflexes that were never anything but violent, who had violence running in his veins, who packed rage against women, who'd committed an array of other ignominious deeds. A guy who was the only other person besides me who thought he saw hands chopping up two women, and thought about it every day of his life. My own detective work had turned up no contrary evidence whatsoever, no indications that he was not guilty, nothing to exonerate him. What are the odds of another individual fitting that description?

Did I hate him? No. I didn't feel hate for him. Not as Dee Dee and Bob Kouns hated their daughter's murderer. I didn't hate him, because after all this, there was an avoidance strategy I'd never entirely let go of: he was only a headless torso, a phantom force I had once struggled with.

Though I felt rage about my missing muscle, and rage on behalf of his other victims, I literally had to remind myself of the magnitude of his crime against me. I was still partially blind, sight disabled in perceiving the enormity of it. I had to remind myself of his truck that had tried and failed to stop my breath, of those percussive blows—of how he had drawn so much blood that Clyde Penhollow had needed a *fire hose* to wash it out of Bill's pickup.

Would I forgive him? No.

He had done nothing to deserve forgiveness. He'd never confessed, and even if he were willing, and he was not, what would that look like? A public confession and an expression of remorse wouldn't expunge his crimes. As the suspect sup-posedly had said himself, in a Bible study group when he was only seventeen, "Some things are unforgivable." As murderer-in-cold-blood Perry Smith said to the Kansas director of penal institutions before he marched to the scaffold, "Mr. McAtee, I'd like to apologize. But to whom? To you? To them? To their relatives? To their friends? . . . And undo what we did with an *apology*?"

In my view, Leo Tolstoy got it right in a story, "The Kreutzer Sonata," about a man who murdered his wife. Just after he dealt her a fatal stab, he cried out, "For-give me!" She answered him as she faded away, "Forgiveness; all that is rubbish. Oh, if I could only keep from dying."

What did he really mean to me, this man, this criminal, this Dirk Duran? What he meant to me had evolved. At first he was a random attacker whose identity never interested me; then he was a character in my drama of self-recovery. He was something else now: I would let this showdown with him stand as a symbol for bringing all tyrants to heel. Dirk Duran did what he did, all of it, because he could get away with it. We need to eliminate from the earth the all-too-common impunity with which perpetrators are able to act.

AT THE OUTCOME of the trial, Bob and Dee Dee and I all shared a levitational feeling, as if we were leaving solid ground. With this malefactor on ice for a while, we could relax. Bob and Dee Dee savored the fruits of this conclusion as deeply as I.

Outside the courtroom, Dee Dee hugged the victim in this case, Tim Bidwell, who had pulled himself up in a heroic way on the stand. In this culture, there are no ego rewards for standing up in public and admitting vulnerability. He further endeared himself to me when he told me—Tim never looked me in the eye, only sideways—that he had decided to show up and testify when he learned that Dirk beat his wife and girlfriend.

The burly boy also said he wanted to show me a place where Dirk told him spooky stories while they drove home from work.

Gallons of Deschutes River water made sure the Redmond cemetery had the thickest green grass carpet the desert could muster. Riding his motorcycle, Tim led me to a grave he knew Dirk was fond of. The grave belonged to a woman born in 1882, who had died a good many decades ago, when Redmond was barely a few crosshatches on the desert. Her gravestone was graced with fairly fresh silk flowers. There was a five-pointed star carved into the granite, and inside the star were little carved ciphers, curiously abstruse, which gave the feeling that the one who lay beneath was a practitioner of the black arts. Around the ciphers were let-ters arranged in a circle. Tim and I picked out the letters one by one: F . . . A . . . T . . . A . . . In unison we chorused, "FATAL."

The one who lay beneath this gravestone had a curious epitaph—either chilling or self-evident, depending on how you looked at it. Tim told me this particular sequence of letters had enchanted Dirk Duran, and he used to trace his fingers over them as you might do a crayon gravestone rubbing.

The abiding question arose again in my mind: Why did he leave me alive? Surely not even he knew why. But I imagined that since he believed he was godly, he enjoyed a godly role, as both death-dealer and life-giver.

I hugged Tim goodbye and set out from the green glen toward the humming traffic of Redmond. En route, I passed a huge frontier grave containing the remains of one of the town patriarchs and founders. It reminded me of a woman with that same last name, one of the man's descendants, no doubt. Her name was Justine, and felon Chris Peterson tipped me off that I should talk to her. I always had a strong hunch that of the dozens of names that remained on my interview list, this was a lead I must follow.

Skinned Alive

What is written with a pen cannot be hacked
away with the axe.

—OLD RUSSIAN PROVERB

For an entire week in late June 1997, on
the twentieth anniversary of the event, the marquee outside the squat *Redmond
Spokesman* office called out in bold letters: "Axe Victim Names Suspect."

The story behind this remarkable signage was the uncanny confluence of three
factors: the anticipated legislation to remove the statute of limitations on attempted murder, the prime suspect's anticipated incarceration, and the twentieth
anniversary of the Cline Falls attack. The time was ripe: on June 22, the Kounses
and I independently sent a press release to media all over the state and held three
press conferences, in Portland, Salem, and in Cline Falls itself, to air allegations
against a suspect in the long-ago Cline Falls case, who was, at that very moment,
in the Deschutes County jail awaiting sentencing for his recent crimes.

My allegations could not be prosecuted in a criminal court of law—which led
to a curious conundrum. If the case were prosecutable, I believed that the suspect's guilt was provable. But since the case was *not prosecutable*—thanks to an
arbitrary law, thanks to this limited statute of limitations—was it then *not provable*? The crime falls into an odd vacuum.

I knew I had the moral high ground. The state had wronged me, and the state
had wronged the public by exposing them to a dangerous man who remained at
large when he should have been apprehended two decades ago. As Jean Amery
writes, "The moral person demands annulment of time—in the particular case
under question, nailing the criminal to the deed."

We conducted our press conference independently, although with private nods
of approval from officials of the state. Deputy District Attorney Pat Flaherty knew
the value of laying to rest this old case. He made it clear that he would have used
resources to prosecute if the statute hadn't expired.

It was a case, as I saw it, that could have been won beyond a reasonable doubt from a stew of circumstantial evidence, along with elliptical statements which Dirk Duran made after his failed polygraph:

The state would have established his patterns of violence, his patterns of deceit, his specific manner of dress and grooming, which matched my memory. His post-attack behavior: heavy use of Valium and alcohol, his murderousness the day after Cline Falls, the missing toolbox, the tire tracks allegedly matching the tracks left at the crime scene. His dangerousness in the months afterward: How he ran people off the road with his truck. How he later sought to soothe his conscience in a Bible study group.

A string of witnesses could have been brought in to form a picture of what likely happened the night of June 22, 1977. Dirk and Janey had a fight at Dirk's house. Dirk was getting violent. Dad stopped the fight and took Janey home. Since Dirk didn't get to finish his fight, he filled himself with drugs and alcohol and flew off into the night, down to Cline Falls. Afterward, late at night, he showed up at Janey's house acting weird. The next day he showed up at her place of work, still on Valium and vodka, and flew into a murderous rage.

The state could have brought his family before a grand jury and asked Mom and Dad a few unusual questions to rattle their well-rehearsed stories: Mom, did Dirk ever wash his own clothes? Did he even know how to use a washing machine? Did you remember your son leaving the house the night of June 22, 1977? And Dad: Was it you who supplied your son with two boy's axes, one with a double blade and one with a single blade? Seems like you paid attention to axes. Wouldn't you have been suspicious when you heard of an axe attack in Cline Falls that took place while you were driving Janey home, just after your son got into an argument with her?

I'd love to see Dirk's sister, Betty, with her hand on a Bible. Maybe Betty had been listening to Dirk and Janey fight. She knew her dad left the house and Dirk stormed out just in time to commit the Cline Falls attack. What else did she know?

The state's ace in the hole: Dirk's behavior after the 1995 failed polygraph. I would like to have watched the faces of the jury as Fred Ackom took the stand: "But after the test, when he was told the results read deceptive, he was a changed man. And what does he do? Does he lash out at me? No. He cowers. He holds his head down. Won't look at me. Starts bawling, tears streaming down his face. I've never had anybody reach out and grab my hand like that. It startled me. And I just grabbed his hands and held on to them."

I could have used the exact wording of the "admissions" Dirk made to the examiner afterward, about how he has pictured the attack every day since it happened. "I know I didn't do it but maybe I don't believe that"; "I swear to God I didn't do it, may God strike me dead right now if I did this."

Dirk made admissions to others as well—Kelly, Donny, Ruby. This hearsay testimony overlapped, and together formed a picture of a man trying to admit a crime. Robert Lee's testimony about Ruby telling him that Dirk confessed the Cline Falls attack "over and over" might have inspired Ruby to come clean about what Dirk really told her.

A string of witnesses could have attested to the shifting nature of the alibi Dirk was trying to put forth. And it could have been proven that he was in the vicinity of the park that night—proximity is a key piece of any prosecutor's story. Bart Firestone could have testified that he remembered Janey telling him, "Dad, he let me off fifteen minutes before the attack." The Firestones lived four miles from Cline Falls. Dirk himself lived less than three miles from the park. Ultimately it could have been proved that Dirk could *not* produce an alibi or an alibi witness. Dirk just couldn't clear himself.

As I wrote my press release, I relished the thought of going public. I meant to flush the hidden secrets from their hiding places. It incensed me that Dirk Duran could continue to lie. I wanted to fight his deceit by piling up evidence, mountains of it. Surely now I would find out if there was a band of conspirators who had helped Dirk cover up. Soon, I felt sure, I'd hear from one of his buddies to whom he had confessed.

I was the soul of courage, until the news got out around the state.

Then I flew into a state of primal terror. I could feel dangerous tremors shaking the county jail. I felt the weight of responsibility. I had exposed not only myself but also others in the community, people who had generously helped me. Nobody knew whether he would remain behind bars.

One night, an intrusive fragment of memory seeped into my dreams: the smell of blood. The olfactory sense bypasses the filters of the brain, goes right to the emotional centers. This fragment of sense memory ignited the past. In some imaginary dimension, I felt locked in mortal combat with him. I was under his control, in his hands, totally vulnerable, exposed on all fronts. Skinned alive.

I drove helter-skelter, escaped the juniper breath of Central Oregon, and hid out in a tiny inn among old-growth trees on the rain forest side of the Cascades. Dee Dee and Bob bolstered my courage. Boo's soothing words coaxed me out of hiding. "Come home," she said to me.

Then, as suddenly as it began, the spell broke. I rejoined the present, calmed down, drove into the desert again, and stayed at the ranch with Boo and her mother.

THE REDMOND SPOKESMAN, the same newspaper that was so tight-lipped in 1977, more than compensated for its past reticence with a two-page story that got most of the details correct. Marlen Hein gladly spoke to the press, confirming that Dirk Duran had been identified as a possible suspect even in 1977. Even Detective Lynn Fredrickson seemed to have come around. He told the reporter that the victim had presented the Oregon State Police with "some pretty powerful stuff that raised a lot of red flags" about Dirk Duran's possible involvement in the attack. The article quoted Detective Fred Ackom's assertion—based on the failed polygraph in July 1995—that "Duran did not answer truthfully when he denied that he had attacked Jentz and Weiss in 1977."

The reporter made a call to the Deschutes County jail, where Dirk was being held before sentencing. Instead of the usual line you read in newspapers, something about "tried to make contact but so-and-so declined our calls," Dirk eagerly took the reporter's call in regard to his guilt or innocence in the Cline Falls attack.

For the record he said, "I had nothing to do with that."

While the marquee was broadcasting the bold news during the last week of June, I drove around the community to make contact with my allies, and found a surround sound of support for my efforts. Dirk's old boss Pat invited me and Boo on a complimentary ride on his murder mystery train. We wound through green fields of emerald alfalfa, past gorgeous canyon country still untouched by encroaching development—until outlaws in black hats with guns stopped the train, jumped aboard, and caused a few passengers to scream in terror.

I even found Lureen, this time in Sisters, in yet another waitress's uniform. She flashed me her final conspiratorial smile.

In keeping with the folkways of 1977, when the sensational story broke again in 1997, the grapevines were quivering, but publicly this community in the American West was as mum as it had been twenty years before. No one wrote a letter to the editor. Nary a one called.

The deeply unsettling feeling came back to me, a mood of mistrust that a dark secret at the heart of the matter was still lurking in this community. No one could miss a big marquee in a small town—why hadn't the news stirred up a public dialogue about how this community had allowed this crime to remain unsolved?

What *had* hindered the pursuit of truth and justice? Had people's unwillingness to falsely accuse trumped their responsibility to protect the safety of their own community? Were the claims that they didn't want to falsely accuse a way of distancing themselves from the circumstances, a way of maintaining a willful ignorance?

Actually (according to the reporter who covered the story) one woman did phone the newspaper—none other than the suspect's mom. Lou Ellen Duran scolded the reporter and the newspaper for implicating her son in something he hadn't done!

Now I felt that I was squaring off against my suspect's mom, and that caused me another irrational fright. I thought of *Beowulf* again. The monster Grendel who arose from his lair to unleash murderous rampages throughout the kingdom didn't arise from a swamp. He had a mother.

My hopes were dashed that I would find a band of Dirk's conspirators, or another buddy to whom Dirk had spilled his guts. No leads emerged whatsoever. A couple of weeks passed. Then Dirk's former boss Mike called me at Boo's ranch to tell me that a guy named Jerry who had been part of Dirk's circle growing up wanted to talk to me.

BOB, DEE DEE, and I sat on the grass with Jerry in front of the Hub Motel along the highway, under the second-oldest willow tree in Redmond—which had had the misfortune to still be alive when the Hub Motel turned into the "Felony Flats" (the same Felony Flats, coincidentally, where my suspect had been living until his recent incarceration, in a tiny room with the curtains drawn tight). I was much relieved to be back in my investigator's skin.

Jerry was a sprite of a man, square-jawed with a cap down over his eyes and a buff, hairless open chest where a cross dangled. He was the one who told us that the majestic tree swaying above us was the second-oldest willow in Redmond, a fact he happened to know because he had been privileged to grow up under the very oldest willow in Redmond. Jerry, tree lover, was a decent guy, he wanted us to know. He did have a small criminal record—got caught once lobbing hand grenades into his own corral. Cops thought he was a terrorist, but apparently he had nothing like terror on his mind. He simply wanted to watch the spectacle of thirty-foot mushroom clouds exploding in the dirt. He laughed in a backwoods-psycho sort of way, and he twitched, but I had a hunch he really was benign. He admitted he was an alcoholic, living on disability.

"Dirk and me. We've been friends for quite a few years. Grew up together. And sometimes I think Dirk was a little touched. 'Specially when he'd been drinkin' and druggin'. And I'm not saying I don't like to drink.

"When that happened back in '77, there were a lot of drugs going around. Methamphetamines. Acid. Opium. Magic mushrooms all starting to hit all at once in the seventies."

"So what did you hear back then when Cline Falls happened?" I asked.

"Quite a few things. There were lots of stories going around. And I talked to Dirk a little while after it happened. I just told him, 'We grew up together. We've been friends a long time. I want you to look me straight in the eye. I want you to tell me the truth.' And he looked me straight in the eye and said, 'I didn't do it.' He said, 'My truck was there.'

"Because we all was in and out of there. And he said, 'I didn't do it.' I believe if he said he didn't do it, I had to go along with the assumption that he didn't actu-ally do the actual whatever. That I don't know. I wasn't there. I didn't see it. I be-lieve he does know who did. I believe he was so messed up that somebody could have been driving his truck. His truck was in and out of there. So was my truck that night. That's where we all went. We's always there and gone and there and gone. That happened five, six nights a week. And he admitted to me that, yes, his truck was there. That he did have a hatchet in the back of his truck, or he had an axe in the back of his truck and a hatchet underneath the backseat of his truck, and admitted getting in a fight with his girlfriend and he did smack her around and he was very abusive."

He did have a hatchet in the back of his truck, or he had an axe in the back of his truck and a hatchet underneath the backseat of his truck? Did this explain the discrepancy in the story? That he carried this hatchet or axe, this boy's axe, in both places?

"And when he gets to drinkin'," Jerry continued, "He gets un-understandable."

Just as I asked him what he meant by "un-understandable," a woman wandered over, Jerry's friend, bombed out of her mind. She'd been pretty once. But her face was puffy and her features were wandering all over her face, not as her DNA had originally prescribed for her. Bob and Dee Dee introduced themselves as my helpmates, people who helped people who'd been hurt by criminals.

"Where were you when I needed you?" she slurred. "I'm serious. I've got scars. I was abused. I was hit in the face and nobody was there for me."

"It's a real common story," Bob said.

"And it's not a good one," said Jerry.

"So you were saying, Jerry," I went on, as lacy branches whipped in a stiff desert wind. "He told you his truck was there and his hatchet was there but he was not there."

"No, I'm saying that he said his truck had been there, and that he was there, but he did not do it. Now that's what he told me. He was there like that day. We'd all been in and out of there. He was there and we were there and there was a whole bunch of other people there."

"Do you think he always tells the truth?" Dee Dee asked.

"As far as I know, he's always been truthful with me."

"Did he show you the axe or hatchet?" I asked.

"Nope. But in my truck, I also had a shovel, a hatchet, a pick. Tools. Everybody did back then. We all had implements of destruction, tools of the trade. If you didn't carry a hatchet or an axe or a shovel or a rack in your truck you must have been from somewhere else. I carry a golf club just for clubbing snakes." Jerry kept talking about how drugs and alcohol can make anyone do anything; then he got more to the point.

"But I thought for a lot of years, he could have been blacked out and not remembered. And it could have been he didn't do it but somebody that was with him might have, and he's not wanting to say. But basically it all comes down to the same. When you do drugs and alcohol, no telling what can happen."

As I spoke with Jerry, the drunk woman kept bending Bob and Dee Dee's ear. She believed Bob and Dee Dee were sent from a divine place to save her. She told them her husband had sex with her child, and another of her children was raped by somebody else. She knew that Bob and Dee Dee had come to save her. She'd seen them in a dream. The two of them looking just like they did now. Dee Dee in her flowing white dress, under this very willow tree.

I wanted to see this drama play out, but Jerry took me aside.

"People always have asked him what happened, what happened, what happened, and it's always been the same: 'I didn't do it.' People would walk blocks to stay away from him. Everybody double-questioning him. And triple-asking him. He's really getting tired. It's starting to upset him because he almost hasn't had a moment's peace since. Because it's still brought up. It's like he's known as the hatchet man. But back when, when everyone was accusing him of doing it, I told him, 'You're not going to lie to me, you tell me the truth.' 'Jerry, I didn't do it.' That's not saying he wasn't there. I took it that he didn't physically do it, but I took it that he knows more than he's saying. If he didn't do it—and I don't know if he did, all I know is what he told me—I have no reason to disbelieve it. And, you know, it could have been anybody. It could have been me."

I put my hand on little Jerry's bony shoulder. "It wasn't you, Jerry."

"I'm just saying I don't know."

As we walked to my car, he looked me straight in the eye and said, "Tell me something. Was it Dirk?"

I said I believed it was Dirk.

"Thanks," Jerry said, dead serious. "I needed to know."

The drunk woman came to my window and looked at me with her one eye that could still see straight ahead. Her other eye wandered off somewhere into the willow branches. She told me she thought I was prettier than she was, and she was jealous.

"You don't look chopped up," she said.

A Scary Guy Goes Down

The sentencing of the guilty party whose penal fate so interested me was set for one month after the trial and I wanted company for that show. I headed to Washington to find Kelly. Though it had been months since our last contact, the screen door flapped open and she grabbed me into a bear hug, surrounding me with protective energy. News traveled fast across state lines. Someone had given Kelly the Redmond newspaper.

At dinner at a country-western steak joint, Kelly told me she wanted to tell Dirk's parents that the best thing for their son and for them would be to have him behind bars for a while. She thought his parents were nice people. They liked her. She was the only girlfriend of Dirk's that passed muster with them. One time Dirk pissed Kelly off, and she threatened to leave him with his parents. His dad Lou got irate. "Oh, no, you brought him down here. You bring him back."

And yet: "In their eyes he was perfect. No room for flaw."

Kelly had a compulsive need to tell more stories about Dirk. She rattled them off, one after the next, examples of his pure spite and treachery. These were not criminally prosecutable acts, but I was compelled to listen anyway, to harvest more examples of his appalling conduct. Because he was still somewhat of an abstraction to me, I needed to bring him before me as a living, detestable presence. Even after all that I knew, I still needed evidence, data, constant confirmation of what I didn't want to believe—that I shared human nature with people like him, who lived life guided by a spirit of perverseness, who did wrong for wrong's sake only.

Something struck me about Kelly: life had dealt her a cruel hand, and she had survived. Because of her strength and toughness, honesty and compassion, she might have thrived—had it not been for the deeply ingrained habit of forgiving the wrongdoings of the tyrants surrounding her. Kelly did a tango between playing the pliant, yielding, forgiving, sentimental female, the redeemer to the bad boy—and fighting back. In the end, she did fight back, managed to clock Dirk enough times to inflict some real pain, made him see some real consequences for his actions.

Yeah, Kelly told me. She would be glad to take a little trip to Bend, Oregon, to accompany me to the penalty phase of Dirk's trial. "At first, I put it behind me. Now I'm angry. I want revenge. But I worry that revenge isn't going to be enough for me. I'll want more and more."

WHEN THE DEFENDANT sauntered into the courtroom on the day of his sentencing in July 1997, his shirt was wrinkled (Mom hadn't been on hand at the jail to iron his clothing), his face puffy with prison pallor, and his eyes bloodshot. He walked with a slight limp. He had gained weight and now emitted none of the slick movie-star radiance of his previous appearance. In fact, this time he looked like the sort of lowlife whom you'd expect to find standing before a judge.

This time his mom was present in the courtroom. Her hair coiffed in tight curls, she was dressed as if she were attending a dinner party, in nice clothes patterned black and white; and she exuded a rather effervescent mood considering the circumstances. Also demonstrating their familial loyalties were his dad, his face looking like the smithy had struck the anvil one too many times, and Dirk's sister, quite a few pounds heavier than when I'd seen her a year before. The family unit sat on the left side of the courtroom behind the defendant's table, along with a few family friends.

The proceedings began. Both lawyers presented their arguments. Mom and sister occasionally shot poison darts my way. The convicted occasionally blew his nose into a red bandanna or scratched notes on a yellow legal pad.

It took some time. But then he caught a glimpse of Kelly over his right shoulder. She was sitting to my right. I noticed that she was shaking. He couldn't turn around and stare, so his eyeball rotated to the right and bulged out of the side of his face. What was he thinking now as he realized I had barged into his life so thoroughly that I had found his ex-girlfriend in another state?

This eye movement was a remarkable feat of facial distortion akin to his lip-licking, reptile-like mannerism. I noticed his eye was startling blue. So blue today, and so dark when I saw him a month before. How does he do it? Could he command his eyes to change color? Could he narrow his pupils to a point where there was almost nothing to see but iris, then open his pupils to pools of darkness?

Kelly made an eat-shit-and-die facial expression back at him: the sweetness of revenge. If only this eat-shit-and-die gesture could speak for all women who would find themselves in the same straits. But alas, I knew only too well that Kelly and Scotty wouldn't be the last women Dirk would hoodwink. His attractiveness was a kind of black art. And I knew with certainty that he would keep the next one between the earth and a stick.

In a bid for the maximum penalty, Prosecutor Flaherty argued that Duran's history showed an escalating pattern of violence tied to the use of alcohol and drugs, and that he persistently denied responsibility for his crimes and showed no remorse for any criminal conduct he was engaged in. Flaherty drew the judge's attention to the pre-sentence investigation, which had proved Duran expressed no remorse whatsoever for his criminal conduct in this case.

The defense, Jock DeKalb, claimed Duran's record showed no escalation in violence. In fact his record consisted mostly of traffic violations or instances in which he was charged with crimes, which were later dismissed, and "you cannot rely upon simply an allegation in a complaint which was later dismissed to find that there's a pattern of escalating violence."

(Actually, there was a lot of truth to what the defense was arguing. Duran was rarely arrested for his deeds. Or he was arrested a total of thirteen times in Oregon, and six in other states—but the charges were dropped, or pled down. When he beat his wife so viciously, in July of 1987, that she was finally able to find the will to escape for good, he ended up with only an "assault in the fourth degree" on his record. And even that charge was dismissed. When Deschutes County finally cleaned up their records files and made them accessible by computer, I was able to peruse Duran's record, and learned that the victim, Ruby, had apparently struck some sort of deal that ended up in an "order of dismissal as a civil compromise." I can imagine the reason why: Ruby didn't want to face the ordeal of a trial.)

With regard to the prosecution's assertion that Mr. Duran showed no remorse, his defense attorney countered, "Yes, there's no remorse. Mr. Duran will tell you he didn't commit these crimes. He is convinced that the alleged victim lied about what took place."

Kelly reached for my hand as we waited for the judge's sentence.

Judge Sullivan said that he would consider the "pre-sentence investigation" in his determination. And thanks to law enforcement, this time Dirk's full criminal history—a chronicle of his misdeeds taken from police reports, along with an in-depth interview with the defendant about his criminal history, was presented to the judge. Criminal histories didn't reach judges' eyes often enough. But this time Dirk wouldn't be sentenced in a vacuum.

Judge Sullivan looked up from the pre-sentence investigation and said with authority, "Mr. Duran, you are a scary guy."

Scary? Dirk hung his head. For a moment he himself looked scared. Then he wagged his head from side to side. Mom and his sister, Betty, were holding themselves in a particularly rapt and erect posture as this pronouncement reached their ears.

When the judge asked Dirk if he had any remarks to make, Dirk stood with his notepad and spoke.

I sat up straight, all antennae alert. In a slow Western cadence with terribly earnest and contrite tones—like a bad soap opera actor's rendition of vulnerability—he talked about how he'd had some troubles in his day, but he wanted a fresh new beginning. He'd like a chance to be a productive member of society, the best person he could be, and there were people in this very room who believed in him, and *who knew his heart* . . .

To my right I could see Kelly nodding *yes!*

I watched the judge. The judge never once looked at Dirk while he was talking. When Dirk sat down, Judge Sullivan shuffled his papers and fell silent a long time. Then he pronounced his sentence: Dirk Duran would spend five years in the state prison (it would be his first visit there), followed by two years of post-prison supervision.

My body erupted in an involuntary emotional release. My scalp was soaking and my eyes were wet as sheriffs squired him away, chained and manacled, walking with his swaggering carriage, one haunch and one shoulder followed by the next haunch and shoulder. Before he left the courtroom he paused, turned back, and glared at Kelly.

Defiantly, she held his gaze.

Part Four

Nowhere else in the United States has nature so dramatically linked these two opposing forces—volcanic fire and glacial ice.

—STEPHEN L. HARRIS, *FIRE MOUNTAINS OF THE WEST*

Memory on Fire

The whole Deity [evil] has in its innermost or beginning
Birth, in the Pith or Kernel, a very tart, terrible *Sharpness*, in
which the astringent Quality is very horrible, tart, hard, dark
and cold Attraction or Drawing together, like Winter, when
there is a fierce, bitter cold Frost, when Water is frozen into
Ice, and besides is very intolerable.

—JACOB BOEHME

The events of the last few weeks had
washed the land innocent—innocent as my paternal grandmother's memory of
it. As a girl of three in 1909, she and her mother journeyed to the Pacific Northwest. Their train steamed through stands of giant pines. When they leaned out
the window to breathe in the fragrance, Margie lost hold of her teddy bear and
started to cry. My great-grandmother knew just what to say: "You dropped your
teddy bear in Santa's garden. Don't worry, he'll bring it back to you one day." As I
looked out the car window at the big trees carpeting the steep Cascade slopes, a
million overlapping triangles in receding folds, I thought of Santa's garden.

The sentencing of Dirk Duran was a culminating hour in my life. The once-
unnamed threat that had shadowed me had now been named and decommis-
sioned for a few years behind bars. An elected judge had entered into the
historical record "Mr. Duran, you are a scary guy" for all the world to know. This
was a liberating moment.

I felt liberated from imagining the shallow graves of murdered women, released from viewing this landscape as a charnel ground. Could I now change my
dark habits of mind? At one point during the peak of my obsession, I had seen a
sign that read, JEAN B. HARRIS MEMORIAL PARK, and imagined that Jean was a
woman who had been slain there. Of course with more sober thought, I had realized that no one wants to commemorate the places where dead women are found.

Perhaps now I could regard this exhilarating landscape as a playground, as
other, normal people did. I could do what other tourists do in Oregon: go fly-
fishing, or skiing, or river rafting, even camping. No, maybe not camping. When

I reached the Cascade summit at the Santiam Pass and slid down into the desert, the moist ocean air turned dry, and the Douglas fir and hemlock were replaced with ponderosa. The messy fragrance morphed into the edgy smell of pine. Once again my pulse quickened, my senses sharpened. My second self felt the death-scape lying farther along the road. I had to accept that this landscape and the synapses of my brain were fused, that the smell of pine and dry air was still linked to juniper and blood. This was my physical makeup, as unmistakable as my quirky patchwork skeleton.

THAT WEEKEND, I stayed on the ranch with Boo's family, and in spite of the babel of animal cries dinning in my ears, I relaxed. Sunday morning I found Boo fixing an irrigation pipe and told her that I was heading to a park somewhere to make notes about the extraordinary events of the past week.

This token trial and sentencing would not slake my tenacious drive to fill in all the gaps of the unfinished story of the summer of '77. Actually, I believed I would never cease wanting every piece, from every perspective.

This story—the story that only I could tell, the story I had to tell before I could tell any other, my rich, searingly extreme narrative—was yielding a compelling sense of purpose, was making me more real to myself. I sensed that the boundaries of this particular tale were infinitely expanding, and therefore possessed an infinite capacity to expand me.

"Where you going? Cline Falls?" Boo called out as I crunched down the driveway. Boo was always teasing—though I didn't admit to her how true it was that I haunted my shrine a good deal more than I would have wanted anyone to know.

I drove beyond Cline Falls, beyond Sisters, and began to climb scenic Highway 242, toward McKenzie Pass, and came to an abrupt halt at a metal fence barricading the road. A knot of angry people with a horse trailer milled about, led by a potbellied fellow with a misshapen felt cowboy hat and a four-day growth of beard, who bleated out in protest at being blocked from the scenic summit.

"This is our country! Sons of bitches gonna hear about it! This is our country!" His anger sweetened to rhapsody. "It's a beautiful country!" he brayed. I did a U-turn and headed to a park deep in an old-growth ponderosa forest. Among the cinnamon giants, I brought out my notebooks and closed my eyes. A few silent minutes passed and then I heard a *chop, chop, chop* sounding from a place in the forest directly in front of me. I opened my eyes to see two boys in the woods, hatchets in their hands, bearing down on a stump. By now I'd begun to believe that when a hatchet appeared in my path, it worked a sympathetic magic. I wondered, was a new piece of story about to show up?

I became fixated now on that pioneer tombstone in the Redmond cemetery, which reminded me of my hunch that I must follow up on finding a woman named Justine to hear whatever tales the felon Chris Peterson had insisted she had to tell. Of all the leads I never followed up on, it possessed me that I must not let this one go unheeded. My quest had taught me to be faithful to instinct and inner voice.

No surprise Justine wasn't listed in phone books. She was no longer living where Detective Fredrickson had tried to interview her during his investigation two summers before, when she had refused to give him any information because, as she told the cop, "Dirk Duran has caused me nothing but trouble." Chris Peterson had dropped a hint for me to check with a friend of Justine's, named Darendia. I found her house in a treeless development southwest of Redmond, and knocked on the door. Darendia's husband got Justine on the phone.

"This is kind of a weird call," I said to the slightly suspicious voice on the other end of the line, trotting out my girl-from-Cline Falls identity. "I want to talk to you about Dirk Duran."

"Is everything all right?" Justine shot back, with peculiar intimacy.

"Everything's fine, there's no problem," I said, thinking I sounded ridiculous to myself.

"He chopped you up. That's a big problem," she shot back again.

I FOLLOWED his white pickup through the grids of Redmond, onto Highway 97 toward Bend, until he turned into Desert Terrace Mobile Homes, the very neighborhood where Dirk Duran pummeled his girlfriend Scotty the year before. Small world.

"I don't know if I can help you." Justine was standing on the porch of her trailer. She stood under five feet tall, a small and round woman in her mid-thirties with shaggy bangs nearly covering her eyes—which followed my gaze to a conspicuous shrine, a circle of whitewashed rocks arranged at the base of a tree, a display of flowers and a sculpture of a squirrel. She forthrightly told me that I was looking at an altar she'd made for her son. It was many years ago when he was killed, at two and half years of age, by her boyfriend's mother, who hadn't seen him playing in the driveway when she backed a car out of it. Justine told me that there's something in the brain that says it's natural to lose a parent, and there's something in the brain that says it's unnatural to lose a child.

"I'm not in posttraumatic stress syndrome. I'm in stress syndrome. There's no *post* about it." She told me how she would lay awake at night and the nightmares would come, always about the death of her son. If only she'd swatted him on the butt and made him go back in, "I'd be a different person today."

I segued to the reason I'd made such effort to seek her out, when she obviously was trying not to be found.

"I know a lot of notorious people, sweetie, and I don't need the trouble it can cause." When I explained my need to investigate my own near murder, she interrupted me, cutting to the quick.

"I know Dirk did it." She quickly began to explain: "I went out with him for about three weeks. He was still married, I don't remember who she was, I don't think I ever met her. It was more of a business arrangement. I dealt dope with him. He had connections I didn't have. I had connections he wanted. That was right after my son was killed, and he was dead in '85, and I started going out with him. But I knew him from before. He's always been bad."

I asked her what went through her mind when she first heard about the Cline Falls attack back in 1977.

"I couldn't believe it. I couldn't believe anybody could do that. I remember I was pregnant with Felicity and I was working at the burger place—Longhorn Burgers had just opened up—and it was on the radio, and they were coming through the drive-through saying, 'You know who did it, you know who did it.' Everybody knew. Honey, within twenty-four hours everybody knew Dirk Duran did it. Everyone knew. There was never a question who did it. Nobody else was even suspected of doing it."

I wondered how she'd ended up in a business arrangement with this suspected axe murderer a few years later? Those were her "drugger" days, she told me. She'd been gravely pained and deeply vulnerable because of the trauma of losing her son. That made sense to me. I knew how Dirk liked to prey on heartsick women. Life was different for Justine now. She was a mother of three and drug-free, avoiding her notorious connections of years before.

"Back then, when this thing happened to you, there were sheets of acid coming through this town like balls o' fire, hon. Dirk was dealin', so probably he was fryin'. That's what I'm thinking. Did he think he killed you, I wonder?"

"He had to think he killed my friend because I put my hand into her brain."

"I had to do that with my son. I held his head together, I know what you mean."

I sensed I could deal in tough realism right off the bat with this oddly compelling woman.

"Yeah. I don't think Dirk planned that. The way he is, it must have been just a spontaneous burst of anger. He get in a fight with Janey that night?"

"She says no. Her friends say yes."

"Because when he'd get in a fight with her, man, he'd get really evil. We had Mountain Charlie's downtown—used to be a pizza parlor and a game room—and Dirk would come down there sometimes looking for Janey. He'd get pissed, he picked up a pool table and set it on its end and it went WHOOF—that's a heavy sucker. All the balls went flyin' everywhere. Dirk Duran is capable of a lot of things. I seen him strangle a puppy at a party one night. The puppy kept crying and he got pissed off and he was drunk, and he reached into the truck and POP. That was it."

If everyone in town knew and nothing was being done, did the town think the police were covering it up?

"Basically, yeah. It was just a hush-hush thing. Supposedly they didn't have enough evidence. Fact of the matter was, they didn't *look* for the evidence. And he's not the only one in this town who's gotten away with crap. And he won't be the last. It's not who you know but what you know about."

I could believe Dirk Duran was an informer, but what could he have known?

"It's what he knew about other people that he could give them. He knew all the dope dealers, was tight with all the homeboys—who was breaking into this and that. Dirk was fencing tools. You can't tell me cops did not know he had hot tools all over the place. He'd hock stolen property, drive to the valley and hock it. He had no visible means of employment, yet he had everything. How does he do that?" She broke off. "That night you got hurt—did the truck drive over the top of your tent? Did he try to stab you?"

"Chopped me up." Again, I intuited that bluntness was the language Justine understood best.

"With an axe. Had *D.D.* on it, huh?"

"I didn't see the *D.D.*, but I saw an axe."

"Well, everything Dirk Duran had had a *D.D.* on it."

We sat on the steps of her trailer and settled in for a long talk. She crackled with energy, as her recall of the past was immediate.

"I seen the friggin' hatchet," she said, a little throaty, below her breath.

"You've seen it?"

"I seen it. I seen him throw it in the woodstove. He burned it up."

I felt an electrical charge at the roots of my hair.

"Then he pulled out the metal and cleaned it out, right. Took all the ashes and everything else and put them in a bag and took it to a Dumpster downtown."

"How did it come up? Out of the clear blue sky, he's throwin' a hatchet in the fireplace!"

"It was right after his wife up and left. Because all the furniture was there, the baby crib was in the bedroom next to the bed. It had something to do with her. He couldn't do it before. He didn't want her to see it or something. And he had been up for a while. After somebody's been up, say, five days, they start to twist and they start telling you their whole life, and they think of things to do. It was like a ceremony, you understand. You had to have a witness. That make any sense? He went out into the garage and he pulled this bundle down from a shelf. He had it stashed way back—you know he's a pretty tall guy, long-armed, lanky. I remember it was way back because he had to reach way back on the shelf to bring it down. It was white T-shirt material. He brought it in the house. He unwrapped it. He had the hatchet wrapped up in this old ripped-up T-shirt material. And I didn't see any blood on it or anything. It was hot, see, it was summertime, and he built a fire. And he burned it. And he dumped it downtown, all the ashes and everything."

"He did it in front of you. He wanted you to see it."

"He wanted me to see it, the hatchet," she said, using, in the manner of so many others, *axe* and *hatchet* interchangeably. "It had *D.D.* cut like this." She drew a picture of that monogram in my notebook, forming each *D* with three straight sides, as though cut by a knife.

"Like triangles?"

"Yeah."

"Didn't you think it was weird he was building a fire on a hot day?"

"Yeah, but considering the state of his mind at that time, I wasn't going to question anything he did. He was in his own little world at that point. He took it down and he took it to the woodstove, and he got a good fire going, and he stuck it in there."

"When did you see it was an axe?"

"When he unwrapped it. That's when I said, 'What are you doing?' He told me, 'I've hurt somebody with this; I have to get rid of it.' I said, 'Well, why now?' And he says, 'Because it's the first time I've gotten a chance.' He had to get rid of it. I said, 'Why do you gotta get rid of it?' And he said, 'Well, you know.' I said, 'No, I don't know,' but I'm not trying to question him. I'm like, 'I don't know because I don't give a shit,' because I don't want him getting off on me, so he had to tell me the whole thing—that basically he used this to hurt someone and that he had to get rid of it. He didn't say he did it to you."

I was mesmerized by this piece of the story that had just made its entrance—the ceremonial burning of an axe. I felt terrifically alive.

In the background Justine's children and their friends were coming and going. Justine interrupted her tale to attend to maternal responsibilities. ("Are you leaving? Bye! Behave! See you later, Alice! You can come back anytime, honey! Have fun!") The instant they were out of the trailer she was again present with me, lucidly absorbed in the details of the past.

"He had that axe for a long time. The cops questioned him about it."

"How do you know they did?"

"Because he told me they did, that they took the tire track prints. And he laughed about that because what he did was, he took the tires and he took the front ones and put them on the back opposites, switched them around, and put them on the opposite sides, so they were balanced weird, and drove them out on a bunch of gravel. Drove on top of lava rocks to mess up 'identifying cracks,' he said. Something about 'identifying cracks.' 'If you can fix the identifying cracks and make them different' they can't prove the truck was there."

New information after all this time? Janey claimed he had mismatched tires. She knew the pattern in which they were mismatched. He knew that tire imprints had been left in the dirt of Cline Falls. That fact was printed in the newspapers.

He knew he had to change the distinctive pattern of his tires—the "identifying cracks." I remembered something Lureen had told me over two years before: "If you're innocent, you don't change your tires and try to destroy them." From what I interpreted from Durr's and Cooley's notes, Dirk's two front tires were worn differently, with the right having better tread than the left. His rear tires were bald. It would make solid sense to move his two treaded front tires to the back, and switch them, to opposite sides.

So the "smoking gun" turned out to be a smoking axe.

From what I knew about homicide investigations, the greatest chance of solving a murder occurs within the first twenty-four hours. I was hearing what sounded to me like a close approximation of a confession, and it was coming to light twenty years after the event, almost to the day.

I wondered aloud to Justine how the events of 1977 had suddenly became relevant on a hot summer morning in the mid-1980s.

"He was all wired. He was on speed. He did heroin and acid."

"Did you ever ask him: 'Did you do the Cline Falls thing?' "

"No, I'm not that dumb. I don't want to get killed. See, you never ask a crazy person a straight-up question like that. You just let them inform you what they want."

"So he's just telling you out of the clear blue sky."

"Oh, yeah. Yes."

"He said the cops investigated him?"

"Oh, yeah, they pulled him in. And after they pulled him in, he got rid of the axe. That axe had been under his pickup seat for the whole time."

"What do you mean, the whole time?" I fired at her, jumping into my prosecutor skin, to home in on this detail I had corroborated now four times.

"The whole time afterwards."

"What did he do with the blood?"

"I have no idea. He didn't tell me."

"It was under the pickup seat?" I asked again, by now accustomed to this fact.

"He threw it under the pickup seat where he always kept it. He had that hatchet a long time. He always had one. Always. The cops know he always did. He kept hatchets. Guns. He was into big swords, that come out of a sheath. He was really into samurai swords—you're damn lucky it was an axe. I can tell you, he's no good. Honey, if you can do something to keep him from hurting somebody else, maybe God will bless you. I'll tell you anything you want to know. I already put another man in jail for the rest of his life. I've got no qualms about it," she said in an especially tough tone of voice.

If I could believe another of my jailhouse sources, Ruby's ex-boyfriend Robert, Dirk had confessed Cline Falls many times to Ruby. But this "confession" was remarkable in that if the hatchet Justine saw was indeed the murder weapon, he had only one opportunity to burn it, and for some reason, he chose to burn it in front of Justine. Why? Justine let out an ironic chuckle.

"Men tell me secrets. I don't know. The only person my ex-husband Terry Abbott confessed to killing his girlfriend to was *moi*! They never found her body. Nicky has a metal plate in her abdomen from a surgery—when she was a child she had a disorder that made her bowels and stomach get all screwed up—and they put this plate in. There were only four or five of these made back East. You find that and you get ten thousand bucks. It's got a serial number and everything. He told me, 'Look between the pines and the junies. Her foot's in the junipers and her head's in the pines.' "

What? I cried with a hysterical edge. No matter how much I might wish to see this patch of Oregon landscape as a playground, wherever I looked I saw bones.

Perhaps your obsessions and your fate actually are one and the same.

"That's what he told me! That's what he told me!"

"Her foot's where?" I wanted to get it right.

"Her foot's in the juniper and her head's in the pines. It's where the pines and junipers meet. Do you know where the pines and juniper meet?"

"Up there in the Cascades," I said, knowing full well where they met—the transition between ponderosa pines into the still-drier zone of the junipers happened to be one of my prevailing obsessions.

"Uh-huh. That's where he wants you to think. There's somewhere else where they meet, too."

I scanned my mental map of Central Oregon.

"Right up there in the Ochoco Mountains," Justine prompted.

"Ahhh," I exclaimed, picturing that choppy landscape I'd ventured into three years before, on my own ceremonial drive along the BikeCentennial route, toward the town of Mitchell in the Ochocos, behind the curtain of where I was allowed to go in '77.

"It's a thought. Everyone has looked all over, scavenged all over for her. Who the heck says he took her out to the Cascades? He never said that. I know what he said. I was scared to death."

"Were you responsible for putting him away?"

"Yes, ma'am. I'm very proud of that fact. I have no remorse. I think Dirk and Terry Abbott, my ex-husband, are two of the most satanic men I ever met."

Justine spewed out in a torrent dozens of names of locals who might provide me with good leads to further my search, then finally began to wind down. She looked tired, but asked me, "Okay. What more do you want to know?"

I asked to hear the story of the ritual just one more time. I wanted to mine her memory for every detail it would yield. I needed her to corroborate her own story, as it seemed unlikely I would ever find supporting evidence for this tale.

"And then he burned it. Then he took all the ashes and the blade and everything and put them in a garbage bag, and he dumped it off downtown in a Dumpster," she repeated, recounting in a steady voice precisely the same details.

"How long did it take to burn?" I asked, for some curious reason. It was as though I was raising the presence of the axe, so that it might burn again—the repetition of the story becoming an incantation, a ritual. He had made her watch. I asked her to tell. I studied the image in my mind's eye, her story alchemizing the weapon from lethality to impotence, the mystery of flame reducing the mono-grammed handle to ashes, the blade to a hunk of white metal.

"I can't tell you exactly how long it took to burn. At that point in my existence, time was irrelevant to life. It didn't matter."

I suggested to Justine that he had performed this ritual in front of her eyes in order to break her down. So that he could prey on her.

"Yeah, because he knew I wasn't afraid of him. Dirk Duran—what's he going to do? Gonna beat me up? He won't be the first. That was my attitude with him. I was thinking about that the other day. Yeah, I did have the attitude with him: 'Screw you, Dirk. I'll blow your head off,' and I was crazy enough around him, be-cause I knew he was crazy. I think he thought he had to go to the extreme to scare me. Because I was always known as a pretty tough cookie. He had to go to the ex-treme with me because I wouldn't let him see the fear—like a dog, they can smell fear. That's the way he is, he can smell fear. Insane people and bad people are like that."

I suggested that maybe because he had already broken Ruby down he didn't need to admit to her that the little axe he had kept stored in the garage wasn't just for chopping wood; it was his special keepsake. Maybe until he met Justine, he'd never found a woman tough enough for whom he needed the magnitude of a full-blown, Gothic, macabre, axe-in-flames ritual to freak her out and break her will.

"That's what I think, too. He wanted me to see everything he was doing. I don't know. Maybe he wanted to confess to somebody but he didn't know how. Maybe the man had a conscience, at that age still. Maybe he wasn't the man he is now. Maybe he really did want to tell somebody. Maybe it really did eat at him. Maybe it got harder and harder as the years went on.

"I'll just never forget the eyes. They were the coldest blue I ever saw. The cold-est blue. Like ice. Like when you see an iceberg, you chop it in half, and the sun hits it just right and it gets that blue; that's the color they get. Like an iceberg chopped in half. Yeah. It reminds me of cold," she said calmly, drawing a glowing tip on her cigarette. "He was a cold man."

A man with eyes like glaciers burning a fire on a hot summer day. By now I knew well the nature of this man. He was indeed a man of fire and ice. Of cold-ness that burns.

I was astonished again at the many searing memories this one man had ignited in so many people. He stood out in relief from the normal narratives of their lives. Was this evil's strategy, to perform breathtakingly brutal acts that so shocked the nervous system and overwhelmed the brain that these traumatic events were not integrated into consciousness, but left disturbing, damaged mosaics of unassimilated memory?

Was this a version of power? Would acts of love have created such numinous memory?

WHEN I headed back to Los Angeles again, I passed through Lake County, Oregon, a primordial landscape with bodies of motionless salt water and fossil deposits filled with bones of prehistoric creatures. I felt compelled to read about this Jurassic place, so I grabbed a guidebook—the same one from which I'd learned, a few years before, that an axe-wielding pioneer crowned Oregon's statehouse. I happened to read:

> An unusual sight in this area is located ten miles northeast of Christmas Valley on a rough but passable Bureau of Land Management road. A 9,000-acre stand of ponderosa pines intermixed with the largest juniper trees in Oregon is all that is left of an ancient grove that dates back thousands of years. This island of green is 40 miles away from the nearest forest, accentuating the isolation and solitude of these stately sentinels. Many of the junipers here are over a thousand years old. On hot summer days, this place is a source of shade. Any time of year, the sound of the desert wind through the trees can stir contemplation.

One thing I knew from traversing the landscape of Oregon: ponderosa pines, which by habit grew in pure stands or with other coniferous trees, seldom kept company with western junipers. One left off where the other began.

"Her head's in the junies and her foot's in the pines," I thought of Terry Abbott's victim, Nicky. Why would her killer have used that catchy nonsensical phrase with incantatory power and a built-in riddle (where do junies and pines grow together?) The Wild West spookiness of the phrase reminded me of that clue supposedly left by the "Lost Dutchman" on his deathbed ("From the tunnel of my mine I can see the Military Trail below, but from the Military Trail you cannot see my mine"), referring to the supposed location of the pure vein of gold in Arizona's Superstition Mountains. Where would a clever murderer bury a body if he wanted to make a puzzle of it? Why not in a place called the "Lost Forest"? In a grove so ancient that ponderosas grow side by side with junies, in a magical forest so out of place in the desert it has earned the descriptive "Lost." This killer knows what I know. Geography is destiny. Landscape defines us, gets inside of us, just as the scenery of Oregon gets replicated inside a thunder egg.

JUSTINE HAD told me she revered the former deputy district attorney of Deschutes County, Josh Marquis. He had had the guts and the heart to put her ex-husband Joel "Terry" Abbott away for murdering Carolann Payne, whom Justine called Nicky. I phoned Marquis, now the DA of Oregon's Clatsop County. He told me he'd taken the seven-year-old case after a former district attorney refused. It was an unusual case. No body had been found. And Carolann Payne had led a twilight existence. With no home, no bank account, no credit cards, she'd left the lightest of footsteps on the earth. So Marquis first had to prove she was dead, and second, that she'd been murdered. In 1993, a unanimous jury convicted Abbott on the evidence of the admissions he made to Justine and to another associate. Abbott was sentenced to a minimum of twenty-five years in prison under Oregon's vintage "matrix" rules, which meant he would eventually be eligible for parole.

I asked Marquis: Was Justine's testimony key to putting Abbott away?

"Absolutely. Two things happened. One is he essentially confessed to killing her, though not directly; he made elliptical statements."

Justine's testimony also proved that Abbott was packing murderous rage against women.

"Joel tried to kill Justine about three years before he tried to kill Carolann. Carolann literally threw herself in front of Justine and got stabbed accidentally by Joel, who was stabbing at Justine."

"Justine told me that Carolann literally saved her life."

"She basically took a knife for Justine. Truth is stranger than fiction."

"Where had they looked for Carolann?" I asked Marquis.

"Two or three distinct sites in the desert over a period of three or four years. We had dogs, we hired psychics. This is a big desert. If somebody really wants to hide a body, we'll never find it."

"Didn't Justine say that Abbott made the statement 'Her foot's in the junies and her head's in the pines'? There aren't that many places where the junies and the pines grow together."

"I don't know if he was speaking literally or not."

"No, one doesn't know with people like that."

BACK IN OREGON in the fall of 1997 to tie up loose ends, I sought Justine out again. I found her on the floor of her trailer, surrounded by a mass of gaudy beads and shiny spangles and fabric of different sorts. She was busily fashioning these into dolls, festooned, she explained, with her very own brown hair—which I had no trouble believing, as her hair had been whacked off at several different levels. She told me she was making a Native American dream catcher specifically for me, her new friend Terri, so that if I hung it above my bed, my night terrors would get caught in the web and couldn't invade my head.

Justine was a strange angel. She went to the hidden core of things. She was a catalyst for bringing up what lay beneath the surface. How else could she have incited two men, by her mere presence, to spontaneously confess their murderous deeds? I amused myself imagining her, with this curious gift, running the FBI from her mobile home in Desert Terrace, off Highway 97 in Central Oregon, as she made dolls with her very own hair.

Justine and I had turned into real friends, with beliefs in common but a different way of expressing them. If I described my belief in the existence of utter evil as a modern revision of Manicheanism, based on my study of gratuitous cruelty in twentieth-century history, Justine described it as: "Humpty Dumpty didn't fall. He was pushed."

Finally I blurted out that I had a growing preoccupation with Nicky, and thought I knew where her body was. "You ever heard of the Lost Forest?" I said, almost breathlessly.

"Uh-huh."

Some part of me was operating in the realm of Nancy Drew titles, into which the "Lost Forest" would have neatly fit. Another part of me was in dead earnest.

"It's one of the few places where the junies and pines grow together."

Justine thought that was a good possibility. Abbott knew that area. He once had a job chopping wood nearby. "I wish you would look for her, for her sister's sake. Nicky was one of the truest women victims I'd ever met. She was one of these people that mean people took advantage of. And she saved my damn life, and I owe her. I owe her."

Nicky, whose last name was Payne, was a victim. And Nicky was a savior, too.

I DROVE SOUTH to the Christmas Valley. Alone in my old BMW sedan, I followed a dirt road, several miles it seemed, until an obscure wooden plaque pointed to the LOST FOREST. I turned down a narrow cinder road that looked like red grease-paint smeared on the earth, stretching out toward the horizon. I was off the tourist beat here. I couldn't imagine that any forest, let alone a primeval forest, lay anywhere near this sun-shot stretch of desert. There was not a tree in sight, no copse of ponderosa and juniper, nothing but sagebrush flats. I checked the Lake County map. No forest was indicated here at all, blank space marked nothing but desert anywhere. I meandered eastward. Drifts of sand appeared on the shoulder, the scent of dry earth in the air. I continued farther still, and the drifts morphed into whole dunes, and then, much to my surprise, the entire road began to undulate and the sand began to overtake the road altogether, until my car wheels plowed into a large dune and stopped. I looked ahead and could still see patches of red cinder road increasingly obscured by sand. If I forded this sand dune there'd be another and another, until perhaps there would be nothing but dunes and I would be alone and unable to move. I would be a woman, with a brave heart, but still alone.

In the distance was a beguiling mirage. The hint of a stand of trees? Junies and ponderosas? Or was it my imagination? I longed to be among those stately sen-

tinels in their isolation and solitude, a source of shade from this wilting sun, the sound of desert wind through their boughs stirring contemplation, so that I might intuit where Nicky was. I stared into the mirage and thought: I am here against my good judgment. Someone should find that metal plate. But not me. An earlier self would have barged ahead. But now I would turn around.

Chopped-up Traveling Angel

The '76 BikeCentennial Trail wound 4,200 miles across eleven American states from coast to coast. There were hundreds of dots along this trail, postage stamps of soil replete with specific flora and fauna, geologic history, and the history of those souls who lived upon it. On the eve of my twentieth birthday, I had intended to sample these little communities of this epic land up close and personal, and stay only as long as my legs would carry me on a bicycle at eleven miles an hour. In a different world, I still might never have reached the end of that trail—a final blowup in some hardpan Western town might well have sent Shayna and me hightailing it to the nearest Greyhound bus station. But a calamitous event had tied me to one dot on the earth and to the concentric rings around it. Now, twenty years later, I was an intimate of the place. The decision to return had been a holy impulse.

It was the fall of '97 and I'd been returning for five years. Five years of journeys were falling into neat patterns. There were the autumn trips, the early-spring trips, the late-summer trips. The year would cycle around and add more layers to my narrative. The passage of time seasoned the story, allowing me to realize the depth of my blood ties. It was impossible to imagine not circulating with the souls in this community. And vice versa. I was their traveling angel, like in those Westerns where the stranger rides into town on a horse and shakes things up or restores the peace—only I was a new twist on the theme: I was a chopped-up traveling angel, female, who came and went, alighted here and there. Told my tales and listened to others tell theirs, checked on old acquaintances, forged new bonds. No one but Boo and a handful of other trusted intimates knew how to find me, knew where I lived when I went away, or when I would ride into town next.

OUT OF MY unquenchable drive to knot together loose threads of the story, I coaxed Linda Shepherd, speaking to me on the phone from Alaska, to resuscitate her memories of that long-ago day in the seed fields. It had taken me two years to track her down, from the time I'd started looking for her, in the scattershot, informal manner of my investigation. Her father had managed the Desert Seed Company in the summer of '77, and the Shepherd family lived in the ranch house on the property. Linda had been the foreman in charge of the teen workers.

I had surprised her with the call. Her memory was spontaneous. She hadn't discussed Cline Falls since she left Oregon.

"We were out in the fields hoeing and pulling weeds. I think it was carrots where we were at. It was mellow. There were three different radios. Because some liked country music. And some liked that noisy stuff. Dirk come out—boy, he was all cleaned up. Spiffy. Looked like he had just showered. Maybe he was up late drinking. Because it was late morning. At least it seemed late morning. We started early."

"So Janey was working, Dirk shows up and it made an impression on you that he was spiffy clean," I said, getting the picture clear in my mind.

"He was dressed cowboy—but you know, usually cowboys have wrinkles in their clothes—somehow it just seemed like later in the morning, and he looked like he'd just stepped out of the shower."

"Did he have wet hair?" I asked.

"Somehow, if his hair wasn't wet, it was slicked down. When somebody puts on nice jeans, they look ironed, fresh ironed, and not even really creased when you sit down. His boots were polished. You know, we're out in the field! His shirt was tucked in, Western style. He just was dressed . . . *really nice.* He looked *good.* A *nice*-looking guy. And if I remember right, he smelled good, too. I was envious of Janey. Good-looking guy wants to talk to Janey."

I never tired of hearing about Dirk Duran's meticulousness. But this description was particularly pertinent, as this was how he'd looked just hours after the Cline Falls attack, and bore a striking resemblance to the way I had always described him. It was late in the morning, but he had just showered. What was he doing all night that he had slept so late?

"He was really polite when he asked could he talk to Janey, and the next thing I know, all hell broke loose." Linda didn't remember when Dirk started thumping on Janey Firestone. She was in another part of the field when she heard the screaming. By the time Linda arrived, Janey had gotten away from Dirk, and he had calmed down.

"He was just so normal. Then he asked to talk to her, and she walked over, and he just cold-cocked her. He just hauled off and hit her. Whoof! Out of nothing! He just KATHUNKED her. Just like in the movies. Where did it come from? I mean, there was no forewarning. Nothing. It's just really bizarre. *Such a clean-cut guy.* I can't get over that!"

The nasty surprise violated normality. Like being asleep in a tent and you wake up with a truck on your body.

"Then what I remember is heading off in the rig with Janey and everyone jumping on the car, and they were all terrified and screaming, like monkeys, just clinging to the car. What amazed me was the fear spreading, because sixteen kids were all piled on the car, so I could barely drive, and I just said I was taking Janey up to the house where my dad could take care of it, removing her from the situation. What was he going to do to these kids? Nothing. But they were totally terrified of him. All I remember is chaos and everybody screaming and hollering. They were utterly rattled. It wasn't even noon. It shot the whole day. I don't know for sure, but I think I sent them on home."

A shocking act of violence the night before—the Cline Falls attack—followed by a shocking act of violence the following day. The kids were "terrified and screaming, like monkeys, just clinging to the car. What amazed me was the fear spreading."

The mark of evil: when an act ruptures all categories of comprehension.

Linda told me that she and Janey were friends, and after that incident she looked after her for a few days. I asked Linda whether, that day in the fields or after, Janey told her anything about her suspicions linking Dirk to Cline Falls?

"Yeah, I believe they had a fight. They had a disagreement, rather. I don't know if it was so much a fight."

"So you remember that."

"I just remember her saying, they were on the outs the night before, and he was upset with her when he left. I don't remember the timing other than she said he was upset when he left and it was the right time—and she lived on the back road on the way to Cline Falls."

I told Linda that, although others whom I'd talked to recalled a fight, Janey Firestone insisted to me that everything had been "hunky-dory" between her and Dirk the night of the Cline Falls attack.

"Oh, really? No. They were on the outs. And I remember Janey told me there was something on his pickup, too, scratch marks or something."

"There were scratch marks!" New information.

"Yeah. If he dresses that nice. Look at his pickup. She was making some comment about something on his pickup. And I don't remember what it was—something was scratched or broken."

I imagined the scratch marks were embedded with special weather-resistant green paint from a Cline Falls picnic table. I remembered the June 25, 1977, article in the Chicago Sun-Times: "Agents see paint as key clue in camp attack," which discussed how green paint from a picnic table could be the key clue to apprehending the attacker. Perhaps this distinctive green paint might have smudged the right side of the assailant's vehicle when he sideswiped it en route to the tent.

This piece of information never appeared in the local news, to plant a seed that could have started a rumor. I knew that the picnic table was missing a sliver of wood. I knew that police tested a portion of the table microscopically to deter-

mine whether traces of the vehicle's body paint had been embedded in it. According to the police report, they'd found nothing. But at that time, the magnificent microscopes of the current Oregon Fish and Wildlife Forensics Laboratory did not exist.

STARS AND STRIPES in profusion billowed in the hot dry breeze, a pole planted every few feet up and down the parallel main streets of Redmond, Oregon. I knew there were six hundred of them, a lot for a small town. It was Labor Day 1997, and I finally was witness to that much-vaunted patriotic display that a long time ago had won Redmond the moniker "Flag City, USA." I headed to the house where Dirk and Ruby had lived together in the 1980s, Ruby's house originally, the place where, in Justine's account, the axe-in-flames ritual had taken place. The house sat on a street named Glacier (a man with eyes so cold they looked like a glacier cut in half lived on a street so named) in the western quadrant of Redmond, near the high school. I expected it to be the neat little box house it was, open to view, with little vegetation, no front fence, and a big picture window— trusting and modest, like so many others in Redmond.

When I drew up in front of this cheerless spot, I wondered why I had pictured it as "normal." This was a house of secrets. Appropriately, a ratty and overgrown, leafy tree covered the picture window and most of the single-story dwelling, which was painted a dirty mustard. The place felt loveless and derelict. If a tract ranch house in the rural American West could be Gothic, like some moldering manse populated by tormented ghosts on the moors of England—this was it.

The garage was attached to the left side, open to view—precisely as I'd pictured it when Justine told her tale. The pull-down garage door had narrow windows, and I was tempted to walk up and look inside—to peer into the deep shadows and make out the outlines of shelves lining the walls, where an axe had lain for many years. But I suppressed this compelling impulse and drove on.

I called to mind a vivid image of Ruby, the tangy woman with the full-bodied sensuality and the face of a Scandinavian model past her prime. I hadn't seen her in some time, and just thinking about her, I noticed my hands were shaking. Ruby scared me because I had been in the presence of a shadow darker than my own. Greater rage, greater fear, a more profound dissociation. As much as I wanted to save Ruby, she shook me.

But I had a score to settle with her. She had betrayed me, in a sense. After we "bonded hard," after I helped her get a restraining order, I'd tried to visit her on every trip I took to her area. And I always found the curtains drawn.

Ruby never told me that she knew Dirk kept a hatchet behind the seat of his pickup, hot at hand, in case the need arose to use it. But I now knew that she had known. I now knew that Dirk had confessed Cline Falls to her, over and over, according to a man who claimed he heard it from her very lips, a man I didn't think had reason to lie. And yet, Dirk hadn't performed the axe-in-flames ritual in front of her. For some reason, that was not for her eyes. I still had the desire to take the fullest measure of Ruby. There was so much more I wanted to talk to her about, although by now I'd figured out how extraordinary it was that she'd opened up to me at all. I also felt obliged to tell her that her ex-husband wouldn't show up on her doorstep for a few years—or if she'd already heard the news, I wanted to celebrate with her.

I was aware that Ruby had changed residences. With a tight band of anxiety stretching across my chest, I drove over the border to Washington, to the neighborhood where she was supposed now to be living—a warren of apartments connected by catwalks that shook. It was a step down from her old place. The whole building was vacant, including her apartment—cleaned out for renovation. An older woman appeared on the catwalk and identified herself as the new owner, telling me which apartments she found to be pigsties and which were not so bad. Ruby's was not so bad. The woman told me she had no way of knowing where the old tenants had gone. I wished her good luck in restoring the apartments back to some semblance of respectability, and headed out of town, relieved after all to leave Washington without having seen Ruby. I realized I didn't feel strong enough to see her just now. I thought I was going to rescue her. But I couldn't. Rescuing Ruby was far beyond me.

NOW THAT Dirk had been in jail for a while, I wondered if his sidekick be willing to sing? It was time, finally, to look for his best friend, Wayne—in fact, Dirk's *only* friend, as far as I knew. "The one lies and the other swears to it," was how Kelly had described the nature of their bond. Boo and I were on our way to the thoroughfare known as the Old Bend–Redmond Highway, which, unlike the newer OR 97, meandered through the desert between the two towns.

We found Wayne, a spare man with a bald head, sprawled on the couch of his clean, well-organized trailer out back on his dad's ranch, his skinny frame draped in a shiny jogging suit. He was watching the hypnotic coverage of Princess Diana's tragic death. We introduced ourselves candidly and he seemed lethargically willing, and even happy, to talk to us.

"So you and Dirk are still friends?" I put to him as I helped myself to a chair, behaving as casually as I could.

"We have been. We've had our differences, but through thick and thin we stuck together. He never really done me harm." Wayne spoke as languidly as his body moved. "A lot of people say he has evil eyes and this and that—I say they never bothered me. I've never known him to bring harm to anybody," Wayne went on. "But he's one of the people I know who's gotten by with more than a lot of people and not have anything happen. To tell you the truth, his parents spoiled him his entire life. His dad is kind of scared of him. Should have beat the shit out of him a couple of times."

So now even Dirk's best blood brother had joined that chorus.

"You saw a lot of the stuff that went down with Ruby, didn't you?" I remembered distinctly Ruby's account of Wayne urging her to leave Dirk when Dirk was away, but sitting by and smoking while Dirk was beating her.

"I was around a lot," Wayne answered me. "I seen them getting in each other's faces, arguing and all of that. I never seen any hand that was laid on anybody. It happened when they were alone. I think he threw her in the bathroom and broke her arm. I never seen the physical violence, but I do believe it was there. I'd never go over there and see her with black eyes or bruises."

Wayne was not a menacing sort. I was feeling comfy in his neat and snug trailer, and so was Boo. I decided I wouldn't ask Wayne point-blank if Dirk had ever confessed Cline Falls. I inverted my usual question: "I know Dirk told a lot of people he didn't do the Cline Falls thing. Did he say that all the time to you?"

Wayne gave a fast response, considering his usual pace. "I've always myself liked to think that . . . ahh . . . he didn't do it."

"You think he's capable?"

"I believe he's capable of anything. Most people are," said Wayne philosophically.

Boo urged him on.

Wayne was feeling more comfortable. He continued. "Tell you the truth, I've had my doubts. Sure. You bet." But he wanted to make clear that he wasn't in Redmond the summer of '77. He had no direct knowledge.

We'd built our rapport with Wayne. It was time to tell the story, a version that spared no detail. He took it all in, his narrow face looking visibly upset.

" 'Meticulously dressed,' " Wayne quoted me, in confirmation, after I brought my story to a close. "I'd like to think myself that it wasn't him, but there's no two ways about looking past my doubts," Wayne confessed, but "I can't condemn him. I have nothing," he insisted.

"Dirk did mention to me once"—he lowered his voice, just as everyone did when they were imitating ole Dirk—'Ted Bundy was through here at that time. Maybe he was the one.' "

A friend of Wayne's named Bob, a big man with a kind face, dropped in and plopped himself on a chair in the trailer. He'd grown up in Redmond and knew the Cline Falls tale, although he wasn't living in the area at the time. Bob told us his sister had gone out with Dirk for a while after Janey left him. Once his sister and Dirk went camping and Dirk was ready to build a fire. Apparently he told her, "I'll get the axe." She was scared to death.

Privately, I worried about a girl who would even go camping with a man whose reputation was such that he could scare her with the line "I'll get the axe."

I WAS STILL keen on finding the Deschutes County sheriff's deputies who showed up at the seed ranch, subdued Dirk, and hauled him off to Bend, or the sheriffs who interviewed him in Bend and escorted him to jail in Prineville—I was hoping they might illuminate for me the final mystery of what happened to the police investigation of Dirk Duran's possible involvement in the Cline Falls case.

I called Linda Shepherd's father and asked him to send his memory back to the seed farm he managed on a June day in 1977.

"A girl named Justine remembered that the sheriff's deputies took a long time to subdue Dirk. Do you remember that?"

"It was only two cops, and I didn't want to get involved with it, because I knew his dad, Lou. And I always thought something was wrong with the boy, or something went wrong with his mind. It happens to people under stress. Because from that day on, he was never rational."

Did he know who those two cops were?

"They was older guys. They could all be dead by now."

Had he heard the rumors that Dirk was connected to the Cline Falls attack?

"Yep."

"What did you think about that?"

"He just slipped another cog."

"Did you believe it?"

"I thought he was capable of it."

When the news about the Cline Falls attack came out, if in his mind he connected Dirk with that incident, wouldn't he have called the cops and said, "Take a good look at this kid?"

"People might have suspicions. But you never act on suspicions. Because it can ruin a person's life . . . so a grand jury indicts someone, and he's ruined for life, and he's never done something wrong."

Did he think that explained why people in the area didn't call the police with their suspicions?

"Yep."

"Because almost nobody did," I informed him, and he fell silent on the other end of the phone. During that pause I could think only about the lava rocks I'd seen in Central Oregon that blocked the roads between neighbors. Isn't that why people moved to the spacious West, to put space between themselves and others so they couldn't see their neighbor's smoke? You don't ask questions. You don't want to falsely accuse or be falsely accused. That's what liberty, what freedom, that sacred American value, was all about.

You'd think if freedom were such a sacred American value people would opt for infinite responsibility and strive to preserve freedom for one another. (Just to take one example: *freedom from bodily harm*. How many women and choirboys have known that?) We're long overdue for a new paradigm: a new cult of individualism—where the ultimate value of the empowered individual is to serve the larger picture.

MAYBE THEY were dead and gone. Maybe the key had been thrown down the well. But I made one last effort to find the cops who picked Dirk up for beating Janey Firestone. I drove to Prineville, Oregon, and saw the single jail cell where Dirk was held for four days, where he apparently climbed the walls, desperate to get out. The police chief of the Prineville Police Department was an old-timer. After I called to make the appointment with him, he'd checked in with Marlen Hein at the state police. Marlen told him to reveal to me anything he knew; the attitude of the state police was complete transparency with regard to my search for what had happened to the '77 investigation.

So the Prineville police chief was honest with me. He had no direct knowledge, but in his opinion, "It would be in the realm of possibility that given what went on then, that money was paid to shut down your investigation." It was well known that big cattle barons paid people off in Crook County back then. For sure, it was possible that influence from Crook County—maybe even that Crook County lawyer Dirk's dad might have an opportunity to hire when Dirk was in the cell in Prineville—could reach in and rearrange some things, could influence police departments all the way over in Deschutes County.

Maybe *cover-up* was too strong a word. Maybe "swept under the carpet" or "looked the other way" or "intentionally let slip through the cracks" was more accurate. Or maybe I should cut the two lead detectives some slack altogether. I never went back to question Durr and Cooley after my allegations to the media. They'd both told their story several times, and I doubted that anything had changed.

The answer to the question of what had specifically happened to the police investigation would remain the riddle wrapped in a mystery inside an enigma.

The Last Sister

Whoever saw you will bear
All your wounds from here on forever.
—ILYA SELVINSKY, "I SAW IT," 1942

I had a list of dozens of names of people in whom memory might still reside, and the invisible elastic bands encircling people touched by this story surely contained others. I could go on, as time seemed to wrinkle as I went along, but I'd been searching since 1992. It was 2000. I supposed I could build this story for the rest of my life, but that plan wouldn't be practical, so I proclaimed this interview to be my last. Four years had transpired since I spoke to the nurses who salved mine and Shayna's wounds with their good hands, but I still hadn't caught up to the third sister of mercy, the one described by the other two as "a great humanitarian woman who brought a dimension of consciousness to the trio." I didn't want to leave the trinity incomplete.

When I originally phoned Lisa in Portland, in the autumn of 1996, she made an appointment to see me, but added enigmatically, "I don't think I want to see your arm." It was an odd remark. I needed her to tell me why she was wary of laying eyes on my arm. I knew she was harboring a story. I spent days anticipating the explosive charge of her memories. Then she had to cancel the appointment.

Finally, four years later, we met at Powell's Books in Portland on a rainy November day. The extra years, now totaling twenty-three intervening years since 1977, had done nothing to dilute the potency of her memory. This, in and of itself, was validating.

A stylish woman in her mid-forties, with straight blond hair pulled back, Lisa regarded me with light blue eyes and empathetic eyebrows that met in an upsweep above her nose. Her face was one of those few that had settled into a permanent attitude of compassion.

"How close in age are we?" she asked right away. She figured that our generational closeness (her twenty-four to my twenty) must have been one reason why she had profoundly identified with me. As she put it, "You were enjoying everything I wanted to do, to bike across, to be outside, to be free . . ."

Lisa had arrived for the day shift in the emergency room in St. Charles Hospital on a hot summer day in June 1977. As she reconstituted that memory, she recalled the faces of the night-shift nurses as flushed red. Crying and angry, barking questions and answers to one another: *"Get that son of a bitch"* on their lips. They were hardly able to do their work.

She walked into the operating theater and remembered the view as spectacular. She made a point of mentioning that the huge windows framed the volcanic spine of Oregon.

And she remembered focusing on a girl's arm, mine.

"I just remember hatchet marks, all the way down your forearm." She indicated the area between elbow and wrist. "And I remembered it was your left."

A *series* of hatchet marks? Not just one? This fact fascinated me. Hadn't I come so far that no new details could catch me by surprise?

The area of flesh so astonishingly marked was surrounded by cool blue surgical drapes. She saw only drapes and the arm. She saw no body the arm was attached to.

I had been collecting images of myself as seen through the eyes of others for many years. Now I'd come to find out that all she saw was an arm. *My arm.* Framed by blue surgical drapes.

"That's what I remember. The slices on your arm. And the axe slice was peeled back. It was unbelievable," she said, full of strong feeling. I mused again on how every individual will unconsciously choose one detail of a memory that blazes in bold relief, a detail as unique as their individual personality.

Lisa was very familiar with bodily mutilation. "Gunshots and knifings and chain saws and putting arms back on from the lumber mills. But to think that a human had done this to a human was an absolutely earthquaking emotional experience."

"Earthquaking" was the word she used, evoking the unsettled tectonic plates. That day, June 23, 1977, divided her beliefs into a before and an after.

Lisa grew up in a family that worked for humanitarian causes. Her grandfather was an old-fashioned country doctor, and as a girl she followed him around the community on his medical rounds. She grew up in Northern California, near San Quentin, and her father volunteered in rehabilitation programs for prisoners. She was inclined to think rehabilitation was always possible.

The moment she saw an arm of one so defenseless, with defensive hatchet marks running along its length, Lisa, a self-described peacemaker and seldom an angry person, had felt her breath sucked in by a tidal wave of an emotion not familiar to her: all-consuming fury.

She told me she could feel her gut tightening at this very moment as she recalled those feelings. Within a few seconds, a belief in radical evil had solidified in her, a belief that some souls were simply unregenerate. There was nothing society could do to rehabilitate them. Those who commit atrocities, she decided then, should be removed from society forever. If that meant giving them the ultimate punishment, she'd think that appropriate. To this day she's never budged from that core belief, although she told me that as a liberal woman she certainly wasn't raised to think that way, and maybe it ran counter to the typical nurse's mission: to try to help absolutely everybody.

It was a process I, too, had undergone, was constantly undergoing—this fundamental realignment. Perhaps I had reached the end of the line in coming to see my own injuries: my own arm as an emblem of suffering, an object of contemplation. What astounded me was that this woman, so like me, had made a journey of understanding, as I had done, which had brought her to an unshakable belief that human nature included souls such as the one who had made these cuts. She'd changed her beliefs because of me. My body, my personal history, had been her object lesson.

"You know that sign to Cline Falls? I've never been there, and I've never wanted to go. All I have to do is see it to bring back the memory of you guys in there. I don't think I've ever been so moved . . . to see you guys, to see what a human can do to another human." She interrupted herself. "It makes my hands sweat just thinking about you that morning."

"It's happening right now?" I asked.

"Yeah, feel my hands. They're both sweating."

Over a table amid the bookshelves of Powell's, I reached out and took Lisa's hands, and let the moisture from her soft palms mingle with my own.

"Because that emotion is just unreal," she said. "Terri, it's a relief to see you. It was a life-altering experience for me. You're always in my thoughts. You guys have just never left. It was one of those things you never forget."

I asked her in what way it was a relief.

"To see you doing well. And to see your arm. It looks great . . . You know, I never went to see you guys after your operation. Usually in something less serious, I would, but I think I didn't because I couldn't control myself. My emotions wouldn't have been too healing for you guys. I think I simply couldn't handle it. I just would have cried. So I never knew your faces. And now I can put a face and personality and a voice to that arm."

I had been dismembered. And she re-membered me. In becoming whole for her, I suppose I was becoming whole for myself. By telling my story, and hearing the answering stories, I was piecing together a split in my being.

I formed an image in my mind of the volcanoes Lisa had seen outside the operating theater, five of them, including the Three Sisters. How remarkable it was that she had conflated the vision of them with her memory of me. Three sisters. Faith. Hope. Charity. This last interview left me feeling wrapped in grace.

The Tale That Came Back to Me

Somewhere in the years of setting my tale to words, in the summer of 1999, I met my own story on the road, recounted in the words of an American poet. I did have a hint that something of the kind existed. I learned—I think from Shayna's family shortly after it happened—that a Boston poet had found the event potent enough to include it in one of his verses. Twenty-two years later, it occurred to me to look for it. What Boston poet? Had the poem been published? A search of Boston-based poets turned up Robert Pinksy, an American Poet Laureate. A book-length poem he had published in 1977, entitled *An Explanation of America*, struck me as a good place to start. Hadn't some small part of my quest in the previous seven years been to find an "explanation of America" through the prism of my own story?

I ordered the paperback, and when it arrived I noted that he had addressed the poem to his daughter. I opened the book, quite at random, to pages 46 and 47, and on those pages I read:

> *Elsewhere along the highway, other limits—*
> *Hanging in shades of neon from dusk to dusk,*
> *The signs of people who know how to take*
> *Pleasure in places where it seems unlikely:*
> *New kind of places, the "overdeveloped" strips*
> *With their arousing, vacant-minded jumble;*
> *Or garbagey lake-towns, and the tourist-pits*
> *Where crimes unspeakably bizarre come true*
> *To astonish countries older, or more savage . . .*
> *As though the rapes and murders of the French*
> *Or Indonesians were less inventive than ours,*

Less goofy than those happenings that grow
Like air-plants—out of nothing, and alone.
. . .

They make us parents want to keep our children
Locked up, safe even from the daily papers
That keep the grisly record of that frontier
Where things unspeakable happen along the highways.
. . .

In today's paper, you see the teen-aged girl
From down the street; camping in Oregon
At the far point of a trip across the country,
Together with another girl her age,
They suffered and survived a random evil.
An unidentified, youngish man in jeans
Aimed his car off the highway, into the park
And at their tent (apparently at random)
And drove it over them once, and then again;
And then got out, and struck at them with a hatchet
Over and over, while they struggled; until
From fear, or for some other reason, or none,
He stopped; and got back into his car again
And drove off down the night-time highway. No rape,
No robbery, no "motive." Not even words,
Or any sound from him that they remember.
The girl still conscious, by crawling, reached the road
And even some way down it; where some people
Drove by and saw her, and brought them both to help,
So doctors could save them—barely marked.   *You see*

. . .

Our neighbor's picture in the paper: smiling,
A pretty child with a kerchief on her head
Covering where the surgeons had to shave it.
You read the story, and in a peculiar tone—
Factual, not unfeeling, like two policemen—
Discuss it with your sister. You seem to feel
Comforted that it happened far away,
As in a crazy place, in Oregon:
For me, a place of wholesome reputation;
For you, a highway where strangers go amok,
As in the universal provincial myth

That sees, in every stranger, a mad attacker . . .
(And in one's victims, it may be, a stranger).

Once I recovered from the shock of finding my own story staring at me from a page I had randomly opened to, in a book I had guessed to order from the title, I read the passages that came before and after this one. What struck me: these verse paragraphs describing my own story were entirely different from the rest, as though the poet had stopped his cryptic prosody at the boundaries of my story—which in comparison, read like an unadorned prose news bulletin, almost as though its shocking nature defied versification. Finding my own story bound in this now twenty-two-year-old book gave it the ring of inevitability, of permanence, of History. (I winced at the detail he got wrong: "by crawling, reached the road." A woman, after an assault such as this, must logically *crawl*, I suppose, not stand up and run and flag down help.) I felt a moment of pride that I had *the* insider's knowledge and that every detail chosen by this poet way back in 1977 I had subsequently exploded and expounded on: the youngish man in jeans, no "motive," the wordless exchange, the pretty girl with kerchief on her head, smiling. Not only had I found out for myself, but I was telling the world a richly annotated version. If there was meaning in this story to begin with, the meaning was larger now.

Now there was a girl being drowned in a pond. A community devastated. A Birdman who lived alone in a shack along that highway where strangers go amok, surveying the soil, saying, *There was a lot of blood there.* There was a woman who remembered a day on Glacier Avenue when snowcapped volcanoes burned against a sunbeaten sky. "*It was hot, see. It was summertime and he built a fire. And he burned it. And he dumped it downtown, all the ashes and everything.*"

Now there were two plastic garbage bags. One on the East Coast. One on the West. One containing ashes and a hatchet blade. The other, a mummy sleeping bag stained with old blood. Now there was a boy who woke up with nightmares. He had seen something he would never forget in a place called Cline Falls State Park.

The Tale That Continues On

On my volcano grows the Grass.

—EMILY DICKINSON

I can see them if I look carefully—through the heat shimmer on a desert road. Two girls on bicycles. They have nearly made their way to Mitchell, Oregon. Two friends are waiting for them there.

We look for poetic justice. Tidy endings. One has pursued a puzzling conflict to its end. To radical transformation? Did the journey into the American desert rescue, resurrect, restore me? I can say I am no longer a marionette in the unsteady hands of a manic and narcoleptic puppeteer. I have spent years willing my scattered energies into a single stream—this story.

Aftermath is a word you hear all the time in therapeutic language. But the word is ancient and its meaning poetic: it refers to the new growth springing up, after the grass is mowed. I like the image. And it fits: as my story has gotten told, there's been a letting-go of cargo, a diminuendo of my hot inner life. The soul in white heat has calmed down, the fire has been transmuted into a little in-dwelling compassion.

The Russian Nadezhda Mandelstam, who endured the Soviet Union's worst horrors, writes in her memoirs: "It always needed a personal misfortune to open our eyes and make us a little more human—and even then the lesson took a while to sink in." To open my eyes and become a little more human won't be the end of my challenge. The greatest challenge for the future will be to keep my eyes open. So I promise no tidy endings.

But little endings for a story, nonetheless:

IN JANUARY 2001, Dee Dee Kouns was tearing at her blond hair with both hands. "Pictures. They come. And they come. And they come."

Picture a human skull atop a sandbar in the middle of a meandering river. That was the image the two sheriffs conjured one warm January day in Portland.

The sheriffs had just left the Kounses' home, and this was the story they had come to tell us—Bob, Dee Dee, their three sons; I had been invited, too. An officer from Ferry County, Washington, leaned on his knees, put his hands together, and said soberly, "I'm here to tell you that your daughter is deceased."

Bob nodded. He'd known this for twenty years.

It was October 23, 1991. A hunter was walking a dry wash of the Kettle River when he spotted a human skull atop a sandbar. Police excavated several layers of silt. They found arms, ribs, a pelvis. There were no remains from the legs down.

For years the Ferry County sheriffs couldn't identify the remains. They entered the dental records in a national database and got no response. They tried again in 1995 and '96. Every time one sheriff went near that part of the river, he prayed. He had a daughter himself. They tried again in '98, and made one last try in the fall of 2000. This time they had a hit. On November 22, 2000, twenty years to the very day after Valerie's killers disposed of her remains, the Department of Justice in California matched records from the skull found in a Washington river with a missing person named Valerie McDonald. Sadness pressed down on the Kounses' living room as the officer described the course of the Kettle River: it flows down from Canada, crosses the U.S. border, makes a loop, then crosses the Canadian border again until it joins the Columbia River. Valerie's skull was found on the American side.

For Bob and Dee Dee, who had figured it all out a long time ago, the discovery was validating, even comforting in a lacerating way. The crime to this day has never been prosecuted. Valerie has emerged to prove that whatever remains unspoken or buried will find a way to the surface—secrets, lies, truths that people refuse to see will come to public light, and that emergence will be sacramental. The currents still flow over what remains of Valeriein that washtub filled with concrete, that time capsule of the late twentieth century.

AWHILE BACK I got inspired to look for that 3-D Viewmaster of my childhood with the image of the headless cowboy torso and the barrel of a revolver trained on me. I found not only the toy, over four decades old, but also the picture disc of 3-D slides, untouched since my childhood. I noted that the disc happened to be manufactured by a company in Oregon.

I rotated the circle of transparencies in front of the light and easily found the image I thought I had remembered: the torso in Western dress training a handgun on me, forcing me to look down its cold, gray barrel—exactly as I had remembered. What I hadn't remembered was its caption: *"Few have seen this view and lived!"*

Was this the moment when the teller met the tale?

We are victims of random circumstance. At the same time, we are living meaningfully in a meaningful universe: telling a story makes it so.

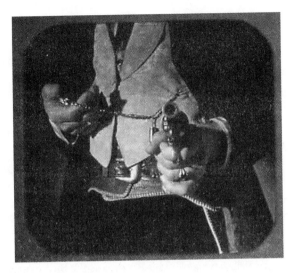

There happened to be another image on that same disc: Mount Hood, with sagebrush desert in the foreground—my strange piece of paradise.

Nostalgia was always waiting for me in that geography that was my destiny. As long as the junipers exhaled their scent, some part of me would inhabit the Central Oregon landscape. As the years went on, I haunted those latitudes less frequently, and finally the day came when paying a visit to Cline Falls would evoke not a chord of emotion in me. The breath of juniper still gave me a sensory alertness, but it was pleasant now. The dangerous feeling of the place went away altogether. A feeling of at-home-ness stayed.

Until the place seemed ever less like itself. Hoards of new people were moving in, and the power of my story—the legend of Cline Falls—became diluted by outsiders. This quirky postage stamp of soil was becoming like every other place. The expanding rims of the three towns that formed a triangle on the desert were coming together with the tide of sprawling subdivisions, lights were filling in the lonesome places even around Cline Falls.

America is constantly in the process of removing its beauty. When the old rodeo and fairgrounds in Redmond were torn down to make way for a Wal-Mart; when acres of junipers gave their gristly old lives for new fairgrounds, without the special provenance of the old center of community life—I began to feel phantom pains. As resident ghost, I felt dismayed and marginalized.

So many new roads crisscrossed Bend that I, like the old-timers, could hardly find my way around anymore. Some of the old-timers' names even wound up on the street signs in the new subdivisions, evoking the past as kind of a ghost town. En route to the Deschutes County Courthouse recently, I found my story on "Poe Sholes Drive."

America's cult of the future can pave over the past, but its ghosts are reminding us that nothing is ever over.

.   .   .

THE WINDING lane down to the Birdman's hovel was barricaded a few years back. He'd been taken off the land, to spend his last days like so many others, in a nursing home. When I found him gone, I deeply regretted that I had never gotten a "bird in the hand." The last time I looked, the shack was still there, but the birds were gone. I wondered how long the chickadees waited before they knew he wasn't coming back. Whenever I thought of the half-crazed soul leaving his little home, my heart got heavy. Recently I learned the mystery of the Birdman's origins. It turned out he had a life divided into a before and after, a couple of times over. When he was a boy named Charlie Weaver in Washington State, his violent father beat his eldest son until he gave him brain damage. The second time Charlie's life divided into a before and after was the day he vanished in 1946, leaving his neighbors to think he'd died in the woods. He changed his name to Abe Johnson, moved to Cline Falls, and started his life over as the Birdman. He hadn't been shell-shocked in World War II. He didn't need a war to come unhinged. One man's cruelty would do.

AS FOR THE axe-wielding cowboy: I hardly think of him, although I dream about him once in a while. He's always nice and polite to me (you can't script dreams). He always has a theatrical, foppish air. And he's always working on my sympathies, trying to convince me he didn't do it. In reality, he lives his life as a free man. Every now and then I get word of him or I check into his court records. I found a restraining order taken out by a bewildered girlfriend who couldn't understand what would make a man put her car in reverse while she was driving sixty miles per hour, all the while threatening her, "I'll mess your face up good." I also heard that the cowboy, biker, son of Elvis, Mafia hit man now wore a new disguise: he is costumed as a meticulous preppie, with khaki pants and a polo shirt. He's still telling members of the community that he was falsely accused of being the Cline Falls hatchet man.

THOSE DREAMS in which I was held captive at the tender age of twenty never have let go. Conscious will has no power over dreams. The unconscious is never a cute and cuddly thing that one can bring to heel. But I'm playful with those dreams now. My psyche has grabbed onto their symbolism. They are like a movie the conscious mind is forced to watch over and over, taking note of subtle new twists on recurring themes, while powerless to affect the narration. So there's a playful and comprehending relationship between my conscious and unconscious mind. My dreams and I, we have an in-joke between us. If I'm lucky, when I'm an ancient crone, I'll have them still. Shayna kept turning up in my dreams. In those night narrations sometimes we were twenty years old, other times we were middle-aged. Sometimes her vision was perfect, other times not. She was polite to me, but restrained. Unspoken matters stood between us. Often we explored landscapes of rare beauty. Twice we began another bike trip.

IN MAY OF 2004, I returned to Yale for a twenty-fifth reunion. The somber buildings of this Eastern establishment institution, seventy-five years older than America itself, were stolidly changeless, impassively looking down upon us mortals as we peered into one another's changed faces and reflected on the midpoint of our passage: had our lives borne out the American promise of an infinitely improving future, as we had once expected? What really constitutes the well-lived life? What have I done, what will I do, with my allotment of time on the earth?

I was silently posing these questions to myself when my former roommate told me that Shayna would be putting in a brief surprise appearance that afternoon. I would never have expected her presence there. It had been twenty-two years. My heart pounded in my chest as though it had been set free.

Only a break in the soggy spring weather could have allowed the perfection of the moment. Sun and breeze had a clarity and freshness that foretold of something vibrating in the air.

Then I spotted her, as though straight from a dream:

In jeans and sneakers, cross-legged on an Indian blanket laid out on the grass, her dark shiny hair falling casually on her shoulders, she was holding court with friends, just like old times. My eyes adjusted to the differences twenty-two years had made on her pretty face, still untouched by makeup. She was physically fit, of good cheer, with a ready laugh. She exuded an aura of self-possession and competence, and if I hadn't known about it, I would never have detected her disability.

Everything had an air of unreality as I approached her. Then I dived into the encounter, kneeling down, announcing my name. We hugged politely. It was but an instant's sensation, but undeniable. The smell of her hair triggered a memory of that most elusive emotional sense: the heavy scents of that long-ago June night.

I thought I detected a flicker of pain on her face as she repeated my name. In another instant the past receded, and we introduced our family members.

Shayna asked me what I was doing, and I answered vaguely, without specifying that I was writing our shared chronicle, because that would have involved catching her up on the story. And I no longer needed to catch her up on the story. Truly, I realized a while back, I had been sated by the other perfect listeners I had found. Then she asked me if I was successful, which I thought was odd, and I asked back, in wonder, "How do you measure success?"

"In your own eyes," she said, and I decided to read her question as encrypted language from her unconscious. I thought, yes, we are successful. We've gotten through this thing. We have willed ourselves to thrive. How resilient we both are, each in our opposite ways. In our own eyes.

It was her birthday. Someone gave her a cake. She made a wish and blew out the candles. I had no idea what contours her wish would take. How little I really knew her. Almost not at all, I mused, as I silently wished her "many more."

Photos were taken, old roommates assembling in pyramids, someone saying, "Hurry up. This picture isn't going to end up in *The New York Times*." This institution, its architecture, its traditions, had performed well. By design, those who had been thrown into physical proximity—those who shared a residential college, an entryway, a floor—were meant to remain in contact forever. Here was the original accident of fate, the one that catalyzed all others: the happenstance of a Yale rooming assignment.

It all came back to me: how she cocked a hip to the side and held her right elbow with her left hand as she talked. I had an insight as I watched her: I was seeing double. For me, there were two Shaynas. I let my perception oscillate between them—the girl of my inner world, and the real woman standing on the grass laughing with friends.

There was no denying the actual flesh-and-blood event we shared: my body had reminded me of this just minutes before. We were connected, this real, live Shayna and I, although our actual friendship had ended long ago, dissolved somewhere in the tensions on that Oregon road—a gradual withering of our simple teenage college bond, until it was as though the whole panorama of desert had gotten pushed in between us.

The second Shayna, that inner, intimately known Shayna suspended in 1977, would always remain in a fantastical realm somewhere at the edges of my consciousness, surrounded by a deep pool of sad tenderness. Our human souls can contain some persons as loved internal objects, who take up residence there, regardless of whether they are present in our world. This phantom wouldn't possess me any more than that other twenty-year-old who ghosted through my dreams. I could negotiate with her there.

I stood on the sidelines of the gathering, my head populated with the many people and places who had entered the circle of the story that I once believed contained only three: Shayna and me and a disappeared axeman.

Boo was still tied to me, as if by blood. Like sister. And just the week before, in a sad, flat Oregon cemetery where American flags flapped in the breeze, I mourned a deep loss as I stood with Dee Dee Kouns while she surrounded a blue marble urn that contained Bob's remains with a circle of red and gold roses—roses as red and gold as the "Orygun" T-shirts Shayna and I had once worn. It all got mixed up in my brain: the volcanoes and the Gothic towers; the cloistered courtyards and the open desert.

I thought back to the heady days of my investigation, those intense encounters when I told my story and heard answering stories. I remembered a time when I was following up on a clue one of the sisters of mercy had told me: the woman who lived above Cline Falls might know something about the mysteries surrounding the summer of '77. The crime scene photos showed a house on the rimrock on the other side of the river from the park. I had found a tiny road that led to the house, knocked on the door, and told my story. The owner had told me that his wife was indeed the woman I was looking for, but she had died, and the clue with her. He himself knew nothing of the story, as he was a pilot, winging his way over some other part of the globe in June 1977. Then he disappeared into another room and returned with a gift for me: an aerial photograph of the land surrounding Cline Falls, a huge acreage he once owned.

Taken on May 6, 1968, the square photograph captured the land eleven years before two twenty-year-old girls would bed down for a tragic night. The desert was cut in curvy halves by the sinuous Deschutes snaking from south to north. Details in the picture were precise enough for me to make out the turbulence in the river, and at five thousand feet, the junipers looked like thousands of little polka dots. It was easy to make out the floodplain along the river that cradled Cline Falls State Park.

I rejoiced at the perfection of the gift: a compassionate pilot could intuit that his uninvited guest would treasure a bird's-eye view of the land where I had left parts of my girl's body, the place in which I had been made over—a missing muscle, a narrowed shoulder span, a remade nose—the place that had once taken control of me. To fly above it struck me as the ultimate way for me to tame it, master it, liberate myself from the day I could not leave by my own power.

It had all been a rejuvenating act of creation, from where I began, breaking out of the claustrophobic confines of my memories, to illuminate little by little what encircled me, the people and the land, from myriad angles of vision, until eventually I knew much about the night of June 22, 1977—as though I had granted myself powers to levitate above Cline Falls, buoyant above the broad land, as Americans in one time zone after the next, safe in their living rooms, watched the CBS-TV premiere of the movie *McCabe and Mrs. Miller* unravel the romantic myth of the West, while the earth turned slowly in the dark on a summer solstice night.

I imagine that's how it'll be, a very long time from now, when I finish the trip that ended early, on a night long ago; I imagine rising like drifting smoke, toward the tremendous frontiers of my own true country, able to see clearly all that lies below, able to see clearly, because all is darkly lit.

Author's Note

I have written a completely factual book. I subjected myself to rigorous standards, checked and cross-checked my facts, and none are invented. The corroboration of the stories in the evolving investigation of the crime is purposely included in the book. If something was said about the commission of the crime or the alleged perpetrator that I was never able to corroborate, it is clear from the reading that this opinion belongs to that speaker alone.

I have included no "probable" dialogue. I took notes during my interviews, and sometimes made audio or video recordings, and I have reconstructed my story through these records. In the case of dialogue spoken decades ago, I have reconstructed it from journal entries, letters, or from my own best memory.

The order of the interviews (either in person or on the telephone) is roughly chronological, though I made small adjustments in the timeline when it better suited the evolving narrative.

I did take what I consider to be small liberties: occasionally, I collapsed two encounters with an interview subject into one. And naturally I edited conversations for brevity, clarity, and occasionally for grammar, but always with scrupulous regard for the original intent and characteristic voice of the speaker.

I have changed many names and some minor identifying details to guard privacy. Not everyone wants to be under public scrutiny, and this is understandable. Changing names does not compromise the veracity of the whole. Most specifically, I have changed the name of the alleged perpetrator. The reason I have done so is that I do not want to feed into the cult of celebrity granted by this culture to charismatic villains.

In order to protect her privacy, I have also changed the name of the woman who appears in these pages as Shayna Weiss. When I wrote to tell her about the publication of our shared story, she wrote back to say that she understood my need to write this book, and gave me her support.

Acknowledgments

The generosities that people have shown me in helping me to understand my personal history stretch back nearly thirty years. From my parents who lived through it with me, to my college friends who were there in the direct aftermath, to my friends and support system in the era when I lived in New York City who listened to me struggle to make sense of the incomprehensible, to my friends, even generous strangers, on the West Coast who listened to every beat of the story as I gradually gained clarity, week by week, year after year. It's impossible to list everyone here, but you know who you are.

I am deeply grateful to every person listed in the pages of this book and to everyone I talked to—the hundreds—during the research and investigation for this book, a period of years between 1992 and 2000. Every one of you contributed enormously to this story. Immense thanks to those who allowed me to profile their personal histories.

Many thanks to the Oregon State Police and the Deschutes County District Attorney's Office for their cooperation, and especially to Marlen Hein, Rich Hein, Fred Ackom, Lorin Weilacher, Dr. John Cochran, Sergeant Tom Kipp, and Deschutes County District Attorney Michael Dugan.

My Friend Patrick Flaherty, Esq., has been a true ally over the years.

I want to express my deep gratitude to Darlene Isaac and Vee Sanders for their tremendous generosity and for treating me like a member of their family. These bonds will last a lifetime.

My bond to Dee Dee and Bob Kouns is profound and abiding. They taught me much, encouraged me to take risks when the stakes were high, and contributed to making me the person I am today. Bob Kouns passed away on April 29, 2004. If we are lucky, we encounter a few human beings in our lifetime who deserve to be described as "noble." Bob was one. In 2005, the Oregon governor, legislature, and senate passed a resolution recognizing him as the founding father of crime victims' rights in Oregon, in honor of his extraordinary twenty-year service to the people of the state.

Thanks to Robin Katz, J'aime ona Pangaia, and Winky Wheeler for accompanying me on my first trip to Cline Falls; to my partner Donna Deitch for her political discernment, and keen insight—honestly and patiently offered on every draft of the manuscript since the very beginning; Jule Talen for reading the earliest draft; Anna Boorstin, Paula Lumbard, and Karen Hall for their patience with the longest possible drafts; Susan Lee Cohen for providing insight into the PTSD narrative and for coming up with the cleverest pseudonyms; Susan Streitfeld for helping make key passages go fathoms deeper; Chris Burrell for performing Photoshop on the images in this book and to Chris Burrell and Anne Russell for their last-minute copyediting.

I am especially indebted to Kirsten Grimstad's generous gift to me of nothing short of devotion to every draft of manuscript. Her literary skills, her sagacity, her ability to pull out the essences, and her willingness to sit down with me for regular discussions about my manuscript has improved this book immeasurably.

When it came time to move an overly long manuscript off my private desk and into the real world, my indomitable agent and friend, Elyse Cheney, with her terrific judgment, deserves credit for launching me into the best possible situation.

After being alone so long with the project, I never would have thought it possible—but my editor Eric Chinski's penetrating and provocative insights, his amazing ability to walk around in my head, have coaxed me to deeper levels of self-understanding. Because his sensibility was in perfect alignment with mine, because he understood the complexity of what I was trying to accomplish, I was able to produce, under his guidance, an infinitely tighter, richer, more nuanced and textured work. His commitment to this book, and his friendship, have touched me deeply, and I am immensely grateful to him.

Thanks to Jenna Dolan and production editor Wah-Ming Chang for deft copyediting and suggestions for streamlining, to Susan Mitchell and Lynn Buckley for translating my photographs into a stunning cover design, and to editorial assistant Gena Hamshaw, whose reassuring support has been especially helpful in easing my way through the publishing process.

The land that I have written about deserves special appreciation. For making and preserving its special character—thank you to the people of the state of Oregon.

Finally I'd like to express my debt to the late author and activist Paul Monette. His first words to me were his parting words, as he died one week after I met him in early 1994. I asked him what single piece of advice he could give me about writing my own story. He told me that every day he sat down to work, he would ask himself to write more honestly than he had the day before. I have tried to keep his counsel.